This book offers a comprehensive survey of the output of American factories during the period 1899-1937. Based on the most extensive data available, it proceeds from a general summary of broad changes in factory production and their significance for the national economy to a detailed presentation of indexes of output of all manufacturing combined, for 15 groups of kindred industries and for 140 individual industries.

Extensive appendices describe and appraise the statistical techniques employed, and provide basic data on the quantity, value and price of hundreds of products.

Publications of the

National Bureau of Economic Research, Inc.

Number 39

The Output of Manufacturing Industries, 1899–1937

RELATION OF THE DIRECTORS
TO THE WORK OF THE NATIONAL BUREAU

1. The object of the National Bureau of Economic Research is to ascertain and to present to the public important economic facts and their interpretation in a scientific and impartial manner. The Board of Directors is charged with the responsibility of ensuring that the work of the Bureau is carried on in strict conformity with this object.

2. To this end the Board of Directors shall appoint one or more Directors of Research.

3. The Director or Directors of Research shall submit to the members of the Board, or to its Executive Committee, for their formal adoption, all specific proposals concerning researches to be instituted.

4. No study shall be published until the Director or Directors of Research shall have submitted to the Board a summary report drawing attention to the character of the data and their utilization in the study, the nature and treatment of the problems involved, the main conclusions and such other information as in their opinion will serve to determine the suitability of the study for publication in accordance with the principles of the Bureau.

5. A copy of any manuscript proposed for publication shall also be submitted to each member of the Board. If publication is approved each member is entitled to have published also a memorandum of any dissent or reservation he may express, together with a brief statement of his reasons. The publication of a volume does not, however, imply that each member of the Board of Directors has read the manuscript and passed upon its validity in every detail.

6. The results of an inquiry shall not be published except with the approval of at least a majority of the entire Board and a two-thirds majority of all those members of the Board who shall have voted on the proposal within the time fixed for the receipt of votes on the publication proposed. The limit shall be forty-five days from the date of the submission of the synopsis and manuscript of the proposed publication unless the Board extends the limit; upon the request of any member the limit may be extended for not more than thirty days.

7. A copy of this resolution shall, unless otherwise determined by the Board, be printed in each copy of every Bureau publication.

(Resolution of October 25, 1926, revised February 6, 1933)

The Output of Manufacturing Industries, 1899–1937

by Solomon Fabricant
with the assistance of Julius Shiskin

National Bureau of Economic Research, Inc.

NEW YORK 1940

Manufactured in the U. S. A. by
Kingsport Press, Inc., Kingsport, Tennessee

Director's Note

THIS report is the first of several dealing with the trends of production and productivity in American industry since the opening of the twentieth century.

The study upon which this volume is based was made possible by funds granted by The Maurice and Laura Falk Foundation of Pittsburgh. The Falk Foundation is not, however, the author, publisher, or proprietor of this publication, and is not to be understood as approving or disapproving by virtue of its grant any of the statements made or views expressed herein.

William J. Carson
Executive Director

National Bureau of Economic Research, Inc.
December 1940

Preface

THE growth of our manufacturing industries—through the comparatively quiet period 1899 to 1914, the war upheaval from 1914 to 1919, the rapid expansion of the 1920's, and the troubled years following 1929—constitutes the material for an exciting tale. The statistics brought together in this volume relate to a single major theme of this story: the long-term changes in the volume and composition of the output of American manufacturing industries between 1899 and 1937. The study is confined to that period chiefly because it is only beginning with 1899 that reasonably adequate data on manufacturing production, collected in the U. S. Census of Manufactures for 1899, 1904, 1909, 1914, 1919 and biennially thereafter through 1937, are available both in detail and at fairly close intervals. These data end with 1937, the latest year for which a Census has been published, and the last peak year of business activity preceding the present war. Our primary interest is in physical output, the actual quantities of goods produced in American factories; we make use of Census data on pecuniary output merely to supplement the available information on physical output.

The first chapter of this book contains a summary of the changes in manufacturing output during the period under discussion, together with a brief consideration of the general economic significance of these events. Some readers may find what they seek to know about manufacturing output within the confines of this single chapter. Others will go on to examine the more complete picture of the changing aspect of manufacturing production outlined in Chapters 3 to 5 of Part One. These readers, we hope, will not find Chapter 2 impassable territory. Because indexes are the medium by which the quantities of the enormous variety of factory products are apprehended and summarized, this volume is peppered with index numbers. Chapter 2 assesses the significance of these measures. Further, since the data basic to this survey originated as answers to Census questionnaires, rather than as observations made in controlled laboratory experiments, we have presented in that chapter a brief statement on the nature of the data, and an appraisal of the economic and statistical biases inherent in them. The impatient reader may derive some comfort from the assurance that a more detailed statement concerning both the data and the statistical techniques has been relegated to an appendix. The changes that have occurred in the physical output of all manufacturing industries combined are described in Chapter 3. Major groups of industries, such as foods, textiles and chemicals, are reviewed in Chapter 4; and a general survey of changes in individual manufacturing industries appears in Chapter 5.

Part Two traces in greater detail the course of output for individual industries and for the groups into which they have been classified. Here, indexes are given for all the separate industries covered by adequate data and for as much of the period 1899–1937 as possible. In addition, the changing relative standing of each industry in its respective group is described. Unfortunately, it has been impossible for us to treat all industries in equal detail. All too frequently the text adds little to the data given in the tables concerning a less important industry. It is probable, too, that there are gaps in the discussion of trends in the output of some important industries. In any case, the uneven allocation of space among the various industries is to be imputed at least in part to the chance distribution of the author's store of information on a subject so variegated and so complex as manufacturing output.

The statistician may merely glance at Chapter 2 and at the charts and tables in the remainder of the text, and concentrate his attention upon the appendices. Appendix A contains a fairly detailed discussion of the nature of the Census data and of the procedure followed in the construction of the indexes of physical output. The basic data on the quantity, value and average price of individual products used in the construction of the indexes of output appear in Appendix B, with footnotes on the extent to which these products cover the output of the respective industries, and on incomparabilities discovered in the Census. Data on dollar values added by manufacturing are assembled in Appendix C, also with footnotes concerning such matters as changes in classification. Finally, Appendix D compares the index numbers constructed by us with those of two other agencies, in respect of methods of construction, industrial coverage, and trends—where these differ greatly.

It will be apparent that the appendices and text tables contain more information than is utilized in the text discussion. The latter deals only with the long-run movements of output; yet the biennial indexes should prove useful also for a study of short-run changes, if supplemented by the less comprehensive data that are available on the annual and monthly volume of manufacturing output. Again, the average prices of individual manufactured products, derived from the Census data and presented in Appendix B, may be of interest to students of wholesale prices.

The description of what has taken place in the productive field of manufacturing, the most important industrial sector of our economy, is the primary object of this volume. But the present study has another purpose: it is designed also to provide a base for an investigation of the changes that occurred during the first four decades of this century in the relationship between manufacturing employment and output, and of the rising efficiency of productive effort in factory establishments. The results of this further study will be published in another volume at a later date. A third volume, dealing with production and productivity in agriculture and other nonmanufacturing industries, will complete the story begun with manufacturing output.

Solomon Fabricant

Author's Acknowledgments

THROUGHOUT the study helpful advice was given by a National Bureau staff committee consisting of Moses Abramovitz, A. F. Burns, N. I. Stone and Leo Wolman, with F. C. Mills as chairman. My obligations to Dr. Burns are especially heavy in this respect. To Dr. Mills I owe, further, the advantage of free use of his extensive unpublished and published work on manufacturing output. The manuscript was read and useful comments were made also by other members of the National Bureau staff, Harold Barger, W. H. Shaw and I. H. Siegel; by several Directors of the National Bureau; and by Witt Bowden of the U. S. Bureau of Labor Statistics and E. W. Browne of the U. S. Bureau of the Census.

T. J. Fitzgerald and H. H. McClure of the U. S. Bureau of the Census replied to many queries concerning the data in the Census of Manufactures; and David Weintraub and Harry Magdoff, of the National Research Project of the Work Projects Administration, permitted me to examine some of their work before publication.

My greatest debt is to my co-workers. Julius Shiskin took charge of most of the computations, helped prepare the text of the appendices, and made substantial suggestions leading to the improvement of the rest of the text. Corolynn L. Lee, Céleste N. Medlicott and Jacob Gould rendered valuable assistance throughout the study not only by participating in the laborious task of computation and preparation of the tables, but also by checking the text and making many helpful comments. I am deeply grateful, in addition, to Maude E. Remey and Mildred G. Uhrbrock, who were of great help in the early stages of the study, and to Hans Landsberg and

Sam H. Schurr, who assisted in many ways in the later stages. In the preparation of Appendix B, Mr. Shiskin was aided by Gerald Fischer, Grace Kastelansky, Fritz Lewy and Francis Pucciani, as well as by other members of our staff. The charts were carefully drawn by H. Irving Forman. The manuscript was edited by Bettina Sinclair, who brought genuine interest and skill to the arduous task of turning a work of the present character into a reasonably readable volume.

S. F.

Contents

APPENDICES

Text Tables

Charts

Part One

The Changing Aspect of Manufacturing Production

Chapter 1

A Summary of the Changes in Manufacturing Output

The economic welfare of the nation is immediately dependent upon the goods and services yielded by its natural resources and creative energies. We live on the products of field, mine and factory, and the measure of our material well-being rises or falls with changes in the amount, kind and quality of those commodities. The present volume, devoted to a consideration of the changes in the product of the factory, has two chief objectives. It seeks first, to gauge the growth in the aggregate output of manufacturing industries in the period 1899–1937; and second, to depict the modifications in the pattern of factory production caused by shifts in the character of goods produced and in the relative positions of the several industries that turn out the same classes of commodities.

We have confined our measurement of the physical output of manufacturing industries to the period 1899–1937 because it is only for these years that the basic source of comprehensive data on manufacturing production, the United States Census of Manufactures, is available in sufficient breadth and detail. Moreover, in tracing the major internal developments of manufacturing production during this 38-year period, we have not considered cyclical changes, but have dealt exclusively with the more persistent shifts of emphasis in production.

MANUFACTURING AND THE NATIONAL ECONOMY

From the founding of the republic to the opening of the present century the manufacturing industries of the United States expanded rapidly. As early as 1791 Alexander Hamilton noted substantial beginnings in his report on manufactures. By 1902 manufacturing industries had progressed to a level undreamed of a century before, and in its report issued in that year the United States Industrial Commission described their status in superlatives. Between the two years a growing proportion of the population had found employment in these industries, and the fraction of the national money income—wages, salaries, dividends and interest—distributed by them had risen sharply. The economy had ceased to be primarily agricultural and had become predominantly industrial.

For some time after 1900 the growth of manufacturing industries, as measured by the rise in the proportion of the national income paid out by them and by their relative contribution to employment, continued at a rapid pace. Although precise figures are available only for the years following 1909, all the evidence at hand indicates that the rate of advance of manufacturing was virtually undiminished during the first 15 years of the present century. In 1913, manufacturing industries distributed 19 percent of the national income, and provided employment for 8,000,000 to 9,000,000 persons—about 20 percent of the total number of workers in the United States with gainful occupations.

The War of 1914–18 supplied a particularly sharp stimulus to the growth of manufacturing industries. From 1913 to 1919 the fraction of national income paid out by them rose from 19 to 25 percent, and the number of workers engaged in manufacturing increased to 10,000,000, from 20 percent of the total in 1913 to 26 percent in 1919.

Since 1919, however, there has been no advance in the relative contribution of this group of industries to the nation's income or employment. On the contrary, the percentage of the national income attributable to manufacturing enterprises declined between 1919 and 1923 to about 22 or 23 percent, and remained at that point during the rest of the post-war decade. From 1929 to 1937, the proportion fluctuated violently, resulting in a slight net rise to 24 percent. As for the number of manufacturing employees, it remained substantially constant during the two decades following the war, except for cyclical fluctuations. Aside from those who replaced or displaced older workers, none of the newcomers to the ranks of the working population found employment in manufacturing industries in the period 1919–37. The working population increased during those years, so that the proportion of wage and salary earners engaged in manufacturing industries fell, during 1919–37, from 26 percent of the total to 22 percent. Manufacturing had apparently reached a plateau, if not a peak, with respect to its relative contributions both to the money income of the nation and to employment.

In terms of actual commodities produced, however, manufacturing industries more than kept pace with the growth in other industries throughout all four decades of the twentieth century. If we may judge from the indexes of manufacturing output computed in the present study, and from the less precise measures of output of all types of commodities—fabricated and unfabricated goods, services and construction—that may be derived from existing series on national income and indexes of the prices paid by consumers, the aggregate physical output of manufacturing industries increased more rapidly than the net national product not only up to 1919, but thereafter as well. From 1899 to 1919 the physical output of manufacturing industries rose about 20 percent more rapidly than the net national product, and from 1919 to 1937 it went up some 35 percent more rapidly. These figures show that there was no cessation of growth during the last two decades in the relative contribution of manufacturing industries to the stream of goods available for consumption. This finding stands in striking contrast to the record of virtual stability in the percentage that wages, salaries, dividends and other money incomes distributed by manufacturing industries constituted of all such payments in the years 1919–37, and to the decline, during the same period, in the proportion of total employment provided by these industries. There is evidence here that advances in manufacturing productivity since the World War have been greater than corresponding advances in the economy at large, which embraces not only manufacturing, but agriculture, mining, public utilities, merchandizing, personal services and a host of other industries.

AGGREGATE MANUFACTURING OUTPUT

Perhaps the outstanding feature of the general measurements presented in this volume is their indication of a rate of advance since the turn of the century higher than the rates shown by other studies of manufacturing output. Most indexes of production have an inherent downward bias because the new and rapidly growing industries either are omitted from the samples studied or are inadequately represented. Electrical gadgets, new chemical products, new machine tools —the variegated and unstandardized products of current invention—cannot readily be included in such indexes. Thus the older industries, usually growing less rapidly as they mature, receive more complete representation than the new and tend to dominate the record. In the present study two procedures were employed in an attempt to lessen, if not to overcome, the downward bias. First, every effort was made to include in the sample as many industries as possible, new and old, large and small. Second, the sample was adjusted for changes in its coverage of all manufacturing industries. The indexes of aggregate manufacturing output thus obtained show an advance of 276 percent between 1899 and 1937. The only other comprehensive index covering this period, that computed by E. E. Day and Woodlief Thomas and extended by other investigators, indicates a rise of 203 percent between 1899 and 1937.

The annual rate of increase of manufacturing output over the 38 years from 1899 to 1937, as averaged over good years and bad, was 3.5 percent, according to the indexes constructed for the present study. At this rate, the total volume of manufactured goods was doubling every 20 years. These figures reveal a notable expansion, yet they take no account of improvements in the quality of goods produced. Although the limitations of the available data have permitted us only to note the unknown territory that remains to be explored, even superficial investigations suggest that the improvements have been so widespread as to affect many standardized as well as unstandardized commodities. If physical output could be measured not merely by volume but also in terms of quality, the average annual rate of increase shown by our index—3.5 percent—would certainly appear as an understatement.

This average is inadequate on still another count, for it fails to indicate the marked changes in the rate of growth of manufacturing production over the years we are reviewing. Between 1899 and 1937 there were actually nine occasions on which manufacturing output suffered an absolute decline. Though often sharp, most of the declines covered only one calendar year. The contraction beginning in 1929 was the most severe as well as the longest in duration: by 1932 manufacturing output had dropped to a point practically equal to that of 1913, according to the indexes we have constructed.

During the period 1899–1937, taken as a whole, the average rate of growth of manufacturing output exceeded by a substantial margin the average rate of increase in the population of the country. While total manufacturing output increased by 276 percent between 1899 and 1937, population rose by 73 percent, so that per capita production of manufactures increased by 120 percent during the 38 years. Per capita manufacturing output rose not only for the entire span of years but also for the greater part of it. There were, however, three periods of five years or more during which there was virtually no net increase in per capita output. Output in 1907 was followed by a slump, and was not substantially exceeded until 1912, and the 1916 peak, for similar reasons, was not surpassed until 1923; but population grew in all these years, as it did indeed in every year from 1899 to 1937. The most recent period, 1929–37, is of particular interest. During that time the population increased by almost 8,000,000, a 6 percent rise, yet by 1937 manufacturing output had registered a net gain of only 3 percent, barely surpassing its 1929 level.

Because output failed to advance appreciably from 1929 to 1937, many persons have concluded, with varying degrees of alarm, that the United States has almost exhausted its capacity for industrial expansion. Others, influenced perhaps by current misconceptions concerning the growth in manufacturing production, have viewed the recent period as one of definite retrogression. The misconceptions, in turn, have originated in the shortcomings of those current measures of total manufacturing output which have been compiled almost exclusively from samples of mature manufacturing industries and have taken little account of the output of the newer, more rapidly growing, industries. Thus the index presented here, which is based on comprehensive Census data, rose 3 percent from 1929 to 1937, while the index of manufacturing production prepared by the Board of Governors of the Federal Reserve System indicated, before its revision in August 1940, a decline from 1929 to 1937 of 8 or 9 percent. To be sure, even the indexes computed in the present study, as well as the revised Federal Reserve index, show only a slight rise in output between 1929 and 1937, and one that certainly failed to keep pace with the increase in population. Yet, if we look beyond the general averages, and observe in detail the changes in production from 1929 to 1937, we find that many industries were making net gains, and that some important new ones were advancing very rapidly. The forces working for growth, though almost completely counterbalanced by the forces making for decline, were not entirely absent even in this disturbed period.

COMPOSITION OF MANUFACTURING OUTPUT

When we turn from the averages and concentrate upon the movements of manufacturing production in individual industries, we find sharp differences in the secular rates of change in the physical output of these industries. In every period some decline, some forge ahead, and only a few industries follow closely the general trend of manufacturing output. These disparate rates of growth affect and are affected by changes in the structure of industry, in technical processes, in the kinds of goods produced and in the distribution of employment.

If related industries are grouped together and the period 1899–1937 is considered as a whole, certain outstanding developments emerge from the general picture. There were, for instance, very large increases, from 1899 to 1937, in the physical output of transportation equipment, petroleum and coal products, chemical products, paper products, and products of the printing and publishing industries. The physical output of each of the first two groups was more than 12 times as large in 1937 as it had been in 1899. Chemical products, paper products, and printing and publishing grew six- or seven-fold during the 38 years under review. In contrast, the physical output of the forest products group actually declined by 7 percent, while leather products rose only 69 percent, less rapidly than population, which increased by 73 percent. Beverages and textile products, which rose 132 and 180 percent respectively, lagged behind total manufacturing output, which increased 276 percent. Moderate advances, approximating the growth in total manufacturing output, are recorded for foods, tobacco products and iron and steel products.

Although accurate data on the output of four other major groups—rubber products, stone, clay and glass products, nonferrous metals, and machinery—are not available, the complete figures on money value added by manufacture (value of products less cost of materials and fuel), and such fragmentary data on physical output as can be obtained, do afford some clues. From them it may be inferred that during 1899–1937 the physical output of stone, clay and glass products rose somewhat less rapidly than total manufacturing output but more rapidly than population; that the output of nonferrous metals increased at the same or at a slightly faster rate than total manufacturing; and that the physical output of machinery and of rubber products rose considerably more rapidly than the aggregate.

The indexes for the entire period 1899–1937 provide a broad background against which recent events may be observed in perspective. For example, there was a severe decline, from 1929 to 1937, in the output of the forest products industries. The physical output of this group fell by 24 percent, as compared with a rise of 3 percent in total manufacturing. The indexes which go back to 1899 show, however, that the resulting relative decline, 26 percent, is not an isolated phenomenon. It reflects, at least in part, trends dating back to the opening of the present century. For the output of forest products declined continuously in relation to total output: 36 percent between 1899 and 1909, 33 percent between 1909 and 1919, and 22 percent between 1919 and 1929.

The changes in the indexes for major groups of manufacturing industries, though marked, are nevertheless slight in comparison with the enormous changes in the output of individual industries from 1899 to 1937. Of the 61 individual industries for which we have adequate measurements for both these years, 11 declined in output and 13 other industries increased less rapidly than population grew. Among the 11 declining industries were virtually all those specializing in transportation equipment other than automobiles and aircraft, i.e., carriages and wagons, locomotives, railroad cars, ships and boats; and also linen goods; turpentine and rosin, and lumber-mill products; clay products; flour; pianos; and chewing and smoking tobacco. At the other extreme there was one industry—automobiles—whose 1937 production was 1,800 times greater than that of 1899, and there were four—cigarettes, petroleum refining, condensed and evaporated milk, and beet sugar—whose 1937 output was more than 15 times as great as it had been in 1899. These were followed in order of speed in growth by cement, canned fruits and vegetables, miscellaneous chemicals, and manufactured ice.

Diversity of trends in the output of individual manufacturing industries is to be expected in a dynamic economy. For in such an economy tastes change, purchasing power fluctuates both in the aggregate and in distribution, technology advances, old natural resources are exhausted and new ones are discovered. Quite naturally, too, the incidence of these changes upon different industries varies. Especially among competitive industries do the alterations in relative status resulting from such developments lead to divergence of trends. The growth in the output of the sugar, confectionery and ice cream industries occurred at the expense of the output of other food industries. Automobiles rose while carriages declined. Cigarettes displaced other tobacco products. Silk and rayon woven goods and knit goods made of all types of yarn rose in relation to cotton and woolen woven goods. Limited forest reserves as well as changes in types of buildings and in methods of construction explain in some measure the relative decline in lumber production and the increases in cement and steel output.

Although displacement of one industry by another was often pronounced, as in the case of automobiles versus carriages, it did not always lead to an actual decline in the output of the less favored industry. The detailed indexes of physical output show, indeed, that comparative retrogression has often consisted merely of a slower rate of growth. Relatively few individual industries, and only one major group, actually declined in physical output from 1899 to 1937. The great increases that occurred in the output of some industries, perhaps at the cost of older competitors, did not prevent the latter from growing also, in a period when the total was rising. Thus butter and oleomargarine both increased; cane sugar as well as beet sugar rose in output; and cotton and woolen woven goods grew although their rates of growth fell below those of silk, rayon, and total knit goods.

Industries producing goods related sequentially or complementarily resembled one another in growth more closely than competitive industries, but the rates were far from identical. One cause of the divergence in the trends of sequentially related industries was a revision of consumers' budgets as standards of living moved upward. With the increase in national income there was a shift from home baking and sewing to corresponding operations in factories; as a consequence, the baking and clothing industries grew more rapidly than the industries producing flour and cloth. Another cause was savings in materials, brought about in large degree by improvements in the productivity of labor and enterprise. The consistently lower rate of growth in blast-furnace products, as compared with steel-mill products, reflected—along with other developments—the more efficient use of ferrous materials in the production of steel, and the increasing substitution of scrap steel for pig iron among the raw materials consumed in steel mills. A third cause of the divergence in rates of growth even among sequentially related industries was a change in the character of our foreign trade, a change that did not apply to related manufacturing industries with equal force. For example, the decline in the export of leather between 1899 and 1937 was not accompanied by any corresponding drop in domestic shoe production.

The divergence of trends in the output of industries related complementarily to one another may be attributed in part to the factors just cited, and to certain others as well. Automobiles, gasoline and rubber tires all made tremendous advances between 1899 and 1937. However, because each of these commodities has a different life span, the advances in output could not progress at identical rates.

For a more complete record of the changes in the output of individual industries, the reader must turn to later chapters of this volume. One set of details is worth anticipating, however. We have already noted that during the final period 1929–37 the aggregate physical output of manufacturing industries scarcely rose. Nevertheless, as our data on separate industries show, the output of about half of them advanced during these years, in some instances by substantial amounts. Refrigerators and rayon, each with an increase of over 200 percent, head the list. There were important gains also in the output of glass and tin cans, each of which rose by about 60 percent; canned fruits and vegetables and lace goods, about 50 percent each; washing machines, radios, miscellaneous chemicals, and wood pulp, 40 percent each; cigarettes, and silk and rayon goods, 30 percent each; cheese, 29 percent; asbestos products, 26 percent; women's clothing, 25 percent; petroleum refining, 19 percent; paper, hosiery, woolen and worsted goods, shoes, leather, paints and varnishes, ice cream, and confectionery, 9 to 15 percent. All these industries produced, in 1937, a physical quantity of goods greater than their output in 1929, sufficiently greater, in fact, to keep pace with or exceed the rise in population during the interval. Unfortunately, deficiencies in the data make it impossible to measure the growth of physical output in certain new industries, notably aircraft manufacture, but despite these gaps it can be observed that the forces making for growth in our economy were not dormant in what is widely viewed as a period of stagnation.

On the other hand, we must not minimize the trends in the opposite direction: half the industries declined absolutely in physical output between 1929 and 1937, and more than half declined in relation to population growth. The output of locomotives, lead, planing-mill products, clay products, pianos, cement, lumber-mill products, dropped in proportions ranging from 57 to 25 percent; of manufactured ice, copper, cigars, tires and tubes, ships and boats, linoleum, from 25 to 17 percent; and of flour, coke, and pig iron, from 14 to 12 percent.

It is sometimes held that a substantial increase in total output can come about only through a direct contribution to that total by a new and rapidly growing industry which gives promise of continuing expansion, and through the indirect stimulation by such an industry of the others which supply it with raw materials or produce goods used jointly with its product. Ranked in order of gains in output, the industries heading the list for the period 1929–37 were rayon and mechanical refrigerators, industries perhaps more limited in potential growth than was, for example, the motor vehicle industry. These industries appear unlikely to expand to the size that the automobile industry had attained by 1930—when it consumed 15 percent of all the steel produced in the United States, 69 percent of the plate glass, 18 percent of the hardwood lumber, 51 percent of the upholstery leather, 15 percent of the copper, and 26 percent of the lead—and cannot therefore be expected to absorb equivalent quantities of other goods. We should not, however, be too easily tempted to forecast our future development. The story of the automobile industry alone should guard us from hasty predictions at close range. In the earlier part of this century it would have been difficult if not impossible to anticipate how great a role automobile manufacture would come to play in the national economy; back in 1899 that industry was not even accorded separate classification in the Census.

The foregoing outline of the course of manufacturing

production gives rise to speculations concerning the mobility of labor and capital. Here also we must refrain from going beyond our statistical materials, although we may point out some of their implications. All industrial systems are characterized by the growth of new industries and the decline of older ones, and labor and capital must always preserve sufficient flexibility for adaptation to these changes. The gravity of the problem of mobility depends, however, on the rate of growth in the whole economy. When the total volume of output, of employment and of capital investment, is rising rapidly, the problem is far less pressing than when the aggregate is stable or declining. The migration and retraining of labor, the formulation of policies relating to the investment of depreciation reserves and corporate savings, take on increasing importance when the rate of growth in total output, employment and capital investment is low or negative. Whether these problems will be of crucial interest depends on the future rate of flow of manufactured goods.

MANUFACTURING OUTPUT AND PRODUCTIVITY

The changes that have occurred in production cannot be appraised in isolation from the concomitant changes in the productivity of labor, capital and business enterprise. An increase as great as that which occurred in manufacturing production between 1899 and 1937 could not have come about without large gains in productivity. Had there been no increase in productivity the rise in output would have been much less than the rise that did in fact occur, even if both population and capital stock had grown at the rates at which they actually did grow. However, without a rise in productivity there would have been a slower growth in capital stock, if not also in population, and output would have been even smaller than in the hypothetical situation just described.

The shifting array of individual products also has been associated with new developments in the efficiency of machines, labor and management. On the one hand, the general advance in productivity, by raising the standard of living and thereby stimulating a demand for luxury goods, has contributed to the divergence of trends in output. On the other hand, the pervasive stimuli to gains in productivity and thereby to change in technical methods have been powerful enough to cause the industries manufacturing the tools of production to grow at a speedier rate than most other manufacturing industries. The more rapid growth of the former is indicated by the statistics for the machinery industries. The machinery group rose, between 1899 and 1909, 2 percent more rapidly (measured in terms of value added by manufacture) than did all manufacturing; between 1909 and 1919, 25 percent more rapidly than the total; and between 1919 and 1929, 18 percent more rapidly than the total. The machinery industries were severely hit by the recession of 1929–33, but revived sufficiently to make the net change in their value added between 1929 and 1937 almost equal to that of total manufacturing, so that in the latter year they reattained the relative position they had held in 1929. The substitution of machine processes for hand labor, of large machines for small, and of complex mechanical devices for simple ones appears to have been—at least up to 1929 if not thereafter as well—a fundamental means of progress. It is true, however, that additions to our stock of capital goods are not the sole means by which productivity is advanced. Thus the discovery and exploitation of new and inexpensive catalytic agents may prove as strategically important in the growth of the chemical industries as the development of mechanical power was in the rise of all manufacturing. And changes in the character of the capital stock, as well as additions to it, have contributed to the growth of output.

Enhanced efficiency in the utilization of raw materials is another factor that bears directly on the course of productivity. Economies in the use of raw materials often lead to large increases in productivity. These economies give rise in turn to economies in the use of labor and capital in the production of the raw materials required for a given number of commodities. The end result is a decline in the total cost of the final product. The saving in raw materials may be far greater than the cost of effecting that saving, and often may lead to a substantial decline in the total cost of the particular manufacturing process in which the saving occurs. In plants in which nonferrous ores are dressed, concentrated and smelted, there have been large economies in the use of raw material; since the latter is an important constituent of cost, the gains in productivity from this source alone have been striking. Significant savings of materials have been made also in the manufacture of beet sugar, in steel mills, and in coke ovens, to cite some of the examples treated in detail below.

Improvements in the quality of goods produced are another cause, as well as a result, of increasing productivity. A bettering of the quality of consumer goods, made possible by more efficient methods of production, brings about an increase in the value and usefulness of the products of industry. Improved capital equipment leads directly to further gains in productivity. Examples of both types of improvement are easily found. Gains in the productivity of the men's hosiery industry have been made possible by the introduction of new knitting machines which require less labor and at the same time produce hose with patterns and designs that could not have been turned out formerly except at prohibitive cost. The improvement in the machine also made possible the improvement in the product. Similar, and more broadly significant, have been the results of the development of standardization, which has enhanced precision and hence quality of product and has been a contributing factor in the rising efficiency of manufacture. This interaction of changes in the quality of goods, in industrial processes and in productivity is a prime characteristic of a developing economy. Progress occurs on all fronts, each advance supporting and stimulating the others. It is true that as population expands pressure upon natural resources may lead to the deterioration of the quality of some raw materials; but the resulting disadvantages are usually more than offset by improvements in the extraction and refinement of these materials, and by discoveries of new sources of supply or of substitutes. The risk of deterioration in the quality of food products, to which urbanization and the increased distance between source of supply and market contribute, is lessened by the improvements resulting from speedy transportation, refrigeration, canning and freezing.

Related to the foregoing considerations is the finding that a decline in the aggregate price received for the services of labor, capital and other agents of fabrication (i.e., value added per unit of physical product, measured in relation to the change in the average value added per unit in all manufacturing) has often been associated with an exceptionally rapid rate of growth in output. Those manufacturing industries which have forged ahead of others in production are usually the ones in which these prices have been cut in relation to the average for all manufacturing. On the other hand, increases in these prices, relative to the average, are commonly found in the laggard industries. There is evidence here that reductions in price have made possible gains in output; and, in turn, that gains in output, perhaps by fostering larger scale production, have promoted reductions in costs and thereby in prices.

Trends in employment and productivity are found to have been similarly related. Many of the industries which cut drastically the amount of labor utilized per unit of product, from 1899 to 1937, expanded so greatly that they actually increased the number of workers employed. Industries in which employment declined or rose only slightly usually effected only moderate reductions in the quantity of labor employed per unit of output. This interrelationship will be considered in detail in the second volume of this study; at this point we shall merely cite one or two outstanding examples. In 1899 the automobile industry employed 2,200 wage earners and produced 3,700 automobiles and trucks. In 1929 the industry employed 447,000 wage earners who turned out 4,360,000 passenger automobiles and 820,000 commercial vehicles. The number of man-years required for the production of one car or truck dropped from six tenths in 1899 to less than one tenth in 1929, yet the number of wage-earner jobs rose by 445,000, an increase running into thousands in percentage terms. Rayon, an industry which between 1929 and 1937 effected one of the most drastic reductions in the number of workers employed per unit of product, nevertheless increased its volume of employment more than 40 percent in this difficult period.

THE GROWTH OF MANUFACTURES: AN ASPECT OF GENERAL ECONOMIC DEVELOPMENT

Manufacturing is but a segment of the entire industrial system. Its output, its productive efficiency, and the changes in them, are only facets of the economic development of the entire nation. We conclude this brief survey, therefore, with some remarks on the interrelations between manufacturing and nonmanufacturing industries, placing particular emphasis on the added significance with which they invest developments in manufacturing itself.

The total product of manufacturing and nonmanufacturing industries combined more than doubled between 1899 and 1937, rising some 30 percent more rapidly than population during the 38 years. One reason for the increase in the per capita national product was, of course, the great advance in manufacturing industries. But the converse is true as well:

the relatively greater rise in manufacturing output was in an important sense a consequence of the growth in the total national product. During the period under consideration the increase in average per capita income led to an even greater rise in average per capita expenditure on factory-made goods. There was a shift from domestic to factory production of such articles as bread, canned food and clothing, as housewives cast off the burden of domestic chores. In some of their household duties women were aided increasingly by manufactured appliances such as washing machines and vacuum cleaners. There is a limit to this sort of development, since eventually there must come a time when all domestic production has been completely transferred to the factory; but that ultimate state of things was not reached during the first four decades of this century. The rise in standards of living was accompanied also by greater fabricational elaboration of consumer goods passing through factories. And an ever larger part of the increased household budget was devoted to such highly processed goods as automobiles and radios. Working in the other direction was the tendency for expenditures on services to rise with standards of living. Apparently, however, the service industries did not progress rapidly enough to cause a decline in the fraction of income expended on manufactured consumer goods. An indirect effect of their advance was the stimulation of the demand for another group of manufactured goods—equipment and materials used by the service industries themselves.

Another set of influences making for growth in manufactures relative to other forms of economic activity may be traced to the forces underlying the increase in productivity, which in turn was responsible in large measure for the rise in total output. The industrial division of labor grew finer. Manufacturing industries took over some of the work formerly done in other industries, and by producing machines and supplies assisted nonmanufacturing industries in their operations. Mechanization in agriculture is a vivid example of this interchange of functions. By producing tractors, agricultural machinery, gasoline and oil, manufacturing undertook a number of tasks formerly relegated to the farm, so that farmers found it less necessary to breed draught animals and grow feed. The increased division of labor is to be observed also in the shift toward factory slaughter of meat animals and toward factory production of butter. Manufacturing itself often profited from assistance of this sort—witness the development of electric power—but the net result seems to have been a gain in the fraction of the total physical output that was contributed by manufacturing industries.

A third reason why manufacturing rose in relation to other industries is connected with the preceding one. The growth of population, and the consequent pressure upon natural resources, exerted a deep influence on the character of our foreign trade. (Tariffs here and abroad also played a part, of course.) Apparently, it became more profitable for us to devote an increasing proportion of our energies to manufacture and a declining proportion to farming. Instead of exporting as much wheat and cotton as formerly, we turned to the export of more automobiles and machinery in order to secure products not made in this country. In 1899 crude foodstuffs and crude materials bulked large in our exports. Together their value accounted for 43 percent of the total value of all exports in that year, but by 1937 the percentage had dropped to 25. Manufactured exports rose from 57 percent to 75, and the greatest rise occurred in finished manufactures, the most highly fabricated type. These constituted, in terms of value, 22 percent of all our exports in 1899 and as much as 49 percent in 1937.

The divergence we have found in the trends of individual manufacturing industries also was a characteristic of the general development of our economy. As we have already observed, changes in consumer budgets, greater division of labor, and modifications in our foreign trade did not affect all manufacturing industries equally. The varying effects of these influences are discussed at greater length in the following chapters and are shown in detail in the basic tables presented in the appendices to this volume.

Chapter 2

Measurement of Output: Method and Material

CHANGES in the volume of output are described in this study mainly by means of index numbers, which summarize data collected for the most part by the United States Census of Manufactures. Because indexes of physical output are rather complex measures, and because in any case the indexes that can be computed from the available Census statistics are often only approximations of the desired measures, some discussion of the methods and materials utilized by us is an essential preliminary to a presentation of the indexes themselves. A more detailed treatment of some of the problems considered here is to be found in Appendix A.

IDEAL INDEXES AND PRACTICABLE INDEXES OF PHYSICAL OUTPUT

The meaning of the indexes computed for this study may be understood most readily if we first describe "ideal" indexes of physical output of a single industry and "ideal" indexes of physical output of all manufacturing industries combined. A comparison of the indexes actually computed from the available data with the "ideal" indexes will then show in what respects they differ.

The aggregate money value of an industry's output changes from time to time because of modifications both in prices and in physical quantities. The index of physical output for the industry should measure the changes in this aggregate value that are attributable exclusively to the changes that actually occurred in physical quantities. To this end prices should be kept constant in the computation of the index of physical output.

The particular physical quantities and prices that are relevant to the measurement of physical output depend upon the definition of output chosen. More specifically, the crucial question to be decided is whether we seek to measure gross output or net output. Considered in economic terms, the output of an industry may be taken either as the total value of the goods it sends to market, or as that portion of the value which the industry has itself added in the process of manufacture. The former is gross output, the latter net output. Now there are a number of concepts of gross output. For example, gross output may be defined simply as the gross proceeds from sales of commodities or it may be enlarged to include capital gains. Most commonly, however, the value of gross output is defined as the aggregate value of goods produced in the ordinary course of business, exclusive of capital gains.

Similarly, there are many concepts of net output, each different from the other in the degree to which the product is net. Payments for materials alone may be subtracted from gross sales to yield a net figure. Fuel expenditures also may be subtracted. The number of deductions may be expanded to cover all payments to other business enterprises for commodities and services, excluding capital equipment. Finally, a net figure may be obtained by a further deduction of expenditures on capital equipment, either immediately or in the form of periodic depreciation charges. Here too, fortunately, there is fairly general acceptance of a single concept: [1] the value of net output is usually defined as the aggregate

[1] The most controversial questions revolve chiefly about the treatment of capital gains and losses, and taxes; see Conference on Research in National Income and Wealth, *Studies in Income and Wealth* (National Bureau of Economic Research) Vol. I (1937), Parts 1, 2, 3, 5; Vol. II (1938), Parts 4 and 5.

value of goods produced (i.e., the value of gross output) less the value of all commodities and services purchased from other business enterprises and consumed in the production process, including periodic allowance for depreciation and depletion and provision for losses by accident. This definition does not allow for deduction of losses on "capital account."

An ideal index of the *gross* physical output of an industry would measure the changes in the aggregate value of gross output due only to changes in the physical quantities of final products, with prices of those products kept constant. Thus if prices are kept constant at the level at which they stood in some selected period, called the "weight base,"[2] the index of gross physical output for the year $(_1)$ on the year $(_0)$ as a "comparison base" is $\frac{\Sigma q_1 p_w}{\Sigma q_0 p_w}$, in which quantities of final products are represented by q and prices of final products by p.

The ideal index of the *net* physical output of an industry would measure the changes in the aggregate value of net output attributable exclusively to changes in the physical quantities of the final products and to changes in the physical quantities of the materials and other commodities consumed in the fabrication of the final products, with prices of final products and of commodities consumed kept constant. The index of net physical output corresponding to the above index of gross physical output would be

$$\frac{\Sigma q_1 p_w - \Sigma Q_1 P_w}{\Sigma q_0 p_w - \Sigma Q_0 P_w},$$

in which Q and P stand for the quantities and prices, respectively, of materials and other commodities consumed.

Whether output is to be defined as gross or net depends on

[2] The "weight base" should be distinguished from the "comparison base." The weight base is the period from which the prices or weights are taken. The comparison base is the period used as the point of reference, i.e., that with which other periods are contrasted. The weight base and comparison base periods need not be identical.

the use to be made of the measure of output. For some purposes, gross output is more satisfactory. Thus, if we wish to study the relation between the output of an industry and the input of materials, labor, equipment, etc.—which is indeed one of our ultimate objectives—the appropriate concept is gross output. Again, the degree of correspondence between the output of certain related industries—wood pulp and paper, for instance—may be of concern, as they are here. In this case, also, gross output is the more suitable measure. For these purposes, then, the ideal index of output of an industry is an index of gross output.

On the other hand, if we wish to obtain an aggregate of the output of several industries, another objective of the present study, net output is the preferable measure. For net output is free from all duplication. In principle, at least, the value of net output of different industries can be combined into a meaningful and unambiguous total, which is equal in fact to the national income. Similarly, an index of the aggregate net physical output of all industries measures changes in the real national income. Such an index, represented algebraically by $\frac{\Sigma(\Sigma q_1 p_w - \Sigma Q_1 P_w)}{\Sigma(\Sigma q_0 p_w - \Sigma Q_0 P_w)}$, is likewise free from all duplication. For example, the gross physical output of the steel industry is included in the first term within the parentheses in the numerator and denominator. Exactly the same item (if exports and imports, transport costs and changes in stocks of steel are ignored, for the sake of simplicity) appears also in the second term in numerator and denominator, as materials consumed by steel-using industries. Unfinished goods are thus canceled out, and only finished goods remain. The quantity of these is equivalent to the real national income.[3] For purposes of combination, then, the ideal index of output of an industry is an index of net output.

[3] Sometimes, all that may be desired is an index of total manufacturing output free only from the duplication that arises from the interchange of semiprocessed goods. For this purpose, the procedure suggested in the text

Having described briefly the computation of ideal indexes of physical output, we may now consider how the nature of available data compels us to modify our procedure when we construct what we call "practicable" indexes. In order to compute the index of gross physical output of an industry we must know the physical quantities and the prices of all the industry's final products. The quantities and prices of substantial samples of final products are readily available for many industries. Because a sample covers incompletely the gross output of an industry, adjustments (described below) must be made for changes in coverage; in this procedure some errors inevitably arise. These errors are slight in most cases, however, since the samples are usually large. Except, then, for the errors that may be introduced because the sample does not cover all the industry's final products, the practicable index of gross output of an industry corresponds to the ideal index described above.

In order to compute the index of net physical output of an industry we must know the physical quantities and the prices not only of the industry's final products but also of the commodities consumed in the making of those final products. As we have already pointed out, data on final products are available. For few industries, however, are there any reliable data on the quantities and prices of commodities consumed in the production process; and for even fewer are these data reasonably complete. The closest possible approximation to the index of net physical output of individual manufacturing industries, therefore, is simply the index of gross physical output.[4] In this case, the practicable index, which covers

is inefficient. A more satisfactory approach is that followed by Simon Kuznets and W. H. Shaw in measuring the output of "finished" processed goods. See Simon Kuznets, *Commodity Flow and Capital Formation* (National Bureau of Economic Research, 1938), and a forthcoming report by Mr. Shaw.

[4] For some industries rough computations of net output were possible. These computations were made for the few scattered industries for which data were available when it appeared that net and gross output had diverged appreciably. The computations are noted below in Part Two. Since indexes of

gross output, and the ideal index of net physical output cannot be expected to correspond very closely. The relation between the two may be expressed algebraically as follows: The index of gross physical output is

(1) $$\frac{\Sigma q_1 p_w}{\Sigma q_0 p_w};$$

the index of physical input of materials, etc., is

(2) $$\frac{\Sigma Q_1 P_w}{\Sigma Q_0 P_w};$$

and the index of net physical output [5] is

(3) $$\frac{\Sigma q_1 p_w - \Sigma Q_1 P_w}{\Sigma q_0 p_w - \Sigma Q_0 P_w}.$$

net output could be computed for a few industries only, and since even for these they were exceedingly rough, no attempt was made to substitute them for the corresponding indexes of gross output.

[5] The numerator, the denominator, or both numerator and denominator of the index of net output for an industry might conceivably be equal to or less than zero. Such an occurrence might reflect the presence of a zero or negative net value added by the industry in the given year, in the weight-base year, or in both years. The presence of a zero or negative net value is unlikely, though not impossible. A zero or negative numerator or denominator could be the result also of a negative correlation between (1) the change, from the initial year ($_0$) to the given year ($_1$), in the average production coefficient, and (2) the corresponding change in the ratio of (a) the average price of materials and other commodities purchased from outside industries to (b) the average selling price of the goods produced by the industry concerned. There are reasons for believing that such a correlation exists. It seems doubtful, however, that the elasticity of the production coefficient with respect to the price ratio that might be derived from the regression line for the purchased goods could often have such a magnitude as to give rise to zero or negative values in the numerator or denominator of the net output index without the appearance also in the net value added in the two years compared of zero or negative values. The paradoxical result of a negative net physical output that might conceivably be obtained even in the absence of a negative net value added reflects the ambiguity inherent in all index numbers of production and prices—an ambiguity which stems from the assumption that the price and production changes underlying a given change in value are independent and can be measured separately. This ambiguity remains the basic problem to be resolved by the still-inchoate economic theory of index numbers.

(3) is not equal to (1) unless (1) = (2); or, if we transpose terms from one side of this equation to the other, unless

$$\frac{\Sigma Q_1 P_w}{\Sigma q_1 p_w} = \frac{\Sigma Q_0 P_w}{\Sigma q_0 p_w}.$$

That is, the weighted average ratio of input to output (the weighted average "production coefficient") in year $(_1)$ must be equal to the weighted average ratio of input to output (the weighted average "production coefficient") in year $(_0)$. As a rule, however, the equality is not attained. Changes in the pattern of production—such as shifts in the relative importance of products requiring more or less elaboration of given materials—will render impossible the equalization of the two average ratios. A concrete case would be an increase in the amount of rolled products and a decrease in the amount of ingots in the final output of steel mills. Changes in the pattern of consumption—such as changes in the relative importance of materials requiring more or less elaboration if they are to yield stated quantities of products—operate in the same way. The reduction in the average tenor of the ore used in copper smelting and refining is an example. Presumably for the industries that use ores as raw materials, the index of gross output is a downward-biased index of net output. The direction of bias is downward also for industries whose final products become subject to an increasing degree of fabrication or improvement in quality. On the other hand, for industries whose raw materials have improved in quality, the indexes of gross output are biased upward as estimates of net output. For industries with a single raw material and a single product, both of fairly constant quality (and there are probably many of them), changes in the pattern of output or input could not give rise to a serious discrepancy between the indexes of gross and net output. The same observation must apply also to industries with relatively homogeneous materials and products, although it is difficult to say how many such industries exist.

The possibility of significant discrepancies between changes in gross and in net output is greatest for industries producing a variety of commodities or utilizing a variety of materials. Many of the Census industry classifications fall into this category since they are usually defined rather broadly, as is noted below. It should be emphasized that differences between indexes of gross and net output of these industries are merely *possible*; we do not know how frequently they occur in significant degree.

Even with the patterns of production and consumption remaining constant, a change in the efficiency with which materials are utilized—e.g., a decline in the amount of pig iron required to produce a ton of steel—will prevent equality of the indexes of net and gross output. Apparently in many industries the quantity of materials and of fuel used has tended to decline in relation to gross output. Such a tendency would cause the index of gross physical output to be biased downward as an estimate of the index of net physical output. It seems unlikely, however, that savings in materials and fuel have been great in all industries. The decline in the amount of fuel used, attributable to greater efficiency in the utilization of fuel, has often been counterbalanced in some degree by increased consumption of fuel arising from the displacement of human power by mechanical power. The trends with reference to other costs per unit of gross output, such as supplies, services purchased from other industries, and capital consumption, are less clear.

Because the indexes obtainable for individual industries relate to gross physical output, the indexes for groups of manufacturing industries and for all manufacturing industries combined cannot serve as accurate indexes of net physical output. Fortunately, however, the indexes for groups of related industries and the index for total manufacturing constitute somewhat more satisfactory approximations to indexes of net physical output than do those for individual industries, because in combining the indexes for various industries we have used, as the price to be kept constant, the Census "value added" (value of products minus cost of materials and fuel) per unit, rather than the gross value of products per unit.[6] The value of net output per unit would be even more satisfactory as the p coefficient, but it, too, is lacking for individual industries.

The use of value added per unit as the p coefficient does not yield an exact index of net output for a group or for all manufacturing combined if the indexes for individual industries are indexes of gross output—as they are in fact. Thus the group or total index we compute is, in simplified form,[7]

$$\frac{\Sigma q_1 \left(p_w - P_w \dfrac{Q_w}{q_w}\right)}{\Sigma q_0 \left(p_w - P_w \dfrac{Q_w}{q_w}\right)}.$$

The parenthetical term is the value added per unit of product. This index will not equal

$$\frac{\Sigma q_1 p_w - \Sigma Q_1 P_w}{\Sigma q_0 p_w - \Sigma Q_0 P_w},$$

the ideal index described earlier, unless

$$\frac{Q_1}{q_1} = \frac{Q_0}{q_0} = \frac{Q_w}{q_w};$$

i.e., unless there have been no changes in the production

[6] Data on value added are available for industries alone, not for individual products. Indeed for an industry in which more than one product is manufactured the value added in the production of any one of the commodities is not theoretically determinable. There are certain materials, like fuel, which are used in the fabrication of all products; the cost of fuel cannot be charged against any particular product except on an arbitrary accounting basis.

[7] The aggregate output of each industry is treated here as a composite quantity, q, and the aggregate input as a composite quantity, Q.

coefficients. It will, however, constitute a closer approximation to the latter than

$$\frac{\Sigma q_1 p_w}{\Sigma q_0 p_w},$$

except in the rare case in which the errors involved in the assumption that the production coefficients are constant happen to be canceled by errors in the opposite direction arising from the use of selling price rather than value added per unit as the p coefficient.

It is impossible to determine accurately the direction, let alone the degree, of bias in our indexes of output for groups and for total manufacturing when these indexes are regarded as estimates of net physical output. For the bias is, so to speak, the net sum of the biases in the component indexes, of which we know little. It is conditioned also by the fact that value added as reported in the Census, which we have used in weighting indexes of individual industries, is not exactly proportionate to the ideal weight, the net value of output as defined above, though this shortcoming is probably not serious. If a guess may be hazarded, the group and total indexes are probably biased downward. It is hardly possible, however, that the various group indexes are all biased in the same degree. To some extent, therefore, group comparisons are distorted.

The import of the preceding discussion may be summarized briefly as follows. For individual industries we should have preferred to present two sets of indexes: one of gross physical output, to be used in a study of the individual industries; and one of net physical output, to be used to obtain composite indexes of net physical output for major industrial groups and for all manufacturing industries combined. However, the nature of our materials permitted us to compute only one comprehensive set of indexes for individual industries, and these only of gross output, although for a small number of industries we have been able to present rough indexes of net output. For major groups and for all manufacturing combined, we should have preferred to present indexes of net physical output. This too was impossible with the available data. Therefore we have followed what appeared to be the next best procedure: we have combined the indexes of gross physical output for individual industries, with value added as the weight, to measure the output of major groups and total manufacturing output. The resulting indexes, despite their shortcomings, are revelatory; although they are not precise measures of net output, they do trace the broad movements of net output for major groups and for manufacturing as a whole.

COMPUTATION OF THE INDEXES OF PHYSICAL OUTPUT

In combining the quantities of output of the different final products of an industry, and in expressing the aggregates as indexes, we used the Edgeworth formula:

$$\frac{\Sigma q_1 (p_0 + p_1)}{\Sigma q_0 (p_0 + p_1)}.$$

The symbol q stands for the quantity of each of the final products of the industry, and p for the corresponding unit value of products. The subscripts identify the year to which these relate.

We employed a mathematically identical formula in combining the indexes of individual industries to obtain the indexes for major manufacturing groups and for total manufacturing. In the construction of the group and total indexes we used the unit value added (value of products minus cost of materials and fuel, per unit of product) rather than the unit value of the products, as the p coefficient.

Our comparison-base periods were 1909 for the 1899 and 1904 indexes, 1919 for the 1909 and 1914 indexes, and 1929 for the remaining indexes. It follows, from the formula chosen, that the weight-base periods were the average of 1909 and 1899 for the 1899 index, the average of 1909 and 1904 for the 1904 index, and so on. We obtained continuous indexes for the entire period 1899–1937 on the 1929 comparison base by splicing the indexes on the 1909 and 1919 bases to those on the 1929 base. In addition, we computed a special set of indexes in which 1899 and 1937 were compared directly. This procedure was designed to check the comparison of these two years made indirectly via the spliced indexes.[8]

The three comparison-base periods, 1909, 1919 and 1929, were selected for two reasons. First, the use of several such periods made it possible for us to utilize the Census data, which tend to become more detailed with each succeeding Census, more effectively than if one period alone had been used. Second, many of our comparisons relate to 1899–1909, 1909–19, 1919–29 and 1929–37. We thought it desirable to construct our indexes in such a manner as to make the average of 1899 and 1909 the weight-base period for the indexes underlying the 1899–1909 comparison, the average of 1909 and 1919 the weight-base period for the indexes underlying the 1909–19 comparison, and so forth.

Only rarely does the Census provide information on the physical quantities of all the products of an industry. The indexes, even for individual industries, were therefore based on samples. When these samples equaled or exceeded 40 percent (in terms of value) of the total output, the index built

[8] In algebraic language, we sought to determine how

$$\frac{\Sigma q_{37}(p_{37}+p_{29})}{\Sigma q_{29}(p_{37}+p_{29})} \times \frac{\Sigma q_{29}(p_{29}+p_{19})}{\Sigma q_{19}(p_{29}+p_{19})} \times \frac{\Sigma q_{19}(p_{19}+p_{09})}{\Sigma q_{09}(p_{19}+p_{09})} \times \frac{\Sigma q_{09}(p_{09}+p_{99})}{\Sigma q_{99}(p_{09}+p_{99})}$$

differs from

$$\frac{\Sigma q_{37}(p_{37}+p_{99})}{\Sigma q_{99}(p_{37}+p_{99})}.$$

(The number and character of the industries whose output is summated are identical for numerator and denominator of each fraction, but vary from one fraction to another.) These special indexes are referred to briefly in the chapters following. For a more extended discussion, see Appendix A.

up from them was considered representative, within a reasonable margin of error, of the output of the industry. Whenever possible we took a further step before accepting an index based on a 40 percent or even greater coverage: we applied the Mills "adequacy adjustment," [9] whereby a correction is attempted for any change that may have occurred in the sample's coverage of the products of the industry. This procedure is based upon the assumption that the average price of all the goods produced in an industry has moved in the same manner as the average price of the goods represented in the index. In the absence of detailed knowledge concerning the reasons for the change in coverage in each industry, such an adjustment seemed preferable to acceptance of the index as it stood. The adjustment has been justified empirically in tests made by us and described in Appendix A. A similar adjustment for changes in coverage was made in the construction of the indexes for groups of manufacturing industries and of the index for all manufacturing industries combined, since these also are based on samples.

SOME DEFICIENCIES OF THE DATA

The most serious deficiency of the data in the Census of Manufactures, the basic source of information on manufacturing production, arises from the fact that its records are available for Census years only: 1899, 1904, 1909, 1914, 1919, and then biennially through 1937. These years cover different phases of business cycles. Some coincide with peaks in general business, some with troughs; some are in expanding phases, some in contracting. The movements from one Census year to another therefore tend to lack consistency with respect to the cyclical phases they bridge, and to that extent are inadequate descriptions of the short-term movements in manufacturing

[9] F. C. Mills, *Economic Tendencies* (National Bureau of Economic Research, 1932), pp. 90, 92–93; and Appendix A, below.

production. Even if it is known that one Census year includes a peak in general business, and that another includes a trough, such knowledge cannot be applied to all individual industries; for this reason it is unjustifiable to draw inferences from the decline in output between these two years concerning the decline from the peak to the trough of a particular industry. For similar reasons, and also because annual data are much less satisfactory than monthly data as indicators of short-term changes,[10] this volume contains no conclusions drawn from these data in respect of cyclical movements in production. We devote our attention almost entirely to the longer-term trends in production, except for a brief discussion of the fluctuations in the annual index for all manufacturing industries combined. The latter index we obtained by interpolating our index for Census years by available annual indexes, which are based on much less comprehensive data. The trends are measured simply by comparisons of good or fairly good years in business activity, mostly ten years apart (1899 with 1909, 1909 with 1919, 1919 with 1929, and 1929 with 1937).[11] The decade trends may be checked by observation of the extent to which the changes between quinquennial and biennial dates confirm or render doubtful the conclusions based on the decade changes. Very long-term movements are more safely traced with the Census data. A good deal of our attention, therefore, is devoted to the net change between 1899 and 1937, a span of 38 years.

A lesser defect in data derived from the Census of Manufactures is attributable to changes in the number of industries covered. On the whole, this number has tended to decline. With the passing of time, the Bureau of the Census has dropped from its list of manufacturing industries several formerly included in it and still in existence. Thus, automo-

[10] See the forthcoming National Bureau report by W. C. Mitchell and A. F. Burns, *Methods of Measuring Cyclical Behavior,* Chapter 11.

[11] The years 1909, 1919 and 1929 were used as bases in the computation of the indexes partly in order to facilitate such comparison.

bile repairing, motion pictures, manufactured gas, and railroad repair shops are no longer considered manufacturing industries. On the other hand, some smaller industries were added to the Census of Manufactures after 1899, e.g., ice cream in 1914. Because of such changes we excluded all industries not covered in 1937,[12] the latest Census year for which data are available, a procedure which enhanced the comparability but not the coverage of the data. The more important doubts concerning the comprehensiveness of the measures presented here arise in connection with the omission of manufactured gas and railroad repair shops, motion pictures, illegal liquor production, and the farm production of processed foods.[13]

Another shortcoming of our indexes of physical output is attributable to lack of detail in the Census quantity data. Sometimes the quantities presented are for relatively heterogenous groups of products—"women's dresses," for example. With such heterogeneous groups, variation in the proportion of complex to simple or of expensive to cheap products within the group are perforce ignored. Since indexes constructed from these statistical materials would be subject to a bias of unknown magnitude, we have sought to avoid the use of excessively heterogeneous groups. The indexes computed for the more recent years are more satisfactory in this respect, because the later Census data are usually more detailed.

Our measures of physical output are subject to still another limitation—changes in the quality of products. The quantity units in the Census reports are the ordinary commercial units. Because of changes in the quality of products these units are not always stable in an economic sense. In some degree, therefore, statements concerning changes in the output of a given commodity are incomplete. Thus an index showing the

[12] Exceptions to this statement are poultry killing and rectified spirits.

[13] Some of these industries will be covered in a later volume dealing with nonmanufacturing output.

increase in the number of radios produced measures the change in only one physical characteristic of radio production: other relevant physical characteristics that remain unmeasured are size of cabinet, type of speaker, range of reception and ease of tuning. Even so-called standardized commodities are likely to change in quality. In our discussion of the indexes of physical output we note relevant quality changes that have come to our attention, although we are unable to take statistical account of them.

DIFFERENTIATION OF INDUSTRIES

Census Classification. The principle basic to the industrial classification used in the Census of Manufactures is formulated by the Bureau of the Census as follows:

> The production of each specific class of finished commodities, however small, might be looked upon as a separate industry; and in some cases certain of the distinct processes in the manufacture of a single commodity might be treated as distinct industries, as, indeed, is sometimes actually done in the Census reports. Manifestly, however, there must be some grouping of commodities and processes, not only in order to bring the number of industries within reasonable compass, but also in order to avoid the extensive overlapping which would result from an attempt to distinguish so large a number of industries. Each establishment must as a rule be treated as a unit and the data reported by it assigned in toto to some one industry. In many cases an establishment manufactures several related articles or commodities, or performs several related operations. The classification should, therefore, if practicable, be broad enough to cover the entire activities of such establishments.
>
> The effort has been made to distinguish, so far as practicable, each well-defined or well-recognized industry. The classification has been based on prevailing conditions as to the actual organization of industry and the distribution of the various

> branches of production among individual establishments. It has been necessary, however, in some cases to combine the data for two or more industries which are usually considered fairly distinct from one another, because of the considerable amount of overlapping among them. . . .[14]

The number of industries distinguished in the Census of Manufactures varies from one Census to another, giving rise to certain complications in the presentation of the data and disturbing the continuity of the industrial series. In order to skirt these difficulties we have followed, as far as possible, the 1929 classification in which 326 industries are differentiated. The classification of that year is one of the least detailed, so that the classifications in other years can readily be adapted to it through combination of subindustries.

Overlapping of Industries. Even after combining what are ordinarily considered to be two or more distinct industries, the Bureau of the Census has not been able to avoid overlapping. Many an establishment produces diverse commodities, some of which constitute the major products of one Census industry while others are classed as the major products of a different Census industry. Yet the firm may keep only one set of books, may transfer workers frequently from one task to another, may use its power plant to feed all machines in the establishment, and so forth. Such considerations make it difficult, if not impossible, to divide the output of an establishment into two categories; invariably the result is overlapping.

Examination of the detailed Census reports reveals that among the 242 industries for which data on degree of specialization were available for 1929, there were at least 16 in which the value of the primary product constituted less than 80 percent of the value of the industry's total output.[15] For example,

[14] U. S. Bureau of the Census, Fifteenth Census of the United States, *Manufactures: 1929* (Washington, 1933), Vol. I, pp. 3–4.

[15] See Appendix A, Table A–2. Because in many cases the Census gives information only for groups of related industries rather than for the individual

in 1929 the lumber-mill products industry devoted only about 61 percent of its energies (measured by value of output) to commodities classified as primary products of that industry: rough lumber, shingles and lath. It produced in addition such items as boxes, flooring, doors and molding, all of which are treated by the Census as primary products of other industries.

Again, the Census reports indicate that of a total of 224 industries, 29 produced in 1929 less than 80 percent of the country's output of the products in which they specialized. For example, the oleomargarine industry as defined by the Bureau of the Census produced in 1929 only 56 percent of all the oleomargarine made in the United States. Most of the remainder was made as a secondary product by establishments classified in the meat-packing industry.

Overlapping of this sort creates an obstacle to the differentiation of industries, especially if a fair degree of detail is desired in the classification. Thus we find in the Census classification several large industries, each with a number of satellites. Meat packing, for example, is closely associated with a group of specialist industries whose primary products are sausage, oleomargarine and shortenings. The relation among these industries may change; there may be a trend toward specialization, so that output in satellite industries will rise at the expense of the major industry. For this reason we cannot safely infer from the movements of output in a specialist industry what has happened to the total output of the product in which the industry specializes. This conclusion is a special and rather extreme development of the general rule that changes in the output of an industry do not measure precisely the changes in the total output of the product to which it is mainly, or even entirely, devoted.

Changes in the Classification. As we have already noted, the number of industries differentiated by the Bureau of the Cen-

---

industries themselves, the statistics quoted in the text understate the amount of overlapping among Census industries.

sus has varied from time to time. One reason for the variation is the growth of new industries. When a branch within an existing industry becomes large enough, the Census promotes it to independent status as a new industry. In consequence, parent industries appear to grow less rapidly than industries that do not propagate themselves in this way. Examples of new offshoot industries are rayon and gases, the former included in "chemicals, not elsewhere classified" prior to 1923, and the latter in the same category prior to 1927; radios, classified with electrical machinery prior to 1931; and mechanical refrigerators, classed with foundry and machine-shop products prior to 1927.

The decisions involved in an attempt to bring "the number of industries within reasonable compass"—and such decisions are necessarily arbitrary—affected not only the number of industries to be differentiated but also the size of each industry. Thus the knit goods industry was divided into four separate branches beginning with 1923; [16] instead of one large industry four relatively small industries were reported thereafter. The effect on size is important because in a sense a large industry is a group of industries and the behavior of its output may be an average behavior and consequently less extreme than the behavior of the output of any of its component branches.

Because of overlapping of industrial functions, the setting of an exact boundary between two industries likewise involves a more or less arbitrary decision. Reconsideration of, and changes in, these decisions by the Bureau of the Census lead to changes in the definition of the Census industries. Establishments devoted to a given product may be classified in a certain industry in one Census year and in another industry in the next Census year, and the continuity of the indexes of output of both industries may be disturbed thereby. Some-

[16] Prior to 1921, also, the group was subdivided into several branches, but these were not exactly comparable with the later divisions.

times this sort of discontinuity is minimized through the provision, by the Census, of two figures for each industry affected, one based on the old definition and one on the new. Often, however, such separate data are not given. The possible effects of these changes should not be disregarded altogether, although their importance is not always susceptible of exact measurement.

Despite the deficiencies inherent in the data, the statistical material assembled by the Census of Manufactures provides the basis for a reasonably trustworthy account of the course of manufacturing output during the period 1899–1937. Many of the difficulties encountered in the differentiation of individual industries do not arise at all when we confine our attention to major groups of industries. Still fewer appear when—as in the following chapter—we deal with the aggregate of all manufacturing industries.

Chapter 3

Changes in Total Manufacturing Output

CHANGES IN PHYSICAL OUTPUT, 1899–1937

According to the indexes presented in Table 1 and in Chart 1, the flow of output from the manufacturing plants of the United States increased 276 percent from 1899 to 1937. Expressed in terms of the change over yearly intervals, the rate of increase during the entire 38-year period, averaged over good years and bad, was 3.5 percent per annum.

Although these indexes show that manufacturing output was nearly four times as great in 1937 as it had been in 1899, they nevertheless understate the actual development of the product of manufacture because, as we have already noted, they do not encompass changes in the quality of the goods produced. Such information as is available concerning changes in quality indicates that improvements have been dominant. If the betterments in quality could be taken into account, the stream of manufactured goods would show a greater rate of increase than is indicated by the indexes presented here. It is probable, furthermore, that manufacturers have tended to require less materials, fuel and other purchased goods per unit of final product. Some manufacturing industries, indeed, have effected sensational reductions in wastage. If the index took account also of the enhanced efficiency in the use of materials, that is, if it were a precise index of the net physical output of manufacturing industries, as defined in Chapter 2, it would show a still greater rise in the contribution of manufacturing industries to the national product.

The average annual rise of 3.5 percent in total manufacturing output between 1899 and 1937 is a summary measure. Like all such measurements, it conceals highly significant variations. During the entire span of 38 years the course of manufacturing production was subject to striking changes of direction. According to the annual record in Table 1, there were actually nine intervals when manufacturing output declined absolutely. Only two of these declines appear to have exceeded

TABLE 1

ALL MANUFACTURING INDUSTRIES COMBINED

Indexes of Physical Output [a]

(1899:100)

Year	*Index*	*Year*	*Index*
1899	100	1919	222
1900	102	1920	242
1901	115	1921	194
1902	129	1922	249
1903	132	1923	280
1904	124	1924	266
1905	148	1925	298
1906	159	1926	316
1907	161	1927	317
1908	133	1928	332
1909	158	1929	364
1910	168	1930	311
1911	161	1931	262
1912	185	1932	197
1913	198	1933	228
1914	186	1934	252
1915	218	1935	301
1916	259	1936	353
1917	257	1937	376
1918	254		

[a] The indexes for Census years have been constructed from basic data in the U.S. Census of Manufactures and other sources, by methods described briefly in Chapter 2 and in detail in Appendix A. Appendix B presents these data, together with the indexes derived from them. The indexes have been adjusted to take account of changes in the coverage of the sample. Interpolations for intercensal years are based on annual indexes, less comprehensive in coverage, computed by F. C. Mills, *op. cit.*, p. 563; W. M. Persons, *Forecasting Business Cycles* (John Wiley, 1931), p. 171; W. W. Stewart, *American Economic Review* (March 1921); and the Board of Governors of the Federal Reserve System, *Federal Reserve Bulletin* (August 1940).

one calendar year in duration: the relatively mild drop between 1916 and 1919, and the severe recession beginning in 1929.[1] Some of the shorter declines were nevertheless sharp. The drop of 1907–08 brought output down almost to the level

Chart 1
ALL MANUFACTURING INDUSTRIES COMBINED
Indexes of Physical Output
(1899 : 100)

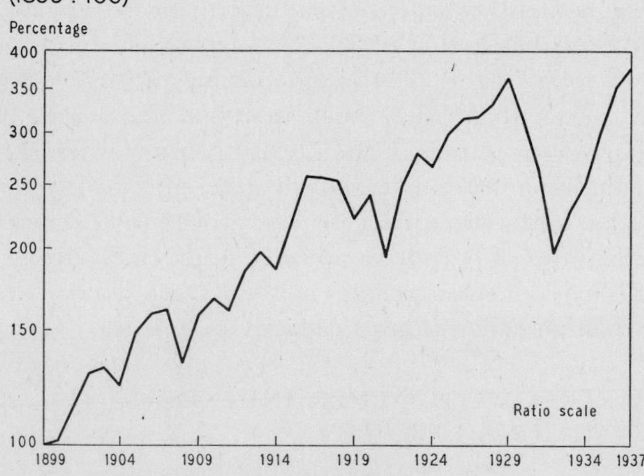

of 1903, and the slump of 1920–21 caused output to fall below that of 1913. Even in comparison with these sharp declines, the 1929–32 recession was extraordinarily severe. It depressed manufacturing output to a point as low as that reached in 1913 and 1921.[2]

The output of the peak year 1907 was barely surpassed in

[1] This conclusion is based on the annual data. Monthly series would probably show different results, as would also annual data representing fiscal rather than calendar years.

[2] The interpolated index is only roughly accurate for intercensal years, particularly with respect to cyclical movements. It is probable that the cyclical fluctuations revealed by the index are greater than would be shown by an index based on a broader sample than is now available for intercensal years. See the comparison, below, of the index constructed by the National Bureau with the old Federal Reserve index.

the following peak year, 1910, and was not exceeded substantially until 1912. The high point immediately following the 1916 peak came in 1920, but was nevertheless lower than that of 1916, a point which was not actually surpassed until 1923. In these two periods, therefore, the slump in the rate of growth of manufactures extended beyond the period of a business cycle. A similar prolongation of depression appears to have occurred in the most recent decade as well. According to available monthly indexes, manufacturing output in 1938 and 1939 was below that of 1937, a year which stands out as the peak following 1929, though output in 1937 was only slightly greater than it had been in 1929. There were, then, three fairly long periods in the present century when the rate of growth in manufacturing output suffered retardation. The retardation in the two earlier periods proved to be temporary, and the failure of output to advance appreciably from 1929 to 1937 may likewise reflect merely a temporary decline rather than an exhaustion of capacity to expand.

COMPARISON WITH OTHER INDEXES OF MANUFACTURING OUTPUT

The changes in manufacturing output outlined by the index presented in this volume differ from those revealed by other indexes. Our index records a more rapid long-term growth than do other indexes, and, contrary to most opinion on production trends, an increase between 1929 and 1937. Such divergences require some explanation.

We begin with an examination of the Day-Thomas index,[3] which, like the National Bureau index presented here, is based primarily on Census data; and follow with the index published monthly by the Board of Governors of the Federal Reserve System.[4] The Day-Thomas index and the index com-

[3] The product of extensive collaboration by W. M. Persons, E. E. Day, Woodlief Thomas and other statisticians. (See footnote a, Table 2.)

[4] Another important index is that computed by the National Research

puted for this study are compared in Table 2 and Chart 2; both have been placed on a common base, 1899. In addition the table and chart show the monthly Federal Reserve indexes, reduced to annual averages and based on the first year for which they are available, 1919, as well as our index for 1919–37, also based on 1919 as 100.

The National Bureau index reveals a distinctly more rapid rate of growth than does the Day-Thomas index. The latter rises 203 percent between 1899 and 1937, whereas our index increases by 276 percent. For 1937 our index is 25 percent higher, in relation to the 1899 base, than the Day-Thomas index. The two indexes run parallel to each other between 1899 and 1909, but then begin to diverge. From 1909 to 1937 our index rises by 140 percent, the Day-Thomas by only 90 percent. The latter appears to be more sensitive to most of the cyclical movements than the National Bureau index: it climbs less rapidly between 1909 and 1914, and more rapidly between 1914 and 1919; it falls and rises more precipitately between 1919 and 1923; between 1925 and 1927 it declines slightly, whereas our index moves upward; and between 1929 and 1933 it declines more sharply than our index. Between 1927 and 1929 and between 1933 and 1937, the Day-Thomas index rises less rapidly than the National Bureau index.

The dissimilarities between our index and the Day-Thomas index originate in many differences of construction and cov-

---

Project of the Work Projects Administration—see H. Magdoff, I. H. Siegel and M. B. Davis, *Production, Employment and Productivity in 59 Manufacturing Industries, 1919–36,* (Report No. S–1, 3 Parts, 1939). The NRP study was directed toward an analysis of changes in employment. Accordingly, the NRP index of "production" is a measure in which the weights used are man-hours of wage labor expended, rather than value of products or value added. Such weights are appropriate to the special purpose for which the index was designed, but the index so constructed is not an index of production in the ordinary sense. For this reason we do not compare our index of total manufacturing output with the NRP index for 59 industries. However, since most of the NRP indexes for individual industries are weighted in the usual manner, we have checked our indexes for individual industries against them. Outstanding differences are noted below in Appendix D.

erage. A complete explanation of these discrepancies would require a detailed comparison of each of the component series, of the weights used, and of the methods of combination. Comparisons of the indexes for the major groups and for some of the more important industries are made below, in Appendix D, but there has been no attempt to detect or to explain all the differences between the two indexes. It is probable, how-

TABLE 2

ALL MANUFACTURING INDUSTRIES COMBINED

Comparison of NBER Index of Physical Output with Indexes Prepared by Other Agencies

Year	*Day-Thomas Index*[a]	*NBER Index*[b]	*Federal Reserve Index*[c] Old	*Federal Reserve Index*[c] New	*NBER Index*[b]
	(1899:100)		*(1919:100)*[c]		
1899	100	100			
1904	122	124			
1909	159	158			
1914	170	186			
1919	214	222	100	100	100
1921	169	194	79	78	88
1923	263	280	120	120	126
1925	275	298	125	125	134
1927	274	317	126	132	143
1929	311	364	142	153	164
1931	206	262	95	103	118
1933	192	228	89	94	103
1935	233	301	107	121	136
1937	303	376	130	157	169

[a] This is the index computed for 1899–1914 by W. M. Persons and E. S. Coyle; for 1914–1925 by E. E. Day and Woodlief Thomas; for 1927–31 by Aryness Joy; for 1933–35 by V. S. Kolesnikoff; and for 1937 by C. L. Dedrick. See E. E. Day and Woodlief Thomas, *The Growth of Manufactures, 1899 to 1923* (Census Monograph VIII, Bureau of the Census, 1928), pp. 23, 34; V. S. Kolesnikoff, "Index of Manufacturing Production derived from Census Data, 1935," *Journal of the American Statistical Association* (Dec. 1937), pp. 713–14; and *Biennial Census of Manufactures: 1937*, Part I (Bureau of the Census, 1939), pp. 12, 17.

[b] Derived from Table 1.

[c] *Federal Reserve Bulletin* (July and August, 1940). The difference between the old and new indexes for 1921 is due entirely to the rounding of the figures, according to M. R. Conklin of the Board of Governors of the Federal Reserve System.

ever, that much of the divergence arises from the lack of identity in the number and character of the manufacturing industries whose output was included in the computations. Our index is based on the greater number: 53 for 1899–1909, 65

Chart 2
ALL MANUFACTURING INDUSTRIES COMBINED
Comparison of NBER Index of Physical Output with Indexes Prepared by Other Agencies
(1899 or 1919 : 100)

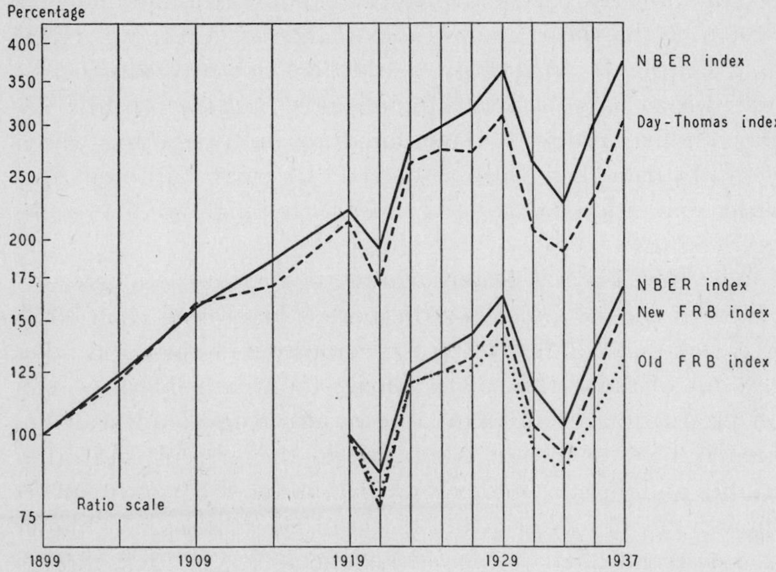

for 1909–19, 74 for 1919–29 and 132 for 1929–37, while the basis of the Day-Thomas index is 26 industries for 1899–1909, 27 for 1909–14, 28 for 1914–19 and 49 for 1919–35.[5] Furthermore, many of the industries which we include, but which the Day-Thomas index omits, are the new and rising industries, such as rayon and rayon goods.

[5] Combinations, such as butter, cheese and canned milk, are treated as one industry in these enumerations. Lists of the industries are given in Appendix D. No information is available concerning the number of industries covered by the Day-Thomas index in 1937.

The old Federal Reserve index, not revised until August 1940, parallels closely the Day-Thomas index for 1919–33, so that it too rises less rapidly than the National Bureau index. From 1919 to 1937 our index goes up 69 percent, as compared with 30 for the unrevised Federal Reserve index. From 1929 to 1933 the old Federal Reserve index moves downward similarly to ours, but rises less rapidly from 1933 to 1937. From 1929 to 1937 our index records a net gain of 3 percent, whereas the old Federal Reserve index drops 8 to 9 percent.

The unrevised Federal Reserve index is fundamentally similar to the Day-Thomas index. Like the latter, it is based on a sample of old industries and does not cover the newer ones which have been advancing more rapidly. Unlike the Day-Thomas index it is confined to industries for which monthly data have been collected currently, although this added limitation has not given rise to any marked divergence between the two.

The new Federal Reserve index is a rather extensive revision of the old index for the period beginning with 1923. It covers many industries not previously included, and takes account of the output of industries for which monthly data on production are not available by utilizing biennial or annual indexes of output computed in the present and other studies and monthly indexes of man-hours of employment. It shows a rate of increase from 1919 to 1937 substantially higher than that indicated by the old Federal Reserve index, though somewhat lower than the rate revealed by the National Bureau index. According to Table 2 the figures are 157, 130 and 169 respectively. From 1919 to 1923 the rise is of course the same as that shown by the old index, and lower than the rise as measured by our index. Between 1923 and 1929 the new index indicates an increase of 27 percent as against 18 percent in the old index and 30 percent in the National Bureau index. The greatest difference between the old and new Federal Reserve indexes is found for 1929–37, with percentage increases of −8.5 and +3 percent respectively. The latter figure is identical with that shown by our index.

During the course of the present study we worked out several different indexes in order to check the trend of manufacturing output indicated by the index in Table 1, which shows a rise of 276 percent from 1899 to 1937. In the alternative indexes, constructed by methods that differ in certain technical respects from the procedure followed in the preparation of the index in Table 1, the rises range from 238 percent to 318 percent for the period 1899–1937.[6] In view of the nature of the data and the length of the period covered, these differences are not large. Even the lowest figure obtained for 1937 is greater than the corresponding quantity shown by the Day-Thomas index. Moreover the test indexes are not all higher or lower than our standard figures; they are distributed around the latter.

COMPARISON OF GROWTH IN PHYSICAL OUTPUT WITH POPULATION GROWTH

The gain in manufacturing output in 1899–1937 becomes still more significant if the advance is measured not merely in absolute terms but in comparison with population growth. The population of the United States increased in each of the 38 years between 1899 and 1937.[7] Since manufacturing output did not rise at a similarly steady rate, but instead moved rapidly upward in some years and downward in others, it is apparent at once that it must at times have fallen below the advance in population. Most of these periods were of short duration, but three of them were fairly long. Thus the advance in manufacturing faltered between 1907 and 1911, between 1916

[6] For a detailed discussion of the several procedures see Appendix A.

[7] The estimates for 1899–1910 are by W. I. King (unpublished) ; for 1910–31 by W. S. Thompson and P. K. Whelpton, *Recent Social Trends* (McGraw-Hill, 1933) , Ch. 1, p. 3; and for 1930–37 by the Bureau of the Census, *Statistical Abstract of the United States, 1939,* p. 10.

and 1922 and between 1929 and 1937. During the last period, population rose 6 percent, whereas manufacturing output increased only 3 percent.

Over the period 1899–1937 taken as a whole, however, the rate of advance in manufacturing output was considerably more rapid than the rate of growth in population. Between the first year and the last the population of the United States increased from 75,000,000 to 129,000,000, or 73 percent. It grew, therefore, at an average annual rate of 1.4 percent. But manufacturing output gained 276 percent over these years, rising on the average 3.5 percent per annum—more than twice the rate of increase in population.

Although the record for the 38 years from 1899 to 1937 reveals a rise of 120 percent in manufacturing output per capita, it does not necessarily follow that there was an equivalent rise in the per capita consumption of finished processed goods, including not only consumers' goods but capital goods as well. As we explained in Chapter 2, our index of manufacturing output is constructed to reflect changes in the *net* output of manufacturing industries. It measures, in short, the changes in the value *added* to the materials consumed in manufacturing that are attributable to changes in the quantities of products and of materials consumed. In this index the output of each individual industry is evaluated by means of the value added per unit. The index does not measure changes in the aggregate quantity of *finished* goods, free of duplication and appraised in terms of the selling price of the final commodities issuing from the factory. It gives much more weight, for example, to a million dollars worth of finished automobiles than to a million dollars worth of meat products, because most of the value of the meat derives from the original value of the livestock slaughtered, whereas most of the value of the automobiles originates in the process of fabrication from relatively cheap iron ore and other products of nonmanufacturing industries.

Our index, then, measures the flow of finished manufactured goods not exactly but approximately. Furthermore, because manufacturing has moved toward increased fabrication of a given quantity of raw material, this index is probably biased upward as a measure of the output of finished goods.[8] In view of these qualifications, it is probable that the rise of 120 percent in the per capita net output of manufacturing industries from 1899 to 1937 overstates the gain in the per capita production of finished processed goods. An estimate of about 100 percent per capita would more closely approximate the increase in finished commodities turned out by our factories in that period, but this estimate is far from precise.[9]

One more reservation should be mentioned at this point: the undoubted rise in the per capita output of finished manufactures does not necessarily imply that the consumption of these goods increased at the same rate. One may infer such a parallelism only if changes in our foreign trade were slight or of negligible importance. Data available from 1913, and given in Table 3, indicate that exports and imports of manufactured goods fluctuated considerably in relation to the domestic production of manufactured goods.[10] The net excess of exports

[8] If the quantity of "fabrication" rises in relation to the quantity of input of raw materials, then the sum of these two quantities—the quantity of output of finished goods—will fall in relation to the quantity of fabrication.

The statement in the text that our index is biased upward as a measure of the output of finished processed goods is not inconsistent with the statement made earlier in this chapter that our index is biased downward as a measure of the net physical output of manufacturing industries.

[9] Figures compiled by W. H. Shaw of the National Bureau indicate that the physical volume of finished goods produced by manufacturing industries—including among finished goods not only consumers' goods but also capital equipment and construction materials—was approximately three and one-half times as great in 1937 as in 1899. Per capita, 1937 output of these goods was twice that of 1899. Mr. Shaw's figures will be published by the National Bureau in a forthcoming report.

[10] The indexes presented here cover semimanufactures as well as finished manufactures. Although the inclusion of semimanufactured goods among the imports is open to some question, the problem is of theoretical rather than of practical significance; the exclusion of semimanufactures would not seriously change either the index of imports or the conclusions drawn therefrom.

over imports rose more rapidly than domestic production between 1913 and 1929, and fell more rapidly between 1929 and 1937, a period when domestic production was rising slightly. Over the period 1913 to 1937, the excess of exports over imports declined in relation to domestic manufactures, and domestic consumption therefore rose more than domestic production. The difference between the trends was slight, however, for both exports and imports constituted relatively small fractions of domestic output and tended to balance each other. In 1914 the value of exports represented about 9 to 10 percent of the value of finished manufactured goods, and in 1929 the percentage was close to 8. The value of manufac-

TABLE 3

MANUFACTURED GOODS

Indexes of Physical Volume of Exports, Imports, and Exports minus Imports[a]

(1923–25:100)

Year	*Exports*	*Imports*	*Exports minus Imports*
1913	72	74	68
1919	124	[b]	[b]
1921	82	66	120
1923	94	98	85
1925	106	105	107
1927	120	112	137
1929	144	135	166
1931	86	93	71
1933	61	83	10
1935	79	103	23
1937	118	136	75

[a] Based on indexes of the U.S. Bureau of Foreign and Domestic Commerce, *Statistical Abstract* (1939), p. 472, and earlier issues of the *Abstract*. In the *Abstract* indexes are given individually for three groups: manufactured foodstuffs, semimanufactures and finished manufactures. These we combined by taking weighted arithmetic means of the individual indexes on the 1923–25 base. The weights were the average value of the exports or imports in the appropriate group in 1923–25 (*op. cit.*, pp. 474–75). The index of exports minus imports we computed by subtracting the weighted index of imports from the weighted index of exports, dividing by the difference between the weights, and multiplying by 100.

[b] Not available.

tured imports was below that of manufactured exports in these years. The difference, exports minus imports, was less than 3 percent of domestic production in 1914 and just about 3 percent in 1929.[11] Thus even considerable upward or downward relative trends in exports and imports would affect the relation between domestic production and domestic consumption only to a minor degree. We may conclude that the rise in the per capita production of finished manufactured goods, about 100 percent, was approximately equivalent to the rise in the per capita consumption of these goods.[12]

From the data thus far presented it is impossible to determine whether or not the gain in manufacturing output between 1899 and 1937 was at the expense of nonmanufacturing production. If manufacturing had simply robbed nonmanufacturing industry, the per capita increase in manufactured goods would represent nothing more than a change either in the character of the goods made available to each person or in the location of the productive process. Conceivably, it might be consistent not with an increase in the actual quantity of available goods but with a decline in that quantity: *total* output, including not only manufactures but also agricultural products, minerals, services of public utilities, construction, domestic services and so on, might have remained constant or even have dropped. We must admit that to some degree the increase in manufactures between 1899 and 1937 does appear to represent such a diversion of resources. Growth in agricultural output and in housewives' activities, for example, lagged behind population increase. These would seem to be the only important factors in the shift, though our information on nonmanufacturing production is too scanty at

[11] These figures are derived from computations by the Bureau of Foreign and Domestic Commerce, published in the *Statistical Abstract* (1938), pp. 435, 450–51.

[12] Although no indexes of the physical volume of exports and imports are available for years prior to 1913, data on their pecuniary volume in the earlier period indicate that this conclusion is valid for the entire period 1899–1937.

this time to warrant precise quantitative statement. Almost certainly, however, the greater part of the increase in manufacturing output reflects the expanding volume of our resources and the enhanced efficiency with which we have used them, and not merely the diversion to manufacturing of resources and energies formerly applied in other fields of industry and in the home. The rise in the per capita output of manufactures may be regarded, then, as a real addition to the volume of goods available to the average person.

Chapter 4

Trends in the Output of Major Groups of Manufacturing Industries

IN THE preceding chapter we were concerned with the aggregate output of American manufacturing industries and with the relationship of that rising volume to a population which also increased, but at a slower annual rate. In this chapter, which deals with the composition of the total volume of factory products, we shall trace the outstanding movements of the output of major groups of industries, and the shifts in production and consumption reflected in the altered makeup of the total.

CLASSIFICATION OF MANUFACTURING INDUSTRIES BY GROUPS

The Census of Manufactures distinguishes more than 300 manufacturing industries. These it classified in 1937 into 15 major groups according to three criteria: first, the primary material utilized in the industry, as in the case of the iron and steel products group; second, the process of manufacture, illustrated by the chemical products group; and third, the use made of the product, as in the case of the foods group. Since these three principles of classification are not mutually exclusive, the Census groups are subject to some degree of overlapping. Furthermore, no industry is placed in more than one group, so that the actual group classification presented in the Census involves some arbitrary decisions. Nevertheless, as it stands it is a valuable "general-purpose" arrangement and can easily be adapted to many specific uses.

The number and composition of the Census groups have varied from time to time. In an effort to keep the composition of each group constant throughout the period 1899–1937, we have shifted a few minor industries from the Census group in which they are now classified back to the group to which they had been allocated formerly. In addition, we have increased the number of groups from 15 to 17, promoting both beverages and tobacco products to group status by breaking down two of the original Census groups. The 17 groupings are listed in Table 4, which contains also brief notes concerning certain inclusions and exclusions.

The relative importance of each of the 17 groups is indicated in the table by its contribution to the total value added in 1923 by manufacturing industry as a whole.[1] Measured by this gauge, the most important group in 1923 was textiles, followed by machinery, and iron and steel products. These three groups, together, accounted for more than one third of the total value added by manufacturing industries in that year. It is well to remember, however, that a combination of iron and steel and nonferrous-metal products into a single group, metal products, or a breakdown of textile products into clothing and textile-mill products, or any one of a number of other changes in the classification would have altered the ranking substantially.

TRENDS IN THE PHYSICAL OUTPUT OF THE MAJOR GROUPS

The reader will note a number of gaps in the indexes for major groups (Table 5 and Chart 3). For two of them, machinery and miscellaneous products, the data were so fragmentary that no separate indexes could be constructed, and for four other groups the data covered only portions of the

[1] Percentages for other years are presented and discussed below.

TABLE 4

MAJOR GROUPS OF MANUFACTURING INDUSTRIES

With Measures of Importance in Terms of Value Added in 1923

Group	Value Added in 1923[a]	
	Millions of Dollars	Percentage of the Total
Foods Including related products, such as feeds, ice, and baking powder; excluding beverages	2,346	9.8
Beverages Including malt	151	0.6
Tobacco products	528	2.2
Textile products Including fur goods, artificial leather, linoleum, and oil cloth	3,829	15.9
Leather products	797	3.3
Rubber products	457	1.9
Paper products Including wood pulp	621	2.6
Printing and publishing Including allied activities, such as book-binding and engraving	1,532	6.4
Chemical products Excluding corn products, petroleum refining, turpentine and rosin, and other industries classified elsewhere	1,148	4.8
Petroleum and coal products Excluding manufactured gas	572	2.4
Stone, clay and glass products	1,050	4.4
Forest products Excluding wood pulp and wood distillation	1,888	7.8
Iron and steel products Excluding machinery and transportation equipment	2,659	11.1
Nonferrous-metal products Excluding machinery, transportation equipment, and aluminum	851	3.5
Machinery Excluding transportation equipment	2,939	12.2
Transportation equipment Excluding railroad repair shops	1,939	8.1
Miscellaneous products Chiefly musical instruments, brushes, professional and scientific instruments, mattresses, photographic supplies, and toys	724	3.0
ALL GROUPS	24,031	100.0

[a] Basic data on value added in all years are given in Appendix C.

TABLE 5

MAJOR GROUPS OF MANUFACTURING INDUSTRIES[a]

Physical Output: Indexes and Percentage Changes[b]

	Foods	*Beverages*[c]	*Tobacco Products*	*Textile Products*	*Leather Products*	*Rubber Products*	*Paper Products*	*Printing and Publishing*
YEAR	INDEX OF PHYSICAL OUTPUT (1929:100)[c]							
1899	30	43	30	38	64	..	18	17
1904	37	55	37	48	74	..	26	26
1909	45	63	43	60	83	..	37	36
1914	53	76	53	72	81	..	46	47
1919	65	23	69	67	90	54	53	54
1921	64	..	66	64	75	43	50	52
1923	80	..	74	82	95	72	70	73
1925	85	..	81	86	85	84	77	82
1927	90	..	90	94	97	92	89	90
1929	100	..	100	100	100	100	100	100
1931	91	..	93	87	80	70	86	84
1933	82	17	88	85	86	69	84	72
1935	92	70	101	99	100	79	102	87
1937	104	100	117	106	108	91	122	102
PERIOD	NET PERCENTAGE CHANGE IN PHYSICAL OUTPUT							
1899–1937	+244	+132	+293	+180	+69	..	+567	+494
1899–1909	+48	+46	+46	+60	+29	..	+100	+108
1909–1919	+45	–63	+60	+11	+9	..	+44	+52
1919–1929	+54	..	+44	+49	+11	+86	+89	+85
1929–1937	+4	..	+17	+6	+8	–9	+22	+2

[a] Groups for which there are no adequate quantity data for any period listed above are machinery and miscellaneous products. These groups are covered by the total.

[b] The indexes have been constructed from basic data in the U.S. Census of Manufactures and other sources, by methods described briefly in Chapter 2 and in detail in Appendix A. Appendix B presents these data, together with

period with which we are concerned.[2] We computed an index of output for an industry only if there were available quantity statistics for at least 40 percent of that industry's products (measured by value of products); and similarly we con-

[2] Because of the inadequacy of data for most groups, no attempt was made to interpolate annual indexes of production between the indexes for Census years.

	Chemical Products	Petroleum and Coal Products	Stone, Clay and Glass Products	Forest Products	Iron and Steel Products	Non-Ferrous Metal Products	Transportation Equipment	Total Manufacturing
YEAR		INDEX OF PHYSICAL OUTPUT (1929:100)[c]						
1899	19	8.7	..	82	21	..	7.3	28
1904	23	10.2	..	76	29	..	7.5	34
1909	31	16	..	83	44	..	10.7	43
1914	42	21	..	82	48	..	20	51
1919	52	39	..	79	59	..	61	61
1921	42	41	..	83	46	..	38	54
1923	64	64	..	91	84	..	76	77
1925	70	75	91	103	87	79	76	82
1927	83	83	100	99	87	84	68	87
1929	100	100	100	100	100	100	100	100
1931	87	84	67	63	54	64	46	72
1933	84	78	47	46	45	47	33	63
1935	101	92	69	59	61	66	72	83
1937	124	114	100	76	89	89	91	103
PERIOD		NET PERCENTAGE CHANGE IN PHYSICAL OUTPUT						
1899–1937	+566	+1206	..	−7	+327	..	+1142	+276
1899–1909	+69	+85	..	+1	+110	..	+47	+58
1909–1919	+64	+143	..	−5	+34	..	+468	+41
1919–1929	+94	+156	..	+27	+70	..	+64	+64
1929–1937	+24	+14	0	−24	−11	−11	−9	+3

the indexes derived from them. The indexes have been adjusted to take account of changes in the coverage of the respective samples.

The percentage changes are not always entirely consistent with the indexes given above because the changes were computed from the indexes in Appendix B, which are carried to one decimal place.

[c] The index for beverages is on the 1937 base.

structed an index for a group only if indexes were available for at least 40 percent of the industries in that group (measured by value added).

Foods, the first group in our list, augmented its physical output by about 50 percent in each of the first three decades of this century. Even in the troubled years from 1929 to 1937

Chart 3

MAJOR GROUPS OF MANUFACTURING INDUSTRIES

Indexes of Physical Output

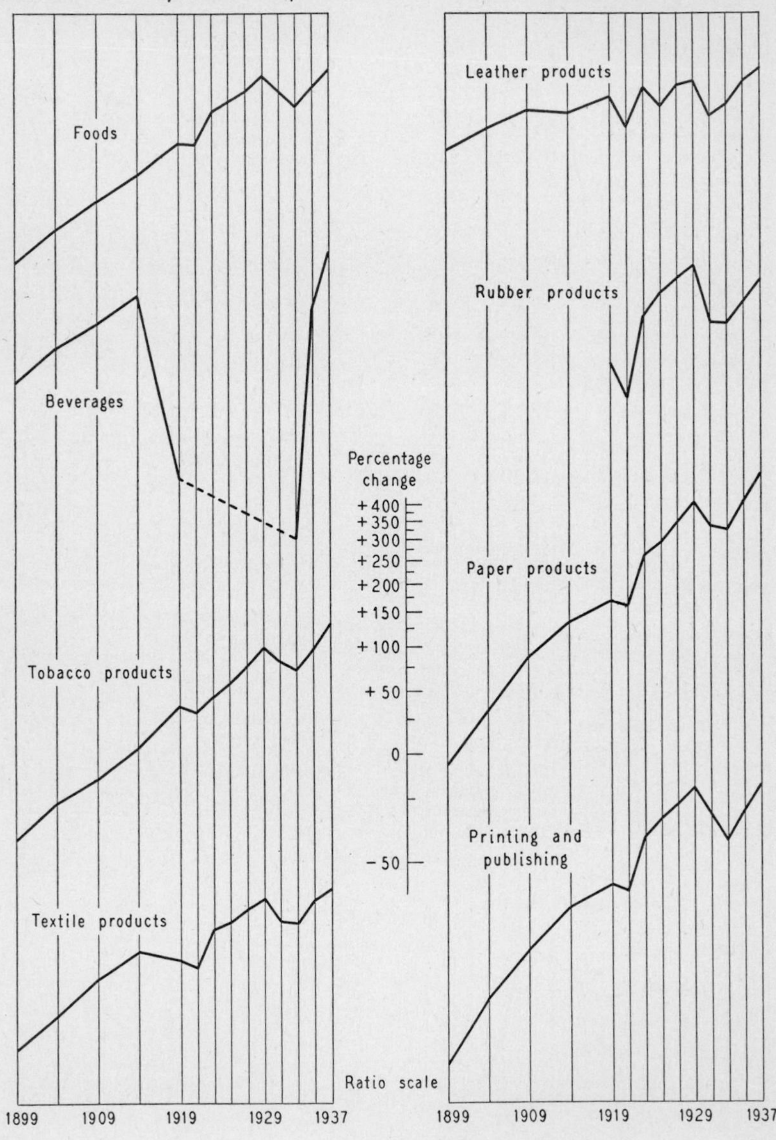

Chart 3 (concl.)

MAJOR GROUPS OF MANUFACTURING INDUSTRIES

Indexes of Physical Output

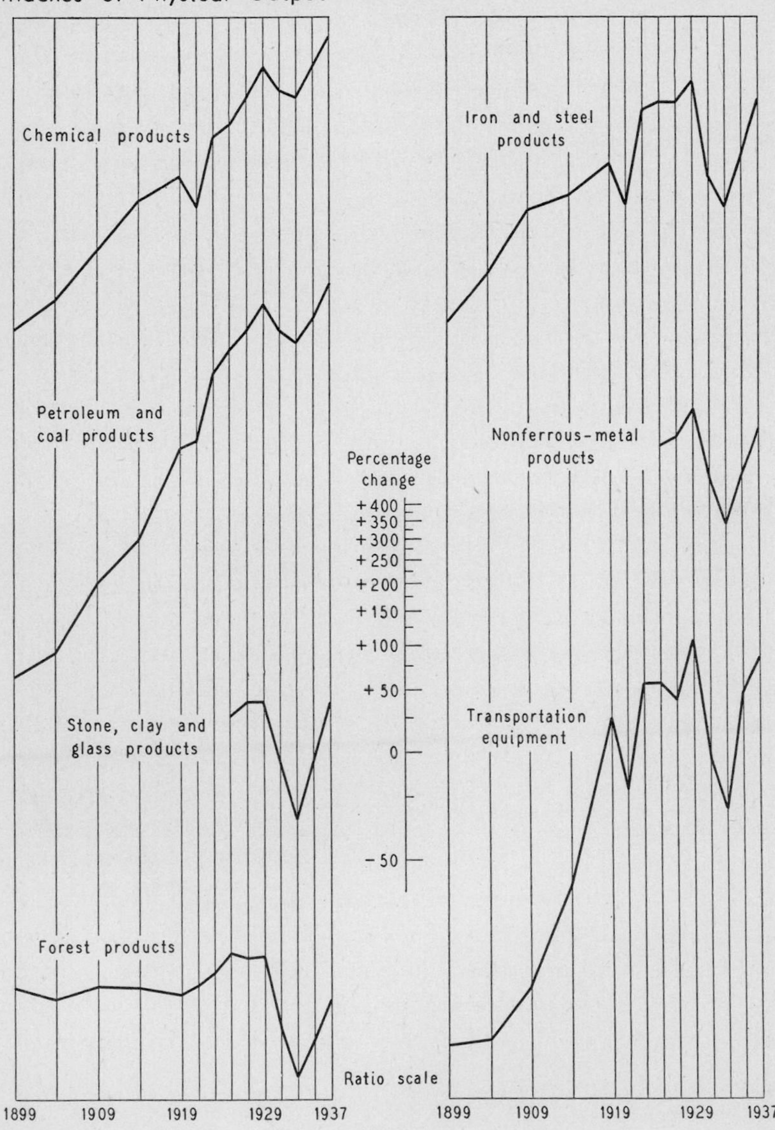

it attained a net increase of 4 percent. For the entire 38-year period the net rise in the factory production of foods reached almost 250 percent, not far short of the percentage gain in total manufacturing.[8] In relation to the population increase of 73 percent from 1899 to 1937, factory food production rose very considerably. This rise does not, however, represent an equivalent increase in the per capita consumption of processed foods. An important factor contributing to the growth in the output of the food manufacturing group was the shift to the factory of food processing formerly carried out on the farm, in retail establishments and in the home. Such shifts were especially pronounced in butter production, canning and preserving, and baking; to a lesser degree they occurred also in the preparation of meats.

The physical output of the *beverages* group rose in the first decade by almost one half, keeping pace with foods and not far behind total manufacturing. The rise continued from 1909 to 1914, but was then followed by a severe decline from 1914 to 1919. The legal production of beverages was greatly affected, of course, by the passage of the prohibition amendment and its subsequent repeal. For the period 1919–33 no adequate index for the group can be computed because quantity data for nonalcoholic beverages, the principal industry of the group in that period, are not available. There is hardly any question, however, that the level of output of the group was exceedingly low during these years. Beginning with 1933 output rose at a very rapid pace. The rise brought production in 1937 to a level one third above that of 1914, the previous high point, and 130 percent above that of 1899. The net rise from 1899 to 1937 fell far short of the corresponding increase in total manufacturing, although it was greater than the growth of population in the same period. It is difficult to draw any conclusion regarding actual per capita consumption

[8] Comparisons with changes indicated by the Day-Thomas indexes are presented in Appendix D.

from these data, since they exclude all illicit production of liquor. Aside from this fact, consumption does not necessarily equal production. Indeed in 1937 the fraction of output that was added to stocks for aging was rather large, much greater than the corresponding fraction in 1899. In other words, consumption was much smaller in relation to production in 1937 than was the case in 1899; therefore the rise in per capita production, in the years 1899 to 1937, was greater than the rise in per capita consumption.

The physical output of the *tobacco products* group rose by about one half in each of the first three decades. In the eight years following 1929 there was a gain of one sixth. The year 1937 found the factory production of tobacco products almost four times as great as it had been in 1899. This increase exceeded slightly the corresponding gains in total manufacturing and foods, and by a wide margin the rise in population. Over the entire period the per capita production of tobacco products more than doubled, although the quantity of tobacco consumed per capita increased by less than 50 percent. The disproportionately large increase in output is to be ascribed largely to a change in the smoking habits of the population. More highly processed tobacco products, especially cigarettes, acquired greater importance in tobacco diets. Factory production, which consists of the fabricational operations on the leaf, therefore rose more rapidly than the quantity of leaf tobacco used.

The *textile products* group, one of the most important of all manufacturing groups measured in terms of value added, made appreciable progress in the first and third decades of the four we are describing. In the last period also, the increase of 6 percent may be considered a fair advance. But the rise of 11 percent between 1909 and 1919 is exceedingly low as compared with the gain in total manufacturing. Even population rose more rapidly in this decade. The increase in textile production in the entire 38-year period, 180 percent, also was slight in relation to total manufacturing. Textile production per capita increased only about 60 percent, surprisingly little in view of the shift from home and custom tailoring to the factory production of clothing.

Leather products advanced even less than textile products. To be sure, the gain of 8 percent from 1929 to 1937 was exceptionally high for a slump period, but in the two preceding decades the output of leather products had risen less than population, and even in the first decade, 1899–1909, the increase (29 percent) had barely exceeded population growth (21 percent). The 38-year gain, 69 percent, fell short of population growth over the same period, and far below that of total manufacturing. The drop in leather exports was one of the factors in the lag in leather output, and it is probable that the decline of saddlery and harness manufacture, the substitution of other materials for leather, and the shift of fashion from high to low shoes contributed even more to the reduction in the per capita production of leather goods.

The *rubber products* group almost doubled its output between 1919 and 1929, the earliest period for which we have adequate data on the physical quantity of rubber products, and decreased it by one tenth in the eight years following. Such clues as we find in data on value added in rubber manufacture, on rubber imports, and on the output of important consumers of rubber products, notably the automobile industry, indicate that the rise between 1909 and 1919 must have been of huge proportions. It is very likely, indeed, that during the 38 years between 1899 and 1937 the rate of increase in rubber goods production was double the rate for total manufacturing, and greatly exceeded the rise in the output of other semidurable goods like textiles and leather products.

The output of the *paper products* group advanced rapidly in each of the four periods. In the first it doubled, and in the third it almost doubled. In the second decade the increase, while moderate, nevertheless exceeded the gain in total manufacturing. In the period between 1929 and 1937, when total manufacturing output rose only 3 percent, the paper group increased its production by more than 20 percent. In relation to population, the output of paper products almost quadrupled between 1899 and 1937. Much of this increase is attributable to the rise in printing and publishing, but other factors were the development of elaborate packaging of consumer goods, the shift from wood to paper in the manufacture of boxes and other containers, and the growing use of such articles as paper napkins and toilet paper.

The *printing and publishing* group also increased its output substantially. Except in the last period, when there was only a slight change, its growth paralleled closely that of paper products. In 1937 the output of the group was six times as large as it had been in 1899, an advance which must reflect in some degree the expansion of advertising during the 38 years.

The *chemicals* group raised its output by two thirds in both the first decade and the second, doubled it in the third, and increased it by a quarter in the last. The total gain from 1899 to 1937 was well over 500 percent. This rise was equivalent to the advance in paper products, considerably greater than the increase in total manufacturing, and very much greater than the growth in population. Most of the additions to the group's output are to be credited to two new industries, rayon and compressed and liquefied gases, to paints and varnishes, and to the collection of other industries whose importance is scarcely hinted at in the Census title "chemicals not elsewhere classified."

The output of the *petroleum and coal products* group rose at a phenomenal rate; it nearly doubled in the first decade, and more than doubled in each of the two following decades. Even in the period 1929–37 it increased 14 percent. In 1937 the group's output was 13 times as great as it had been in 1899. On the demand side this spectacular growth reflected primarily the development of the automobile; and on the supply side it resulted from important technological advances in the extraction of gasoline from crude petroleum.

The output of the *stone, clay and glass products* group, on which data are available only from 1925, rose 9 percent from 1925 to 1927, and stood at the 1927 level in 1929 and 1937. It is difficult to estimate the long-period growth in the group's output not alone because of the inadequacy of the data, but also because the group includes rapidly growing industries like cement, and declining industries like clay products (brick) and marble and granite. From the incomplete evidence it appears that the declines in the latter industries, resulting from shifts in the types of materials used in building, were more than counterbalanced by the growth in cement and glass products. It is not unreasonable to conclude, therefore, that the group's output rose somewhat less rapidly than total manufacturing, though perhaps not so slowly as population.

The *forest products* group is outstanding because its output not only lagged behind that of total manufacturing but actually was smaller in 1937 than it had been in 1899. It failed to advance appreciably during the first decade and declined slightly during the second. Beginning with 1919, there set in a rise which culminated by 1925 in an increase of one third. There was little change from 1925 to 1929, but from 1929 to 1937 output fell by one fourth; in the latter year it was 7 percent below the 1899 level. Undoubtedly the chief cause of the decline in forest products was the displacement of lumber by other materials. In construction, and to some extent in furniture manufacture, lumber was supplanted in large measure by metal and other products. These substitutions, in turn, were set in motion by the depletion of forest reserves, the rapid technological developments in such competitive products as steel and cement, and the growing demand for materials sturdy enough for use in large structures.

Iron and steel products, which rank high among the basic materials used by contemporary industry, more than doubled in output in the first ten years of the century, rose by one third in the second decade, and by two thirds in the post-war decade. From 1929 to 1937 the group's output declined by a tenth. The net increase between 1899 and 1937 surpassed substantially the corresponding rise in total manufacturing. In this entire period the dominant position of iron and steel remained unchallenged because the declines in industries using the products were offset by the emergence of new industries that required these fundamental materials.

For the *nonferrous-metal products* group adequate data are available beginning only with 1925. From that year to 1929 the output of the group rose by one fourth, and from 1929 to 1937 it declined 10 percent. For the period 1899–1937 as a whole the statistical materials for a rough estimate of the trend in the group's output are somewhat more adequate than in the case of stone, clay and glass products. The industries for which we have data on physical output—the three primary smelting and refining industries, copper, zinc and lead—increased their combined physical output by 200 percent during the 38 years. It is probable, however, that the products of the fabricational processes following upon the primary smelting and refining stage, and carried on by other industries in the group, grew more rapidly than the products of the primary process. The occurrence of this growth is indicated, though not measured exactly, by the decline in exports of primary metals and the increase in the output of secondary metals, and is revealed also by the data on value added. It is probable that the total output of the group rose more than 200 percent.

For *machinery* too our data are incomplete. The great number of machinery products, their vast complexity, and the rapid changes in their quality have made impossible the construction of an adequate index of output. If we may judge from rough estimates by W. H. Shaw, who deflated the value of machinery production by the few price series that could be obtained, the group increased its physical output about 30 percent more rapidly between 1899 and 1937 than did all manufacturing industries combined. Data on value added indicate a relative rise of 50 percent. According to estimates similarly derived, the machinery group rose by the same amount as total manufacturing from 1929 to 1937; that is, machinery output in 1937 was only slightly higher than it was in 1929. Though the precision of the figures quoted is open to question, there can be little doubt that the output of the machinery industries increased, from 1899 to 1937, more rapidly than the output of most other manufacturing groups, and that output in 1937 was relatively as high as it had been in 1929.

The output of *transportation equipment,* which includes automobiles, railroad equipment, ships and boats, and a few other industries, increased at a highly varying rate. In the first decade the rise was somewhat less than that in total manufacturing. In the following ten years, however, transportation equipment more than quintupled, whereas total manufacturing rose less than one half. Between 1919 and 1929 the group kept pace with the total; both increased by about two thirds. From 1929 to 1937, a period when total manufacturing was increasing slightly, there was a decline of almost 10 percent in the group's output. By 1937 the physical output of transportation equipment was more than 12 times as great as it had been in 1899.[4] The behavior of this group was determined

[4] It should be remembered that the indexes in Table 5 are chains of four links, 1899–1909, 1909–19, 1919–29 and 1929–37. If output in 1899 and in 1937 were compared directly, with the average of the two years as the weight-base (see Chapter 2), the percentage change in the output of transportation equipment between 1899 and 1937 thus derived would be +750 instead of +1,140 as Table 5 shows. The discrepancy is attributable to the extreme diversity, among the component industries, of trends in physical output and in value added per unit of physical output. No discrepancy of this magnitude appears when the index of any other group is computed by both methods. The differences are discussed in Appendix A.

primarily by the course of automobile production. Indeed, of the five transportation-equipment industries for which we have complete indexes, the automobile industry was the only one that showed a net increase in output from 1899 to 1937. Part of the great rise from 1914 to 1919 was due also to the war-time development of the shipbuilding industry; the decline in that industry and in railroad equipment served to moderate the gain in the output of the group in the post-war decade.

The substantial differences among the trends in the physical output of the major groups of manufacturing industries are shown in bold relief in Chart 4, where the indexes for the period 1899–1937 are started from a common point—1899. This view of the trends in the component elements of manufacturing output, restricted though it is to major groups, nevertheless shows wide variety. Yet, as we shall see in the next chapter, this amazing diversity does not even approach the divergence in the trends of individual industries.

In the most recent period, 1929–37, when the aggregate output of all manufacturing industries rose only 3 percent, the greatest percentage increase for any single group was attained by beverages as a result of the repeal of prohibition.[5] Chemical products came next, with a gain of about 25 percent, followed closely by paper products, with an increase of 22 percent. Tobacco products rose 17 percent, and petroleum and coal products 14 percent. Leather products, textile products, foods, and printing and publishing all gained between 2 and 8 percent. It is probable that machinery output increased slightly between 1929 and 1937.[6] The six remaining groups declined. Stone, clay and glass products were affected but slightly. More serious were the decreases of around one tenth in rubber products, iron and steel, nonferrous metals, and transportation equipment. Most severe was the drop in forest products:

[5] No exact figures are available.
[6] For this group, too, no exact figures can be given.

Chart 4

GROUPS OF MANUFACTURING INDUSTRIES

Indexes of Physical Output

(1899 : 100)

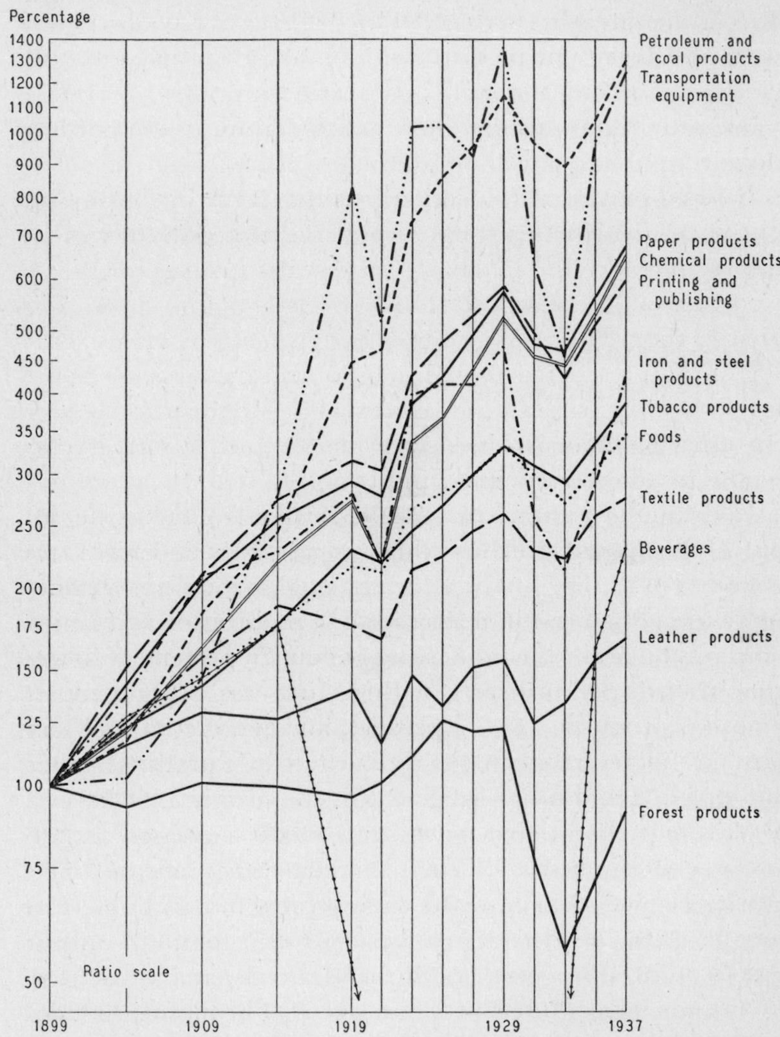

the output of this group fell by almost one fourth. With the exception of rubber products, all the industrial groups whose output declined from 1929 to 1937 were those engaged largely in the production of building materials and metal products. Most of the durable goods industries appear to have been the losers in this period; it is noteworthy, however, that machinery was not among them.

Forest products was the only major manufacturing group whose output was lower in 1937 than it had been in 1899. Only forest products and leather products lagged behind population growth in this long period; the rest exceeded it in varying degree.

CHANGES IN THE RELATIVE IMPORTANCE OF THE MAJOR MANUFACTURING GROUPS

The divergence of the trends in the output of the several groups of manufacturing industries resulted in profound changes in the pattern of output of all manufacturing industries combined. Declines in forest products and low rates of growth in leather products, on the one hand, and extremely high rates of increase in transportation equipment and petroleum products, on the other, meant that in the flow of goods from manufacturing plants in 1937 there was a larger representation of automobiles, gasoline and coke than there had been in 1899, and a smaller proportion of lumber, leather and shoes. The change is depicted graphically in Chart 5, which shows the indexes given in Table 5 expressed as percentages of the index of total manufacturing output. The relative changes thus brought out are presented in numerical form in Table 6. The relative movements in physical output may be checked by corresponding indexes derived for pecuniary output, as measured by value added. These also are cited in the chart, and in numerical form in Table 7. The measures of value added supply approximate information on the rela-

Chart 5

CHANGING PATTERN OF MANUFACTURING OUTPUT

Indexes of Physical Output and of Value Added for Major Groups Expressed as Percentages of the Corresponding Indexes for Total Manufacturing

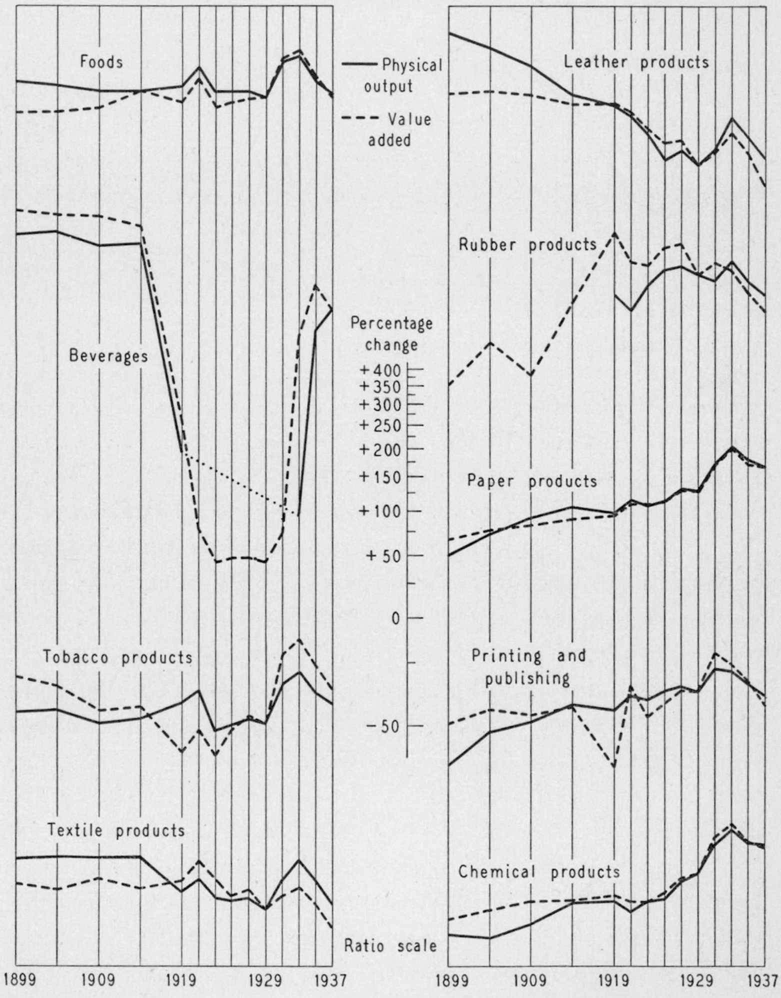

Chart 5 (concl.)

CHANGING PATTERN OF MANUFACTURING OUTPUT

Indexes of Physical Output and of Value Added for Major Groups Expressed as Percentages of the Corresponding Indexes for Total Manufacturing

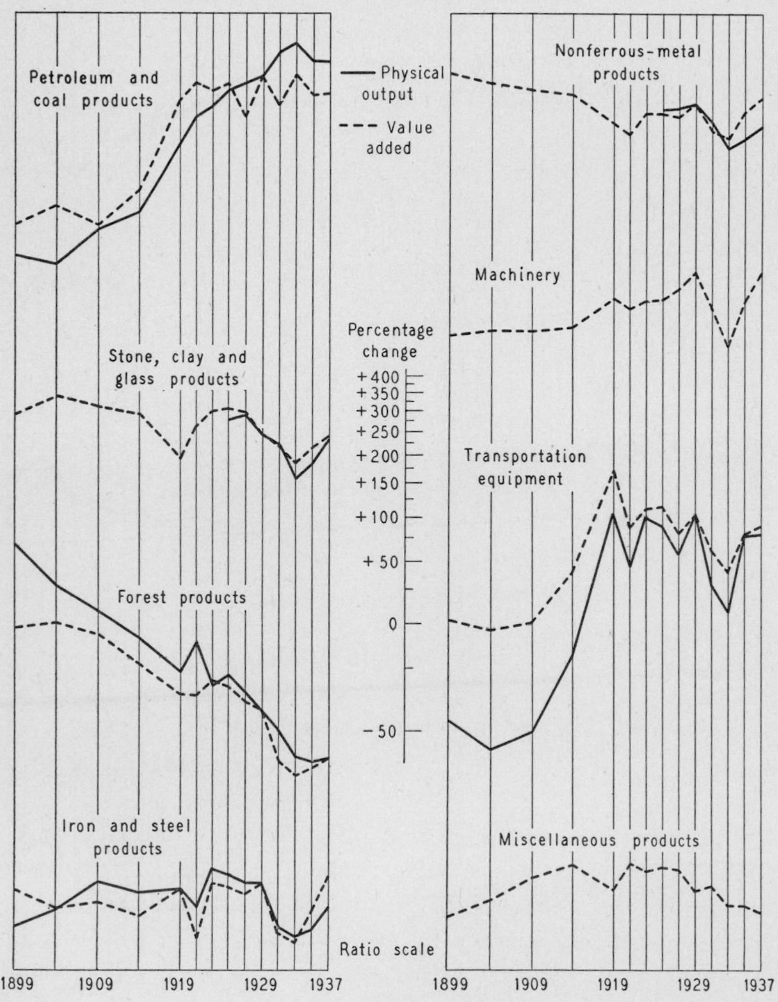

TABLE 6

CHANGES IN THE PATTERN OF MANUFACTURING OUTPUT

Indexes of Physical Output for Major Groups Expressed as Percentages of the Corresponding Index for Total Manufacturing[a]

	Foods	*Beverages*[b]	*Tobacco Products*	*Textile Products*	*Leather Products*	*Rubber Products*	*Paper Products*	*Printing and Publishing*
YEAR				INDEX (1929:100)[b]				
1899	110	162	108	138	233	..	66	62
1904	108	165	109	140	216	..	76	77
1909	104	151	100	139	191	..	85	82
1914	104	153	103	141	158	..	91	92
1919	107	39	114	110	148	88	87	88
1921	121	..	124	121	139	80	94	98
1923	104	..	96	107	123	94	91	95
1925	104	..	99	105	103	103	94	100
1927	104	..	103	107	111	106	102	104
1929	100	..	100	100	100	100	100	100
1931	126	..	129	120	111	96	120	117
1933	131	26	140	136	137	110	135	115
1935	112	88	122	120	120	96	123	105
1937	101	100	114	103	105	88	118	98
PERIOD				NET PERCENTAGE CHANGE[c]				
1899–1937	–8	–38	+5	–25	–55	..	+78	+58
1899–1909	–6	–7	–8	+1	–18	..	+27	+32
1909–1919	+3	–74	+14	–21	–23	..	+2	+8
1919–1929	–6	..	–12	–9	–32	+14	+16	+13
1929–1937	+1	..	+14	+3	+5	–12	+18	–2

[a] Derived from Table 5.
[b] For beverages the base is 1937.
[c] The percentage changes are not always entirely consistent with the indexes

tive growth of machinery and miscellaneous products, for which we have no precise measures of physical output, and also on the relative growth of the groups for which our indexes of physical output are incomplete.

The long-run relative trends in physical output and in the value added in the fabrication of that output are in close correspondence in respect of rank, as the table at the top of

	Chemical Products	Petroleum and Coal Products	Stone, Clay and Glass Products	Forest Products	Iron and Steel Products	Nonferrous Metal Products	Transportation Equipment
YEAR				INDEX (1929:100)[b]			
1899	68	32	..	298	76	..	26
1904	66	30	..	224	84	..	22
1909	72	37	..	191	101	..	25
1914	83	42	..	161	94	..	40
1919	84	64	..	129	97	..	100
1921	78	76	..	156	85	..	71
1923	84	83	..	118	110	..	98
1925	85	92	111	126	106	97	93
1927	95	96	114	114	100	97	78
1929	100	100	100	100	100	100	100
1931	121	117	94	88	76	89	64
1933	133	124	75	74	71	75	53
1935	122	111	83	72	74	80	87
1937	120	110	96	74	86	87	88
PERIOD			NET PERCENTAGE CHANGE[c]				
1899–1937	+77	+248	..	−75	+14	..	+231
1899–1909	+7	+17	..	−36	+33	..	−7
1909–1919	+17	+73	..	−33	−4	..	+304
1919–1929	+18	+56	..	−22	+4	..	0
1929–1937	+20	+10	−4	−26	−14	−13	−12

given above because the changes were computed from indexes carried to one decimal place.

page 80 shows.[7] Despite the absence of quantity indexes, this correspondence provides some ground for the supposition that the fraction of the aggregate of manufacturing output repre-

[7] The coefficient of rank correlation is +0.97.

The indexes of physical output are the indexes adjusted, on the basis of value added, for changes in the coverage of the samples. The adjustment did not result in a spurious correlation between physical output and value added. If we correlate the unadjusted indexes with value added, we obtain a coefficient only slightly less, +0.96.

TABLE 7

CHANGES IN THE PATTERN OF VALUE ADDED IN MANUFACTURING

Indexes of Value Added for Major Groups Expressed as Percentages of the Corresponding Index for Total Manufacturing[a]

	Foods	*Beverages*[b]	*Tobacco Products*	*Textile Products*	*Leather Products*	*Rubber Products*	*Paper Products*	*Printing and Publishing*	*Chemical Products*
YEAR				INDEX (1929:100)[b]					
1899	91	191	136	118	160	49	74	82	75
1904	91	184	126	113	162	65	78	89	79
1909	94	183	109	122	158	52	80	86	83
1914	105	172	112	114	149	84	84	90	84
1919	98	49	82	120	149	131	86	62	87
1921	113	24	96	136	140	109	93	104	84
1923	94	19	81	121	129	107	92	86	83
1925	98	20	97	108	116	120	94	94	88
1927	100	20	106	113	118	122	102	101	97
1929	100	19	100	100	100	100	100	100	100
1931	129	24	157	109	109	108	120	129	127
1933	136	84	174	115	124	103	134	120	138
1935	113	116	146	104	108	90	119	109	123
1937	100	100	125	89	89	79	118	94	118
PERIOD				NET PERCENTAGE CHANGE[c]					
1899–1937	+10	−48	−8	−24	−44	+61	+60	+14	+58
1899–1909	+3	−4	−20	+4	−1	+7	+9	+5	+11
1909–1919	+4	−73	−24	−2	−5	+150	+7	−28	+5
1919–1929	+3	−60	+21	−17	−33	−24	+17	+62	+14
1929–1937	0	+416	+25	−11	−11	−21	+18	−6	+18

[a] Derived from data collected in the U. S. Census of Manufactures. See Appendix C.

[b] For beverages the base is 1937.

sented by nonferrous-metal products [8] and by stone, clay and glass products declined; that the fraction represented by miscellaneous products remained approximately constant; and that the fraction represented by machinery and rubber products rose.

[8] Note, however, the preceding discussion, p. 69.

	Petroleum and Coal Products	Stone, Clay and Glass Products	Forest Products	Iron and Steel Products	Nonferrous-Metal Products	Machinery	Transportation Equipment	Miscellaneous Products
YEAR				INDEX (1929:100)[b]				
1899	38	115	172	96	122	67	50	85
1904	43	128	178	85	114	68	47	94
1909	38	120	164	89	109	68	50	109
1914	48	115	135	82	106	70	68	118
1919	85	86	111	96	89	85	132	101
1921	96	106	110	71	82	79	91	119
1923	91	117	122	101	94	83	103	114
1925	96	119	117	98	94	84	104	116
1927	78	116	106	94	92	90	88	115
1929	100	100	100	100	100	100	100	100
1931	83	94	72	72	84	80	79	103
1933	102	83	66	69	80	62	69	91
1935	89	92	68	85	95	81	87	91
1937	90	99	74	105	103	100	93	87
PERIOD				NET PERCENTAGE CHANGE[c]				
1899–1937	+133	−13	−57	+9	−15	+50	+85	+3
1899–1909	0	+5	−5	−8	−11	+2	−1	+28
1909–1919	+123	−28	−32	+8	−18	+25	+166	−7
1919–1929	+17	+16	−10	+4	+13	+18	−24	−1
1929–1937	−10	−1	−26	+5	+3	0	−7	−13

[c] The percentage changes are not always entirely consistent with the indexes given above because the changes were computed from indexes carried to one decimal place.

The dispersion in the two columns of the tabulation on page 80 is worth noting also. With three exceptions, the relative changes in value added are smaller, without regard to sign, than are the relative changes in physical output. This finding, together with the positive correlation, suggests that net pecuniary receipts rose less rapidly than physical output in

Group	Percentage Change in Relation to Total Manufacturing, 1899 to 1937 — Physical Output	Value Added
Forest products	−75	−57
Leather products	−55	−44
Beverages	−38	−48
Textile products	−25	−24
Nonferrous-metal products	..	−15
Stone, clay and glass products	..	−13
Foods	−8	+10
Tobacco products	+5	−8
Miscellaneous products	..	+3
Iron and steel products	+14	+9
Printing and publishing	+58	+14
Machinery	..	+50
Chemical products	+77	+58
Paper products	+78	+60
Rubber products	..	+61
Transportation equipment	+231	+85
Petroleum and coal products	+248	+133

the growing industrial groups; and fell less rapidly than physical output in the laggard groups.[9]

The relative contribution of any group to the aggregate physical output of manufacturing industries in a particular year may be expressed as a percentage of the total in that year. Such percentages describe the pattern of output in a given year, and changes in them measure changes in the pattern.[10] Comparison of these percentages (as in Table 8) is

[9] The implication is considered in greater detail in Chapter 5.

[10] See A. F. Burns, *Production Trends in the United States since 1870* (National Bureau of Economic Research, 1934), pp. 49–50. The various kinds of physical output are rendered commensurate by means of the unit value added. By physical output, therefore, we mean value added to output, at fixed prices. These fixed prices are the averages or sums (the result is the same) of the prices prevailing in the two years that are compared with each other; for this reason the percentage contribution to total output computed for an industry for a particular year depends on the other year with which it is compared.

In symbols, the physical output of an industry in any year, say 1919, comparable with any other year, say 1929, is

$$\Sigma q_{19} (p_{19} + p_{29}) \, .$$

The physical output of any group is the sum of the physical output of the component industries, and is indicated by the prefixing of another summation

Table 8

Relative Contributions of Major Groups of Manufacturing Industries to the Physical Output of All Manufacturing Industries Combined[a]

Group	Percentage Distribution, Comparable Pairs of Years									
	1899	1937	1899	1909	1909	1919	1919	1929	1929	1937
Foods	10.0	9.6	9.7	9.1	9.6	9.9	10.6	9.9	10.4	10.4
Tobacco products	3.5	3.6	3.5	3.2	2.3	2.6	2.6	2.3	2.8	3.2
Textile products	16.2	11.5	15.8	15.9	18.8	14.4	15.3	13.8	12.4	12.7
Leather products	4.6	2.1	4.6	3.7	4.6	3.6	3.8	2.6	2.4	2.5
Paper products	1.9	3.4	1.9	2.4	2.3	2.3	2.4	2.8	2.8	3.3
Printing and publishing	5.1	8.3	5.6	7.4	4.9	5.3	5.5	6.2	7.3	7.2
Chemical products	4.0	7.1	4.4	4.7	4.4	5.1	5.0	5.9	5.7	6.8
Petroleum and coal products	0.8	2.7	0.9	1.1	1.2	2.0	2.0	3.1	2.4	2.6
Forest products	16.4	4.2	14.0	9.0	10.5	7.1	7.6	5.9	6.4	4.7
Iron and steel products	10.0	11.5	8.7	11.6	10.4	9.9	10.4	10.8	11.9	10.3
Transportation equipment	3.4	8.0	4.1	3.8	2.9	11.9	9.3	9.3	8.1	7.1
Rubber products							2.0	2.3	1.7	1.5
Stone, clay and glass products									3.8	3.7
Nonferrous-metal products	18.6	24.3	20.4	22.1	22.0	24.3			4.1	3.6
Machinery							23.5	25.1		
Miscellaneous products									17.8	20.4
Beverages	5.5	3.7	6.5	6.0	6.1	1.6				
TOTAL[b]	100.0	100.0	100.0	100.0	100.0	100.0	100.0	100.0	100.0	100.0

Grouped values, bracketed in the original:

- 1899–1937, 1899–1909 and 1909 columns: Rubber products through Miscellaneous products.
- 1919 (1909–1919 pair) column: Rubber products through Miscellaneous products.
- 1919–1929 columns: Stone, clay and glass products through Beverages.
- 1929–1937 columns: Machinery through Beverages.

[a] Derived from Table 5. For an explanation of the derivation of the measurements see footnote 10 above.

[b] The columns do not add up to 100.0 in every instance because they contain rounded percentages.

in some respects more satisfactory than comparison of rates of growth, because the importance of each component is taken into account in the former procedure.[11] A moderate change in the relative contribution of an important group should, for some purposes, receive as much weight as a large change in the relative contribution of a small group, or possibly even more weight.

The arithmetic changes in the percentages between 1899 and 1937, given in Table 8, are ranked in order of magnitude in the tabulation on page 83. They are accompanied by the percentage changes in the percentages, given in the last column.[12] The latter summarize the sort of information that can be obtained from a comparison of rates of growth like that presented in Table 6.[13] According to Table 8, transportation

---

sign to the preceding expression. The 1919 physical output of an industry that is comparable with 1909 is

$$\Sigma q_{19}\,(p_{19} + p_{09})\,.$$

The percentage contribution of the industry in 1919, then, is

$$100 \cdot \frac{\Sigma q_{19}\,(p_{19} + p_{29})}{\Sigma\Sigma q_{19}\,(p_{19} + p_{29})},$$

which is comparable with similar percentages computed for 1929; or

$$100 \cdot \frac{\Sigma q_{19}\,(p_{19} + p_{09})}{\Sigma\Sigma q_{19}\,(p_{19} + p_{09})},$$

which is comparable with 1909.

[11] The importance of each component depends to some extent, however, on the classification. Thus beverages might be combined with foods into a single group called "foods, including beverages." The latter would then be more "important," in terms of value added, than either of the two now treated separately.

[12] Thus the relative contributions of transportation equipment in 1899 and 1937 are given in Table 8 as 3.4 and 8.0, respectively. The arithmetic change from 1899 to 1937 is $8.0 - 3.4 = +4.6$; the percentage change from 1899 to 1937 is

$$100\,\frac{8.0 - 3.4}{3.4} = +135.$$

[13] They differ from the percentages given in Table 6, slightly in most cases, and considerably in the case of transportation equipment. The 1899–1937 percentage changes given in Table 6 were derived from chains of four links: 1899–1909, 1909–1919, 1919–1929 and 1929–1937. The first two columns in Table 8 were derived from a direct comparison of 1899 and 1937. See footnote 4, above. For a more detailed explanation see Appendix A.

equipment achieved a larger increase than any other group: its output rose from 3.4 to 8.0 percent during the 38 years between 1899 and 1937. The printing and publishing group was second, with a rise of 3.2 points. The comparison of rates of

Group	*Change in Relative Contribution, 1899–1937* Arithmetic	Percentage
Transportation equipment	+4.6	+135
Printing and publishing	+3.2	+63
Chemical products	+3.1	+77
Petroleum and coal products	+1.9	+238
Paper products	+1.5	+79
Iron and steel products	+1.5	+15
Tobacco products	+0.1	+3
Foods	−0.4	−4
Beverages	−1.8	−33
Leather products	−2.5	−54
Textile products	−4.7	−29
Forest products	−12.2	−74

growth shows, however, that petroleum and coal products came first and transportation equipment second. Among the declines, the fall in the contribution of textile products, although slower than the drop in leather and beverages, appears to have had a greater effect upon the pattern of total manufacturing output than the declines in the two latter groups. The percentage contributions for 1899 and 1937 are shown in graphic form in Chart 6.[14]

A rough notion of the relative position of machinery and

[14] Comparison of the two 1909 columns, the two 1919 columns, and the two 1929 columns in Table 8 reveals that the values in the second column are higher than those in the first in as many as 17 instances. Of these, 11 are associated with declines in the percentages during the decade ending in the year to which the columns relate. For example, the second 1909 percentage for foods is 9.6, which is higher than the first 1909 percentage, 9.1; and this is associated with a decline during the decade 1899–1909. The values in the second column are lower in 15 instances, and 10 of these are associated with rises in the decade ending in the year to which the columns refer. These relations reflect a negative correlation between direction of movement of physical output and direction of movement of value added per unit. This finding is closely connected with the point made earlier concerning the less marked dispersion of relative changes in value added than of relative changes in physical output. The correlation is studied in a more direct manner in Chapter 5.

Chart 6

PATTERN OF PHYSICAL OUTPUT OF MANUFACTURING INDUSTRIES, IN TERMS OF MAJOR GROUPS

Percentage Distribution of Total Physical Output

1899 and 1937

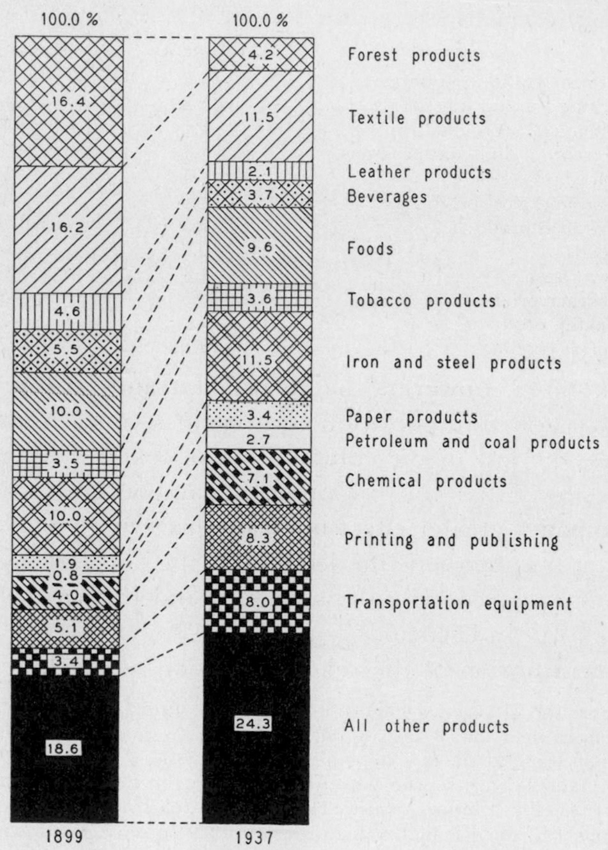

miscellaneous products in all years, and of beverages, rubber products, stone, clay and glass products, and nonferrous-metal products in those years for which physical quantities are lacking, may be obtained from data on value added (Table 9). The contributions to value added confirm, in broad outline, the movements noted for physical output. Among the largest declines in both sets of measures are those in forest products, textiles and beverages; and among the largest rises are the gains in transportation equipment and in chemical products.

The most interesting information to be found in Table 9 relates to the machinery group. According to the figures, the

TABLE 9

Relative Contributions of Major Groups of Manufacturing Industries to the Value Added by All Manufacturing Industries Combined[a]

Group	Percentage Distribution, Comparable Pair of Years							
	1899	1909	1909	1919	1919	1929	1929	1937
Foods	9.2	9.5	9.7	10.1	10.1	10.1	10.4	10.4
Beverages	6.3	6.1	6.1	1.6	1.6	0.6	0.6	3.3
Tobacco products	3.7	3.0	3.0	2.3	2.2	2.7	2.7	3.4
Textile products	15.5	16.1	16.0	15.8	15.9	13.2	13.2	11.8
Leather products	4.1	4.1	4.0	3.8	3.8	2.6	2.6	2.3
Rubber products	0.9	0.9	0.9	2.3	2.3	1.8	1.8	1.4
Paper products	2.0	2.2	2.2	2.4	2.4	2.8	2.8	3.3
Printing and publishing	6.2	6.5	6.5	4.7	4.6	7.4	7.4	7.0
Chemical products	4.3	4.8	4.8	5.0	5.0	5.8	5.8	6.8
Petroleum and coal products	1.0	1.0	1.0	2.2	2.2	2.6	2.6	2.3
Stone, clay and glass products	4.3	4.5	4.5	3.2	3.2	3.7	3.7	3.7
Forest products	11.2	10.6	10.6	7.2	7.1	6.4	6.4	4.7
Iron and steel products	10.4	9.6	9.7	10.5	10.4	10.8	10.8	11.3
Nonferrous-metal products	4.6	4.1	4.1	3.3	3.3	3.8	3.8	3.9
Machinery	10.0	10.2	10.0	12.5	12.6	14.9	14.9	14.8
Transportation equipment	4.0	3.9	3.9	10.3	10.4	7.9	7.9	7.3
Miscellaneous products	2.2	2.9	2.9	2.7	2.6	2.6	2.6	2.3
TOTAL[b]	100.0	100.0	100.0	100.0	100.0	100.0	100.0	100.0

[a] Basic data are given in Appendix C.

[b] The columns do not add up to 100.0 in every instance because they contain rounded percentages.

relative importance of the group rose in each of the first three decades and declined only minutely in the last period. Indeed, if we go beyond the table to the detailed data available for each Census year,[15] we find that the relative contribution of the machinery group rose in as many as 9 out of 13 pairs of contiguous Census years. The exceptions were 1904–09, when the contribution remained constant, and the cyclical recessions 1919–21, 1929–31 and 1931–33, when there were declines. There was a net rise, from 1899 to 1937, of close to five points, which was greater than the net rise between these two years in any other group. In terms of value added, machinery was definitely more important among our manufactures in 1937 than it had been in 1899; and the probabilities are that it was more important also in terms of physical output. In the advance of this group of industries we find one basic reason for the growth in total manufacturing and in the economy at large.

[15] Appendix C.

Chapter 5

Trends in the Output of Individual Manufacturing Industries

THE account of the changes in the aggregate output of the seventeen groups of manufacturing industries, presented in the preceding chapter, provides a broad outline of the course of manufacturing production in the 38 years from 1899 to 1937. But any group classification must necessarily gloss over the rich variety of trends, since each group is composed of industries that have grown more or less rapidly than the group aggregate. Indeed, few industries have advanced, even approximately, at the same rate as the group of which they are part. In many instances new industries have displaced their older competitors within the same group. Even industries engaged in successive stages of fabrication of the same materials have diverged. In the present chapter we treat first the more important changes that have occurred within each of the groups of manufacturing industries, and then cut across group lines to trace similarities and differences in trends of output for a number of industries which, though classified in separate groups, are related to one another.

A CONSPECTUS OF CHANGES IN OUTPUT, 1899–1937

In Table 10 the 61 individual industries for which we have indexes of physical output for the entire period are arranged in order of percentage change in physical output from 1899 to 1937. Here the divergence of individual industries is shown to have been greater than the variation from group to group brought out in Chapter 4. The group of industries classified under transportation equipment increased in output by more than 1,000 percent from 1899 to 1937, but this aggregate change included automobiles, which rose 180,000 percent, and at the other extreme, carriages and wagons, which declined 95 percent. Whereas the output of only one *group*, forest products, decreased absolutely over the long period, 11 out of the 61 individual *industries* for which we have indexes suffered actual declines in output.[1] These are found in the following groups: transportation equipment; textiles; stone, clay and glass products; foods; tobacco products; forest products; and miscellaneous products. There were only two groups—forest products and leather products—whose aggregate output increased less rapidly than population, but the growth of 24 out of the 61 individual industries for which we have complete indexes fell short of the population increase of 73 percent.

The table shows, moreover, certain interrelations among the trends of separate industries. The automobile industry stands at the top of the list and the carriage industry at the bottom. Automobiles are followed closely by petroleum refining. Paper and pulp are not far from each other. On the other hand the differences in the ranking of what might be expected to be closely related industries seem more striking, in some instances, than the similarities. For example, blast-furnace products and steel-mill products are rather far apart in the list.

[1] Some industries are not listed in Table 10 because the indexes for them do not cover the entire period 1899–1937. Among these, high points were reached in Census years prior to 1927 in the series for organs, motorcycles and bicycles, phonographs, charcoal, planing-mill products and lime. These industries, therefore, appear to have been declining in recent years. (The recent revival in bicycle output may indicate a change in the trend of that industry.) The high point in clay products occurred in 1927, and the decline from 1899 to 1937 may reflect the severity of the fall in building construction from 1927 to 1937, rather than a true secular decline.

TABLE 10

INDIVIDUAL MANUFACTURING INDUSTRIES[a]

Ranked According to Percentage Change in Physical Output, 1899–1937[b]

Industry	*Percentage Change*	*Industry*	*Percentage Change*
Automobiles	+180,100	Cotton goods	+101
Cigarettes	+4,226	Cane-sugar refining	+101
Petroleum refining	+1,920	Fish, canned	+96
Milk, canned	+1,810	Hats, wool-felt	+90
Beet sugar	+1,688	Shoes, leather	+87
Hosiery, knit	+1,202	Salt	+82
Cement	+838	Cane sugar, not elsewhere made	+67
Fruits and vegetables, canned	+792	Meat packing	+66
Chemicals, not elsewhere classified	+741	Cottonseed products	+63
Ice	+668	Leather	+61
Silk and rayon goods	+512	Woolen and worsted goods	+60
Pulp	+505	Liquors, malt	+60
Printing and publishing	+494	Underwear, knit	+52
Paper	+465	Carpet and rugs, wool	+52
Rice	+416	Lead	+51
Outerwear, knit	+393	Cordage and twine	+38
Paints and varnishes	+391	Hats, fur-felt	+26
Coke-oven products	+380	Gloves, leather	+16
Zinc	+318	Cigars	0
Liquors, distilled	+315	Pianos	−5
Steel-mill products	+313	Tobacco products, other	−6
Butter	+309	Flour	−8
Tanning and dye materials	+292	Clay products	−15
Copper	+272	Ships and boats	−17
Explosives	+267	Cars, railroad, not elsewhere made	−22
Wood-distillation products	+259	Lumber-mill products, not elsewhere classified	−32
Fertilizers	+248	Turpentine and rosin	−32
Blast-furnace products	+171	Linen goods	−44
Cheese	+158	Locomotives, not elsewhere made	−79
Jute goods	+134	Carriages, wagons and sleighs	−95
Wool shoddy	+116		

[a] The industry titles are short. Full titles appear in the index at the end of this volume.

[b] The indexes of physical output have been constructed from basic data in the U. S. Census of Manufactures and other sources, by methods described briefly in Chapter 2 and in detail in Appendix A. Appendix B presents these data, together with the indexes derived from them. The indexes have been adjusted to take account of changes in the coverage of the respective samples, except when such adjustment has been impossible.

CHANGES IN THE COMPOSITION OF THE MAJOR GROUPS OF INDUSTRIES [2]

Some of the component industries of the first major group, foods, are found among the first ten industries listed in Table 10; others are much farther down the list. Canned milk and canned fruits and vegetables, beet sugar and ice all augmented their output by more than 600 percent during the 38 years, whereas flour production dropped by 8 percent and meat packing and cane sugar increased less rapidly than population grew. Reflecting these diverse trends, the composition of manufactured food output changed markedly between 1899 and 1937. The major declines occurred in the relative importance of the flour and meat-packing industries. In 1899 flour and meat packing together contributed almost half of the physical output of the entire foods group; in 1937 their contribution was not quite one fifth. Canned fruits and vegetables, bakery products and dairy products were the chief gainers. An important factor in this shift in relative contributions to the group total was the change in the diet of the American people. Per capita consumption of grain products and meats declined, but consumption of fruits, dairy products and sugar rose. Another factor was the varying rate of shift from farm and domestic production to factory production. In some food industries, notably flour and cheese, the transfer of processing to the factory had been substantially completed by the opening of the twentieth century; for others, especially butter, baking, and canned fruits and vegetables, a large part of the growth must be ascribed to the substitution of factory for home and farm processing. Declines in the export of flour and meat products also contributed to the transformation in the group's output.

[2] This section is a brief summary of portions of Part Two, Chapters 6–22, to which the reader is referred for complete indexes and more detailed discussion.

In the beverage group the most important industry both in 1899 and in 1937 was malt liquors, including beer. Distilled liquors came second, and nonalcoholic beverages third, with minor industries in the group trailing after. During the postwar decade nonalcoholic beverages ranked first in importance as a result of the prohibition legislation. Although nonalcoholic beverages reverted to third place after the repeal of prohibition, the position of this industry, measured by its contribution to the group's value added, improved between 1914 and 1937, probably because of a change in drinking habits, and also of a shift from home-made to factory-bottled soft drinks. The increase in the output of distilled liquors from 1899 to 1937, over 300 percent, was much greater than the corresponding rise in malt liquors, only 60 percent. The marked variance results in large part from the consignment to warehouse stocks of a substantial proportion of the 1937 output of distilled liquors.

The several tobacco products show wide divergence of trends. The gain in the group's output between 1899 and 1937 is attributable entirely to cigarettes: this industry ranks second among the 61 manufacturing industries listed in order of percentage increase in output. Cigars remained almost constant while smoking and chewing tobacco actually declined. Cigarettes, the minor industry of 1899, accounted for four fifths of the output of the group in 1937.

The most important changes in the composition of the textile group's output, so far as we can tell from available data, occurred in the relative standing of cotton and woolen and worsted woven goods on the one hand, and silk and rayon woven goods and knit goods on the other. Hosiery and silk and rayon goods rose by more than 500 percent from 1899 to 1937. Cotton goods merely doubled in output, and woolen and worsted goods rose 60 percent. Knit underwear too made a poor record, but this was more than offset by the gains in the other knit goods divisions, and as a result the aggregate output of the entire knit goods industry increased 500 percent. Stated in other terms, the contribution of cotton goods to the physical output of the textile group fell from 22 percent in 1899 to 17 percent in 1937. Woolen and worsted goods, which contributed 14 percent in 1899, accounted for only 8 percent in 1937. The relative contribution of silk and rayon goods rose from 3 to 7 percent, and of knit goods, from 5 to 11 percent. There were mild increases also in the output of wool carpets and rugs, cordage and twine, and fur-felt hats. Since they were of minor importance, these industries had slight effect upon the general character of the group's output. No quantitative data on the physical output of the major clothing industries (other than knit goods) are available for the entire period. In terms of value added, men's clothing declined in relative importance (from 15 to 12 percent of the group total) between 1899 and 1937, and women's clothing rose sharply (from 10 to 16 percent of the total).

The modifications in the composition of the textile group's output are attributable in part to changes in the fibers utilized. The consumption of flax, hemp, jute and similar fibers actually declined; the amount of wool used rose, but less than did the total consumption of all fibers; cotton went up both absolutely and in relation to the total; silk, never an important fraction of the total quantity of fibers, increased at a very rapid rate; rayon, introduced in 1909, constituted 5 percent by weight of all fibers used in textile mills in 1937. Another significant cause of the change in the composition of textile production was the shift from home and retail fabrication to the factory. No figures measuring this shift are available, but it is probable that a large part of the rise in knit goods represented such a transfer, and that the increase in the factory production of women's and children's clothing is to be credited to it.

No especially important changes occurred in the composition of the output of the leather products group. It is noteworthy, however, that shoe output increased 87 percent from 1899 to 1937, whereas leather rose only 61 percent. One reason for the disparity was the decline in leather exports. Another was the relatively slow rise in other leather-consuming industries. Leather gloves rose only 16 percent from 1899 to 1937; and there was an actual decline in the output of the saddlery and harness industry, an important consumer of leather at the opening of the century.

None of the rubber products industries is listed in Table 10, since our indexes for this group do not go back to 1899. According to available figures, the increase in the output of rubber shoes was rather moderate from 1914 to 1937—only 39 percent. Tires and tubes rose at a very much faster rate; during these 23 years their output increased more than 500 percent. Other rubber products appear to have made substantial gains, though they fell short of the tremendous advance in tires and tubes. The growth in tires and tubes, attendant as it was upon the development of the automobile, quite transformed the output of the rubber group. In 1899 tires and tubes accounted for a very minor fraction of the group's production. In 1937, however, these products constituted over one half of the entire output of the group. The relative importance of the other industries naturally declined.

No radical changes occurred within the paper products group despite the fact that the two basic industries, pulp and paper, are not tied together very closely. A fair fraction of the wood pulp consumed in domestic paper mills is imported, and pulp itself constitutes less than two thirds of the materials consumed in paper mills, the remainder consisting of rags, old and waste paper, and straw. It is rather surprising, therefore, that the output of both pulp and paper rose from 1899 to 1937 by substantially similar amounts, 505 and 465 percent respectively.

The industries within the printing and publishing group also maintained a rather stable interrelationship. Book and job printing and publishing rose only slightly in relative importance, from 28 percent of the total in 1899 (in terms of value added), to 29 percent in 1937. Periodical printing and publishing fell from 57 to 56 percent. Although most of the subsidiary industries, like engraving and lithographing, kept their positions unchanged, photo-engraving increased its relative contribution from 1 to 4 percent.

Despite the very great gain in the aggregate output of the chemicals group, which far exceeded the rise in total manufacturing, most of the industries in the group failed to grow as rapidly as that total. However, these industries, which include cottonseed products, fertilizers, explosives, wood distillation products, and salt, among others, are the less important members of the group when measured in terms of value added. The large Census industries, "chemicals, not elsewhere classified," and paints and varnishes, gained 700 and 400 percent, respectively. Although rayon did not come into use until around 1909, it soon became one of the larger industries of the group, and by 1937 its output was 150 times that of 1914. Compressed and liquefied gases, and carbon black (an important material in rubber manufacture), also made very substantial gains. The pattern of production for the entire chemicals group clearly reflects this great divergence of trends. "Chemicals, not elsewhere classified," rayon, and gases contributed only 10 percent to the group's output in 1899, and as much as 42 percent in 1937.

In the petroleum and coal products group both the principal component industries rose, but the increase in petroleum refining, almost 2,000 percent from 1899 to 1937, exceeded by far the increase in coke-oven products, 380 percent. The more rapid growth of petroleum reflects, of course, the rising demand for gasoline and lubricants. As a consequence, petroleum refining raised its contribution to the group's output from less than half in 1899 to eight tenths in 1937.

The stone, clay and glass products group includes rapidly

growing industries like cement, which increased by more than 800 percent from 1899 to 1937, and glass, for which no exact figure can be given; and declining industries like marble and granite and clay products (brick). The output of the last industry fell by 15 percent in the 38-year period. Cement and glass increased their contributions to the group's output, as did several smaller industries, pulp goods, asbestos products and concrete products. On the other hand marble and granite, clay products, and pottery declined in relative importance: in 1899 these industries accounted for well over half the group's value added, but in 1937 for only one quarter.

The decreasing use of lumber as a building material (output fell 32 percent from 1899 to 1937), and the growing substitution of metal for wood in furniture, caused lumber to decline in relation to the total output of the forest products group. Lumber-mill products contributed three fifths of the group's value added in 1899 but only two fifths in 1937. The major part of the rise occurred in furniture.

Steel-mill products increased in physical output by more than 300 percent from 1899 to 1937. In contrast, blast-furnace products rose only 170 percent. This is a surprisingly wide difference, since iron, practically the only product of blast-furnaces, constitutes the essential material in steel manufacture. The principal cause of the divergence was the displacement of pig iron by iron and steel scrap, made possible by the development of the open-hearth process of steel manufacture. A contributing factor was the increased efficiency in the utilization of iron for steel production, and the decline in the fraction of total iron output absorbed by foundries.

Within the nonferrous-metal products group, too, the increased use of secondary or scrap metal helped to bring about a divergence of trends. The primary smelting and refining industries accounted for 36 percent of the group's value added in 1899 but for only 13 percent in 1937. The nonferrous-metal products industries using copper, lead and zinc rose in importance. Also contributing to the divergence was the decline in the percentage of domestically produced nonferrous metals exported to other countries. Although all three primary nonferrous-metal industries were subject to these influences, the rate of increase in their physical product nevertheless varied. Zinc and copper are in the upper half of the list in Table 10, whereas lead is in the lower half.

The machinery industries are not listed in Table 10. No adequate indexes of physical output are available for most of these industries, and for none do the indexes cover the entire period 1899–1937. The data on value added do, however, provide some information on changes in the composition of the group's output. The major decrease came in agricultural implements, which contributed one eighth of the group's value added in 1899, but less than one thirtieth in 1937. Sewing machines also declined in relative importance. The major increase occurred in the relative contribution of electrical machinery, which rose from 9.5 percent of the group's total value added to 25 percent. Pumps, business machinery and refrigerators likewise gained in relative importance. The largest machinery industry, foundry and machine-shop products, remained in the same position in the group over the long period.

The most striking divergence of trends is found in the transportation equipment group. We have already noted that automobiles head the list in Table 10, while carriages, wagons and sleighs are at the foot. The decline in railroad cars and locomotives, too, is closely bound up with the development of the motor car. It is interesting to trace the course of the displacement of carriages and railroad equipment by the automobile. According to the figures given in the tabulation on page 97, automobile production rose by 3,500 percent during the decade 1899–1909. It must be remembered that though this growth was immense, it started from a very low level. In 1899 the value added in automobile manufacture was $3,000,000, less than one tenth of one percent of the total value added in all manufacturing industries. In the manufacture of carriages, wagons and sleighs the value added in 1899 was $60,000,000; and in the fabrication of railroad cars and

	Percentage Change in Physical Output				
	1899–1937	1899–1909	1909–1919	1919–1929	1929–1937
Automobiles (incl. bodies and parts)	+180,100	+3,500	+1,467	+255	−10
Carriages, wagons and sleighs	−95	+1	−52	−84	−29
Cars, railroad, not elsewhere made	−22	−5	+50	−41	−7
Locomotives, not elsewhere made	−79	+7	+14	−69	−45

	Value Added as a Percentage of Value Added by All Manufacturing Industries				
	1899	1909	1919	1929	1937
Automobiles (incl. bodies and parts)	.06	1.47	4.88	6.66	5.86
Carriages, wagons and sleighs	1.31	.78	.16	.03	.02
Cars, railroad, not elsewhere made	.70	.61	.81	.35	.42
Locomotives, not elsewhere made	.33	.21	.36	.10	.13
TOTAL	2.40	3.07	6.21	7.14	6.43

locomotives $32,000,000 and $15,000,000, respectively. The 3,500 percent rise in automobile production during the decade left these competitor industries relatively untouched. The railroad equipment industries were not notably affected, and carriages and wagons simply stopped growing. In the next decade, although automobile production rose at a slower rate (the percentage increase from 1909 to 1919 was about 1,500) the rise started from a much higher point: in 1909 the value added in the automobile industry already constituted one and a half percent of the grand total, almost as much as the aggregate percentage of value added contributed by the carriage and railroad equipment industries together. Thus in 1909–19 the output of the carriage industry suffered a decline of 50 percent, while the output of the railroad equipment industries failed to grow.[3] During the third decade of the century automobile output rose 250 percent. Now the industry was full-grown and one of the most important in all manufacturing. In those ten years the output of carriages fell by 84 percent, of railroad cars by 41 percent, and of locomotives by 69 percent. The decline in the two latter industries is exaggerated somewhat because quality improvements are not taken into account; but no corrections for quality changes would seriously alter the basic relations among the trends in output. In the last period, 1929–37, the output of all four industries fell. The competitive interrelation was overshadowed by more general forces affecting the industries, yet the output of carriages fell 29 percent, while automobile production declined only 10 percent. The development of the automobile resulted not only in the displacement of the other types of transportation equipment, but also in the growth of the group aggregate. The group total rose also in relation to total manufacturing, as is indicated by the increase in value added by the four industries as a percentage of total value added: from 2.4 in 1899 to 6.4 in 1937.

Another important member of the transportation equipment group, ships and boats, passed through an extraordinary development during the war of 1914–18. Shipbuilding rose 650 percent from 1909 to 1919, but fell 82 percent from 1919 to 1929.

In the miscellaneous products group only one industry, pianos, appears in Table 10. The data on value added for the industries in this group show a large decline in the relative importance of all the musical instruments industries, and in

[3] The rise in the output of railroad equipment from 1909 to 1919 must be ascribed to the depression in the industry in 1909. See Chapter 21, footnote 14.

brooms and brushes, artificial flowers, feathers and plumes, and umbrellas and canes. The outstanding rises occurred in the manufacture of professional instruments used in surveying, navigation and industrial measurement and control; photographic supplies; signs; and toys and games.

INTERRELATIONS OF INDUSTRIAL TRENDS

The preceding discussion has provided abundant illustration of the diversity in the movements of output among individual manufacturing industries. This diversity, to be sure, is far from unexpected. Industries that compete with one another would naturally grow at diverse rates, and changes in income, tastes and fashion would accentuate the tendency toward differentiation. Even if demand were unchanged, modifications of the conditions of supply would affect competing industries in diverse degree. Differences in rates of advance in technology and in industrial organization, as well as variations in the drain upon natural resources, must inevitably result in uneven changes in cost, which in turn lead to differences in price trends and hence in output trends.

There are many examples of divergence in the trends of competing manufacturing industries. Since many of the major groups are composed of industries devoted to commodities satisfying the same or similar needs, a good deal of the divergence of trends within groups reflects shifts among competing commodities. Thus, rises in sugar, ice cream and cereal preparations have been at the expense of other food industries. Beet sugar increased many-fold, while cane sugar barely doubled. Nonalcoholic beverages rose more rapidly than population, but total alcoholic beverages barely kept pace with the gain in population. Cigarettes displaced cigars and other tobacco products. Fashion changes, in conjunction with differing rates of technological advance and the development of new fibers, were responsible for the rapidity of the growth in silk, rayon goods and knit goods as compared with the slower rise in output of cotton and woolen goods. The vinegar and cider industry declined because its products were displaced by the vinegar and cider produced as secondary products in the growing canned fruits and vegetables industry. A similar development probably lies behind the decline in the charcoal industry: there was an increase in the output of the wood-distillation products industry, and with it an increase in the output of by-product charcoal. Industries refining nonferrous metals from scrap increased more rapidly than those smelting ores. Phonographs tended to decline when radios increased. Cement production grew, but brick and stone production dropped off. Most spectacular, of course, was the divergence between automobile and carriage production.

Cutting across group lines, we find that leather rose relatively slowly as compared with various substitute textile products. Ice-boxes and manufactured ice declined during the last decade, whereas mechanical refrigerators grew at a rapid pace. Structural steel and cement increased at the expense of lumber, brick and stone. The output of phonographs, itself declining in relation to that of radios, nevertheless increased in relation to organs and pianos. Paper boxes displaced wooden boxes. Wood-distillation products rose, turpentine and rosin fell.

Divergence of trends is found not only among competitively related industries but among sequentially related industries as well. It is true that there is some similarity of trend among related industries in the latter group. Both malt and malt liquors fell together upon the enactment of prohibitive legislation and increased rapidly after its repeal. Shoe, glove and leather production all rose at moderate rates. Printing kept pace, approximately, with paper, and paper with pulp. Steel-mill products, blast-furnace products and coke-oven products are found together near the middle of the list in Table 10. Rayon production in chemical factories and the output of rayon goods in textile factories both rose at high rates. Carbon black and rubber products increased rapidly. Tin can production and food canning advanced together.

Nevertheless there is a noticeable degree of diversity in trend even among these closely related industries. Industries sequentially related have diverged in output because of changes in foreign trade; because of inventions and other improvements conducive to savings in materials; because of changes in domestic tasks brought about by higher standards of living; and because of shifts in the kind and quality of products made from given materials. The drop in the production of flour, attributable to a fall in exports, was not accompanied by a corresponding decline in domestic bakery output. The consistently slower rate of growth in blast-furnace products, as compared with steel-mill products, reflected the increasing use of scrap steel as a raw material in steel mills; the same influence is apparent in the diversity between the growth of the primary nonferrous-metal industries and the development of the industries using these metals. Rising incomes and the entry of women into industry caused the clothing and baking industries to increase in output more rapidly than the industries producing commodities such as cloth and flour. Further, sequentially related industries are not always tightly articulated. While blast-furnaces transfer three quarters of their product to steel mills, they also supply pig iron to foundries. Coke-oven products rose more rapidly than blast-furnace products because many of the increasingly important by-products of the coke process are not sold to blast furnaces.

Industries producing goods related complementarily to one another also tended to grow or decline together. Two outstanding examples are presented in the following tabulation:

	Value Added as a Percentage of Value Added in All Manufacturing Industries				
	1899	1909	1919	1929	1937
Automobiles and related industries					
Automobiles (incl. bodies and parts)	.06	1.47	4.88	6.66	5.86
Petroleum refining	.46	.47	1.65	2.02	1.90
Lubricants, not elsewhere made	.01	.01	.02	.10	.07
Tires and tubes, and other rubber products	.46	.68	2.05	1.57	1.29
Carriages and related industries					
Carriages, wagons and sleighs	1.31	.78	.16	.03	.02
Carriage and wagon materials	.26	.21	.05	.00	[a]
Saddlery, harness and whips	.33	.29	.14	.03	.02
Horse blankets	.01	.02	.01	.00	[a]

[a] No longer shown separately.

An expansion of petroleum refining, lubricants, and tires and tubes accompanied the growth of automobiles. Conversely, obsolescence of carriages, wagons and sleighs dragged down the related industries producing carriage materials, harness and horse blankets. Similar relations are found among other complementary industries. Cigars and cigar boxes both declined. Smoking tobacco and pipes fell together. The rise in printing and publishing stimulated such subsidiary industries as engraving, lithographing, stereotyping, and printers and engravers' materials. Shoes, shoe-cut stock, shoe findings and lasts moved together. Watches and watch cases fell in relative importance. Manufactured ice, ice-boxes, fresh meat and refrigerator cars all rose together; and in the recent period, with the advent of mechanical refrigeration, the first two industries both declined. As in the case of industries related sequentially, the rates of growth or decline in the output of industries complementarily related were not identical. Foreign trade and the manufacture of secondary products helped to cause the divergence. There was, however, another feature peculiar to this group of industries—a difference in durability of product. This difference may be illustrated by reference to automobile, tire, and gasoline production. These all made tremendous advances, but because of variation in their life spans the advances were not maintained at the same pace. Automobile tires do not last as long as automobiles, and gasoline, of course, is consumed at once. Thus the output of gasoline would be expected to change with the number of automobiles in use rather than with the number produced. Another factor making for change in the degree of divergence of these related industries was the increase in the length of life of some of the products. Automobiles now last longer and tires are much more durable. In addition, the changing economy of gasoline utilization has affected the degree of divergence in the rates of growth of these industries.

The rapid advance in total manufacturing output between 1899 and 1937 and the divergence of trends of the individual industries are not unrelated. We have already noted that a rise in total production brings about a reallocation of consumer purchasing power. Foods came to occupy a smaller place in the consumer's budget, while other commodities grew in importance. The housewife rid herself of domestic chores and factories increasingly took over these activities. The rise in total output and in population exerted pressure on natural resources, which vary in abundance. Technological progress helped to make possible the rise in the aggregate national product, but its effects were far from uniform in all industries. Finally, increased division of labor among industries, which also contributed to the rise in the total, necessarily caused divergence in the rates of growth. Thus "the very causes which have determined the rapid advance of general production in this country . . . have also determined the divergence in the trends of its separate industries." [4]

[4] A. F. Burns, *Production Trends in the United States since 1870* (National Bureau of Economic Research, 1934), p. 63. The causes of divergence are systematically discussed by Dr. Burns in Chapter 3, Sec. 1–2. Divergence in trends may be expected also in a retrogressive economy, as Dr. Burns points out. In this case, the forces determining the decline in general output would be those which also determine the divergence in trends, but the divergence would be different from that which characterizes a progressive economy.

THE RELATION BETWEEN GROWTH IN OUTPUT AND CHANGE IN THE PRICE OF FABRICATIONAL SERVICES

Divergence in the trends of physical output of American manufacturing industries was accompanied by divergence in the trends of pecuniary output, selling price, employment, wage rates, capital investment, and so on. It is safe to say that few of the industries that make up the manufacturing sector of our economy changed in any important characteristic at the same or approximately the same rate. In respect of each of these economic quantities the relations among them were subject to continued flux: patterns of production, employment and capital investment, and the structure of prices and wage rates did not remain rigid.

The likenesses and dissimilarities among these long-term changes require investigation. Since comprehensive and reliable data are lacking, an extensive study along these lines is a long and difficult task beyond the scope of the present survey. The relations between trends in physical output and in employment will be considered in a separate volume devoted entirely to them. In this volume it is possible only to point out rather briefly what we can learn from the indexes of physical output and from the Census data on value added concerning the relation between the trends in physical output on the one hand, and on the other, the trends in pecuniary output, particularly in the average pecuniary receipts per unit of output (the average price obtained for the services of fabrication).

Along with the changes in the industrial pattern of the physical output of manufacturing, described above, there were similar changes in the industrial pattern of the money received for the fabricational services involved in the making of the physical product—that is, the value added by manufacturing, which is equal to the value of products minus the cost of materials and fuels. This correspondence has already been shown for major groups of industries in Chapter 4. It may easily be illustrated also in terms of individual industries. Thus the automobile industry increased its physical output 1,800 times from 1899 to 1937, more than any other manufacturing industry for which data are available. The rise in the value added by the industry was considerably less, for it increased only 500 times, but this figure too surpasses the records of other industries. At the other extreme we find the industry producing carriages, wagons and sleighs; its physical output fell 95 percent from 1899 to 1937, and the value added by it dropped 90 percent—greater declines than have been observed in any other industry for which we have comparable information. Table 11 shows the same sort of correspondence between the two figures for other industries. It is because of this correspondence that we have felt justified in utilizing the data on value added, not only in the preceding discussion but also even more extensively in Part Two (below), to throw some light on the more pronounced changes in the physical output of those industries for which no adequate direct indexes of physical output can be computed.[5]

The relation between the indexes of output and those of value added is significant on still another count. A careful study of the changes in the pattern of physical output and in that of value added reveals that the changes in the former differ among themselves more widely than do the corresponding changes in value added. In particular, there is a tendency for

[5] The correlation between the ranks of the indexes of physical output and of value added is measured by a coefficient of +.84. The coefficient of correlation between the logarithms of the indexes is +.88. It is true, of course, that even if the correlation coefficients were equal to unity, there might be some risk of error if we inferred from the change in the value added by an industry what had happened to the physical output of that industry. Because the correlation is in fact imperfect, this is almost a certain risk. But while in a particular case an inference of the kind mentioned might well be wrong, it is probable that the number of such inferences that are right, within reasonable margins of error, considerably outweighs the number that are wrong.

TABLE 11

INDIVIDUAL MANUFACTURING INDUSTRIES

Indexes of Value Added, Physical Output, and Value Added per Unit of Physical Output, 1937 relative to 1899[a]

Industry	Index			Rank		
	Value Added	Physical Output	Value Added per Unit of Physical Output	Value Added	Physical Output	Value Added per Unit of Physical Output
	(1)	(2)	(1) ÷ (2) × 100			
Foods						
Meat packing	391	166	236	26½	32	9
Flour	183	92	200	41	43	16½
Rice	727	516	141	12½	13	30
Fish, canned	426	196	217	23	27	11
Fruits and vegetables, canned	1,020	892	114	6	5	40
Butter, cheese and canned milk	644	560	115	15	11	38½
Beet sugar	1,536	1,788	86	4	4	44
Cane sugar and cane-sugar refining	385	186	207	28	30	14
Ice	1,047	768	136	5	6	32½
Beverages						
Liquors, malt	314	160	196	35	35½	18
Liquors, distilled	92	415	22	48	17	50
Tobacco products						
Cigarettes and cigars	800	554	144	10	12	29
Tobacco products, other	122	94	130	46	42	34
Textile products						
Cotton goods	346	201	172	31	26	25
Woolen and worsted goods	324	160	202	34	35½	15
Silk and rayon goods	410	612	67	25	8	45
Knit goods	760	605	126	11	9	36
Carpets and rugs, wool	379	152	249	29	37	7
Cordage and twine	254	138	185	36	39	20½
Jute goods	517	234	221	18	25	10
Linen goods	144	56	256	45	48	6
Hats, fur-felt	227	126	180	38	40	23
Hats, wool-felt	467	190	246	22	28	8

Leather products						
Leather	236	161	147	37	34	28
Shoes, leather	391	187	209	26½	29	12
Gloves, leather	212	116	183	40	41	22
Paper products						
Paper and pulp	852	618	138	8	7	31
Printing and publishing	652	594	110	4	10	42
Chemicals						
Chemicals, not elsewhere classified, including rayon and compressed gases	2,713	2,600	104	2	2	43
Cottonseed products	340	163	208	32½	33	13
Wood-distillation products	592	359	165	16	22	26½
Explosives	500	367	136	20	21	32½
Fertilizers	418	348	120	24	23	37
Paints and varnishes	913	491	186	7	14	19
Salt	472	182	260	21	31	5
Tanning and dye materials	504	392	129	19	19	35
Petroleum and coal products						
Petroleum refining	2,319	2,020	115	3	3	38½
Coke-oven products	532	480	111	17	15	41
Forest products						
Lumber-mill products	180	68	267	42	46½	4
Turpentine and rosin	112	68	165	47	46½	26½
Iron and steel products						
Blast-furnace products	170	271	62	43	24	46
Steel-mill products	727	413	176	12½	18	24
Nonferrous-metal products						
Copper	164	372	44	44	20	47
Lead	63	151	41	49	38	48
Zinc	835	418	200	9	16	16½
Transportation equipment						
Automobiles, including bodies and parts	52,123	180,200	29	1	1	49
Carriages, wagons and sleighs	10.0	5.4	185	50	50	20½
Cars, railroad, not elsewhere made	340	78	434	32½	45	3
Locomotives, not elsewhere made	219	21	1,049	39	49	1
Ships and boats	366	83	440	30	44	2

[a] The indexes of value added are derived from data in the U.S. Census of Manufactures, given in detail in Appendix C.

The indexes of physical output have been constructed from basic data in the Census of Manufactures and other sources by methods described briefly in Chapter 2 and in detail in Appendix A. Appendix B presents the data on physical output together with the indexes derived from them. The indexes have been adjusted to take account of changes in the coverage of the respective samples, except when such adjustment was impossible.

Because the data on value added are available in some cases only for combinations, such as butter, cheese and canned milk, the number of separate indexes shown here is smaller than the number given in Table 10.

the change in the physical output of an industry to be further away from the average change in physical output than the change in the industry's value added is from the average change in value added. This divergence is well illustrated by the figures for automobiles and carriages. Value added rose less than physical output in the case of automobiles; it fell less than physical output in the case of carriages.[6]

The same finding may be expressed more significantly in terms of the relation between physical output and value added *per unit* of physical output (third column of Table 11). Greater-than-average rises in physical output were accompanied, more often than not, by less-than-average rises in value added per unit of output; and, correspondingly, less-than-average rises in physical output were accompanied, more often than not, by greater-than-average rises in value added per unit of physical product. For example, the large increase in the number of automobiles produced was accompanied by a relative decline in the amount of money received per automobile (after deduction of cost of materials).[7] And a concomitant of the drastic decline in the number of carriages, wagons and sleighs manufactured was a greater-than-average rise in the value added in the production of each carriage, wagon or sleigh. Other examples are to be noted in Table 11. Thus, the second largest rise in value added per unit is credited to lumber-mills, which declined in output 32 percent.

It is not invariably true, however, that an inverse relation exists between the rate of growth in output and the change

[6] The degree of variation about the mean for all the items in Table 11 may be measured by the standard deviation. The standard deviation of the value added relatives, after conversion to logarithms, is .51; of the physical output indexes, .62.

[7] It is important to remember that value added per unit is simply the selling price minus the cost of materials and fuel per unit of product. It is a pecuniary quantity, not the utility added to the raw materials. The physical unit—one auto—was a far more efficient machine and more valuable in that sense in 1937 than in 1899, although both its price and the value added per unit were much lower in 1937 than in 1899.

in value added per unit. Lead production rose only 51 percent, yet the value added per pound of lead fell drastically in relation to the average. Nevertheless, there appears to have been a definite tendency, over the long run, for an industry with a greater-than-average growth in physical output to have had a lower-than-average increase in value added per unit of output, and vice versa.[8]

Still closer examination of the relation between output and value added per unit shows up certain interesting details. Table 12 and Chart 7 bring together the complete series for

[8] If the indexes of physical output are correlated with value added per unit of physical output for the longest period, 1899–1937, a coefficient of rank correlation equal to —.66 is obtained.

There is, of course, a danger of spurious correlation between changes in physical output and changes in value added per unit of physical output. Thus if our estimate of the true index of output of an industry is too high, the derived estimate of value added per unit for that industry will be too low; if the estimate of output is too low, the derived estimate of value added per unit will be too high. It was impossible to avoid this danger entirely although every effort was made to compute accurate estimates of output. The probability of spurious correlation may be reduced by exclusion from the correlation of the industries with the more doubtful indexes of physical output. After such exclusion we obtained about the same degree of correlation as we had by using the entire sample.

The present finding is supported, further, by the statistical relation between output and value added per unit that can be derived from the regression lines obtained in the correlation, mentioned in footnote 5 above, of the logarithms of physical output and value added. (For a discussion of the meaning and the method of derivation of the regression lines see F. C. Mills, *Statistical Methods* [Henry Holt, 1938], pp. 359–66.) The two regression lines are:

$$\log y = a + .93 \log x, \text{ and}$$
$$\log y = A + .72 \log x,$$

in which y is the index of value added, x is the index of physical output, and a and A are constants which need not be specified in numerical form. These equations may be transformed into:

$$\log \left(\frac{y}{x}\right) = a - .07 \log x, \text{ and}$$

$$\log \left(\frac{y}{x}\right) = A - .28 \log x.$$

Since the coefficients of log x are both negative, $\log \left(\frac{y}{x}\right)$ and log x are related inversely in both equations. The relation thus obtained between output and value added per unit of output also is negative. Since it is not subject to spurious correlation it confirms the inverse relation found by direct correlation of output and value added per unit.

TABLE 12

SELECTED MANUFACTURING INDUSTRIES

Indexes of Physical Output and of Value Added per Unit of Physical Output[a] (1929:100)

Industry and Index	*1899*	*1904*	*1909*	*1914*	*1919*	*1921*	*1923*	*1925*	*1927*	*1929*	*1931*	*1933*	*1935*	*1937*
Rayon														
Physical output	..	..	..	2.0	6.7	12	28	40	60	100	138	201	253	310
Value added per unit	..	..	..	..	..	..	143	149	120	100	60	48	41	48
Radios[b]														
Physical output	..	..	..	..	..	..	2.6	33	28	69	51	52	74	100
Value added per unit	..	..	..	..	..	..	..	..	..	..	84	51	78	100
Refrigerators, mechanical														
Physical output	..	..	..	..	..	0.6	2.0	8.4	44	100	118	130	212	317
Value added per unit	..	..	..	..	..	..	..	..	138	100	78	46	42	44
Washing and ironing machines														
Physical output	..	..	..	..	..	..	..	..	73	100	79	92	132	146
Value added per unit	..	..	..	..	..	..	..	..	117	100	80	53	46	47
Automobiles, including bodies and parts														
Physical output	0.05	0.25	1.8	8.5	28	25	63	72	63	100	44	35	74	90
Value added per unit	200	320	328	162	202	154	116	121	116	100	108	92	76	84
Petroleum refining														
Physical output	5.9	7.2	11	17	34	40	56	73	81	100	91	86	99	119
Value added per unit	59	82	56	69	186	141	109	110	79	100	57	60	60	68
Beet sugar														
Physical output	6.7	23	45	68	67	96	68	100	84	100	107	151	111	120
Value added per unit	98	116	122	82	245	48	184	120	82	100	58	90	57	85
Milk, canned														
Physical output	7.2	10.9	18	36	84	69	73	76	88	100	100	98	115	128
Value added per unit	..	85	103	83	149	142	100	90	102	100	87	77	78	76
Ice														
Physical output	9.8	17	30	44	60	67	77	88	88	100	96	74	72	75
Value added per unit	62	62	62	57	91	93	90	95	96	100	96	88	81	85

Industry and Index	1899	1904	1909	1914	1919	1921	1923	1925	1927	1929	1931	1933	1935	1937
Fruits and vegetables, canned														
Physical output	17	24	29	42	55	38	67	82	82	100	91	88	127	151
Value added per unit	59	58	54	59	119	118	112	97	92	100	73	68	66	67
Paints and varnishes														
Physical output	22	28	38	41	52	45	67	76	87	100	69	62	87	109
Value added per unit	48	48	52	59	101	97	99	99	103	100	97	93	90	88
Flour														
Physical output	94	98	102	108	114	94	106	102	100	100	91	80	82	86
Value added per unit	41	50	59	60	116	103	80	89	92	100	79	87	87	81
Lumber-mill products, n.e.c.[c]														
Physical output	107	96	105	96	97	80	99	106	97	100	51	40	55	72
Value added per unit	31	44	51	50	107	74	107	92	86	100	65	65	72	84
Cars, railroad, n.e.m.[d]														
Physical output	119	122	114	154	171	96	229	139	101	100	31	..	30	93
Value added per unit	26	32	41	42	106	129	80	86	98	100	122	..	126	112
Carriages, wagons and sleighs														
Physical output	1,317	1,392	1,333	1,123	647	182	300	216	173	100	36	40	59	71
Value added per unit	52	54	54	56	70	82	78	70	64	100	114	92	83	96
Clay products														
Physical output	77	85	102	83	63	57	99	106	107	100	48	28	40	66
Value added per unit	..	..	..	52	106	104	109	104	97	100	87	74	85	91
Linen goods														
Physical output	137	..	200	192	86	72	125	117	120	100	68	72	73	77
Value added per unit	29	..	27	31	72	114	94	91	92	100	88	68	67	75

[a] The indexes of physical output have been constructed from basic data in the U. S. Census of Manufactures and other sources, by methods described briefly in Chapter 2 and in detail in Appendix A. Appendix B presents these data, together with the indexes derived from them. The indexes of physical output have been adjusted to take account of changes in the coverage of the respective samples, except when such adjustment was impossible.

The indexes of value added per unit have been derived from the Census data on value added, given in Appendix C, and the indexes of physical output, given in Appendix B.

[b] Base is 1937.

[c] Not elsewhere classified.

[d] Not elsewhere made.

Chart 7

SELECTED MANUFACTURING INDUSTRIES

Indexes of Physical Output and of Value Added per Unit of Physical Output Expressed as Percentages of the Corresponding Indexes for All Manufacturing Industries Combined

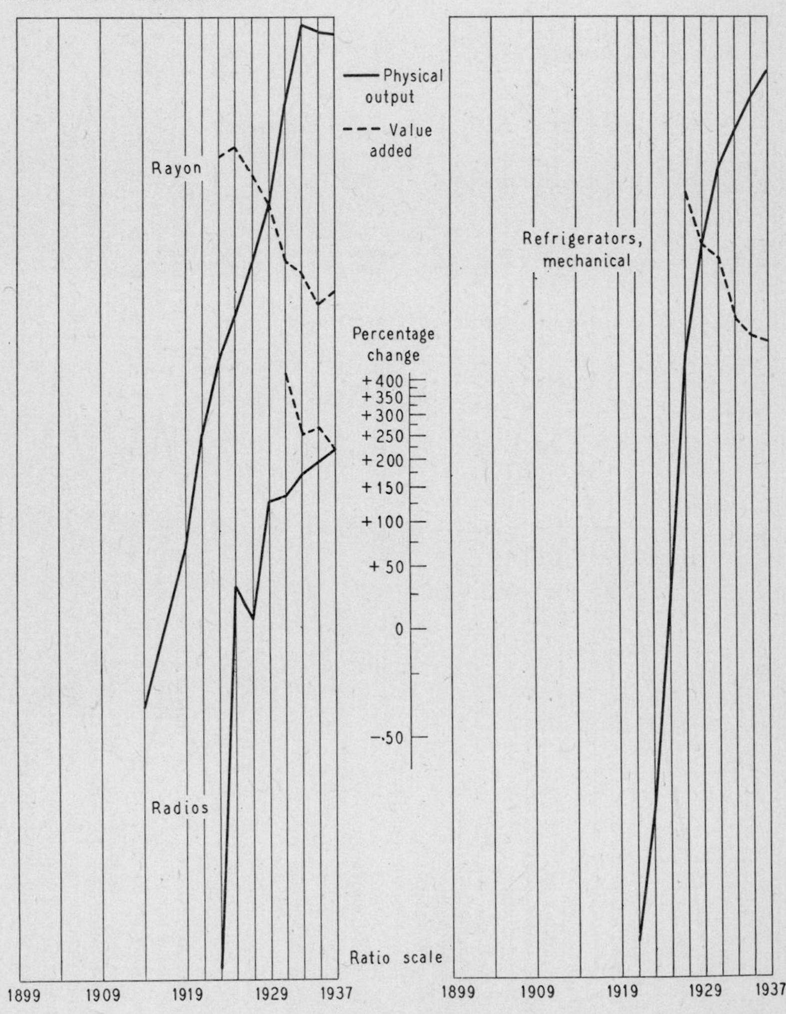

Chart 7 (cont.)

SELECTED MANUFACTURING INDUSTRIES

Indexes of Physical Output and of Value Added per Unit of Physical Output Expressed as Percentages of the Corresponding Indexes for All Manufacturing Industries Combined

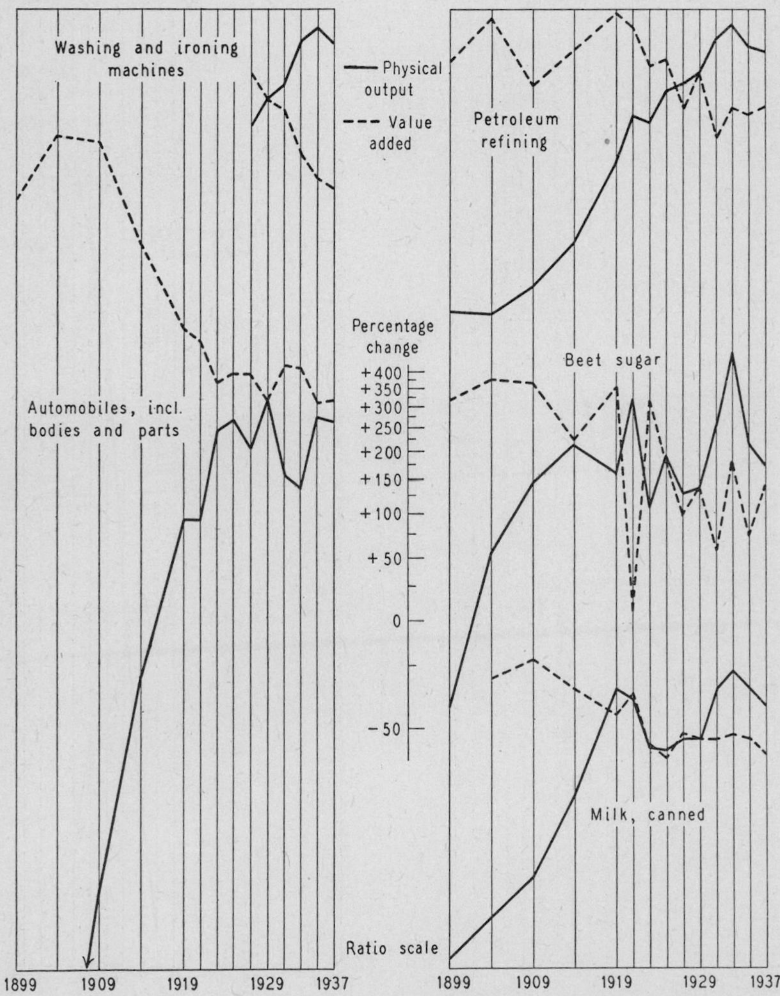

Chart 7 (cont.)

SELECTED MANUFACTURING INDUSTRIES

Indexes of Physical Output and of Value Added per Unit of Physical Output Expressed as Percentages of the Corresponding Indexes for All Manufacturing Industries Combined

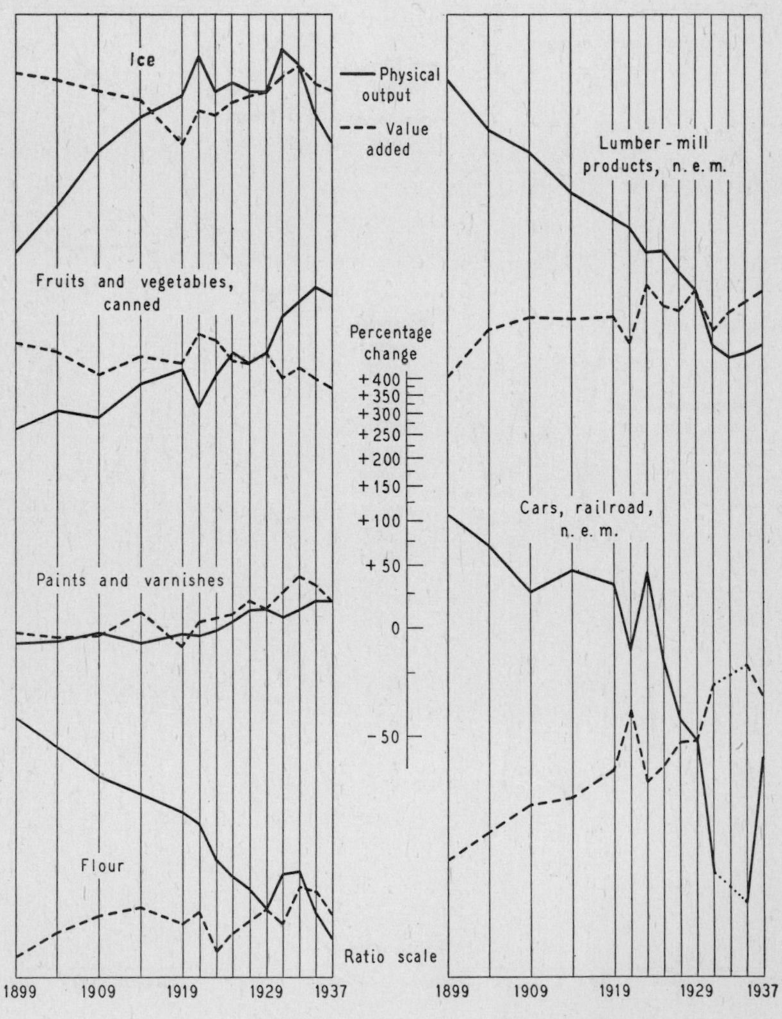

Chart 7 (concl.)

SELECTED MANUFACTURING INDUSTRIES

Indexes of Physical Output and of Value Added per Unit of Physical Output Expressed as Percentages of the Corresponding Indexes for All Manufacturing Industries Combined

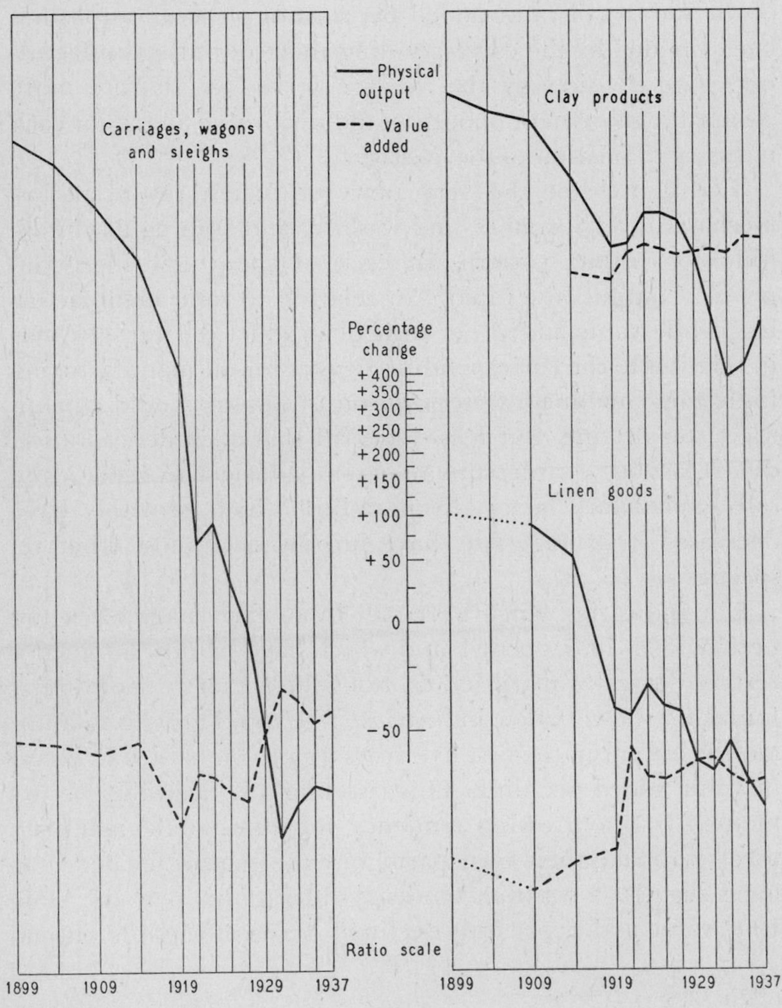

several industries. Included are some industries that came into existence after 1899 and are therefore not listed in Table 11. The selection consists of industries growing very rapidly, or very slowly, or actually declining. Each of the indexes of physical output in the chart has been divided by the corresponding index for all manufacturing combined, and similarly, each of the indexes of value added per unit of physical output has been divided by the corresponding index for all manufacturing. The division by the average serves to indicate more clearly the movement of output and unit value added for each industry in relation to the average.

The figures for the very new industries, rayon, radios, mechanical refrigerators, and washing and ironing machines, follow a distinct pattern. In each of these new industries physical output rose rapidly in relation to total manufacturing, while value added per unit of product fell rapidly, also in relation to the corresponding figures for all manufacturing industries combined. Deterioration of quality would explain the latter decline. But it is doubtful that such deterioration did in fact occur, at least to an extent sufficient to make it the sole explanatory factor. Even radios, which probably have decreased in average size, have improved in most other respects.

The industries which were still in an early stage when the period 1899–1937 opened, and which have by now attained a certain degree of maturity, do not follow exactly the pattern found for the very new industries. The rapid growth in automobile output in the first five years was accompanied by a rise in value added per unit. This rise might conceivably be explained by the growing tendency for automobile manufacturers to make their own parts, but the meager evidence at hand suggests a contrary tendency during this period.[9] After 1904 value added per unit declined drastically, while output

[9] See Chapter 21 below.

continued to rise at a rapid pace. These steep movements persisted until 1923, by which time the industry had more or less reached a state of maturity. Between 1923 and 1937 the changes in both series were slight in comparison with earlier trends. If the trends were adjusted for improvements in quality, both the rise in output and the fall in value added per unit from 1899 to 1937 would be even sharper than the present indexes indicate.

In petroleum refining, too, the relation between trends in output and in the price of fabricational services is complex. During the period when output was rising most rapidly, 1909–19, value added per unit also climbed in relation to total manufacturing. The demand for gasoline was increasing at an accelerated pace during this period, and it stimulated attempts to extract, even at high cost, additional quantities of gasoline from given quantities of crude petroleum. As noted in Chapter 15, below, commercial use of the revolutionary cracking process was still in its infancy in 1914. During the 18 years after 1919, however, when output continued to rise, value added per unit fell, reaching a level lower than that prevailing in the pre-war period. By 1930 about 38 percent of the total production of gasoline was made by the cracking process, whereas in 1920 only 13 percent had been so treated. Over the 38-year period, taken as a whole, output rose and unit value added fell.

Value added per unit by the beet sugar industry changed but little during the first decade of the century, when output rose very rapidly not only in relation to total manufacturing output, but also in relation to cane sugar. This relative growth, despite the absence of a decline in relative costs, has been ascribed to the sugar tariff.[10] During the succeeding two decades, output fluctuated about an approximately horizontal

[10] R. K. Adamson and M. E. West, *Productivity and Employment in Selected Industries: Beet Sugar,* Report No. N-1 (National Research Project, October 1938), pp. 47–53.

trend while value added per unit declined. In this industry, also, the net relative movement from 1899 to 1937 was upward for physical output and downward for value added per unit.

The next four industries, canned milk, manufactured ice, canned fruits and vegetables, and paints and varnishes, are all characterized by relative increases in physical output, though none is a new industry in the ordinary sense of the term. In three of the four, value added per unit fell from 1899 to 1937 in relation to value added per unit for all industries combined. Paints and varnishes is a distinct exception. Even in the other industries, however, no continuous decrease is found in unit value added.

Flour, lumber-mill products, railroad cars, linen goods, clay products and carriages have all been declining industries. In each one, over the long period as a whole, value added per unit has risen in relation to the corresponding index for total manufacturing. However, the rise in the series for carriages has developed only since 1927, whereas the rise in linen goods occurred mainly between 1909 and 1921. A significant part of the upswing in railroad cars must be ascribed to improvements in quality.

The relation between trends in physical output and in the money received by agents of fabrication per unit of product is not completely uniform, as is now apparent. The most distinct inverse relation[11] appears when output is rising

[11] A similar inverse relation appears to hold true also for all manufacturing industries combined in comparison with the economy at large. Thus the aggregate physical output of manufacturing industries increased in relation to the total national output (real national income). Between 1899 and 1937 manufacturing output rose 276 percent, while the rise in real national income was somewhat over 100 percent. This relative growth in total manufacturing output was accompanied also by an increase in the net value added by manufacturing industries in relation to the total net value added by all industries. But the latter relative increase was not of corresponding amount; it was smaller than the former. The fraction of national income (the best available measure of net value added) paid out by manufacturing industries was about 17 percent in 1899 and 24 percent in 1937. Reflecting this

rapidly, especially in a new industry, though here too there are exceptions.

It is impossible, of course, to determine merely from an examination of the summary indexes why, in particular industries during particular periods, growth or decline in output was associated with decline or growth in the price received by fabricational agents for their services. Still less is it possible to determine in this way whether in any particular case growth in output followed or preceded a decline in price. These questions can be answered, if at all, only after an intensive study of the detailed records not only of the industry concerned, but also of related industries.

Many economists have speculated about the more general factors involved in the relation between long-term trends in physical output and in unit prices of fabrication. Some have stressed the causal influence of invention and other technological advances upon costs, hence upon prices, and ultimately upon output. This chain of relationship is not a simple one, however. It is affected, in varying degree, by the character of the product and the elasticity of demand for it. A disturbing factor is the price of related commodities. The product of every manufacturing industry is used, in some sense, in conjunction with the product of another industry—for example, the industry supplying the raw materials. A rise (or decline) in the price of the related product may more than counterbalance a decline (or rise) in the price of the product under consideration. The state of the markets in which labor, capital and other agents are traded is relevant also, since a given technological advance may lead not to a lowering of costs but to a rise in the prices paid for labor or other agents of production. Still another complicating factor is the degree of monopoly enjoyed by the business enterprise

difference is the relative decline in the price of fabricational services (value added per unit of output). This price rose less, between 1899 and 1937, than did the general price level as measured by the cost of living, by wholesale price indexes, or by Snyder's index of the general price level.

whose costs are cut: a decline in selling price may not follow upon a decline in cost.

Causal influences running in the other direction have been emphasized in some discussions. Lower prices, by leading to increases in output, eventuate in economies of large-scale production. There are limits to these economies, however, because there are also diseconomies of large-scale output. While these limits have been noted not only in such fields as agriculture and mining, but also in manufacturing, their magnitudes have not been measured in specific terms.

The possible causal relations just mentioned are circular. Technological progress induces growth, and growth leads to lower costs and thereby to further growth which may stimulate additional technological advances, and so on. If any factor has been taken as prime it is technological progress in the early stages of an industry's growth—particularly as the consequence of invention.[12] This consideration suggests, in turn, that a more or less typical chronological pattern of the cost and price of an industry's output may be followed during an industry's growth and maturity. Since growth is most rapid in the early stages of an industry's life, declines in unit costs and prices also tend to be greatest at that time. As the industry approaches maturity, its unit costs and values decline less rapidly and tend to become subject to influences more important, at that stage, than technological progress.

At this time we cannot tell how closely the complex of hypotheses outlined here resembles the facts. The relation between the size of an industry or a business enterprise and the level of costs, the relation between costs and prices, and the relation between prices and sales are all largely matters of conjecture, and a resolution of these problems still waits upon the future.

[12] See Simon Kuznets, *Secular Movements in Production and Prices* (Houghton Mifflin, 1930), pp. 11–41.

Part Two

The Output of Individual Manufacturing Industries

Chapter 6

Foods

THE foods group comprises almost all industries that manufacture foods and kindred products. It includes the related industries producing baking powder, manufactured ice, and feeds, but excludes beverages, which are classified separately, and drugs possessing food value, which are treated as chemical products. Thus defined, the foods group in 1937 ranked fourth among all manufacturing groups listed according to their contributions to total value added. It was exceeded in this respect by textile products, machinery, and iron and steel products.

TRENDS IN THE PHYSICAL OUTPUT OF THE FOOD INDUSTRIES [1]

Indexes of physical output of processed foods and related products are presented numerically in Table 13 and graphically in Chart 8. Although there are as many as 29 food industries, only 26 are represented by quantity data even for that comparatively recent year. Of these, 12 have been covered by indexes for all four decades listed; one more by data for the second and third decades; and an additional 13 for the period 1929–37. Some of the most important food in-

[1] The tables in this and later chapters contain data on the output of all industries for which figures are available in reasonably adequate form. The discussion in the text, however, is usually limited to those individual industries concerning whose development we could add information to supplement the indexes.

Substantial differences between the indexes presented here and those constructed by E. E. Day and Woodlief Thomas and their collaborators, and by the National Research Project, are noted in Appendix D.

TABLE 13

FOODS[a]

Physical Output: Indexes and Percentage Changes[b]

	Meat Packing	Sausage, n.e.m.[c]	Oleomargarine, n.e.m.[c]	Shortenings	Flour	Feeds	Cereals	Rice	Macaroni	Bread and Cake	Biscuits and Crackers	Fish, Canned	Fruits and Vegetables, Canned	Milk, Canned
YEAR	INDEX OF PHYSICAL OUTPUT (1929:100)													
1899	56	..	..	..	94	..	..	21	..	..	..	53	17	6.7
1904	64	..	..	..	98	..	..	51	..	..	..	65	24	10.9
1909	72	..	..	..	102	..	..	52	..	..	..	78	29	18
1914	71	..	..	..	108	..	..	55	..	..	..	73	42	36
1919	93	..	..	..	114	..	..	88	..	..	..	85	55	84
1921	77	..	..	..	94	..	..	94	..	..	..	45	38	69
1923	97	..	..	..	106	..	..	95	..	75	81	59	67	73
1925	92	..	72	..	102	56	70	76	..	78	86	73	82	76
1927	95	..	79	99	100	74	80	100	91	90	91	77	82	88
1929	100	100	100	100	100	100	100	100	100	100	100	100	100	100
1931	94	108	71	100	91	76	100	102	97	92	86	64	91	100
1933	95	..	63	98	80	70	79	90	..	74	78	69	88	98
1935	85	154	94	134	82	90	70	96	116	86	96	103	127	115
1937	94	182	126	148	86	111	77	106	123	96	106	104	151	128
PERIOD	NET PERCENTAGE CHANGE IN PHYSICAL OUTPUT													
1899–1937	+66	..	..	..	−8	..	..	+416	..	..	..	+96	+792	+1,812
1899–1909	+28	..	..	..	+9	..	..	+152	..	..	..	+47	+69	+167
1909–1919	+29	..	..	..	+11	..	..	+70	..	..	..	+9	+92	+371
1919–1929	+7	..	..	..	−12	..	..	+13	..	..	..	+18	+82	+19
1929–1937	−6	+82	+26	+48	−14	+11	−23	+6	+23	−4	+6	+4	+51	+28

TABLE 13 (Concluded)

	Butter	Cheese	Ice Cream	Beet Sugar	Cane Sugar, n.e.m.[c]	Cane-Sugar Refining	Confectionery	Chocolate	Corn Products	Flavorings	Baking Powder	Ice	Total: Un-adjusted	Total: Adjusted
YEAR					INDEX OF PHYSICAL OUTPUT (1929:100)									
1899	26	50	..	6.7	115	44	..	..	..	..	..	9.8	40	30
1904	33	56	..	23	113	50	..	..	..	..	..	17	48	37
1909	40	55	..	45	168	55	..	..	47	..	..	30	57	45
1914	50	66	..	68	132	66	..	..	50	..	..	44	64	53
1919	60	86	..	67	125	79	..	..	69	..	..	60	79	65
1921	72	77	..	96	129	74	..	60	57	..	..	67	68	64
1923	84	101	77	68	88	87	..	82	76	..	..	77	82	80
1925	92	100	84	100	69	106	91	90	76	..	..	88	86	85
1927	97	97	88	84	36	100	94	96	92	..	88	88	90	90
1929	100	100	100	100	100	100	100	100	100	100	100	100	100	100
1931	102	92	83	107	91	87	80	98	76	101	96	96	91	91
1933	110	95	60	151	125	77	79	105	84	..	74	74	82	82
1935	104	126	82	111	174	83	100	140	68	103	73	72	92	92
1937	105	129	109	120	192	89	111	124	84	174	63	75	103	104
PERIOD					NET PERCENTAGE CHANGE IN PHYSICAL OUTPUT									
1899–1937	+309	+158		+1,688	+67	+101	..	..	..	..	..	+668	+156	+244
1899–1909	+55	+11	..	+578	+46	+24	..	..	..	..	..	+203	+41	+48
1909–1919	+51	+56	..	+48	–26	+45	..	..	+48	..	..	+101	+40	+45
1919–1929	+67	+16	..	+48	–20	+26	..	..	+44	..	..	+67	+26	+54
1929–1937	+5	+29	+9	+20	+92	–11	+11	+24	–16	+74	–37	–25	+3	+4

[a] Industries for which there are no adequate quantity data for any period listed above are: vinegar and cider; chewing gum; and food, not elsewhere classified. These industries are covered by the adjusted total.

[b] The indexes have been constructed from basic data in the U.S. Census of Manufactures and other sources, by methods described briefly in Chapter 2 and in detail in Appendix A. Appendix B presents these data, together with the indexes derived from them. The indexes cited here for individual industries have been adjusted to take account of changes in the coverage of the respective samples, except when such adjustment was impossible. The percentage changes are not always entirely consistent with the indexes given above because the changes were computed from the indexes in Appendix B, which are carried to one decimal place.

[c] N.e.m. denotes not elsewhere made.

Chart 8
FOODS
Indexes of Physical Output

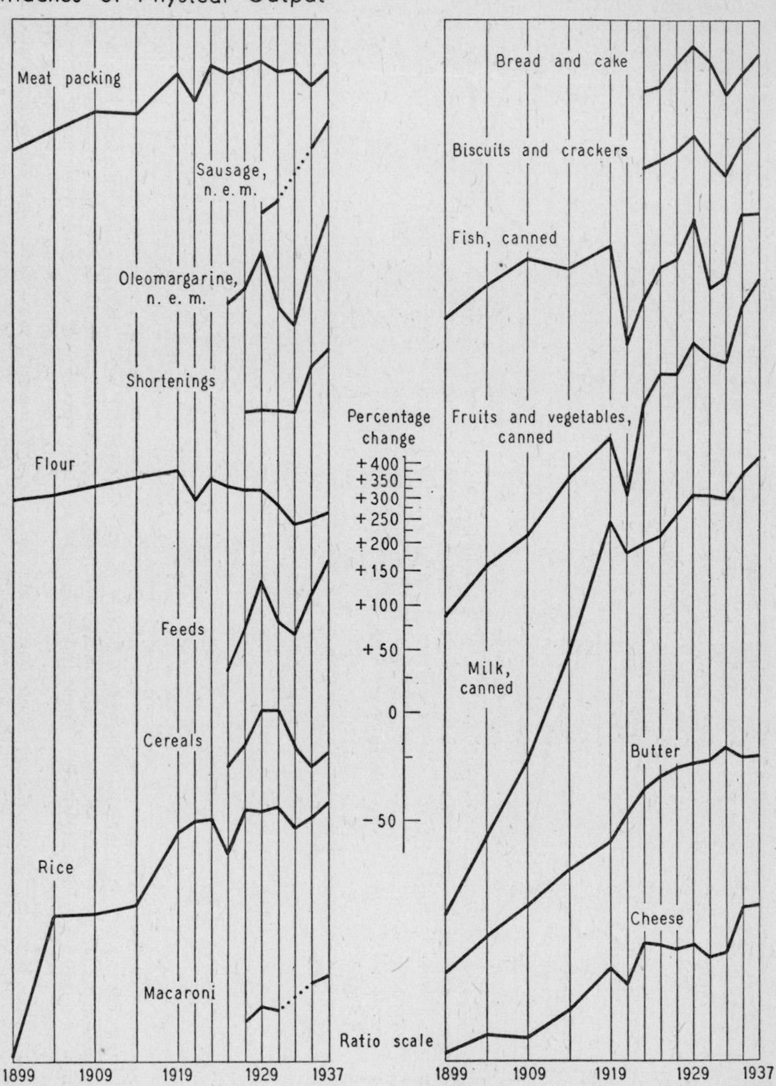

Chart 8 (concl.)
FOODS
Indexes of Physical Output

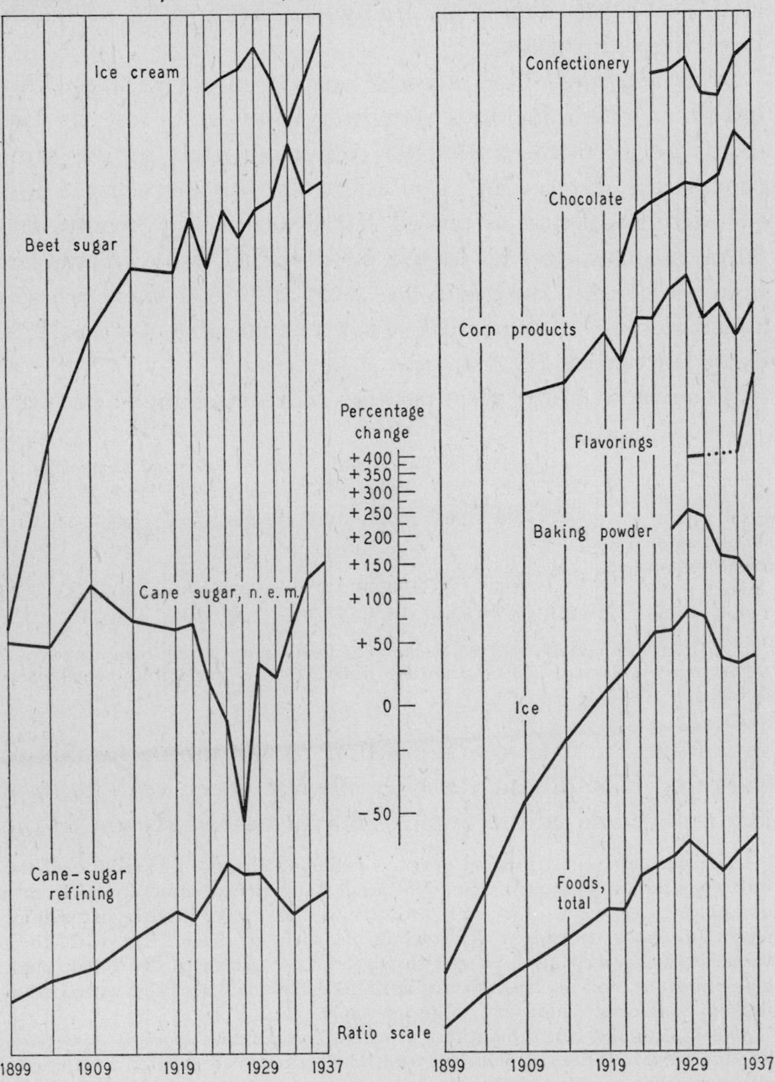

dustries—biscuits and crackers, bread and cake, confectionery, and ice cream—are those for which the indexes are incomplete; nevertheless, the foods group is more adequately covered by Census data than are most other groups of manufacturing industries.

Meat Packing. The physical output of the meat-packing industry, which includes slaughtering as well, rose by two thirds between 1899 and 1937, approximately at the same pace as the increase in population. During each of the first two decades output advanced fairly steadily, approximating 30 percent per decade. In the third period the gain was less than 10 percent, and between 1929 and 1937 there was an actual decline of 6 percent. Peak output, reached in 1929, exceeded that of 1923 by only 3 percent.

The output of the meat-packing industry changed not only

	Quantity (billion pounds)					*Percentage Distribution*				
	1899	1909	1919	1929	1937	1899	1909	1919	1929	1937
Fresh meat[a]	4.7	6.8	8.4	9.8	10.0	58	69	60	67	73
Cured, canned and other preserved meats	3.4	3.1	5.5	4.9	3.7	42	31	40	33	27
TOTAL	8.1	9.9	13.9	14.7	13.7	100	100	100	100	100

[a] Includes fresh meat sold to packers to be manufactured into cured and other preserved meats. The resulting duplication is negligible; see Appendix B.

in volume but also in composition, as the tabulation above indicates.[2] The production of fresh meat (beef, veal, mutton, lamb, pork and edible organs) fluctuated in relation to the

[2] The percentage distribution portrays inadequately the composition of the industry's output because a pound of fresh meat is not equal in value to a pound of cured meat. However, no attempt was made, in this and similar text tabulations, to weight the various products in accordance with their value. Weights were used, of course, in the construction of the index numbers of output, and in the preparation of all tables showing relative contributions of component industries to group totals.

This and similar text tabulations relating to output are based on data given in Appendix B. Other tabulations and information incorporated in the text, and not otherwise reproduced in this volume, are derived from data in the Census of Manufactures unless a different source is mentioned.

output of cured meat (including canned and other preserved meats). Over the 38-year period as a whole, the output of fresh meat more than doubled, whereas the output of cured meat scarcely increased at all. The shift from preserved to fresh meats reflects in some degree improved methods of refrigeration in the factory, in transit and in the home. The large output of cured meats in 1919 suggests, however, that this improvement is not the sole explanation of the change in the composition of meat-packing products.

There were shifts not only in the composition of the industry's output but also in the composition of its input. The proportions of the several species of animals slaughtered in factory establishments varied as follows:

	Weight on Hoof (billion pounds)					*Percentage Distribution*				
	1899	1909	1919	1929	1937	1899	1909	1919	1929	1937
Cattle	5.9	8.3	9.9	9.0	10.9	44	50	46	38	49
Calves	0.1	0.4	0.8	0.9	1.4	1	3	4	4	6
Sheep and lambs	0.8	1.0	1.1	1.3	1.7	6	6	5	6	8
Hogs	6.7	6.9	9.7	12.3	8.1	49	41	45	52	37
TOTAL	13.5	16.6	21.5	23.5	22.1	100	100	100	100	100

Over the entire 38-year period there was a net decline in the relative importance of hogs. The relative importance of cattle, sheep and lambs increased moderately, while that of calves rose rapidly. Since the fraction of pork that is cured is greater than the fraction of beef, veal, mutton or lamb,[3] these changes in the composition of the industry's input are not unrelated to the changes in the composition of its output. Because of differences in the anatomical characteristics of the various species of animals slaughtered, and particularly in the ratio of dressed to live weight,[4] the shift in the character of input should be observable also in the amount and type of labor employed and in the processes utilized in the industry.[5]

[3] The meat cured in 1909 consisted almost entirely of pork, with a small amount of beef and no cured veal, mutton or lamb reported.

[4] The dressed weight yield, per pound of live weight, varies from one species to another: in 1929 it averaged 75 percent for hogs, 59 percent for calves, 54 percent for cattle and 47 percent for sheep and lambs.

[5] Slaughtering plants are divided into highly specialized departments—

Although it is impossible from the data at hand to trace the causal relationship in detail, the changes in the types of commodities produced and in the species of animals slaughtered must have contributed to the divergence in trend between gross output and net output in the meat-packing industry.[6] During the 38 years between 1899 and 1937 gross output (including not only the meat products but also lard, skins, etc.) appears to have risen more rapidly than the input of materials (animals to be slaughtered). As a consequence, net output (the difference between gross output and input, expressed in fixed prices) probably increased somewhat faster than gross output.[7]

The changes in the composition of both the input and the output of the meat-packing industry are undoubtedly related to differences in the rate of shift, from farm and retail establishment to the factory, of the slaughter of different species of animals. These variations are illustrated by the percentage distributions on the opposite page:

---

cattle killing, hog killing, fresh beef cutting, and fresh pork cutting. Within each of these there is a fine division of labor. See the bulletins of the Bureau of Labor Statistics on this industry, especially *Bulletin No. 252,* pp. 1075–1114.

[6] See Chapter 2 above, for an explanation of net physical output.

[7] A slight discrepancy between the change in gross output and in input has an important effect on net output, chiefly because the cost of materials in meat packing accounts for a very large percentage of the value of the final product (as much as 85 percent in 1937). As a consequence, the index of net output is highly sensitive even to small errors in either of the two indexes from which it is derived, and for this reason the following estimates of net output must be regarded as very rough approximations.

	Percentage Change				
	1899–1937	1899–1909	1909–1919	1919–1929	1929–1937
Gross output (meat and other products)	+66	+28	+29	+7	–6
Input (animals slaughtered)	+61	+20	+28	+11	–5
Net output	+118	+110	+38	–13	–14

The index of input is a weighted index; it therefore differs somewhat from the index that might be derived from the figures given in the text relating to the total weight on the hoof of all animals slaughtered.

	Percentage of Total Slaughter[a]	
	1899	1937
Cattle		
In wholesale establishments	61	83
In retail establishments and on farms	39	17
Total	100	100
Calves		
In wholesale establishments	28	77
In retail establishments and on farms	72	23
Total	100	100
Hogs		
In wholesale establishments	67	69
In retail establishments and on farms	33	31
Total	100	100
Sheep and lambs		
In wholesale establishments	87	91
In retail establishments and on farms	13	9
Total	100	100
Total (weighted average)[b]		
In wholesale establishments	64	77
In retail establishments and on farms	36	23
TOTAL	100	100

[a] See U.S. Department of Agriculture, *Agricultural Statistics* (1939), pp. 318, 329, 347.
[b] Weighted by total live weight, in pounds.

The shift to factory slaughtering was most pronounced in the case of calves, which it will be recalled also rose more rapidly than other meat animals slaughtered within factories from 1899 to 1937. The transfer of hog slaughter to the factory was slight in comparison, a finding consonant with the decline in the relative importance of hogs in the total slaughter within meat-packing plants.

Even as early as 1899 the weight of animals slaughtered inside factory walls was close to two thirds of the aggregate weight of all animals slaughtered, so that the shift thereafter from retail establishments and farms to factory plants was necessarily moderate. It was, however, a continuing process: by 1937 factories accounted for more than three quarters of the total slaughter.

Although factory production of meats rose, between 1899

and 1937, about as rapidly as did population, the total domestic production of meats, in and out of factories, actually declined in relation to population. The drop in per capita production reflects primarily a decrease in per capita consumption of meats during the period under discussion. In 1899 each person consumed, on the average, 163 pounds of meat products (beef, veal, lamb, mutton, pork and lard) whereas in 1937 the average amount consumed was 136 pounds.[8] But the decline in domestic per capita consumption did not exactly parallel the decrease in domestic per capita production. Because of a shift in the balance of imports versus exports, the former decline was less marked than the latter. In 1899 domestic consumption was less than domestic production because we exported more meat products than we imported. As the accompanying tabulation shows, exports in

	Imports minus Exports as a Percentage of Domestic Production[a]	
	1899	1937
Beef	−9	+5
Veal	0	0
Lamb and mutton	0	+1
Pork	−15	+3
Lard	−44	−5

[a] Derived from figures given in source cited in footnote 8, above.

that year exceeded imports of three meat products and equaled the imports of two. By 1937, however, the relationship was reversed. In that year we exported less than we imported, so that domestic consumption was greater than domestic production; the imports of three products exceeded exports, balanced exactly for one product and fell below exports only for the fifth.

Sausage, Oleomargarine and Shortenings. These industries are closely related to the meat-packing industry since they produce commodities made also to a great extent in meat-

[8] U.S. Bureau of Agricultural Economics, *Livestock, Meats, and Wool Market Statistics and Related Data, 1939* (May 1940), p. 100.

packing plants. Of the total amount of sausage made in 1929, the sausage industry proper accounted for 30 percent, while meat packers produced 70 percent. In 1929, 56 percent of the total output of oleomargarine was manufactured in specialist plants, 29 percent in meat-packing plants and 15 percent elsewhere. Shortenings produced by the shortenings industry in 1929 constituted 66 percent of the total; most of the remainder came from meat-packing establishments.

The indexes presented in Table 13 for the three specialist industries relate only to their own output and not to the total production of sausage, oleomargarine or shortenings. The three industries increased their physical output in substantial proportions between 1929 and 1937: by 82, 26 and 48 percent, respectively.

The increase in the output of the sausage industry is by no means ascribable to sausage alone, which rose only 11 percent between 1929 and 1937. Other products of the industry, not specified in detail in the Census, advanced much more rapidly; they constituted 19 percent (by value) of the total output in 1929 and as much as 50 percent in 1937. There was a similar change in the composition of the output of the oleomargarine industry. Thus oleomargarine rose only 15 percent between 1929 and 1937, while total output, including salad dressing and shortenings made in the same industry, increased by 26 percent.

Despite the large percentage increases in the three small satellite industries, the combined physical output of all four industries—meat packing, sausage, oleomargarine and shortenings (each weighted by value added)—remained almost constant between 1929 and 1937: the net rise was less than 1 percent, for the 6 percent decline in meat packing almost counterbalanced the increases in the three smaller industries.

Flour. The flour industry consists of merchant mills which purchase the grain, mill it and sell the products. Custom milling is excluded from the data, except for the portion attributable to mills engaged also in merchant milling.[9] The industry decreased its physical output by 8 percent between 1899 and 1937. The drop was the net result of a moderate rise up to 1919, the peak year, and a decline thereafter. As in the case of meats, there was a definite decrease in the per capita consumption of flour-mill products, coupled with a decline in exports. Exports, minus imports, amounted to 18 percent of domestic flour production in 1899, but to only 4 percent in 1937.[10]

The output of the flour-milling industry changed in composition as well as in volume during the 38 years between 1899 and 1937, as may be observed from the data in the following tabulation:

		1899	*1909*	*1919*	*1929*	*1937*
Wheat flour	Mil. bbls.	99.8	105.8	132.5	120.1	105.3
Feeds, screenings, bran and middlings[a]	Mil. tons	7.2	9.2	9.3	7.2	5.8
Corn meal and flour	Mil. bbls.	27.8	21.6	10.7	11.1	7.3
Buckwheat flour	Mil. lbs.	143	176	90	38	27

[a] Includes, for the period 1899–1919, "prepared feeds for stock" not separately reported.

The output of wheat flour, the most important component, rose slightly from 1899 to 1937, with a peak in 1919. Feeds, screenings, bran and middlings, also of importance, declined nearly 20 percent during the 38 years. The production of corn meal and flour fell off much more seriously; in 1937 it was little more than one-quarter of the output in 1899. The greatest decline, more than 80 percent, was in the production of buckwheat flour, which reached its peak in 1909. This product was, however, a relatively small component of the industry's output, even in 1899 and 1909.

[9] Custom mills accounted for only 5.9 and 4.4 percent of the combined output of merchant and custom mills in 1909 and 1919, respectively, according to the Census data for these years. See Magdoff, Siegel and Davis, *Production, Employment, and Productivity in 59 Manufacturing Industries* (National Research Project, 1939), Part II, p. 74.

[10] For 1899 see *Commerce Yearbook, 1929,* p. 227. The figure for 1937 was computed by us from data in the *Statistical Abstract.*

Feeds, an industry which specializes chiefly in the manufacture of prepared feeds for livestock and fowl from purchased materials or from grain ground by the industry itself, is covered by the Census data from the year 1925 on. Between that year and 1929 output increased by 80 percent. In the most recent period, 1929–37, the industry boosted its output 11 percent. The total gain from 1925 to 1937 was 100 percent. On the other hand, prepared feeds, made in this and other industries, rose less than 50 percent in the same period. A large portion of the increase in the output of the industry proper is attributable, therefore, to a change in the fraction that feeds made within the industry constituted of total feeds, and to an increase in the industry's output of products other than feeds.[11]

Cereals. The output of the cereals industry, which produces prepared feeds as secondary products, rose more than 40 percent between 1925 (the first year for which we have data) and 1929, but declined 25 percent from the latter year to 1937. From 1925 to 1937 the output of breakfast foods made from oats declined 22 percent, while cereals made from corn rose 70 percent and prepared flour went up 85 percent.

Rice. This industry is a rather small one, when gauged by value added; it is engaged merely in cleaning and polishing threshed rice. Between 1899 and 1937 the industry's output quintupled, chiefly as a result of a large net increase up to 1919. After 1919 the gains were slight. In 1899 domestic requirements were satisfied only in part by domestic production of rice; imports, minus exports, came to nearly a quarter of domestic production. By 1927 the growth of the domestic rice industry had turned the balance in the other

[11] The 1925 index for feeds is unadjusted; i.e., because of lack of data, no account could be taken of changes in the coverage of the sample from 1925 to 1927; see Appendix B. Because the adjusted and unadjusted indexes of the industry do not correspond closely, the 1925 figure must be considered as merely a rough estimate of the industry's output.

direction, for in that year exports, minus imports, amounted to 47 percent of domestic production.[12]

Bakery Products. For these industries, highly significant in terms of value added, data on output are available only from 1923. Between that year and 1929 the physical output of bread and cake rose by as much as one third, but from 1929 to 1937 it declined 4 percent. The output of biscuits and crackers increased 25 percent in 1923–29, and another 6 percent in 1929–37. When these two bakery industries are considered together, their combined output is found to have risen 30 percent between 1923 and 1929 and to have dropped 3 percent between 1929 and 1937. The contrast with flour milling is striking. The latter industry decreased its output by 6 percent between 1923 and 1929, and by 14 percent between 1929 and 1937.

Canned Fish. This classification covers the canning and curing of fish, crabs, shrimp, oysters, clams and other sea foods. The physical output of the industry almost doubled between 1899 and 1937. In the first decade of the century it increased by one half, in the second by only about one tenth. There was a severe decline between 1919 and 1921, followed by recovery which more than counterbalanced the slump and resulted in a net gain of nearly a fifth for 1919–29. The rise from 1929 to 1937 was only 4 percent.

An outstanding change in the composition of the output of the industry resulted from the decline in cured fish (salted, pickled and smoked). The output of this commodity had dropped by 1937 to less than half the volume produced in 1899. Canned fish products rose as a group despite declines in the canning of salmon and oysters.

Canned Fruits and Vegetables, one of the most important industries in the foods group with respect to value added,

[12] U.S. Bureau of Foreign and Domestic Commerce, "Apparent Per Capita Consumption of Principal Foodstuffs in the United States," *Domestic Commerce Series, No. 38* (1930), pp. 10–11.

augmented its physical product at a very rapid rate. From 1899 to 1937 output increased by almost 800 percent; in the first decade it rose some 70 percent, in the second 90, in the third 80, and in the last period 50 percent. Although there was no serious slackening in the rate of growth of total output, there was a slowing down in the rate of growth of individual products of the industry. Deceleration in the rate of growth is observable for virtually all the products covered by comparatively long-term data. This does not mean, however, that the output of these products had actually begun to decline; few of them had even approached peak output. Thus in Census years preceding 1931 highest points were reached only in the production of canned hominy (1929), canned apples (1929), dried peaches (1919) and dried raisins (1925).

Much of the rise in the output of canned fruits and vegetables reflects a shift from home cooking and preserving to factory canning, though no statistical data concerning this change are available. There is little question, however, that total production of canned and preserved fruits and vegetables, prepared in both home and factory, rose rapidly in relation to population.

Canned Milk. Data on the canned milk industry, which produces condensed and evaporated milk, show that it rose even more rapidly than canned fruits and vegetables. Its output in 1937 was more than 19 times as large as that of 1899.[13] Within the period there was a noticeable acceleration after 1909, and a pronounced retardation in the post-war years. Figures on the movement of individual products, available largely from 1925, reveal a drop between 1925 and 1937 in the output of sweetened condensed milk; a rise in the output of unsweetened condensed and evaporated milk, casein, dried and powdered milk, cream and buttermilk, and ice-

[13] The 1899 index for canned milk could not be adjusted for changes in the coverage of the sample (see Appendix B). For this reason, it is not an altogether precise measure of the industry's output of that year.

cream mix; and a rather slight decline in the production of condensed and evaporated buttermilk.

Butter. The enterprises included in this classification (which does not cover farm production) increased their aggregate output by over 300 percent between 1899 and 1937. The industry's product gained over 50 percent in each of the first three decades, and 5 percent between 1929 and 1937. The largest output recorded by the Census for any single year through 1937 was that of 1933.

While factory butter production just about quadrupled, from 1899 to 1929, total production, including farm output, rose less than 50 percent. In other words, factories accounted for an increasingly greater share of a total which grew much less rapidly. The great shift from farm to factory is illustrated in part by the following figures, available only through 1929:

	Butter Production[a] On Farms	In Factories (million pounds)	Total	*Factory Production as a Percentage of Total Production*
1899	1,072	420	1,492	28
1909	995	627	1,622	39
1919	708	939	1,647	57
1929	542	1,618	2,160	75

[a] *Statistical Abstract, 1931,* p. 686; *1935,* p. 603; and reports of the Census of Manufactures.

In 1899 little more than a quarter of all domestic butter was made in factories; by 1929 the fraction had risen to three quarters, and farm families were consuming most of their own product.[14]

Cheese. Among the industries manufacturing milk products, the cheese industry had the smallest increase in output —160 percent—between 1899 and 1937. Within those 38 years there were two periods, 1904–09 and 1923–29, during which there was no growth at all in cheese production. The

[14] In 1929 only 135 million pounds were sold, out of the 542 million made on farms. (*Statistical Abstract, 1935,* p. 603.)

shift from farm to factory production of cheese (unlike that of butter) was almost complete by the opening of the present century; in 1899 over 90 percent of the total domestic production of cheese was ascribed to factories.[15]

Ice Cream made in factories rose 9 percent between 1929 and 1937. The Census records reveal a larger increase, amounting to 30 percent, between 1923 (the first year for which we have adequate data) and 1929. Ices, sherbets, and such specialties as cups and sticks, rather than plain ice cream, accounted for most of the added output.

Beet Sugar. The beet sugar industry, which is so closely connected with the cultivation of sugar beets that it is practically part of an agricultural industry, increased its output by almost 1,700 percent between 1899 and 1937 despite marked fluctuations within that period. During the first decade output rose almost 600 percent; in each of the next two decades the increase was about 50 percent, and in the last period 20 percent.

The rise in physical output is to be attributed only in part to an increase in the quantity of sugar beets treated, for it resulted in large measure from an increase in the amount of sugar extracted from each pound of beets. As a consequence, the net physical output of the industry (the output of beet sugar and by-products minus the input of sugar beets) rose more rapidly than its gross physical output (beet sugar and by-products).[16]

[15] *Twelfth Census of the United States,* Vol. IX, pp. 437–38.

[16] Percentage changes in these indexes follow:

	Percentage Change				
	1899–1937	1899–1909	1909–1919	1919–1929	1929–1937
Gross output (beet sugar and by-products)	+1,688	+578	+48	+48	+20
Beets treated (tons)	+965	+400	+42	+23	+21
Net output	+3,360	+920	+56	+88	+18

The index of net output thus computed tends to overstate the rise since it takes no account of improvements in the quality of the beets. The increase in the sugar extracted per pound of beets reflects not only improved methods of

Cane Sugar. Both of the cane sugar industries distinguished by the Census were characterized by slower rates of advance than was beet sugar manufacture. Cane sugar, not elsewhere made, which covers the production of sugar from domestic sugar cane, increased in output by only two thirds between 1899 and 1937, the net result of a rise up to 1909, a serious fall from 1909 to 1927, and a rapid upswing from 1927 to 1937. The decline to the low point in 1927 has been attributed to the destructive effects of the mosaic disease, and the rise since then to a new development—the utilization of bagasse, a pulpy by-product of cane crushing, in the manufacture of celotex [17]—which incidentally stimulated the growth of domestic cane-sugar production.

The cane-sugar refining industry, which refines purchased, and for the most part imported, raw cane sugar, doubled its output between 1899 and 1937. This industry followed a pattern quite different from that of the industry treated in the preceding paragraph. It reached peak output, for example, in 1925, a year when cane sugar, not elsewhere made, was dropping rapidly.

The combined output of the three sugar industries, which we have obtained by weighting the output of each by its value added, rose 250 percent from 1899 to 1937, the net result of a gain of 93 percent between 1899 and 1909; of 34 percent between 1909 and 1919; of 30 percent between 1919 and 1929; and of 4 percent between 1929 and 1937. Most of the violent fluctuations in the three component series offset one another.

Corn Products, including sirup, sugar, oil and starch, increased in output between 40 and 50 percent during each of the second and third decades, and fell 16 percent in the most

manufacture but also new methods of cultivation which yield greater sucrose content. On this point see R. K. Adamson and M. E. West, *Productivity and Employment in Selected Industries: Beet Sugar* (National Research Project in co-operation with National Bureau of Economic Research, 1938), p. 38.

[17] E. W. Zimmermann, *World Resources and Industries* (Harpers, 1933), pp. 771–72.

recent period. Among the important individual products of the industry, for which data are available in some detail beginning with 1923, increases are recorded for corn oil, and starch (corn, potato and other) ; and declines for corn sirup and mixtures of corn and other sirups, and corn sugar.

Baking Powder. Although not strictly a food industry (it is classified by the Census among chemicals), we have placed the baking powder industry in the foods group because it produces compounds, including yeast and baking powder, that are used for leavening purposes. It is one of the few industries in the group whose output declined substantially: between 1929 and 1937 there was a net drop of nearly 40 percent in the products in this industry.

Manufactured Ice, classified perhaps arbitrarily as a food industry, made large gains in physical output. The net increase between 1899 and 1937 was almost 700 percent. In the first decade output rose 200 percent; in the second 100 percent; and in the third 67 percent. After 1929 output fell, so that in 1937 it stood 25 percent below the level reached in 1929. The retardation in growth has materialized into a downward trend in recent years; mechanical refrigeration has undoubtedly been a primary factor in this decline.

Summary of Changes in Individual Industries. The trends in the physical output of the food manufacturing industries are summarized in Table 14. Out of 12 industries covered for the entire period 1899–1937, only one, flour, declined in output. Three industries rose less rapidly than population: flour, meat packing and cane sugar. These three, and canned fish, cane-sugar refining and cheese, rose less rapidly than all manufacturing industries combined.

If we compare the four periods, we find that the most recent, 1929–37, differed from the other three in several respects. Eight out of 26 industries declined in output between 1929 and 1937; in none of the earlier periods was the proportion as large. Ten of the 26 industries rose less rapidly than population grew in the years 1929–37; in this respect, also, the latest period is outstanding. Eight of the 26 industries rose less rapidly than all manufacturing industries combined; a similar proportion is found for the period 1909–19.

TABLE 14

FOODS

Summary of Changes in Physical Output[a]

	Number of Industries				
	1899–1937	1899–1909	1909–1919	1919–1929	1929–1937
Industries for which there are indexes of physical output	12	12	13	13	26
Industries with rising output	11	12	12	11	18
Industries with falling output	1	0	1	2	8
Industries with output rising in relation to population	9	10	10	8	14
Industries with output constant in relation to population				1	2
Industries with output falling in relation to population	3	2	3	4	10
Industries with output rising in relation to total manufacturing output	6	5	9	3	18
Industries with output falling in relation to total manufacturing output	6	7	4	10	8

[a] Derived from data in Table 13 and the following figures on changes in population and in total manufacturing output:

	Percentage Change				
	1899–1937	1899–1909	1909–1919	1919–1929	1929–1937
Population of the United States	+73	+21	+16	+16	+6
Physical output of all manufacturing industries combined	+276	+58	+41	+64	+3

The Group Total. The unadjusted weighted average index for the food group, based on the available individual indexes, rose between 1899 and 1937 by 156 percent—the net result of an increase of two fifths in each of the first two decades, one quarter in the third decade and 3 percent in the last period. The statistical coverage of this average is, however, incomplete. In 1899 it related to only 63.5 percent of the group's output (in terms of value added), and in 1937 to 92.8 percent. Further, the industries included in the sample appear, from the data on value added, to have grown at rates differing from those of the industries not covered by the index. When the index is corrected for bias of this sort it becomes an adjusted index.[18] The adjusted index for the entire foods group rose 244 percent between 1899 and 1937, considerably more than the unadjusted index (156 percent). Moreover, the adjusted index shows a greater rise than the unadjusted index in each of the four periods into which we have divided the 38 years from 1899 to 1937.

The rise of 244 percent in the physical output of processed foods and related products, as compared with an increase of 73 percent in population, indicates a considerable gain in the per capita production of factory-made foods. It must be remembered, however, that there was a substantial transfer of production from the home, the farm or the retail establishment to the industrial plant. For this reason the consumption of processed foods would tend to rise less rapidly than factory production. On the other hand, exports of manufactured foods appear to have declined and imports to have risen, as is indicated by the indexes on page 144, available beginning with 1913. Such a change in our export-import balance would have caused consumption to rise more rapidly than production. It is difficult to determine the net effect of these opposing tendencies. It seems likely that the changes in the relation between exports and imports of processed foodstuffs were, on the whole, of less importance than the shifts to the factory. Exports of manufactured foodstuffs (including beverages) amounted to 305 million dollars in 1899 and 178 mil-

[18] The assumptions and methods basic to the derivation of the adjusted index are described briefly in Chapter 2 and in detail in Appendix A.

Manufactured Foodstuffs[a]
Indexes of Physical Volume
(1923–25:100)

Year	Imports	Exports
1913	74	73
1919	[b]	183
1921	74	114
1923	90	107
1925	118	88
1927	111	81
1929	137	87
1931	97	62
1933	102	49
1935	137	37
1937	172	39

[a] Including beverages. Calculated by the Bureau of the Census. See *Statistical Abstract, 1938,* p. 448; *1935,* p. 418; *1934,* p. 404; *1933,* p. 399.
[b] Not available.

lion in 1937, and imports of manufactured foodstuffs (also including beverages) were valued at 123 million in 1899 and 440 million in 1937.[19] These amounts are probably small in relation to the value of the output transferred to the factory; the latter must have been a substantial fraction of the domestic production of processed foods, valued at some 1,800 million dollars in 1899 and 8,000 or 9,000 million in 1937.[20] We may conclude, therefore, that the increase in the per capita consumption of processed foodstuffs is overstated by the change in the ratio of factory-made foods to population. It is scarcely to be doubted, however, that there was a considerable rise in the per capita consumption of processed foods.[21]

Little that is definite can be said about changes in the quality of processed foodstuffs. Insofar as the contribution of

[19] *Statistical Abstract, 1938,* pp. 450–51.

[20] The 1899 figure is an average of maximum and minimum estimates published in *Statistical Abstract, 1938,* p. 435. The 1937 figure is based on the value added in 1937 and 1929, and the net value of processed foods produced in 1929. Both figures exclude duplication arising from the consumption of processed foodstuffs by factories engaged in further fabrication.

[21] In order to combine the different types of foods, we multiplied their respective quantities by the appropriate value added per unit in the weight-base period. If caloric content, rather than value added per unit, had been used as the coefficient, it is possible that no increase in per capita consumption would have been found.

the fabricational process is concerned, it is probable that the net trend has been toward improvements. Perfection of preserving techniques and better control of them, as well as improved sanitary conditions, have certainly helped to raise the quality of factory-produced meats.[22] Of greater importance, however, have been the innovations in packing, which have resulted in the preservation of flavor, in enhanced cleanliness and in reduction of breakage and damage. The increase in the output of paper products (see Chapter 12, below) is a reflection of this trend.

CHANGES IN THE INDUSTRIAL PATTERN OF FOOD PRODUCTION

The most outstanding feature of the industrial pattern of food manufacturing, as sketched in the foregoing pages, is the slow rate of growth in the output of the great staple food industries, flour and meat packing, and the rapid rate of growth in the output of canned milk, canned fruits and vegetables, and ice. It is because of this divergence in rates of development that the composition of the physical output of the food group became virtually transformed in the 38 years from 1899 to 1937. In order clearly to depict the composition of the group in various years we express the physical output of each industry as a percentage of the total physical output of the entire group (Table 15).[23]

In 1899 the meat-packing industry contributed 28 percent of the physical output of the entire foods group. Flour accounted for 18 percent. Together, these industries made up more than two fifths of the total. Other industries, for which we have separate figures, constituted 18 percent, and the balance, 36 percent, came from the remaining food industries.

[22] See V. S. Clark, *History of Manufactures in the United States* (McGraw Hill, 1929), Vol. III, p. 264.

[23] For an algebraic statement on the method of derivation of the percentages in Table 15 see footnote 10, Chapter 4.

Table 15

FOODS

Relative Contributions of Component Industries to the Physical Output of the Entire Group[a]

Industry	Percentage Distribution, Comparable Pairs of Years									
	1899	1937	1899	1909	1909	1919	1919	1929	1929	1937
Meat packing	28.0	13.1	24.6	21.2	21.9	19.1	20.3	14.1	15.5	13.9
Flour	17.8	4.6	19.1	14.1	14.4	10.8	10.7	6.1	6.0	5.0
Rice	0.2	0.3	0.2	0.4	0.5	0.5	0.5	0.4	0.3	0.3
Fish, canned	1.8	1.0	1.5	1.5	1.4	1.1	1.1	0.9	1.0	1.0
Fruits and vegetables, canned	5.0	12.5	5.8	6.7	6.1	7.8	7.9	9.4	8.4	12.1
Butter					3.0	3.0	3.1	3.3	3.2	3.3
Cheese	3.8	6.0	4.9	5.3	0.6	0.6	0.7	0.5	0.5	0.7
Milk, canned					0.8	2.7	2.2	1.7	1.4	1.7
Beet sugar	0.4	1.9	0.6	2.7	2.6	2.6	2.0	1.9	1.2	1.4
Cane sugar, n.e.m.[b]	4.5	2.4	4.5	4.0	1.1	0.6	0.5	0.3	0.2	0.3
Cane-sugar refining					2.9	2.9	2.8	2.3	2.4	2.1
Ice	2.0	4.4	2.2	4.6	3.3	4.5	4.4	4.9	5.5	4.0
Corn products					2.0	2.1	2.2	2.1	1.9	1.5
Sausage, n.e.m.[b]									0.8	1.4
Oleomargarine, n.e.m.[b]									0.5	0.6
Shortenings									0.7	1.0
Cereals									2.9	2.1
Feeds									2.5	2.7
Macaroni									0.6	0.7
Biscuits and crackers	36.5	53.8	36.5	39.5	39.4	41.8	41.7	52.1	4.7	4.8
Bread and cake									21.5	19.8
Ice cream									5.2	5.5
Chocolate									1.1	1.3
Confectionery									5.0	5.4
Baking powder									1.0	0.6
All other products									6.1	7.1
TOTAL[c]	100.0	100.0	100.0	100.0	100.0	100.0	100.0	100.0	100.0	100.0

[a] Derived from Table 13. For an explanation of the derivation of the measurements see footnote 10, Chapter 4.

[b] N.e.m. denotes not elsewhere made.

[c] The columns do not in fact add up to 100.0 in every case, since rounding of the separate percentages has caused some columns to total more, and others less, than this figure.

In 1937 the situation was quite different. Meat packing contributed only 13 percent to the total physical output of the group, and flour only 5 percent. The two together made up less than one fifth of the total, whereas in 1899 they accounted for over two fifths. Rice, butter, cheese and milk, and ice provided larger shares of the total than they had in 1899, and there was a substantial increase (almost 8 percent) in canned fruits and vegetables. The beet-sugar industry augmented its relative contribution, but the two cane-sugar industries decreased theirs, so that all three together declined slightly. Canned fish decreased its contribution also. The industries for which we do not have separate data, and which together accounted for 36 percent of the group's output in 1899, increased their relative contribution to 54 percent in 1937.

Similar data are provided in the table for other years. Two sets of figures are given for 1909, 1919 and 1929, one comparable with an earlier year, the other comparable with a later year. Continuous declines are to be noted in the relative contributions of the flour and meat-packing industries.

By employing data on value added (Table 16) we may obtain a rough notion of the changing contribution to the total made by the industries for which separate figures on physical output are lacking, and at the same time confirm the evidence of Table 15. Interesting differences between the changes in the figures in this table and the changes in the figures in Table 16 are explored elsewhere.[24] The similarities, too, are striking, and validate our use of the data on value added to indicate major changes in the pattern of physical output. The bakery industries—biscuits and crackers, and bread and cake—increased their contribution to value added from 19 percent in 1899 to 26 percent in 1937. All of the increase occurred, however, between 1919 and 1937. There was another fairly large increase in the combined contributions of food, not elsewhere classified, feeds, shortenings, ce-

[24] Chapter 5, above.

TABLE 16

FOODS

Relative Contributions of Component Industries to the Value Added by the Entire Group[a]

Industry	*Percentage Distribution* 1899	1909	1919 Comparable with earlier years	1919 Comparable with later years	1929	1937
Meat packing	24.6	21.6	20.2	19.6	14.7	14.9
Sausage, n.e.m.[b]	0.3	0.5	0.6	0.5	0.9	1.2
Oleomargarine, n.e.m.[b]	1.2	0.2	0.6	0.6	0.5	0.5
Flour	17.5	15.2	11.0	10.7[c]	6.1	4.9
Rice	0.3	0.4	0.6	0.6	0.3	0.3
Biscuits and crackers	19.2 (with Bread and cake)	20.8 (with Bread and cake)	4.4	4.2	5.4	4.1
Bread and cake			14.7	14.2	19.9	21.8
Fish, canned	1.7	1.4	1.1	1.1	0.9	1.1
Fruits and vegetables, canned	6.8	5.8	8.2	8.0	9.2	10.7
Vinegar and cider	0.7	0.5	0.4	0.4	0.1	0.1
Butter	5.2 (Butter, Cheese, Milk)	3.3	3.0	2.9	3.5	3.0
Cheese		0.7	0.6	0.6	0.6	0.6
Milk, canned		1.1	2.5	2.4	1.4	1.6
Ice cream			d	3.1	5.5	5.1
Beet sugar	0.6	2.7	2.7	2.6	1.2	1.4
Cane sugar, n.e.m.[b]	4.4 (with Cane-sugar refining)	1.2	0.6	0.6	0.2	0.3
Cane-sugar refining		2.9	3.0	2.9	2.2	2.3
Chewing gum	6.0 (with Confectionery)	7.0 (with Confectionery)	1.1	1.1	1.2	1.5
Confectionery			8.5	8.2	5.7	4.6
Chocolate	0.7	0.9	1.6	1.6	1.3	1.0
Corn products	2.2	1.6	2.4	2.4	2.0	1.5
Food, n.e.c.[b]	3.6 (Food n.e.c. through Macaroni)	5.4 (Food n.e.c. through Macaroni)	2.3	2.2	2.4	2.9
Feeds			0.9	0.9[c]	2.4	2.8
Shortenings			0.5	0.4	0.5	1.3
Cereals			1.8	1.8	2.4	2.6
Macaroni			0.5	0.5	0.6	0.6
Flavorings	0.9	1.1	1.2	1.1	2.4	2.6
Baking powder	1.8	1.5	0.9	0.8	1.0	0.6
Ice	2.5	4.1	4.1	4.0	5.5	4.0
TOTAL[e]	100.0	100.0	100.0	100.0	100.0	100.0

[a] Basic data are given in Appendix C.

[b] N.e.m. denotes not elsewhere made; n.e.c. denotes not elsewhere classified.

[c] Between 1925 and 1927 certain establishments were shifted from the flour to the feeds industry.

[d] Not treated as a manufacturing industry prior to 1914.

[e] The columns do not add up to 100.0 in every instance because they contain rounded percentages.

reals and macaroni, from less than 4 percent in 1899 to 10 in 1937. (The increase is overstated somewhat because of a shift of establishments from flour to feeds following a revision of the definitions of the two industries.) The contribution of the flavorings industry rose from 1 percent in 1899 to 2.6 in 1937.

Changes in the industrial composition of the physical output of the foods group represent the net result of variation in the degree to which certain types of changes have affected the output of the several food-processing industries. These have already been noted above: first, a shift in the proportion of each food produced in and out of factories; second, a change in the proportion of imports or exports of each food; and third, a change in the amount of each kind of food consumed per capita.

The general tendency, of course, was toward greater factory production of foods and less processing on farms, in retail establishments or in homes. But the rate of shift varied from product to product, determined as it was by the relation between costs (including transport charges) in the factory and outside it, by changes in this relation, and by fluctuations in wants and in family incomes. In some food-processing industries, notably flour-milling and cheese, the shift to the factory had been virtually completed by the opening of the present century. In meat packing, the transfer was more moderate in extent, although it had a marked effect on the output of the foods group because of the importance of the industry itself. In the case of butter, the shift from farm to factory production was accomplished largely in the period under discussion. Other food industries that probably moved in the same direction, but in varying degree, were bakery products, cereals, macaroni, canned fruits and vegetables, ice cream, confectionery and ice.

There was variation also in the degree to which changes in foreign trade affected the different food industries. We have already noted the increased export of rice, and the decreased export of flour and meat products.

Differences in the rate of change in the distribution of output as between factory and nonfactory production, and in the export-import balance as well, account only in part for the shifting composition of the food group. There were also appreciable modifications in the diet of the people of the United States, and these too helped to condition the composition of the output of the food manufacturing group. The per capita consumption of meats and grain products declined. The consumption of sugar, dairy products, and fruits, went up.[25] These trends, based on production, export and import data, are confirmed by studies of family budgets. The latter provide, in addition, information on another aspect of food consumption. They indicate that usually the same sort of change in diet occurred at each income level. Thus the annual consumption of meats, fish and poultry, per capita, was 123 pounds in 1885–1904 and 85 pounds in 1935–37 for persons spending between $1.25 and $1.87 per week on food; 169 and 106 pounds, respectively, for those spending $1.88 to $2.49; and 204 and 139 pounds, respectively, for persons in a position to expend $2.50 to $3.12 for food.[26] At each income level the per capita consumption of meat, fish and poultry declined rather considerably between 1885–1904 and 1935–37. The decline at each level, however, was at a rate greater than that indicated by the data on average per capita consumption of meat products.[27] The rise in incomes accounts for the discrepancy, for there was always more meat consumption at high income levels than at low. Since the high income

[25] See U.S. Bureau of Foreign and Domestic Commerce, *op. cit.*, p. 1.

[26] These expenditure levels are expressed in fixed (1935) prices. See U.S. Department of Agriculture, "Present-Day Diets in the United States," by H. K. Stiebeling and C. M. Coons, *Yearbook of Agriculture, 1939,* p. 313.

[27] For all income levels combined the average consumption of meat products (not including fish and poultry) declined per capita from 163 pounds in 1899 to 136 pounds in 1937. See above, p. 132.

groups had greater weight in 1935–37 as a result of upward shifts in income, the considerable declines that occurred at each income level were in part counterbalanced, and the net result was a more moderate decline in the average per capita consumption of meats than would have occurred if incomes had remained stable.

Chapter 7

Beverages

THE beverage group includes one industry making nonalcoholic drinks, three industries producing spirituous beverages (malt, vinous and distilled), and one related industry manufacturing malt. The importance of the beverages group has fluctuated tremendously as a result of the enactment and repeal of prohibition laws. In 1899 the group accounted for a larger percentage of the total value added by manufacturing industries than 11 of the 16 other major groupings, but by 1937 its share of this total had diminished, and it stood among the lowest six instead of the highest.

TRENDS IN THE PHYSICAL OUTPUT OF THE BEVERAGE INDUSTRIES

Data on physical output are available for malt liquors and distilled liquors for the entire period; for vinous liquors, beginning with 1923; for malt, beginning with 1925; and for nonalcoholic beverages, beginning with 1931 (Table 17 and Chart 9).

Malt Liquors. The malt liquors industry, which embraces the factory production of beer, near beer, and similar beverages, made a net gain in output of only 60 percent from 1899 to 1937. There was a considerable rise during the first 15 years, culminating in a peak in 1914; after that date output fell rapidly until a low was reached in 1931. Following repeal output rose again, but even in 1937 it was more than 10 percent below the level attained in 1914.

Radical changes occurred not only in the aggregate quan-

Table 17

BEVERAGES

Physical Output: Indexes and Percentage Changes[a]

	Liquors, Malt	Malt	Liquors, Vinous	Liquors, Distilled	Beverages, Non-alcoholic	Total[b] Un-adjusted	Total[b] Adjusted
YEAR	INDEX OF PHYSICAL OUTPUT (1937:100)						
1899	62	..	..	24	..	53	43
1904	82	..	..	27	..	66	55
1909	96	..	..	31	..	77	63
1914	112	..	..	40	..	91	76
1919	47	..	..	1.0	..	24	23
1921	16	..	..	1.1	..	..	..
1923	9.0	..	11	0.9	..	..	..
1925	8.7	34	3.0	0.5	..	..	..
1927	7.4	33	3.6	0.4	..	..	..
1929	6.6	41	9.3	0.9	..	..	..
1931	5.3	36	5.4	0.9	66	..	..
1933	19	51	15	3.0	35	17	17
1935	77	87	75	65	52	70	70
1937	100	100	100	100	100	100	100
PERIOD	NET PERCENTAGE CHANGE IN PHYSICAL OUTPUT						
1899–1937	+60	..	..	+315	..	+89	+132
1899–1909	+54	..	..	+30	..	+45	+46
1909–1919	−51	..	..	−97	..	−69	−63
1919–1929	−86	..	..	−10	..	..	..
1929–1933	+185	+25	+64	+233	..	..	..
1933–1937	+432	+96	+554	+3,233	+183	+492	+492

[a] Legal production only. The indexes have been constructed from basic data in the U.S. Census of Manufactures and reports of the U.S. Bureau of Internal Revenue, by methods described briefly in Chapter 2 and in detail in Appendix A. Appendix B presents these data, together with the indexes derived from them. The indexes cited here for individual industries have been adjusted to take account of changes in the coverage of the respective samples, except when such adjustment was impossible. The percentage changes are not always entirely consistent with the indexes given above because the changes were computed from the indexes in Appendix B, which are carried to one decimal place.

[b] No indexes are given for 1919–33 because of inadequate data. The 1899–1919 indexes were computed on the 1909 and 1919 bases, as usual, and the 1935 and 1937 indexes were computed on the 1933 base. The segments were chained by the computation of an index for 1919 on the 1937 base.

Chart 9
BEVERAGES
Indexes of Physical Output

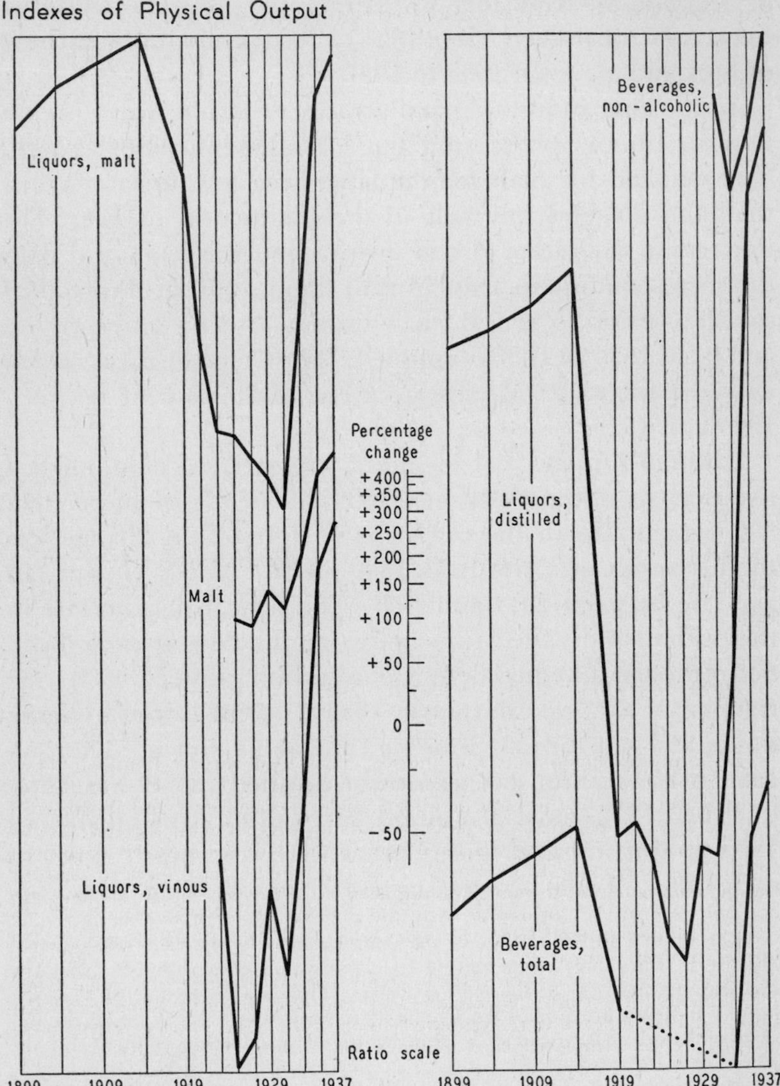

tity of the output of the industry but also in its character. The products of the malt liquors industry consisted entirely of beer and ale from 1899 to 1919; entirely of so-called cereal beverages (near beer) from 1921 to 1931; and almost entirely of beer and ale from 1933 to 1937.

Malt. This industry manufactures malt not only for use in malt liquors production but for other purposes as well. The demand for malt for the latter rose less, in later years, than the demand for malt in the production of beer. For this reason the recent rise in malt output was less rapid than the corresponding increase in malt liquors output. From 1929 to 1933, prior to repeal, malt output rose by one quarter, and from 1933 to 1937 it doubled.[1] The Census figures, which extend back to 1925, indicate a rise of 20 percent between 1925 and 1929.

Distilled Liquors, not including industrial alcohol, made a net gain in output, between 1899 and 1937, of more than 300 percent. As in the case of malt liquors, the change was the net result of a rise from 1899 to 1914, and a violent fall and rise between 1914 and 1937. The substantial increase in the output of distilled liquors during the 38-year period did not represent an equivalent rise in consumption. A very large fraction of the legal output in 1933–37 went into warehouse stocks and not directly into bars and retail stores.[2] Thus, although 259 million tax gallons of distilled spirits were produced in 1937, only 99 million were withdrawn for sale. In 1899 production and consumption were very much closer to each other. These figures suggest, therefore, that consump-

[1] The growth in the output of the malt industry is somewhat exaggerated because in 1935 the Census shifted its classification of malthouses from the malt liquors industry to the malt industry. The data on output of the malt liquors industry are unaffected by the shift since the index is based on Bureau of Internal Revenue data relating to the production of malt liquors wherever made.

[2] Measurement of output of the industry at the time of distillation takes no account of the important productive process involved in aging. Unfortunately, no more satisfactory measure is readily available.

tion per capita changed but little from 1899 to 1937. The inclusion of imports does not materially affect this conclusion. If, however, illegal production constituted an appreciably larger fraction of total production in 1937 than it did in 1899 —as may have been true—consumption per capita must have risen.

Nonalcoholic Beverages. This classification covers the factory production of soft drinks, including cereal beverages. (Because of the inclusion of the latter, the output of the industry overlaps the output of the malt liquors industry.) Retail production, and the bottling of natural waters or purchased manufactured beverages, are not included. The physical output of the industry as just defined rose 50 percent from 1931 to 1937. During this 6-year period the output of cereal beverages (near beer) fell from 96 million gallons to 3 million gallons, while carbonated beverages rose from 291 million gallons to 565 million.

Summary. The physical output of the group taken as a whole cannot be measured satisfactorily for the entire period 1899–1937. For the first two decades we have data covering the two most important industries, malt liquors and distilled liquors. Their combined output rose 45 percent in the first decade and fell 69 percent in the second. For the years 1919 to 1931 data are lacking for the nonalcoholic beverages industry, which in that period was the most important industry in the group, and was probably rising in output. For the period 1933–37 we have complete coverage of the output of the entire group. The figures indicate a gain of nearly 500 percent in the 4 years. Since in 1937 malt liquors and distilled liquors again constituted a large part of the total, we may compute a reasonably accurate group index, relating output in 1937 with output in 1919, and thereby with output in 1899. The unadjusted index reveals a rise, between 1899 and 1937, of 89 percent; the adjusted index, which reflects the increase in the importance of nonalcoholic beverages, shows a rise of 132 percent.

Over the long period taken as a whole, the output of malt liquors rose less rapidly than population, and much less rapidly than total manufacturing output. In contrast, the output of distilled liquors increased much more rapidly than population and slightly more rapidly than total manufacturing. The group total increased at a faster pace than population but was surpassed by total manufacturing output.

CHANGES IN THE INDUSTRIAL PATTERN OF BEVERAGE PRODUCTION

The composition of the physical output of the beverages group is given for selected years in Table 18. In the first decade there were only minor changes in the relative contributions of the individual industries to the group total. Malt liquors contributed more to the group's output than the

TABLE 18

BEVERAGES

Relative Contributions of Component Industries to the Physical Output of the Entire Group[a]

Industry	*Percentage Distribution, Comparable Pairs of Years*[b]							
	1899	1937	1899	1909	1909	1919	1933	1937
Liquors, malt	78.1	51.5	58.6	61.5	55.9	75.0	54.3	48.9
Liquors, distilled	14.2	24.2	33.7	30.1	35.6	3.1	5.2	29.4
Liquors, vinous							4.4	4.9
Beverages, nonalcoholic	7.7	24.3	7.7	8.4	8.5	21.9	31.9	15.3
Malt							4.2	1.4
TOTAL	100.0	100.0	100.0	100.0	100.0	100.0	100.0	100.0

(In the 1899–1937, 1899–1909 and 1909–1919 columns, a brace groups Liquors, vinous; Beverages, nonalcoholic; and Malt under the single figure shown.)

[a] Derived from Table 17. For an explanation of the derivation of the measurements see footnote 10, Chapter 4.

[b] Taxes are included in the value added per unit used to evaluate the physical output of malt, distilled liquors and vinous liquors in the 1899–1909, 1909–1919 and 1899–1937 comparisons; and are excluded in the 1933–37 comparison.

other beverage industries combined. In the second decade malt liquors not only retained its preeminent position but actually rose in importance; the relative contribution of distilled liquors declined severely in this period, whereas the remaining beverage industries (including nonalcoholic beverages) augmented their relative contributions. For the period 1919–33 no exact data on physical output are available. In the last period the share of the malt liquors industry in the group's output was largest again, though it declined slightly; the contribution of distilled liquors rose rapidly, and that of nonalcoholic beverages dropped off.

TABLE 19

BEVERAGES

Relative Contributions of Component Industries to the Value Added by the Entire Group[a]

Industry	Percentage Distribution					
	1899	1909	1919 Comparable with earlier years	1919 Comparable with later years	1929	1937
Beverages, nonalcoholic						
Excluding near beer	5.1	5.5	17.5	17.0	..	..
Including near beer	..	..	..	..	86.7	28.5
Liquors, malt						
Including near beer	64.1	57.0	74.8	75.3	..	..
Excluding near beer and tax	..	..	..	..	b	58.1
Malt	1.6	1.6	2.0	2.0	2.4[c]	3.2
Liquors, vinous	1.0	1.3	2.4	2.4	0.9	..
Excluding tax	..	..	..	..	..	3.3
Liquors, distilled	28.2	34.6	3.2	3.2	10.0	..
Excluding tax	..	..	..	..	..	6.9
TOTAL[d]	100.0	100.0	100.0	100.0	100.0	100.0

[a] Basic data are given in Appendix C.

[b] No legal production.

[c] Between 1929 and 1937 malthouses were shifted from the malt liquors to the malt industry.

[d] The columns do not add up to 100.0 in every instance because they contain rounded percentages.

Between 1899 and 1937 the relative contribution of malt liquors to total beverage output (both evaluated to include taxes) fell from more than 75 percent to about 50; the contribution of distilled liquors rose from 14 percent to 24; and that of all other beverage industries from 8 percent to 24.

The incomplete information on physical output is supplemented by data on value added (in Table 19). During the prohibition era nonalcoholic beverages and malt liquors (largely near beer) naturally accounted for most of the legal beverage production. Although the nonalcoholic beverages industry declined in relative importance between 1929 and 1937, it was nevertheless much more significant in 1937 than it had been before the war—even after liberal allowance is made for the discontinuity in the data arising from the exclusion of internal revenue taxes from value added in 1937.

Chapter 8

Tobacco Products

THE tobacco products group consists of three industries—cigars, cigarettes, and miscellaneous processed tobacco products. Tobacco curing and stemming and establishments engaged solely in tobacco packing are not included. Although it contains comparatively few industries, the group in 1937 contributed a larger share of the value added by all manufacturing industries than six other groups.[1]

TRENDS IN THE PHYSICAL OUTPUT OF THE TOBACCO PRODUCTS INDUSTRIES

Cigars. The physical output of the cigar industry was practically the same in 1937 as it had been in 1899 (Table 20 and Chart 10). During the first decade output rose by two fifths, but most of the rise occurred in the first five years. Between 1909 and 1919 the net gain was only 1 percent. The high point in the series for Census years was reached in 1914. Following 1919 a moderate decline set in, and by 1929 output was 11 percent below the 1919 level. From 1929 to 1937 the net decline was steeper, amounting to 20 percent.

Mechanization was widely introduced in cigar manufacture during the second half of the long period. Price reductions resulted, but apparently these served only to prevent cigar production from declining even more than it did. Another consequence of mechanization was the increase in the relative importance of short-filler cigars which brought down the

[1] The value added by the tobacco products group includes internal revenue taxes, an exceedingly important item.

average quality of cigars produced: these cigars, which tend to shred in the mouth during smoking, were originally made from scrap and cuttings discarded in the manufacture of long-filler cigars. They constituted 11 percent of the 1920 output, but after the introduction of the short-filler machine, which requires less labor than the hand or machine long-filler proc-

Table 20
TOBACCO PRODUCTS
Physical Output: Indexes and Percentage Changes[a]

	Cigarettes	*Cigars*	*Tobacco Products, Other*	*Total*
YEAR	INDEX OF PHYSICAL OUTPUT (1929:100)			
1899	3.1	80	89	30
1904	2.8	106	106	37
1909	5.6	111	130	43
1914	14	119	133	53
1919	43	112	128	69
1912	42	107	116	66
1923	54	108	124	74
1925	67	100	124	81
1927	81	100	114	90
1929	100	100	100	100
1931	96	82	96	93
1933	96	66	81	88
1935	113	70	82	101
1937	134	80	83	117
PERIOD	NET PERCENTAGE CHANGE IN PHYSICAL OUTPUT			
1899–1937	+4,226	0	−6	+293
1899–1909	+81	+39	+46	+ 46
1909–1919	+670	+1	−2	+60
1919–1929	+132	−11	−22	+44
1929–1937	+34	−20	−17	+17

[a] The indexes have been constructed from basic data in the U.S. Census of Manufactures and reports of the U.S. Bureau of Internal Revenue, by methods described briefly in Chapter 2 and in detail in Appendix A. Appendix B presents these data, together with the indexes derived from them. The indexes cited here for individual industries have been adjusted to take account of changes in the coverage of the respective samples, except when such adjustment was impossible. The percentage changes are not always entirely consistent with the indexes given above because the changes were computed from the indexes in Appendix B, which are carried to one decimal place.

ess, the proportion increased rapidly, reaching 27 percent in 1936. On the other hand there was an improvement in cigar wrapping: many more cigars are individually wrapped today than was the case in the past.[2]

Cigarettes. The course of cigarette production stands in sharp contrast to the record of cigar output. Cigarettes rose

Chart 10
TOBACCO PRODUCTS
Indexes of Physical Output

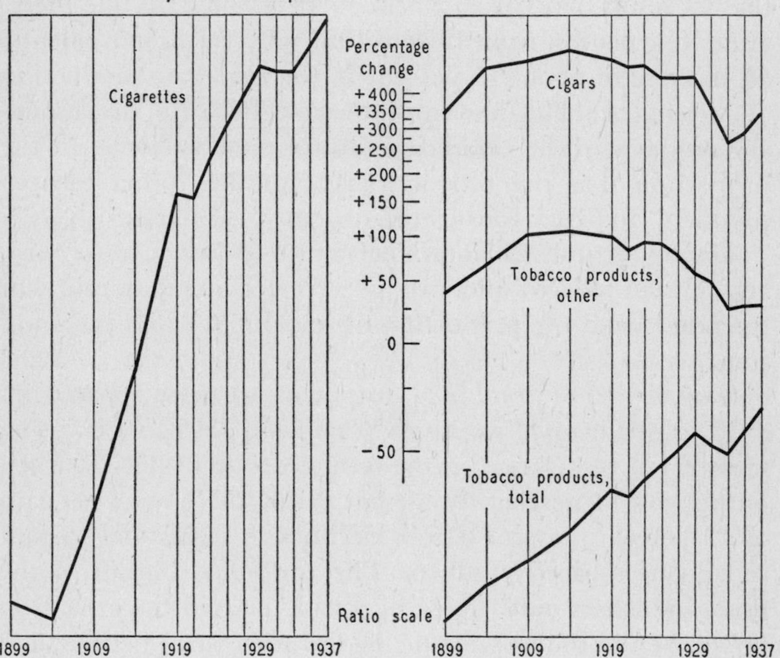

from 1899 to 1937 at a rate that resulted in an increase of over 4,000 percent. After a decline in 1899–1904, output rose rapidly, so that by 1909 it had made a net gain of 80 percent over output in 1899. In the next decade the rate of growth

[2] U.S. Department of Labor, Bureau of Labor Statistics, "Mechanization and Productivity of Labor in the Cigar Manufacturing Industry," by W. D. Evans, *Bulletin No. 660* (1939), pp. 3, 4, 20, 53–54.

was greatly accelerated, and the increase approached 700 percent. From 1919 to 1929 the rate of growth in cigarette production was slower, but output more than doubled. There was only a slight retardation in the recession years 1929–33, and by 1937 cigarette output was one third above the 1929 level.

Other Tobacco Products, including chewing and smoking tobacco and snuff, followed a time pattern roughly similar to that of cigars. Between 1899 and 1937 output fell 6 percent, the net result of a rise to a peak in 1914 and a decline thereafter. The net loss from 1899 to 1937 reflects two movements: an increase of about 15 percent in the aggregate production of chewing, smoking and snuff tobacco, including the secondary products of the cigarette industry; and a decline in the proportion that the products made in the "other tobacco products" industry constituted of total production.[3]

Among the individual products of the industry, plug, twist, and fine-cut tobacco underwent severe declines in output. On the other hand the production of smoking tobacco and snuff rose.[4]

Summary. The combined output of all three tobacco industries quadrupled in the 38 years from 1899 to 1937. The growth was most rapid in the second decade, 1909–19, when output rose 60 percent. In the last period there was a net gain of 17 percent, despite serious declines in cigars and in miscellaneous tobacco products. The combined output of the three industries outstripped by a wide margin the growth in population in the first decade. In the other three periods, and during the period 1899–1937 as a whole, the rise in population was exceeded only by the rate of increase in cigarette output. Cigarettes alone rose more rapidly than total manu-

[3] An adjustment for this second movement could not be made for the years 1899–1923 inclusive. Because the adjusted and unadjusted indexes fail to correspond closely for 1925–37, the unadjusted index for 1899–1923 must be considered only an approximate measure of the output of the industry.

[4] *Statistical Abstract, 1938,* p. 802.

facturing output in every period. The output of the entire group increased at about the same rate as total manufacturing in the entire period 1899–1937, although its rise was more rapid in the second and fourth periods, and less rapid in the first and third.

CHANGES IN THE INDUSTRIAL PATTERN OF TOBACCO MANUFACTURE

As Table 21 shows, there was wide variation over the years in the relative contributions of the three individual tobacco products industries to the output of this major group. In

Table 21

TOBACCO PRODUCTS

Relative Contributions of Component Industries to the Physical Output of the Entire Group[a]

Industry	*Percentage Distribution, Comparable Pairs of Years*									
	1899	1909	1909	1919	1919	1929	1929	1937	1909	1937
Cigarettes, Cigars (combined)	62.8	62.6								
Cigarettes			9.0	43.2	40.2	64.7	68.1	77.9	10.3	80.3
Cigars			58.2	36.6	37.2	23.0	18.7	12.7	49.5	11.4
Tobacco products, other	37.2	37.4	32.8	20.1	22.6	12.3	13.2	9.4	40.1	8.3
TOTAL[b]	100.0	100.0	100.0	100.0	100.0	100.0	100.0	100.0	100.0	100.0

[a] Derived from Table 20. For an explanation of the derivation of the measurements see footnote 10, Chapter 4.

[b] The columns do not add up to 100.0 in every instance because they contain rounded percentages.

1909 (the earliest year for which we have accurate data on which to base a detailed distribution), the cigarette industry accounted for only 10 percent of the group's output. Cigars contributed almost 50 percent, and miscellaneous tobacco products the remaining 40 percent. By 1937 the pattern had changed almost beyond recognition: the cigarette industry, contributing four fifths of the total, was now predominant, whereas cigars and miscellaneous products accounted for only 11 and 8 percent respectively. Corresponding figures, based on value added and given in Table 22, serve to confirm the account presented in Table 21.

Table 22

TOBACCO PRODUCTS

Relative Contributions of Component Industries to the Value Added by the Entire Group[a]

Industry	Percentage Distribution 1899	1909	1919 Comparable with earlier years	1919 Comparable with later years	1929	1937
Cigarettes	59.8	10.7	39.3	39.2	65.7	79.9
Cigars		55.0	40.1	40.0	21.2	10.7
Tobacco products, other	40.2	34.3	20.6	20.8	13.1	9.4
TOTAL	100.0	100.0	100.0	100.0	100.0	100.0

[a] Basic data are given in Appendix C.

It should not be assumed that the changes in the industrial distribution of output, as indicated by the figures in Tables 21 and 22, represent the pattern of tobacco consumption, for which quantitative data are presented below:

	Leaf Tobacco Consumed (million pounds)[a] 1899	1909	1914	1919	1929	1937	*Percentage Distribution* 1899	1909	1914	1919	1929	1937
Cigars	93	137	159	165	152	129	25	27	29	25	19	15
Cigarettes	15	24	62	198	347	480	4	5	11	29	44	55
Tobacco products, other	259	344	334	308	298	264	71	68	60	46	37	30
TOTAL	367	505	555	671	797	873	100	100	100	100	100	100

[a] *Statistical Abstract, 1920*, p. 566; *1922*, p. 490; *1938*, p. 803.

Although the cigarette industry accounted for about 80 percent of processed tobacco output in 1937, it consumed only about half the leaf tobacco in that year. At the beginning of the century, the manufacture of chewing and smoking tobacco absorbed almost three quarters of the leaf tobacco, but even then these products contributed only two fifths of the output of the group as a whole.

There is another important difference between consumption by the tobacco products industries and their output. Although the group's physical output quadrupled between 1899 and 1937, the amount of tobacco it used did not even triple. It is true that the per capita consumption of tobacco rose fairly rapidly, but there was an even more rapid rise in the output of manufactured tobacco products. The divergence reflects two shifts: first, a change in the kind of product (cigarettes containing a pound of tobacco are worth more in dollars and cents than a pound of smoking tobacco) and second, a movement of processing to the factory from the home (cigarettes made in the factory have a greater money value than the "makings" purchased by the man who rolls his own).

Chapter 9

Textile Products

THE textile products group includes all manufacturing industries whose chief materials are animal and vegetable fibers or fiber products; to these we have added industries engaged in the processing of furs. The manufacture of rayon yarn from cotton and wood pulp is treated as a chemical process and is therefore classified in the chemical products group. The activities covered by the textile group include preparation of fibers; spinning of yarns; weaving, knitting, or braiding of yarns into cloth, finished garments or other products; cutting and sewing of garments from woven or knitted fabrics; and processing of embroideries, artificial leather, oilcloth, linoleum, and the like. While most of the products are eventually transformed into articles of apparel, other important articles are used for furnishings (carpets, rugs, upholstery materials and curtains), wrapping materials (bags and twine), and industrial materials (tire fabrics, belting and cordage).

TRENDS IN THE PHYSICAL OUTPUT OF THE TEXTILE PRODUCTS INDUSTRIES

During the greater part of the period 1899–1937 the textile manufacturing industries, measured in terms of value added, constituted the most important manufacturing group. It is fortunate, therefore, that the data on physical output for this group are fairly extensive. Complete data on the physical output of textile products are available for most of the less advanced stages of production; and the final stages of manufacture are covered in the most recent period (Table 23, Chart 11).[1]

Cotton Goods, an industry which surpasses all the others in the group with respect to value added, includes establishments engaged in weaving broad cotton goods from yarn either made in the same establishments or purchased; in producing cotton felts; and in spinning yarns and thread for sale. The physical output of the industry doubled in the years 1899–1937. Most of the rise occurred in the first decade, when output rose 38 percent. From 1909 to 1919 output increased only 15 percent, slightly less rapidly than population. In the next decade there was a rise of 28 percent, and in the last period a decline of 1 percent. The peak was reached in 1927, with output 4 percent above that of 1929.

There were significant changes also in the composition of the output of the cotton goods industry. During the first 20 years, when total output rose 60 percent, napped fabrics and twine remained practically unchanged; the combined output of sheetings, shirtings and muslin increased only 14 percent; and waste rose only 16 percent.[2] Plushes and corduroys, however, went up by 400 percent. In the years 1919–37 total output rose 27 percent, yet declines are recorded for the output of numbered duck (—30 percent), drills (—10 percent), muslins (—51 percent), twills and sateens (—22 percent), yarns for sale (—13 percent),[3] and denims, including pin checks, tickings and ginghams (—46 percent). In contrast

[1] Between 1933 and 1935, and between 1935 and 1937, considerable revisions were made by the Census in the classification of textile establishments. As a result, the changes in output noted in Table 23 are somewhat inaccurate for silk and rayon goods, carpets and rugs, men's clothing, textile gloves, elastic woven goods, cloth hats, knit hosiery, and men's shirts and collars. These errors are presumably minor, though no exact information is available. Details concerning these changes in classification are to be found in the footnotes in Appendix C. For the group as a whole the errors tend to cancel out; the group index is therefore only slightly affected by these shifts.

[2] The sale of waste and yarns to other establishments in the industry results in some duplication in the industry's output. This does not appear to be serious; see Appendix B.

[3] See footnote 2.

TABLE 23

TEXTILE PRODUCTS[a]

Physical Output: Indexes and Percentage Changes[b]

	Cotton Goods	Lace Goods	Woolen and Worsted Goods: Total	Woolen and Worsted Goods: Woolen Goods	Woolen and Worsted Goods: Worsted Goods	Silk and Rayon Goods	Knit Goods: Total	Knit Goods: Hosiery, Knit	Knit Goods: Underwear, Knit	Knit Goods: Outerwear, Knit	Knit Goods: Cloth, Knit
YEAR					INDEX OF PHYSICAL OUTPUT (1929:100)						
1899	49	..	71	..	..	22	19	8.8	67	24	8.9
1904	54	..	86	..	..	30	24	13	74	32	12
1909	68	..	103	78	123	40	33	19	95	59	7.5
1914	73	74	102	83	118	49	45	34	103	57	13
1919	78	87	98	92	104	64	55	43	109	61	38
1921	70	67	93	80	105	58	59	47	90	84	57
1923	93	101	120	115	130	73	75	57	103	119	58
1925	93	90	108	112	106	86	77	68	107	85	64
1927	104	96	103	105	103	92	83	78	102	84	74
1929	100	100	100	100	100	100	100	100	100	100	100
1931	78	80	81	70	88	92	92	88	78	108	148
1933	87	..	87	..	..	84	100	92	98	119	..
1935	78	143	116	..	..	133	111	102	99	142	..
1937	99	154	114	..	..	135	116	115	102	117	..
PERIOD					NET PERCENTAGE CHANGE IN PHYSICAL OUTPUT						
1899–1937	+101	..	+60	..	..	+512	+505	+1,202	+52	+393	..
1899–1909	+38	..	+44	..	..	+79	+73	+117	+42	+148	−16
1909–1919	+15	..	−5	+18	−15	+61	+67	+125	+14	+3	+402
1919–1929	+28	+15	+3	+9	−4	+57	+80	+133	−8	+65	+165
1929–1937	−1	+54	+14	..	..	+35	+16	+15	+2	+17	..

For footnotes see end of table, p. 171.

TABLE 23 (concluded)

	Carpets and Rugs, Wool	Asphalted-Felt-Base Floor Covering	Linoleum	Cordage and Twine	Jute Goods	Linen Goods	Clothing, Men's[e]	Gloves, Textile, n.e.m.[d]	Shirts and Collars, Men's	Clothing, Women's, n.e.c.[e]	Corsets
YEAR	INDEX OF PHYSICAL OUTPUT (1929:100)										
1899	61	..	..	67	61	137	..	..	..	..	..
1904	65	..	32	..	..	..	..	..	..	..	..
1909	78	..	59	82	109	200	..	..	..	..	..
1914	71	..	83	98	138	192	..	..	..	..	..
1919	62	23	66	93	117	86	..	..	..	..	..
1921	59	24	82	75	77	72	..	..	..	..	..
1923	101	56	99	96	104	125	..	..	..	..	..
1925	96	74	86	95	105	117	..	..	..	..	..
1927	89	105	92	95	97	120	96	104	101	84	99
1929	100	100	100	100	100	100	100	100	100	100	100
1931	63	78	45	69	79	68	75	67	99	103	111
1933	61	84	42	71	89	72	79	..	79	91	109
1935	86	113	60	72	100	73	100	61	91	109	..
1937	92	144	83	92	143	77	99	97	93	125	129
PERIOD	NET PERCENTAGE CHANGE IN PHYSICAL OUTPUT										
1899–1937	+52	..	..	+38	+134	−44	..	..	..	..	..
1899–1909	+29	..	..	+23	+78	+46	..	..	..	..	..
1909–1919	−21	..	+14	+13	+7	−57	..	..	..	..	..
1919–1929	+62	+332	+50	+8	−14	+16	..	..	..	..	..
1929–1937	−8	+44	−17	−8	+43	−23	−1	−3	−7	+25	+29

	Handker-chiefs	Elastic Woven Goods, n.e.m.[d]	Hats, Fur-Felt	Hats, Cloth	Hats, Straw, Men's	Hats, Wool-Felt	Artificial Leather	Oilcloth	Wool Shoddy	Total Unadjusted	Total Adjusted
YEAR					INDEX OF PHYSICAL OUTPUT (1929:100)						
1899	..	..	79	..	..	135	..	..	55	43	38
1904	..	..	106	..	..	68	..	36	75	50	48
1909	..	..	126	..	..	101	..	62	68	64	60
1914	..	..	91	..	..	64	..	61	82	72	72
1919	..	..	94	..	..	79	..	38	98	75	67
1921	..	..	81	..	..	50	..	46	46	69	64
1923	..	..	93	..	..	72	102	61	100	91	82
1925	..	..	86	..	..	73	109	66	110	91	86
1927	99	76	104	97	122	87	104	79	71	94	94
1929	100	100	100	100	100	100	100	100	100	100	100
1931	75	62	78	59	99	84	59	77	59	85	87
1933	..	..	..	..	..	..	..	..	87	86	85
1935	78	69	94	71	143	185	91	76	109	101	99
1937	86	63	100	53	158	256	118	66	118	110	106
PERIOD					NET PERCENTAGE CHANGE IN PHYSICAL OUTPUT						
1899–1937	..	..	+26	..	..	+90	..	..	+116	+153	+180
1899–1909	..	..	+59	..	..	–25	..	..	+24	+47	+60
1909–1919	..	..	–25	..	..	–21	..	–39	+44	+17	+11
1919–1929	..	..	+6	..	..	+26	..	+163	+2	+34	+49
1929–1937	–14	–37	0	–47	+58	+156	+18	–34	+18	+10	+6

[a] Industries for which there are no adequate quantity data for any period listed above are: cotton small wares; haircloth; wool pulling; wool scouring; dyeing and finishing; carpets and rugs, rag; mats and matting; furnishings, men's, not elsewhere classified; embroideries, millinery and trimmings; hat and cap materials; fur goods; furs, dressed; awnings; bags, textile, not elsewhere made; belting, woven, not elsewhere made; house furnishings, not elsewhere classified; horse blankets; felt goods; flags and banners; regalia; nets and seines; upholstering materials, not elsewhere classified; and waste. These industries are covered by the adjusted total.

[b] The indexes have been constructed from basic data in the U. S. Census of Manufactures by methods described briefly in Chapter 2 and in detail in Appendix A. Appendix B presents these data, together with the indexes derived from them. The indexes cited here for individual industries have been adjusted to take account of changes in the coverage of the respective samples, except when such adjustment was impossible.

The percentage changes are not always entirely consistent with the indexes given above because the changes were computed from the indexes in Appendix B, which are carried to one decimal place.

[c] Includes clothing, men's, work; clothing, men's, n.e.c.; clothing, men's, buttonholes; and cloth sponging and refinishing.

[d] N.e.m. denotes not elsewhere made.

[e] N.e.c. denotes not elsewhere classified.

Chart 11
TEXTILE PRODUCTS
Indexes of Physical Output

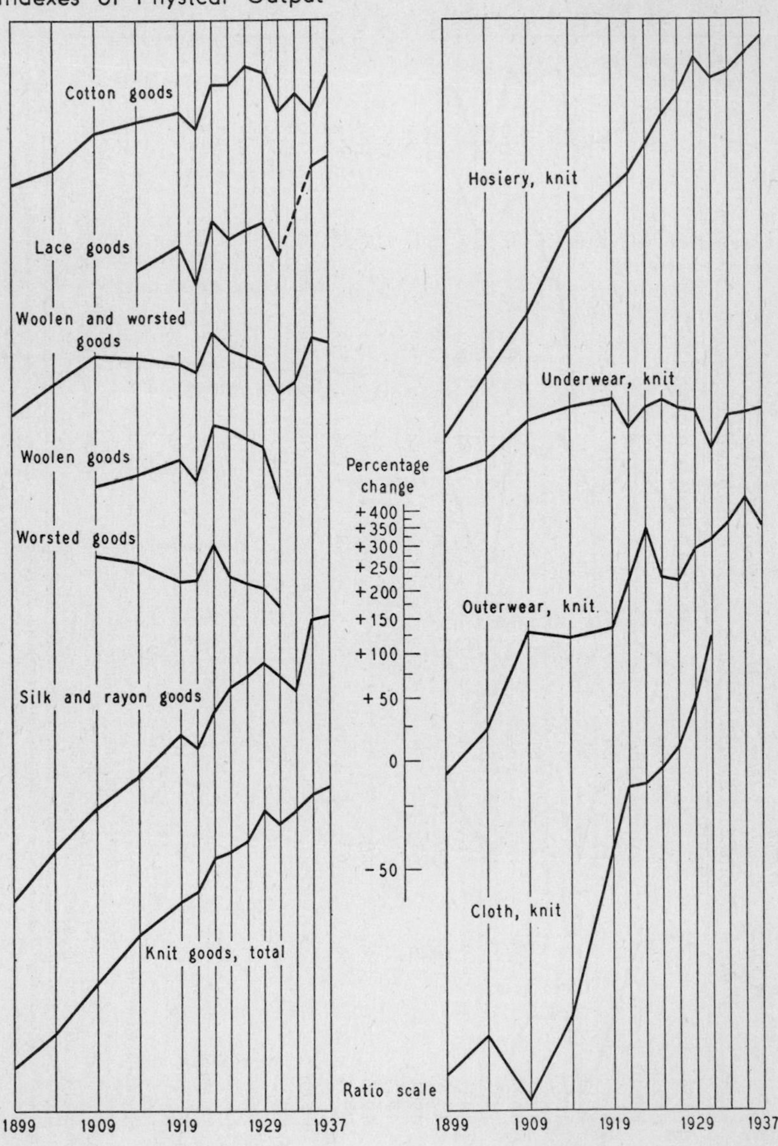

Chart 11 (cont.)
TEXTILE PRODUCTS
Indexes of Physical Output

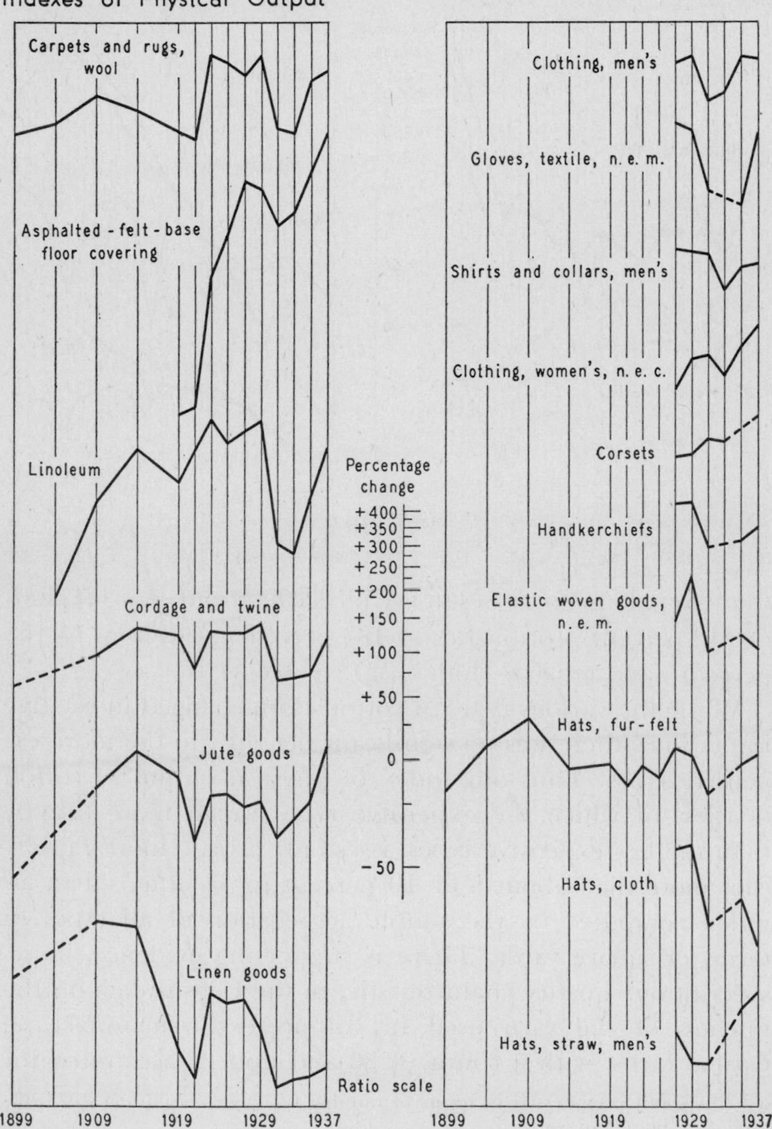

Chart 11 (concl.)
TEXTILE PRODUCTS
Indexes of Physical Output

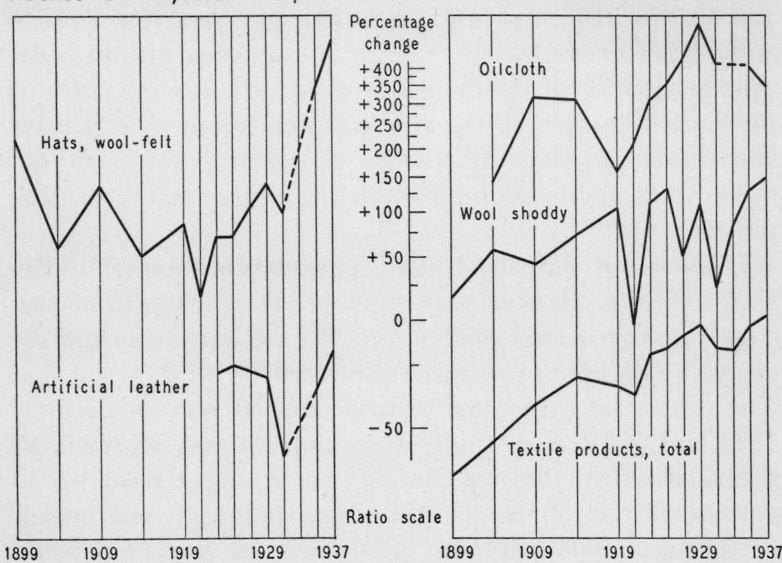

there were large increases in the physical output of print cloth (+112 percent), cottonades (+183 percent), towelings (+168 percent), and tobacco cloth (+275 percent).

While the various types of cotton cloth changed in relative importance there was no significant net shift to the more expensive types. Thus our index of physical output of cotton textiles, in which the expensive types weigh more heavily than the less expensive types, rises only a little more rapidly (not more than about 5 or 10 percent in 38 years) than an index computed by the simple aggregation of all types in terms of square yards. There is supporting evidence, in respect of one quality characteristic, in the Census data on the fineness of the yarn used in cotton textile manufacture. Coarse yarns, with a count of 20 and under,[4] accounted for

[4] The count is expressed in terms of number of hanks containing 840 yards each, per pound of yarn.

57.9 percent of all cotton yarns produced for consumption and sale in 1899, 47.8 in 1919 and 55.2 in 1937; medium yarns (21's to 40's) for 36.8 percent in 1899, 45.3 in 1919 and 38.3 in 1937; and fine yarns (61's and over) for 5.3, 6.9, and 6.5 percent in the three years, respectively. Although the average quality of cotton goods produced was not affected by marked changes in the relative proportions of expensive and cheap varieties, the quality of each type of cloth was raised as a result of improvements in the manufacturing process.[5]

Woolen and Worsted Goods. This classification comprises woven fabrics, blankets and other products made from purchased or transferred woolen and worsted yarns or from the original raw wool, and yarns produced for sale or transfer. The output of this industry rose only 60 percent between 1899 and 1937, less rapidly than population.[6] Most of the rise occurred in the first decade, when output went up 44 percent. In the following two decades there were only minor net changes, but in the last period output rose 14 percent. The peak in the series came in 1923, when output was about 5 percent above the level it was to reach 14 years later, in 1937.

The woolen and worsted goods industry turns out an enormous variety of fabrics. These differ from one another not only with respect to the basic fiber and type of yarn—e.g., all-wool cloth, made of worsted yarn, woolen yarn, or a combination of both types of yarn; woolen- or worsted-

[5] "For example, the 64 × 60 print cloth produced today under conditions of controlled humidity, with feeler motion and on automatic looms, is definitely superior to that sold twenty-five years ago. Weak spots have been reduced through far greater uniformity in the yarns." *Textile Markets,* Report of the Committee on Textile Price Research to the Conference on Price Research (National Bureau of Economic Research, Price Studies No. 2, 1939), p. 92.

[6] Even 60 percent is a slight overstatement, because there was an increase in the amount of duplication in the total product of the industry made from yarns originating in the industry and sold to other establishments within the same classification.

filled cloth, made with warp yarns of cotton, rayon, etc.—but also with respect to purpose—e.g., men's suitings, men's overcoatings, shirtings, etc. Unfortunately, continuous data on the output of individual products are not given in the Census reports. It is possible to distinguish only between woolen and worsted goods, and even this breakdown applies only to the two middle decades. These limited data show increases, from 1909 to 1919, and from 1919 to 1929, in the output of woolen fabrics made of rough fleecy yarns spun from carded short-staple wool; and decreases in the output of worsted fabrics made of smooth-surfaced yarns spun from combed long-staple wool. We know also that there have been changes in the weight per unit of area in wool fabrics: men's suitings in 1932 weighed 8 to 12 ounces per square yard, whereas a few years earlier they weighed 12 to 16 ounces. Similarly, men's overcoatings, which formerly ran from 16 to 20 ounces, in 1932 seldom weighed over 16 and more often were as low as 12 ounces. Women's fabrics showed even more striking reductions in weight.[7]

Silk and Rayon Goods. This industry, which manufactures cloth and yarn from silk and rayon fibers, experienced much more rapid growth in output than the industries using cotton and wool. Output of silk and rayon goods in 1937 was six times as great as it had been in 1899.[8] Acceleration of production was most pronounced in the first decade, when output rose almost 80 percent; in the second and third decades the gains were close to 60 percent and even in the troubled years 1929–37 output rose by one third.[9] The major change in the composition of the industry's output is at-

[7] P. T. Cherington, *Commercial Problems of the Woolen and Worsted Industries* (Textile Foundation, 1932), p. 28.

[8] Duplication in the aggregate output of the industry did not change sufficiently to affect this index to an appreciable degree. See Appendix B.

[9] Owing to changes in the Census industrial classification no precise index for this industry can be computed for 1929–37. However, the index presented here is the best that can be constructed from the available data and is believed to be reasonably accurate.

tributable, as the following tabulation shows, to the tremendous increase in the amount of rayon used in the industry,[10] and to the far less rapid rise in the quantity of silk absorbed by it. Up to 1919 the products of the industry consisted

	Quantity Consumed (million pounds)	
	Silk	Rayon
1914	29	2
1919	37	3
1929	64	33
1935	32	140

almost entirely of silk goods. From 1919 to 1929, however, rayon goods rose in importance at a rate exceeding the growth in silk goods. And from 1929 to 1935 silk goods actually declined in output while rayon goods continued rapidly upward. In 1937, according to the detailed Census data, the output of rayon broad goods amounted to 950 million square yards; rayon-mixture broad goods to 55 million; silk broad goods to 110 million; and silk-mixture broad goods to 30 million.

Knit Goods is another textile industry which made rapid and continuous progress during the 38 years covered by our indexes. The total gain in output between 1899 and 1937 exceeded 500 percent.[11] The hosiery branch of the knit goods industry rose much more rapidly than the total: the 38-year gain was 1,200 percent. Knit underwear, on the other hand, rose only 50 percent between 1899 and 1937, and knit outer-

[10] The increase in rayon consumption during 1929–35 in the silk and rayon goods industry exceeds the increase in total rayon consumed in all textile industries. The disparity is accounted for chiefly by a decline in the quantity of rayon consumed in the cotton textile industry, as the latter is defined in the Census: from 35 million lbs. in 1929 to 19 million in 1935.

[11] The National Bureau index for the entire industry is adjusted for changes in coverage over the full period 1899–1937. The indexes for the separate branches are not so adjusted except for 1923–37. The figures (Appendix B) suggest that inaccuracies arising from this source might be expected to appear in the indexes for outerwear and underwear alone.

wear also failed to increase in output more rapidly than the group as a whole. The increase of the latter branch of knit goods production, close to 400 percent, was distributed irregularly among the four periods. Data on knit cloth are not available for the entire period: during the first decade there was a net decline of 16 percent, in the next decade production quintupled and in the third period it rose 165 percent. In 1929 output was more than ten times as great as it had been in 1899.

Within each of the branches of the knit goods industry there were changes also in the composition of output. In hosiery production, for example, the output of seamless hose in 1937 was no greater than it had been in 1919, but the output of full-fashioned hosiery was five times greater. Since the two types of hosiery are products of different machines, the change in the character of the industry's output is closely bound up with basic changes in the industry's equipment and labor force. The greater variety of designs woven into men's hose reflects changes in equipment too. In addition, there were marked shifts from one material to another in the manufacture of hosiery. Cotton declined in relative importance, while silk and rayon grew.[12] In the underwear branch of the knit goods industry also there were changes in the relative importance of different types of garments and of the several materials used. Shirts and drawers declined in output while the production of union suits rose; consumption by underwear factories of cotton and wool materials dropped but the use of silk and rayon increased.

In the knit outerwear branch there were striking increases in dress and suit production, and declines in the output of scarfs and shawls, neckties, and gloves and mittens.

[12] Because silk, cotton, and rayon stockings are each weighted by their appropriate values, rather than simply aggregated in terms of number, the shift to the more expensive silk hose causes the index of output to rise from 1919 to 1921, although the aggregate number of stockings produced actually declined.

Wool Carpets and Rugs. This classification covers establishments engaged in the manufacture from wool yarns of carpets and rugs made with jute, cotton or linen backs; it does not include the manufacture of rag carpets. The physical output of wool carpets and rugs rose from 1899 to 1937 by only 50 percent, the net effect of rises in the first and third decades, and declines in the second and fourth periods. The peak in the series was reached in 1923. The output of carpets and rugs appears to have risen in relation to the input of materials during the first two decades and to have fallen during the third and fourth periods.[13] The difference is probably associated with the great changes that occurred in the composition of the output of the carpets and rugs industry. Axminster and moquette carpets and rugs increased enormously, as did tapestry velvet and Wilton, while the output of Brussels, tapestry Brussels, and ingrain carpets and rugs fell off.

Other Floor-Coverings Industries. Asphalted-felt-base floor covering, an industry which competes to some extent with the carpets and rugs industry, made greater gains than the latter in the short period for which we have data. Between 1919 and 1929 its output more than quadrupled, and in the eight years following 1929 it rose 44 percent.[14]

Linoleum, a related industry, increased its output by 160 percent from 1904 (the first year for which we have data) to

[13] As a consequence, the net output of the industry advanced more rapidly (or fell less rapidly) than the gross output prior to 1919, and rose less rapidly (or fell more rapidly) after 1919:

	Percentage Change				
	1899–1937	1899–1909	1909–1919	1919–1929	1929–1937
Output of carpets and rugs	+52	+29	–21	+62	–8
Input of wool and yarns	+37	+18	–33	+81	–4
Net output	+79	+43	–2	+43	–10

Over the 38-year period, net output rose in relation to gross output.

[14] The index for 1919 is not precise because it could not be adjusted for change in coverage from 1919 to 1921; see Appendix B.

1937. From 1914 to 1919 output fell, but in 1923 it reached a high point exceeded only in 1929.[15] Within the industry there was a rise in the output of inlaid and linoleum rugs, and a decline in the output of plain and printed linoleum.

Cordage and Twine made but slight progress in the two more recent periods. The output of this industry rose 38 percent over the years 1899–1937, but almost all of the gain occurred between 1899 and 1914. Output in 1929 was not far above that of 1914, and from 1929 to 1937 it actually declined 8 percent. Within the industry there was a shift in the materials utilized. Cotton consumption rose, while the use of most other fibers declined. One of the most important products, binder twine, fell in output by as much as 30 percent between 1899 and 1937.[16]

Clothing. Of the five clothing industries (men's clothing, gloves, men's shirts and collars, women's clothing, and corsets) two are extremely important in terms of value added, and a third is of more than average importance. It is unfortunate, therefore, that data on quantity of output are not available for these industries for the years prior to 1927. Even the available data are probably affected seriously by quality changes. The quality of clothing is frequently modified in order that the merchandise may be adapted to rather stable retail price lines. The manufacturer and retailer can "adjust for raw material price fluctuations by shifting from one standard [cloth] construction to another without changing the retail price of the finished article. A rise in the price of 80 x 80 gray cloth, for example, from 7½ to 10 cents per yard would throw printed percales made from this construction out of the range the dollar dress cutter could pay. After the supply of goods he had purchased in expectation of that

[15] The 1904–19 indexes are unadjusted and susceptible to some error on that account; see Appendix B.

[16] Our figures do not include the considerable output of binder twine made in penal institutions.

price rise had been exhausted, he would be obliged to turn to the next cheaper construction of percales for his dollar dress line; i.e., 68 x 72s and so on. Over the last 15 years all these constructions have been used for the dollar dress at one time or another." [17]

The output of men's clothing, including youths' and boys' suits, coats, trousers and overalls, changed only slightly between 1927 and 1929 and again between 1929 and 1937. In the entire decade there was a net rise of only 2 percent. In considerable contrast to these minor changes are the important increases in the output of the women's clothing industry. Women's clothing, which includes children's and infants' wear, as well as women's coats, suits, dresses, skirts, underwear and nightwear, rose almost 50 percent from 1927 to 1937.[18] There were especially large increases from 1929 to 1937 in the output of women's suits, ensembles, separate skirts, blouses and shirtwaists, washable service apparel, kimonos and bathrobes, aprons and hoovers. Textile gloves (made of cloth or cloth and leather combined) declined 7 percent from 1927 to 1937. Men's shirts and collars fell 8

[17] *Textile Markets,* pp. 90–91.

[18] These percentage changes are exceedingly rough measures of output since they reflect merely changes in the number of garments of each general type. For example, one of our series is "dresses, 1-piece," of which 163 million were produced in 1929. The figure is the sum of the following quantities, each relating to a particular retail price line:

Retail Price Line	*Quantity (Millions)*
Under $1.00	23
$1 to $1.99	36
$2 to $2.99	16
$3 to $4.99	14
$5 to $9.99	35
$10 to $24.99	31
$25 and over	8
	163

These price differences reflect variations not only in the amount and quality of materials and trimmings, but also in the labor utilized in the process of fabrication.

percent in the same period. Collar output decreased steadily, from 8 million dozen in 1927 to 1.2 million in 1935 (the last year covered by the data on this product). The corsets industry increased its output by 29 percent from 1929 to 1937. There were increases in the production of brassieres, and of corsets, girdles and garter belts, and decreases in combinations or one-piece garments.

The two clothing accessory industries listed in Table 23, handkerchiefs and elastic woven goods, decreased their output from 1929 to 1937. Output in the former industry fell by 14 percent. Elastic woven goods, including suspenders and garters, declined by 37 percent.

Hats. The four hat industries distinguished by the Census differed greatly with respect to rate of increase in output. Fur-felt hats, made from hatters' fur, rose by one fourth between 1899 and 1937, and wool-felt hats almost doubled in the same period. Neither of these net percentages can be considered an accurate reflection of the trend, however. The output of fur-felt hats reached a peak in 1909. In wool-felt hat production a low point occurred in 1921, and 1909, 1919 and 1929 were all below the initial (1899) and final (1937) levels. For the period 1929–37 indexes are available for all four industries: wool-felt hats rose 156 percent, and men's straw hats 58 percent; fur-felt hats remained constant, and cloth hats (silk hats, caps, industrial hats, etc.) fell 47 percent. Within the fur-felt hats industry the output of finished hats fell slightly from 1899 to 1937, while hat bodies and hats in the rough rose many-fold.[19] A similar change in composition characterized the output of wool-felt hats. In 1899, 56,000 dozen hat bodies and 811,000 dozen finished hats were produced, but in 1937 the corresponding quantities were 2,428,000 dozen hat bodies and 372,000 dozen finished hats.

[19] An increasing degree of duplication in the output of the fur-felt hats industry causes our index to overstate the rise in the industry's output; see Appendix B.

Summary of Changes in Individual Industries. The trends in physical output are summarized in Table 24. Over the period 1899–1937 as a whole only one of the textile industries for which we have data, linen goods, declined in physical output. In the first decade, 1899–1909, there were two declining textile industries, knit cloth and wool-felt hats. The number with declining output rose to six in 1909–1919: worsted goods, wool carpets and rugs, linen goods, fur-felt and wool-felt hats, and oilcloth. Between 1919 and 1929, however, only three textile industries declined in output: worsted goods, knit underwear, and jute goods. In the last period, 1929–37, almost half the industries decreased their output.

TABLE 24
TEXTILE PRODUCTS
Summary of Changes in Physical Output[a]

	Number of Industries				
	1899–1937	1899–1909	1909–1919	1919–1929	1929–1937
Industries for which there are indexes of physical output	13	14	17	19	27
Industries with output rising	12	12	11	16	14
Industries with output constant	..	..	..	..	1
Industries with output falling	1	2	6	3	12
Industries with output rising in relation to population	7	12	5	10	13
Industries with output falling in relation to population	6	2	12	9[b]	14
Industries with output rising in relation to total manufacturing output	3	5	4	5	13
Industries with output falling in relation to total manufacturing output	10	9	13	14	14

[a] Derived from data in Table 23, and from figures on changes in population and in total manufacturing output given in footnote a, Table 14.
[b] Includes one industry with output constant in relation to population.

Measured in relation to population growth during the 38 years, almost half the industries for which indexes are available declined in output. Besides linen goods, which fell absolutely, there were relative declines in the output of woolen and worsted goods, knit underwear, wool carpets and rugs, cordage and twine, and fur-felt hats. In the first decade the rate of output of 2 out of 14 industries fell below the rate of population growth; in the second, 12 out of 17 suffered a similar decline; in the third, 8 out of 19; and in the last period, 14 out of 27.

In relation to the growth in the output of all manufacturing industries combined, more textile industries declined than rose. This was true of the period as a whole and of each of the periods into which we have divided it.

The Group Total. The index of physical output of the entire textile products group, based on available samples, rose 153 percent between 1899 and 1937. But according to the data on value added the importance of the sample declined somewhat in that period. After correction for this downward bias the index shows an increase of 180 percent. Both adjusted and unadjusted indexes rose most rapidly in the first decade, more slowly in the third decade, and much more slowly in the second and fourth periods. The decline in the adjusted index from 1914 to 1919 is especially striking.

CHANGES IN THE INDUSTRIAL PATTERN OF TEXTILE PRODUCTION

There was a radical transformation of the industrial pattern of textile production in the period 1899–1937. That pattern is depicted, insofar as the data permit, in Table 25, which gives the percentage contributions of each industry to the physical output of the entire group for selected years. In 1899 the cotton goods industry contributed 22.4 percent to the physical output of the entire group, but by 1937 the

TABLE 25

TEXTILE PRODUCTS

Relative Contributions of Component Industries to the Physical Output of the Entire Group[a]

Group	Percentage Distribution, Comparable Pairs of Years									
	1899	1937	1899	1909	1909	1919	1919	1929	1929	1937
Cotton goods	22.4	16.6	22.5	19.3	21.1	22.0	21.0	17.9	17.0	15.8
Silk and rayon goods	3.3	7.4	5.4	6.0	5.1	7.4	6.9	7.2	5.8	7.3
Woolen and worsted goods	14.3	8.4	12.7	11.4	12.2	10.4	11.3	7.7	8.5	9.1
Knit goods	5.1	11.4	6.2	6.7	5.5	8.2	8.1	9.8	9.9	10.5
Carpets and rugs, wool	3.8	2.1	3.0	2.4	2.2	1.6	1.8	1.9	2.6	2.2
Cordage and twine	1.7	0.8	1.4	1.1	1.1	1.1	1.2	0.9	1.0	0.8
Jute goods	0.4	0.3	0.3	0.4	0.4	0.4	0.4	0.3	0.3	0.4
Linen goods	0.3	0.1	0.2	0.2	0.2	0.1	0.1	0.1	0.1	0.1
Hats, fur-felt	2.1	1.0	2.0	2.0	1.8	1.2	1.4	1.0	1.2	1.1
Hats, wool-felt	0.3	0.2	0.3	0.1	0.1	0.1	0.1	0.1	0.1	0.2
Wool shoddy			0.3	0.2	0.2	0.2	0.2	0.1	e	e
Oilcloth					0.2	0.1	0.1	0.2	0.2	0.1
Lace goods							0.5	0.4	0.4	0.6
Linoleum							0.7	1.0	0.8	0.6
Asphalted-felt-base floor covering									0.4	0.6
Gloves, textile, n.e.m.[b]									0.4	0.3
Clothing, men's									11.6	10.8
Clothing, women's, n.e.c.[c]	46.2	51.7							14.8	17.3
Corsets			45.8	50.1	49.9	47.2			1.0	1.3
Shirts and collars, men's									2.6	2.4
Handkerchiefs							46.1	51.4	0.3	0.3
Elastic woven goods n.e.m.[b]									0.3	0.2
Hats, cloth									0.4	0.2
Hats, straw, men's									0.2	0.3
Artificial leather									0.3	0.3
All other products									19.8[e]	17.2[e]
TOTAL[d]	100.0	100.0	100.0	100.0	100.0	100.0	100.0	100.0	100.0	100.0

[a] Derived from Table 23. For an explanation of the derivation of the measurements see footnote 10, Chapter 4.

[b] N.e.m. denotes not elsewhere made.

[c] N.e.c. denotes not elsewhere classified.

[d] The columns do not add up to 100.0 in every instance because they contain rounded percentages.

[e] Wool shoddy is included in all other textile industries.

percentage had fallen to 16.6. There were declines in the relative contribution of this industry in three of the four subperiods as well. The relative contribution of woolen and worsted goods fell also, from 14.3 percent in 1899 to 8.4 in 1937, and only in the last period, 1929–37, was there a rise in that industry's share of total output. Declines between 1899 and 1937 are to be noted also for wool carpets and rugs, cordage and twine, and fur-felt hats. On the other hand there were important and consistent advances in the relative contributions of silk and rayon goods. Industries for which no separate data are available increased their aggregate relative contribution from 46.2 to 51.7 percent.

The data on value added (Table 26) serve to fill in a number of gaps in the record of physical output. The most interesting supplementary information relates to the clothing industries. Men's clothing decreased in relative importance between 1899 and 1937: its contribution fell from 14.9 to 11.6 percent of the total value added by the group. Men's collars and shirts fell also, from 4.4 to 2.6 percent. On the other hand, women's clothing rose sharply, from 9.8 to 15.9 percent. Less important changes also are to be noted: declines in cloth and straw hats; rises in dyeing and finishing, in embroideries, trimmings, millinery, and house furnishings. Surprisingly enough, the relative contribution of silk and rayon goods in terms of value added rose from 1899 to 1929, then fell to a point lower than that of 1899.[20] In most

[20] The 1929–37 movement of the industry's share of value added contrasts sharply with the trend of the industry's contribution to physical output for the same years. This variation brings into question the accuracy of the index of physical output of silk and rayon goods for 1929–37 (and particularly for 1933–35), as well as the accuracy of the data on value added for the same period. In this connection, see footnotes 1 and 9, above. If errors exist, they probably arise from changes in the definition of the industry, and are counterbalanced—so far as the group index is concerned—by changes in the opposite direction in other textile industries. While the exact magnitude of the rise in the physical output of silk and rayon goods between 1929 and 1937 may be in doubt, there can hardly be any question that a substantial rise did occur, since non-Census data tend to support such a view.

Table 26

TEXTILE PRODUCTS

Relative Contributions of Component Industries to the Value Added by the Entire Group[a]

Industry	*Percentage Distribution*[b]					
	1899	1909 Comparable with 1899	1909 Comparable with 1919	1919	1929	1937
Cotton goods	22.3	19.7	19.5	22.8	15.6	17.8
Cotton small wares	0.5	0.5	0.5	0.5	0.8	0.7
Lace goods	. .	. .	[c]	0.4	0.5	0.6
Woolen goods	6.7	3.2	3.2	4.0	3.2	4.1
Worsted goods	6.1	8.2	8.1	6.8	5.0	5.4
Haircloth	[d]	*	0.1	*	*	
Wool pulling	0.1	0.1	0.1	0.1	0.1	0.1
Wool scouring	0.1	0.1	0.1	0.2	0.1	0.1
Silk and rayon goods	5.4	6.0	6.0	6.9	7.1	5.1
Dyeing and finishing	3.8	3.8	3.8	4.0	5.8	5.1
Hosiery, knit	6.1	6.9	6.8	7.5	6.8	6.6
Underwear, knit					1.8	1.8
Outerwear, knit					1.7	1.7
Cloth, knit					0.5	0.8
Carpets and rugs, rag	0.2	0.1	0.2	0.1	0.1	*
Carpets and rugs, wool	3.0	2.5	2.4	1.5	2.3	2.6
Mats and matting	0.1	0.1	0.1	0.1	0.1	0.1
Asphalted-felt-base floor covering	0.4	0.4	0.4	0.6	0.4	0.5
Linoleum					0.8	0.7
Cordage and twine	1.6	1.0	1.0	1.2	0.9	0.9
Jute goods	0.3	0.4	0.4	0.4	0.2	0.4
Linen goods	0.2	0.2	0.2	0.1	0.1	0.1
Clothing, men's, work	14.7	15.1	14.9	12.1	1.3	2.3
Clothing, men's, n.e.c.[e]					9.6	9.3
Clothing, men's buttonholes	0.1	0.1	0.1	*	*	
Cloth sponging and refinishing	0.1	0.1	0.1	0.1	0.1	
Furnishings, men's, n.e.c.[e]	1.5	1.2	1.2	1.2	1.7	1.1
Gloves, textile, n.e.m.[f]				0.3	0.3	0.4
Shirts	3.0	2.5	2.5	1.8	2.4	2.6
Collars, men's	1.4	0.9	0.9	0.8	0.1	
Clothing, women's, n.e.c.[e]	9.8	13.0	12.9	12.8	15.7	15.9
Corsets	1.1	1.4	1.4	1.0	1.0	1.3
Embroideries	1.9	3.2	3.2	3.3	0.5	0.4
Millinery					2.5	1.6
Trimmings, n.e.m.[f]					0.6	0.6
Handkerchiefs				[g]	0.3	0.2
Elastic woven goods, n.e.m.[f]		[g]	0.9	0.7	0.3	0.2

For footnotes see end of table, p. 188.

TABLE 26 (concluded)

Industry	*Percentage Distribution*[b]					
	1899	1909 Comparable with 1899	1909 Comparable with 1919	1919	1929	1937
Hats, fur-felt	2.0	2.0	2.0	1.2	1.2	1.1
Hats, cloth	1.5	0.5	0.5	0.6	0.5	0.2
Hats, straw, men's		0.8	0.8	0.4	0.2	0.2
Hats, wool-felt	0.2	0.1	0.2	0.1	0.1	0.2
Hat and cap materials	0.2	0.2	0.2	0.3	0.2	0.2
Fur goods	1.6	1.9	1.9	1.8	2.6	1.6
Furs, dressed	0.1	0.1	0.1	0.4	0.6	0.5
Artificial leather	0.2	0.2	0.1	0.2	0.3	0.3
Awnings	0.6	0.5	0.5	0.5	0.6	0.4
Bags, textile, n.e.m.[f]	0.4	0.7	0.7	1.0	0.6	0.9
Belting, woven, n.e.m.[f]	*	0.1	0.2	0.2	*	
Housefurnishings, n.e.c.[e]	0.7	0.5	0.5	0.6	1.3	1.7
Horse blankets	0.1	0.1	0.1	0.1	*	
Felt goods	0.4	0.4	0.4	0.4	0.5	0.4
Flags and banners	0.1	0.1	0.1	0.1	0.1	0.1
Regalia	0.2	0.3	0.3	0.1	0.1	
Oilcloth	0.1	0.2	0.2	0.1	0.2	0.1
Nets and seines	0.1	*	*	*	0.1	*
Upholstering materials, n.e.c.[e]	0.4[d]	0.2	0.2	0.1	0.1	0.4
Wool shoddy	0.3	0.2	0.2	0.2	0.1	0.4
Waste	0.1	0.2	0.2	0.2	0.3	
TOTAL[h]	100.0	100.0	100.0	100.0	100.0	100.0

* Less than half of one percent.
[a] Basic data are given in Appendix C.
[b] Incomparabilities arising from changes in definitions of industries are noted in footnote 1 of this chapter, and cited in detail in Appendix A.
[c] Included in cotton goods and cotton small wares.
[d] Haircloth is included in upholstering materials, n.e.c.
[e] N.e.c. denotes not elsewhere classified.
[f] N.e.m. denotes not elsewhere made.
[g] Included in various other (chiefly textile) industries.
[h] The columns do not add up to 100.0 in every instance because they contain rounded percentages.

other respects the figures in Table 26 are consistent with those in Table 25.

The change in the industrial composition of textile manufactures may be gauged also in terms of the fibers utilized

(Table 27). Judged by the rather crude measure of weight, the changes in the character of the fibers consumed in textile manufacture appear to have been slight. Hemp, jute and similar fibers declined in importance, whereas rayon rose

TABLE 27
TEXTILE PRODUCTS
Raw Fibers Consumed in Textile Mills[a]

Type of Fiber	*1899*	*1909*	*1919*	*1929*	*1937*
	QUANTITY (million pounds)				
Cotton	1,923.7	2,465.2	2,905.8	3,635.3	3,784.0
Wool[b]	251.9	358.3	299.7	389.8	391.8
Animal hair[c]	34.8	41.6	55.4	84.1	85.4
Silk	9.8	17.7	27.9	64.2	54.4
Flax	17.0	28.1	12.8	14.5	10.7
Hemp, jute, etc.	507.8	632.8	570.5	528.1	478.8
Rayon yarn		0.9	8.0	128.3	254.9
Rayon staple fiber and waste					43.6
Other, not given in detail					3.9
TOTAL	2,745.0	3,544.6	3,880.1	4,844.3	5,107.5
	PERCENTAGE DISTRIBUTION				
Cotton	70.1	69.5	74.9	75.0	74.1
Wool[b]	9.2	10.1	7.7	8.1	7.7
Animal hair[c]	1.3	1.2	1.4	1.7	1.7
Silk	0.3	0.5	0.7	1.3	1.0
Flax	0.6	0.8	0.4	0.3	0.2
Hemp, jute, etc.	18.5	17.9	14.7	10.9	9.4
Rayon yarn		0.0	0.2	2.7	5.0
Rayon staple fiber and waste					0.8
Other, not given in detail					0.1
TOTAL	100.0	100.0	100.0	100.0	100.0

[a] Derived from data given in the U.S. Census of Manufactures.
[b] Scoured weight.
[c] Includes some hatters' fur.

rapidly. The decline in wool and flax, and the rise in animal hair and silk, were all of minor significance, although the use made of these fibers changed considerably. The consumption of silk rose many-fold between 1899 and 1937, but in terms of its effects on fiber consumption by the group as a whole, the changes were small.[21]

The character of textile manufacture changed in still another respect—basic technical processes. Factory knitting is more important today than it was in 1900, an advance achieved partly at the expense of weaving. Thanks to the shift of clothing production from the home and retail tailorshop to the factory, more textile manufacturing is devoted today to the cutting of cloth and the sewing of garments than was the case at the opening of the century. "Men's clothing, an industry that at first catered almost exclusively to slaves and sailors, and to the least exacting class of common laborers, now competes with the best custom tailors." [22] The movement from home and custom dressmaking to factory dress production has probably been of even greater magnitude than the corresponding transfer of men's clothing production.

[21] The data on consumption of fibers do not agree in every respect with corresponding data on production because consumer reports to the Census of Manufactures have been incomplete. See, on this point, *Rayon Organon* (Dec. 1937), p. 177. Any minor errors present in Table 27 would scarcely affect the conclusions we have drawn from it.

[22] V. S. Clark, *History of Manufactures in the United States* (McGraw Hill, 1929), Vol. III, p. 224.

Chapter 10

Leather Products

THE leather products group consists of industries which either process leather or use leather as the principal material in the fabrication of other products, such as shoes and gloves. Measured in terms of value added, the group was less than a fourth as important as textiles in 1929.

TRENDS IN THE PHYSICAL OUTPUT OF THE LEATHER PRODUCTS INDUSTRIES

Of the 11 leather products industries distinguished in the Census of Manufactures, quantity indexes are available for only four (Table 28 and Chart 12). Fortunately, two of these, leather and shoes, are the most important in the group.

Leather. The output of the primary leather industry, in which hides and skins are tanned, and the resulting leather is curried and finished, rose 61 percent between 1899 and 1937. In the last period, 1929–37, the leather industry achieved a net gain in output amounting to 12 percent. The peak in the series was reached in 1923. Declining exports accounted only in small degree for the retardation in the rate of growth in leather output: in 1899, 89 percent of the leather produced in this country went for domestic consumption, and in 1937 the percentage was 99. The output of leather was probably affected more by the decline in the manufacture of certain leather products and by the substitution for leather of such materials as cloth, rubber and artificial leather.

The leather industry is far from homogeneous. Indeed, it

TABLE 28

LEATHER PRODUCTS[a]

Physical Output: Indexes and Percentage Changes[b]

	Leather	Shoes, Leather	Gloves, Leather	Belting, Leather	Total Unadjusted	Total Adjusted
YEAR	INDEX OF PHYSICAL OUTPUT (1929:100)					
1899	70	60	85	..	64	64
1904	82	68	97	..	73	74
1909	89	78	98	..	82	83
1914	84	81	91	..	82	81
1919	104	89	105	..	94	90
1921	88	76	65	..	78	75
1923	120	93	..	..	99	95
1925	101	84	..	..	88	85
1927	106	96	91	80	98	97
1929	100	100	100	100	100	100
1931	81	84	74	46	82	80
1933	85	94	..	48	90	86
1935	104	103	102	76	103	100
1937	112	112	98	86	111	108
PERIOD	NET PERCENTAGE CHANGE IN PHYSICAL OUTPUT					
1899–1937	+61	+87	+16	..	+75	+69
1899–1909	+28	+31	+16	..	+29	+29
1909–1919	+17	+14	+7	..	+15	+9
1919–1929	−4	+12	−5	..	+6	+11
1929–1937	+12	+12	−2	−14	+11	+8

[a] Industries for which there are no adequate quantity data for any period listed above are: shoe cut stock, not elsewhere made; shoe findings, not elsewhere made; leather goods, not elsewhere classified; luggage; pocketbooks; saddlery and harness; and whips. These industries are covered by the adjusted total.

[b] The indexes have been constructed from basic data in the U.S. Census of Manufactures and other sources, by methods described briefly in Chapter 2 and in detail in Appendix A. Appendix B presents these data, together with the indexes derived from them. The indexes cited here for individual industries have been adjusted to take account of changes in the coverage of the respective samples, except when such adjustment was impossible.

The percentage changes are not always entirely consistent with the indexes given above because the changes were computed from the indexes in Appendix B, which are carried to one decimal place.

is really a group of about ten independent subindustries,[1] because the various types of leather are prepared by proc-

[1] J. R. Arnold, "Labor Productivity in the Leather Industry," *Monthly Labor Review* (July 1937), p. 68; Allen Rogers, "The Leather Industry," in *Representative Industries in the United States,* ed. by H. T. Warshow (Henry Holt, 1928), Chapter 12.

Chart 12
LEATHER PRODUCTS
Indexes of Physical Output

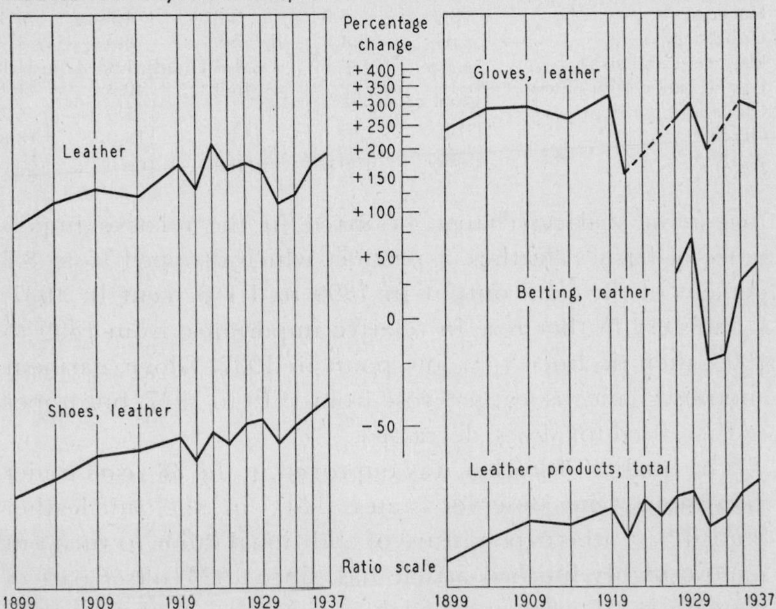

esses which differ markedly from one another. In Chapter 6 we noted shifts in the relative importance of the several species of animals slaughtered in meat-packing establishments. Such changes alone would have given rise to differences in the rates of growth in the output of the various branches of leather fabrication. In addition, there have been variations in the imports of hides and skins, and changes in the uses to which leather has been put. For example, there was a large demand for leather for automobile upholstery at one period, and a subsequent decline when the closed car superseded the open car and cloth materials came into use instead. Some of the changes in the composition of the industry's products are shown in the following figures, based on value of output:

Type of Leather	*Percentage Distribution of Total Value of Output* 1899	1909	1919	1929	1937
Sole	28.2	28.1	25.8	30.6	29.6
Belting	3.6	3.5	3.9		
Harness	8.7	8.0	2.8	1.3	1.1
Upholstery	3.1	4.5	3.8	3.3	1.9
Bag, case, and strap			1.4	1.5	1.3
Upper, other than patent	56.4	55.9	46.9	40.3	41.1
Glove and garment			15.4	5.0	6.2
Other				18.0	18.8
TOTAL	100.0	100.0	100.0	100.0	100.0

The most striking change occurred in the relative importance of harness leather, a product which dropped from 8.7 percent of the total output in 1899 to 1.1 percent in 1937. Upholstery leather rose in relative importance from 1899 to 1909, then declined to a low point in 1937. Glove, garment and miscellaneous leathers rose from 1919 to 1937, but upper leather, used for shoes, decreased.

The quality of leather was improved in the 38 years under discussion. One observer states that "in the side-leather branch . . . the expenditure of additional labor to turn out a more highly finished article has, since 1923, offset part of the gain in the efficiency of labor." [2] Moreover, the development of new tannages and treatments and the opening of new fields of use for leather have resulted in a far greater variety of leather products.[3] The increased variety represents, of course, a real improvement in the "quality" of leather in general.

Shoes made of leather rose at a somewhat more rapid rate than the output of leather alone. From 1899 to 1937 the net increase in the physical quantity of shoes produced was 87 percent, a rise slightly in excess of population growth during the period. In this industry, as in leather production, there was a gain of 12 percent from 1929 to 1937.

Among the types of shoes distinguished by the Census,

[2] J. R. Arnold, *op. cit.*, pp. 76–77.
[3] V. S. Clark, *op. cit.*, p. 228.

youths' and boys' and misses' and children's shoes changed but little in output between 1899 and 1937, whereas men's shoes rose 50 percent and women's shoes more than 130 percent. Since women's shoes are quite different from men's shoes in size, construction and design, the change in the composition of the industry's output reflects a considerable shift in manufacturing processes. The following tabulation classifies the number of shoes according to method of construction:

	Percentage Distribution			
Type of Shoe	1909	1919	1929	1937
Welted	32.3	38.0	33.5	32.7
Turned	16.4	18.6	15.1	6.4
McKay	41.5	36.3	34.2	20.0
Wood-and-metal-fastened	9.8	4.0	5.9	5.6
Stitchdown	..	3.2	10.6	13.2
Cemented	..	..	0.7	22.0
TOTAL	100.0	100.0	100.0	100.0

The welted shoe retained its place over the years 1909–37. Turned, McKay, and wood-and-metal-fastened shoes declined in relative importance. Stitchdown and cemented shoes, comparatively new in 1919, together accounted for 35 percent of the total output in 1937.

Though no exact figures can be given, there is some evidence that savings in materials caused the net output of the shoe industry to rise more rapidly than the gross output.[4]

Summary. The unadjusted index for the entire leather products group rose 75 percent between 1899 and 1937. Since the index is based on the output of the most important industries in the group, adjustment for industries omitted

[4] "Since 1923 specially designed mulling cabinets or rooms in which the upper leathers are hung before lasting have become increasingly general. The condition of the uppers can now be suitably and positively controlled to meet the requirements of different kinds of leather in different seasons—without excessive moisture in the work rooms and with benefit to the quality of the finished shoe. The result is economy in the amount of material used in each shoe and a saving in the number and cost of 'cripples' or spoiled shoes." Boris Stern, "Labor Productivity in the Boot and Shoe Industry," *Monthly Labor Review* (February 1939), p. 287.

affects it but slightly, reducing the gain between 1899 and 1937 to 69 percent. The growth during the 38 years was relatively slow but fairly continuous. There were increases in all four periods, ranging from 29 percent in the first to 8 percent in the last.

Two of the three leather industries for which we have data increased their output less rapidly than population grew between 1899 and 1937. The same trend may be observed in the adjusted total. All the leather products industries fell behind the 276 percent rise in total manufacturing for the entire 38 years. Only in 1929–37 did the output of the leather group grow more rapidly than the output of all manufacturing industries combined.

CHANGES IN THE INDUSTRIAL PATTERN OF LEATHER PRODUCTS MANUFACTURE

The data in Table 28 indicate that leather and leather glove production advanced less rapidly than the output of the group, and that shoe production went up more rapidly. The effects of these differing rates of growth on the composition of the group's output are shown in Table 29. In 1899 the primary leather branch contributed 23 percent of the group's output; by 1937 the relative contribution of the industry had fallen to 21 per cent. The leather gloves industry reduced its contribution from 3.9 to 2.6 percent. All other leather industries, excluding shoes, also decreased their contributions to the total. The shoe industry alone increased its relative contribution, from 52 to 57 percent.

Data on the relative contributions of individual industries to the value added by the leather group are presented in Table 30. These are not inconsistent with the trends indicated by the data on physical output: the trends in value added are somewhat steeper, but they move in the same direction as the trends in physical output. The value data provide some additional information on "all other" leather industries. The most noteworthy changes occurred in the contributions of industries producing saddlery, harness and whips. These industries together contributed 8.2 percent of the value added in 1899 but only 0.9 percent in 1937. Pocketbooks, and the two shoe supply industries, shoe cut stock and

TABLE 29

LEATHER PRODUCTS

Relative Contributions of Component Industries to the Physical Output of the Entire Group[a]

Industry	*Percentage Distribution, Comparable Pairs of Years*									
	1899	1937	1899	1909	1909	1919	1919	1929	1929	1937
Leather	22.6	21.3	25.3	25.2	27.9	30.0	27.2	23.5	18.6	19.3
Shoes, leather	52.1	57.0	49.5	50.0	48.0	50.1	53.0	53.5	57.7	59.8
Gloves, leather	3.9	2.7	3.7	3.3	2.6	2.5	2.5	2.2	2.6	2.4
Belting, leather									2.2	1.8
All other (Belting, leather and all other products combined)	21.4	19.0	21.4	21.5	21.5	17.3	17.3	20.8		
products									18.8	16.8
TOTAL[b]	100.0	100.0	100.0	100.0	100.0	100.0	100.0	100.0	100.0	100.0

[a] Derived from Table 28. For an explanation of the derivation of the measurements see Chapter 4, footnote 10.

[b] The columns do not add up to 100.0 in every instance because they contain rounded percentages.

shoe findings, improved their relative standing over the same period.

The fact that shoe production increased in relation to leather production may be explained by the decline in leather exports, the fall in harness and related leather products, the shift from retail to factory-made shoes, the growing use of rubber and cloth materials in shoe production, and the drift to half-shoes which require less leather per shoe. Indeed, in view of the presumptive importance of these trends, it is rather surprising that there is not a more pronounced

TABLE 30

LEATHER PRODUCTS

Relative Contributions of Component Industries to the Value Added by the Entire Group[a]

Industry	Percentage Distribution				
	1899	1909	1919	1929	1937
Leather	26.2	24.5	31.5	18.6	19.4
Shoes, leather	48.4	50.8	49.0	58.2	59.1
Shoe cut stock, n.e.m.	2.9	2.4	3.0	3.3	6.2
Shoe findings, n.e.m.	1.5	2.2	2.5	3.4	
Belting, leather	1.7	2.5	1.4	1.9	2.1
Gloves, leather	4.0	3.2	2.3	2.4	2.6
Leather goods, n.e.c.	3.0	2.6	2.5	2.3	6.7
Pocket books	0.6	0.5	0.8	4.3	
Luggage	3.5	4.1	3.4	4.2	3.0
Saddlery and harness	7.4	6.5	3.4	1.2	0.9
Whips	0.8	0.7	0.2	*	
TOTAL[b]	100.0	100.0	100.0	100.0	100.0

* Less than half of one percent.

[a] Basic data are given in Appendix C. N.e.m. denotes not elsewhere made; n.e.c. denotes not elsewhere classified.

[b] The columns do not add up to 100.0 in every instance because they contain rounded percentages.

difference between the rates of growth of leather output and of shoe production.[5]

[5] If the rise in shoe production is compared with the rise in leather output, the latter being measured by simple aggregation of the quantities of various leathers produced, as in the Day-Thomas index (Appendix D), the discrepancy is greater. Our index of shoe production increased by 72 percent from 1899 to 1935, while the Day-Thomas index of leather output rose by 12 percent.

Chapter 11

Rubber Products

THE rubber products group is composed of establishments which use natural, reclaimed or synthetic rubber or gutta-percha as an important constituent in the manufacture of their products. In 1937 this group made a smaller contribution to value added by all manufacturing than any other group of industries.

TRENDS IN THE PHYSICAL OUTPUT OF THE RUBBER PRODUCTS INDUSTRIES

No index of physical output for any of the rubber products industries is available for the years prior to 1914. Two begin in that year and one begins in 1927 (Table 31 and Chart 13).

Tires and Tubes. Rubber tires and inner tubes increased in output more than six-fold from 1914 to 1937. The gain between 1899 and 1937 must have been very much greater than this, because of the advent of the automobile, but no exact figures are available.[1] Output in 1919 was almost four times the 1914 output, and 1929 production was more than

[1] Automobile production rose 3,500 percent between 1899 and 1909, and 1,500 percent between 1909 and 1919. (See Chapter 21, below.) From 1899 to 1937 the increase in automobile output was 180,000 percent. Corresponding increases must have occurred in the output of tires used as original equipment on new cars. Total tire production includes tires used for replacements, and the quantity of these is difficult to estimate. Rather rough estimates for 1910–14 prepared by the U.S. Bureau of Foreign and Domestic Commerce (Special Circular No. 3500—Rubber Section, Table III) and extended back to 1904 by W. H. Shaw of the National Bureau, indicate the following production of pneumatic tires and casings: 1904: 250,000; 1909: 1,500,000; 1914: 8,021,000.

twice the 1919 output. Between 1929 and 1937, however, there was a decrease of 19 percent.

Production of some types of tires reached a peak before 1929. According to the Census solid and cushion tires fell

TABLE 31

RUBBER PRODUCTS

Physical Output: Indexes and Percentage Changes[a]

	Shoes, Rubber	*Tires and Tubes*	*Rubber Goods, Other*	*Total*
YEAR	INDEX OF PHYSICAL OUTPUT (1929:100)			
1914	69	12	..	..
1919	115	49	..	54
1921	91	39	..	43
1923	111	69	..	72
1925	91	88	..	84
1927	120	91	80	92
1929	100	100	100	100
1931	58	67	83	70
1933	71	65	80	69
1935	83	72	96	79
1937	95	81	112	91
PERIOD	NET PERCENTAGE CHANGE IN PHYSICAL OUTPUT			
1914–1937	+39	+556	..	..
1914–1919	+68	+297	..	..
1919–1929	–13	+103	..	+86
1929–1937	–5	–19	+12	–9

[a] The indexes have been constructed from basic data in the U.S. Census of Manufactures, by methods described briefly in Chapter 2 and in detail in Appendix A. Appendix B presents these data, together with the indexes derived from them. The indexes cited here for individual industries have been adjusted to take account of changes in the coverage of the respective samples, except when such adjustment was impossible.

The percentage changes are not always entirely consistent with the indexes given above because the changes were computed from the indexes in Appendix B, which are carried to one decimal place.

from 1.5 million in 1919 (the first year for which separate data are available) to .3 million in 1937, a decline of 80 percent. Output of pneumatic tires, casings and inner tubes used for motorcycles and bicycles changed but slightly between 1914 and 1929 (rising from 3.73 million to 3.74 million), then went

Chart 13
RUBBER PRODUCTS
Indexes of Physical Output

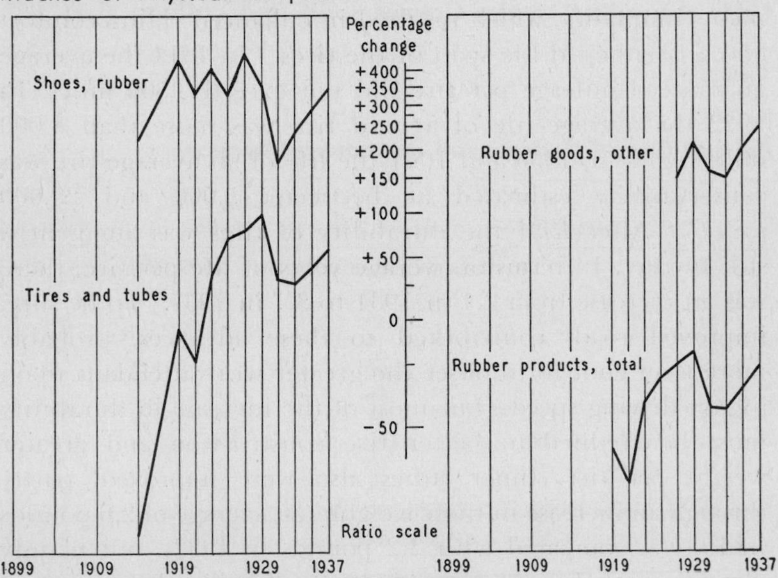

up sharply to 8.5 million in 1937. From a non-Census source [2] we have obtained data on important changes in the types of automobile casings (the output of each is expressed as a percent of total output):

	Construction		
	High Pressure		
Year	Fabric	Cord	Balloon
1910	100	0	0
1915	95	5	0
1920	65	35	0
1925	14	52	34
1930	0	17	83
1933	0	11	89

In addition to the displacement of high pressure tires by balloon tires, there was a considerable increase in the average

[2] Rubber Section of the Bureau of Foreign and Domestic Commerce.

weight of rubber tires, from 16 pounds in 1922 to 22 pounds in 1931.[3]

These two changes were accompanied by great improvements in quality, which resulted in enhanced riding comfort and a lengthened life span of the tires. "In 1914 the average guaranteed mileage per tire did not exceed 3,500 miles. In 1922 the average life of a cord tire was more than 8,000 miles, while in 1930 and 1931 the life of an average tire was conservatively estimated at between 15,000 and 20,000 miles."[4] After 1931 the durability of tires was augmented still further. In terms of average years of life per tire, there was an increase from 2.4 in 1931 to 3.1 in 1937.[5] To be sure, improved roads contributed to these advances, probably more than enough to offset the greater wear attendant upon higher driving speeds, but most of the increase in durability must be credited to better tire construction and greater weight per tire. Inner tubes also were improved, partly through an increase in their weight (an average of 2.6 pounds in 1931 as compared with 2.2 pounds in 1922), but mainly as a result of the adoption of the "molded" tube process of manufacture, which yields a smooth and perfectly fitting tube, less susceptible to dangerous wrinkling and creasing.[6]

Rubber Shoes. This industry—which produces rubber-soled canvas shoes, rubber boots, arctics and rubbers—progressed also, but at a much slower rate than the tires and

[3] Boris Stern, "Labor Productivity in the Automobile Tire Industry," U.S. Bureau of Labor Statistics, *Bulletin No. 585* (July 1933), pp. 2, 7.

Our measure of output is based on the number of tires and tubes. An alternative measure of the physical output of the tires and tubes industry could be constructed on the basis of the weight of the rubber, textiles and chemicals consumed. Such an index has been prepared by the National Research Project for the period 1921–36 (*op. cit.,* Part II, p. 198). This index, of course, rises more rapidly than ours.

[4] Boris Stern, *op. cit.,* p. 2.

[5] U.S. Bureau of Foreign and Domestic Commerce, *Rubber News Letter* (Oct. 15, 1939).

[6] Boris Stern, *op. cit.,* p. 67.

tubes industry. The physical output of rubber shoes increased only 39 percent between 1914 and 1937. The most important rise occurred in the years 1914–19. Between 1919 and 1927 the trend seems to have been horizontal, and since 1927, downward. Among the industry's products, rubber-soled canvas shoes rose in output between 1919 and 1937, while rubber boots fell considerably.

Other Rubber Goods. The third rubber products classification, which covers all other rubber goods, increased its output 40 percent from 1927 to 1937. The output of automobile and carriage fabrics declined, but there were rises in the production of rubber soles, certain types of rubberized fabrics, rubber belting (except for transmission), rubber bands and cement, and rubber gloves.

Summary. The index for the group rose almost 100 percent between 1919 and 1929, but fell 9 percent in the most recent period. Although no group index is available for the years prior to 1919,[7] it is probable that between 1899 and 1937 the output of the rubber products group rose at a much faster rate than population grew and perhaps twice as rapidly as total manufacturing. In the third decade the relative growth in the group's output was slower, though it was nevertheless rapid. In the latest period, 1929–37, the group's output fell 9 percent, while both population and total manufacturing output rose.

[7] An index of the group's output in the period prior to 1919 was not computed because the data were inadequate. Rubber imports, a rather crude index of the output of rubber products, rose 73 percent from 1899 to 1909, 496 percent from 1909 to 1919, 122 percent from 1919 to 1929, and 12 percent from 1929 to 1937. The imports index does not agree well with our index of output, or with annual figures of rubber consumption available since 1922. It should be noted that the imports series is defective as a measure of rubber consumption since it does not include reclaimed rubber. The latter is a fairly important item: in 1937 the consumption of purchased reclaimed rubber amounted to 101,000 tons; the consumption of all reclaimed rubber, to 156,000 tons; and the consumption of all rubber, crude and reclaimed, to 687,000 tons.

CHANGES IN THE INDUSTRIAL PATTERN OF RUBBER PRODUCTS MANUFACTURE

The advance in tires and tubes transformed the industrial composition of the rubber group's output. In terms of relative contributions (Table 32), rubber shoes fell from 14.5 percent in 1919 to 7.0 percent in 1937, whereas all other rubber products, including tires and tubes, increased. In the last period, 1929–37, rubber tires and tubes declined while "other rubber goods" rose. If separate data for tires and tubes were available, they would undoubtedly show a rise in the tire industry's contribution from almost zero in 1899 to more than 50 percent in 1937.

TABLE 32

RUBBER PRODUCTS

Relative Contributions of Component Industries to the Physical Output of the Entire Group[a]

Industry	*Percentage Distribution, Comparable Pairs of Years*					
	1919	1937	1919	1929	1929	1937
Shoes, rubber	14.5	7.0	17.0	7.9	11.3	11.9
Tires and tubes	85.5	93.0	83.0	92.1	63.2	56.7
Rubber goods, other					25.4	31.4
TOTAL[b]	100.0	100.0	100.0	100.0	100.0	100.0

[a] Derived from Table 31. For an explanation of the derivation of the measurements see footnote 10, Chapter 4.

[b] The columns do not add up to 100.0 in every instance because they contain rounded percentages.

The shifts in the pattern of pecuniary output, as revealed by the data on value added in Table 33, do not coincide with the changing pattern of physical output. Between 1919 and 1937 there was only a slight decline in the relative value contribution of the rubber shoes industry, but there was a large decline in its relative contribution to the physical output of the group. If the data on physical output are accurate, the discrepancy indicates a considerable rise in the value added per unit of physical output in the rubber shoes industry in relation to the corresponding price of fabricational services

TABLE 33

RUBBER PRODUCTS

Relative Contributions of Component Industries to the Value Added by the Entire Group[a]

<table>
<tr><th rowspan="3">Industry</th><th colspan="6">Percentage Distribution</th></tr>
<tr><th rowspan="2">1899</th><th rowspan="2">1909</th><th rowspan="2">1919</th><th colspan="2">1929
Comparable with</th><th rowspan="2">1937</th></tr>
<tr><th>earlier years</th><th>later years</th></tr>
<tr><td>Shoes, rubber</td><td>46.5</td><td>26.9</td><td>12.2</td><td>12.7</td><td>12.6</td><td>10 1</td></tr>
<tr><td>Tires and tubes</td><td rowspan="2">53.5</td><td rowspan="2">73.1</td><td rowspan="2">87.8</td><td rowspan="2">87.3</td><td>63.2</td><td>56.6</td></tr>
<tr><td>Rubber goods, other</td><td>24.2</td><td>33.3</td></tr>
<tr><td>TOTAL</td><td>100.0</td><td>100.0</td><td>100.0</td><td>100.0</td><td>100.0</td><td>100.0</td></tr>
</table>

[a] Basic data are given in Appendix C.

of the rubber group considered as a whole. This suggestion does not appear unreasonable: technological developments in the tires and tubes industry, which were exceptionally rapid, could easily account for the divergence of trends in value added per unit.

Chapter 12

Paper Products

THE industries in this group manufacture pulp, paper and paperboard from pulp, and converted paper products (boxes, bags, etc.) from paper and paperboard. In terms of value added, the group has risen steadily in importance. By 1937 its contribution to total value added by all manufacturing exceeded that of leather products, rubber products, petroleum and coal products, beverages and miscellaneous products.

TRENDS IN THE PHYSICAL OUTPUT OF THE PAPER PRODUCTS INDUSTRIES

Pulp. This basic industry embraces establishments engaged primarily in the manufacture of pulp from wood and other fibers, many of which transfer their output to closely affiliated paper mills. The physical output of the pulp industry increased at a rapid rate during the 38-year period (Table 34 and Chart 14). From 1899 to 1937 it achieved a net rise of over 500 percent. In the first ten years output more than doubled. While growth was less rapid in the later periods, output increased in each of them by about two fifths.

Among the individual products of the pulp industry, sulphate-fiber pulp is outstanding because of its particularly rapid growth. In 1914, the first year in which the output of this type of pulp reached such proportions that it had to be shown separately, production totaled 50,000 tons; by 1937 it had climbed to 2,140,000 tons. Another kind of pulp, sulphite-fiber, which accounted for 35 percent of all pulp in 1899, moved so slowly that its 1937 output was no greater than that of sulphate pulp—2,140,000 tons. The output of the unbleached variety of sulphite-fiber pulp was 770,000 tons in 1914 (the first year for which separate data are avail-

TABLE 34

PAPER PRODUCTS[a]

Physical Output: Indexes and Percentage Changes[b]

	Pulp	*Paper*	*Wall Paper*	*Total* Unadjusted	*Total* Adjusted
YEAR	INDEX OF PHYSICAL OUTPUT (1929:100)				
1899	23	20	..	19	18
1904	38	29	..	28	26
1909	50	39	..	36	37
1914	55	49	..	44	46
1919	68	57	..	53	53
1921	56	50	..	44	50
1923	74	73	..	66	70
1925	78	82	..	75	77
1927	86	88	..	88	89
1929	100	100	100	100	100
1931	88	85	81	86	86
1933	89	83	77	84	84
1935	107	96	93	98	102
1937	141	115	110	120	122
PERIOD	NET PERCENTAGE CHANGE IN PHYSICAL OUTPUT				
1899–1937	+505	+465	..	+516	+567
1899–1909	+116	+92	..	+88	+100
1909–1919	+36	+45	..	+44	+44
1919–1929	+46	+76	..	+90	+89
1929–1937	+41	+15	+10	+20	+22

[a] Industries for which there are no adequate quantity data for any period listed above are: bags, paper, not elsewhere made; boxes, paper, not elsewhere classified; cardboard, not elsewhere made; card cutting and designing; envelopes; labels and tags; paper goods, not elsewhere classified; and stationery goods, not elsewhere classified. These industries are covered by the adjusted total.

[b] The indexes have been constructed from basic data in the U.S. Census of Manufactures, by methods described briefly in Chapter 2 and in detail in Appendix A. Appendix B presents these data, together with the indexes derived from them. The indexes cited here for individual industries have been adjusted to take account of changes in the coverage of the respective samples, except when such adjustment was impossible.

The percentage changes are not always entirely consistent with the indexes given above because the changes were computed from the indexes in Appendix B, which are carried to one decimal place.

Chart 14
PAPER PRODUCTS
Indexes of Physical Output

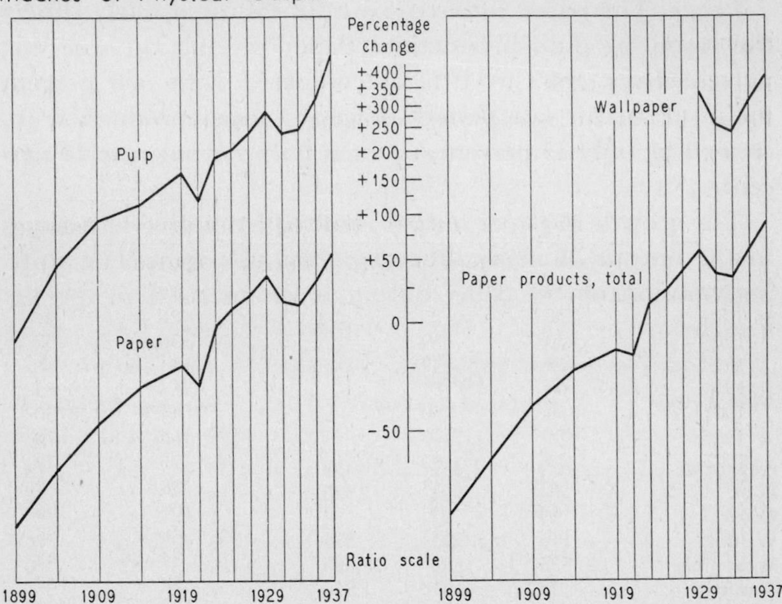

able) and 790,000 tons in 1937, while bleached sulphite-fiber pulp rose from 380,000 to 1,350,000 tons.[1] Soda-fiber pulp rose from 180,000 to 510,000 tons between 1899 and 1937. The increase in mechanical pulp was the smallest: in 1899 the output of this product amounted to 590,000 tons, 50 percent of the total, and in 1937, to 1,600,000 tons.[2] The slow growth of mechanical pulp, as well as of unbleached sulphite-fiber pulp, reflects the relative decline in the domestic production of newsprint, one of the principal types of paper made from these pulps.[3] Since each of these types of

[1] In 1937 this product included 354,000 tons of superpurified pulp intended for use in rayon and other special chemical products.

[2] The 1899 figures are taken from J. D. Studley, *United States Pulp and Paper Industry,* U.S. Bureau of Foreign and Domestic Commerce, Trade Promotion Series No. 182 (1938), Table 9.

[3] Studley, *op. cit.,* p. 28.

pulp is the product of a special manufacturing process, the marked shifts in the industry's output reflect corresponding changes in its techniques, equipment and labor skills.[4]

Paper. The paper industry's output followed fairly closely the trend in pulp production. Paper production rose 465 percent from 1899 to 1937 as compared with 506 percent for pulp. In the last period, however, paper production increased by only 15 percent, whereas pulp output rose 41 percent.

The growth in paper output resulted from diverse changes in the output of many different types of paper. The shifting composition of paper output is summarized in the figures below:

Type of Paper	*Output* (thousand short tons)			*Percentage Distribution*		
	1899	1919	1937	1899	1919	1937
Newsprint	624	1,474	1,494	30	25	12
Book	304	961	1,520	14	16	12
Cover	19	22	24	1	*	*
Writing	113	325	578	5	6	5
Wrapping	535	858	2,053	25	15	16
Tissue	28	191	540	1	3	4
Building	97	195	608	5	3	5
Paperboard	394	1,867	5,802	19	32	46
TOTAL	2,114	5,893	12,619	100	100	100

* Less than half of one percent.

The most striking facts to be noted in the tabulation are the relative decline of newsprint and wrapping paper as contributors to the total, and the huge rise in the contribution of tissue paper and paperboard. The failure of newsprint to

[4] Perhaps a more vivid illustration of the transformation in the industry's output is to be found in the profit and loss statements of paper manufacturers. The "displacement of sulphite pulp by the cheap and strong sulphate pulp for the manufacture of coarse wrapping papers and paper bags" was accompanied by profits in sulphate pulp manufacture and losses in sulphite pulp manufacture: "The difficulties of the Union Bag and Paper Corporation and of the Continental Paper and Bag Corporation can be ascribed mostly to the displacement of sulphite paper by sulphate paper." See C. E. Fraser and G. F. Doriot, *Analyzing Our Industries* (McGraw-Hill, 1932), p. 325.

increase rapidly in output is accounted for by the great rise in the quantity of newsprint imported. In 1914 about 15 percent of our domestic requirements were met by imports, but in 1936 the proportion was as high as 75 percent.[5]

Summary. The output of the entire paper products group rose 516 percent, according to the index based on the three industries for which we have data, and 567 percent if we adjust this index for changes in the relative importance of the sample. In the first decade, according to the adjusted index, output doubled; in the second decade it rose by almost one half; in the third decade it nearly doubled; and in the last period it increased almost a fourth. Similar changes are shown by the unadjusted index.

The group index rose more rapidly than total manufacturing in three of the four subperiods. The exception was the decade 1909–19, during which paper products output merely kept pace with the grand total. In relation to population, the output of paper products forged ahead in each of the four subperiods.

CHANGES IN THE INDUSTRIAL PATTERN OF PAPER PRODUCTS MANUFACTURE

The pulp and paper industries are not closely related technically, since much of the pulp consumed in the paper industry is imported, and since the paper industry uses a considerable amount of rags and old or waste paper as well as pulp. In 1929 the tonnage of various materials consumed by the paper industry, expressed as percentages of the total quantity, stood approximately as follows: [6]

[5] Studley, *op. cit.*, p. 85.

[6] Data on the quantity of materials consumed are not available for the years preceding 1929. According to data on the cost of materials, rags declined in relative importance between 1899 and 1929 while old and waste paper rose; there was little change in the relative importance of the aggregate of these materials.

		Percentage
Wood pulp		55
Domestic	39	
Imported	16	
Rags		6
Old or waste paper		33
Manila stock		1
Straw		5
TOTAL		100

The trends in pulp and paper production are nevertheless surprisingly close to one another.

The relation between pulp and paper is expressed in terms of relative contributions, in Table 35, for the years 1929–37 only; no separate data on value added per unit are available for these industries for earlier years. Since the output of the paper and pulp industries rose at about the same rate as the group total, no other important change in the composition of the group's physical output is revealed by the table. Paper and pulp combined accounted for 61 percent of the total physical output of the group in 1899, and for 56 percent in 1937. This slight decline was accompanied, of course, by an increase in the combined relative importance of the other industries in the group.

Table 35
PAPER PRODUCTS
Relative Contributions of Component Industries to the Physical Output of the Entire Group[a]

<table>
<tr><th rowspan="2">Industry</th><th colspan="10">Percentage Distribution, Comparable Pairs of Years</th></tr>
<tr><th>1899</th><th>1937</th><th>1899</th><th>1909</th><th>1909</th><th>1919</th><th>1919</th><th>1929</th><th>1929</th><th>1937</th></tr>
<tr><td>Paper</td><td rowspan="2">60.8</td><td rowspan="2">56.3</td><td rowspan="2">60.8</td><td rowspan="2">57.0</td><td rowspan="2">57.0</td><td rowspan="2">57.3</td><td rowspan="2">57.3</td><td rowspan="2">57.4</td><td>47.3</td><td>44.7</td></tr>
<tr><td>Pulp</td><td>10.1</td><td>11.7</td></tr>
<tr><td>Wall paper</td><td rowspan="2">39.2</td><td rowspan="2">43.7</td><td rowspan="2">39.2</td><td rowspan="2">43.0</td><td rowspan="2">43.0</td><td rowspan="2">42.7</td><td rowspan="2">42.7</td><td rowspan="2">42.6</td><td>1.9</td><td>1.8</td></tr>
<tr><td>All other</td><td>40.6</td><td>41.9</td></tr>
<tr><td>TOTAL[b]</td><td>100.0</td><td>100.0</td><td>100.0</td><td>100.0</td><td>100.0</td><td>100.0</td><td>100.0</td><td>100.0</td><td>100.0</td><td>100.0</td></tr>
</table>

[a] Derived from Table 34. For an explanation of the derivation of the measurements see footnote 10, Chapter 4.

[b] The columns do not add up to 100.0 in every instance because they contain rounded percentages.

The data on the industrial pattern of pecuniary output of the paper products group (Table 36) add information concerning some of the industries for which we have no data on physical output. The relative contributions of the container industries (bags and boxes), and of miscellaneous pa-

TABLE 36

PAPER PRODUCTS

Relative Contributions of Component Industries to the Value Added by the Entire Group[a]

Industry	*Percentage Distribution*					
	1899	1909	1919	1929 Comparable with earlier years	1929 Comparable with later years	1937
Paper	60.8	57.0	57.3	46.6	50.2	46.3
Pulp				10.7	11.5	11.1
Bags, paper, n.e.m.[b]	2.5	3.0	2.5	2.5	2.7	3.4
Boxes, paper, n.e.c.[c]	16.7	16.0	18.8	16.0	17.2	20.3
Cardboard, n.e.m.[b]	0.6	0.6	0.7	0.4	0.4	0.3
Card cutting and designing	0.3	0.4	0.5	1.2	1.3	1.4
Envelopes	2.8	3.3	3.2	3.7	4.0	3.1
Labels and tags	0.8	1.6	2.3	2.1	d	
Paper goods, n.e.c.[c]	7.5	9.4	7.5	9.8	10.5	12.3
Stationery goods, n.e.c.[c]	3.1	5.0	5.4	5.0	d	
Wall paper	4.9	3.8	1.8	2.0	2.1	1.8
TOTAL[e]	100.0	100.0	100.0	100.0	100.0	100.0

[a] Basic data are given in Appendix C.
[b] N.e.m. denotes not elsewhere made.
[c] N.e.c. denotes not elsewhere classified.
[d] Distributed among paper, printing and other industries.
[e] The columns do not add up to 100.0 in every instance because they contain rounded percentages.

per goods (waxed, toilet, and coated-book paper; napkins, cups, and spoons; towels; playing cards; adding machine paper, and other products) rose appreciably between 1899 and 1937. Card cutting and designing also increased. Wall paper, on the other hand, declined rather considerably, from 4.9 to 1.8 percent.

Chapter 13

Printing and Publishing

THE printing and publishing group includes establishments engaged in printing, in publishing, in printing and publishing, and in allied activities such as bookbinding and engraving. In terms of value added, the group is much more important than paper products, and in this respect compares favorably with most other manufacturing groups as well. In 1937 the relative contribution of the printing and publishing group to total value added was exceeded only by foods, textiles, iron and steel products, machinery, and transportation equipment.

TRENDS IN THE PHYSICAL OUTPUT OF THE PRINTING AND PUBLISHING INDUSTRIES

The Group Total. A reasonably adequate measure of the physical output of the printing and publishing industries may be obtained only by recourse to data on paper consumption. Since these data relate to paper consumption in all printing and publishing industries combined, it is impossible to determine from them the trends in the physical output of the individual industries included in the group.[1] We have therefore regarded the available figures on paper consumption as rough indicators of change in the physical output of

[1] The volume of paper consumption can be broken down by types of paper—newsprint, book paper, and fine paper. Each of these would seem to relate to a different kind of printing. In fact, however, a considerable volume of newsprint is consumed in the job printing of catalogues and circulars; and a large amount of book paper is used in magazine printing.

TABLE 37

PRINTING AND PUBLISHING

Physical Output: Index and Percentage Changes[a]

	Printing and Publishing, Total[b]
YEAR	INDEX OF PHYSICAL OUTPUT (1929:100)
1899	17
1904	26
1909	36
1914	47
1919	54
1921	52
1923	73
1925	82
1927	90
1929	100
1931	84
1933	72
1935	87
1937	102
PERIOD	NET PERCENTAGE CHANGE IN PHYSICAL OUTPUT
1899–1937	+494
1899–1909	+108
1909–1919	+52
1919–1929	+85
1929–1937	+2

[a] The index has been constructed from basic data presented in Appendix B by methods described in the text.

The percentage changes are not always entirely consistent with the index given above because the changes were computed from the index in Appendix B, which is carried to one decimal place.

[b] Indexes for individual industries are not available.

the entire printing and publishing group (Table 37 and Chart 15).[2]

The physical output of the entire group was almost six times as large in 1937 as it had been in 1899. The greatest advance occurred in the first decade, when output more

[2] No attempt was made to weight one type of paper more than another. Any set of weights based on the meager materials available would be excessively arbitrary. Nor could changes in the relative space allotted to editorial and advertising matter be taken into account. Because of these shortcomings, the index is far from precise.

than doubled; in the period 1909–19 output rose 50 percent; in the next decade, 85 percent; and in 1929–37, barely 2 percent.

The growth over the long period surpassed the rise in total manufacturing and exceeded by far the increase in population.

Chart 15
PRINTING AND PUBLISHING
Indexes of Physical Output

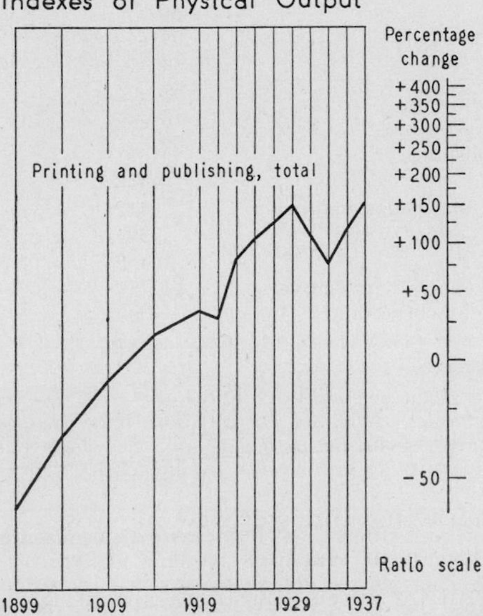

Only in the latest period, 1929–37, did the output of the group fail to rise more rapidly than either population or total manufacturing output.

Individual Industries. Some information on the trends in the output of individual printing and publishing industries is provided by the data on value added (Table 38). The two major printing industries, the first embracing book, music and job printing, and the second periodical printing, increased their pecuniary output by approximately the same percentage in the years 1899–1937, and at about the same rate as the group as a whole. Bookbinding and blankbook manufacture declined about 25 percent in relation to the group. Steel, copper, wood and other engraving industries

TABLE 38

PRINTING AND PUBLISHING

Changes in Value Added, 1899–1937[a]

Industry	*Percentage Change in Value Added*	*Percentage Change in the Ratio of Value Added to Total Value Added by the Group*
Printing and publishing, book, music, and job	+570	+3
Printing and publishing, periodical	+538	−3
Bookbinding and blankbook making	+412	−25
Engraving, steel, copper, wood	+391	−29
Engraving, other	+438	−21
Photo-engraving, not elsewhere done	+1,751	+217
Sterotyping, not elsewhere done	+780	+41
TOTAL[b]	+552	0

[a] Basic data are given in Appendix C.

[b] Industries for which there are no adequate data include: engravers' materials; lithographing; printing materials, not elsewhere classified; and type founding. These industries are covered by the total.

fell. Photo-engraving and stereotyping rose.

Some indication of changes in the character of the products of the printing and publishing industries is provided by the following tabulation, available beginning with 1909:

	Value of Products (million dollars)			
	1909	1919	1929	1937
Newspapers				
Subscriptions and sales	84	193	276	288
Advertising	149	374	797	574
Periodicals other than newspapers				
Subscriptions and sales	51	85	184	172
Advertising	54	155	323	236
Books and pamphlets	63	133	199	168
Commercial printing[a]			738	555

[a] Not given separately in 1909 and 1919. Excludes printing of periodicals, books, pamphlets, etc. for publication by others.

The most interesting development revealed by these data is the growing importance of advertising. In 1929 receipts from advertising constituted almost three quarters of the total revenue of newspapers, and two thirds of the revenue of other periodicals. Advertising receipts rose more rapidly than subscriptions and sales, from 1909 to 1929, and fell more rapidly from 1929 to 1937. Books and pamphlets lagged behind periodicals throughout the rise that characterized the industry in the period 1909–29.

CHANGES IN THE INDUSTRIAL PATTERN OF PRINTING AND PUBLISHING

No statistical data are available on the composition, or the changes in the composition, of the physical output of the printing and publishing group. A rough notion of the internal composition of the group's output may be obtained from the data on value added, which are brought together in Table 39.

The most important industry in the group, the periodical printing and publishing industry, accounted for over half the value added by the group. Next in order is the book and job printing and publishing industry, with a contribution averaging over 30 percent. Together, these industries were responsible for about 85 percent of the pecuniary output of the entire group. This percentage remained stable throughout the 38 years from 1899 to 1937. The other industries in the group are all small, and therefore no significant changes occurred in their contributions to the group as a whole. Among the minor industries, photo-engraving achieved a noteworthy gain, raising its contribution from 1.2 to 3.6 percent of the value added by the entire group of printing and publishing industries.

TABLE 39

PRINTING AND PUBLISHING

Relative Contributions of Component Industries to the Value Added by the Entire Group[a]

Industry	Percentage Distribution				
	1899	1909	1919	1929	1937
Printing and publishing, book and job	27.6	31.2	32.7	30.4	29.1
Printing and publishing, music	0.5	0.7	0.9	0.5	
Printing and publishing, periodical	56.9	54.8	52.2	55.6	55.5
Bookbinding and blankbook making	4.6	3.8	4.0	3.2	3.7
Engravers' materials	*	0.1	0.1	0.1	[b]
Engraving, steel and copper	1.4	1.4	1.6	1.6	1.2
Engraving, wood	0.2	0.1	0.1	*	
Engraving, other	0.5	0.4	0.4	0.4	0.3
Lithographing	5.1	4.2	4.2	3.7	5.1[c]
Photo-engraving, n.e.d.[d]	1.2	1.8	2.3	3.0	3.6
Printing materials, n.e.c.[e]	0.2	0.2	0.3	0.3	[b]
Type founding	0.7	0.3	0.1	0.1	[b]
Stereotyping, n.e.d.[d]	1.0	0.9	1.1	1.3	1.5
TOTAL[f]	100.0	100.0	100.0	100.0	100.0

* Less than half of one percent.

[a] Basic data are given in Appendix C.

[b] Included in foundry and machine-shop products (classified in the machinery group).

[c] Includes some establishments formerly classified in labels and tags (paper products group).

[d] N.e.d. denotes not elsewhere done.

[e] N.e.c. denotes not elsewhere classified.

[f] The columns do not add up to 100.0 in every instance because they contain rounded percentages.

Chapter 14

Chemical Products

THE chemical products group comprises all industries manufacturing chemicals, as ordinarily defined, and industries using chemical processes in their operations. There are a few exceptions which are classified in other groups: baking powder and corn products, placed in the foods group; and beverages and petroleum and coal products, which are classified separately. The chemical group is rather heterogeneous in respect of the use made of its products. Numbered among them are industrial materials, construction materials, fertilizers, and such final consumer goods as drugs.

The chemical industries have grown in relative importance, as measured by value added; in 1899 this group was exceeded by eight others, in 1937 by six.

TRENDS IN THE PHYSICAL OUTPUT OF THE CHEMICAL PRODUCTS INDUSTRIES

Of the 30 industries included in the chemicals group, we have adequate quantity statistics for 15. For only eight, however, do the indexes extend over the entire period 1899–1937 (Table 40 and Chart 16).

Chemicals, not elsewhere classified, the most important industry in the group, consists of establishments producing acids, nitrogen compounds, sodium and potassium compounds, aluminum compounds and alum, coal-tar products, and plastics. Prior to 1923 this classification included also rayon manufacture, and prior to 1927, compressed and liquefied gases. The growth of the industry has been phenomenal.

TABLE 40

CHEMICAL PRODUCTS[a]

Physical Output: Indexes and Percentage Changes[b]

	Chemicals, n.e.c.[c] (including Compressed Gases and Rayon)								
	Total	Chemicals, n.e.c.,[c] (excl. gases and rayon)	Gases, Compressed	Rayon	*Cottonseed Products*	*Linseed Products*	*Carbon Black*	*Soap*	*Wood-Distillaton Products*
YEAR					INDEX OF PHYSICAL OUTPUT (1929:100)				
1899	6.6	17	..	..	51	..	..	..	28
1904	8.3	22	..	..	74	..	..	46	40
1909	12	30	3.3	..	73	..	..	61	54
1914	20	29	9.2	2.0	134	..	10.0	70	58
1919	36	48	33	6.7	111	..	23	89	75
1921	27	34	31	12	80	..	24	79	31
1923	55	64	52	28	70	83	47	87	80
1925	56	65	55	40	108	100	70	86	85
1927	70	74	68	60	121	95	67	93	92
1929	100	100	100	100	100	100	100	100	100
1931	92	81	82	138	86	67	75	98	56
1933	102	80	71	201	94	..	74	98	..
1935	130	105	95	253	66	63	94	100	73
1937	172	141	138	310	83	86	133	109	101
PERIOD					NET PERCENTAGE CHANGE IN PHYSICAL OUTPUT				
1899–1937	+2,500	+741	..	..	+63	..	..	..	+259
1899–1909	+89	+78	..	..	+45	..	..	..	+92
1909–1919	+190	+61	+906	+235[d]	+51	..	..	+46	+38
1919–1929	+176	+108	+201	+1,393	−10	..	+337	+12	+34
1929–1937	+72	+41	+38	+210	−17	−14	+33	+9	+1

	Charcoal	Explosives	Fertilizers	Glue and Gelatin	Paints and Varnishes	Salt	Tanning and Dye Materials	Total	
								Unadjusted	Adjusted
YEAR				INDEX OF PHYSICAL OUTPUT (1929:100)					
1899	..	25	30	..	22	53	26	17	19
1904	..	45	37	..	28	57	38	20	23
1909	..	62	60	..	38	67	54	30	31
1914	..	70	88	..	41	72	79	42	42
1919	..	94	80	..	52	88	82	54	52
1921	192	61	60	..	45	71	69	42	42
1923	132	94	76	..	67	87	95	66	64
1925	238	92	87	..	76	88	87	70	70
1927	144	96	90	96	87	92	88	82	83
1929	100	100	100	100	100	100	100	100	100
1931	39	67	78	85	69	91	78	85	87
1933	..	58	60	..	62	84	74	87	84
1935	46	68	78	110	87	87	100	106	101
1937	43	93	106	139	109	97	101	135	124
PERIOD				NET PERCENTAGE CHANGE IN PHYSICAL OUTPUT					
1899–1937	..	+267	+248	..	+391	+82	+292	+696	+566
1899–1909	..	+143	+97	..	+69	+26	+107	+80	+69
1909–1919	..	+52	+34	..	+39	+31	+52	+79	+64
1919–1929	..	+7	+24	..	+92	+13	+22	+84	+94
1929–1937	−57	−7	+6	+39	+9	−3	+1	+35	+24

[a] Industries for which there are no adequate quantity data for any period listed above are: druggists' preparations; patent medicines; toilet preparations; drug grinding; oils, essential; ammunition; fireworks; blackings; bluing; candles; cleaning preparations; grease and tallow; ink, printing; ink, writing; and mucilage. These industries are covered by the adjusted total.

[b] The indexes have been constructed from basic data in the U. S. Census of Manufactures, reports of the U. S. Bureau of Mines and other sources, by methods described briefly in Chapter 2 and in detail in Appendix A. Appendix B presents these data, together with the indexes derived from them. The indexes cited here for individual industries have been adjusted to take account of changes in the coverage of the respective samples, except when such adjustment was impossible.

The percentage changes are not always entirely consistent with the indexes given above because the changes were computed from the indexes in Appendix B, which are carried to one decimal place.

[c] N.e.c. denotes not elsewhere classified.

[d] Percentage change from 1914 to 1919.

Chart 16
CHEMICAL PRODUCTS
Indexes of Physical Output

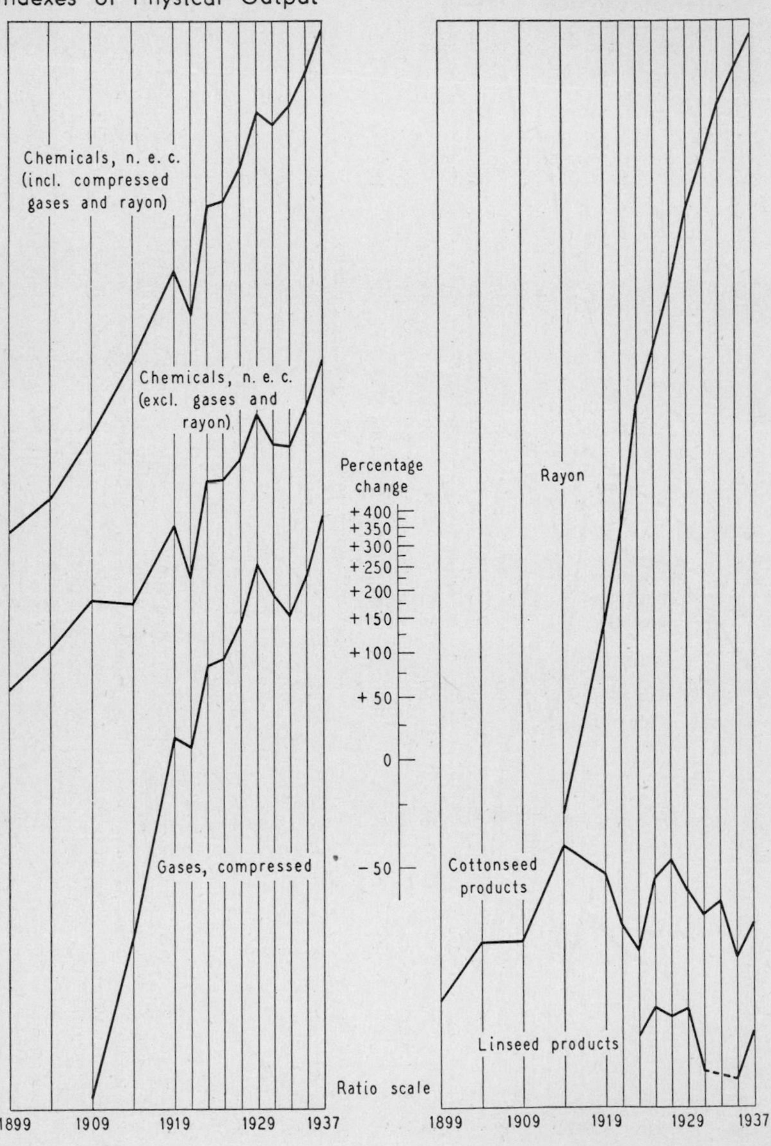

Chart 16 (concl.)
CHEMICAL PRODUCTS
Indexes of Physical Output

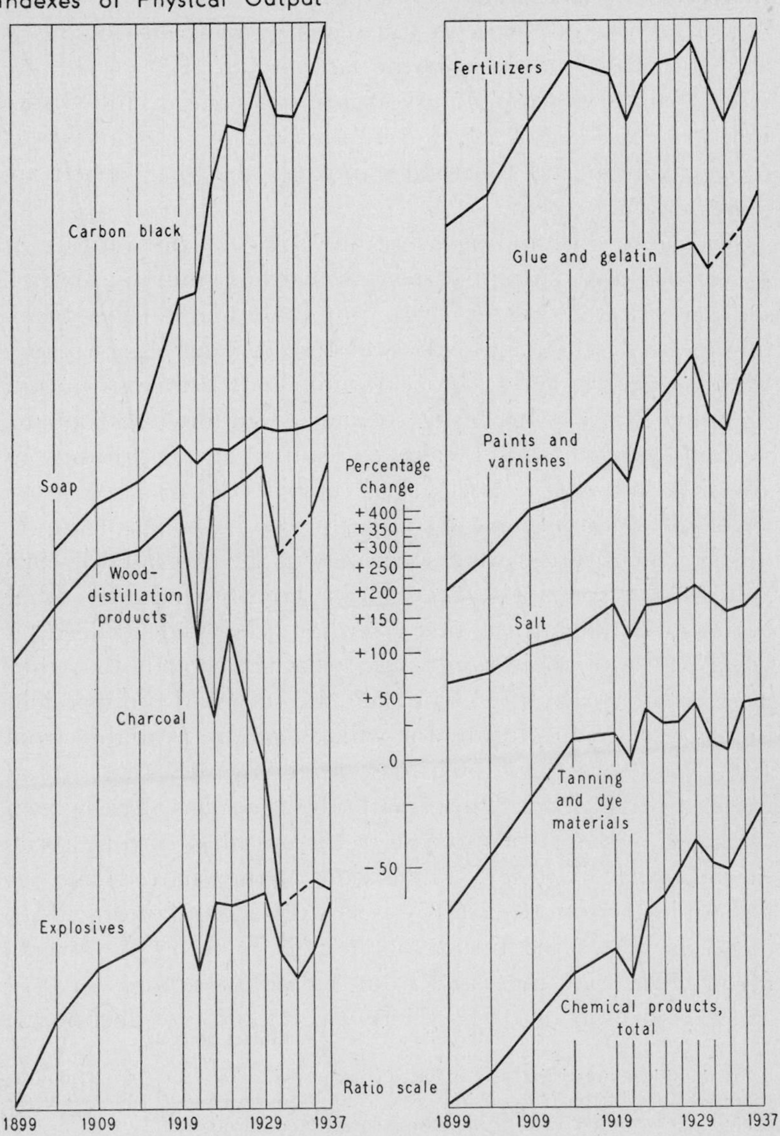

Between 1899 and 1937 chemicals, not elsewhere classified (including the two branches separated out in 1923 and 1927), increased production by 2,500 percent. In the first decade output almost doubled, in the second and third decades it almost tripled, and even in the last period, 1929–37, it rose more than 70 percent. If rayon and gases are excluded, the industry's rise is less rapid, but the rate is nevertheless exceedingly high and the total gain over the long period approaches 750 percent.[1]

Especially outstanding were the rises in the output of phosphoric acid, sulphuric acid, anhydrous ammonia, borax, sodium silicate, coal-tar dyes, butyl acetate, carbon bisulphide, ethyl ether, and ethyl acetate. Among the products which appear to have been constant or declining in output for some length of time are oleic acid, sodium bicarbonate, sodium sulphate (niter cake), cream of tartar, aluminous abrasives, pyroxylin plastics, and refined sulphur.

Rayon and Compressed Gases, the two branches of the industry which were treated separately in the Censuses of 1923 and 1927, respectively, grew more rapidly than the other branches of chemicals, not elsewhere classified. Indeed, it was because of their rapid and sustained growth that they were promoted by the Census to the status of independent industries. Rayon output, for which data are available from 1914, was more than 150 times greater in 1937 than it had been 23 years earlier. The extent of the gain has already been indicated by the great increase in the output of rayon fabrics in the textile industry. The ascent of the charted line for rayon production (Chart 16) is so steep that it is difficult to comprehend the magnitude of the rise. In terms of volume, rayon production increased from 2.4 million pounds in 1914 to 321.7 million in 1937. There was no absolute decline be-

[1] It should be noted that the index is unadjusted, except for 1927–37, and is therefore subject to error arising from changes in coverage. The index for chemicals, including rayon and gases, is adjusted throughout.

tween any two Census years, although very recently a slackening in the rate of growth has been apparent.

The rapid increases in the quantity of rayon produced were accompanied by improvements in the quality of rayon yarn. The average denier spun fell from 151 in 1929 to 137 in 1938,[2] indicating a trend to a finer product. Tensile strength, dry, increased from 1.5 grams per denier for commercial 150-denier viscose yarn rayon in 1922, to 2.0 grams per denier in 1932; wet tensile strength increased from 0.5 grams to 1.0 grams. In addition, delustering processes have been developed, dyeing properties have been improved, and greater uniformity in many respects has been effected.[3]

Compressed and liquefied gases also increased at a phenomenal rate, though not as rapidly as rayon. Output in 1937 was 42 times as great as it had been in 1909. The growth has been subject to some retardation, as is apparent from the chart. Even in the most recent period, however, there was a substantial increase of 38 percent.

Cottonseed and Linseed Products. The cottonseed products industry comprises establishments which crush cottonseed and produce from it oil, cake and meal. The further processing of cottonseed oil in the manufacture of lard substitutes and cooking oils is treated as a food manufacturing process. The output of oil, cake and meal rose by less than two thirds from 1899 to 1937. The peak in the series came in 1914, but 1927 output was only 10 percent lower. Two by-products of the industry, cotton linters, and cottonseed cake and meal, increased more rapidly than the output of cottonseed oil; and a third, cottonseed hulls, changed but slightly between 1899 and 1937.

Linseed products are made by methods similar to those employed in the processing of cottonseed. The output of the lin-

[2] *Rayon Organon* (January 23, 1939), p. 19.

[3] Department of Agriculture, mimeographed "Report on Development and Use of Rayon and Other Synthetic Fibers," by a committee appointed by the Secretary of Agriculture (October 1938), pp. 28–29.

seed products industry rose 20 percent between 1923 (the first year for which adequate data are available) and 1929. From 1929 to 1937 output fell 14 percent.

Carbon Black. In addition to carbon black, this industry manufactures bone black, and lampblack from natural gas, bone, petroleum, etc. Almost half of its chief product, carbon black, is used in the manufacture of rubber products, particularly tires and tubes, a fact which helps to explain the rapid rise in the output of the industry: between 1914 and 1937 there was a 13-fold increase. From 1914 to 1919 the rise exceeded 100 percent; from 1919 to 1929, 300 percent; and from 1929 to 1937, 33 percent. Although today carbon black is the major product of the industry, in 1914 bone black was the principal product. Since 1914 the output of bone black has declined, as has also that of lamp black.

Soap. This industry, one of the most important in the entire chemicals group in terms of value added, includes establishments manufacturing soap and soap products, such as granulated soap and cleansers. The output of the industry moved upward at a comparatively slow rate: from 1904 to 1937 the increase was 140 percent. Data on the products of the industry are supplied in detail beginning with 1923. Since that year decreases have occurred in the output of foots soap, white and yellow laundry soap, miscellaneous hard soaps, soap powders, and soft soap. There are large rises in the series for soap chips, and for granulated and powdered soap.

Wood-Distillation Products. This classification covers establishments engaged in distilling wood for methanol, acetate of lime, turpentine and rosin, etc. Charcoal is the principal by-product of the industry. The total output of the industry rose 259 percent from 1899 to 1937, but the rate of increase slowed down from decade to decade. In the first period there was a rise of 92 percent, in the second 38 percent, in the third 34 percent and in the last only 1 percent. The hardwood-distillation branch of the industry fell off in relation to the softwood-distillation branch, effecting declines in the output of the hardwood products (methanol and acetate of lime) in relation to the softwood products (turpentine, rosin, pine oil, tar, and tar oils). Charcoal, a by-product of both branches, rose less rapidly than all the primary products combined.

Charcoal. The only products of the charcoal industry proper are charcoal and wood tar. The volatile substances, which constitute the chief products of the wood-distillation industry, are driven off and lost in the manufacture of charcoal. The output of the charcoal industry declined at a rapid pace. After a rise from 1921 to 1925, it fell sharply from 1925 to 1929, and again from 1929 to 1937 by more than 50 percent.

Explosives. Among the products of the explosives industry are gunpowder, dynamite and nitroglycerine. Ammunition and fireworks are classified in other industries. The output of the explosives industry increased 267 percent between 1899 and 1937, but retardation in its rate of growth is shown by the record of declines in the percentage increases in successive decades. There were large rises in the output of permissible explosives (approved by the Bureau of Mines for use in mines), and decreases in the output of blasting and pellet powder, and gun powder.

Fertilizers. This category encompasses the manufacture of commercial fertilizers, not including fertilizer materials for use in the natural state, or unprocessed tankage from meat-packing plants. The industry's physical output rose 250 percent between 1899 and 1937.[4] Most of the rise occurred from 1899 to 1914.

Paints and Varnishes, a very important industry when judged by value added, increased its output almost five times in the years 1899–1937. Even in the most recent period, 1929–37, production increased by 9 percent. Among the in-

[4] The index for the industry is affected, though only slightly, by duplication arising from intra-industry sales of superphosphates. See Appendix B.

dustry's individual products relatively small increases or even declines are found in the output of dry white lead pigments, zinc oxide, iron oxides, pulp colors, paints in paste form, japans and fillers. The output of water paints and calcimine, spirit varnishes, and pyroxylin products (lacquer and lacquer enamels) rose substantially.[5]

Salt, a laggard industry in the chemical group, increased in output only 82 percent in the 38 years between 1899 and 1937. From the detailed data available since 1921, it appears that there have been changes in the relative importance of each type of salt-making process. The amount of salt produced by evaporation in open pans or grainers has declined, but the amount produced by evaporation in vacuum pans has increased. The output of salt in brine, sold as such, advanced more rapidly than that of any other salt product.

Tanning and Dye Materials, the last industry in the group for which we have quantitative data, comprises establishments engaged in the production of tanning extracts and solutions, natural dyestuffs, mordants, assistants, and sizes. Artificial dyestuffs are classed with "chemicals not elsewhere classified." The output of the tanning and dye materials industry rose almost 4-fold between 1899 and 1937. The greater part of the rise occurred in the first 15 years, when output increased by over 200 percent. In contrast, the increase from 1914 to 1937 was less than 30 percent. Natural dyes and extracts all declined in absolute output: logwood, from 39 million pounds in 1899 to 8 million in 1937; fustic, from 4.5 million pounds in 1914 to 1.2 million in 1937; and quercitron, from 3.8 million pounds in 1914 to 2.4 million in 1929. On the other hand, the output of artificial dyestuffs rose.

Summary of Changes in Individual Chemical Industries. In only one period, 1929–37, did more than one chemical industry decline in output (Table 41). Even in that period,

[5] Intra-industry sales of dry colors and pigments result in duplication of part of the industry's output. See Appendix B.

however, ten out of the fifteen industries for which we have data increased their output. Over the long period 1899–1937 all but one of the chemical industries reported increases in output more rapid than the growth of population. For 1899–1909 all eight industries for which we have data surpassed population growth, and for 1909–19, all ten. In the third pe-

TABLE 41

CHEMICAL PRODUCTS

Summary of Changes in Physical Output[a]

	Number of Industries				
	1899–1937	1899–1909	1909–1919	1919–1929	1929–1937
Industries for which there are indexes of physical output	8	8	10	12	15
Industries with rising output	8	8	10	11	10
Industries with falling output	0	0	0	1	5
Industries with output rising in relation to population	7	8	10	8	7
Industries with output falling in relation to population	1	0	0	4	8
Industries with output rising in relation to total manufacturing output	3	6	6	5	8
Industries with output falling in relation to total manufacturing output	5	2	4	7	7

[a] Derived from data in Table 40 and from figures on changes in population and in total manufacturing output given in footnote a, Table 14.

riod, 1919–29, eight out of twelve industries increased output more rapidly than population grew; the exceptions were soap, explosives, salt, and cottonseed products. In the last period, only seven out of fifteen industries managed to exceed the rise in population.

Between 1899 and 1937 only three out of the eight individual industries covered increased their output more rapidly than did total manufacturing; these were chemicals, n.e.c., paints and varnishes, and tanning and dye materials. Nevertheless, the increase in the output of the first was so great, and the combined importance of the three industries so considerable, that the group total, discussed below, advanced in relation to the grand total.

The Group Total. The index of physical output of the entire chemical products group, based on the sample of industries given in Table 40, rose almost 700 percent between 1899 and 1937. The rise exceeded 75 percent in each of the first three decades and came to about 35 percent for the period 1929–37. Unfortunately, the sample is incomplete. Data are lacking on the physical output of several important chemical products industries—drugs, patent medicines, and toilet preparations. If we may judge from the movements of the value added by the sample in relation to the value added by the entire group, which includes industries for which no quantity data are available, the sample increased in relative importance. Using the differential movement revealed by value added to correct the unadjusted group index, we obtain an adjusted index that rose somewhat less rapidly in three of the four subperiods, increasing by 566 percent for the entire 38-year span.

CHANGES IN THE INDUSTRIAL PATTERN OF CHEMICAL PRODUCTION

We have already noted the divergence of trends in the output of several industries in this group. That divergence reflects a far-reaching transformation in the character of the total group output (Table 42). The industry producing chemicals, rayon and gases, which contributed only 10 percent to the group output in 1899, accounted for 42 percent in 1937. The relative contributions of all other industries declined; among these we may mention the drop in cottonseed products, from 8 to 2 percent, and in fertilizers, from 7 to 4 percent. Even paints and varnishes contributed a declining share to the total, al-

TABLE 42

CHEMICAL PRODUCTS

Relative Contributions of Component Industries to the Physical Output of the Entire Group[a]

Industry	Percentage Distribution, Comparable Pairs of Years									
	1899	1937	1899	1909	1909	1919	1919	1929	1929	1937
Chemicals, n.e.c.[b]									22.2	25.4
Gases, compressed	10.4	42.2	13.2	14.9	15.0	26.7	24.1	34.2	2.1	2.4
Rayon									5.4	13.5
Cottonseed products	8.4	2.1	7.8	6.6	7.7	7.1	6.7	3.1	3.3	2.2
Wood-distillation products	1.3	0.7	1.1	1.2	1.2	1.0	1.1	0.8	0.9	0.7
Explosives	3.2	1.8	3.3	4.7	4.4	4.0	4.1	2.2	2.4	1.8
Fertilizers	6.9	3.7	7.8	9.1	9.6	7.9	7.4	4.7	4.2	3.6
Paints and varnishes	14.2	10.8	12.2	12.2	12.2	10.4	11.8	11.6	13.8	12.1
Salt	3.3	0.9	2.2	1.7	2.0	1.6	2.0	1.2	1.4	1.1
Tanning and dye materials	1.2	0.7	1.3	1.6	1.7	1.6	1.5	0.9	0.9	0.7
Soap					8.4	7.5	9.3	5.3	7.4	6.5
Carbon black							0.3	0.6	0.6	0.7
Linseed products									1.2	0.8
Charcoal	51.1	36.9	51.1	47.9	37.7	32.2	31.7	35.3	*	*
Glue and gelatin									0.8	0.9
Other chemical products									33.4	27.6
TOTAL[c]	100.0	100.0	100.0	100.0	100.0	100.0	100.0	100.0	100.0	100.0

* Less than half of one percent.

[a] Derived from Table 40. For an explanation of the derivation of the measurements see footnote 10, Chapter 4.

[b] N.e.c. denotes not elsewhere classified.

[c] The columns do not add up to 100.0 in every instance because they contain rounded percentages.

TABLE 43

CHEMICAL PRODUCTS

Relative Contributions of Component Industries to the Value Added by the Entire Group[a]

Industry	*Percentage Distribution*				
	1899	1909	1919	1929	1937
Chemicals, n.e.c.[b]				21.6	27.1
Gases, compressed	13.0	15.1	26.7	2.2	2.4
Rayon				6.7	9.9
Druggist preparations	6.0	6.8	5.1	4.7	16.1
Patent medicines	20.8	14.8	10.4	13.0	
Toilet preparations	2.0	2.2	2.8	7.8	4.4
Drug grinding	0.5	0.7	0.4	0.2	0.2
Cottonseed products	6.9	7.3	7.4	2.9	2.6
Linseed products	1.4	1.5	1.7	1.1	0.9
Oils, essential	0.1	0.1	0.2	0.2	0.1
Ammunition	2.8	2.8	4.3	1.4	1.4
Fireworks	0.6	0.4	0.2	0.2	
Blackings	1.2	1.1	1.0	0.9	0.6
Bluing	0.2	0.2	0.1	0.1	0.1
Carbon black	0.2	0.2	0.3	0.6	0.7
Candles	10.2	0.3	0.1	0.2	0.2
Soap		10.2	6.7	7.5	6.6
Charcoal	0.4	0.1	*	*	*
Wood-distillation products	1.3	1.0	1.1	0.9	0.8
Cleaning preparations	0.6	0.9	1.2	1.8	1.9
Explosives	3.5	4.5	4.0	2.4	1.9
Fertilizers	8.0	9.0	8.2	4.2	3.7
Glue and gelatin	0.8	1.6	1.1	0.8	1.0
Grease and tallow	1.6	2.1	1.6	1.2	1.1
Ink, printing	0.8	1.2	1.0	1.4	1.3
Ink, writing	0.4	0.4	0.3	0.2	0.1
Mucilage	0.5	0.4	0.4	0.2	0.1
Paints and varnishes	12.6	12.0	10.5	13.6	12.8
Salt	2.3	1.6	1.8	1.4	1.2
Tanning and dye materials	1.3	1.6	1.6	0.8	0.7
TOTAL[c]	100.0	100.0	100.0	100.0	100.0

* Less than half of one percent.

[a] Basic data are given in Appendix C.

[b] N.e.c. denotes not elsewhere classified.

[c] The columns do not add up to 100.0 in every instance because they contain rounded percentages.

though in physical output this industry rose more rapidly than all but one other in the group. In the latest period,

1929–37, the contribution of rayon went up spectacularly, from 5 to 13 percent.

The data on value added, expressed in terms of percentage contributions, indicate changes in the relative standing of industries for which no data on physical output are available (Table 43). Outstanding declines are to be noted in drugs and patent medicines, which fell from 26.8 percent in 1899 to 16.1 in 1937. The contribution of toilet preparations rose from 2.0 percent in 1899 to 7.8 in 1929, then dropped to 4.4 in 1937. Ammunition reached a peak in 1919 and declined in the ten years following.

Chapter 15

Petroleum and Coal Products

THE petroleum and coal products group consists of five industries: petroleum refining; lubricants, not elsewhere made; oils, not elsewhere classified; [1] coke-oven products; and fuel briquettes. The manufactured gas industry, formerly included in this group, was dropped from the Census of Manufactures in part after 1931, and entirely after 1935. We have excluded it from the data for all years.

Although the group's output increased at a rapid rate, in 1937 it surpassed only beverages, leather products, rubber products and miscellaneous products in terms of value added.

TRENDS IN THE PHYSICAL OUTPUT OF THE PETROLEUM AND COAL PRODUCTS INDUSTRIES

Petroleum Refining is an industry engaged in the refining of crude petroleum by distillation. The classification does not cover the compounding of refined petroleum products or the production of gasoline from natural gas at the wells. The output of the industry increased at an extremely rapid rate (Table 44 and Chart 17); in 1937 it was more than 20 times as great as it had been in 1899. In the first decade output came close to doubling; it tripled in each of the next two decades, and rose by a fifth even in the latest period.

[1] Oils, not elsewhere classified, is placed by the Bureau of the Census in the chemical products group. We have classified it under petroleum and coal products because prior to 1929 it included establishments producing lubricants (see Table 46, below).

The acceleration of the rate of output of the petroleum refining industry in the early part of the century, and the later retardation, reflect the influence of automobile development. The advent of the automobile contributed also to a revolu-

TABLE 44

PETROLEUM AND COAL PRODUCTS[a]

Physical Output: Indexes and Percentage Changes[b]

	Petroleum Refining	Coke-Oven Products	Fuel Briquettes	Total	
				Unadjusted	Adjusted
YEAR	INDEX OF PHYSICAL OUTPUT (1929:100)				
1899	5.9	18	..	7.5	8.7
1904	7.2	23	..	9.3	10.2
1909	11	38	7.9	15	16
1914	17	38	16	20	21
1919	34	61	21	38	39
1921	40	43	29	41	41
1923	56	89	54	62	64
1925	73	81	59	74	75
1927	81	84	72	82	83
1929	100	100	100	100	100
1931	91	55	50	83	84
1933	86	43	37	78	78
1935	99	58	64	91	92
1937	119	87	79	113	114
PERIOD	NET PERCENTAGE CHANGE IN PHYSICAL OUTPUT				
1899–1937	+1,920	+380	..	+1,408	+1,206
1899–1909	+86	+110	..	+97	+85
1909–1919	+209	+60	+166	+155	+143
1919–1929	+194	+63	+376	+165	+156
1929–1937	+19	−13	−21	+13	+14

[a] Industries for which there are no adequate quantity data for any of the above periods are: lubricants, not elsewhere made; and oils, not elsewhere classified. These industries are covered by the adjusted total.

[b] The indexes have been constructed from basic data in the U.S. Census of Manufactures and in reports of the U.S. Bureau of Mines, by methods described briefly in Chapter 2 and in detail in Appendix A. Appendix B presents these data, together with the indexes derived from them. The indexes cited here for individual industries have been adjusted to take account of changes in the coverage of the respective samples.

The percentage changes are not always entirely consistent with the indexes given above because the changes were computed from the indexes in Appendix B, which are carried to one decimal place.

Chart 17

PETROLEUM AND COAL PRODUCTS

Indexes of Physical Output

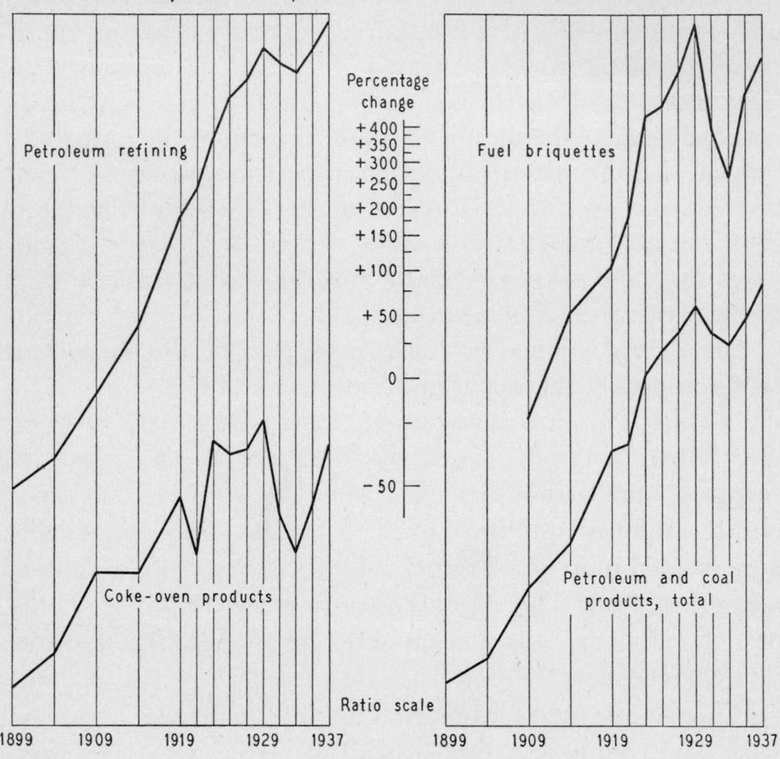

tionary transformation of the composition of the industry's output. The chief products, in selected years, were:

	Quantity (billion gallons)					*Percentage Distribution*				
	1899	1909	1919	1929	1937	1899	1909	1919	1929	1937
Light products of distillation (incl. gasoline)	0.28	0.54	4.11	18.4	22.9	14	12	27	48	50
Illuminating oils (incl. kerosene)	1.26	1.67	2.31	2.34	2.51	63	38	15	6	5
Fuel oils	0.30	1.70	7.77	16.4	19.2	15	38	52	42	42
Lubricating oils	0.17	0.54	0.82	1.55	1.52	8	12	6	4	3
TOTAL	2.01	4.45	15.0	38.7	46.2	100	100	100	100	100

In 1899 the most important products were kerosene and other illuminating oils. The latter rose in output between each of the years specified; yet in 1909 and later years illuminating oils were exceeded in quantitative importance by the more rapidly growing fuel oils, and in 1919 and subsequently by light products of distillation as well. By 1929 the light products had become the most important segment of the industry's output. In 1937 the output of light products was over 80 times the 1899 output; the 1937 output of fuel oils was 64 times the 1899 output; the 1937 output of lubricating oils was nine times the 1899 output; and the 1937 output of illuminating oils was twice the 1899 output.

The radical change in the composition of the industry's products came about through successive improvements in the technical processes employed. In the very early years of the century a rather simple distilling operation, known as "topping" or "skimming," was generally employed to separate the light oil products from the heavy. This process seldom yielded more than 10 percent of gasoline from each barrel of crude oil. The skimming process was improved upon by "straight run" distillation. First introduced successfully in 1899, the new method separated some 25 percent of the gasoline at the maximum. In 1914 the "cracking" process came into commercial use. Instead of merely separating out the gasoline, this process actually creates more gasoline by breaking down the nongasoline molecules into lighter molecules (gasoline) and heavier molecules. The maximum proportion of gasoline obtainable was now raised to between 60 and 65 percent of the crude oil used, and the product itself was greatly improved in quality.[2]

[2] Zimmermann, *op. cit.*, pp. 510–13; Fraser and Doriot, *op. cit.*, pp. 425–30; B. Guthrie, Herbert Schimmel, *et al.*, "Technology, Employment, and Output per Man in Petroleum and Natural-Gas Production," *Report No. E–10* (National Research Project in cooperation with the Bureau of Mines, July, 1939), Chapter 10.

The rise of the cracking process contributed also to the industry's net output by decreasing the amount of purchased fuel consumed in its operations. By-products of the cracking process, such as refinery gas and fuel oil, replaced in large measure the outside fuels formerly purchased. The saving thus effected, plus other savings of fuel arising from the use of improved refining techniques which require less heat per barrel of oil treated, may be gauged by the decline in fuel used per barrel of oil. In 1909, 860,000 British thermal units of fuel were consumed per barrel of crude oil run to stills; in 1937 the corresponding figure was 607,000.[3]

Coke-Oven Products. In comparison with the progress made in the petroleum refining industry, the rise in the output of coke-oven products seems moderate, despite the increase of 380 percent between 1899 and 1937. Output doubled in the first decade (rising more rapidly than petroleum refining), rose 60 percent in each of the next two decades, and fell 13 percent in the period 1929–37.

Coke manufacturing affords a striking illustration of the trend toward increased utilization of by-products. In 1904 (the first year for which such data appear in the Census), "beehive" ovens produced close to 90 percent of all the coke made in the industry and thereby wasted 90 percent of the volatile constituents of all the coal distilled. Only one tenth of the coke produced in 1904 was made in ovens which retained the by-products. By 1937 the proportions were reversed, and over 90 percent of the coke was produced in by-product ovens. As a consequence of this change in the method of manufacture, the entire output of the industry, including coke and by-products, increased 380 percent from 1899 to 1937, whereas its output of coke alone rose only 150 percent. This trend toward better utilization of the fuel consumed by the industry was furthered also by more efficient operation of by-product ovens. Thus, of the total number of British ther-

[3] Guthrie, Schimmel, *et al.*, *op. cit.*, p. 343.

mal units in the coal charged into by-product ovens in 1913, 80 percent was recovered in the form of coke and by-products; in 1936 the percentage was 86. Reflecting both this improvement and the shift from the beehive to the by-product oven are the percentages for the recovery from coal charged into all types of coke ovens: 62 in 1913 and 85 in 1936.[4] Coal is, of course, an extremely important material in the coke industry: in 1914 the cost of coal used amounted to 65 percent of the total value of products. Savings of the magnitude indicated by the above figures suggest that the index of net output of the industry rose considerably more rapidly than the index of gross output given in Table 44.[5]

Summary. The output of the petroleum and coal products group as a whole increased at an accelerating rate between 1899 and 1929, then leveled out somewhat in the last period. Since the unadjusted group index includes the output of the petroleum-refining industry, which was gaining very rapidly, adjustment of the index for the industries omitted reduces the rise shown by the index for 1899–1937 from 1,400 percent to 1,200 percent.

Both petroleum refining and coke-oven products increased their output more rapidly than total manufacturing over the period 1899–1937 taken as a whole. In the last period coke-oven products and fuel briquettes fell in relation to the total. When compared with population growth, the output of each industry rose in every period except the last.

CHANGES IN THE INDUSTRIAL PATTERN OF PETROLEUM AND COAL MANUFACTURE

Since the petroleum refining industry grew in output more rapidly than the entire group, it effected an appreciable

[4] N. Yaworski, V. Spencer, G. A. Saeger and O. E. Kiessling, "Fuel Efficiency in Cement Manufacture," *Report No. E-5* (National Research Project, April 1938), pp. 6–7, 70–71.

[5] Indeed it may be estimated roughly that from 1914–19 to 1933–35 net physical output rose some 40 percent more rapidly than gross physical output.

TABLE 45

PETROLEUM AND COAL PRODUCTS

Relative Contributions of Component Industries to the Physical Output of the Entire Group[a]

<table>
<tr><th rowspan="2">Industry</th><th colspan="10">Percentage Distribution, Comparable Pairs of Years</th></tr>
<tr><th>1899</th><th>1937</th><th>1899</th><th>1909</th><th>1909</th><th>1919</th><th>1919</th><th>1929</th><th>1929</th><th>1937</th></tr>
<tr><td>Petroleum refining</td><td>47.1</td><td>80.4</td><td>46.9</td><td>47.1</td><td>56.0</td><td>71.5</td><td>71.0</td><td>81.5</td><td>77.1</td><td>80.9</td></tr>
<tr><td>Coke-oven products</td><td>34.8</td><td>14.1</td><td>35.2</td><td>39.9</td><td>30.8</td><td>20.4</td><td>21.0</td><td>13.4</td><td>17.5</td><td>13.4</td></tr>
<tr><td>Fuel briquettes</td><td rowspan="2">18.0</td><td rowspan="2">5.4</td><td rowspan="2">17.9</td><td rowspan="2">13.0</td><td>0.1</td><td>0.2</td><td>0.2</td><td>0.3</td><td>0.5</td><td>0.3</td></tr>
<tr><td>All other</td><td>13.0</td><td>8.0</td><td>7.9</td><td>4.8</td><td>4.9</td><td>5.3</td></tr>
<tr><td>TOTAL[b]</td><td>100.0</td><td>100.0</td><td>100.0</td><td>100.0</td><td>100.0</td><td>100.0</td><td>100.0</td><td>100.0</td><td>100.0</td><td>100.0</td></tr>
</table>

[a] Derived from Table 44. For an explanation of the derivation of the measurements see footnote 10, Chapter 4.

[b] The columns do not add up to 100.0 in every instance because they contain rounded percentages.

TABLE 46

PETROLEUM AND COAL PRODUCTS

Relative Contributions of Component Industries to the Value Added by the Entire Group[a]

<table>
<tr><th rowspan="2">Industry</th><th colspan="6">Percentage Distribution</th></tr>
<tr><th>1899</th><th>1909</th><th>1919</th><th></th><th>1929</th><th>1937</th></tr>
<tr><td>Petroleum refining</td><td>46.8</td><td>47.1</td><td>74.2</td><td></td><td>77.5</td><td>80.5</td></tr>
<tr><td>Lubricants, n.e.m.[b]</td><td>0.9</td><td>0.9</td><td>0.8</td><td rowspan="2">c</td><td>4.7</td><td>3.1</td></tr>
<tr><td>Oils, n.e.c.[d]</td><td>17.1</td><td>12.1</td><td>7.2</td><td>1.5</td><td>2.2</td></tr>
<tr><td>Coke-oven products</td><td>35.2</td><td>39.6</td><td>17.8</td><td></td><td>15.8</td><td>13.9</td></tr>
<tr><td>Fuel briquettes</td><td>e</td><td>0.2</td><td>0.1</td><td></td><td>0.4</td><td>0.4</td></tr>
<tr><td>TOTAL[f]</td><td>100.0</td><td>100.0</td><td>100.0</td><td></td><td>100.0</td><td>100.0</td></tr>
</table>

[a] Basic data are given in Appendix C.

[b] N.e.m. denotes not elsewhere made.

[c] Between 1927 and 1929 establishments producing lubricating oils were transferred from oils to the lubricants industry.

[d] N.e.c. denotes not elsewhere classified.

[e] Not shown separately.

[f] The columns do not add up to 100.0 in every instance because they contain rounded percentages.

change in the pattern of the group's output (Table 45). In 1899 the petroleum refining industry accounted for less than half of the group's physical output. In 1937 the fraction had risen to eight tenths. The contribution of coke-oven products fell from 35 to 14 percent, and of the other industries, from 18 to 5 percent. The most marked changes in group composition occurred in the second decade.

Data on the relative contributions of the individual industries to the value added by the group, shown in Table 46, tend to reproduce the pattern outlined in Table 45.

Chapter 16

Stone, Clay and Glass Products

THE industries in this group all derive their principal materials from the earth in the form of stone, clay and sand, and most of them are located close to their sources of supply. Indeed, in some of the establishment reports, mining and quarrying operations are included because they are inseparable from the manufacturing activities. The processes employed in the industries comprising the group range from the simple cutting of stone to the manufacture of complex glass instruments. The resulting array of products is rather heterogeneous.[1]

In terms of value added the group was as important, in 1899, as leather products or chemical products, and in 1937, as important as nonferrous-metal products.

TRENDS IN THE PHYSICAL OUTPUT OF THE STONE, CLAY AND GLASS PRODUCTS INDUSTRIES

Data on physical output of the industries in the group are fragmentary (Table 47 and Chart 18). From 1899 we have indexes for only two of the 23 industries distinguished by the Census. Even for the recent period, 1929–37, indexes are available for no more than nine industries.

Asbestos Products. This classification embraces establishments manufacturing asbestos textiles, asbestos building materials, and other asbestos products. Steam and other packing,

[1] We include roofing in this group (although it is classified in the miscellaneous products group in the 1929 Census) because in the earlier years this industry made asbestos products.

STONE, CLAY AND GLASS PRODUCTS[a]

Physical Output: Indexes and Percentage Changes[b]

	Asbestos Products	Roofing	Cement	Lime	Wall Plaster and Board	Concrete Products	Sand-Lime Brick	Clay Products	Glass	Total: Unadjusted	Total: Adjusted
					INDEX OF PHYSICAL OUTPUT (1929:100)						
YEAR											
1899	..	..	7.3	..	..	..	..	77	..	..	..
1904	..	..	19	81	..	..	..	85	..	..	..
1909	..	..	43	91	..	..	..	102	..	..	..
1914	..	..	61	95	..	..	59	83	..	..	..
1919	..	..	57	77	..	..	52	63	..	..	..
1921	..	..	60	58	..	..	34	57	..	..	..
1923	..	..	77	93	..	..	76	99	..	..	..
1925	..	..	94	102	..	75	114	106	84	93	91
1927	73	..	100	101	100	94	115	107	92	98	100
1929	100	100	100	100	100	100	100	100	100	100	100
1931	68	62	75	78	65	61	54	48	81	66	67
1933	56	..	36	..	..	25	8.7	28	78	46	47
1935	78	83	44	67	64	57	26	40	118	67	69
1937	126	110	68	102	112	92	66	66	163	100	100
					NET PERCENTAGE CHANGE IN PHYSICAL OUTPUT						
PERIOD											
1899–1937	..	..	+838	..	..	..	..	–15	..	..	..
1899–1909	..	..	+493	..	..	..	..	+32	..	..	..
1909–1919	..	.	+32	–15	..	..	..	–38	..	..	..
1919–1929	..	..	+75	+30	..	..	+92	+59	..	..	..
1929–1937	+26	+10	–32	+2	+12	–8	–34	–34	+63	0	0

[a] Industries for which there are no adequate quantity data for any of the periods listed above are: steam and other packing; marble and granite; emery wheels; hones; sandpaper; pulp goods; china firing and decorating, not elsewhere done; pottery; crucibles; graphite; minerals and earths; statuary and art goods; glass products, not elsewhere made; and mirrors. These industries are covered by the adjusted total.

[b] The indexes have been constructed from basic data in the U.S. Census of Manufactures and other sources, by methods described briefly in Chapter 2 and in detail in Appendix A. Appendix B presents these data, together with the indexes derived from them. The indexes cited here for individual industries have been adjusted to take account of changes in the coverage of the respective samples, except when such adjustment was impossible.

The percentage changes are not always entirely consistent with the indexes given above because the changes were computed from the indexes in Appendix B, which are carried to one decimal place.

Chart 18
STONE, CLAY AND GLASS PRODUCTS
Indexes of Physical Output

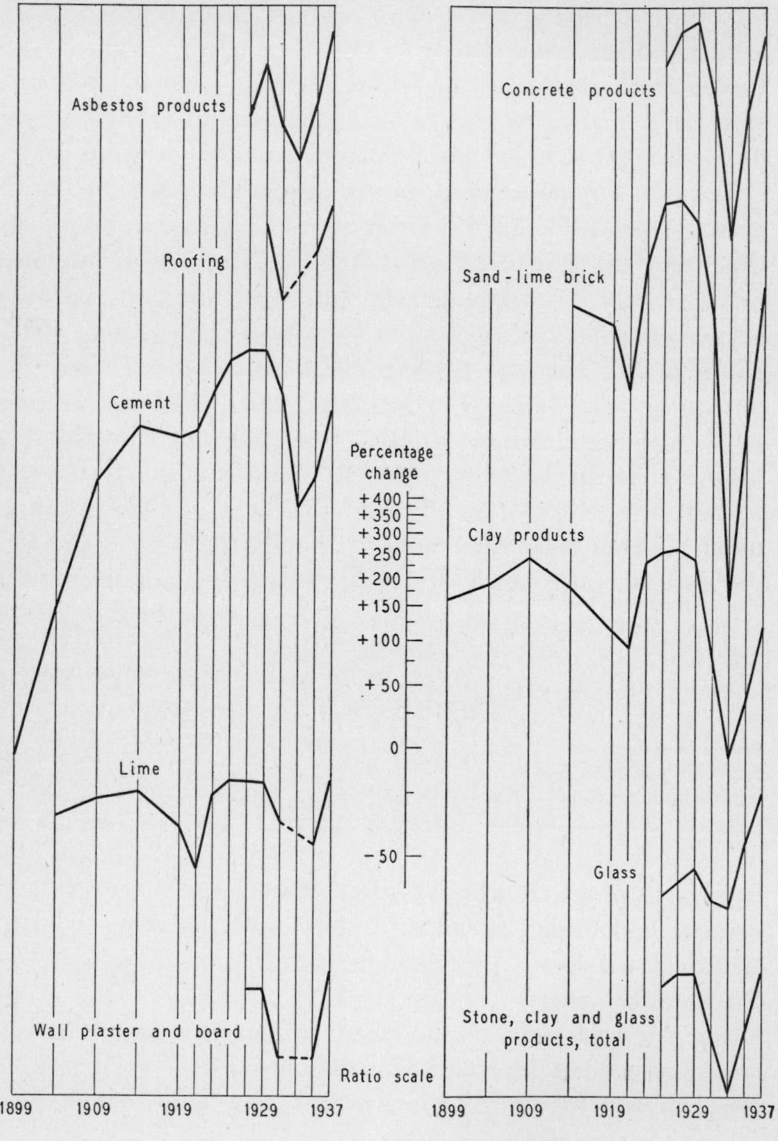

pipe and boiler covering and gaskets are treated elsewhere. The output of the asbestos products industry increased 38 percent from 1927 to 1929, and 26 percent from 1929 to 1937; in the entire decade it rose over 70 percent. Within the industry some products either failed to rise, or actually declined—asbestos cloth, brake lining (not molded), asbestos lumber, and table mats. On the other hand asbestos shingles and molded-asbestos brake lining made tremendous gains.

Cement. For the cement industry our data cover the entire period 1899–1937. In the latter year output was almost ten times as great as it had been in 1899. In the first decade output rose six-fold; between 1909 and 1919 the gain was only 32 percent, and the 1919 level was lower than that of 1914. In the decade between 1919 and 1929 output rose 75 percent, but in the years 1929–37 it fell 32 percent. The peak came in 1927, although output in that year was only fractionally higher than in 1929. A principal theme in the history of cement production from 1899 to 1937 is the gradual displacement of other types of cement by the Portland type. In 1899 the natural, puzzolan and masonry cements made up almost

	Quantity (million barrels)					*Percentage Distribution*				
	1899	1909	1919	1929	1937	1899	1909	1919	1929	1937
Portland cement	5.7	65.0	80.8	170.6	116.2	36	98	99	99	98
Natural, puzzolan and masonry cement	10.2	1.7	0.5	2.2	1.9	64	2	1	1	2
TOTAL	15.9	66.7	81.3	172.8	118.1	100	100	100	100	100

two thirds of the industry's output. Within ten years Portland cement had forged ahead so rapidly, and the other cements had declined so sharply, that the industry was dominated by Portland cement.

Even a relatively standardized commodity like Portland cement has been improved over the years with respect to both strength and hardening properties. Compression strength of seven-day-old concrete, in which standard cement is used, increased from 1,460 pounds per square inch in 1916–20 to 3,390 in 1931–35. In six-month-old concrete the compression strength increased from 4,430 to 6,560 pounds per square inch. One cause of this improvement was the enhanced fineness of standard Portland cement. During the period 1916–20 the average fineness of Portland cement, judged by the percentage of cement passing through a 200-mesh-per-inch sieve, was 82; in 1931–35, the corresponding percentage was 93. There was not only a marked quality improvement in standard Portland cement, but also an increase in the percentage that special cements comprised of all Portland cement production. These special cements, characterized by high-early-strength, quick-set, water-proof, color, low-heat, or other properties, constituted less than 2 percent of all cement produced in 1927; in 1937 the percentage was almost eight. Improvements in the quality of standard cements and the development of special cements served to augment the effective construction capacity of a given volume of cement; less cement was required per cubic yard of concrete of a given strength.[2]

The industry also decreased the amount of fuel used per barrel of cement. In 1909, 186 pounds of coal and coal equivalent were needed to turn out a barrel of hydraulic cement, but in 1935 only 159 pounds were required.[3] This reduction, of course, meant that the industry's net output rose even more rapidly than the actual number of barrels of cement produced.

Lime increased in output at a very moderate rate from 1904 to 1937. The net rise over the 33 years amounted to only 26 percent. As in cement production, there was a drop

[2] G. Perazich, S. T. Woal and H. Schimmel, "Mechanization in the Cement Industry," *Report No. M-3* (National Research Project, Dec. 1939), pp. 13, 17–19.

[3] N. Yaworski, *et al., op. cit.*, pp. 70–71.

between 1914 and 1919. The output in both 1925 and 1927 was fractionally higher than the 1929 volume, and about equal to that attained in 1937. Hydrated lime rose rapidly between 1909 (the first year for which data on the output of this product are available) and 1937; during the same period the combined output of quicklime and agricultural lime declined.

Wall Plaster and Board. This industry utilizes lime and gypsum to manufacture its chief products. Its output remained constant between 1927 and 1929, then made a net gain of 12 percent from 1929 to 1937. Among the individual products, gypsum plaster-board and lath, fiber wallboard, insulating board and flexible insulations rose rapidly in output, although most of the plasters declined.

Concrete Products (building materials, pipe and conduit, piling, etc.) rose 33 percent from 1925 to 1929, and fell 8 percent from 1929 to 1937. The net gain from 1925 to 1937 was 21 percent. Between 1929 and 1937 culvert pipe, pressure pipe, vaults, and paving materials increased in output. All other products declined, and some of these—brick, cast stone, circular structures, electric conduits, and septic tanks—dropped precipitously.

Clay Products, a very important industry in the group, consists largely of brick and tile enterprises. (Pottery is classified separately.) The output of the industry declined 15 percent from 1899 to 1937. In the first decade it rose 32 percent, then declined between 1909 and 1919 by 38 percent.[4] Following the recession of 1919–21 it rose sharply to a peak in 1927. In that year, however, output was only 4 percent higher than it had been in 1909. From 1919 to 1929 it gained 59 percent, and in the next period, 1929–37, dropped 34 percent. The only products of the industry which still appear to be rising in output are enameled and faience tile, magnesite and

[4] Because the 1899–1909 indexes are not adjusted for changes in the coverage of the underlying sample, they are subject to some error. See Appendix B.

chrome brick, and refractory cement. The 1937 output of common brick was two fifths the 1899 production. Vitrified brick fell even more drastically: the 1937 output of this product was only about one sixth as large as the volume turned out in 1899.

Glass, the last industrial category in the list, is represented by establishments engaged in manufacturing glass and glass products. Enterprises which manufacture glassware from purchased glass "blanks" are classified in other industries. Adequate data for the industry as a whole are available only from 1925. Output rose from 1925 to 1929 by 19 percent, and from 1929 to 1937 by 63 percent. There were especially large increases in beverage bottle production. For three products the records go back to 1899: polished plate glass rose from 17 million square feet in 1899 to 177 million in 1935 (the latest year for which separate data are given); window glass, from 217 million square feet in 1899 to 617 million in 1937; and obscured glass, from 13 million square feet to 28 million. All three, as well as polished wire glass (for which data are available beginning with 1914), declined from 1914 to 1919. Rough wire glass is the only product on which we have data that showed a rise between those two years.

Summary. Our index for the entire stone, clay and glass products group dates only from 1925. Total output rose between 1925 and 1929 by 7 percent according to the unadjusted index, and according to the adjusted index by 10 percent. From 1929 to 1937 the group's physical output changed less than 1 percent.

In relation to population growth the output of the cement industry rose over the period 1899–1937. Clay products fell absolutely, and in relation to population as well. As compared with total manufacturing, the clay products industry lagged behind not only in each subperiod but in the entire span of 38 years.

CHANGES IN THE INDUSTRIAL PATTERN OF STONE, CLAY AND GLASS MANUFACTURE

Because the coverage of the group's industries is inadequate, we must confine our examination of the changes in the composition of the group's physical output to the period beginning in 1925. Between that year and 1937, the cement industry decreased its contribution to the group's output from 17 to 11 percent (Table 48). The decline in the relative contribution of the clay products industry was even more severe: from 22 to 12 percent. Glass raised its share of the total from 15 to 27 percent. These changes occurred for the most part between 1929 and 1937, when the output of the construction-material industries was declining.

From data on value added, available as far back as 1899, it

Table 48

STONE, CLAY AND GLASS PRODUCTS

Relative Contributions of Component Industries to the Physical Output of the Entire Group[a]

Industry	*Percentage Distribution, Comparable Pairs of Years*					
	1925	1937	1925	1929	1929	1937
Cement	17.0	11.2	16.3	15.7	16.0	11.0
Lime	2.6	2.4	2.5	2.2	2.1	2.1
Concrete	4.0	4.4	4.3	5.2	4.9	4.5
Sand-lime brick	0.2	0.1	0.2	0.2	0.2	0.1
Clay products	21.9	12.3	21.3	18.4	19.5	12.9
Glass	15.4	27.0	16.3	17.7	16.7	27.3
Asbestos products	38.8	42.5	39.1	40.6	2.8	3.5
Roofing					3.7	4.1
Wall plaster and board					4.1	4.6
All other products					30.0	29.8
TOTAL[b]	100.0	100.0	100.0	100.0	100.0	100.0

[a] Derived from Table 47. For an explanation of the derivation of the measurements see footnote 10, Chapter 4.

[b] The columns do not add up to 100.0 in every instance because they contain rounded percentages.

TABLE 49

STONE, CLAY AND GLASS PRODUCTS

Relative Contributions of Component Industries to the Value Added by the Entire Group[a]

Industry	*Percentage Distribution, Comparable Pairs of Years*							
	1899	1909	1909	1919	1919	1929	1929	1937
Asbestos products					1.5	2.7	2.7	3.5
Steam and other packing	4.5	3.4	3.3	6.9	2.4	2.1	2.0	1.8
Roofing					4.4	3.7	3.7	4.1
Cement		9.4	9.4	12.9	12.8	15.3	15.1	11.6
Lime	9.0	3.1	3.1	2.6	2.6	2.0	1.9	2.2
Wall plaster and board		1.9	1.9	2.0	2.0[b]	3.8	3.8	5.2
Concrete products	21.6	3.2	3.2	2.7	2.4	5.2	5.2	4.2
Marble and granite		21.0	20.9	10.7	10.4	12.0	11.8	5.4
Emery wheels	0.5	1.1	1.1	2.5	2.5	1.8		
Hones	0.1	0.1	0.1	0.1	0.1	*	2.5[c]	5.0
Sand paper	0.3	0.6	0.6	0.6	0.6	0.8		
Pulp goods	0.3	0.2	0.2	1.6	1.6[b]	1.4	2.7	4.7
Sand-lime brick				[d]	0.1	0.2	0.2	0.1
China firing and decorating, n.e.d.[e]	0.2	0.1	0.1	0.1	0.1	0.1	0.1	0.1
Pottery	16.6	15.1	14.9[f]	7.3	7.2	7.4	7.3	7.1
Clay products	20.7	19.2	19.0	19.2	19.0	19.0	18.9	13.1
Crucibles	0.5	0.2	0.2	0.1	0.1	0.2		
Graphite	0.1	0.2	0.2	0.1	0.1	0.2	0.2	*
Minerals and earths	1.1	0.7	0.7	4.0	4.0[g]	0.8	0.7	1.6
Statuary and art goods		[h]	0.8	0.5	0.5	0.7	0.7	0.2
Glass	20.4	16.7	16.5	23.0	22.8	17.8	17.6	25.3
Glass products, n.e.m.[i]	2.7	2.8	2.7	1.9	1.8	1.5	2.9	4.8
Mirrors	1.5	1.0	1.0	1.1	1.1	1.4		
TOTAL[j]	100.0	100.0	100.0	100.0	100.0	100.0	100.0	100.0

* Less than half of one percent.

[a] Basic data are given in Appendix C.

[b] Between 1921 and 1923 there was a shift of some establishments from pulp goods to wall plaster.

[c] Not comparable with 1937, owing to a shift in the classification of an important establishment.

[d] Prior to 1914, included in clay products.

[e] N.e.d. denotes not elsewhere done.

[f] Between 1909 and 1914 there was an important shift from pottery to clay products.

[g] Including mining operations before 1929, but not in 1929 or later years.

[h] Included in several other industries in 1899.

[i] N.e.m. denotes not elsewhere made.

[j] The columns do not add up to 100.0 in every instance because they contain rounded percentages.

is possible to sketch the rough outlines of the movements in the composition of the entire group. As Table 49 shows, there was a pronounced rise in the relative contribution of cement, from 9 percent in 1909 to 15 percent in 1929, followed by a decline from 1929 to 1937. The contribution of the glass industry fell from 1899 to 1909 (4 points), rose sharply from 1909 to 1919 (6.5 points), fell again from 1919 to 1929 (5 points), then rose from 1929 to 1937 (8 points). The net rise was 5 percent. In pulp goods also there was a substantial increase of over 4 points. Asbestos products, concrete products, emery wheels, and minerals and earths all increased their relative contributions, but in smaller degree.

The largest relative decline was that of marble and granite. The contribution of this industry fell from 21 percent of the total value added by the group in 1909 to 5 percent in 1937. Pottery and clay products also dropped off. The combined contribution of these two industries declined from 37 percent in 1899 to 20 percent in 1937.

Chapter 17

Forest Products

The forest products group encompasses all industries engaged in the manufacture of lumber and lumber products, and certain related industries, notably turpentine and rosin. The wood-distillation industries are classified in the chemical products group; and the wood pulp industry is grouped with paper products.

The relative importance of the forest products group declined almost without interruption from 1899 to 1937. In the first year it contributed more to the value added by all manufacturing industries than any other group but one, textile products. In contrast, its contribution to total value added in 1937 was smaller than that of each of seven other groups.

TRENDS IN THE PHYSICAL OUTPUT OF THE FOREST PRODUCTS INDUSTRIES

For the entire period 1899–1937 we have data on physical output for only two of the forest products industries (Table 50 and Chart 19). One of these, lumber-mill products, is the dominant industry in the group.

Lumber-Mill Products. This classification includes logging camps, merchant sawmills, combined sawmills and planing mills, veneer mills, and cooperage-stock mills. Planing mills and box factories not operated in conjunction with sawmills are classified with other industries in the group. The physical output of the lumber-mill products industry fell by 32 percent between 1899 and 1937. During the first three decades output fluctuated about a fairly horizontal trend. The decade

FOREST PRODUCTS[a]

Physical Output: Indexes and Percentage Changes[b]

	Lumber-Mill Products, n.e.c.[c]	Planing-Mill Products, n.e.m.[d]	Boxes, Wooden, Cigar	Cooperage	Caskets and Coffins	Excelsior	Turpentine and Rosin	Total Unadjusted	Total adjusted
YEAR				INDEX OF PHYSICAL OUTPUT (1929: 100)					
1899	107	..	..	..	..	..	119	108	82
1904	96	..	..	..	..	..	97	96	76
1909	105	..	..	..	..	..	90	104	83
1914	96	..	..	..	..	..	82	95	82
1919	97	..	..	..	..	..	76	96	79
1921	80	..	..	..	..	..	74	80	83
1923	99	..	..	..	..	..	88	98	91
1925	106	119	..	..	..	99	91	108	103
1927	97	97	98	98	77	97	107	97	99
1929	100	100	100	100	100	100	100	100	100
1931	51	55	84	68	89	63	78	55	63
1933	40	32	65	56	..	51	82	40	46
1935	55	46	64	60	97	60	78	55	59
1937	72	64	83	63	104	70	81	72	76
PERIOD				NET PERCENTAGE CHANGE IN PHYSICAL OUTPUT					
1899–1937	−32	..	..	..	..	..	−32	−33	−7
1899–1909	−2	..	..	..	..	..	−24	−3	+1
1909–1919	−7	..	..	..	..	..	−16	−8	−5
1919–1929	+3	..	..	..	..	..	+32	+4	+27
1929–1937	−28	−36	−17	−37	+4	−30	−19	−28	−24

[a] Industries for which there are no adequate quantity data for any of the periods listed above are: window and door screens; wood turned and shaped; baskets; boxes, wooden, other; furniture; billiard tables; mirror and picture frames; cork products; lasts; matches; and wood preserving. These industries are covered by the adjusted total.

[b] The indexes have been constructed from basic data in the U.S. Census of Manufactures and other sources, by methods described briefly in Chapter 2 and in detail in Appendix A. Appendix B presents these data, together with the indexes derived from them. The indexes cited here for individual industries have been adjusted to take account of changes in the coverage of the respective samples, except when such adjustment was impossible.

The percentage changes are not always entirely consistent with the indexes given above because the changes were computed from the indexes in Appendix B, which are carried to one decimal place.

[c] N.e.c. denotes not elsewhere classified.

[d] N.e.m. denotes not elsewhere made.

Chart 19
FOREST PRODUCTS
Indexes of Physical Output

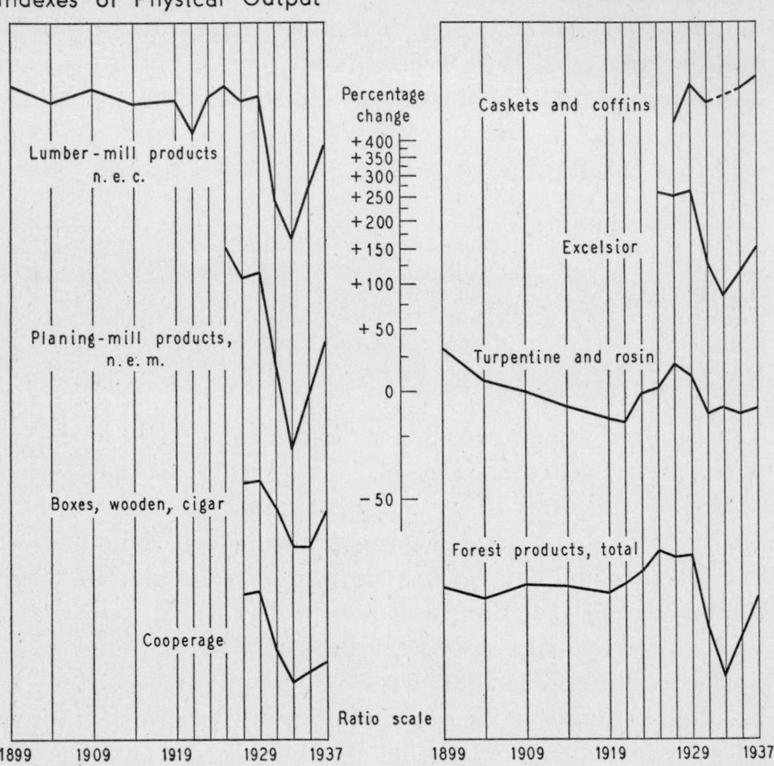

changes were −2, −7, and +3 percent, respectively.[1] From 1929 to 1937, however, output fell 28 percent. The industry's product was largest in 1899, although the level in that year was only slightly greater than that reached in 1909 or 1925.

Of the four lumber-mill products for which we have detailed data from 1899 onward, softwood lumber declined least. Its output in 1899 was 26 billion feet (board measure),

[1] The 1914 index is unadjusted and therefore may contain some error attributable to changes in the coverage of the sample. See the coverage percentages for other years, given in Appendix B.

and in 1937, 22 billion. Hardwood lumber output fell from 9 billion feet to 4 billion. The production of lath dropped more than 65 percent, from 2.5 billion feet in 1899 to 0.8 billion in 1937. Shingles declined more drastically: from 15 million squares in 1899 to 6 million in 1937. For the period beginning with 1925 we have more detailed data:

Product	*Unit*	*Quantity* 1925	1937	*Percentage Change*
Rough lumber sold	Bil. ft.	17.2	11.3	–34
Lath	Bil.	3.1	0.8	–74
Shingles	Mil. sq.	9.2	5.6	–39
Dressed lumber	Bil. ft.	14.3	11.6	–19
Doors	Mil.	8.0	2.4	–70
Sash	Mil.	7.2	1.6	–78
Window and door frames	Mil.	2.0	0.5	–75

The declines in lath, doors, sash, and frames made in the industry were particularly severe.

Despite the drop in its output, lumber has improved in quality with the passage of time, thanks to better methods of manufacture and drying. Kiln-drying, for example, has made lumber stronger, lighter, and less subject to sap stains, and has reduced spoilage resulting from air seasoning.[2]

The enormous declines we have found in the output of building materials made in the lumber-mill products industry tell only half the story, for they relate to the quantities of the products made in this industry alone, and not to total production.

Planing-Mill Products, another industry that manufactures some of these commodities, is covered by data beginning with 1925. Its output dropped 16 percent from that year to 1929, and then another 36 percent from 1929 to 1937. There were sharp declines between 1925 and 1937 in the output of all the individual products for which we have data:

[2] A. J. Van Tassel, *Mechanization in the Lumber Industry* (National Research Project, March 1940), p. 25.

Product	Unit	Quantity 1925	1937	Percentage Change
Dressed lumber	Bil. ft.	4.8	2.4	−50
Doors	Mil.	15.1	9.1	−40
Sash	Mil.	40.7	29.6	−27
Window and door frames	Mil.	10.8	5.3	−51

The output of the last three products listed fell less in this industry than in the lumber-mill products industry. Only the first product, dressed lumber, declined more sharply.

Turpentine and Rosin. This industry differs from the wood-distillation products industry in that its products are derived through distillation of the resinous exudation of the pine, rather than by distillation of the wood itself. The industry has been a declining one, in contrast to the growing wood-distillation industry. Between 1899 and 1919 the output of turpentine and rosin fell steadily.[3] After 1919 there was an increase which brought output in 1927 to a point higher than that of any other year except 1899. There was a decline of 7 percent from 1927 to 1929, and then another decline, from 1929 to 1937, of 19 percent. The net loss from 1899 to 1937 was 32 percent.

Summary. The unadjusted group average follows closely the index for lumber-mill products. For the important planing-mill products industry data are available for the most recent period only; and for the important furniture industry no satisfactory quantity data are available at all. If we take into account these and the other industries omitted, the group index is greatly affected, particularly for the post-war decade. The net decline of 33 percent between 1899 and 1937 changes to a decline of only 7 percent.[4] Gauged by either index, how-

[3] The 1899–1909 indexes are not as precise as the indexes for later years because they could not be adjusted for change in coverage.

[4] The adjustment for industries omitted from the unadjusted index is especially drastic for 1919–21. The unadjusted index fell between these two years, while the adjusted index rose. The cause of this variation is the large drop in 1919–21 in value added by lumber-mill products and by turpentine and rosin, in relation to the value added by the group as a whole. The adjustment therefore causes the index of physical output to rise. This is not

ever, the group's output has grown slowly, both absolutely and in relation to the output of other manufacturing groups so far studied and to the change in population. The peak in the adjusted index appears in 1925.

The group total and all the individual industries for which we have data (with the exception of caskets and coffins) failed to increase as rapidly as total manufacturing in any of the four periods; and only in 1919–29 did the group total and turpentine and rosin rise more rapidly than population.

Presumably the relative position of the group reflects the displacement of lumber by other materials in construction and even in furniture manufacture. This displacement resulted in part from the increasing pressure on our forest reserves; and in part from rapid technological developments in the industries producing substitutes for wood. The need for building materials that can be used in large structures, and the substitution of wood by more resistant and more handsome materials, have exerted a similar influence upon the course of the forest products industries.

CHANGES IN THE INDUSTRIAL PATTERN OF FOREST PRODUCTS MANUFACTURE

The major change in the composition of the physical output of the forest products group is attributable to the decline in the output of the lumber-mill products industry. The industrial pattern of the group's production in selected years is shown in terms of relative contributions in Table 51. Lumber-

---

necessarily an incorrect result: the post-war building boom began before 1921; and a decline in the output of lumber need not be associated with a decline in the output of industries using lumber, since stocks can be drawn upon. Interestingly enough, the NRP index of the output of planing-mill products rose between 1919 and 1921 (see Appendix D).

We may secure an alternative adjusted index of output for the group by utilizing, in addition to the indexes listed, the NRP index of furniture output (obtained by deflation of the value of furniture production by an index of furniture prices—see Appendix D). This alternative index also shows a rise of 27 percent between 1919 and 1929.

mill products contributed almost three fifths of the entire output of the group in 1899, but only about two fifths in 1937. Most of the decline occurred in the third decade. The decline in the relative contribution of turpentine and rosin was of minor importance because of the small size of the industry.

No data are available on the physical output of the individual industries grouped together as "other forest products,"

TABLE 51

FOREST PRODUCTS

Relative Contributions of Component Industries to the Physical Output of the Entire Group[a]

<table>
<tr><th rowspan="2">Industry</th><th colspan="10">Percentage Distribution, Comparable Pairs of Years</th></tr>
<tr><th>1899</th><th>1937</th><th>1899</th><th>1909</th><th>1909</th><th>1919</th><th>1919</th><th>1929</th><th>1929</th><th>1937</th></tr>
<tr><td>Lumber-mill products, n.e.c.[b]</td><td>59.1</td><td>42.8</td><td>55.7</td><td>53.8</td><td>53.5</td><td>52.4</td><td>52.4</td><td>42.4</td><td>43.0</td><td>40.7</td></tr>
<tr><td>Turpentine and rosin</td><td>2.0</td><td>1.4</td><td>3.0</td><td>2.3</td><td>2.6</td><td>2.3</td><td>1.8</td><td>1.9</td><td>1.3</td><td>1.4</td></tr>
<tr><td>Planing-mill products, n.e.m.[c]</td><td rowspan="6">38.9</td><td rowspan="6">55.8</td><td rowspan="6">41.2</td><td rowspan="6">43.9</td><td rowspan="6">43.9</td><td rowspan="6">45.4</td><td rowspan="6">45.8</td><td rowspan="6">55.7</td><td>13.3</td><td>11.2</td></tr>
<tr><td>Boxes, wooden, cigar</td><td>0.4</td><td>0.4</td></tr>
<tr><td>Cooperage</td><td>1.4</td><td>1.2</td></tr>
<tr><td>Caskets and coffins</td><td>2.4</td><td>3.3</td></tr>
<tr><td>Excelsior</td><td>0.1</td><td>0.1</td></tr>
<tr><td>Other forest products</td><td>38.1</td><td>41.7</td></tr>
<tr><td>TOTAL[d]</td><td>100.0</td><td>100.0</td><td>100.0</td><td>100.0</td><td>100.0</td><td>100.0</td><td>100.0</td><td>100.0</td><td>100.0</td><td>100.0</td></tr>
</table>

[a] Derived from Table 50. For an explanation of the derivation of the measurements see footnote 10, Chapter 4.

[b] N.e.c. denotes not elsewhere classified.

[c] N.e.m. denotes not elsewhere made.

[d] The columns do not add up to 100.0 in every instance because they contain rounded percentages.

but the figures on value added presented in Table 52 afford a clue to their relative contributions. The decline in the contribution of the planing-mill products industry indicates that the drop in lumber-mill products was not merely the result of a separation of planing mills from sawmills. The most important industry in the "other forest products" group shown in Table 51, furniture, accounted for almost the entire gain in the relative contribution of that group. Furniture's contribution increased from 14 percent of the total in 1899 to 29 in 1937. Minor rises occurred also in the contributions of wood preserving and caskets and coffins.

The increase in furniture and the decrease in lumber-mill

TABLE 52

FOREST PRODUCTS

Relative Contributions of Component Industries to the Value Added by the Entire Group[a]

Industry	*Percentage Distribution*						
	1899	1909		1919		1929	1937
		Comparable with 1899	Comparable with 1919	Comparable with 1909	Comparable with later years		
Lumber-mill products, n.e.c.[b]	56.2	53.7	53.6	52.3	51.9	43.0	40.8
Planing-mill products, n.e.m.[c]	13.4 (incl. window and door screens)	15.4 (incl. window and door screens)	15.4 (incl. window and door screens)	12.0	12.0	13.3	11.2
Window and door screens				0.4	0.4	0.7	0.6
Wood turned and shaped	2.1	2.2	2.2	1.8	1.8	2.1	3.0
Baskets	0.5	0.4	0.4	0.4	0.4	0.7	0.8
Boxes, wooden, cigar	0.6	0.5	0.5	0.4	0.4	0.4	0.4
Boxes, wooden, other	3.0	3.4	3.4	4.4	4.5	3.2	3.3
Cooperage	3.2	2.1	2.1	1.8	1.8	1.2	1.4
Furniture	14.2	15.2	15.2	18.7	18.9	27.0	28.6
Billiard tables	0.2	0.3	0.3	0.6	0.6	0.3	0.3
Mirror and picture frames	1.2	0.9	0.9	0.7	0.7	0.7	0.6
Caskets and coffins	1.4	1.5	1.5	2.0	2.0	2.5	3.1
Cork products	0.4	0.3	0.3	0.4	0.4	0.5	0.7
Excelsior		d	0.1	0.1	0.1	0.1	0.1
Lasts	0.3	0.3	0.3	0.5	0.5	0.3	0.3
Matches	0.5	0.8	0.8	0.7	0.7	0.4	0.9
Turpentine and rosin	2.8	2.4	2.4	2.3	2.3	1.3	1.3
Wood preserving	0.1	0.6	0.6	0.6	0.6	2.2	2.6
TOTAL[e]	100.0	100.0	100.0	100.0	100.0	100.0	100.0

[a] Basic data are given in Appendix C.
[b] N.e.c. denotes not elsewhere classified.
[c] N.e.m. denotes not elsewhere made.
[d] Included in artificial leather.
[e] The columns do not add up to 100.0 in every instance because they contain rounded percentages.

and planing-mill products are apparently inconsistent developments. We may note, however, that more than half the lumber produced is used in industries other than furniture. In 1929, for example, the entire cost of all materials consumed in the furniture industry was 426 million dollars, while the value of goods turned out by the lumber-mill products industry alone equaled 1,273 million. Again, a large and increasing fraction of all furniture manufactured is made from metal rather than from wood. The proportion of metal furniture was as high as 12 percent in 1925 (the earliest Census year for which information is available), and had reached 27 percent by 1937.

Chapter 18

Iron and Steel Products

THE iron and steel products group consists of industries which manufacture crude iron and steel, and those which use iron and steel as principal materials in the fabrication of other products. It does not include the important machinery and transportation equipment industries, which are classified separately.

One of the most important of the manufacturing groups, iron and steel products stood among the first three, ranked according to value added, both in 1899 and in 1937.

TRENDS IN THE PHYSICAL OUTPUT OF THE IRON AND STEEL PRODUCTS INDUSTRIES

Indexes of physical output of the two basic iron and steel industries, blast-furnace and steel-mill products, are available for the entire period 1899–1937; of two specialist industries, wire and wrought pipe, for 1909–37 and 1925–37, respectively; and of four other industries for varying periods, none longer than 1914–37 (Table 53 and Chart 20).

Blast-Furnace Products. This industrial category includes establishments engaged in the first stage of iron and steel processing: the manufacture from ore and scrap of pig iron and ferro-alloys. (Ferro-alloys made in electric furnaces are classified as products of the chemical industry.) The output of blast-furnace products rose 171 percent from 1899 to 1937. The sharpest increase came in the first ten years, when output went up by 79 percent; in the next decade production rose

TABLE 53

IRON AND STEEL PRODUCTS[a]

Physical Output: Indexes and Percentage Changes[b]

	Blast-Furnace Products	Steel-Mill Products	Wire, n.e.m.[c]	Wrought Pipe, n.e.m.[c]	Cast-Iron Pipe	Files	Firearms	Tin Cans and Tinware, n.e.c.[d]	Total: Unadjusted	Total: Adjusted
YEAR				INDEX OF PHYSICAL OUTPUT (1929: 100)						
1899	32	24	..	..	..	..	..	..	25	21
1904	38	29	..	..	..	..	..	..	30	29
1909	58	43	66	..	..	..	..	..	46	44
1914	53	44	64	..	62	..	..	..	46	48
1919	70	63	69	..	44	..	..	..	64	59
1921	39	38	51	..	48	..	52	..	39	46
1923	93	81	97	..	93	..	77	..	83	84
1925	84	82	92	77	113	..	70	..	83	87
1927	84	81	98	68	114	..	93	87	83	87
1929	100	100	100	100	100	100	100	100	100	100
1931	44	47	50	63	69	63	56	92	50	54
1933	32	43	46	31	31	65	56	94	45	45
1935	51	64	67	56	46	72	72	119	65	61
1937	88	97	90	91	68	106	107	160	98	89
PERIOD				NET PERCENTAGE CHANGE IN PHYSICAL OUTPUT						
1899–1937	+171	+313	..	..	..	..	..	..	+294	+327
1899–1909	+79	+84	..	..	..	..	..	..	+83	+110
1909–1919	+20	+46	+4	..	..	..	..	..	+40	+34
1919–1929	+43	+58	+45	..	+129	..	..	..	+57	+70
1929–1937	–12	–3	–10	–9	–32	+6	+7	+60	–2	–11

[a] Industries for which there are no adequate quantity data for any period listed above are: bolts and nuts, not elsewhere made; forgings, not elsewhere made; galvanizing, not elsewhere done; nails and spikes, not elsewhere made; springs, steel, not elsewhere made; structural metal work, not elsewhere made; wirework, not elsewhere classified; doors, metal; heating apparatus; stoves and ranges; plumbers' supplies, not elsewhere classified; screw-machine products; cutlery, not elsewhere classified; saws; tools, other; hardware, not elsewhere classified; and safes and vaults. These industries are covered by the adjusted total.

[b] See the discussion of the sources and methods of computation in Chapter 2 and in detail in Appendix A. Appendix B presents these data, together with the indexes derived from them. The indexes cited here for individual industries have been adjusted to take account of changes in the coverage of the respective samples, except when such adjustment was impossible.

The percentage changes are not always entirely consistent with the indexes given above because the changes were computed from the indexes in Appendix B, which are carried to one decimal place.

[c] N.e.m. denotes not elsewhere made.

Chart 20
IRON AND STEEL PRODUCTS
Indexes of Physical Output

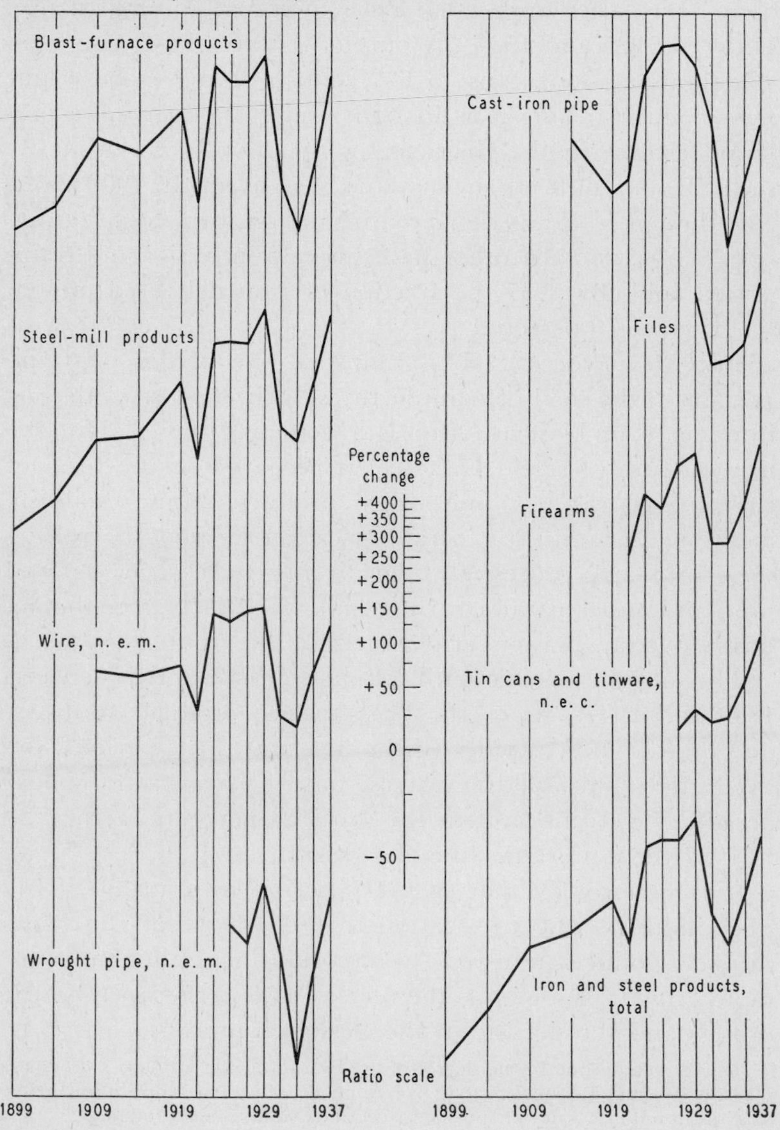

only 20 percent; in the third it increased 43 percent; but in the last period it declined 12 percent.

Of the two principal products, ordinary pig iron and ferro-alloys, the latter appears to have increased in importance. Between 1925 and 1937 the output of ferro-alloys rose from 430 thousand long tons to 629 thousand; pig iron output was 36 million long tons in both years. A much more profound change in the character of the industry's output resulted from a shift to new methods of delivery. In 1909 about half the pig iron was delivered in molten form to adjoining steel works, and the other half was cast into pigs and transported cold. By 1937 the fraction of iron delivered molten had risen to 70 percent.

Steel-Mill Products. This industry, one of the most important in the field of manufactures, utilizes most of the pig iron made in blast-furnaces as a principal material in the manufacture of steel. The steel is prepared in the form of steel ingots, castings, and rolled products. Some establishments in the industry carry fabrication beyond the rolling stage into such processes as tin dipping, wire drawing, and pipe and tube manufacturing, and for this reason the industry overlaps a number of others in the group.

The output of steel-mill products quadrupled between 1899 and 1937.[1] As in the blast-furnace products industry, output rose most rapidly in the first and third periods. Between 1899 and 1909 the increase was 84 percent; in the next decade 46 percent, and in the third 58 percent. From 1929 to 1937 there was a decline of 3 percent.

It is noteworthy that in every period the output of the steel industry rose in relation to the output of the blast-furnace products industry. An important reason for the more rapid growth of steel was the relative rise in the open-hearth process and the decline in the Bessemer process:

[1] Owing to a decline in the degree of duplication in the industry's products, the rise is somewhat understated; see Appendix B. The duplication arises from intra-industry sales of unrolled steel and semifinished products.

Process	*Production of Steel Ingots and Castings* (million long tons)					*Percentage Distribution*				
	1899	1909	1919	1929	1937	1899	1909	1919	1929	1937
Open-hearth	3.0	14.2	26.7	48.2	47.0	28	60	79	86	91
Bessemer	7.5	9.2	6.9	7.1	3.5	71	39	20	13	7
Other	0.1	0.1	0.3	0.8	1.1	1	1	1	1	2
TOTAL	10.7	23.5	34.0	56.2	51.6	100	100	100	100	100

The open-hearth process, although it is slower and requires more expensive equipment than the Bessemer process, yields a product of better quality, permits the use of high phosphorus ore, and—most important in the present connection—utilizes scrap iron and steel.[2] The increase in the proportion of steel made in open-hearth furnaces, from 28 percent in 1899 to 60 percent in 1909 and 91 percent in 1937, was accompanied by a rise in the ratio of scrap to pig iron charged to steel furnaces. In 1909 (the first year for which Census data become available) 10 million tons of scrap and 19 million tons of pig iron were consumed in steel works. In 1937 the amount of scrap used was 27 million tons, and the amount of pig iron (including ferro-alloys) 30 million.

Technological developments in the steel industry led also to savings in materials. The economies are indicated by the following figures, given for all the years for which they are available:

	1909	*1914*	*1919*	*1929*	*1935*	*1937*
1. Materials consumed: pig iron (including ferro-alloys) and scrap (million long tons)	29.0	28.1	40.8	64.8	38.5	57.5
2. Products: ingots and castings (million long tons)	23.5	23.4	34.0	56.2	34.4	51.6
3. Ratio, 2 ÷ 1	.81	.83	.83	.87	.89	.90

In 1937 about 10 percent less ferrous materials were used in the production of a ton of steel than were required in 1909.[3]

[2] E. D. McCallum, *The Iron and Steel Industry in the United States* (P. S. King, 1931), pp. 77–78.

[3] Some iron ore is used also, but it is not quantitatively important.

Improved furnace design and increased knowledge of the equilibrium relationship between slag and metal helped to reduce the amount of metal lost in the slag. Again, improved tapping and teeming practice cut down pit losses and skull losses in ladles.[4] As a result of these technological advances, the net output of the steel industry rose in relation to its gross output.[5]

Steel-mill products are so numerous that we can list only the more important ones in attempting to show the changing composition of the industry's output. Continuous data are available only beginning with 1909:

Product	*Quantity* (million long tons)				*Percentage Change*[a]
	1909	1919	1929	1937	1909 to 1937
Unrolled steel					
Ingots	.14	.71	.66	.64	+350
Direct steel castings	.45	.68	1.21	1.04	+132
Semifinished rolled products					
Blooms, billets and slabs	4.97	6.23	7.63	7.65	+54
Sheet and tinplate bars	1.65	2.86	5.06	2.64	+60
Muck and scrap bar	.17	.17	.07	.022	−87
Finished rolled products					
Rails	2.84	2.08	2.67	1.41	−50
Rail joints and fastenings, tie plates, etc.	.39	.46	.87	.46	+17
Structural steel, light and heavy	2.10	2.45	4.47	3.11	+49
Concrete reinforcing bars	.19	.30	.97	.81	+325
Merchant bars, mill shafting, wire rods, etc.	4.13	5.34	7.70	5.52	+34
Plates, no. 12 and thicker, not coated	}		{ 5.21	3.34 }	
Sheets, no. 13 and thinner, not coated	} 2.87	5.47	{	}	+183
Plain automobile body	}		{ 3.90	4.79 }	
Black for tinning	.63	.56	.14	.78	+23

[4] We are indebted to Walter S. Tower, of the American Iron and Steel Institute, for this information.

[5] It may be estimated, roughly, that as a result of the savings in materials, net output rose about 25 percent more than gross output from 1909 to 1937.

Product	Quantity (million long tons)				Percentage Change
	1909	1919	1929	1937	1909 to 1937
Strips, bands, flats, scroll and hoops, narrower than 24 inches	.34 (strips and cotton ties combined)	.74	2.01	2.29	+589 (strips and cotton ties combined)
Cotton ties, for sale		.043	.038	.062	
Skelp	.68	.92	1.27	1.14	+68
Axles, rolled and forged	.094	.098	.150	.13	+35
Armor plate and ordnance, for sale	.027	.10	.01	.020	−26
Scrap iron and steel	1.24	2.11	2.83	2.94	+138
Rerolled or renewed rails	.11	.10	.057	.032	−70

[a] The percentage changes are not always entirely consistent with the quantities given above because the changes were computed from the data in Appendix B, which are carried to more decimal places.

All the quantities listed are those sold or transferred; commodities produced and consumed in the same plant are not included. It is noteworthy that only a small fraction of the total volume of ingots produced was sold. Of 50 million tons produced in 1937, 49 million were consumed in the same works in the manufacture of rolled and finished products, 0.5 million were transferred to other plants of the same company, and only 0.2 million tons were sold.

Between 1909 and 1937 the aggregate output of the industry almost doubled. Individual products which rose much more rapidly than the aggregate were ingots for sale, concrete reinforcing bars, thick and auto plates, and narrow strips and bands. In the same period there were declines in the output of muck and scrap bar, rails (new and renewed), and armor plate and ordnance.

Marked improvements in the quality of steel and steel products have been noted in testimony by the United States Steel Corporation before the Temporary National Economic Committee.[6] During the last 15 years steel sheets used in making automobile bodies have had their "deep drawing

[6] "Improved Quality of Steel as a Price Reduction," a pamphlet published by the United States Steel Corporation (November 1939).

qualities" increased by 30 to 40 percent; this means that sharply rounded shapes may be stamped deeper. Again, sheets are now made wider. As a result of these improvements, a front fender can be stamped out of one sheet, whereas formerly a fender was made of two sheets separately formed and then joined together. Moreover, because of the fine grain and dense polished surface of modern sheet steel, the time required to apply paint to automobile body parts has been reduced from a minimum of 48 hours to 6.

Tin plates also have been improved remarkably. Higher corrosion resistance now makes possible the canning of certain types of acid fruits and the storing of cans of such fruits for longer periods. Other advances are noted in the following quotation: [7]

> The purchaser of modern tin plate has less waste in trimming the sheets to the size and shape required for his purposes since modern tin plate is made more accurate in its dimensions than was the tin plate of fifteen years ago. Increased uniformity of thickness has contributed to the economical use of high speed machines with automatic feeders in the can-making industry, by eliminating the necessity of frequent adjustment in the machines, and has also resulted in a reduction in sheet damage. It is estimated that, due to the improved quality of modern tin plate, the average weight of tin plate used for any given purpose has decreased about 10 percent. . . . Formerly, a relatively high number of sheets of the tin plate were damaged in transit to the purchaser's plant due to twisted and bent edges. The modern, much more compact and better protected packages, made possible by the almost perfect uniformity of the sheets, have greatly reduced these losses.

Improved quality of output in the steel industry has contributed on many counts to greater productivity in the steel-consuming industries.

Wire. This industry manufactures wire and wire products

[7] *Ibid.*, pp. 4–5.

from purchased rods. These products are made also to a large extent in the steel-mill products and nonferrous-metal products, n.e.c. industries, from rods manufactured in the same plant: in 1929 the wire industry turned out only 34.8 percent of all wire and wire products.

The output of the specialist wire industry, which we are considering here, rose only 4 percent from 1909 to 1919. Between 1919 and 1923 it increased over 40 percent, reaching a level which it maintained until 1929. From 1929 to 1937 output fell 10 percent. The net increase between 1909 and 1937 was 35 percent. Detailed statistics concerning the products of the industry are available in continuous form from 1909 to 1929. Between these two years there were declines in coated iron and steel wire, nails and spikes, and barbed wire.

Wrought Pipe. This industry, too, specializes in products made to a large extent also in the steel-mill products industry. Only 27 percent of all the wrought pipe produced in 1929 was made in the specialist industry, whose output rose 30 percent from 1925 to 1929, and fell 9 percent from 1929 to 1937.

Cast-Iron Pipe output fell almost 30 percent from 1914 to 1919, a decline reminiscent of those occurring in this period in the other industries devoted largely to construction materials. From 1919 to 1929 there was a rise of 129 percent (with a peak in 1927) and from 1929 to 1937 a decline of 32 percent. The net increase between 1914 and 1937 was only 11 percent. Between these two years bell and spigot pipe, flanged pipe, and culvert pipe declined. Gas and water-pipe fittings made an especially large gain, from 42 thousand tons to 163 thousand.

Tin Cans and Other Tinware, not elsewhere classified, the last industry in the list for which we have quantity data, attained a particularly large increase in output. From 1927 to 1929, the product of this industry rose 15 percent, and from 1929 to 1937, 60 percent, a net increase of 84 percent in ten years. All the individual products of the industry for which we have data increased, particularly packers' cans. As was noted above, savings of materials were effected in the tin can industry through reductions both of the wastage involved in the trimming of tin plates to prescribed sizes and shapes, and of the weight of tin plate required for any given purpose.

Summary. Among the individual industries, blast-furnace products lagged behind total manufacturing, except in the period 1899–1909. This was true also of wire in the three periods for which we have data.

In all the industries the increase in output was more rapid than the rise in population, except in 1929–37, when only two industries outstripped population growth, and in 1909–19, when wire rose only 4 percent.

The output of the iron and steel group as a whole followed fairly closely the trend of the important steel-mill products industry. The net gain between 1899 and 1937 was 294 percent according to the unadjusted index, and 327 percent according to the adjusted index. In the last period, 1929–37, output fell 2 percent according to the unadjusted index and 11 percent according to the adjusted index. The group index rose about as rapidly between 1899 and 1937 as the index for all manufacturing combined. In the first and third periods the group index rose faster, in the second and fourth periods more slowly.

CHANGES IN THE INDUSTRIAL PATTERN OF IRON AND STEEL PRODUCTS MANUFACTURE

We have noted that the output of blast-furnace products rose less rapidly than that of steel-mill products; and that the average output of these two industries rose less rapidly than the group total. The effect of these varying trends upon the composition of the group's output is brought out in Table 54. The relative contribution of blast-furnace products fell

TABLE 54

IRON AND STEEL PRODUCTS

Relative Contributions of Component Industries to the Physical Output of the Entire Group[a]

Industry	Percentage Distribution, Comparable Pairs of Years									
	1899	1937	1899	1909	1909	1919	1919	1929	1929	1937
Blast-furnace products	10.5	6.8	13.7	11.7	8.5	7.6	6.7	5.7	4.7	4.6
Steel-mill products	48.8	48.1	45.9	40.2	42.7	46.6	47.8	44.5	45.8	49.7
Wire, n.e.m.[b]					3.1	2.4	2.8	2.3	2.7	2.7
Cast-iron pipe							1.0	1.4	1.5	1.1
Wrought pipe, n.e.m.[b]									1.6	1.6
Files									0.3	0.3
Firearms	40.7	45.1	40.4	48.1					0.5	0.6
Tin cans and tinware, n.e.c.[c]					45.7	43.4	41.7	46.1	2.6	4.7
All other products									40.3	34.5
TOTAL[d]	100.0	100.0	100.0	100.0	100.0	100.0	100.0	100.0	100.0	100.0

(Bracketed figures: 40.7, 45.1, 40.4, 48.1 cover Wire through All other products; 45.7, 43.4 cover Cast-iron pipe through All other products; 41.7, 46.1 cover Wrought pipe through All other products.)

[a] Derived from Table 53. For an explanation of the derivation of the measurements see footnote 10, Chapter 4.

[b] N.e.m. denotes not elsewhere made.

[c] N.e.c. denotes not elsewhere classified.

[d] The columns do not add up to 100.0 in every instance because they contain rounded percentages.

from 10 percent in 1899 to 7 percent in 1937, and there were declines in each of the four subperiods distinguished in the table. The contribution of steel-mill products to the group's output was practically the same in 1937 as it had been in 1899, although it fluctuated from one period to another. Our data are most detailed for the last period, 1929–37, when there were substantial rises in steel-mill products, in tin cans and in tinware not elsewhere classified; appreciable declines in cast-iron pipe and in the total of "all other" industries; and minute changes in the few remaining industries in the group for which we have figures.

TABLE 55

IRON AND STEEL PRODUCTS

Relative Contributions of Component Industries to the Value Added by the Entire Group[a]

Industry	Percentage Distribution						
	1899	1909		1919		1929	1937
		Comparable with		Comparable with			
		1899	1919	1909	later years		
Blast-furnace products	17.6	10.1	9.1	7.4	7.5	5.0	4.3
Steel-mill products	48.2	46.6	42.2	46.8	47.6	44.9	50.9
Bolts and nuts, n.e.m.[b]	1.4	1.7	1.5	1.8	1.9	1.8	1.8
Forgings, n.e.m.[b]	1.3	1.5	1.4	3.8	3.9	2.6	2.0
Galvanizing, n.e.d.[c]	0.2	0.2	0.2	0.2	0.2	0.1	0.1
Nails and spikes, n.e.m.[b]	1.4	0.6	0.5	0.4	0.4	0.2	0.2
Springs, steel, n.e.m.[b]	0.6	0.6	0.6	1.0	1.0	0.6	0.5
Structural metal work, n.e.m.[b]	6.8	8.0	7.3	5.1	5.2	7.1	4.3
Wire, n.e.m.[b]	0.6	3.4	3.1	2.4	2.5	2.7	2.8
Wirework, n.e.c.[d]	2.1	2.5	2.2	1.6	1.6	2.4	3.0
Wrought pipe, n.e.m.[b]	1.4	1.1	1.0	1.2	1.3	1.7	1.5
Cast-iron pipe		[e]	1.3	1.0	1.0	1.4	1.2
Doors, metal	0.1	0.2	0.2	0.3	0.3	1.3	1.0
Heating apparatus	2.8	4.5	4.0	3.6	3.7	4.8	8.9 (Heating apparatus and Stoves and ranges combined)
Stoves and ranges	0.5	0.7	6.4	5.0	5.1	5.2	
Plumbers' supplies, n.e.c.[d]	1.8	3.2	2.9	1.3	1.3	2.5	2.2
Screw-machine products	0.7	0.8	0.8	1.4	1.4	2.0	2.1
Cutlery, n.e.c.[d]	2.3	2.2	2.0	1.9	2.0	2.0	1.7
Files	0.5	0.6	0.5	0.6	0.6	0.3	0.4
Saws	0.9	0.9	0.8	0.8	0.8	0.5	0.4
Tools, other	2.0	2.7	2.5	4.0	2.4	2.1	1.7
Firearms	1.0	0.9	0.8	0.9	0.9	0.6	0.6
Hardware, n.e.c.[d]	5.5	6.1	5.5	4.3	4.4	4.7	4.5
Safes and vaults	0.5	0.7	0.6	0.4	0.4	0.4	0.1
Tin cans and tinware, n.e.c.[d]		[f]	2.5	2.8	2.8	3.1	3.9
TOTAL[g]	100.0	100.0	100.0	100.0	100.0	100.0	100.0

[a] Basic data are given in Appendix C.
[b] N.e.m. denotes not elsewhere made.
[c] N.e.d. denotes not elsewhere done.
[d] N.e.c. denotes not elsewhere classified.
[e] Included in foundry and machine-shop products prior to 1909.
[f] In 1899, included in sheet metal work, not elsewhere classified.
[g] The columns do not add up to 100.0 in every instance because they contain rounded percentages.

The contributions of the component industries to the value added by the iron and steel products group as a whole are summarized in Table 55. From this tabulation, it appears that the relative contribution of the blast-furnace industry to the value added by the group declined between 1899 and 1937 much more than its relative contribution to the physical output of the group. The only other outstanding decline between 1899 and 1937 was in the relative contributions (to value added) of nails and spikes and structural metal work. Wire, metal doors, heating apparatus, stoves and ranges, and screw-machine products rose rather sharply.

The most interesting change in the group's composition is the decline of the blast-furnace products industry in relation to the steel-mill products industry. This relative decline persisted not only throughout the period 1899–1937 considered as a whole, but also in each of the subperiods. We have already remarked upon the displacement of pig iron by scrap and upon the savings effected in the quantity of all ferrous materials consumed in the production of steel. Another factor that made for divergence was the increased share obtained by the steel-mill products industry of the pig iron produced by blast furnaces:

	1899	*1909*	*1919*	*1929*	*1937*
1. Pig iron and ferro-alloy production, blast-furnace products industry (millon long tons)	14.4	25.7	30.9	42.5	36.8
2. Pig iron and ferro-alloy consumption, steel-mill products industry (million long tons)	10.4	19.1	24.4	35.4	30.2
3. Ratio, (2) ÷ (1)	.72	.74	.79	.83	.82

The share of steel-mills increased from 72 to 82 percent between 1899 and 1937, and the share of the other industries declined correspondingly.[8]

[8] Of the 36.8 million long tons of pig iron produced in 1937, 29.5 million were used in the steel-mill products industry, 1.9 million in the foundry and machine-shop products industry, 0.6 million in the cast-iron pipe industry, and 4.8 million in other industries.

Chapter 19

Nonferrous-Metal Products

THE nonferrous-metal products group includes industries producing nonferrous metals from the ore or recovering them from scrap; refining or alloying these metals; and producing commodities for which the metals or their alloys constitute the principal material. Large quantities of nonferrous metals and alloys are used in industries classified in other groups, particularly iron and steel products, chemicals, machinery, and transportation equipment. Establishments engaged in the primary production of aluminum are classified in the chemicals industry and not in the nonferrous-metals group.

In 1937 the value added by the nonferrous-metals group was about one third as great as that added by the iron and steel products group.

TRENDS IN THE PHYSICAL OUTPUT OF THE NONFERROUS-METAL PRODUCTS INDUSTRIES

Data on the output of the three basic smelting and refining nonferrous-metals industries—copper, lead and zinc—are available for the entire period 1899–1937 (Table 56 and Chart 21).[1] For the important industry in the next stage of production, "nonferrous-metal products, not elsewhere classified," and two minor industries, the data begin only in 1925, and for clocks and watches in 1927. Data on a number of important industries in the group are entirely lacking.

[1] The indexes for the three smelting and refining industries are unadjusted for changes in the coverage of the underlying samples. Excessive duplication in the output of these industries made it impossible to calculate a reasonably accurate adjustment. See Appendices A and B.

NONFERROUS-METAL PRODUCTS[a]

Physical Output: Indexes and Percentage Changes[b]

	Copper	Lead	Zinc	Secondary Metals, Nonprecious	Collapsible Tubes	Nonferrous-Metal Products, n.e.c.[c]	Clocks, Watches and Materials	Total: Unadjusted	Total: Adjusted
YEAR				INDEX OF PHYSICAL OUTPUT (1929:100)					
1899	22	38	21	..	..	..	..	..	..
1904	31	51	30	..	..	..	..	..	..
1909	47	63	41	..	..	..	..	..	..
1914	52	72	57	..	..	..	..	..	..
1919	60	63	74	..	..	..	..	..	..
1921	34	60	34	..	..	..	..	..	..
1923	69	83	82	..	..	..	..	..	..
1925	78	99	90	78	94	70	..	76	79
1927	82	101	94	84	103	72	113	82	84
1929	100	100	100	100	100	100	100	100	100
1931	54	58	48	58	102	59	64	58	64
1933	30	36	50	67	108	43	48	43	47
1935	48	43	64	87	110	62	78	62	66
1937	80	58	86	124	124	88	139	92	89
PERIOD				NET PERCENTAGE CHANGE IN PHYSICAL OUTPUT					
1899–1937	+272	+51	+318	..	..	..	..	..	..
1899–1909	+117	+64	+98	..	..	..	..	..	..
1909–1919	+28	0	+82	..	..	..	..	..	..
1919–1929	+67	+59	+35	..	..	..	..	..	..
1929–1937	−20	−42	−14	+24	+24	−12	+39	−8	−11

[a] Industries for which there are no adequate quantity data for any period listed above are: secondary metals, precious; aluminum manufactures; tin and other foils; electroplating; fire extinguishers; gold leaf and foil; lighting equipment; needles and pins; plated ware; silverware; sheet metal work, not elsewhere classified; stamped and enameled ware; watch-cases; and jewelry and jewelers' findings. These industries are covered by the adjusted total.

[b] The indexes have been constructed from basic data in the U.S. Census of Manufactures and reports of the U.S. Bureau of Mines, by methods described briefly in Chapter 2 and in detail in Appendix A. Appendix B presents these data, together with the indexes derived from them. The indexes cited here for individual industries have been adjusted to take account of changes in the coverage of the respective samples, except when such adjustment was impossible.

The percentage changes are not always entirely consistent with the indexes given above because the changes were computed from the indexes in Appendix B, which are carried to one decimal place.

[c] N.e.c. denotes not elsewhere classified.

Chart 21

NONFERROUS-METAL PRODUCTS

Indexes of Physical Output

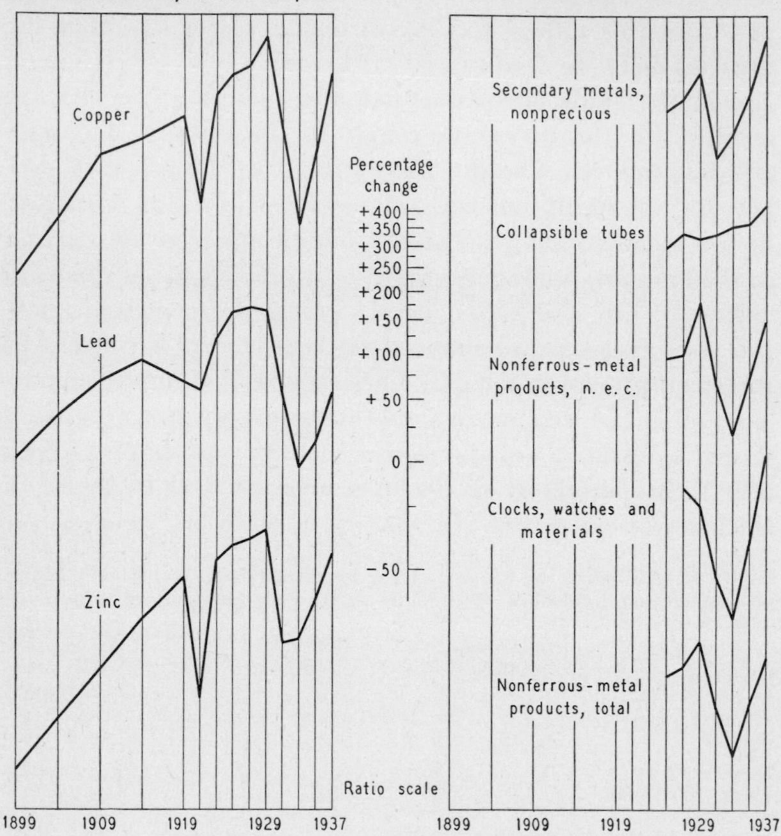

Copper. This smelting and refining industry came close to quadrupling its output between 1899 and 1937. Most of the rise occurred in the decade 1899–1909, when production more than doubled; in the next decade the net gain was less than one third; from 1919 to 1929 it amounted to two thirds, but in the final period it declined as much as one fifth.

By-products like gold and silver increased at a rate somewhat slower than that which characterized copper production. One reason for the disparity may be the inclusion, in the industry's copper output, of some secondary copper refined from scrap (which yields neither gold nor silver); copper from this source was increasing more rapidly than the primary metal derived directly from ore. There were changes also in the grade of ore smelted, and these too may help to account for the divergent trends in the output of copper and by-products. The downward trend in the grade of copper ore was significant on still another count, for reduction in the metal content of the ore mined involved an increase in the amount of effort required to produce a given quantity of metal. On the other hand, advances in metallurgical processes gave rise to enhanced efficiency in the extraction of the metal present in the ore. These and related improvements have offset the decline in grade only in part, however, as is shown by estimates of the copper yield per ton of ore, which reflect the net result of declines in grade and increases in efficiency of extraction.[2] In 1889 each ton of ore yielded over

[2] No general figures are available for a measurement of the individual force of each of these influences. The following figures relate to three mills:

	Utah Copper Mill		*Ray Mill (Hayden)*		*Miami Mill*	
	1911	1930	1911	1930	1911	1930
	(pounds of copper per ton of ore)					
Yield	21	17	23	17	37	12
Metal content	30	19	36	20	50	15
Unextracted metal	9	2	13	3	13	3

In the Utah Mill, for example, the yield per ton declined from 21 lbs. in 1911 to 17 lbs. in 1930. Total metal content fell from 30 lbs. to about 19. Unextracted metal, therefore, was nine lbs. in 1910 and two lbs. in 1930. The decline of 11 lbs. in metal content, which measures the deterioration in the quality of the ore, was largely but not entirely counterbalanced by a rise of seven lbs. in metal extracted, which measures the increased efficiency of extraction. See A. V. Corry and O. E. Kiessling, *Grade of Ore,* Report No. E–6 (National Research Project in cooperation with the Bureau of Mines, Aug. 1938), p. 52. The data are cited from T. O. Chapman, Bureau of Mines *Bulletin No. 392,* pp. 10–11, and A. B. Parsons, *The Porphyry Coppers,* p. 200. A large fraction of the increased efficiency of extraction should probably be credited to copper concentrators, which are not treated by the Census as manufacturing establishments.

65 pounds of copper. The yield per ton dropped to about 53 pounds in 1902, 40 pounds in 1909, 33 pounds in 1919 and 28 pounds in 1929. During the recession following 1929 the yield rose, as a result of a deliberate avoidance of the leaner ores, reaching a level of about 42 pounds per ton in 1933.[3]

Lead increased in output at a very much lower rate than copper. The rise from 1899 to 1937 was only 51 percent, the net result of large gains in the first and third decades, a minute decline in the second decade, and a drastic one in the last period. The peak output came in 1927. The drop from that point brought output in 1937 to a very low level.

As in the copper industry, gold and silver by-products declined in relation to the output of the primary product, lead. Although lead production rose much less rapidly, between 1899 and 1937, than did copper output, the percentage decline in yield per ton of ore treated was about as great: in 1910 the number of pounds of lead obtained from a ton of ore averaged 110, and in 1930 the corresponding yield was 85 pounds.[4]

Zinc. In this industry output rose more rapidly than it did in the other two smelting and refining industries. From 1899 to 1937 the net gain amounted to 318 percent. In the first decade production doubled; from 1909 to 1919 it rose at a rate only slightly lower; and from 1919 to 1929 it increased by about a third. From 1929 to 1937 output fell almost one seventh.

Here too, gold by-products declined in relation to the main product; however, silver changed irregularly, with a net relative rise. The downward trend in the grade of zinc ore was offset in part by shifts to higher-tenor ore deposits. These, together with improvements in metallurgy, served to prevent a serious drop in the average yield per ton of ore. Yields in the Joplin region, the largest source of domestic production,

[3] Corry and Kiessling, *op cit.*, p. 2.
[4] *Op. cit.*, p. 71.

actually rose from 1910 to 1930. In the Eastern and Western regions, however, there were definite reductions in yield.[5]

The declines in the grade of the nonferrous ores treated in the smelting and refining industries, and the increases in the percentage of metal extracted in smelting and refining operations, suggest that the net physical output of these industries advanced more rapidly than their gross physical output. The extraction of 30 pounds of copper metal from two tons of a given grade of ore represents a greater *net* contribution to the national output than does the extraction of 30 pounds of metal from one ton of an ore of much higher tenor. Again, a yield of 20 pounds of copper metal from a single ton of a given grade of ore represents a greater net contribution than 20 pounds of copper metal extracted from two tons of the same grade of ore. Since the cost of materials in the smelting and refining industries constitutes a very large fraction of the value of products, even slight savings in materials must have meant large increases in the net output in relation to the gross output. Unfortunately, data adequate enough for a reasonably accurate computation of net output are not available.[6]

Secondary Metals, Nonprecious. This classification includes establishments engaged *primarily* in the recovery from scrap and dross of copper, lead, zinc, nickel and their alloys. As we have noted, a certain amount of secondary metals is produced by refineries engaged principally in the refining of metals from newly smelted ores. The output of the secondary

[5] *Op. cit.*, pp. 72, 75.

[6] If there were a rise in the percentage of copper extracted, say, from 80 percent in 1910 to 95 in 1930 (compare the Calumet and Hecla figures cited by Corry and Kiessling, *op. cit.*, p. 10), and if the cost of materials constituted 90 percent of the 1910 value of copper (see the 1909 Census), then the index of net output (1930 on the 1910 base) would be two and a half times as great as the index of gross output. However, as stated in footnote 2 above, the rise in the percentage of copper extracted is in part due to improvements in concentration processes that are performed before the ore reaches the smelter. Therefore the index of net output could not have risen as rapidly, relatively to the index of gross output, as this computation would suggest.

metals industry rose 28 percent from 1925 to 1929, and 24 percent from 1929 to 1937, a net gain of 59 percent. This trend contrasts with the movement of the output of the primary refineries.

Nonferrous-Metal Products, not elsewhere classified, the most important industry in the group, comprises establishments manufacturing nonferrous alloys and products made from nonferrous alloys and metals (except aluminum). Many important products made from nonferrous metals and alloys are classified elsewhere: in wire, wire products, electrical machinery, structural metal work, hardware, and screw-machine products. The output of the present industry rose 43 percent from 1925 to 1929, and fell 12 percent from 1929 to 1937. The net gain between 1925 and 1937 was 26 percent. Of the more important products of the industry for which we have data, those whose output rose between 1925 and 1937 were copper sheets and plates, brass and bronze rods, copper rods, and brass and bronze tubing, and those with seriously declining output were lead tubing, antifriction-bearing metal, and brass and bronze rough castings.

Clocks, Watches and Related Materials fell 12 percent from 1927 to 1929, but made a net gain of 39 percent from 1929 to 1937. There were notable rises, over the entire decade, in the output of electric clocks, which increased from 87,000 to 4,269,000. Clock movements for use in recording instruments and gauges, time stamps, time switches, and time locks, rose from 239,000 in 1929 to 1,131,000 in 1937. The final products, time stamps, time switches, etc., increased from 129,000 in 1929 to 429,000 in 1937.[7] There were only moderate gains in the output of ordinary alarm clocks and nonjeweled watches.

Summary. Two of the three nonferrous smelting and refining industries increased their output between 1899 and

[7] The duplication of clock movements does not affect our index in any serious degree.

1937 less rapidly than all manufacturing industries combined. The output of one of these, lead, lagged even behind population growth. In the period 1929–37, three out of seven industries increased their output.

For the nonferrous-metal products group as a whole we have an index of physical output only for the period beginning in 1925. The low coverage for earlier years precludes the calculation of an adequate index for those years.[8] According to the unadjusted index, the group's output rose 32 percent in 1925–29, and fell 8 percent in 1929–37, a net gain of 21 percent. The adjusted index shows that output increased somewhat less rapidly between 1925 and 1929, fell more sharply between 1929 and 1937, and made a smaller net gain (13 percent) between 1925 and 1937.

CHANGES IN THE INDUSTRIAL PATTERN OF NONFERROUS METAL MANUFACTURE

The zinc industry rose in relation to copper, and copper rose in relation to lead, during the period 1899–1937 considered as a whole. In 1929–37 zinc, secondary metals, collapsible tubes, and clocks and watches, increased their relative contributions to the group's output, while copper, lead, and nonferrous-metal products (not elsewhere classified) lost ground.

These changes in the pattern of the group's output are examined from another point of view in Table 57, in which we present the relative contributions, in percentage form, for

[8] We decided not to accept the combined index of output of the three smelting and refining industries—copper, lead and zinc—as representative of the group. The dangers inherent in such a procedure are revealed by the figures for the recent period: our group index, based on fairly adequate coverage, fell only 8 or 10 percent from 1929 to 1937. The combined index for copper, lead and zinc fell over 20 percent between these two years.

An index for the group based on nonferrous-metal consumption is unacceptable also because a large (and perhaps variable) fraction of these metals is consumed in the iron and steel, chemicals, machinery and transportation-equipment groups.

TABLE 57

NONFERROUS-METAL PRODUCTS

Relative Contributions of Component Industries to the Physical Output of the Entire Group[a]

Industry	*Percentage Distribution, Comparable Pairs of Years*					
	1925	1937	1925	1929	1929	1937
Copper	8.8	8.4	8.4	8.5	7.2	6.4
Lead	3.4	1.8	3.1	2.5	2.7	1.8
Zinc	4.3	3.8	4.2	3.7	3.9	4.0
Secondary metals, nonprecious	1.4	2.0	1.7	1.7	1.7	2.3
Collapsible tubes	0.4	0.5	0.4	0.3	0.3	0.4
Nonferrous-metal products, n.e.c.[c]	22.7	26.4	23.0	25.8	27.6	27.2
Clocks, watches and materials } All other products	59.0	57.1	59.2	57.4	4.4	6.8
					52.3	51.2
TOTAL[b]	100.0	100.0	100.0	100.0	100.0	100.0

[a] Derived from Table 56. For an explanation of the derivation of the measurements see footnote 10, Chapter 4.

[b] The columns do not add up to 100.0 in every instance because they contain rounded percentages.

[c] N.e.c. denotes not elsewhere classified.

selected years. Here we note that between 1925 and 1937 there was a substantial decline in the relative contribution of the lead industry, from 3.4 to 1.8 percent. Copper and zinc declined less markedly. The contribution of nonferrous-metal products (not elsewhere classified) increased from 22.7 percent to 26.3, but the remaining industries in the group declined in this respect.

The data on relative contributions to the physical output of the group are available for a very limited period, and for only a few industries. Some information on the industrial pattern of output of the group in other years, and covering a broader representation of industries, is provided by the data on value added. These are presented in Table 58.

The relative contributions to the group's value added of two of the three smelting and refining industries fell drasti-

TABLE 58

NONFERROUS-METAL PRODUCTS

Relative Contributions of Component Industries to the Value Added by the Entire Group[a]

Industry	Percentage Distribution						
	1899	1909		1919		1929	1937
		Comparable with 1899	Comparable with 1919	Comparable with 1909	Comparable with later years		
Copper	19.4	12.9	13.8	8.8	8.6	6.6	6.9
Lead	14.1	4.4	4.7	2.3	2.2	2.5	1.9
Zinc	2.2	2.6	2.7	4.5	4.4	3.9	4.0
Secondary metals, nonprecious	0.9	1.4	1.5	1.9	1.9	2.0	1.9
Secondary metals, precious	0.4	0.5	0.5	0.8	0.7	0.6	0.7
Aluminum manufactures				[b]	3.3	5.2	6.9
Collapsible tubes	0.2 (with Tin and other foils)	0.3 (with Tin and other foils)	0.3 (with Tin and other foils)	0.6 (with Tin and other foils)	0.6 (with Tin and other foils)	0.3	0.4
Tin and other foils						0.6	0.6
Electroplating	0.9	0.9	1.0	1.0	1.0	1.7	2.0
Fire extinguishers	0.1	0.1	0.1	0.4	0.4	0.4	0.5
Gold leaf and foil	0.5	0.3	0.3	0.2	0.2	0.2	0.1
Lighting equipment	5.4	7.0	7.5	5.5	5.3	7.7	6.0
Needles and pins	0.9	1.3	1.3	2.5	2.4	1.4	2.6
Nonferrous-metal products, n.e.c.[c]	13.7	16.1	17.2	25.4	24.6	27.4	27.6
Plated ware	3.0	2.9	3.1	3.2	3.1	3.4	3.4 (with Silverware)
Silverware	3.5	3.9	4.1	2.1	2.1	1.8	
Sheet metal work, n.e.c.[c]	12.8	18.6	12.9	10.5	9.9	9.7	7.3
Stamped and enameled ware	5.4	7.7	8.2	10.6	10.3	10.3	14.6
Clocks	1.8	2.4	2.6	2.1	2.1	2.8	5.9 (with Watch and clock materials and Watches)
Watch and clock materials	0.1	0.1	0.2	0.1	0.1	0.1	
Watches	2.5	2.7	2.9	3.4	3.3	2.1	
Watch cases	1.5	1.6	1.7	1.5	1.5	0.8	0.6
Jewelry	10.8 (with Jewelers' findings)	12.4 (with Jewelers' findings)	13.3 (with Jewelers' findings)	12.4 (with Jewelers' findings)	11.9 (with Jewelers' findings)	8.6 (with Jewelers' findings)	5.3
Jewelers' findings							0.7
TOTAL[d]	100.0	100.0	100.0	100.0	100.0	100.0	100.0

[a] Basic data are given in Appendix C.
[b] Included in various other industries.
[c] N.e.c. denotes not elsewhere classified.
[d] The columns do not add up to 100.0 in every instance because they contain rounded percentages.

cally between 1899 and 1937. The contribution of copper declined from 19 percent in 1899 to about 13 in 1909, to 9 in 1919, and finally to 7 in both 1929 and 1937. Lead fell from

14 percent in 1899 to 4 in 1909, then to 2 in 1919–37. The contribution of zinc rose from 2 to 4 percent. The three industries combined accounted for 36 percent of the group's value added in 1899 but for only 13 in 1937. Large relative declines are found also in the contributions of silverware, sheet-metal work, and jewelry (including findings), industries for which we have no data on physical output.

The most important rise occurred in the relative contribution of nonferrous-metal products (not elsewhere classified). In 1899 this industry accounted for 14 percent of the group's value added; the percentage rose steadily until by 1937 it had reached 28, an increase of 14 points. Stamped and enameled ware increased its contribution from 5 percent in 1899 to 15 in 1937. There were other, but less important, rises in the contributions of nonprecious secondary metals, aluminum manufactures, electroplating, needles and pins, and clocks.

It is difficult to determine whether the decline in the combined value contribution of the industries engaged in the smelting and refining of the primary nonferrous metals and the rise in the value contribution of the other industries during the period 1899–1937, reflect closely corresponding changes in the group's pattern of physical output. A fair correspondence is indicated by the data available since 1925. If a similar correspondence prevailed also during the period preceding 1925, as seems likely, we must conclude on the basis of the value added data that the output of the entire nonferrous-metal products group rose considerably more than the 225 percent recorded for the combined output of the three smelting and refining industries in the period 1899–1937.

To some extent the relative decline in smelting and refining was due to an increase in the production of secondary metals (not refined in primary plants) at the expense of both primary and secondary metals passing through the three smelting and refining industries. The following figures, not available for the earlier years, indicate such a trend:

	1919	*1929*	*1937*
Copper (million pounds)			
1. Production at primary refineries	1,841	3,074	2,447
2. Secondary production, not at primary refineries	503	919	751
3. Ratio, 2 ÷ 1	.27	.30	.31
Lead (thousand short tons)			
1. Production at primary refineries	495	840	497
2. Secondary production, not at primary refineries	110	246	279
3. Ratio, 2 ÷ 1	.22	.29	.56
Zinc (thousand short tons)			
1. Production at primary refineries	477	637	581
2. Secondary production, not at primary refineries	29	54	58
3. Ratio, 2 ÷ 1	.06	.08	.10

In every case we find an increase in secondary production relative to primary refinery output of new and recovered metal.

A second important factor making for a drop in the output of the smelting and refining industries in relation to the output of the industries engaged in the further fabrication of nonferrous-metal products was the comparative decline in the volume of exports of domestically-produced refined nonferrous metals:

	1909	*1919*	*1929*	*1937*
Copper (million pounds)				
1. Total production	1,480	2,345	3,993	3,198
2. Exports minus imports	622	403	770	605
3. Ratio, 2 ÷ 1	.42	.17	.19	.19
Lead (thousand short tons)				
1. Total production	488	604	1,085	776
2. Exports minus imports	82	46	72	15
3. Ratio, 2 ÷ 1	.17	.08	.07	.02
Zinc (thousand short tons)				
1. Total production	289	505	690	639
2. Exports minus imports	–7	122	14	–37
3. Ratio, 2 ÷ 1	–.02	.24	.02	–.06

The data on secondary (hence on total) production are not available for 1899, but it is probable that larger fractions of each of the metals were exported in 1899 than in 1909.

Other factors may be involved in the change in the pattern of output of the nonferrous group, for example an increase in the percentage of available nonferrous metals utilized in further fabrication in the nonferrous group itself; or an increase in the degree of fabrication of given quantities of nonferrous metals. These factors it is impossible to appraise, since no measures of the increases can be obtained.

Chapter 20

Machinery

THE machinery industries make as primary products not only machinery itself, but also parts for use in the manufacture of machinery.[1] Industries producing transportation equipment are classified in a separate group. In terms of value added, the machinery industries constituted the most important of all manufacturing groups in 1937, having risen from fourth place in the years following 1899.

TRENDS IN THE PHYSICAL OUTPUT OF THE MACHINERY INDUSTRIES

The task of measuring the physical output of machinery is complicated by two serious difficulties. In the first place, few of the machinery industries are covered by adequate quantity data on output; and in the second place, the available statistics are ambiguous because the products are not divided into homogeneous subclasses.[2] Inadequacy of data and of subclassification are almost inevitable when the variety of items produced is as wide as it is in the case of machinery, and no classification, no matter how detailed, could be expected to resolve the problem conclusively. The enormous variety of machines[3] illustrates rather pointedly the extent to which

[1] In order to keep the composition of the machinery group constant, we have treated carbon paper and steel barrels as machinery industries. See Appendix C.

[2] For examples of inadequate classification, see Appendix A.

[3] The Bureau of the Census cites, in 1937, more than 20 major classes of machine tools (including the ubiquitous "all other" class)—bending machines, boring machines, boring mills, broaching machines, drilling machines, etc. The classes are broken down further into more than 90 subclasses. Thus,

our industrial processes are both specialized and mechanized. The continuing improvements in our productive equipment, tools and machines, reflect the drive toward faster, better, cheaper production—a basic factor in our economic progress.[4] In other words, some of the very factors that have made this a machine era also make it impossible for us to measure in a straightforward manner the degree to which the physical

---

under the caption "drilling machines" are differentiated horizontal, vertical and radial drilling machines, and the vertical machines are subclassified into multiple-spindle (other than sensitive), standard, sensitive (including bench-type) single spindle, sensitive (including bench-type) multiple spindle, etc.

[4] It is scarcely necessary to offer a long list of improvements in machinery. Even simple tools and dies have had their usefulness extended 3 to 20 times by chromium plating. See David Weintraub, *Effects of Technological Developments upon Capital Formation* (Report No. G-4, National Research Project, March 1939; reprint from *American Economic Review*), p. 8. Sizes of equipment have changed. Industrial-type gasoline locomotives increased in average size from 7.4 tons in 1924–27 to 11.4 in 1932–36 (*ibid.*, p. 3). The dipper capacity of power shovels sold to mining industries by a sample of representative companies rose from 1.7 cubic yards in 1920–23, to 3.3 cubic yards in 1932–36 (*ibid.*, p. 3). Driers used in phosphate-rock mining increased in length from 12–25 feet in 1895 to 30–60 feet in 1936; in diameter, from 30–36 inches in 1895 to 42–90 inches in 1936; in capacity from 6–10 long tons of dried rock per drier-hour in 1895 to 20–110 tons in 1936. See A. P. Haskell, Jr., and O. E. Kiessling, *Technology, Employment, and Output per Man in Phosphate-Rock Mining, 1880–1937* (Report No. E-7, National Research Project, Nov. 1938), p. 36. Further illustrations of increases in the size of individual equipment units will be found in Harry Jerome's *Mechanization in Industry* (National Bureau of Economic Research, 1934), p. 245. Machines have been made safer and therefore less expensive to operate: in 1913, the frequency of accident per million hours' exposure, caused by machinery in a sample of six iron and steel plants, was 7.3. The corresponding figure for 1931 was 1.7; "Accident Experience in the Iron and Steel Industry to the End of 1931," *Monthly Labor Review* (March 1933), p. 533. Machines have become more economical of fuel, as we have noted elsewhere in this volume. Other improvements have been effected; witness the adoption of caterpillar traction in shovels used in strip mining, and the supplanting of steam by electricity in this and in many types of equipment. Because of these changes, and also because of increases in size and power, the average tonnage handled per stripping shovel per day rose from 164 in 1915 to 276 in 1928; "Employment in Relation to Mechanization in the Bituminous Coal Industry," *Monthly Labor Review* (February 1933), p. 264.

Shifts in the relative importance of different machines performing the same general functions are relevant also. For example, there is the automatic bottle machine, making half-ounce prescription ovals. The Owens A. V. (15 arms) single, with conveyor, produced 20.3 bottles per hour in 1918, 24.8 in 1920.

volume of output of machines has risen, and the size of the existing stock of mechanical instruments.

All but one of the indexes for the few machinery industries for which there are adequate quantity statistics (Table 59 and Chart 22) begin with 1921 or an even later year. Because of the deficiencies in the data which we have already noted, no index for the group as a whole could be computed by us. (An index computed by W. H. Shaw is described below.)

Agricultural Implements. The output of this industry fell 10 percent from 1921 to 1925. From 1925 to 1929 there was a rapid rise of 64 percent, but from 1929 to 1937 there was a drop of 2 percent, the net effect of an extremely severe decline from 1929 to 1931, and a sharp rise from 1931 to 1937.[5] Most of the products of the industry evidence a trend toward tractor-drawn, and away from horse-drawn, machinery. Between 1929 and 1937 horse-drawn plows fell from 504 thousand to 316 thousand, while tractor plows rose from 123 thousand to 149 thousand.

Phonograph output is covered by data for the period 1899–1929. The absence of more recent statistics is not to be ascribed simply to a deficiency in Census coverage, for the industry lost its independent status in 1931, when it was

The Owens A. V. (15 arms) double, with conveyor, produced 43.4 bottles per hour in 1925. In the same year the Owens A. N. (ten arms) double, with conveyor, produced 33.0 bottles per hour; while the Owens C. A. (ten arms) double triplex, with conveyor, produced 79.5 bottles per hour; U.S. Bureau of Labor Statistics, "Productivity of Labor in the Glass Industry," *Bulletin 441*, p. 60. Shifts in the relative numbers of such machines produced result in broad changes in the "quality" of the general class of automatic bottle machines.

[5] For 1933 the coverage of our data is only 27 percent—not extensive enough to justify the construction of an index. These data suggest, however, that in the year 1933 output was at an even lower point than it had been in 1931.

The indexes for 1935 and 1937 are unadjusted for changes in the coverage of the sample from 1931 to 1935 and 1937 (see Appendix B). If such changes occurred, they were probably upward, because repair and similar work—not covered by the available quantity data—must have declined in relative importance as revival proceeded. If this assumption is correct, the index we present for 1937 is too high, perhaps by as much as 25 percent; in other words, the 1937 output of the industry may have been 20 or 25 percent below that of 1929, and not approximately equal to it.

TABLE 59

MACHINERY[a]

Physical Output: Indexes and Percentage Changes[b]

	Agricultural Implements	*Phonographs*	*Radios*	*Refrigerators, Mechanical*	*Scales and Balances*	*Sewing Machines*	*Typewriters*	*Washing and Ironing Machines*
YEAR				INDEX OF PHYSICAL OUTPUT (1929:100)				
1899	..	8.3	..	..	..	..	..	..
1904	..	..	..	..	..	..	..	..
1909	..	29	..	..	..	..	..	..
1914	..	38	..	..	..	..	..	..
1919	..	182	..	..	..	..	..	..
1921	68	80	..	0.6	..	..	51	..
1923	64	105	3.8	2.0	..	..	73	..
1925	61	80	47	8.4	..	..	78	..
1927	73	114	40	44	83	101	91	73
1929	100	100	100	100	100	100	100	100
1931	30	..	74	118	60	49	54	79
1933	..	..	75	130	35	26	43	92
1935	50	..	106	212	62	57	83	132
1937	98	..	144	317	87	100	109	146
PERIOD				NET PERCENTAGE CHANGE IN PHYSICAL OUTPUT				
1899–1937	..	..	..	..	..	..	..	..
1899–1909	..	+253	..	..	..	..	..	..
1909–1919	..	+520	..	..	..	..	..	..
1919–1929	..	−45	..	..	..	..	..	..
1929–1937	−2	..	+44	+217	−13	0	+9	+46

[a] Industries for which there are no adequate quantity data for any period listed above are: foundry and machine-shop products, not elsewhere classified; business machines; carbon paper; electrical machinery; engines and tractors; windmills; steel barrels; machine tools; machine-tool accessories, not elsewhere classified; pumps; textile machinery; gas machines and meters; and refrigerators, non-mechanical.

[b] The indexes have been constructed from basic data in the U.S. Census of Manufactures and other sources, by methods described briefly in Chapter 2 and in detail in Appendix A. Appendix B presents these data, together with the indexes derived from them. The indexes have been adjusted to take account of changes in the coverage of the respective samples, except when such adjustment was impossible.

The percentage changes are not always entirely consistent with the indexes given above because the changes were com puted from the indexes in Appendix B, which are carried to one decimal place.

classed as a branch of the radio industry; the phonograph was now regarded largely as an adjunct of the radio-phonograph combination. The output of the phonograph industry rose rapidly from 1899 to 1909 and from 1909 to 1919, gaining 250 and 520 percent in these two periods, respectively. After reaching a peak in 1919 it declined sharply to 1923, then underwent some fluctuations until 1929. From 1919 to 1929 the net loss was 45 percent.

Between 1899 and 1929 the output of the phonograph industry increased by 1100 percent. The output of the chief product, phonograph machines, rose from 151 thousand to 755 thousand between these two years. Phonograph records and blanks increased in output from 2.8 million in 1899 to 105 million in 1929.

Radios. This industry was not shown separately in the Census until 1931, but information is available on radio production from 1923 on.[6] In that year 190 thousand receiving sets were built (excluding crystal and short-wave sets). By 1929 output had reached almost 5 million sets, a rise of 2,500 percent. From 1929 to 1937 the net increase was 44 percent. The retardation in rate of growth is rather surprising when we consider the brief span of the period covered. The composition of the industry's output changed as the result of an extremely rapid rise in automobile sets between 1931 and 1937 (from 93 thousand to two million sets), and a decline in radio-phonograph combinations between 1929 and 1937.

Mechanical Refrigerators rose spectacularly from 5,000 units in 1921 to 900,000 in 1929 and to 2,800,000 in 1937.[7] The percentage increase in the first period was huge, of course. In the last period the rise exceeded 200 percent. These great increases, as might have been expected, caused a drastic decline in the output of nonmechanical refrigerators. Manufac-

[6] These data are not derived from the Census, and are unadjusted for change in coverage. See Appendix B.

[7] These data, also, are derived from sources other than the Census, and are unadjusted for change in coverage.

Chart 22
MACHINERY
Indexes of Physical Output

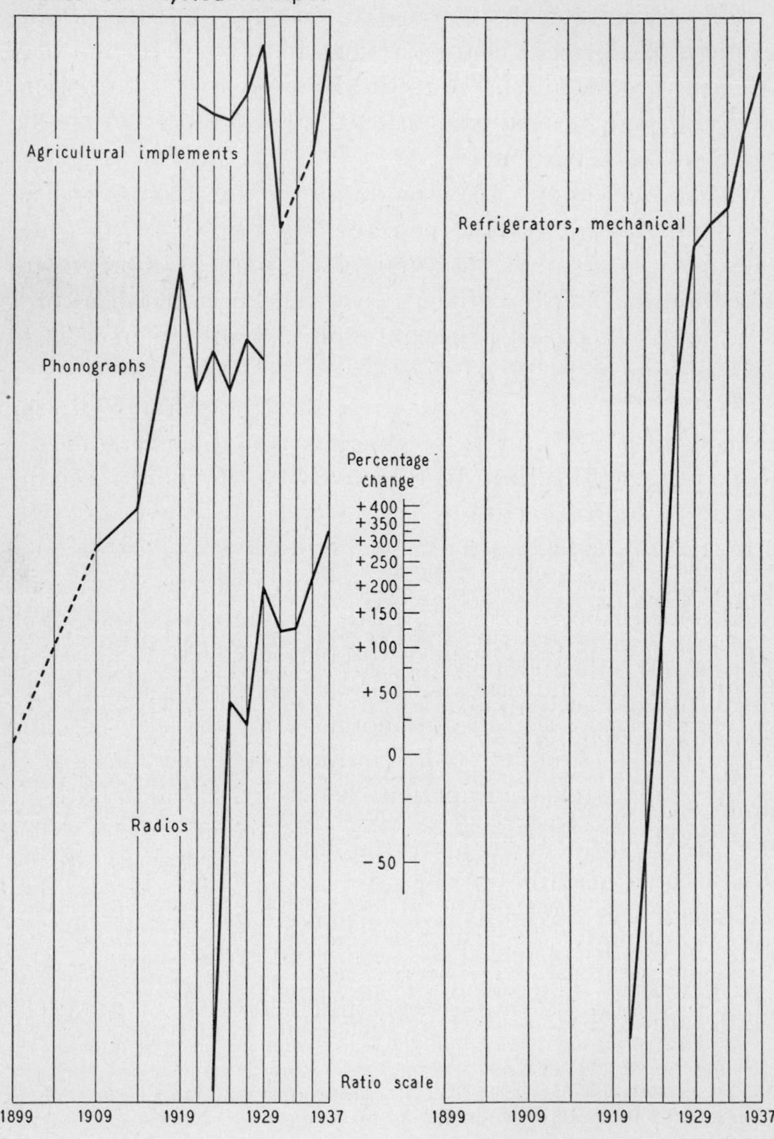

Chart 22 (concl.)

MACHINERY

Indexes of Physical Output

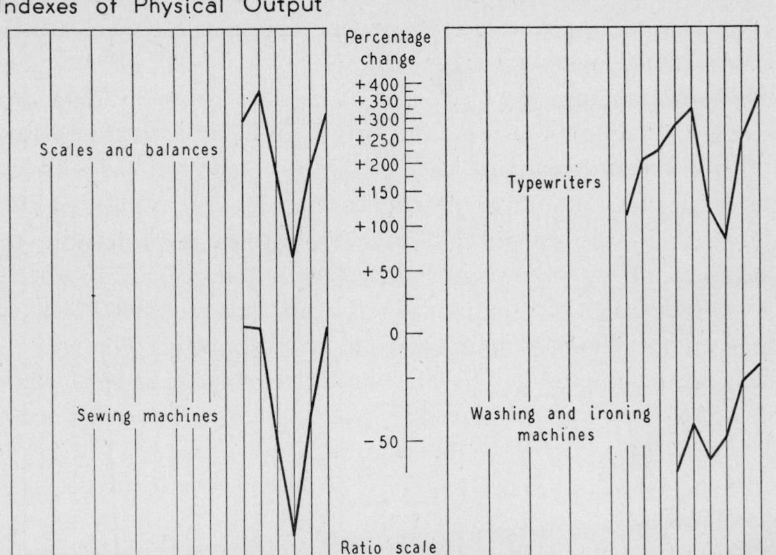

turers' sales of ice-boxes reached their Census year peak in 1925. In 1937 ice-box sales totaled less than a third of the 1929 volume and only about a tenth of 1925 sales.[8] The decline in the output of manufactured ice from 1929 to 1937 has already been noted (Chapter 6).

Sewing Machines declined from 1927 to 1929, but to a very minor extent, and rose in similarly small degree from 1929 to 1937. Machines of the industrial type gained at the expense of household machines in the entire decade 1927–37; this development was obviously a reflection of the changes noted above in the discussion of the textile industries (Chapter 9).

Typewriters. The output of the typewriter industry moved rapidly upward from 1921 to 1929.[9] The gain from 1923 (a

[8] *Refrigeration and Air Conditioning Market Data* (Business News Publishing Co., Detroit, 1935), p. 64. The data do not cover all plants.

[9] The index for 1921–29 is unadjusted for changes in coverage.

peak year in general business activity and therefore more comparable with 1929) to 1929 was 36 percent, and from the latter year to 1937 output increased again by 9 percent. The output of portable typewriters rose in these years while that of standard typewriters fell.

Other Machinery Industries. Adequate quantity data are not available for the most important industries in the group —foundry and machine-shop products, electrical machinery, and engines and tractors. Since even a rough notion of the changes in the output of these industries is preferable to none at all, we present in Table 60 the data on value added expressed as percentage changes from 1899 to 1937, and as percentage changes in relation to corresponding changes in the total value added by all manufacturing industries combined.

TABLE 60

MACHINERY

Changes in Value Added, 1899–1937[a]

Industry	*Percentage Change in Value Added*	*Percentage Change in the Ratio of Value Added to Total Value Added by All Manufacturing Industries*
Foundry and machine-shop products, n.e.c.[b]	+548	+13
Agricultural implements	+153	–56
Business machines	+1,956	+259
Typewriters and carbon paper	+633	+28
Electrical machinery	+2,548	+362
Pumps	+3,263	+487
Scales and balances	+227	–43
Sewing machines	+144	–57
Washing and ironing machines	+1,694	+213
TOTAL	+752	+49

[a] Basic data are given in Appendix C.

[b] N.e.c. denotes not elsewhere classified. This classification includes the following industries shown separately in Censuses after 1899: cast-iron pipe, engines and tractors, windmills, steel barrels, textile machinery, and machine tools.

Foundry and machine-shop products, the basic industry, increased its value added by over 500 percent. Electrical machinery exceeded this rise, augmenting its value added by 2,500 percent. Business machines increased in this respect almost 2,000 percent; typewriters and carbon paper, over 600 percent; pumps, 3,200 percent; and washing and ironing machines, 1,700 percent. Agricultural implements, scales and balances, and sewing machines made slighter gains, ranging from 144 to 227 percent. The entire group increased its value added by 750 percent. The last three industries fell below total manufacturing in rate of increase in value added, and the other six surpassed the total.

Even the value data for the machinery group are inadequately classified by industries. In the 1899 Census the foundry and machine-shop products industry included engines, machine tools and textile machinery. These are shown separately for the period 1919–37:

	Percentage Change in Value Added, 1919–37	*Percentage Change in the Ratio of Value Added to Total Value Added by All Manufacturing Industries, 1919–37*
Engines, tractors, and windmills	–33	–40
Steel barrels	+83	+64
Machine tools	+32	+18
Textile machinery	–6	–15
Foundry and machine-shop products (excluding above)	+8	–4

Steel barrels and machine tools increased their value added more rapidly between 1919 and 1937 than did all manufacturing industries combined. Foundry and machine-shop products, excluding the four industries listed separately, rose in value added by 8 percent, but fell behind total manufacturing by 4 percent. Engines and textile machinery declined both absolutely and in relation to total manufacturing.

The great rise in the output of electrical machinery reflects, among other things, the increased utilization of power equipment in business establishments. This trend is revealed by the figures cited below, which relate to the aggregate horsepower of power equipment reported by manufacturing plants alone:

Year	Prime Movers (nonelectrical)	Electric Motors: Driven by Energy Generated in Reporting Establishment	Electric Motors: Driven by Purchased Energy
	(*Unit: Million Horsepower*)		
1899	9.8	0.3	0.2
1909	16.8	3.1	1.7
1919	20.0	7.0	9.3
1929	20.2	12.4	22.8

All three types of equipment rose between 1899 and 1929, the latest year for which the data are available. But the rate of increase in the horsepower of electrical equipment far exceeded that of such nonelectrical prime movers as steam engines, internal-combustion engines, and water-wheels and turbines. The rate of output of new electrical equipment is indicated more clearly by the net increments. During the decade between 1899 and 1909 there was a net increase of 4.3 million horsepower for all electric motors used in manufacturing. In the second decade, 1909–19, the increase was 11.5 million; and in the third, 18.9 million, a rise more than four times as great as that occurring in the first decade.

These figures are much more significant than their effect on a single industry, electrical machinery, would seem to show. The most important inference to be drawn from them concerns the application of power in manufacturing. Clearly, more mechanical power was utilized in 1929 than at the opening of the century. The three columns of figures are not additive,[10] but there is hardly any question that the

[10] See W. L. Thorpe, "Horsepower Statistics for Manufactures," *Journal of the American Statistical Association* (Dec. 1929).

capacity of the power equipment used in factories increased much more rapidly than the number of workers, and—though this is less certain—somewhat more rapidly than the total quantity of output. The bearing of this development upon trends in productivity, and thereby in production, needs no emphasis.

Scarcely less significant is the fact that factories have transferred some of their functions to nonmanufacturing industries. A growing fraction of the power used in manufacturing is being purchased from the electric light and power industry, and a declining fraction is being made on the premises. During the decade 1919–29 there was virtually no increase in the horsepower of prime movers owned by factories, whereas motors driven by purchased current more than doubled in horsepower capacity. The increasingly fine division of labor also has been conducive to increases in productivity in manufacturing, since central power production is more efficient than local production. At the same time, it is difficult to interpret the usual measures of productivity, since the increases in employment in central power stations are not reflected in the employment figures for manufacturing plants.

Still another bit of general information may be extracted from the statistics on horsepower. The increase in the horsepower of electric motors driven by energy produced in the reporting establishment has proceeded at a greater rate than the increase in the horsepower of the prime mover. This divergence suggests that increasingly widespread use has been made of a highly flexible method of transmitting power from the prime mover to the point of application. A development of this sort must have had a far-reaching effect not only upon plant layout, but also upon manufacturing production and efficiency.

The Group Total. The machinery group as a whole increased its value added almost 50 percent more than did all manufacturing industries combined. This finding indicates that there must have been a substantial relative rise in the group's physical output, though the exact amount cannot be determined. A rough check on this conclusion is provided by estimates of machinery output, made by W. H. Shaw and presented below. Mr. Shaw arrived at these estimates by deflating the value of production of machinery by whatever appropriate price series could be secured.[11] The price data are necessarily fragmentary, and the indexes of physical output thus obtained must therefore be regarded only as approximate measures. They indicate that machinery output rose,

	Indexes (1929:100)	
	Machinery Production	Machinery Production in Relation to Total Manufacturing Production
1899	22	79
1904	28	81
1909	37	85
1914	40	78
1919	67	109
1921	43	80
1923	71	93
1925	73	89
1927	77	89
1929	100	100
1931	54	75
1933	29	46
1935	65	79
1937	107	103

between 1899 and 1937, about 30 percent more rapidly than total manufacturing output. The estimates, then, tend to confirm the trend indicated by the data on value added. Of particular interest is the movement from 1929 to 1937 as shown by the indexes. There appears to have been an appreciable gain in machinery output between these two years, exceeding the corresponding rise in total manufacturing.

[11] These figures will be presented and discussed in a report by Mr. Shaw to be published by the National Bureau of Economic Research.

To persons living in an age characterized by increasing mechanization on all fronts, the relative gain of 30 or even 50 percent indicated by the data presented here may appear slight rather than otherwise. It must be remembered, however, that increasing mechanization has been a causal factor in the augmented output of other goods; and further, that mechanization results from improvements in the quality and performance of machines, and not merely from increases in their number.

CHANGES IN THE INDUSTRIAL PATTERN OF MACHINERY OUTPUT

The data on the physical output of the machinery group are so inadequate that we must turn to data on value added (Table 61) for information on changes in composition.

As the table shows, the largest industry in the group, foundry and machine-shop products, made only a slight change in its contribution to the value added by the entire group. This contribution includes the value added by a number of offspring industries, and it is obvious that a declining trend would emerge if we were to treat the parent industry separately. Agricultural implements lost considerable ground. In 1899 this industry contributed 12.6 percent of the group's value added, but in 1929 less than 4 percent. A relatively minor decline characterized the movement of value added by the sewing-machine industry.

The contribution of electrical machinery increased substantially, from 9.5 percent to over 25 percent of the group total. An appreciable rise occurred also in the contribution of pumps and business machines. The value added by phonographs rose until 1919, then declined as a fraction of the total. The relative increase in mechanical refrigerators is noteworthy even in the last period, the only one for which we have data on this industry.

TABLE 61

MACHINERY

Relative Contributions of Component Industries to the Value Added by the Entire Group[a]

Industry	Percentage Distribution, Comparable Pairs of Years							
	1899	1909	1909	1919	1919	1929	1929	1937
Foundry and machine shop products, n.e.c.[b]	69.8	64.5	61.8	64.0	46.0	41.2	39.1	38.6
Business machines	1.1	2.5	2.7	2.5	2.5	2.3	2.2	2.6
Typewriters } Carbon paper	1.2	1.9	2.1	1.2	1.3	1.5	1.2	0.8
Carbon paper							0.2	0.2
Electrical machinery, incl. radios	9.5	13.8	14.9	19.6	19.9	31.2	29.7 }	28.9
Phonographs	0.3	1.0	1.1	3.4	3.4	1.4	1.3 }	
Agricultural implements	12.6	10.5	11.3	5.5	5.6	3.8	3.7 }	
Engines and tractors				[b]	8.6	6.0	5.7 }	10.2
Windmills	0.5	0.4	0.4	0.2	0.2	0.1	0.1 }	
Steel barrels				[c]	0.3	0.4	0.4	0.5
Machine tools				[c]	4.8	4.2	4.0	4.8
Machine-tool accessories, n.e.c.[b]						[d]	2.6	3.1
Pumps	0.2	0.4	0.4	0.4	1.7	2.3	2.2	2.5
Textile machinery				[b]	2.6	2.0	1.9	1.9
Gas machines and meters	0.5	1.0	1.1	0.5	0.5	0.6	0.6	[e]
Refrigerators, nonmechanical	0.6	0.7	0.8	0.5	0.5	0.8	0.8 }	4.4
Refrigerators, mechanical						[c]	2.2 }	
Scales and balances	0.8	0.8	0.8	0.5	0.5	0.5	0.5	0.3
Sewing machines	2.6	2.1	2.2	1.1	1.1	0.8	0.6	0.7
Washing and ironing machines	0.4	0.4	0.4	0.6	0.6	1.0	0.9	0.7
TOTAL[f]	100.0	100.0	100.0	100.0	100.0	100.0	100.0	100.0

[a] Basic data are given in Appendix C.

[b] N.e.c. denotes not elsewhere classified.

[c] Included in foundry and machine-shop products.

[d] Included in foundry and machine-shop products, machine tools, and tools, other.

[e] Included in foundry and machine-shop products and electrical machinery.

[f] The columns do not add up to 100.0 in every instance because they contain rounded percentages.

Chapter 21

Transportation Equipment

THE transportation equipment group consists of industries engaged primarily in the manufacture of aircraft, vehicles for land transportation, and watercraft. Railroad equipment manufactured in repair shops operated by railroads is not included.

In 1899 the transportation equipment group was one of the less important manufacturing groups. Ranked according to value added, it stood among the lowest six. In 1937, however, the contribution of transportation equipment to total value added was greater than that of twelve other groups.

TRENDS IN THE PHYSICAL OUTPUT OF THE TRANSPORTATION EQUIPMENT INDUSTRIES

Automobiles increased in output at a phenomenal rate (Table 62, Chart 23). Output in 1937 was 1,800 times as great as it had been in 1899. In the first decade it increased 3,500 percent, in the next almost 1,500 percent, and in the third about 250 percent; in the last period, 1929–37, it declined 10 percent.[1] The speed with which an important industry can attain maturity in our economic system cannot be illustrated more strikingly than here.

[1] The index is based on the output of new cars and chassis only; replacement parts are not included. It is probable, therefore, that the trend shown by the index understates the trend in the total output of the industry. Perhaps more important in terms of general economic significance, are the cyclical defects of the index, which is biased downward for recession periods and upward for recovery periods: replacement parts do not fall off in output as much as new cars do during recession, nor do they rise as much during recovery. No adequate data on the production of parts for replacement are available; for rough estimates see Magdoff, Siegel, and Davis, *op. cit.*

TABLE 62

TRANSPORTATION EQUIPMENT[a]

Physical Output: Indexes and Percentage Changes[b]

	Automobiles, incl. Bodies and Parts	*Carriages, Wagons and Sleighs*	*Cars, Railroad, n.e.m.*[c]	*Locomotives, n.e.m.*[c]	*Ships and Boats*[d]	*Motorcycles and Bicycles*	*Carriages and Sleds, Children's*	*Total*	
								Unadjusted	Adjusted
YEAR				INDEX OF PHYSICAL OUTPUT (1929:100)					
1899	0.05	1,317	119	264	97	141	..	6.9	7.3
1904	0.2	1,392	122	366	80	32	..	7.1	7.5
1909	1.8	1,333	114	282	74	64	..	10.2	10.7
1914	8.5	1,123	154	204	74	121	..	20	20
1919	28	647	171	321	551	180	..	62	61
1921	25	182	96	175	213	81	..	38	38
1923	63	300	229	412	99	128	..	76	76
1925	72	216	139	137	90	98	92	77	76
1927	63	173	101	105	110	87	90	68	68
1929	100	100	100	100	100	100	100	100	100
1931	44	36	31	23	78	..	71	45	46
1933	35	40	..	..	23	..	59	34	33
1935	74	59	30	..	..	..	70	71	72
1937	90	71	93	55	80	..	89	89	91
PERIOD				NET PERCENTAGE CHANGE IN PHYSICAL OUTPUT					
1899–1937	+180,100	−95	−22	−79	−17	..	..	+1,186	+1,142
1899–1909	+3,500	+1	−5	+7	−24	−55	..	+48	+47
1909–1919	+1,467	−52	+50	+14	+646	+181	..	+504	+468
1919–1929	+255	−84	−41	−69	−82	−44	..	+62	+64
1929–1937	−10	−29	−7	−45	−20	..	−11	−11	−9

[a] Industries for which there are no adequate quantity data for any period listed above are aircraft and carriage and wagon materials. These industries are covered by the adjusted total.

[b] The indexes have been constructed from basic data in the U.S. Census of Manufactures and other sources, by methods described briefly in Chapter 2 and in detail in Appendix A. Appendix B presents these data, together with the indexes derived from them. The indexes cited here for individual industries have been adjusted to take account of changes in the coverage of the respective samples, except when such adjustment was impossible.

The percentage changes are not always entirely consistent with the indexes given above because the changes were computed from the indexes in Appendix B, which are carried to one decimal place.

[c] N.e.m. denotes not elsewhere made.

[d] Does not include government-owned shipyards.

There were far-reaching changes in both the composition and the total of the automobile industry's output:

	1904	1909	1919	1923	1929	1937
			Quantity (thousand units)			
Passenger cars						
Open	19	117	1,400	2,215	444	20
Closed }	[a]	5 {	157	1,202	3,917	3,826
Public conveyances }			2	13	26	12
Trucks	0.4	3	120	281	386	602
All other types	2.6	2	209	190	520	172
All types	22	127	1,888	3,901	5,293	4,632
			Percentage Distribution			
Passenger cars						
Open	86	92	74	57	8	*
Closed }	[a]	4 {	8	31	74	83
Public conveyances }			*	*	1	*
Trucks	2	2	7	7	7	13
All other types	12	2	11	5	10	4
All types	100	100	100	100	100	100

[a] No data.
* Less than half of one percent.

In 1904 (the earliest year for which we have detailed data), open passenger cars accounted for nearly the entire output of the industry. This type of vehicle increased at a rapid rate until a peak was reached in 1923 with the production of more than 2,000,000. From then on open cars declined so rapidly that by 1937 only 20,000 were manufactured, about as many as in 1904. Virtually the entire history of the growth and decline of the product is compressed within the brief span of time covered in the tabulation just presented. Closed cars began to increase notably only in 1919, and even in 1923 their output was far below that of open cars. Within six years, however, they had largely displaced the latter, and by 1937 the process was just about completed. Public conveyances (taxicabs and busses) rose from 2,000 to 26,000 in the ten years between 1919 and 1929, and fell to 12,000 in 1937.

Chart 23
TRANSPORTATION EQUIPMENT
Indexes of Physical Output

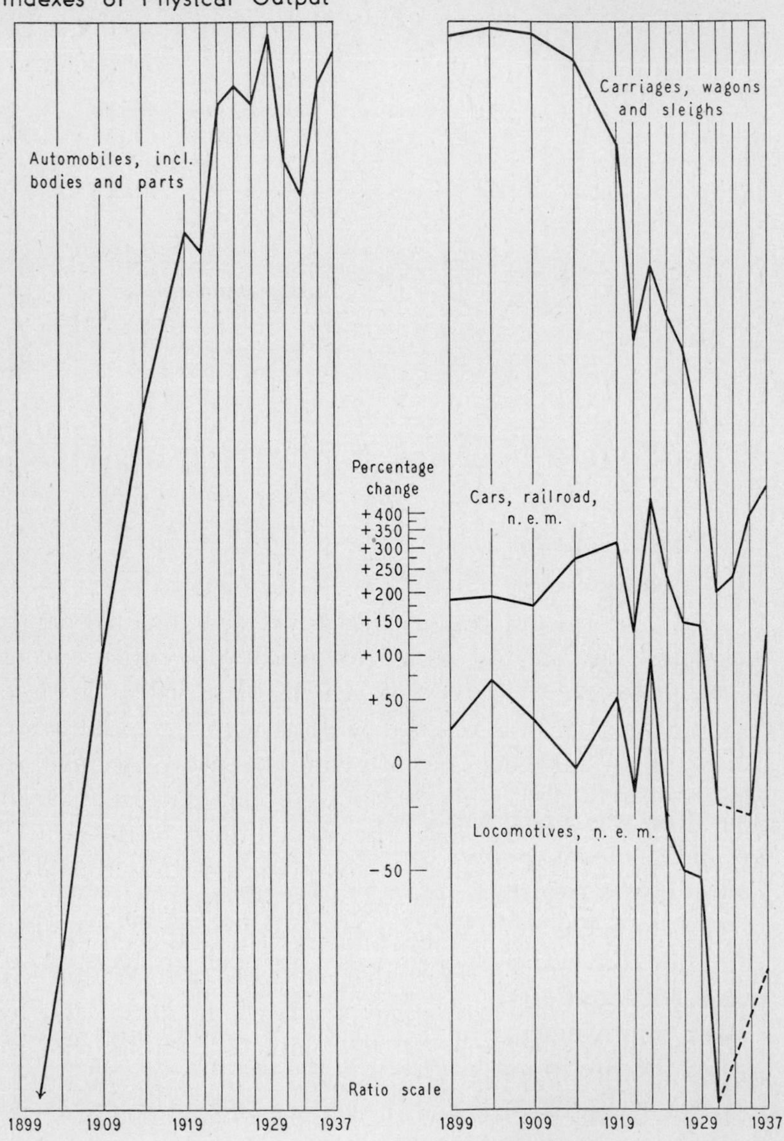

Chart 23 (concl.)
TRANSPORTATION EQUIPMENT
Indexes of Physical Output

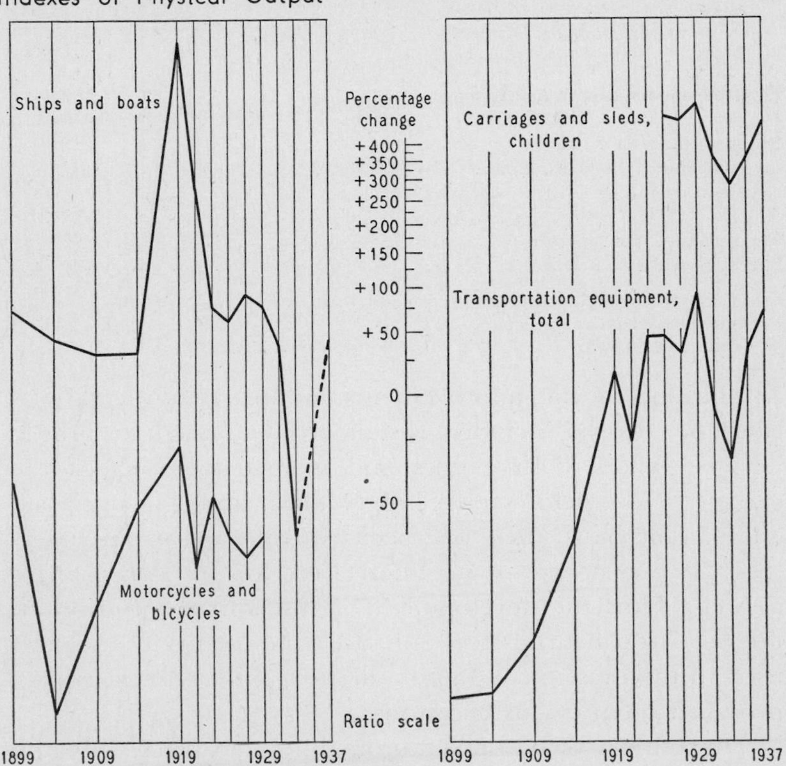

The drop was attributable entirely to a decline in taxicabs, in miscellaneous public conveyances and in small busses. Larger busses (seating 21 or more passengers) rose from 3,400 in 1929 to 6,400 in 1937. Trucks, unlike passenger cars and all public conveyances, continued to increase rapidly even between 1929 and 1937.

Vast improvements in the quality of automobiles accompanied the rise in output. Even in the last decade, when output was declining, the quality changes continued. Below we compare some of the specifications for the 1925 and the 1935 models of a leading make of passenger car: [2]

Description	*1925*	*1935*	*Percentage Change*
Wheelbase, inches	100	112	+12
Horsepower, maximum developed	20	90	+350
Weight (two door sedan), pounds	1,900	2,700	+42
Piston displacement, cu. in.	177	221	+25
Front spring frequencies, o.p.m.[a]	160	85	−47
Acceleration, max. 10–25 m.p.h.,[c] f.p.s.[b]	1.8	4.1	+128
Deceleration, max., f.p.s.[b]	12	21	+75
Speed, maximum, m.p.h.[c]	40	80	+100

[a] Oscillations per minute under normal load.
[b] Feet per second per second.
[c] Miles per hour.

In addition to the improvements indicated by the tabulation, the 1935 car included as standard equipment anti-rattle devices, braces, dash gauges and meters, locks, shock absorbers, windshield wipers, safety glass, and a counterbalanced crankshaft. These had been available to car purchasers in 1925, but at extra cost. There were less obvious changes as well. Thus the development of instrumental control in the heat treatment of steel enhanced the quality of the steel used in the present-day motor car to a point only rarely approached on previous occasions.[3]

The output of finished automobiles measures only the gross output of the motor vehicles industry. The true net output of the industry must be related to the operations it performs on the materials it purchases and assembles into finished cars. A modification of the materials utilized may imply a change in the degree of fabrication within the in-

[2] A. T. Court, "Hedonic Price Indexes with Automotive Examples," *The Dynamics of Automobile Demand* (General Motors Corporation, 1939), p. 102. The make of the car is not given. The specifications are derived from a variety of unofficial sources. They are believed to be approximately correct.

[3] G. Perazich, H. Schimmel and B. Rosenberg, *Industrial Instruments and Changing Technology*, Report No. M-1 (National Research Project, October 1938), pp. 54, 86.

dustry, and hence a change in net output, although gross output may remain unaltered. For example, the net output of an automobile plant which purchases readymade parts and merely assembles them, is less than the net output of a factory which manufactures and assembles the parts. And if a factory simply puts automobiles together with purchased parts in one year, and then subsequently takes to manufacturing the parts and assembling the automobiles, its net output will rise more than its gross output. There are strong indications that important changes of this sort have occurred. Until about 1900 the industry was in an experimental stage, and the automobile was a crude product of home or workshop. The manufacturer then had to make most of his own parts, since he could not secure them elsewhere.[4] Shortly after the turn of the century the automobile industry passed the purely experimental stage. The manufacturers were able to purchase a substantial portion of the parts required, and many of them now merely assembled purchased parts.[5] The 1905 Census states: "While some of the larger plants turn out all the parts, the smaller establishments, and by far the greater number, do not, but purchase more or less material in fully or partially manufactured form. In fact, there is a strong tendency in this direction. . . ." [6] In 1903, even the Ford enterprise was not much more than an assembly plant for parts purchased elsewhere, mainly from the Dodge Brothers' machine shop.[7] The tendency to restrict activities to the assembly of parts became most pronounced in the period 1908–14 when "the cars of nearly all manufacturers were in large measure assembled, a few of even the leading makes almost entirely so." [8] About 1915 there were signs of a re-

[4] R. C. Epstein, *The Automobile Industry, Its Economic and Commercial Development* (A. W. Shaw, 1928), p. 28.

[5] *Ibid.*, p. 39.

[6] 1905 Census, Part IV, p. 275.

[7] L. H. Seltzer, *A Financial History of the American Automobile Industry* (Houghton Mifflin, 1928), p. 89.

[8] Epstein, *op. cit.*, p. 51.

versal in tendency; the larger manufacturers now began to make their own parts, particularly engines. Among the numerous factors contributing to the change the most important were the need for certainty of supply for the sake of continuity of plant operation; the possibility of lower production costs; and the enhanced prestige and advertising advantage which was supposed to accrue from manufacture of the parts themselves.[9] By 1918–20 the shift was almost complete, and most manufacturers were making the majority of the important parts.

About 1927, however, there was a revival of the old tendency to purchase outside parts because manufacturers began to put out a large variety of models.

> The marketing advantages of a variety of models are opposed, however, to the manufacturing economies of standardized production. . . . One result of this antagonism promises to be a partial reversal, at least temporarily, of the tendency toward integration of manufacture: the delays and expense incident to frequent readjustment of integrated establishments for changes in models are likely to lead to increased reliance, once more, upon the more elastic organizations of the parts-makers.[10]

With the increase in the number of models produced it became more economical for a manufacturer to buy parts outside than to produce the large assortment needed within his plant. This factor, it should be noted, has always been of more importance in truck manufacture than in passenger car production.

Information on very recent tendencies is not available. Observers writing in 1932 remarked that automobile manufacturers were adopting machines which could be used for a wider range of cars than those they had previously employed. These writers noted, in addition, that there was an increasing

[9] *Ibid.*, pp. 51–53.
[10] Seltzer, *op. cit.*, p. 61.

tendency toward use of the same parts in different makes and models.[11] Both these developments may have presaged a return to more extensive parts manufacture by the automobile makers themselves.

The limited summary of changes in automobile production presented above touches upon only a few aspects of the relation between gross and net output in the Census industry, "automobiles, including bodies and parts." This relation is complicated further by the fact that so long as the parts plants are segregated, and their output is reported separately, the Census classifies them in such industries as engines, springs, stamped metal, etc., even though their products ultimately find their way into the automobile factory, and even if they are owned by the automobile manufacturers. Only the integration of a parts factory with an automobile assembly plant in a manner designed to make possible a single Census report can affect the Census industry with which we are here concerned; i.e., can cause a divergence between its gross and net output. This does seem to have occurred, according to the meager evidence relating to engines: [12]

Year	*Motor Vehicle Internal Combustion Carburetor Engines Made in the Engines Industry (1,000)*		*Motor Vehicles and Chassis Made in the Automobile Industry (1,000)*		*Percentage of Engines Made in the Engines Industry*	
1914	72		573		12.5	
1919	223		1,893		11.8	
1921	160		1,603		10.0	
1923	385		3,902		9.9	
1925	304		4,178		7.3	
1927	325		3,356		9.7	
1929	280		5,316	5,294	5.3	
1931	130	116		2,295	5.6	5.0
1933		33		1,848		1.8
1935		69		3,923		1.8
1937		105		4,733		2.2

[11] Fraser and Doriot, *op. cit.*, pp. 45, 50.

[12] Changes in classification make necessary the overlapping series.

The percentage of engines made in the automobile industry rose from 87.5 in 1914 to 97.8 in 1937. These data indicate that the rise in the number of finished automobiles definitely understates the rise in the net physical output of the automobile industry, if all other factors remained constant.

Carriages, Wagons and Sleighs, in extreme contrast to the automobile industry, decreased in output almost continuously after 1904, the peak year in the Census series. From 1899 to 1937 the net decline was 95 percent. From 1899 to 1904 there was a slight increase, and from 1904 to 1909 a slight decline; in the next five years there was another drop, amounting to 15 percent. The decline became disastrous only in 1914, when the industry suffered from the competition of the large and rapidly-growing automobile industry. From 1914 to 1919 there was a decline of 42 percent, from 1919 to 1929 another drop, 84 percent, and from 1929 to 1937 still another decline, 29 percent. From 1899 to 1937 every product of the industry declined, although the decrease in farm wagons and trucks was least severe.

Locomotives, measured simply by the number of standard-gauge steam locomotives,[13] decreased by 79 percent between 1899 and 1937. The trends in the series are overshadowed by violent cyclical movements, but it is clear that most, if not all, of the decline occurred in the second half of the long period. The Census peak year came in 1923, when 3,100 locomotives were produced. In 1937 the number was only 380.

Railroad Cars fell much less drastically, declining 22 percent from 1899 to 1937. In the first and fourth periods the changes were slight. In the second decade there was a rise of 50 percent, and in the third, a fall of 41 percent. The peak came, as in the case of locomotives, in 1923.[14] Within the in-

[13] No adjustment for coverage could be made for 1899–1923; the index therefore fluctuates more violently than it should.

[14] The railroad car and locomotive industries suffer immense fluctuations in output which are associated primarily with business cycles. For this reason the figures in Table 62 portray inadequately the trends in output of cars

dustry there were increases in the output of cabooses, gondola cars and refrigerator cars. Passenger cars, flat cars, hopper cars and stock cars were subject to the most serious declines.

The output of both railroad equipment industries was greatly affected by quality improvements. As the accompanying figures indicate, the average tractive power of existing steam locomotives more than doubled in the 30 years from 1905 to 1935, and the average capacity of existing freight cars rose more than 50 percent. The corresponding rates of change in the power and capacity of *new* locomotives and freight cars were considerably lower. But even the higher

Railway Equipment in Service[a]

Year	Average Tractive Power, Steam Locomotives (thousand pounds)	Average Capacity, Freight Cars (tons)
1905	23.7	30.8
1910	27.3	35.9
1916	32.9	40.8
1920	36.4	42.4
1925	40.7	44.8
1930	45.2	46.6
1935	48.4	48.3

[a] From data collected by the Interstate Commerce Commission, and published in the *Statistical Abstract, 1938,* p. 381, and *1931,* p. 415.

figures, when multiplied by the quantity indexes, indicate no rise between 1899 and 1937 in the aggregate tractive power of new locomotives built, and suggest only a moderate increase in the aggregate capacity of new freight cars.

Ships and Boats underwent extraordinarily violent changes in output. Over the 38 years there was a net decline of 17 percent. Between 1899 and 1909 the industry's output de-

---

and locomotives. From the available annual data, the trend in output of railroad cars and locomotives appears to have been upward only until 1907, and downward thereafter. The decline in car production between 1899 and 1909 and the rises in both series between 1909 and 1919 reflect the fact that 1909 was a depressed year in railroad equipment output.

clined 24 percent. From 1909 to 1914 output remained constant, then shot up at a tremendous rate to a peak in 1919, registering a gain of 650 percent.[15] After 1919 there was a drastic fall, to a level somewhat above the pre-war output. Output in 1929 was approximately the same as it had been in 1923, but 1927 output was higher than that of either year. Finally, from 1929 to 1937 output fell 20 percent.

Steel ships grew in relation to wooden vessels. In 1899 the latter were most important (in terms of gross tonnage), but in 1909 and later years the production of steel ships exceeded that of the wooden ones. The fraction of output devoted to repair work fluctuated also. In 1899 the percentage (in terms of value) was 31; in 1909 it was 36; in 1919 it was 11; in 1929 it was 50; and in 1937 it was 38.[16]

Motorcycles and Bicycles also fluctuated in output. From 1899 to 1904 production fell sharply, then rose to a peak in 1919, when it stood 180 percent above the 1909 level and 27 percent above the 1899 level. From 1919 to 1929 output

[15] The classification, ships and boats, does not cover government-owned shipyards. These shipyards did 29 million dollars worth of work in 1914, as compared with 90 million in private establishments; and 240 million dollars worth of work in 1919, as compared with 1,622 million in private yards. If we may judge from these figures, the combined output of private and government yards rose somewhat less rapidly from 1914 to 1919 than the output of private yards alone. No data on government-owned shipyards are available after 1919.

[16] The index of physical output of the ships and boats industry is a rather rough measure, scarcely more satisfactory as a gauge of physical output than is value added. Several difficulties were involved in the construction of the index of physical output:

(1) The Census data on quantity of output relate to vessels launched, rather than to work done during the year, while the Census data on value of output relate to value of work done during the year, and not to value of vessels launched. For this reason no completely satisfactory weighting scheme can be devised. Further, the chronological reference of the quantity series is ambiguous. (2) The quantity data, which are given in terms of tonnage of vessels launched, are unsatisfactory measures of output because the tonnage unit is unstable, including as it does both gross tons and displacement tons; further, the relation between the two is neither fixed nor determinable. (3) The value of repair work done (for which there are no corresponding quantity data) constitutes a large and variable percentage of the total value of output. Our adjustment compensates only in part for this defect.

fell again, this time by 44 percent. For 1929 to 1937 the data on motorcycles are inadequate, so that no index is available for the recent period, but it is highly probable that total output rose as a result of a revival in the bicycle branch of the industry. The output of bicycles in 1937 was higher than in any preceding year.

Aircraft. Owing to changes in the Census schedules, the Census data on airplane production are inadequate. Moreover, there have been vast changes in the size and character of airplanes manufactured. We are therefore unable to present an index of physical output for the aircraft industry.[17]

The Group Total. The great diversity of trends within the group subjects any index of output for the group as a whole to considerable error, for slight changes in the weighting scheme used would have an important effect on the group index obtained. But while the index we present cannot be accepted as entirely accurate, there can scarcely be any doubt that its record of a mild rise in the first decade, a sharp increase in the second, a moderate gain in the third, and a decline in the fourth period, portrays the trend of the group as a whole. There is certainly no question that transportation equipment advanced more rapidly between 1899 and 1937 than most, if not all, other manufacturing groups.

Although, except for the petroleum and coal products

[17] Data collected by the Bureau of Air Commerce of the Department of Commerce indicate that the following number of airplanes were produced in the United States from 1919 to 1937:

Year	*Number*	*Year*	*Number*
1919	660	1929	6,190
1921	300	1931	2,800
1923	590	1933	1,320
1925	790	1935	1,750
1927	1,990	1937	3,760

These include commercial planes, military planes, and planes for export, with average prices ranging in 1935 from $3,700 for small single-engine airplanes to $56,000 for multi-engine airplanes. Since the average size of planes has undoubtedly increased, the decline in number from 1929 to 1937 exaggerates the decline in the output of the aircraft industry.

group, the transportation equipment group made the largest net gain between 1899 and 1937, its output declined in the most recent period. Indeed, of the six component industries for which there are data, none achieved a net rise in output between 1929 and 1937.

TABLE 63

TRANSPORTATION EQUIPMENT

Relative Contributions of Component Industries to the Physical Output of the Entire Group[a]

Industry	*Percentage Distribution, Comparable Pairs of Years*									
	1899	1937	1899	1909	1909	1919	1919	1929	1929	1937
Automobiles, incl. bodies and parts	0.4	89.7	1.6	38.1	23.1	62.9	41.0	88.5	82.2	81.7
Carriages, wagons and sleighs	19.3	0.1	30.6	21.2	16.7	1.4	2.1	0.2	0.4	0.3
Cars, railroad, n.e.m.[b]	19.4	1.8	21.0	13.6	21.1	5.5	8.8	3.1	4.9	5.1
Locomotives, n.e.m.[b]	19.5	0.5	7.7	5.6	11.0	2.2	4.4	0.8	2.0	1.2
Ships and boats[c]	25.1	2.5	24.3	12.6	19.9	25.9	41.2	4.6	7.4	6.6
Motorcycles and bicycles	}	}	6.9	2.2	1.8	0.9	1.2	0.4	d	d
Carriages and sleds, children's	} 16.3	} 5.5	}	}					0.6	0.5
All other products	}	}	} 7.9	} 6.7	6.4	1.2	1.2	2.4	2.4[d]	4.5[d]
TOTAL[e]	100.0	100.0	100.0	100.0	100.0	100.0	100.0	100.0	100.0	100.0

[a] Derived from Table 62. For an explanation of the derivation of the measurements see footnote 10, Chapter 4.

[b] N.e.m. denotes not elsewhere made.

[c] Does not include government-owned shipyards.

[d] Motorcycles and bicycles included in "All other products."

[e] The columns do not add up to 100.0 in every instance because they contain rounded percentages.

CHANGES IN THE INDUSTRIAL PATTERN OF TRANSPORTATION EQUIPMENT OUTPUT

Of the five industries in the transportation group for which we have complete data, only one, the automobile industry, advanced in output between 1899 and 1937. This advance proceeded at an astonishingly rapid rate, effecting an enormous change in the composition of the group's output, as Table 63 shows.

In 1899 the two railroad equipment industries accounted for 43 percent of the group's output, ships and boats for 27 percent, and carriages, wagons and sleighs for 21 percent. All other industries made up the balance of 9 percent. In that year automobiles contributed less than 1 percent to the

TABLE 64

TRANSPORTATION EQUIPMENT

Relative Contributions of Component Industries to the Value Added by the Entire Group[a]

Industry	*Percentage Distribution*				
	1899	1909	1919	1929	1937
Aircraft	8.4 (Aircraft and Motorcycles and bicycles combined)	1.8 (Aircraft and Motorcycles and bicycles combined)	0.3	1.8	3.7
Motorcycles and bicycles			1.1	0.5	0.9
Automobile bodies and parts	0.0	10.0	13.6	29.1	42.4
Automobiles	1.6	27.4	33.4	55.6	36.9
Carriage and wagon materials	6.7	5.3	0.5	0.1	[b]
Carriages and sleds, children's	1.3	1.5	0.5	0.6	0.5
Carriages, wagons and sleighs	33.2	19.9	1.6	0.3	0.2
Cars, railroad, n.e.m.[c]	17.8	15.4	7.8	4.4	5.7
Locomotives, n.e.m.[c]	8.3	5.3	3.5	1.3	1.7
Ships and boats[d]	22.8	13.4	37.7	6.2	7.9
TOTAL[e]	100.0	100.0	100.0	100.0	100.0

[a] Basic data are given in Appendix C.

[b] Abandoned as a separate classification in 1931. Included in carriages, wagons, and sleighs; and in wood turned and shaped.

[c] N.e.m. denotes not elsewhere made.

[d] Does not include government-owned shipyards.

[e] The columns do not add up to 100.0 in every instance because they contain rounded percentages.

group's output. In 1937 the picture was altogether different. The group was now dominated by a single industry, since automobiles accounted for 92 percent of its output.

Data on the industrial pattern of value added in the transportation equipment group add little to the picture presented in Table 63. Thus Table 64 records the comparative rise of the aircraft industry and the decline of the carriage and wagon industry. The distinction between automobiles and bodies and parts is of doubtful value, since the line of separation between the two industries is continually shifting.[18]

[18] According to a preliminary statement, the Bureau of the Census has abandoned the distinction between these two industries, and in the 1939 Census report they will be combined.

Chapter 22

Miscellaneous Products

THIS group includes all industries which are not properly classifiable in the 16 groups treated in the preceding chapters and are not important enough to be allocated to independent groups. Within this heterogeneous collection are the industries producing musical instruments; brooms and brushes; professional, scientific and other instruments; mattresses and bed springs; photographic supplies; signs; and toys and games. The group is small and has always ranked low in terms of value added.

TRENDS IN THE PHYSICAL OUTPUT OF THE MISCELLANEOUS PRODUCTS INDUSTRIES

The data on the physical output of the miscellaneous products industries are very inadequate (Table 65 and Chart 24). Only seven are represented, and only for one of these is there a series covering the entire period 1899–1937.

Organs. This industry, which includes establishments engaged in producing pipe and reed organs, declined in output from 1899 to 1935 by 78 percent. A peak in the production of pipe organs was reached in 1927, when 2,471 were turned out. In 1935 only 479 were produced, less than in 1899, when the number manufactured totaled 564. The output of reed organs was highest in 1904 (113,000 units). Thereafter output declined steadily until 1931. From that year to 1935 output rose somewhat, although it never exceeded a total of 2,000 in any of the four years.

Pianos declined 5 percent from 1899 to 1937. Output rose

TABLE 65

MISCELLANEOUS PRODUCTS[a]

Physical Output: Indexes and Percentage Changes[b]

	Organs	Pianos	Buttons	Brooms	Pencils	Pens and Points	Sporting Goods, n.e.c[c]
YEAR			INDEX OF PHYSICAL OUTPUT (1929:100)				
1899	143	69	..	..	..	..	..
1904	168	114	..	..	..	..	..
1909	124	156	..	..	..	..	..
1914	130	156	96	..	..	..	..
1919	92	189	121	..	..	..	..
1921	125	128	78	..	..	..	..
1923	96	210	113	..	..	..	..
1925	104	198	111	..	..	..	..
1927	125	151	91	93	..	..	..
1929	100	100	100	100	100	100	100
1931	54	43	88	88	74	83	96
1933	..	..	..	76	..	..	..
1935	31	40	121	90	134	144	69
1937	..	66	126	81	130	221	91
PERIOD			NET PERCENTAGE CHANGE IN PHYSICAL OUTPUT				
1899–1937	..	–5	..	..	..	..	..
1899–1909	–13	+125	..	..	..	..	..
1909–1919	–26	+21	..	..	..	..	..
1919–1929	+8	–47	–18	..	..	..	..
1929–1937	..	–34	+26	–19	+30	+121	–9

[a] Industries for which there are no adequate quantity data for any period listed above are: organ and piano parts; musical instruments, not elsewhere classified; artificial flowers; feathers and plumes; artists' materials; brushes; dairymen's supplies; dental goods and equipment; miscellaneous articles; ivory work; combs, not elsewhere classified; foundry supplies; hair work; hand stamps and stencils; instruments, professional; optical goods; jewelry and instrument cases; lapidary work; mattresses and bed springs, not elsewhere classified; models and patterns, not elsewhere classified; paving materials; photographic supplies; pipes, tobacco; signs; soda-water apparatus; surgical equipment; theatrical equipment; toys and games, not elsewhere classified; umbrellas and canes; and window shades.

[b] The indexes have been constructed from basic data in the U. S. Census of Manufactures, by methods described briefly in Chapter 2 and in detail in Appendix A. Appendix B presents these data, together with the indexes derived from them. The indexes have been adjusted to take account of changes in the coverage of the respective samples, except when such adjustment was impossible.

The percentage changes are not always entirely consistent with the indexes given above because the changes were computed from the indexes in Appendix B, which are carried to one decimal place.

[c] N.e.c. denotes not elsewhere classified.

Chart 24
MISCELLANEOUS PRODUCTS
Indexes of Physical Output

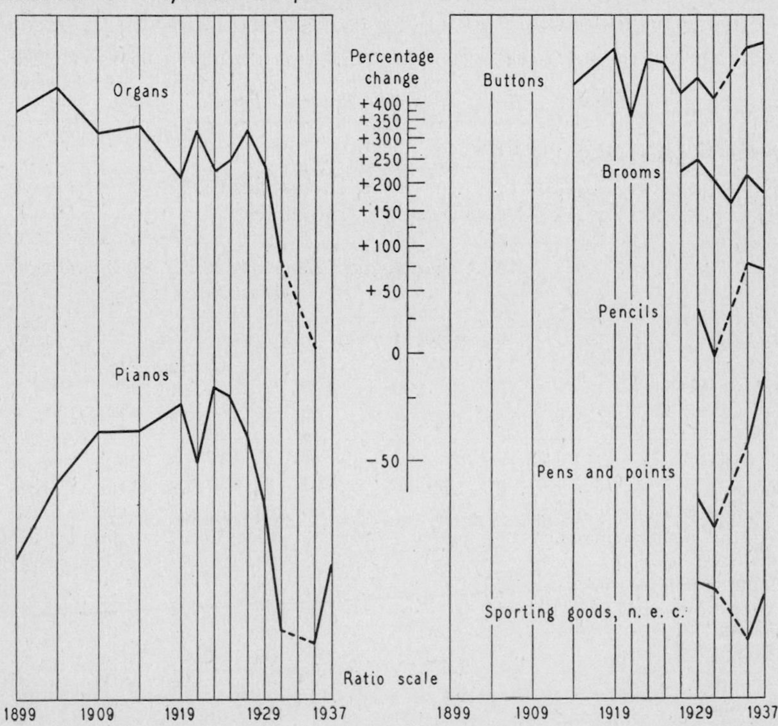

in the first two decades, reached a peak in 1923, and declined in the third and fourth periods. According to the detailed data on products, all uprights except player pianos reached their peak in 1909; player uprights touched a high only in 1923, and grand pianos in 1925.

CHANGES IN THE INDUSTRIAL PATTERN OF MISCELLANEOUS PRODUCTS MANUFACTURE

Because of the heterogeneity of the group, we note the changes in the relative contributions of the component industries to the production of all manufacturing industries combined, rather than to the group total. The only comprehensive figures relating to the group's output are, of course, those on value added, presented in Table 66. A great decline is to be noted in the relative contribution of the

TABLE 66

MISCELLANEOUS PRODUCTS

Relative Contributions of Component Industries to the Value Added by All Manufacturing Industries[a]

Industry	Percentage of Value Added by All Manufacturing Industries					
	1899	1909	1919	1929 Comparable with earlier years	1929 Comparable with 1937	1937
Organs		.04	.02	.03	.03	.01
Pianos	.52	.42	.23	.08	.08	.05
Organ and piano parts		.12	.09	.02	.02	.01
Musical instruments, n.e.c.[b]	.05	.03	.03	.04	.04	.03
Artificial flowers	.08	.06	.04	.03	.03	.03
Feathers and plumes		.07	.04	*	*	*
Artists' materials	*	.01	.01	.02	.02	.01
Pencils	.03	.05	.06	.06	.06	.05
Brooms	.19	.08	.05	.03	.03	.02
Brushes		.09	.08	.08	.08	.08
Buttons	.11	.16	.11	.06	.06	.07
Dairymen's supplies	[c]	.12	.08	.09	.09	[c]
Dental goods and equipment	.04	.03	.06	.06	.06	.07
Miscellaneous articles	.11	.09	.13	.17	.17	
Ivory work	.02	.01	.01	*	*	.12
Combs, n.e.c.[b]	.02	.06	.02	.01	.01	
Foundry supplies	.01	.01	.02	.02	.02	.02
Hair work	.02	.06	.01	*	*	.01
Hand stamps and stencils	.04	.03	.03	.04	.04	.03
Instruments, professional	.08	.10	.16	.20	.20	.26
Optical goods	.07	.09	.15	.10	.10	.13
Jewelry and instrument cases	.02	.02	.02	.02	.02	.03
Lapidary work	.02	.03	.04	.01	.01	*
Mattresses and bed springs, n.e.c.[b]	.17	.19	.15	.21	.21	.19
Models and patterns, n.e.c.[b]	.07	.08	.08	.08	.08	.07
Paving materials	.05	.04	.13	.05	.03	.04
Pens and points	.03	.04	.05	.08	.08	.06

TABLE 66 (concluded)

Industry	Percentage of Value Added by All Manufacturing Industries					
	1899	1909	1919	1929 Comparable with earlier years	1929 Comparable with 1937	1937
Photographic supplies	.10	.20	.23	.24	.24	.31
Pipes, tobacco	.03	.04	.03	.01	.01	.02
Signs	[c]	.11	.12	.27	.27	.19
Soda-water apparatus	.04	.05	.04	.05	.05	.03
Sporting goods, n.e.c.[b]	.04	.07	.05	.11	.11	.09
Surgical equipment	.07	.09	.10	.12	.12	.12
Theatrical equipment		[d]	*	.01	.01	.01
Toys and games, n.e.c.[b]	.05	.06	.11	.15	.15	.14
Umbrellas and canes	.12	.07	.04	.02	.02	.02
Window shades	.06	.07	.05	.06	.06	.04
TOTAL MISCELLANEOUS PRODUCTS[e]	2.23	2.88	2.67	2.61	2.56	2.34
TOTAL MANUFACTURING	100.00	100.00	100.00	100.00	100.00	100.00

* Less than .005 percent.
[a] Basic data are given in Appendix C.
[b] N.e.c. denotes not elsewhere classified.
[c] Included in various other industries.
[d] Not treated as a manufacturing industry prior to 1914.
[e] The columns do not add up to the total shown in every instance because they contain rounded percentages.

musical instruments industry, which fell from .52 percent of the grand total in 1899 to .07 percent in 1937. Brooms and brushes, artificial flowers, feathers and plumes, and umbrellas and canes also declined, but less severely.

On the other hand there were outstanding rises in the relative contributions of professional instruments (such as those used by surveyors and laboratory workers, and commercial and industrial measuring and control apparatus); photographic supplies; signs; toys and games; dental goods and equipment; optical goods; sporting goods; and surgical equipment.

Appendices

Appendix A

Technical Notes on Data and Methods

Tables

Appendix A

Technical Notes on Data and Methods

COVERAGE OF THE CENSUS OF MANUFACTURES

THE United States Census of Manufactures, our basic source, has been taken quinquennially from 1899 to 1919, and biennially since the latter year.[1] Because it has never attempted to include all types and sizes of manufacturing establishments, and because of changes in the particular sizes and types of establishments canvassed, the coverage of the Census has varied from one Census year to another.

General Changes in Coverage: the $500–$5,000 Lower Limit

The Census of Manufactures excludes from its count all establishments with a value of products below a certain minimum.[2] For the Census years 1899–1919 this limit was $500; for the years since 1919 it has been $5,000.[3] The change in the minimum between the years 1919 and 1921 resulted in a decline in the coverage of the Census data. This decline appears to have been

[1] The data collected in the Censuses are tabulated and published by the Bureau of the Census as part of the decennial Censuses, as special reports for the quinquennial periods, and as individual volumes under the title *Biennial Census of Manufactures* for the two-year periods.

[2] In the lumber-mill products industry the minimum is expressed in terms of a physical quantity of product.

[3] For the Census year 1921 data were collected also from establishments with a value of products of $500 to $5,000. The data, published in Table 1,041 in the 1921 Report, are limited to number of establishments, number of wage earners, and value of products. They are not included in any general tables in the reports for 1921 or later years. For the Census years 1923 and 1925 data on products alone were collected in certain industries from establishments with products valued at less than $5,000, but since these were not tabulated they were excluded from the published figures (1925 Report, pp. 5–6). Certain establishments engaged chiefly in nonmanufacturing activities and only secondarily in manufacturing are canvassed only if the value of their products is $20,000 or more. There are many such establishments in such industries as ice cream and confectionery (see 1927 Report, p. 6). Note, also, awnings and other industries listed in Appendix C, below.

of minor importance for the coverage of manufacturing as a whole and for that of most individual industries as well. In any case, the provision by the Bureau of the Census of overlapping figures for the year 1919—one comparable with earlier years and the other comparable with later years—avoids any difficulties that might arise from the change. Only seven industries in 1919 embraced establishments whose value of products was below $5,000 and yet were so relatively numerous that they accounted for more than 5 percent of the value added by the industry as a whole. These were: carpets and rugs, rag; clothing, men's, buttonholes; engraving, other; engraving, wood; charcoal; china firing and decorating; and concrete products. Most of these industries are unimportant in terms of value added.

Apart from the *change* in the minimum from $500 to $5,000, the mere *existence* of the minimum would result in variation in the coverage of the Census, for two reasons:

1. A decline in the relative importance (measured in terms of physical output) of establishments whose value of products falls below the minimum will, of itself, cause an increase in the coverage of the Census. A rise in the relative importance of these establishments will effect a decrease in the Census coverage.
2. A change in the prices of manufactured goods will likewise bring about an increase in the Census coverage (if the change is a rise in prices) or a decrease (if it is a decline).

If there exists no extraordinarily dense concentration of establishments (in terms of the aggregate value of their products) in the size groups under the minimum value of output imposed in each Census, as compared with the corresponding frequency shown by the Census for the size group immediately above the minimum, the incomparabilities introduced by either of these two factors are not at all serious, so far as the total is concerned. That such a dense concentration is unlikely to occur may be observed in the upper half of Table A-1, and even more readily in the lower half of the table, in which the percentages are expressed as ratios to the corresponding class interval (i.e., as average frequencies per unit of class interval) in order to avoid the obscuring effect of the differing class intervals. In all years but three the unit frequency in the smallest value-of-products or value-added size class shown was equal to or less than the unit frequency in the higher contiguous class. In other words, the

TABLE A-1

ALL MANUFACTURING INDUSTRIES COMBINED

Relative Importance of Small Establishments, 1904–37

Census Year	*As Measured by Value of Products* Establishments with Products Valued at			*As Measured by Value Added* Establishments with Products Valued at		
	$500–$5,000	$5,000–$20,000	$20,000–$100,000	$500–$5,000	$5,000–$20,000	$20,000–$100,000
	PERCENTAGE OF TOTAL[a]					
1904	1.2	5.1	14.4	1.8	6.7	17.3
1909	1.1	4.4	12.3	1.7	6.0	14.8
1914	1.0	3.7	10.5	1.5	5.1	..
1919	0.3	1.5	5.7	0.4	2.2	..
1921	0.3	1.8	7.6	..	..	..
1919	..	1.4	5.2	..	2.0	..
1921	..	1.8	5.7	..	..	..
1923	..	1.2	7.6	..	..	..
1925	..	1.0	5.6	..	..	..
1929	..	1.1	2.1[b]	..	1.5	2.8[b]
1937	..	0.9	2.0[b]	..	1.3	2.6[b]
	PERCENTAGE OF TOTAL, PER 1000 UNITS OF CLASS INTERVAL[c]					
1904	.27	.34	.18	.40	.45	.22
1909	.24	.29	.15	.38	.40	.18
1914	.22	.25	.13	.33	.34	..
1919	.07	.10	.07	.09	.15	..
1921	.07	.12	.10	..	..	..
1919	..	.09	.06	..	.13	..
1921	..	.12	.07	..	..	..
1923	..	.08	.10	..	..	..
1925	..	.07	.07	..	..	..
1929	..	.07	.07[b]	..	.10	.09[b]
1937	..	.06	.07[b]	..	.09	.09[b]

[a] Including $500 and over in 1904–21; including $5,000 and over in 1919–37. No data by size are available for 1899, 1927, and 1931–35.

[b] Class interval: $20,000 to $50,000.

[c] The percentage shown above, divided by the class interval expressed in thousands (e.g., 15 for the class $5,000–$20,000).

maximum frequency point had been passed, and a further decline was to be expected. Even if a rise were to occur it could not be great, since the lowest class includes the low frequencies near the zero point.

The existence of the minimum will have quite a different effect on the figures for those individual industries in which small establishments are relatively important. On the basis of the available Census data we may infer that the figures for only a few individual industries could be affected. Those few would be the seven listed above, in addition to the following: whips, electroplating, hair work, and models and patterns.

General Changes in Coverage: Biennial Canvasses

"Since the canvasses for the biennial years intervening between decennial years are made largely by mail, whereas in making the canvasses for the decennial years it is possible to employ a large field force, it is impossible to make as close an approach to absolute completeness for the biennial years as for the decennial years." [4] The biennial Census of 1935 is an exception, however; in this canvass a large field force of Federal works project employees was used.

The extent to which the biennial Censuses are incomplete has been indicated in only two Census volumes. A special note appears in the 1933 Report [5] concerning the 1933 Census:

> Because of the necessity of making the canvass with a field force considerably smaller than the field forces employed on former censuses of manufactures, the 1933 coverage of some of the industries was not quite complete; but the degree of incompleteness was not sufficient to have any material effect on the comparableness of the 1933 figures with those for earlier years, except in the case of the "Number of establishments" item. That is to say, the establishments that were active in 1933 but were not accounted for in the canvass were of little or no industrial importance.
>
> Of the 175,325 establishments that had reported for 1931, 8,595 failed to supply any information in regard to their status

[4] Letter from LeVerne Beales of the Bureau of the Census, dated February 29, 1932.

[5] Page 3.

(active, idle, out of business, etc.) or their activities in 1933, but these establishments had contributed only nine-tenths of 1 percent of the aggregate number of wage earners employed by all establishments reporting for 1931. For a very few industries the degree of incompleteness, thus measured, exceeded 3 percent, but in the great majority of cases it did not exceed 1.5 percent. Moreover, it is certain that some of the establishments that reported for 1931 but not for 1933 were idle or out of business in the later year, or made products valued at less than $5,000. . . .

Although, as explained above, the field force employed on the 1933 canvass was comparatively small, returns were nevertheless received from approximately 3,000 establishments that had not reported at previous censuses.

The Bureau of the Census estimates that only for seven industries did the reported 1933 totals of value of products or number of wage earners constitute less than 97 percent of the true totals. These seven industries are noted in Appendix C. The Bureau reported no case in which less than 94 percent of an industry was covered in the 1933 Census.

In the 1937 Census a statement similar to the following is to be found in some of the textile industry reports: "Because of the fact that some establishments such as those engaged in making women's, misses', and children's clothing lose their identity during a 2-year period through change of name, ownership, and location and, therefore, may be missed by a canvass made largely by mail, the 1937 statistics for the women's, misses', and children's apparel not elsewhere classified industry are not complete." [6] The Bureau of the Census believes that five of the needle trade industries were affected, mainly because of the inadequacy of trade directories and trade association lists.[7, 8]

---

[6] *Biennial Census of Manufactures, 1937,* Part I, p. 419, Table 1 (headnote).

[7] Letter from T. J. Fitzgerald, Chief Statistician for Manufactures, January 10, 1939. Notes concerning the inadequacy are appended to the data for these industries in Appendix C.

[8] Brief mention may be made of a third possibility of change in coverage. The Census for any year is taken, of course, in the following year. For example, the 1929 Census schedules were mailed in January 1930 (1929 Report, Vol. I, p. 1). Any establishment that went out of business at any time during 1929 (or even in the first few months of 1930) might not have filled in the schedule at all, despite the efforts of the Bureau of the Census. Be-

Changes in the Coverage of Individual Industries

Changes in the coverage of particular industries are frequently mentioned in the published volumes of the Census of Manufactures for 1899–1937. (Here the expression "change of coverage" refers not to a change resulting from the shift of establishments from one Census manufacturing industry to another consequent upon a change in the definition of the industry, but to a shift of establishments from manufacturing to nonmanufacturing or vice versa.) Such transfers are noted in Appendix C. Many of them result from the fact that the Census of Manufactures has been decreasing its coverage by eliminating operations that are doubtfully included in manufacturing—for example, operations closely related to mining, quarrying, servicing and repairing. We have accepted the definition of manufacturing implied in the 1937 Census,[9] excluding from the data for earlier years figures for industries abandoned in or before 1937.

Absolute Coverage

In discussing changes in the coverage of the Census of Manufactures we have touched only incidentally on the absolute coverage. The absolute coverage of a collection of statistical data can be assessed only by examination of the methods of collection, of the reliability of the personnel utilized, of the experience gained through repetition of the collecting process, etc.; by comparison with other, independently collected, bodies of data; and by tests of the data for internal consistency. It is obvious that a detailed consideration of the absolute coverage is impossible here.[10] We

---

cause the number of defunct establishments varies from year to year according to business conditions, changes in the degree of coverage result. However, data collected by the Bureau of the Census for 1929 and 1933 and analyzed by Tracy Thompson and Daniel Creamer indicate that "deaths" during Census years are of minor importance (Tracy Thompson, *Location of Manufactures, 1899–1929* [U.S. Bureau of the Census, 1933], p. 59; and Daniel B. Creamer, "Is Industry Decentralizing?" *Study of Population Redistribution, Bulletin No. 3* [University of Pennsylvania Press, 1935], Chapter 3 and Table 30).

[9] Except that we regard as nonmanufacturing industries two industries covered in the 1937 Census: rectified spirits and poultry killing. These were not consistently covered in the Censuses for years prior to 1937.

[10] Comparisons with the 1930 Census of Occupations, in respect of employment, and with the Treasury compilation of 1937 *Statistics of Income*, in respect of compensation of corporate officers and of inventories, yield rea-

have therefore assumed that the coverage of the Census is practically complete. It must be remembered that the Census of Manufactures has been collected decennially for one hundred years, quinquennially since 1899, and biennially since 1919. In the course of the years there has been brought together a trained personnel that has accumulated experience in phrasing schedules, locating establishments, editing replies [11] and tabulating results. The Bureau of the Census is not only well aware of the likelihood of an undercount but has itself sometimes evaluated such undercounts.[12]

While it is a huge task to assess the coverage of all of the hundreds of manufacturing industries, an investigator interested in one or two particular industries should find it not only possible but desirable to check the Census data for those industries, especially by comparison with other sources and by tests for internal consistency.

INDUSTRIAL CLASSIFICATION OF THE CENSUS OF MANUFACTURES

Census Definition of Manufacturing

"The Census of Manufactures is confined in general to manufacturing establishments conducted under the so-called factory system as distinguished from the neighborhood, hand, and building industries. No precise definition of a factory, for census purposes, can be given, but the following instructions relative to the

sonably close agreement for total manufacturing, after allowance for differences in scope and classification. Comparisons by industries or industrial groups show less favorable results, perhaps because differences in classification become more pronounced when lesser categories are considered.

[11] Schedules in all the Censuses from which we have taken our data have been edited, with one exception: the 1909 Census. See H. Parker Willis, "The Thirteenth Census," *Journal of Political Economy* (July 1913).

[12] See, for example, the remarks on coverage appended to the 1937 statistics for some of the needle-trade industries. See also footnotes to the table on products of the tobacco industries in the 1935 Census, in which discrepancies between the Census and the Internal Revenue statistics on number of cigarettes produced are explained (1935 Census, p. 1,265, footnote 1). The Bureau of the Census has, of course, enjoyed the cooperation of various business associations. Thus its figures are subjected to the close scrutiny of those who not only have access to other sources of data, but also are willing to share their knowledge with the Bureau.

omission of certain classes of establishments will show the general line of division." [13] Manufacturing carried on in educational, eleemosynary and penal institutions are not included. Other exclusions are:

Custom work on wearing apparel
Establishments, except publishers, having goods made for them, but not furnishing the materials
Hand trades: automobile repairing,[14] multigraph work, jewelry engraving, photography, etc.
Cotton cleaners, rehandlers, compressors, and ginners
Electric light and power stations
Floral designers
Kindling-wood producers
Rectifiers and blenders of liquor [15]
Hide salters
Tobacco stemmers and rehandlers
Manufacturing on farms, except canning and preserving of fruits, vegetables, etc., and where materials are purchased from others
Beneficiating processes applied to minerals
Custom flour and feed mills, if entirely custom work

Certain inclusions are of interest: mining and quarrying operations carried on in conjunction with manufacturing are covered by the Census of Manufactures if they consist of the digging of clay by manufacturers of clay products; the quarrying of cement rock or limestone by manufacturers of cement or lime, respectively; and the quarrying of stone by establishments dressing and finishing stone for monumental, ornamental and construction work. Logging camps also are included in the Census of Manufactures.

In order to follow the latest Census classifications we have excluded several industries listed at various times by the Census; the most important of these are motion pictures, manufactured gas, and railroad repair shops. Certain industries included in the 1937 Census but omitted from some of the earlier Censuses also

[13] Instructions for Preparing Reports, Census of Manufactures: 1929.
[14] Included in the 1909 Census, in combination with automobiles.
[15] Included beginning with the 1935 Census.

have been excluded by us; among these are poultry killing and rectified spirits. A full list appears in the reconciliation of our totals for value added by manufacturing industries with the corresponding Census totals, the last tabulation in Appendix C.

Detail of the Census Classification of Industries

The Bureau of the Census has presented the data on manufactures by industries in varying degree of detail. In the 1929 Census it distinguished 326 separate industries, whereas in the 1919 Census it had listed over 550 (including subindustries). Although the number of industries changed somewhat between every pair of Census years, it dropped sharply in 1925 from the higher level of earlier years. Since 1935 there has been a revival of the subindustry designation and a corresponding increase in detail. In presenting the industrial statistics taken from the Censuses we have accepted the 1929 classification and have combined the subindustries presented in earlier and later Censuses in almost every case.[16] We have used the 1929 breakdown, with its less detailed classification, in order to present continuous data for as long a period as possible.

Overlapping of Industries

Because establishments (with few exceptions) are assigned by the Bureau of the Census as units to one or another industry according to the product or group of products of chief value, and because establishments sometimes turn out a variety of products, overlapping of industries often results. In Table A-2 we present a systematic statement of the overlapping. This tabulation answers two questions. First, to what extent does the given industry make only products described by the name of the industry? That is, what percentage of the total value of products of the industry is represented by its primary (normal) product? Second, of the total production of the commodities described by the name of the industry, what percentage is made within the industry itself?[17] That is, what percentage of a given group of

[16] All industries listed in the 1937 Census are indexed at the end of the present volume; and for subindustries references are given to the industries of which they are components.

[17] The overlapping takes into account only manufacturing industries. We

TABLE A-2

MANUFACTURING INDUSTRIES[a]

Degree of Specialization and Extent of Overlapping of Products, 1929 and 1931

Percentage Class	*Degree of Specialization* Value of Primary Products as Percentage of Total Value of Output of the Industry — Number of Industries or Industrial Groups Reporting		*Extent of Overlapping* Value of Primary Products as Percentage of Value of Total Output of These Products[b] — Number of Industries or Industrial Groups Reporting	
	1929	*1931*	*1929*	*1931*
100.0–95.1	116	113	102	107
95.0–90.1	61	62	46	40
90.0–85.1	35	24	29	25
85.0–80.1	14	21	18	19
80.0–75.1	7	8	12	9
75.0–70.1	5	3	3	7
70.0–65.1	..	..	1	..
65.0–60.1	2	3	2	2
60.0–55.1	..	..	2	1
55.0–50.1	2	1	3	2
50.0– 0.0	..	..	6[c]	6[c]
No data	43	50	61	67
TOTAL	285	285	285	285

[a] Among these 285 industries are included 23 which represent not single industries but groups of industries. For example, "butter," "cheese," and "milk, canned" are counted as one industry; "hosiery," "underwear," "outerwear," and "knit cloth" are counted as one industry; "bags, paper," "boxes, paper," "cardboard," "card-cutting and designing," "envelopes," "labels and tags," "wall paper," and "paper goods, n.e.c." are counted as one industry; "copper," "lead," and "zinc" are counted as one industry; and so forth. The total number of industries included in the 23 combinations is 64.

[b] In some cases where data were lacking we had to take total value of products of the industry as a percentage of value of total production.

[c] The industries in this open-end class, together with the percentages reported by them, are given in detail in Table A-3.

products is produced in the industry specializing in those goods? The two questions are interrelated. If a given industry devotes half its energies to its primary product, the other half will be

disregard such products as butter manufactured on farms. Certain products made and consumed in the same establishment also are disregarded, e.g., cut stock made in the shoe industry and consumed immediately by the plant producing it.

given over to commodities that are primary in another industry. Obviously, then, the sum of all "other" products reported in the Census should equal the sum of all "secondary" products.[18]

In 16 of the 242 industries or groups for which we have data on degree of specialization in 1929, the value of the primary product constituted less than 80 percent of the total output of the industry; in 1931 the number was 15 out of 235. More important was the extent of overlapping. In 1929 out of 224 industries, 29 produced less than 80 percent of the total value of the products in which they specialized; in 1931 the proportion was 27 out of 218. The industries referred to here are listed in detail in Table A-3. Some of the interrelations are obvious. Establishments classified in the cereals industry produce some feeds as well; establishments classified in the feeds industry make some cereal preparations also. Another type of interrelation, where a large industry is surrounded by satellite specialist industries, is illustrated by the meat-packing, oleomargarine, sausage, and shortenings industries.

The percentages are not absolutely consistent in level from year to year, as is revealed by a comparison of the figures for 1929 and 1931. The correlation is rather high, however, and there seems to be no systematic change from the former year to the latter.

It should be remembered that the statistics understate considerably the true amount of overlapping because many of the units relate to groups of industries (see Table A-2, footnote a). Indeed, the combination into particular groups is probably attributable to the large degree of overlapping among these industries.

Changes in Classification

There are two kinds of change in classification. First, establishments may be shifted from one industry-classification to another because of a change from one primary product to another. We consider such cases as analogous to the closing of old plants and

[18] Except where one or the other represents a nonmanufacturing activity, and barring discrepancies in Census coverage and absence of detailed statements of products of certain industries (in 1929 there were more than 50 such cases).

the opening of new ones and therefore disregard them. Second, the Census Bureau has changed the definitions of some industries. Sometimes it has provided an overlap for such cases, and if so, we have reproduced it. Pulp goods, for example, includes molded plastics from 1931 on. In 1931 the industry's value added that is comparable with earlier years is 8.1 million dollars, and in the same year the value added that is comparable with later

TABLE A-3

INDUSTRIES WITH MARKED OVERLAPPING OF PRODUCTS, 1929 AND 1931[a]

A. Indicated by Degree of Specialization

Industry	*Primary Products as a Percentage of Total Output of the Industry*		*Nature of "Other" Products*[b]
	1929	1931	
Cereals	75.0	79.8	Prepared feeds and miscellaneous food products
Oleomargarine	76.3	64.8	Shortenings
Mats and matting	77.9		
Collars, men's		73.6	
Elastic woven goods, other		78.0	
Lumber-mill products	61.0	62.1	Planing-mill products and boxes
Druggists' preparations	75.8	70.8	Patent and proprietary medicines, perfumes, cosmetics, etc.
Grease and tallow	52.9	53.2	
Ink, writing	63.6	53.5	
Liquors, vinous	75.2		
Tanning materials	78.2		
Coke-oven products	62.2	61.6	Illuminating gas
Abrasives		78.8	
Firearms		75.8	
Saws		73.9	
Springs, steel	76.8		
Nonferrous-metal products, not elsewhere classified	79.5		Wire, plumbers' goods, spun and stamped goods, etc.
Machine tools		79.4	
Carriages, wagons and sleighs		77.1	Carriage materials
Locomotives		71.3	Clay machinery, heating equipment, castings, etc.
Miscellaneous articles	79.7		
Paving materials	79.7		
Pencils, lead	70.8		
Pens		75.6	

Table A-3 (continued)

B. Indicated by Extent of Overlapping

Industry	*Primary Products as a Percentage of Total Output of These Products*		*Other Industries Contributing to Output of These Products*[b]
	1929	1931	
Cereals	77.9		Feeds
Feeds	74.1	75.2	Cereals
Oleomargarine	58.8	57.6	Meat packing principally
Sausage	29.9	35.1	Meat packing principally
Shortenings	70.8	75.3	Meat packing principally
Vinegar and cider	53.6	50.7	Fruits and vegetables, canned
Horse blankets		75.1	Woolen and worsted goods
Mats and matting	73.8	79.7	
Boxes, wooden	63.3	64.2	Principally lumber products and planing-mill products
Planing-mill products	51.1	56.2	Lumber products principally
Window and door screens	75.3	76.8	
Converted paper products	78.1	77.9	Paper principally
Candles	75.6	78.9	
Cleaning and polishing preparations	76.5		
Compressed gases	72.4	73.1	
Druggists' preparations	75.6	72.2	Patent and proprietary medicines, perfumes and cosmetics
Perfumes and cosmetics		77.7	Druggists' preparations, patent medicines
Grease and tallow	48.1	47.7	Meat packing principally
Ink, writing	62.5	53.4	
Mucilage	70.7	51.6	
Lubricants	16.7	15.9	Petroleum refining
Leather goods, not elsewhere classified	76.1		
Bolts and nuts		77.0	Steel-mill products
Nails and spikes	24.5	24.7	Wire; steel-mill products
Springs, steel	71.3	66.4	Steel-mill products
Wire	34.8	30.2	Steel-mill products; nonferrous-metal products, not elsewhere classified
Wrought pipe	27.4	37.5	Steel-mill products
Machine-tool accessories	73.6		Tools; foundry and machine-shop products; machine tools
Carriages, wagons and sleighs		79.4	
Combs and hairpins	77.8		
Foundry supplies		72.3	
Hand stamps		65.0	
Models and patterns	77.9		
Paving materials		78.8	
Pencils, lead		75.1	

[a] Not including groups, like that combining butter; cheese; and milk, canned. See footnote a to Table A-2.

[b] If specified in the Census reports.

years is 16.4 million dollars. When no overlap is provided, we have at least noted changes in definition whenever they are mentioned or discussed in the Census reports. Further, we have indicated, in footnotes to the basic table in Appendix C, which of the changes in classification appeared to cause a serious disturbance in the continuity of the series for the industries concerned. On this point, unfortunately, the Census usually contains little information.

Major Groups

The 1937 Census classifies manufacturing industries into 15 major groups (excluding railroad repair shops).[19] We have found it convenient to increase this number to 17 by setting up as separate groups both beverages and tobacco products, and to shift a few individual industries from one major group to another to preserve continuity of classification throughout the period 1899–1937.

DATA ON VALUE ADDED

Since value added is the difference between value of products and cost of materials and fuel, the character of value added as reported by the Census is best described by separate discussion of the minuend and the subtrahend.

Value of Products

Items included. Value of products represents not only the value of physical commodities produced in factories but also the value of certain services rendered. Among these services are contract work (important in printing and in the garment industries), custom work (flour mills and slaughtering), repair work (sheet-metal, shipyards, railroad equipment), and advertising (publishing).

Repair work is included only when carried on by plants engaged primarily in the manufacture of physical commodities. Custom work is reported only when accompanied by operations

[19] According to preliminary information there will be 20 major groups in the 1939 Census.

on the plant's own account; when flour mills do custom work even to the extent of more than half of their total business, they are treated as merchant mills and included, whereas custom mills that do not work on their own materials are excluded. In the earlier years of the period 1899–1937, the Census did cover both custom flour mills and shops engaged in auto repairing; since they were dropped many years ago we have excluded them from the figures for the entire period.

Value of products, as reported in the Census, does not include the value of construction, repairs and maintenance undertaken within the manufacturer's plant by his own force.[20]

Method of evaluation. Value of products represents the selling value, f.o.b. factory, of the products manufactured; or, for some industries, receipts for work done. If separate sales departments are maintained, or if transfers are made to other establishments under the same management, the values are the assigned transfer values at which the products are turned over to the other departments or establishments. In the latter case, the Census states, "the transfer value is usually based on market prices or on the cost of manufacture, but sometimes it is purely arbitrary." The differences between transfer values and selling prices do not appear to be great for the few products (pig iron, iron and steel wire, steel ingots, and sheet and tin-plate bars) for which we have computed them.

Period covered. The value of products reported in the Census represents the selling value of the products finished during the year, which may be a fiscal and not a calendar year ending on December 31 of the Census date.[21] Value added to work not

[20] However, maintenance employees and their wages are probably included in the Census data on employment and payrolls.

[21] Fiscal-year reports have been permitted for all industries, and have been requested, for specified fiscal years, for certain industries closely associated with farming, e.g., the beet sugar and cane sugar industries. No information concerning the number of fiscal-year reports is given in the Census of Manufactures, except for the latter industries. Data for corporations, published in *Statistics of Income* by the Statistical Unit of the Bureau of Internal Revenue, indicate that in 1929, 14 percent of all corporate reports on manufactures were on a fiscal year basis, and the "fiscal year" corporations reported 12 percent of the total net income of all manufacturing corporations and 18 percent of all manufacturing deficits. Statisticians at the Bureau of the Census believe that these figures do not apply to the Census reports. "It is definitely the opinion of those who are familiar with the manufacturers' re-

completed by the end of the year is not considered part of the output of the year except in the specific cases of ships and boats and aircraft; in these industries the value of products represents only the value of work done during the year. As a rule, then, the Census value includes some of the value added in the preceding year, and excludes some of the value added in the Census year. For this reason the figures may be somewhat too small during periods of expansion and too large during periods of contraction. It is unlikely, however, that this error will have significant effect upon the figures for more than a few industries.[22]

It is important to note that the increasing tendency of manufacturers to take over distributive functions from wholesalers or retailers has not affected the Census data on value added. The Census figures on value added relate to the value added in the factory proper, since value added is the difference between value of products, f.o.b. factory, and cost of materials delivered to the factory. Value added in manufacturers' sales agencies or warehouses is therefore not represented by the statistics in the present volume.

The value of all goods manufactured is included in the value of products, whether the goods are sold or added to stock. There is one exception to this rule. For the Census year 1929 the value of products for the majority of industries was the selling value, f.o.b. factory, of products shipped or delivered during the year. But for 76 industries, including some of the most important, it represented products manufactured, whether sold or not.[23] The

---

turns" that the number of fiscal-year reports would amount to "considerably less than 14 percent of all corporate reports." But because no tabulation to determine the exact percentage has been made, "it is impracticable to support this statement with any statistical evidence." (Excerpts from a letter by H. H. McClure, Acting Chief Statistician for Manufactures, November 19, 1938).

The schedules sent out in 1900 requested that the "information returned should cover the business year of the establishment most nearly conforming to and preceding the Census year which ends June 1, 1900." However, as is noted in the Census, "a very large proportion of the reports made in the Twelfth Census actually related to the business of the calendar year 1899."

[22] These are industries in which the manufacturing process is a long one, or in which the fluctuations in output are severe.

If the "natural business year" is used as the fiscal year, then inventories at the end of the year will be rather small, and the carry-over from one year to another will be less important than if the calendar year is used.

[23] These 76 industries were excepted "for special reasons, and in most cases at the request of the associations representing the industries in question, or

Bureau of the Census believes, however, "that the change in question had very little effect on the comparableness of the statistics for 1929 with those for 1931 and those for 1927 and preceding biennial-census years, since it is likely that the excess of sales over production in some establishments and the excess of production over sales in others counter-balanced each other in large measure." [24] In the absence of any empirical support it is difficult to appreciate the basis for this belief. For 52 of the 76 industries mentioned, the Census does present data showing the difference between production and sales, i.e., the net increase or net decrease in inventory of finished goods.[25] In 26 of these industries there was a net increase in inventory during 1929; in 26, a net decrease. Most of these changes constituted small fractions of value of products. However, in nine of the 52 industries the fraction exceeded 5 percent.[26] If we may judge from this meager sample, about one sixth of all industries were affected rather appreciably by the change in the definition of value of products between 1927 and 1929, and between 1929 and 1931.

Cost of Materials

Cost of materials represents the outlay not only for materials but also for containers for goods produced, fuel and purchased

---

of important manufacturers in the industries" (1929 Report, Vol. I, p. 3). It is not clear whether these industries were excepted because their own inventory changes were especially large.

[24] 1931 Report, p. 5.

[25] *Distribution of Sales of Manufacturing Plants, 15th Census,* Table 3. In the case of the ships and boats industry, the inventory covers unfinished goods also.

[26] These industries are:

	Change in Inventory of Finished Goods, as a Percentage of Total Value of Products
Agricultural implements	+5.5
Aircraft	+7.2
Planing-mill products, not elsewhere made	−6.8
Sand-lime brick	−5.9
Sausage	−8.6
Ships and boats	+9.5
Sugar, beet	+9.1
Sugar, cane	+5.2
Vinegar and cider	−5.4

Since the figures reported for these industries represent output rather than sales, it is unnecessary to correct them for these changes in inventories.

electric energy consumed during the year (including transfers of such items from other plants under the same ownership), and freight and haulage costs (excluding the cost of haulage performed by the plant's own employees and equipment if the latter costs can be segregated).

Treatment of mill and shop supplies. In all years except 1929, 1931 and 1933, cost of materials included mill and shop supplies (such as lubricating oil and minor replacements). The Bureau of the Census holds that the change between 1927 and 1929 was "slight and unimportant. In the reports for the few industries in which the cost of supplies formerly constituted a considerable part of the cost-of-materials item, special attention is called to this fact."[27] The "few industries" number 11, and all of them produce metals and metal products. To these we may add four other industries mentioned in another Census report.[28] The 15 industries are: cast-iron pipe, cutlery, n.e.c., files, firearms, steel-mill products, saws, stoves and ranges, business machines, gas machines and meters, textile machinery, typewriters, automobiles, automobile bodies and parts, foundry and machine-shop products, n.e.c., and hardware, n.e.c.

No evidence is provided in the Census reports on the exact extent to which the figures for these industries were affected by the exclusion of mill and shop supplies between 1927 and 1929 or by the re-inclusion of these supplies in 1935. The sole clue to the quantitative significance of these items is found in the 1904 Census which reports "mill supplies" separately. In 1904 cost of mill supplies, as a percentage of value added (with these supplies excluded), did not exceed 3 percent for any industry, exceeded 2 percent for only one (steel-mill products) and exceeded 1 percent for only five industries. If we may judge by that early Census, none of the figures on value added by the industries listed above would have been seriously affected by the changes between 1927 and 1929, and between 1933 and 1935.

Treatment of contract work and internal revenue taxes. To obtain the value added by manufacturing in the years 1899–1933,

[27] 1929 Report, Vol. I, p. 3.

[28] Tracy Thompson, *Materials Used in Manufacture, 1929* (U.S. Bureau of the Census, 1933), p. 14, footnote 11.

the Bureau of the Census deducted from value of products the cost of materials, excluding payments for contract work. For 1935 the Bureau of the Census computed the value added in some industries by deducting from the value of their products the payments for contract work as well as those for costs of materials. Beginning with 1937 the Bureau of the Census followed this procedure in determining the value added by all industries. We have used this method for all years, wherever possible, for the industries (chiefly textiles and printing and publishing) in which contract work is important, and have made special note of the industries so affected (Appendix C). Moreover, when necessary we adjusted the 1935 and 1937 Census data on the value added by all other industries to render them comparable with the data for earlier years. Such adjustment involved the addition of payments for contract work, if these had been deducted by the Census.

Internal-revenue taxes are similar neither to cost of materials nor to cost of contract work. From the economic standpoint, it might be argued that they should be treated as part of the net output of an industry, rather than as payment for commodities or services purchased from another industry. Subscribing to this view, we have made an effort to include these taxes in the value added data for every year. In order to do so we have had to revise the Census data for 1931–37, since internal-revenue taxes have been included by the Census in value of products in all years and, beginning with 1931, also in cost of materials. We have indicated the industries for which such revision was necessary—chiefly those engaged in tobacco manufacture and liquor production (Appendix C). For one or two of the more recent Census years, however, when it was impossible to obtain the necessary information, we have provided overlaps.

Period covered. For all years except 1929, cost of materials relates to the amount consumed during the year, and not to the amount purchased or paid for.[29] In 1929 manufacturers were given the option of reporting either the amount consumed or the amount purchased, but where amounts reported purchased appeared to be out of line with reports for earlier years in the opin-

[29] Concerning fiscal-year reports, see above, footnote 21.

ion of the Bureau of the Census, data on materials consumed were requested by correspondence. "It is therefore unlikely that the comparableness of the statistics has been affected appreciably by the use of data for materials purchased." [30] The 1931 Census resumed the practice of requiring information on the amount consumed.

Method of evaluation. Both cost of materials consumed and cost of materials purchased are evaluated in terms of the prices paid. If they were to be expressed in terms of the prices prevailing at the time of use rather than at the time of purchase, the data on value added would be different from the Census figures. In a period of rising prices value added would be smaller, and in a period of falling prices, larger; consequently, the cyclical amplitude of fluctuation would be reduced. In Table A-4 are presented estimates of value added by all manufacturing industries combined, computed on the basis of current rather than original cost of materials, and comparisons with the value added as reported in the Census of Manufactures. The adjustments are large for 1921, 1931 and 1933, when there were substantial changes in prices.

Value Added

Because it is computed as the difference between two items, value added is subject to all the qualifications attaching to the minuend and subtrahend, except to the extent that these cancel one another. Some of the qualifications do cancel out in a certain sense. For example, if assigned transfer values are too high or too low, they influence cost of materials in the same manner as value of products affects such costs (unless the transfers are to nonmanufacturing industries), and thus leave the aggregate value added by all manufacturing industries untouched; on the other hand, the value added by particular industries is necessarily affected by assigned transfer values.

Data on value added are free from the defects in aggregates of value of products and cost of materials that tend to arise from the integration of industrial plants. For example, the Bureau of the

[30] 1929 Report, Vol. I, p. 3.

TABLE A-4

VALUE ADDED BY MANUFACTURING, 1919–33

Census Totals, Before and After Adjustment for Inventory Revaluation[a]

Year	*Unadjusted Total ($1,000,000)* (1)	*Inventory Revaluation ($1,000,000)* (2)	*Adjusted Total ($1,000,000)* (3)	*Unadjusted Total as a Percentage of Adjusted Total* (1÷3)
1919	23,313	+902	22,411	104
1921	16,879	−2,813	19,692	86
1923	24,031	+129	23,902	101
1925	25,162	+51	25,111	100
1927	25,769	−383	26,152	99
1929	30,062	−362	30,424	99
1931	18,597	−1,517	20,114	92
1933	14,119	+1,111	13,008	109

[a] The inventory revaluation data, available for 1919–33 alone, are derived from estimates by Simon Kuznets, some of which were published in his *Commodity Flow and Capital Formation* (National Bureau of Economic Research, 1938), Vol. I, Part VII.

Census draws attention to the duplication in the latter two items which is attributable to the fact that smelters, classified in the smelting and refining industry, sell crude metals to independent refiners, also classified in this industry. More serious than the degree of duplication is the possibility of a change in its relative importance. An increase in the proportion of smelting and refining plants that are integrated will affect not only the aggregate amounts of the industry's value of products and cost of materials but also their movements in time.

Value added is not free from all duplication, however. It includes many items which should be deducted if a truly net value added is to be obtained. These are mainly overhead items, such as depreciation, taxes, rent, interest on short-term debt, maintenance and repairs, and other purchased supplies and services (advertising, light, office supplies, professional services).[31] The ratio of

[31] For manufacturing as a whole the magnitudes of these items in 1929 may be estimated roughly as follows:

the net value added to the Census value added is .63 for 1929.[32] For the six major divisions of manufacturing for which we have figures, the 1929 ratios vary from .49 to .69, five being between .60 and .70 (Table A-5).

Not all the overhead items included in value added are inflexible in the short run, but a comparison of the Census value added and estimates of net value added [33] by major manufacturing divisions in the Census years 1919–37, and by all manufacturing combined in 1909–37, shows that the total of these overhead items is relatively inflexible (Table A-5). As a consequence net value added falls more rapidly during business recessions than does the Census value added, and rises more sharply during advances in business. Further, the amplitude of cyclical changes in the ratio of net value added to the Census value added varies from major group to major group: the greater the cyclical amplitude of changes in value added, the greater seems to be the cyclical amplitude of the ratio. Reference to the table shows that value added is a poor approximation to net value added so far as short-term changes are concerned.

The two values are somewhat closer in respect of movements

	Billion dollars	
Value of products		67.9
Cost of materials and fuel		37.8
Value added		30.1
Other deductions		
Depreciation	1.9	
Depletion	.3	
Provision for fire losses	.1	
Maintenance and repairs	3.0	
Interest on short-term debt	.5	
Taxes	1.3	
Bad debts	.3	
Rent (net)	.3	
Advertising	.5	
Other deductions, and errors of estimate	3.0	11.2
NET VALUE ADDED		18.9

These estimates are derived from data in *Statistics of Income,* an annual publication of the Bureau of Internal Revenue; from Solomon Fabricant, *Capital Consumption and Adjustment* (National Bureau of Economic Research, 1938); and from the Census of Manufactures.

[32] If taxes, interest and rent are considered as income originating in manufacturing, the ratio becomes .70.

[33] The net value added in an industry, as defined here, is of course identical with the portion of the national income produced in the industry.

TABLE A-5
COMBINATIONS OF MAJOR GROUPS
Net Value Added as a Percentage of Census Value Added,[a] 1919–37

Combined Group	*1919*	*1921*	*1923*	*1925*	*1927*	*1929*	*1931*	*1933*	*1935*	*1937*
Foods, beverages and tobacco products	58	47	58	52	51	49	41	41		
								43	46	
									49	52
Textile and leather products	75	61	69	66	66	61	50	65	66	64
Forest, stone, clay and glass products	77	67	79	76	72	69	52	48	61	64
Paper products and printing and publishing	68	62	66	65	64	62	56	55	59	62
Metal products	72	54	68	67	64	65	46	48	62	68
Chemical and petroleum products	61	45	56	61	54	64	32	39	55	58
TOTAL[b]	72	57	69	66	64	63	48	51	60	
									61	65

[a] The Census data on value added are to be found in Appendix C. The figures on net value added are those computed by Simon Kuznets for the National Bureau (1919–35), by R. R. Nathan for the Department of Commerce (1935–37), and by W. I. King for the National Bureau (1909–19). The figures for 1919–37 relate to "national income," while those for 1909–19 refer to "payments to individuals."

[b] Includes a miscellaneous group. For earlier years the corresponding percentages for total manufacturing are: 68 for 1909; 75 for 1914; and 68 for 1919. These are not available by groups.

from peak to peak. For all manufacturing the ratio of net value added to the Census value added changed but slightly from 1909 to 1919 and from 1919 to 1923, about 10 percent from 1923 to 1929, and 2 percent from 1929 to 1937. The shift ranged from zero to 15 percent for the major groups from 1919 to 1923, 1923 to 1929, and 1929 to 1937. Over longer periods, the discrepancies in trend between net value added and the Census value added often cumulate. From 1919 to 1937 the relation of these two series changed about 11 percent for all manufacturing, 20 percent for foods, 15 percent for textiles and leather, 17 percent for forest, stone, clay and glass products, 9 percent for paper and printing, 6 percent for metal products, and 5 percent for chemical and petroleum products. In all groups value added rose in relation to net value added, a fact which indicates the growing importance of the overhead items. It should be noted that these conclusions based on major groups cannot be applied without reservation to the interpretation of the data on value added by individual industries.

DATA ON PHYSICAL OUTPUT

The figures on physical volume are subject to almost all the qualifications outlined above, and in addition, to certain other reservations.

"Primary" and "Secondary" Products

The first difficulty encountered in any attempt to use the Census data on physical output arises from the fact that the Census tables seldom give the quantities of individual products made in an industry.[34] Instead, the Census usually publishes the amounts of each individual product wherever made. That is, it lumps together primary and secondary output, as these are defined above (pp. 336–37). Thus the amount of butter produced in factories in 1929 was reported in the Census as 1.6 billion pounds. But this quantity includes not only butter made in the "butter" industry proper, but that made as a secondary product in the "cheese" and other industries. Because this sort of combination is frequently encountered we have had to treat all of the product reported (e.g., the 1.6 billion pounds of butter) as if it were made in the industry of which it is a primary product (in this instance the "butter" industry). Usually secondary output accounts in fact for only a small proportion of the total made (see Table A-2 above), though for a few industries secondary output is rather important. In the case of the latter industries the method of treatment just described may sometimes lead to the result that the sum of the values of the specified individual products (including secondary production outside the industry) exceeds the total value of products of the industry proper.[35] Such a result

[34] The tables supply this information for only a few products, among which are wire and oleomargarine. It is possible that in the earlier years the data in the Census tables were restricted to primary products; but whether this is true cannot be ascertained.

[35] Another possible result is overstatement of the "coverage ratio" (see below).

is not necessarily a grave matter, since changes in the ratio of these two values, whatever the cause, are taken into account by means of the "coverage ratio adjustment" discussed below.

Also of concern is the fact that it is often impossible to tell exactly to what the Census data refer. Occasionally they relate to different products in different years. For example, in the canned fish industry the product data prior to 1925 include clam chowder manufactured by canners of vegetables and fruits, whereas the figures for the later years do not. Difficulties of this sort also are most commonly resolved by the coverage ratio adjustment.

Degree of Coverage

Another defect of the Census data on physical quantities arises from incomplete coverage of products. For many industries no data on physical quantities are reported at all, and consequently no index of physical output can be computed for them. When we come to compute indexes for major groups and for "total" manufacturing, we have prominent gaps in our list. Our efforts to overcome this handicap are described in a later section. In the case of many other industries, data on physical output are reported, but these do not cover all the products of the industry. It then becomes necessary to try to answer two important questions: First, for what industries is adequate coverage of output provided? Second, what is the effect of a change in the percentage of coverage?

The answer to the first question depends primarily on the relation between the products for which we have quantity data and those for which we do not have quantity data. In other words, it depends on the character and size of the sample. There is little that we can say concerning the character of the sample because an adequate opinion requires an intimate knowledge of the particular industry under discussion. The size of a sample, however, can readily be measured. We have had to form our judgments, therefore, on the basis of the second criterion alone; for this reason our calculations for particular industries are subject to revision by experts familiar with them. In this study we have regarded a coverage of 40 percent as sufficient to warrant the computation of an index of physical output for an industry.[36] A coverage of 40 percent is not very high, especially since the percentages at hand usually overstate the true coverage because "secondary" products are counted in as if they were primary products.[37] However, the indexes of but a few industries cover as little as 40 percent of the products.

The coverage ratios are given in detail in the tables in Appendix B. If the reader chooses he may raise the standards and refuse to accept as reliable the indexes based on less than 60, 70 or even 80 percent coverage. It is apparent from the summary of the coverage ratios that appears in Table A-6 that for most of the indexes the coverage is high. Thus, out of 129 indexes available for 1937, 82 are based on a coverage of 80 percent or more. Only 11 are based on less than 60 percent coverage.

Another problem arises from changes in the degree of coverage. If an industry consistently reported the physical quantities of 60 percent of its products, we could confidently assume that the index of physical volume of output that could be computed would

[36] For a few industries (for example, chemicals, not elsewhere classified), we computed indexes of physical output even when the coverage fell slightly below 40 percent for a few years, provided that we could build up fairly long series of index numbers for the industries concerned.

[37] The computed coverage ratio equals the total value of products of the industry (most often excluding "other products" of the industry but usually including "secondary products" of other industries) that are covered by quantity statistics, divided by the total value of products of the industry. The "true" coverage ratio excludes from its numerator the secondary products. In symbols, let $V =$ the total value of products of a given industry, as reported in the Census; $O =$ value of "other products not normally belonging to the industry"; $S =$ value of secondary products of other industries; and let the subscript q indicate coverage by quantity statistics. Then the computed coverage ratio is commonly equal to

$$\frac{(V - O)_q + S_q}{V}$$

and the true coverage ratio is equal to

$$\frac{(V - O)_q}{V}.$$

Thus, the computed coverage ratio is equal to or greater than the true ratio, most frequently the latter. It follows that a 40 percent coverage ratio is normally somewhat less conservative than it would appear to be. It may also happen occasionally that the coverage ratio will exceed 100 percent.

More important than the relation between the computed and true coverage ratios is the relation between the changes in the prices of the "secondary products" and the corresponding changes in the prices of the "other products." But this also is a question concerning the *character* of the sample, about which we can say nothing here.

TABLE A-6

COVERAGE OF INDEXES OF PHYSICAL OUTPUT

Frequency Distribution of Manufacturing Industries by Percentage of Coverage, Selected Years[a]

Percentage of Coverage	Number of Industries				
	1899	1909	1919	1929	1937
Below 40.0	1	..	..	1	2
40.0–49.9	2	3	2	5	4
50.0–59.9	1	3	3	4	5
60.0–69.9	2	1	6	10	10
70.0–79.9	7	8	8	24	26
80.0–89.9	6	8	12	28	28
90.0–99.9	17	24	25	46	39
100.0 and above[b]	2	6	8	15	15
TOTAL NUMBER OF INDUSTRIES	38	53	64	133	129

[a] Not including industries for which the exact percentage of coverage is not known. For most of these the coverage is undoubtedly close to 100 percent. Two or more coverage ratios are available for most industries for most of the years listed. For example, for 1919 there is a 1919 coverage ratio for the 1919 index relative to 1909, and one for the 1919 index relative to 1929. The ratios in this table apply to the indexes relative to the latest year (e.g., 1919 relative to 1929).

[b] See footnote 37, above.

represent adequately the total output of the industry. But often the products not covered in the index of production increase or decrease in importance. We are then less justified in considering our index of output as representative. Obviously an adjustment is called for. This adjustment, as made in the present study, is described at a later point in this section. When no adjustment could be made, the unadjusted index was used. When adjustment was possible only for part of the index, the adjusted index was interpolated or extrapolated by the unadjusted index.

Homogeneity of Product Classes

The detail in which products have been covered in the Census of Manufactures has varied from time to time. On the whole, there has been a secular trend toward an increase in detail: the classes of products shown in the Census have become more homogeneous. For this reason our indexes for the more recent years are superior to those for the earlier years of the period 1899–1937. For example, the 1899–1927 index for cheese is based on one output series ("all varieties"), and is therefore somewhat inferior to the 1929–37 index which is based on 4 or 5 series.

The difference between an index derived from detailed data and one derived from less detailed data may be very great. It will depend upon the relative magnitudes of the prices and quantities of the several products and the relative magnitude of the changes in the prices and quantities. If, for example, the output of the more expensive products of an industry is increasing in relation to the output of the less expensive products, an index based on the more detailed data will rise more rapidly than an index based on the less detailed data. The degree of disparity between the two indexes will be determined by the relation between the values of the two groups of products. Some of the differences that may be found when indexes based on detailed data are compared with indexes based on broad groups of data are illustrated by figures on carpet and rug production computed by Dr. Mills.[38] Additional empirical tests made in the present study yield the results shown in Table A-7. Here it is apparent that the differences are rather pronounced for some of the industries. On the basis of this limited evidence, and of a consideration of the assumptions implicit in the acceptance of indexes based on inadequate detail, we decided to use fairly detailed data in computing our indexes whenever it was possible to do so.[39]

For some industries for all years, and for some industries for certain years, no indexes were computed at all because it was felt that the available Census data were insufficiently detailed. Thus it is impossible to compute satisfactory indexes of physical output for most of the machinery industries because of the extremely heterogeneous classifications of their products. In the 1929 report for the electrical machinery industry, for example, alternating-current generators "under 2,000 kv-a" are combined with alternating-current generators "2,000 kv-a and over." According to detailed data available in the 1935 Census, these two

[38] F. C. Mills, *Economic Tendencies* (National Bureau of Economic Research, 1932), p. 32, footnote.

[39] The most detailed data were not used if, after inspection of the Census reports, homogeneous combinations could be constructed or had been published by the Census. Severity of judgment as to what constituted homogeneity varied, perhaps, as the work proceeded. The combinations we have used appear in the basic tables in Appendix B.

TABLE A-7

Ratios Of Indexes Constructed From More Detailed Data To Indexes Constructed From Less Detailed Data, 1919–37

Year	*Baking Powder*	*Cheese*	*Linoleum*	*Boxes, Wooden, Cigar*	*Blast-Furnace Products*	*Pianos*	*Tin and Other Foils*	*Hosiery, Knit*	*Carpets and Rugs, Wool*
1919	..	..	..	..	1.01	..	..	..	0.78
1921	..	..	..	..	..	..	..	..	0.80
1923	..	..	1.12	..	..	..	..	0.67	0.88
1925	..	..	1.09	..	1.01	..	..	0.77	0.97
1927	1.02	..	1.08	1.01	1.00	0.98	1.13	0.87	0.97
1929	1.00	1.00	1.00	1.00	1.00	1.00	1.00	1.00	1.00
1931	1.00	1.01	0.94	1.01	0.99	1.08	..	1.03	1.07
1933	1.06	1.00	..	..	0.99	..	..	1.08	1.02
1935	1.05	1.00	0.94	1.01	0.99	0.97	..	1.08	1.01
1937	1.04	1.00	0.92	1.00	1.00	..	..	1.09	0.99

types were valued at $660 each and $151,025 each, respectively, in the later year. Another example of heterogeneity is found in the organs industry. In 1937 only one series was given for this industry—a combination of pipe, reed, and electronic organs—to avoid disclosure of output by individual establishments. According to the more detailed data available for 1931, such a combination involved a lumping together of pipe organs valued in that year at $5,761 each, and reed organs valued at $131 each.

Continuity of Series

Difficulties related to changes in degree of detail are encountered also when one tries to secure chronological comparability in the series for individual products. From time to time the Census changes its definition of a series so that the data for the given year are not strictly comparable with those for the base year. When this sort of change in a series appeared to be slight, we used the series in constructing our index; when large, we did not use the series. Sometimes, when revisions of data for earlier years were made by the Census, we found that the series could be broken into segments, each of which was usable.

Another type of difficulty arises from changes in titles. Occasionally the Census alters the title of a series but fails to give definite information as to whether a real change in the composition of the series has taken place. We had to assume in such cases that the change was confined to the title alone.

In the data for the washing and ironing machines industry we find an example of the sort of incomparability described above. Figures on electric washing machines for household use (standard size) include apartment-size washing machines for 1927 and 1929 but not for other years. Changes in title are encountered in the data on the steel-mill products industry: the series listed in 1904 as "splice bars, including all patent splices and rail joints" was called in 1919 "rail joints, fastenings, etc." and in 1929 "rail joints and fastenings, tie plates, etc."

Incomparabilities in old series may be suspected when "new" series appear. A separate series was listed for automobile chassis in 1919 for the first time, but there was no statement concerning the classification of chassis in earlier years. It is likely, however, that they were combined with some of the other products presented in earlier Census reports. In the pulp industry a new series, "screenings," is listed in 1914. Here, however, there is a statement that prior to 1914 "screenings" were included in "sulphite-fiber, soda-fiber, and mechanical pulp." We sought to resolve the attendant difficulties in accordance with the following policy: where there was no statement regarding the classification in earlier years of products included in a new series, the series from which the products might have been taken were considered comparable as between the years in question. Where a definite statement was made, the resulting incomparabilities were, of course, taken into account. Fortunately, the incomparability from this source is not likely to be serious, because a product is usually segregated by the Census before it has acquired any great importance. In 1914, the value of screenings, for example, was less than one-half of one percent of the total value of the products among which it had previously been included.

Non-Census Data

While we have made no effort to compute index numbers for non-Census years, we have tried to secure index numbers for all the Census years for each industry. To this end we have sometimes had to seek data from sources outside the Census.

When Census data were not available for a particular industry for all the Census years, related series taken from other sources were spliced to the index based on Census data. Two criteria were applied in an attempt to determine whether a series was related closely enough for this purpose: (1) theoretical grounds for expecting conformity of movement; (2) statistical conformity over the period for which both sets of data were available. When a series which met these requirements was found, the incomplete index based on Census data was extrapolated backward or forward on the basis of the related series. For instance, the Willett and Gray series for sugar meltings which appears in the *Statistical Sugar Trade Journal* moves very similarly to our cane-sugar refining index for the period 1914–37. An index based on the Willett and Gray series was therefore constructed for the period 1899–1914 and spliced to our index for 1914. While it was often possible to obtain statistical series which might be expected to conform closely to our corresponding indexes, series which did in fact conform were seldom found.

Non-Census data were used mainly for the construction of indexes for industries for which no Census data at all were available. Bureau of Internal Revenue figures published in *The Annual Report of the Commissioner of Internal Revenue* were employed for the tobacco industries and for most of the beverage industries. In a few of these, as in the case of cigarettes, Census data also could be obtained for one or two years. In such instances index numbers based on data from both sources were constructed and compared. Data collected by the Bureau of Mines and published in the *Minerals Yearbook* were employed likewise. Sometimes the Census itself reproduced these data, as in the case of cement, but usually they were to be found only in the *Yearbook,* as was true for copper, lead and zinc. Whenever no source is mentioned in Appendix B, it may be assumed that the figures were collected in the Census of Manufactures; otherwise the source is specifically indicated in footnotes to the tables in that Appendix.

METHOD OF CONSTRUCTION OF THE INDEXES OF PHYSICAL OUTPUT

Formula and Bases

The aggregate physical volume of output in a given year may be defined as the output of that year evaluated at weight-base prices. Thus we multiply the number of tons of steel ingots produced for sale or shipment by steel mills in a given year (designated by q_1) by the price of steel ingots per ton in the weight-base period (p_w); do the same for steel sheets and for other products of steel mills; then add these computed values to obtain the physical output of steel mills. In algebraic language, this is $\Sigma q_1 p_w$. We secure these values for each year and, to compute the index of output, express them as relatives on a comparison-base period: $\Sigma q_1 p_w / \Sigma q_o p_w$. When the comparison base and weight base are identical, we have $\Sigma q_1 p_o / \Sigma q_o p_o$. When the weight base is the "given" year, we have $\Sigma q_1 p_1 / \Sigma q_o p_1$. A combination of both years as the weight base yields the Edgeworth formula, which we have used:

$$\frac{\Sigma q_1 (p_o + p_1)}{\Sigma q_o (p_o + p_1)}.$$

In short, to determine the change in physical output between any two years we use price coefficients taken from both years. The formula we employ gives results that fall between those yielded by the other two formulas cited.

According to the theory underlying the Edgeworth formula, a separate index number must be computed for each pair of years compared. Thus, if we wish to determine the changes in output between any two of the 14 Census years, 1899–1937, we require 91 separate index numbers. It is common experience, however, that only a minor degree of inaccuracy is likely to be introduced if the number of separate index numbers is reduced, and several comparisons are made indirectly. If only 13 index numbers were computed, say those comparing output in 1899 with output in each of the years 1904–37, comparisons of indexes for any other two years, e.g., 1904 and 1937, would be made by division of the 1937 index number (relative to 1899) by the 1904 index number (relative to 1899). Such a procedure would yield, in algebraic symbols,

$$\frac{\Sigma q_{37}(p_{99}+p_{37})}{\Sigma q_{99}(p_{99}+p_{37})} \div \frac{\Sigma q_{04}(p_{99}+p_{04})}{\Sigma q_{99}(p_{99}+p_{04})},$$

as an approximation to the desired index number,

$$\frac{\Sigma q_{37}(p_{04}+p_{37})}{\Sigma q_{04}(p_{04}+p_{37})}.$$

In this study we computed the following index numbers: 1899 and 1904 on a 1909 base; 1909 and 1914 on a 1919 base; and 1919 through 1937 on a 1929 base.[40] This selection proved helpful on two counts. First, it provided us with direct comparisons of 1899 with 1909, of 1909 with 1919, of 1919 with 1929, and of 1929 with 1937; we have used these comparisons in Parts One and Two of the text. Second, since the Census data usually increased progressively in detail, the use of 1909, 1919 and 1929 as successive bases enabled us to take advantage of the available detail. For the major groups of industries and for total manufacturing we com-

[40] Exceptions, made necessary by the character of the data in certain industries, are noted in Appendix B. The most common exception is the use of 1931 as a base for the 1933 index. For many industries the quantity data for 1933 are incomplete. Because of a smaller appropriation in that year the Bureau of the Census found it necessary to use an abridged schedule in canvassing the smaller establishments in many industries. The Bureau writes: "With a very few exceptions, the establishments in any industry for which this [the abridged] schedule was used did not contribute more than 10 percent of the total value of products for the industry, and in most cases the percentage was considerably smaller. So far as practicable, the data returned on the abridged schedule were distributed among the proper items in the tables giving detailed production statistics. . . . Where this could not be done, two sets of detailed production figures are given for 1931, one comparable with 1929 and the other adjusted for comparison with the 1933 figures derived from the standard schedules; or—especially in the cases of the less important industries—the total value of products reported on the abridged schedule for 1933 is carried as a single item at the end of the table and only one set of figures is given for 1931." (Census of Manufactures, 1933, p. 4.)

Where two sets of detailed production statistics were given for 1931, we treated that year as an additional base year. The 1933 index number we constructed on 1931, using the two sets of comparable figures; the 1931 index number we constructed on 1929, using the 1931 figures comparable with those of 1929; we then spliced the two segments together.

puted, in addition, index numbers comparing output in 1899 directly with output in 1937 (see below).

Computation of the Indexes for Individual Industries

The computation of the indexes for individual industries may be illustrated by reference to the 1929–31 index for cane-sugar refining.

The first step was the transcription in full detail of the quantities and values of individual products made in this industry in the most recent year, 1937 (taken from the Census of Manufactures, 1937), and the computation of average prices:

		1937
Refined sugar, hard		
Quantity	th. tons	4,251.3
Value	th. $	395,142
Price	$ per ton	92.946
Refined sugar, soft or brown		
Quantity	th. tons	264.30
Value	th. $	22,603
Price	$ per ton	85.520
Refiners' sirup, edible		
Quantity	th. gal.	2,735.5
Value	th. $	546.83
Price	¢ per gal.	19.990
Refiners' blackstrap and nonedible sirup		
Quantity	th. gal.	23,380
Value	th. $	1,399.0
Price	¢ per gal.	5.9837

On the basis of a study of this table, we could determine the amount of detail to be used in our computations. Because the prices of both types of refined sugar were close to each other, and because the two products appeared to be similar in character, we decided to combine their output into a single series for our index; and because the prices of the next two items were rather dissimilar, we decided not to combine them.[41]

A subsequent step was the assembly of products data in the degree of detail thus decided upon, for all available Census years.

[41] If one were making a detailed study of the output of the sugar industry he might, of course, find it more rewarding to distinguish between the two types of sugar—because of their importance—than between the two types of by-products—which are relatively unimportant. In the present study, however, it was necessary to combine similar products whenever possible (similarity being judged by character of product and by average price) in order to lessen the labor of calculation.

These are given in the basic table for cane-sugar refining in Appendix B, p. 387. We took the data from the latest Census volumes, working backwards: the 1937 volume for 1937–31 data; the 1931 report for 1931–27 data; and so on. The quantity and value data were given in the Census; we derived the per-unit values (indicated by p)[42] by dividing the values by the corresponding quantities.

Next, we combined the basic data into the unadjusted index, in accordance with the following form (showing 1929 and 1931 only):

	1931/1929	
	$q_{31}(p_{29}+p_{31})$	$q_{29}(p_{29}+p_{31})$
1 Refined sugar	827,270	955,306
2 Refiners' sirup, edible	1,444	1,835
3 Refiners' blackstrap and nonedible sirup	3,066	4,723
4 $\Sigma(1+2+3)$	831,780	961,864
5 Index, unadjusted	86.476	100.000
6 Coverage ratio	.99673	.99799
7 Coverage adjustment factor	.99874	1.00000
8 Index, adjusted (5÷7)	86.585	100.00

We computed the ratios of coverage by adding up the values of the three products shown and dividing their sum by the industry's total value of products. These ratios we then transformed into coverage adjustment factors by dividing by the base year ratio (.99673 ÷ .99799 = .99874). Next we divided the unadjusted index for 1931 (86.476) by the coverage adjustment factor, to derive the adjusted index (86.585). Finally we linked together the unadjusted and adjusted indexes on the various bases (1909, 1919 and 1929) and arrived at the indexes given in Appendix B.

The procedure illustrated above was followed whenever possible, but not invariably. Sometimes quantity data were reported for only part of the total output of a particular product, whereas value was reported both for this part and for the total. In such a case an additional step was introduced: we estimated the total quantity of the product by deriving a price obtained from the in-

[42] Although we use the symbol p and the term "price" for the per-unit value, it does not represent a price in a strict sense. It is the average realized price for the entire country's output, f.o.b. many different factories, of a class of goods which is sometimes rather heterogeneous.

complete figures and dividing this price into the total value. This, as well as other deviations from the procedure outlined, are noted in footnotes to the tables in Appendix B.

Adjustment for Changes in Coverage

The coverage adjustment requires further examination, particularly since there are three possible assumptions concerning the cause of a variation in coverage.

(1) It might be assumed that the prices of the goods not represented by physical quantity data have fluctuated in the same manner as the prices of the goods represented. If this were so, a decline or rise in the coverage of the index of output would be entirely the result of a decline or rise in the physical quantity of output of the represented goods in relation to the physical quantity of output of the unrepresented goods. Thus, a decline in coverage means that the index of output overstates the actual decline in the industry or understates the actual rise; and a rise in coverage means that the index understates the actual decline or overstates the actual rise. If the assumption concerning the identical price movements is valid, we can correct for the overstatement by deflating the unrepresented portion of the value of products of the industry by an index of the prices of the represented portion, and by then combining this physical output with the physical output of the represented portion; or we can follow an equivalent procedure and deflate the entire value of products of the industry by this price index. (The price index is obtained by division of the value relatives of the represented goods by the corresponding quantity indexes.) This adjustment, identical with Frederick C. Mills' adequacy adjustment,[43] may be accomplished easily by way of an algebraic short cut. The procedure is illustrated in the following hypothetical example, in which we assume that there has been no change in the true total output:

	1929	*1933*
1 Index of output based on selected products	100	70
2 Coverage ratio	.80	.56
3 Index of output adjusted for change in relation between the value of the selected products and the total value of products of the industry	100	100

[43] *Op. cit.*, pp. 90, 92–93.

The index of output based on partial coverage in 1929 and 1933 declined from 100 to 70. This drop represents merely a decline in the importance of certain of the products of the industry in relation to the other products. Such a movement must be eliminated. Knowing the change in the coverage, we can apply a correction factor to obtain an adjusted index. In the present example, this adjustment involves multiplication of the uncorrected index, 70, by the coverage adjustment factor, .80/.56.[44]

(2) A second assumption concerning the reason for changes in coverage is that the quantity of output of the unrepresented goods has changed in the same degree as the quantity of the represented goods. This would mean that the decline in the coverage of the index of output is a result entirely of a decline in the prices of the represented commodities relative to the prices of the unrepresented goods. It follows then that the computed index of output correctly reflects the movements of physical output of the entire industry. We need make no adjustment.

[44] The equivalence of this simplified procedure to the deflation process mentioned can be demonstrated algebraically. If the symbols p_1, p_0, q_1, q_0, are used in the usual sense, the simplified procedure involves the following operations. (The unprimed quantities relate to the represented commodities, the primed to the unrepresented commodities.)

(1) Index of output based on partial coverage, $\frac{\Sigma p_0 q_1}{\Sigma p_0 q_0}$.

(2) Coverage of index of output in current year, $\frac{\Sigma p_1 q_1}{\Sigma (p_1 q_1 + p'_1 q'_1)}$.

(3) Index of total output adjusted for change in coverage,

$$\frac{\Sigma p_0 q_1}{\Sigma p_0 q_0} \div \frac{\dfrac{\Sigma p_1 q_1}{\Sigma (p_1 q_1 + p'_1 q'_1)}}{\dfrac{\Sigma p_0 q_0}{\Sigma (p_0 q_0 + p'_0 q'_0)}}.$$

The deflation procedure involves the following operations:

(4) Index of output based on partial coverage, $\frac{\Sigma p_0 q_1}{\Sigma p_0 q_0}$.

(5) Index of prices of the covered items, $\frac{\Sigma p_1 q_1}{\Sigma p_0 q_0} \div \frac{\Sigma p_0 q_1}{\Sigma p_0 q_0}$.

(6) Index of total output adjusted for change in coverage,

$$\frac{\Sigma (p_1 q_1 + p'_1 q'_1)}{\Sigma (p_0 q_0 + p'_0 q'_0)} \div \left[\frac{\Sigma p_1 q_1}{\Sigma p_0 q_0} \div \frac{\Sigma p_0 q_1}{\Sigma p_0 q_0}\right].$$

It is clear that both procedures yield the same results: (3) and (6) are identical. This equality stands also if the Edgeworth or the Fisher ideal index formula is used.

This assumption is implicit when changes in the coverage ratio are ignored.

(3) Third, it might be assumed that both the quantity and the price of the group of unrepresented goods have behaved differently from the quantity and price of the represented goods. Any adjustment, therefore, must be adapted to the particular case and based on the widest possible survey of the facts. Thus, the value of products of an industry, say copper smelting and refining, may involve duplication, in the sense that the products (e.g., blister copper) made by establishments within that industry are sold for further processing (refining) to other establishments within that industry. The duplication, furthermore, may change in relative importance. Now if our index of physical volume of output is measured at one or the other stage of the process—blister copper or refined copper—then the coverage ratio will change merely because of a modification in the degree of duplication. In this case, no correction for the change in coverage is desirable; indeed, a complete coverage of *both* stages of production, with a coverage ratio of 1.00, will yield an incorrect index of physical volume which will have to be adjusted for the changing amount of duplication.

After considering the three possible assumptions outlined above, we decided that in the absence of specific and detailed knowledge the first was the least objectionable and we therefore adopted it for this study.[45] Its use is justified by the fact that prices probably move together within closer limits than do quantities, which may rise one-hundredfold or fall to zero. With but a few exceptions, we make the adjustment only when the coverage ratio in both years compared is at least .40, and in this way limit the possibility of error. For most industries the adjustment has only a slight effect upon the index. It scarcely needs to be repeated that expert knowledge of each industry might suggest other, less mechanical, methods of adjustment.

It is well to explore the implications of our use of the 40 percent minimum coverage. These implications can be brought out

[45] For a few industries, such as copper and automobiles, no adjustment for coverage was made, chiefly because of changes in the degree of duplication within the industries. These exceptions are noted in Appendix B.

if we make certain simplifying assumptions. Let us suppose that the ratio of coverage, *c,* remains constant between the two years compared, and let us use Laspeyres' formula, $\Sigma q_1 p_o / \Sigma q_o p_o$, to compute the output index. We define *k* as the ratio of the price index of the products for which we have quantity data (derived by division of the index of value by the index of output) to the price index of the products for which we do not have quantity data (similarly derived). Then the ratio, *r,* of the correct total to the estimated total (adjusted) quantity index, is $r = c + (1 - c)k$. The ratio, *r,* varies with *c* or *k*. If we limit *c,* then *r* depends only on *k;* i.e., the accuracy of the index is determined by the validity of the assumptions we make about *k*. This is the logical basis of the 40 percent minimum. Suppose we define a correct quantity index as one falling within 5 percent of the true index. Then to obtain at least the accuracy implied by this definition, values of *k* and *c* must satisfy the following inequality:

$$1.05 > c + (1 - c)\,k > .95.$$

Let us consider the .95 and 1.05 and the .90 and 1.10 lines; that is, the lines described by

$$c + (1 - c)\,k = .95 \text{ or } 1.05, \text{ and } c + (1 - c)k = .90 \text{ or } 1.10.$$

For these lines, we have:

c	*k* (r=.90)	*k* (r=.95)	*k* (r=1.05)	*k* (r=1.10)
.0	.90	.95	1.05	1.10
.1	.89	.94	1.06	1.11
.2	.88	.94	1.06	1.12
.3	.86	.93	1.07	1.14
.4	.83	.92	1.08	1.17
.5	.80	.90	1.10	1.20
.6	.75	.88	1.12	1.25
.7	.67	.83	1.17	1.33
.8	.50	.75	1.25	1.50
.9	0	.50	1.50	2.00
1.0	$-\infty$	$-\infty$	$+\infty$	$+\infty$

If the ratio of coverage is only .3, then the derived quantity index can be within 5 percent of the true index only if the value of *k* is not less than .93 or more than 1.07; i.e., the ratio of the price index of the covered products to the price index of the other products must not be less than .93 or more than 1.07. If the derived index is to come within 10 percent of the true indexes, the value of k must be between .86 and 1.14. For $c = .4$, so long as k lies between .92 and 1.08 our derived index will be correct within 5 percent, and if k lies between .83 and 1.17 it will be correct within 10 percent. It is clear that sometimes we shall be in error when we assume that an index based only on a 40 percent coverage reflects correctly the change in the total output of an industry.[46] We may point out in this connection some comforting considerations. First, only a few of the industries considered here are characterized by low coverage, as we have seen in Table A–6. Second, the indexes for industries with low coverage ratios are merely *subject* to error. The evidence at hand suggests that the dispersion of prices in general is not very large; and within industries we may expect even less dispersion.[47] The probability that values of k may differ widely from unity is therefore relatively slight,[48] though it is likely that as the period between the years compared increases, k also moves farther from unity.

The validity of the coverage adjustment was tested empirically (Table A–8, pp. 368–69). We sought to determine whether adjusted indexes based on low coverage tend to be more accurate than unadjusted indexes based on the same coverage. We took industries for which we had indexes (1937 relative to 1929) based on at least 80 percent coverage. These are listed in Table A–8, together with the percentage coverage (column 2). In lieu

[46] As was noted earlier (footnote 37, above), sometimes c exceeds unity because the secondary products of other industries cannot be separated from the primary products of the industry for which c is computed. Consequently, there should be imposed also an upper limit on c, which will lessen the probability of an incorrect index. However, because the number of industries for which c exceeds unity is small, we have ignored this possibility of error.

[47] Dr. Mills' measures of price dispersion (the approximate percentage limits, measured from the mean, within which 50 percent of the price relatives would fall if the distribution of price relatives were normal) range from 7.1 to 23.0 for fixed-base relatives, and from 5.4 to 18.0 for link relatives. (These are measured about the weighted arithmetic means in both cases.) The modal values of the measures are about 12 to 15 and 9 to 12, respectively. See F. C. Mills, *The Behavior of Prices* (National Bureau of Economic Research, 1927), pp. 257–59.

[48] It is difficult to be precise in this context because weights are used in the actual computation of our indexes, and because k is not entirely a matter of chance.

of other information we regarded the adjusted indexes (column 4) as the "correct" indexes for the industry in one set of our computations, and the unadjusted indexes (column 6) as the "correct" ones in a second set of computations. For these same industries we then computed new indexes based on low coverage, discarding sufficient data to reduce the coverage by at least 15 percent but not to fall below a coverage of 45 percent.[49] The "new" coverage is given in column 3 and the new indexes, adjusted and unadjusted, are shown in columns 5 and 7. We then computed our measures of accuracy of these new indexes: these appear in columns 8–11. The final comparisons between the degree of accuracy of the new adjusted indexes and the new unadjusted indexes are presented in the last two columns. In 37 of the 47 industries, the adjusted indexes based on low coverage are more accurate than the unadjusted indexes based on identically low coverage, if the adjusted index based on high coverage is taken to be the "correct" one. The proportion is 30 out of 47 if the unadjusted index based on high coverage is regarded as "correct." The evidence is clear that in most cases, although not in all, the adjusted indexes are more accurate than the unadjusted. Inspection of columns 8–11 reveals that the unadjusted indexes tend to be higher than the correct indexes (30 out of 47 are higher in one case and 32 out of 47 in the other), while the adjusted indexes are almost evenly divided (23 out of 47 being higher in one case and 22 out of 47 in the other). The magnitudes of the percentage differences given in columns 8–11 are large for some industries, but no frequency distribution for all the industries may be worked out since the original percentage coverages vary, as do also the new percentage coverages (columns 2 and 3). For the 5 industries with an original coverage of 90–94.9 percent and a reduced coverage of 55–59.9 percent, the percentage differences between the new adjusted and the old adjusted indexes are +4.7, +3.2, −2.9, −1.9, and −1.8. The percentage differences between the new unadjusted and the old adjusted indexes are −4.2, +23.6, +5.9, +32.3 and −8.3.

[49] We discarded the less important items, such as by-products, because when coverage is small the quantity of the chief products is usually reported by the Census.

TABLE A–8

SELECTED MANUFACTURING INDUSTRIES

Comparison of Accuracy of Adjusted and Unadjusted Indexes of Physical Output

(1)	(2)	(3)	(4)	(5)	(6)	(7)
Industry	Percentage Coverage in 1937		Index, Adjusted (1937 on 1929 as 100)		Index, Unadjusted (1937 on 1929 as 100)	
	Old	New	Old	New	Old	New
Meat packing	89.7	50.9	93.8	103.0	89.2	101.1
Shortenings	91.9	58.2	147.8	154.8	141.8	141.6
Milk, canned	103.8	65.1	128.1	128.1	126.9	137.7
Cheese	102.4	69.4	128.8	128.0	131.0	127.9
Fish, canned	86.8	51.6	103.7	102.9	99.6	107.7
Flour	96.7	72.1	85.8	84.6	84.6	87.7
Macaroni	99.6	78.5	122.7	118.4	122.8	113.2
Chocolate	99.6	78.3	123.5	123.6	124.0	119.1
Ice cream	101.8	85.1	109.0	108.4	109.7	96.1
Cotton goods	87.4	58.9	98.9	97.6	102.9	103.4
Hats, fur-felt	97.4	66.2	100.0	101.6	104.3	96.9
Carpets and rugs, wool	86.5	57.8	92.4	82.2	87.1	119.3
Linoleum	83.0	56.3	82.7	85.6	80.6	95.3
Asphalted-felt-base floor covering	105.8	54.7	144.1	161.1	131.5	126.1
Clothing, women's, n.e.c.	81.8	58.3	124.7	130.6	117.0	105.7
Corsets	98.9	50.8	129.4	131.2	134.8	156.0
Hats, wool-felt	86.6	62.5	256.0	310.4	249.9	485.0
Linen goods	93.9	55.4	77.2	79.7	89.6	95.4
Artificial leather	81.5	47.1	118.1	123.2	104.2	86.5
Handkerchiefs	95.2	54.1	85.6	78.3	84.4	85.2
Hosiery, knit	97.3	63.1	114.6	118.2	113.5	128.6
Boxes, wooden, cigar	90.7	67.2	82.9	85.0	79.9	89.6
Turpentine and rosin	99.6	76.6	80.6	70.0	85.4	86.5
Caskets and coffins	85.6	60.7	104.1	98.2	108.0	94.3
Wood-distillation products	84.1	63.4	101.3	77.4	99.1	119.7
Paper	92.7	56.8	115.2	111.9	114.3	122.0
Pulp	90.3	56.1	141.0	138.3	137.3	186.6
Soap	82.8	63.9	109.0	108.8	109.2	115.0
Linseed products	89.9	66.2	86.0	77.9	83.5	86.1
Glue and gelatin	91.7	61.9	138.7	130.4	128.6	115.6
Gases, compressed	107.4	64.7	138.1	139.4	143.3	154.2
Explosives	83.8	60.3	92.8	93.9	89.6	93.4
Fertilizers	88.6	65.8	105.9	104.7	98.0	94.8
Paints and varnishes	98.6	58.6	109.0	102.1	109.5	120.7
Clocks, watches and materials	81.8	52.3	139.2	180.6	152.0	212.0
Roofing	83.5	62.7	110.4	100.5	100.9	83.2
Tin cans and tinware, n.e.c.	89.5	51.6	160.2	152.8	153.0	163.9
Shoes, leather	89.1	56.5	112.3	118.3	109.5	113.0
Shoes, rubber	90.4	56.5	95.1	93.4	79.2	87.2
Petroleum refining	97.4	57.7	119.2	131.8	117.6	124.7
Coke-oven products	96.3	62.6	87.3	81.7	89.1	91.1
Clay products, n.e.c.	83.7	61.8	65.7	62.2	60.6	58.0
Cast-iron pipe	108.3	58.6	68.5	78.1	69.3	94.3
Scales and balances	90.0	63.3	86.9	108.2	106.3	127.3
Carriages and sleds, children's	82.3	62.3	88.7	92.9	98.2	108.3
Pianos	90.2	48.3	66.0	67.3	73.1	110.9
Brooms	105.2	77.8	81.4	82.6	87.4	78.9

(8)	(9)	(10)	(11)	(12)	(13)
Percentage Difference from Old Adjusted Index		*Percentage Difference from Old Unadjusted Index*		*Comparison between New Adjusted and New Unadjusted Indexes: Difference between Absolute Percentage Differences*	
New Adjusted	New Unadjusted	New Adjusted	New Unadjusted	|(8)| − |(9)|	|(10)| − |(11)|
+9.8	+7.8	+15.5	+13.3	+2.0	+2.2
+4.7	−4.2	+9.2	−0.1	+0.5	+9.1
0	+7.5	+0.9	+8.5	−7.5	−7.6
−0.6	−0.7	−2.3	−2.4	−0.1	−0.1
−0.8	+3.9	+3.3	+8.1	−3.1	−4.8
−1.4	+2.2	0	+3.7	−0.8	−3.7
−3.5	−7.7	−3.6	−7.8	−4.2	−4.2
+0.1	−3.6	−0.3	−4.0	−3.5	−3.7
−0.6	−11.8	−1.2	−12.4	−11.2	−11.2
−1.3	+4.6	−5.2	+0.5	−3.3	+4.7
+1.6	−3.1	−2.6	−7.1	−1.5	−4.5
−11.0	+29.1	−5.6	+37.0	−18.1	−31.4
+3.5	+15.2	+6.2	+18.2	−11.7	−12.0
+11.8	−12.5	+22.5	−4.1	−0.7	+18.4
+4.7	−15.2	+11.6	−9.7	−10.5	+1.9
+1.4	+20.6	−2.7	+15.7	−19.2	−13.0
+21.2	+89.5	+24.2	+94.1	−68.3	−69.9
+3.2	+23.6	−11.0	+6.5	−20.4	+4.5
+4.3	−26.8	+18.2	−17.0	−22.5	+1.2
−8.5	−0.5	−7.2	+0.9	+8.0	+6.3
+3.1	+12.2	+4.1	+13.3	−9.1	−9.2
+2.5	+8.1	+6.4	+12.1	−5.6	−5.7
−13.2	+7.3	−18.0	+1.3	−5.9	+16.7
−5.7	−9.4	−9.1	−12.7	−3.7	−3.6
−23.6	+18.2	−21.9	+20.8	+5.4	+1.1
−2.9	+5.9	−2.1	+6.7	−3.0	−4.6
−1.9	+32.3	+0.7	+35.9	−30.4	−35.2
−0.2	+5.5	−0.4	+5.3	−5.3	−4.9
−9.4	+0.1	−6.7	+3.1	+9.3	+3.6
−6.0	−16.7	+1.4	−10.1	−10.7	−8.7
+0.9	+11.7	−2.7	+7.6	−10.8	−4.9
+1.2	+0.6	+4.8	+4.2	+0.6	+0.6
−1.1	−10.5	+6.8	−3.3	−9.4	+3.5
−6.3	+10.7	−6.8	+10.2	−4.4	−3.4
+29.7	+52.3	+18.8	+39.5	−22.6	−20.7
−9.0	−24.6	−0.4	−17.5	−15.6	−17.1
−4.6	+2.3	−0.1	+7.1	+2.3	−7.0
+5.3	+0.6	+8.0	+3.2	+4.7	+4.8
−1.8	−8.3	+17.9	+10.1	−6.5	+7.8
+10.6	+4.6	+12.1	+6.0	+6.0	+6.1
−6.4	+4.4	−8.3	+2.2	+2.0	+6.1
−5.3	−11.7	+2.6	−4.3	−6.4	−1.7
+14.0	+37.7	+12.7	+36.1	−23.7	−23.4
+24.5	+46.5	+1.8	+19.8	−22.0	−18.0
+4.7	+22.1	−5.4	+10.3	−17.4	−4.9
+2.0	+68.0	−7.9	+51.7	−66.0	−43.8
+1.5	−3.1	−5.5	−9.7	−1.6	−4.2

Computation of the Indexes for Major Groups and for the Total

The method of computation of the major group indexes is identical, in principle, with that for individual industries. The component series used were the adjusted indexes for the industries comprising the group, or the unadjusted indexes, if adjusted indexes were not available. Instead of value of products per unit of product, the price coefficient was value added per unit. To avoid unnecessary computation we employed the following formula, in which Q is the given year index (on the base year as 100) for each individual industry, V_1 is the value added in the given year, and V_0 is the value added in the base year: $\frac{\Sigma (V_1 + QV_0)}{\Sigma (V_0 + \frac{V_1}{Q})}$. This formula yields results identical with those obtained by the usual form of the Edgeworth formula. The index derived by such combination of the adjusted individual industry indexes is the *unadjusted* index for the group. This index, of course, is based on a sample only: its coverage is incomplete and changing in amount, as the coverage ratios collected in Appendix B will show.[50] Adjustment identical in principle with that used for the individual industry indexes yields the adjusted indexes.

For two groups, machinery and miscellaneous products, no index was computed for any year; and for a few other groups, no index was computed for certain years. The reason in all instances was inadequacy of coverage (under 40 percent).

We computed an unadjusted index for total manufacturing by using the available adjusted group indexes and the adjusted industry indexes for the few industries (machinery and others) for which no group indexes were available. This index was then adjusted for changes in coverage. For checking purposes we computed an additional set of indexes for all industries combined. In this supplementary computation we used the adjusted individual industry indexes (rather than the group indexes) to obtain the unadjusted index for total manufacturing, and then

[50] In a few groups of industries the coverage is complete.

made an adjustment for changing coverage to obtain the adjusted index for total manufacturing. The two sets of indexes are presented in Appendix B.

In these adjustments of the total indexes for changes in coverage of the underlying samples there is implied a relationship between changes in value added and in physical output. In Chapter 5 we noted that the relationship in our sample was both close and significant.[51] We must assume, of course, a corresponding relationship for industries not in the sample; i.e., we must take the sample to be representative of the entire population of industries in respect of the relation between changes in value added and in physical output. Such an assumption appears reasonable. Examination of the sample does not suggest that those included industries which may be considered similar in character to the industries not in the sample are different, in this particular respect, from the other industries included. For major industrial divisions the adjustment is less easily justified; too few series are available for individual groups to invest the empirical test with appreciable significance.[52] We must simply assume that for each industrial division changes in value added are closely related to changes in physical output. We have made this assumption reluctantly and offer the results without claiming great accuracy for them. We believe, however, that the adjusted group indexes are probably better estimates than the unadjusted group indexes.[53]

[51] The correlation noted in Chapter 5 relates to the indexes for 1937 on the 1899 base. Similar correlations were calculated for other periods: 1909 relative to 1899, 1919 relative to 1909, 1929 relative to 1919, and 1937 relative to 1929. In all, the coefficients were fairly high: none fell below .6.

[52] A related difficulty lies in the fact that the empirical test ignores the importance of the industries covered. This is not a serious matter when we test our entire sample, but it is important for a test of group samples, in which the number of items is small.

[53] The adjustment does more than correct for the bias of a limited sample. It tends to avoid another common fault of indexes, which may be illustrated by reference to the data on forest products. For 1923 we have indexes for only two of the industries in the group—lumber-mill products and turpentine and rosin. The weighted average of these two indexes, on 1929 as 100, is 98.4. For 1925, we have indexes for four industries, the two mentioned plus planing-mill products and excelsior. The average of these four indexes, on 1929 as 100, is 108.5. If we compare 1923 and 1925 by means of these unadjusted indexes we find a change of 10 percent between the two years. The question arises whether this result does not reflect mainly the fact that the 1925 index for planing-mill products was on a relatively high level (ex-

Our adjustment is derived from that employed by F. C. Mills[54] for the adjustment of his index of total manufacturing output. We have extended its use to individual groups as well as to the total; and have adopted as its basis value added alone, whereas Mills uses number of wage earners as well. An alternative method of passing from indexes based on a sample of manufacturing industries to an index representative of total manufacturing involves the use of imputed weights.[55] According to such a procedure the unadjusted index for a given group is not corrected for changing coverage, but when it is combined with other indexes into a grand average it is given the weight of the entire group to which it refers, including the industries it fails to cover. Here too are involved several assumptions; in this particular procedure the assumptions relate to the ratio of materials consumed per unit of gross output, imports and exports of semimanufactured goods, and changes in inventories of semimanufactured goods. These assumptions seem less valid than those underlying our own adjustment.

Still another method of covering the output of industries for which data on physical volume cannot be obtained is to deflate their value of products by suitable price indexes. However, very few indexes of prices of homogeneous products of these industries are available. It is true that the adjustment we have used is similar in principle to the deflation process mentioned, but there is a fundamental difference also: we do not present indexes for the individual industries not included in our sample. Our objective has been to estimate the aggregate, including the indexes for the industries not covered, rather than the individual indexes themselves. In view of the nature of the available data this approach seems the more defensible of the two.

---

celsior may be disregarded because of its slight importance). The indexes of the two industries for which we have data for both 1923 and 1925 rose only 7 and 3 percent respectively. This ambiguity in the 1923–25 comparison of the *unadjusted* indexes cannot be avoided except by construction of a new index that compares the two years directly. The ambiguity is obviated, however, by the *adjusted* indexes, which are designed to represent the movements of the *entire* forest products group and therefore do not suffer from incomparabilities arising from changes in the size of the sample.

[54] *Economic Tendencies*, pp. 39–43.

[55] See E. E. Day and Woodlief Thomas, *Growth of Manufactures, 1899 to 1923*, pp. 101–02. This index is described below, in Appendix D.

Since our indexes are relatively short links, which must be chained together for long-period comparisons, a question arises concerning the results that might have been obtained if we had constructed indexes comparing directly years that are far apart.

TABLE A–9

INDEX NUMBERS OF PHYSICAL OUTPUT, 1937 RELATIVE TO 1899

Direct Comparisons and Chains of Three Series of Indexes on Different Bases

Group	*Direct Indexes*		*Chained Indexes*		*Ratio of Chained to Direct Indexes*	
	Unadjusted	Adjusted	Unadjusted	Adjusted	Unadjusted	Adjusted
Foods	257	354	256	344	1.00	0.97
Beverages	200	243	189	232	0.95	0.95
Tobacco products	375	375	393	393	1.05	1.05
Textile products	245	273	253	280	1.03	1.03
Leather products	176	171	175	169	0.99	0.99
Paper products	618	667	616	667	1.00	1.00
Printing and publishing[a]	594	594	594	594	1.00	1.00
Chemical products	830	643	796	666	0.96	1.04
Petroleum and coal products	1,365	1,183	1,508	1,306	1.10	1.10
Forest products	68	94	67	93	0.99	0.99
Iron and steel products	388	419	394	427	1.02	1.02
Transportation equipment	959	849	1,286	1,242	1.34	1.46
Total manufacturing	338	363	339	376	1.00	1.04

[a] The index for this group is based on a single series which represents the entire group output.

In order to answer this question we constructed special indexes, unadjusted and adjusted, for groups as well as for total manufacturing, comparing 1899 and 1937 directly with each other.[56] These are shown in Table A–9, where they are also compared with the chained indexes. The differences found are relatively

[56] In computing these direct indexes we assumed that the indexes of individual industries were fully comparable for any pair of years covered; in fact, however, the indexes for individual industries are also chains of links for the various periods.

slight except for the transportation equipment group. Here the differences between the direct and indirect unadjusted and adjusted indexes are 34 and 46 percent, respectively. For all manufacturing industries combined, the two unadjusted indexes are close to each other, and the two adjusted indexes are less than 5 percent apart.

The indexes for total manufacturing given in Table A–9 are those obtained by a combination of the adjusted group indexes. The indexes derived by combination of the adjusted indexes of individual industries are as follows:

Indexes	*Direct*	*Chained*	*Ratio of Chained to Direct Indexes*
Unadjusted	371	354	0.95
Adjusted	418	416	1.00

Here also we find substantial correspondence between the direct and indirect indexes.

BUSINESS-CYCLE PHASES COVERED BY THE CENSUS YEARS

The detailed data we have assembled on production relate to quinquennial and biennial Census years. The picture they draw of the entire 1899–1937 period is necessarily incomplete, because they fail to depict the developments in the years for which we have no data and to show the relation of the years covered to those for which no information is available. They cannot be interpreted intelligently, therefore, without some description of the setting from which they are taken. That background is sketched in broad outline in Table A–10, which shows the relative position of the several Census years in the business cycles of the period.

The period 1899–1937 is characterized by two severe business cycles, 1920–23 and 1929–37; and by eight comparatively mild cycles, with troughs in 1900, 1904, 1908, 1911, 1914, 1919, 1924 and 1927. Five of the Census years contain cyclical troughs, four contain peaks, four are years of expansion and one is a year of contraction.

TABLE A–10

CYCLICAL POSITION OF GENERAL BUSINESS IN THE UNITED STATES

Calendar Years 1899–1938 [a]

Stage of Cycle	*Calendar Year*
Peak	1899
Mid-contraction	1899–1900
Trough	1900
Mid-expansion	1901–1902
Peak	1903
Mid-contraction	1903–1904
Trough	1904
Mid-expansion	1905–1906
Peak	1907
Mid-contraction	1907–1908
Trough	1908
Mid-expansion	1909
Peak	1910
Mid-contraction	1910–1911
Trough	1911
Mid-expansion	1912
Peak	1913
Mid-contraction	1913–1914
Trough	1914
Mid-expansion	1915–1916–1917
Peak	1918
Mid-contraction	1918–1919
Trough	1919
Mid-expansion	1919–1920
Peak	1920
Mid-contraction	1920–1921
Trough	1921
Mid-expansion	1922
Peak	1923
Mid-contraction	1923–1924
Trough	1924
Mid-expansion	1925
Peak	1926
Mid-contraction	1926–1927
Trough	1927
Mid-expansion	1928
Peak	1929
Mid-contraction	1930–1931
Trough	1932
Mid-expansion	1934–1935
Peak	1937
Mid-contraction	1937–1938
Trough	1938

[a] Taken from unpublished data compiled at the National Bureau of Economic Research by W. C. Mitchell and A. F. Burns.

Appendix B

Indexes of Physical Output, with Basic Data on Quantity, Value and Price of Products, Census Years, 1899–1937

Appendix B

Indexes of Physical Output, with Basic Data on Quantity, Value and Price of Products, Census Years, 1899–1937

EXPLANATORY NOTE

This appendix consists of a set of tables giving unadjusted and adjusted indexes of the physical output of individual manufacturing industries, of major groups of manufacturing industries, and of all manufacturing industries combined; and basic underlying data on the quantity, value and price of the products of the individual industries.

The method of construction of the indexes has been described briefly in Chapter 2 and in detail in Appendix A. The basic data on products are presented in a form as detailed as that used in the computation of the indexes. Footnotes to the tables indicate the percentages of coverage in each industry (the aggregate value of the products included in the computation of the indexes, expressed as a percentage of the total value of the products of the industry), specify the base-periods used in the computation of the indexes,[1] and mention incomparabilities, gaps and other limitations of the data. The data on products listed for an industry cover not only the output of the industry concerned but also the output of the same commodities in other industries, unless otherwise noted.[2]

The quantities of output of some products, as the footnotes indicate, are "estimated in part." In such cases the quantity of only a portion of a particular product was reported, and the entire quantity of the product was estimated by division of the entire value of the product by the average price of the portion of the product for which the quantity was reported. Occasionally the estimate was worked out in this way by the Bureau of the Census itself.

In most instances we give values in millions of dollars, with a sufficient number of decimals to provide at least 3 significant figures.

[1] We chose the years 1909, 1919 and 1929 as base-periods, except when the nature of the available data made it necessary or more convenient to use other years.

[2] See Appendix A for a discussion of "primary" and "secondary" products.

Quantities and average prices also are shown with a sufficient number of decimals to provide at least 3 significant figures. In our original computations we used 5 significant figures.

In the 1933 Census a short schedule was used for small establishments in many industries, and as a consequence the 1933 data on their products are not altogether complete. Since the Bureau of the Census published two sets of 1931 data for these industries, one complete and comparable with the data for all years except 1933, and one incomplete and comparable with the data for 1933, we computed the 1933 index on the 1931 base and spliced it to the 1931 index on the 1929 base. The 1933 figures, and the 1931 figures comparable with them, were published by the Bureau of the Census in round thousands; for this reason some of these data are expressed in our tables in a fewer number of significant figures than are the data for other years.

The tabulations for individual industries are arranged by industrial groups and are presented in alphabetical order within each group. A table at the end of all but two groups gives the adjusted and unadjusted group indexes and the underlying percentages of coverage. The exceptions are machinery and miscellaneous products, for which no adequate group indexes could be computed. The value added weights, which we have used in combining the indexes of individual industries in order to derive the group indexes, appear in Appendix C, below.

The last tabulation in this appendix presents the adjusted and unadjusted indexes for all manufacturing industries combined, computed in two different ways, with notes on percentages of coverage.

The following abbreviations recur frequently both in the tables and in the footnotes to them:

n.e.c.	not elsewhere classified
n.e.m.	not elsewhere made
n.e.d.	not elsewhere done
q	physical quantity of product
v	value of product
p	value of product per unit of physical quantity $(v \div q)$
th.	thousand
mil.	million
bil.	billion
gr.	gross
t.	ton
l.t.	long ton
c.	case

std.c.	standard case
lin.	linear
sq.	square
ea.	each
pr.	pair
b.m.	board measure
equiv.	equivalent

Other abbreviations, such as lb., gal., yd., doz., bbl., are used in the customary sense. Long tons are specified as indicated above; all other references to tons apply to short tons, or to tons not defined by the Census.

FOODS

Indexes of Physical Output, with Basic Data on Quantity, Value and Price of Products

BAKING POWDER		1927	1929	1931	1933	1935	1937
Adjusted index		88.4	100.0	96.4	73.5	73.0	63.3
Unadjusted index[a]		85.4	100.0	93.2	70.5	72.0	68.6
Product	*Item*						
Baking powder	q Mil. lb.	163		170	147	160	142
	v Mil. $	30.7		22.7	17.0	15.0	15.4
	p $ per lb.	.189	q 541	.134	.116	.0940	.109
			v 49.9				
Yeast and other leavening compounds	q Mil. lb.	288	p .0923	335	214	210	216
	v Mil. $	20.6		20.7	12.3	15.4	15.9
	p $ per lb.	.0714		.0617	.0572	.0734	.0736

(The 1929 figures q 541, v 49.9, p .0923 cover both products combined, as bracketed; the 1927 and 1931 figures are likewise bracketed.)

[a] Percentages of coverage: Given year 1927: 92.1, 1929: 95.4, 1933: 91.6 — Base year 1931: 92.3; Given year 1935: 94.1, 1937: 103.5 — Base year 1931: 92.3

BEET SUGAR		1899	1904	1909	1914	1919	1921	1923	1925	1927	1929	1931	1933	1935	1937
Adjusted index		6.7	22.6	45.4	68.5	67.4	96.2	68.5	100.5	83.7	100.0	107.0	151.4	111.3	119.8
Unadjusted index[a]		7.0	23.8	47.3	70.0	67.6	96.2	70.4	101.7	83.7	100.0	107.5	152.4	111.4	119.9
Product[b]	*Item*														
Sugar, granulated	q Th. t.	57.8	248	497	739	719	1,023	749	1,076	893	1,068	1,156	1,626	1,178	1,286
	v Mil. $	5.58	23.5	45.6	58.4	138	128	112	124	98.1	100	81.5	121	88.8	99.6
	p $ per t.	96.5	94.6	91.9	78.9	192	125	150	115	110	93.8	70.5	74.3	75.3	77.4
Sugar, unfinished	q Th. t.	23.9	5.61	4.88	4.24	2.49	6.72	5.01	7.27	6.18	17.8	9.32	10.5	8.12	10.5
	v Mil. $	1.64	.431	.292	.239	.247	.722	.409	.388	.443	.518	.338	.360	.345	.434
	p $ per t.	68.7	76.8	59.9	56.4	99.4	107	81.7	53.3	71.7	29.1	36.3	34.2	42.5	41.2

BEET SUGAR (concluded)		1899	1904	1909	1914	1919	1921	1923	1925	1927	1929	1931	1933	1935	1937
Product[b]	*Item*														
Molasses	*q* Th. t.[d]	20.8	56.2	122	155	110	158	105	143[c]	76.4	77.8	86.5	175	87.9	93.8
	v Mil. $	.0484[e]	.221	1.13	1.54	2.36	2.36	1.29	2.25	.692	1.17	.394	.877	.797	1.07
	p $ per t.	2.33	3.93	9.28	9.93	21.5	15.0	12.3	15.7	9.06	15.0	4.55	5.01	9.06	11.4
Beet pulp, dried, excl. molasses pulp	*q* Th. t.								134	79.2	87.5	83.8	133	132	42.7
	v Mil. $								3.27	1.97	2.13	.984	1.83	1.53	1.09
	p $ per t.								24.4	24.9	24.3	11.7	13.8	11.6	25.4
Beet pulp, moist[f]	*q* Mil. t.								1.36	1.15	1.30	1.21	1.75	1.28	1.62
	v Mil. $								.823	.996	1.12	.904	.870	.928	1.23
	p $ per t.								.604	.862	.866	.749	.496	.724	.757
Molasses pulp	*q* Th. t.								54.5	73.8	75.7	85.2	130	133	158
	v Mil. $								1.44	1.44	1.98	.945	1.52	1.73	2.74
	p $ per t.								26.4	19.6	26.2	11.1	11.7	13.0	17.3

[a] Percentages of coverage:

Given year	Base year	Given year	Base year	Given year	Base year	Given year	Base year
1899:99.3	1909:97.8	1914:96.0	1919:94.2	1923:96.4	1929:93.9	1933:99.3	1929:98.7
1904:99.0	1909:97.8	1919:94.2	1929:93.9	1925:99.9	1929:98.7	1935:98.9	1929:98.7
1909:97.8	1919:94.2	1921:94.0	1929:93.9	1927:98.8	1929:98.7	1937:98.8	1929:98.7
				1931:99.3	1929:98.7		

[b] Figures for 1931 to 1937 were requested by the U.S. Bureau of the Census for the seasons beginning in the respective Census years, and for earlier Census years for the seasons ending in those years. Thus the figure given for 1931 applies to the season 1931–32, whereas the figure for 1921 refers to the season 1920–21. In 1925, 1927 and 1929, however, some of the establishments in the beet sugar industry reported for the seasons 1925–26, 1927–28 and 1929–30, instead of 1924–25, 1926–27 and 1928–29.

[c] Because of a change in the method of reporting molasses, the figures for 1925 and earlier years are not strictly comparable with those for 1927 and later years.

[d] Reported in gallons, 1899–1923; converted to tons calculated at 171 gallons per ton.

[e] Estimated in part.

[f] The figures for 1927–37 include data for a small quantity of pressed beet pulp.

Indexes of Physical Output, with Basic Data on Quantity, Value and Price of Products

BISCUITS and CRACKERS		*1923*	*1925*	*1927*	*1929*	*1931*	*1933*	*1935*	*1937*
Adjusted index		81.4	85.6	91.4	100.0	85.5	77.8	95.5	105.9
Unadjusted index[a]		84.4	86.3	91.9	100.0	85.4	77.9	96.6	106.9
Product	*Item*								
Biscuits, crackers, and cookies	*q* Mil. lb.	1,120	1,167	1,243	1,323	1,115	1,011	1,260	1,407
	v Mil. $	208	238	241	259	196	137	171	197
	p $ per lb.	.186	.204	.194	.196	.176	.136	.136	.140
Bread, rolls, and coffee cake	*q* Mil. lb.	9.13	30.3	25.2	22.1	48.0	35.2	39.1	37.3
	v Mil. $	.662	2.32	1.78	1.54	2.05	1.74	2.39	2.38
	p $ per lb.	.0726	.0765	.0707	.0699	.0426	.0493	.0611	.0639
Pretzels	*q* Mil. lb.		.688	8.54	43.9	44.2	48.9	56.8	48.2
	v Mil. $		.108	1.69	7.01	6.25	7.00	6.44	5.35
	p $ per lb.		.157	.198	.160	.141	.143	.114	.111
Doughnuts, crullers, and other fried cakes	*q* Th. doz.				699	289	396	153	834
	v Th. $				140	52.2	71.6	23.0	99.0
	p $ per doz.				.200	.181	.181	.151	.119

[a] Percentages of coverage:

Given year	Base year	Given year	Base year
1923:98.5	1929:95.0	1933:97.7	1929:97.6
1925:98.3	1929:97.5	1935:98.7	1929:97.6
1927:98.2	1929:97.5	1937:98.5	1929:97.6
1931:97.5	1929:97.6		

BREAD and CAKE		*1923*	*1925*	*1927*	*1929*	*1931*	*1933*	*1935*	*1937*
Adjusted index		75.3	78.0	89.5	100.0	92.1	73.6	86.4	95.5
Unadjusted index[a]		76.6	82.7	92.8	100.0	92.2	80.3	91.0	98.7
Product[b]	*Item*								
Bread, rolls, and coffee cake	*q* Bil. lb.	8.44	8.99	10.16	11.00	10.21	8.94	9.89	10.58
	v Mil. $	631	730	803	850	668	577	752	841
	p $ per lb.	.0747	.0812	.0791	.0773	.0655	.0646	.0760	.0795

BREAD and CAKE (concluded)		1923	1925	1927	1929	1931	1933	1935	1937
Product[b]	*Item*								
Biscuits, crackers,	*q* Mil. lb.	12.9	37.9	14.7	29.2	24.6	36.8	67.7	103
and cookies	*v* Mil. $	1.89	6.15	2.76	4.81	3.06	4.71	8.79	15.6
	p $ per lb.	.146	.162	.188	.165	.125	.128	.130	.152
Doughnuts, crullers, and	*q* Mil. doz.				224	184	129	217	273
other fried cakes	*v* Mil. $				44.7	33.8	22.5	36.0	47.0
	p $ per doz.				.200	.184	.175	.166	.172
Pretzels	*q* Mil. lb.		33.1	36.3	1.61	1.07	.892	3.31	2.28
	v Mil. $		5.92	6.13	.300	.189	.135	.514	.414
	p $ per lb.		.179	.169	.187	.177	.151	.155	.182

[a] Percentages of coverage:

Given year	Base year	Given year	Base year
1923:69.4, 1925:72.5, 1927:70.9	1929:68.3	1933:78.5, 1935:75.7, 1937:74.3	1929:71.9
1931:72.0	1929:71.9		

[b] Detailed data on products were not reported by all establishments. Estimates of the products of all establishments were made by us for 1925–37 and by the Bureau of the Census for 1923 according to the following procedure: the percentages that the value of products of establishments reporting detailed data constituted of the total value of products of the entire industry were computed, and these percentages were then divided into the reported detailed data. The percentages are: 79.3 for 1923; 81.1 for 1925; 86.2 for 1927; 89.5 for 1929; 88.6 for 1931; 91.4 for 1933; 93.7 for 1935; and 94.4 for 1937.

BUTTER		1899	1904	1909	1914	1919	1921	1923	1925	1927	1929	1931	1933	1935	1937
Adjusted index		[b]	32.6	39.7	50.2	60.0	71.8	84.4	91.5	97.2	100.0	101.9	109.8	104.4	105.0
Unadjusted index[a]		26.0	33.0	38.8	48.2	58.0	69.9	81.6	90.0	96.7	100.0	102.3	107.8	102.2	102.3
Product	*Item*														
Butter,	*q* Mil. lb.	420	533	627	780	939	1,132	1,320	1,456	1,564	1,618	1,656	1,744	1,653	1,655
creamery	*v* Mil. $	84.1	114	180	221	533	443	586	637	696	707	441	358	465	544
and whey	*p* $ per lb.	.200	.213	.287	.284	.568	.391	.444	.437	.445	.437	.266	.205	.281	.329

[a] Percentages of coverage:

Given year	Base year	Given year	Base year	Given year	Base year	Given year	Base year
1904:95.9	1909:92.4	1919:91.5, 1921:92.3, 1923:91.5	1929:94.7	1925:93.1, 1927:94.1, 1931:95.1	1929:94.7	1933:92.9, 1935:92.7, 1937:92.3	1929:94.7
1909:92.4, 1914:90.9	1919:91.5						

[b] No adjusted index for 1899 could be computed because the industry is not shown separately in the Census for that year. The adjusted index given above, extrapolated by the unadjusted index, is 25.7 for 1899.

Indexes of Physical Output, with Basic Data on Quantity, Value and Price of Products

CANE SUGAR, not elsewhere made		1899	1904	1909	1914	1919	1921	1923	1925	1927	1929	1931	1933	1935	1937
Adjusted index				167.9	132.5	124.7	129.2	87.5	68.9	36.3	100.0	91.2	124.8	173.6	192.1
Unadjusted index[a]		122.8[c]	120.1[c]	178.9	147.1	134.0	134.2	91.1	70.6	36.4	100.0	91.5	124.9	173.2	192.3
Product[b]	*Item*														
Sugar	*q* Th. t.			327	265	225	260	170	116	56.5	180	176	237	351	392
	v Mil. $			26.1	18.9	46.7	20.4	22.9	9.67	5.12	13.8	11.7	15.3	23.1	25.7
	p $ per t.			79.8	71.6	207	78.6	135	83.3	90.5	76.5	66.4	64.5	65.8	65.6
Sirup	*q* Mil. gal.			1.45	2.42	6.74	2.33	3.36	5.70	3.89	4.63	3.55	3.40	3.44	2.95
	v Mil. $			.366	.610	4.19	.682	1.55	1.77	1.34	1.34	.924	.869	.864	.911
	p $ per gal.			.252	.252	.622	.292	.459	.310	.345	.290	.260	.255	.251	.309
Molasses, other than blackstrap	*q* Mil. gal.			24.6	20.7	20.1	9.65	6.11	5.52	3.28	7.96	5.10	8.07	5.44	4.30
	v Mil. $			2.85	2.02	4.87	1.31	1.83	1.13	.927	1.37	.761	1.04	.664	.533
	p $ per gal.			.116	.0978	.243	.136	.300	.205	.282	.172	.149	.130	.122	.124
Blackstrap molasses	*q* Mil. gal.						12.2	9.62	9.65	2.30	10.9	10.5	9.64	19.9	26.4
	v Mil. $						.421	.825	.621	.193	1.09	.405	.507	1.18	1.36
	p $ per gal.						.0345	.0858	.0643	.0837	.100	.0387	.0526	.0589	.0514
Bagasse, for sale as such	*q* Th. t.									69.4	134	44.2	272	116	180
	v Th. $									416	684	158	453	279	500
	p $ per t.									6.00	5.10	3.58	1.66	2.41	2.78

[a] Percentages of coverage:

Given year	Base year	Given year	Base year	Given year	Base year	Given year	Base year
1909:95.7 1914:99.7	1919:96.5	1921:99.5 1923:99.7 1925:98.2	1929:95.8	1927:99.8 1931:99.8 1933:99.6	1929:99.5	1935:99.3 1937:99.6	1929:99.5
1919:96.5	1929:89.8						

[b] Figures for 1931 to 1937 were requested by the Bureau of the Census for the seasons beginning in the respective Census years, and for earlier Census years for the seasons ending in those years. Thus the figure given for 1931 applies to the season 1931–32, whereas the figure given for 1921 applies to the season 1920–21. In 1925, 1927 and 1929, however, most of the establishments in the cane sugar industry reported for the seasons 1925–26, 1927–28 and 1929–30 instead of 1924–25, 1926–27 and 1928–29. It is not indicated in the Census volumes whether a similar qualification applies to the data for earlier years.

[c] We obtained the indexes for 1899 and 1904 by splicing the 1909 index to an index of domestic raw cane sugar production which appears in *Yearbook of the Department of Agriculture, 1910*, p. 603. The movements of this series approximate closely those of our index during the years for which our index is available. The figures for U.S. raw cane sugar production in th. tons are as follows: 284 for 1899; 278 for 1904; 414 for 1909. The adjusted index given above, extrapolated by the unadjusted index, is 115.2 for 1899; 112.7 for 1904.

CANE-SUGAR REFINING		*1899*	*1904*	*1909*	*1914*	*1919*	*1921*	*1923*	*1925*	*1927*	*1929*	*1931*	*1933*	*1935*	*1937*
Adjusted index					65.6	79.2	73.9	86.6	105.9	100.1	100.0	86.6	77.1	82.6	89.0
Unadjusted index[a]		44.2[b]	50.3[b]	54.7[b]	65.5	79.1	73.8	86.7	106.0	100.3	100.0	86.5	76.9	82.2	88.2
Product	*Item*														
Refined sugar	q Mil. t.				3.33	4.02[c]	3.77	4.43	5.41	5.13	5.12	4.43	3.94	4.21	4.52
	v Mil. $				285	714	462	722	600	594	502	392	334	373	418
	p $ per t.				85.7	177	123	163	111	116	98.2	88.5	84.9	88.5	92.5
Refiners' sirup, edible	q Mil. gal.								8.54	5.54	4.32	3.40	3.69	2.89	2.74
	v Mil. $								2.15	1.25	.920	.720	.559	.599	.547
	p ¢ per gal.								25.2	22.5	21.3	21.2	15.1	20.8	20.0
	q				35.8	44.1	31.8	41.1							
	v				3.28	15.3	2.91	3.34							
	p				9.17	34.8	9.15	8.12							
Refiners' blackstrap and nonedible sirup	q Mil. gal.								37.4	31.0	32.2	20.9	19.6	22.3	23.4
	v Mil. $								3.86	2.17	3.04	1.09	.842	1.32	1.40
	p ¢ per gal.								10.3	7.00	9.46	5.22	4.29	5.92	5.98

[a] Percentages of coverage:

Given year	Base year	Given year	Base year	Given year	Base year
1914:99.8	1919:99.7	1925:99.9	1929:99.8	1933:99.6	1929:99.8
1919:99.7	1929:99.8	1927:99.9		1935:99.3	
1921:99.7		1931:99.7		1937:98.8	
1923:99.9					

[b] We obtained the indexes for 1899, 1904 and 1909 by splicing our 1914 index to the Willett and Gray sugar meltings series which appears in the *Statistical Sugar Trade Journal*. The movements of the sugar meltings series closely approximate those of our index during the years for which our index is available. The figures for sugar meltings in mil. tons are as follows: 1.68 for 1899; 1.91 for 1904; 2.08 for 1909; and 2.49 for 1914. The adjusted index given above, extrapolated by the unadjusted index, is 44.3 for 1899; 50.4 for 1904; 54.8 for 1909.

[c] The 1919 Census figure for quantity of refined sugar production was discarded as inaccurate. The figure used was that estimated by the Bureau of Labor Statistics on the basis of the Willett and Gray sugar meltings series; see U.S. Bureau of Labor Statistics, "Productivity of Labor in the Cement, Leather, Flour, and Sugar-Refining Industries, 1914–1925," *Monthly Labor Review* (October 1926), p. 19.

Indexes of Physical Output, with Basic Data on Quantity, Value and Price of Products

CEREALS		1925	1927	1929	1931	1933	1935	1937
Adjusted index		69.8	80.1	100.0	100.1	78.8	69.5	77.2
Unadjusted index[a]		66.6	76.9	100.0	103.2	79.2	66.3	72.2
Product[b]	*Item*							
Breakfast foods								
Made from oats	*q* Mil. lb.	642	817	707	832	639[c]	526	503[c]
	v Mil. $	32.8	38.7	35.9	29.5	18.9	26.3	25.1
	p $ per lb.	.0510	.0474	.0509	.0354	.0296	.0500	.0500
Made from corn	*q* Mil. lb.	136	166	297	310	214[c]	178	230[c]
	v Mil. $	19.7	19.5	23.7	19.7	16.6	18.6	24.8
	p $ per lb.	.145	.118	.0798	.0636	.0775	.104	.107
Prepared flour	*q* Mil. lb.	170	119	466[d]	415[d]	376[d]	287	315[d]
	v Mil. $	9.43	6.05	18.3	17.8	15.5	17.1	18.3
	p $ per lb.	.0553	.0508	.0393	.0429	.0411	.0595	.0579
Coffee substitute	*q* Mil. lb.	36.5	29.7	19.8	12.3	8.63		
	v Mil. $	5.76	6.26	5.25	2.61	1.82		
	p $ per lb.	.158	.211	.265	.212	.211		

[a] Percentages of coverage:

Given year	Base year	Given year	Base year
1925: 45.1 1927: 45.4 1931: 48.8 1933: 47.5	1929: 47.3	1935: 42.2 1937: 41.4	1929: 44.3

[b] Data relate to products of the cereals industry alone, except where otherwise noted.

[c] For 1933 and 1937 the Census data relate to breakfast foods made from oats or corn, wherever produced. We have estimated the amount made in the cereals industry: for 1933, on the basis of the average of the fractions of the total that was made in the cereals industry in 1931 and in 1935; and for 1937, on the basis of the fraction in 1935.

[d] Includes a small amount of prepared flour made in other industries.

CHEESE		1899	1904	1909	1914	1919	1921	1923	1925	1927	1929	1931	1933[b]	1935	1937
Adjusted index		[c]	56.0	55.2	65.9	86.1	77.2	100.9	100.4	96.6	100.0	92.1	94.8	126.5	128.8
Unadjusted index[a]		48.0	53.9	52.9	63.1	80.8	72.1	96.5	92.8	88.1	100.0	93.0	95.4	128.5	131.0
Product	*Item*														
All varieties of cheese	*q* Mil. lb.	282	317	311	371	475	424	567	546	518	588	552	562	756	778
	v Mil. $	26.5	28.6	43.3	50.5	137	77.9	125	112	110	113	70.2	58.9	103	118
	p $ per lb.	.0940	.0902	.139	.136	.289	.184	.219	.205	.213	.192	.127	.105	.136	.151
American or cheddar	*q* Mil. lb.										375	339	357	492	480
	v Mil. $										76.9	44.2	38.0	70.5	78.3
	p $ per lb.										.205	.130	.107	.143	.163
American or cheddar and Swiss, brick, Münster and limburger (combined)	*q*								464	414					
	v								100	93.6					
	p								.216	.226					
Swiss, brick, Münster and limburger	*q* Mil. lb.										58.1	63.3	69.8	81.8	78.8
	v Mil. $										12.1	8.68	8.75	12.7	13.3
	p $ per lb.										.208	.137	.125	.156	.169
Italian varieties, Jack, and Monterey	*q* Mil. lb.								2.77	4.30	8.58	8.38	7.10	14.7	17.6
	v Mil. $								.614	1.00	1.96	.159	.898	2.31	3.10
	p $ per lb.								.222	.234	.229	.190	.127	.157	.176
Cream and Neufchatel	*q* Mil. lb.								22.8	26.4	42.0	36.6	32.6	42.3	
	v Mil. $								6.13	8.03	11.1	7.53	5.09	8.15	
	p $ per lb.								.269	.304	.265	.205	.156	.193	
Cream and Neufchatel and Cottage, pot, and bakers' cheese (combined)	*q*														190
	v														20.9
	p														.110
Cottage, pot, and bakers' cheese	*q* Mil. lb.							39.4	51.0	68.8	101	100	90.7	118	
	v Mil. $							3.51	4.23	5.94	9.43	7.27	5.37	7.60	
	p $ per lb.							.0890	.0829	.0864	.0936	.0723	.0592	.0646	

[a] Percentages of coverage:

Given year	Base year	Given year	Base year	Given year	Base year	Given year	Base year
1904:98.2	1909:97.7	1919:95.7	1929:101.9	1925:94.2	1929:101.9	1933:101.4	1929:100.8
1909:97.7	1919:95.7	1921:95.2	1929:101.9	1927:93.0	1929:101.9	1935:102.4	1929:100.8
1914:97.7	1919:95.7	1923:97.5	1929:101.9	1931:101.8	1929:100.8	1937:102.4	1929:100.8

[b] The 1933 Census of this industry is considered by the Bureau of the Census to be somewhat incomplete.

[c] No adjusted index could be computed for 1899 because the industry is not shown separately in the Census for that year. The adjusted index given above, extrapolated by the unadjusted index, is 49.9 for 1899.

Indexes of Physical Output, with Basic Data on Quantity, Value and Price of Products

CHOCOLATE		*1921*	*1923*	*1925*	*1927*	*1929*	*1931*	*1933*	*1935*	*1937*
Adjusted index		60.0	82.2	89.8[c]	95.6	100.0	98.5	104.6	139.5	123.5
Unadjusted index[a]		55.3	81.8	98.3[c]	96.1	100.0	98.0	103.1	139.6	124.0
Product[b]	*Item*									
Chocolate, incl. coatings	*q* Mil. lb.	218	339	418	406	420	401	410	568	500
	v Mil. $	58.7	79.2	97.0	99.1	97.1	69.7	51.2	73.4	80.1
	p $ per lb.	.269	.233	.232	.244	.231	.174	.125	.129	.160
Cocoa, powdered, in cans	*q* Mil. lb.	32.3	38.7	33.3	34.7	44.7	45.3		53.3	49.8
	v Mil. $	8.31	6.87	7.82	8.53	9.61	7.33		5.58	5.96
	p $ per lb.	.258	.178	.235	.246	.215	.162	*q* 119	.105	.120
								v 10.4		
Cocoa, powdered, in barrels	*q* Mil. lb.	30.3	42.1	52.0	56.2	61.0	63.8	*p* .0874	73.1	81.1
	v Mil. $	2.24	2.34	3.22	5.24	5.44	4.36		4.66	5.79
	p $ per lb.	.0739	.0556	.0621	.0932	.0892	.0683		.0637	.0714
Cocoa butter	*q* Mil. lb.	17.8	19.8	25.4	22.8	19.2	23.7	29.9	41.8	23.5
	v Mil. $	4.81	5.23	6.82	8.56	5.43	3.61	3.30	5.31	4.74
	p $ per lb.	.271	.264	.269	.376	.283	.152	.110	.127	.202
Chocolate sirup	*q* Mil. gal.					.855	1.26	1.81	3.74	5.31
	v Mil. $					.985	1.16	1.29	3.41	5.34
	p $ per gal.					1.15	.921	.712	.910	1.01

[a] Percentages of coverage:

Given year	Base year	Given year	Base year
1921:90.6	1929:98.4	1931:98.7	1929:99.2
1923:98.0		1933:97.7	
1925:107.7		1935:99.3	
1927:98.9		1937:99.6	

[b] After 1923 products normally originating in the industry but made as secondary products in other industries are included.

[c] Chocolate departments operated by confectionery manufacturers are classified under chocolate. Prior to 1927 some confectionery manufacturers failed to make separate returns for their chocolate departments; the latter, consequently, were included in confectionery. A similar situation existed in 1935; however, according to the Bureau of the Census, the resulting incomparability is negligible.

CONFECTIONERY		1925	1927	1929	1931	1933	1935	1937
Adjusted index		91.1[b]	94.0	100.0	80.1	79.1	100.2	111.0
Unadjusted index[a]		75.9[b]	90.7	100.0	83.0	80.0	98.4	108.3
Product[c]	*Item*							
Chocolate, fancy package	*q* Mil. lb.	125	132	149	104	94.1	139	168
	v Mil. $	63.2	69.0	73.6	47.2	30.8	38.9	50.7
	p $ per lb.	.507	.523	.493	.455	.328	.280	.301
Other candy[d]	*q* Mil. lb.	670		921				
	v Mil. $	135		173				
	p $ per lb.	.201		.188				
Other candy[e]	*q* Mil. lb.		1,151	1,258	1,099	1,075	1,258	1,345
	v Mil. $		218	224	176	131	154	175
	p $ per lb.		.189	.178	.160	.122	.123	.130

[a] Percentages of coverage:

Given year	Base year	Given year	Base year
1925:52.2	1929:62.7	1933:76.5	1929:75.7
1927:73.1	1929:75.7	1935:74.3	
1931:78.5		1937:73.9	

[b] The figures for 1925 include data on chocolate departments operated by some confectionery manufacturers who failed to make separate returns for their chocolate departments.

[c] The data are not strictly comparable from year to year because a varying number of manufacturers failed to report their products in detail.

[d] Includes chocolate in bulk, candy bars, hard candy, and pan work.

[e] Includes, in addition to the items specified in footnote d, caramels, gum work, marshmallows, lozenges, and miscellaneous chocolates.

CORN PRODUCTS		1904	1909	1914	1919	1921	1923	1925	1927	1929	1931	1933	1935	1937
Adjusted index			46.8	50.4	69.4	57.4	76.4	76.0	92.4	100.0	76.3	83.6	67.7	84.3
Unadjusted index[a]		b	41.3	42.1	49.6	52.8	77.9	78.9	93.8	100.0	80.2	88.7	70.1	83.4
Product[c]	*Item*													
Corn sirups, and mixtures of corn and other sirups	*q* Mil. lb.						1,174	1,146	1,124	1,165	980	1,066	997	1,114
	v Mil. $						34.1	41.3	32.5	40.6	25.8	24.3	31.3	37.0
	p $ per lb.						.0290	.0361	.0289	.0348	.0263	.0228	.0313	.0332
Corn sugar	*q* Mil. lb.		159	174	157	152	528	580	905	896	802	827	351	468
	v Mil. $		3.62	3.77	9.32	4.54	16.8	19.5	25.6	30.2	20.4	18.0	11.0	15.7
	p $ per lb.		.0228	.0216	.0592	.0299	.0318	.0336	.0283	.0337	.0255	.0218	.0313	.0336

For footnotes see next page.

Indexes of Physical Output, with Basic Data on Quantity, Value and Price of Products

CORN PRODUCTS (concluded)		1904	1909	1914	1919	1921	1923	1925	1927	1929	1931	1933	1935	1937
Product[c]	*Item*													
Corn oil, total	*q* Mil. lb.[d]		65.3	70.9	100	94.2	116	111	148	176	142	129	137	163
	v Mil. $		2.80	3.69	20.3	11.2	14.8	15.2	18.3	20.2	12.2	8.40	14.7	16.6
	p $ per lb.		.0429	.0521	.203	.119	.128	.138	.123	.114	.0861	.0654	.107	.101
Starch, corn, potato, and other	*q* Mil. lb.	357	678	621	784	898	863	878	1,038	1,123	795	1,020	833	1,006
	v Mil. $	10.9	17.5	15.8	44.4	25.6	29.9	35.1	33.9	42.8	25.6	29.6	30.0	39.2
	p $ per lb.	.0306	.0259	.0254	.0567	.0285	.0346	.0399	.0327	.0381	.0322	.0290	.0360	.0390
Corn-oil cake and meal	*q* Th. t.[e]			71.5	30.8	16.7	32.3	33.3	23.6	36.0	20.3	26.0	19.3	35.6
	v Mil. $			1.83	1.84	.621	1.32	1.32	.797	1.45	.423	.390	.453	.953
	p $ per t.			25.6	59.8	37.3	40.8	39.5	33.8	40.3	20.8	15.0	23.4	26.8

[a] Percentages of coverage:

Given year	Base year	Given year	Base year	Given year	Base year	Given year	Base year
1909:49.1	1919:39.8	1919:40.7	1929:57.0	1925:84.6	1929:81.5	1933:86.4	1929:81.5
1914:47.6	1919:40.7	1921:52.4		1927:82.6		1935:84.3	
		1923:83.1	1929:81.5	1931:85.6		1937:80.6	

[b] No index was computed for 1904 because of the low coverage in that year.

[c] After 1919 products normally originating in the industry but made as secondary products in other industries are included.

[d] Reported in gallons, 1909–21; converted to pounds calculated at 8 pounds per gallon.

[e] Reported in pounds, 1914–21; converted to tons calculated at 2,000 pounds per ton.

FEEDS		1925	1927	1929	1931	1933	1935	1937
Adjusted index		b	74.3	100.0	75.6	69.7	90.4	111.2
Unadjusted index[a]		70.2	93.5	100.0	76.3	74.7	84.2	102.1
Product	*Item*							
Prepared feeds, made chiefly from grain[c]	*q* Mil. ton	5.16	6.89	7.35	5.64	5.56	6.22	7.47
	v Mil. $	250	313	331	175	144	223	314
	p $ per ton	48.5	45.4	45.0	31.1	25.9	35.8	42.0
Alfalfa	*q* Mil. ton		.259	.314	.186	.124	.207	.391
	v Mil. $		5.16	8.23	2.94	1.77	3.81	7.50
	p $ per ton		19.9	26.2	15.8	14.2	18.4	19.2

[a] Percentages of coverage:

Given year	Base year	Given year	Base year
1927:106.1	1929:84.3	1933:90.3	1929:84.3
1931: 85.0		1935:78.5	
		1937:77.4	

[b] Because of a serious change in the definition of the industry between 1925 and 1927, no adjusted index for 1925 was computed. The adjusted index given above, extrapolated by the unadjusted index, is 55.8 for 1925.

[c] Includes prepared feeds, wherever made.

FISH, CANNED		1899	1904	1909	1914	1919	1921	1923	1925	1927	1929	1931	1933	1935	1937
Adjusted index		52.8	65.4	77.8	73.0	84.8	44.7	58.9	73.3	77.3	100.0	63.9	68.6	103.1	103.7
Unadjusted index[a]		64.8	84.0	98.3	86.3	95.6	47.1	63.4	78.7	84.5	100.0	65.2	71.1	99.4	99.6
Product	*Item*														
Canned fish															
Tuna fish	*q* Mil. std.c.				.437	.874	.360	.818	1.10	1.26	1.54	1.19	1.44	2.82	3.14
	v Mil. $				1.64	5.71	2.58	6.91	8.50	8.37	10.8	7.21	6.93	11.9	19.0
	p $ per std.c.				3.75	6.53	7.17	8.46	7.71	6.66	7.01	6.06	4.81	4.21	6.04
Salmon	*q* Mil. std.c.	1.31	1.00	2.08	1.51	2.19	1.25	1.37	1.56	1.50	1.56	1.19	1.14	.918	.885
	v Mil. $	5.68	4.25	8.72	8.71	19.1	8.63	12.7	15.4	15.7	14.3	7.62	7.87	6.29	8.39
	p $ per std.c.	4.35	4.24	4.19	5.76	8.74	6.90	9.26	9.87	10.4	9.16	6.42	6.92	6.85	9.47
Sardines, pilchard	*q* Mil. std. c.[b]										3.78	1.68	1.54	2.69	2.81
	v Mil. $										11.3	4.50	3.81	6.28	8.59
	p $ per std.c.										2.98	2.68	2.47	2.33	3.06
Sardines, herring	*q* Mil. std. c.[b]										2.02	.900	.981	1.59	1.68
	v Mil. $										6.94	2.62	2.40	5.10	5.00
	p $ per std.c.										3.44	2.91	2.44	3.22	2.97
Sardines, total	*q* Mil. std.c.[b]	1.99	3.86	4.01	5.01	5.78	1.70	3.38	5.16	6.18	9.27[b]				
	v Mil. $	4.21	4.38	4.93	6.24	20.3	6.65	9.90	13.1	14.5	18.2				
	p $ per std.c.	2.12	1.13	1.23	1.24	3.51	3.91	2.92	2.54	2.35	1.96				
Shrimps	*q* Mil. std.c.			.172	.460	.322	.633	.700	.736[c]	.853	.980	.818	.860	1.10	1.27
	v Mil. $			.690	1.73	1.86	3.68	4.38	3.78	5.32	5.54	3.39	3.48	4.44	7.04
	p $ per std.c.			4.01	3.75	5.79	5.82	6.26	5.14	6.24	5.65	4.15	4.04	4.03	5.55
Oysters	*q* Mil. std.c.		3.95	1.88	.945	.718	.464	.525	.568	.447	.455	.351	.348	.533	.690
	v Mil. $		3.80	2.44	2.68	3.51	2.02	2.72	3.01	2.37	2.17	.989	1.07	2.13	2.84
	p $ per std.c.		.962	1.30	2.83	4.89	4.35	5.19	5.30	5.29	4.78	2.82	3.09	3.99	4.12
Clams and clam chowder, juice, bouillon and broth	*q* Mil. std.c.				.185	.158	.195	.303[d]	.348	.494	.464	.400	.380	.596	.746
	v Mil. $				.670	.773	1.12	1.43	1.67	2.60	2.17	1.99	1.44	1.98	2.77
	p $ per std.c.				3.62	4.90	5.73	4.72	4.81	5.26	4.69	4.97	3.80	3.32	3.72
Mackerel	*q* Mil. std.c.										.575	.148	.748	1.73	.841
	v Mil. $										2.32	.393	1.87	4.60	2.67
	p $ per std.c.										4.03	2.66	2.50	2.66	3.18

For footnotes see next page.

Indexes of Physical Output, with Basic Data on Quantity, Value and Price of Products

FISH, CANNED (concluded)		1899	1904	1909	1914	1919	1921	1923	1925	1927	1929	1931	1933	1935	1937
Product	*Item*														
Cured fish	*q* Th. lb.	142	150	174	160	144	83.0	80.7	88.3	91.2	99.8	66.4		77.3	69.4
	v Th. $	6.03	8.94	10.3	10.9	23.6	9.70	10.3	11.2	13.3	17.5	10.3		10.0	11.8
	p $ per lb.	.0426	.0595	.0590	.0684	.164	.117	.127	.126	.146	.176	.155		.130	.169

[a] Percentages of coverage:

Given year	Base year	Given year	Base year	Given year	Base year	Given year	Base year
1899:82.0	1909:84.4	1914:97.7	1919:93.2	1923:86.7	1929:80.6	1931:92.1	1929:90.3
1904:94.4	1909:93.0	1919:90.9	1929:80.6	1925:86.5	1929:80.6	1933:71.2	1929:68.6
1909:95.5	1919:85.1	1921:85.0	1929:80.6	1927:95.6	1929:87.4	1935:87.1	1929:90.3
						1937:86.8	1929:90.3

[b] For 1929–37 standard cases represent various sized cans converted to standard cases calculated at 100 ¼-lb. cans to the case of herring sardines, and at 48 1-lb. cans to the case of pilchard sardines; for 1929 and previous years all types of sardines were converted to standard cases calculated at 100 no. ¼ cans (3½ oz.) to the case. For this reason, the number of standard cases of pilchard sardines and herring sardines do not add up to the total given for the year 1929.

[c] Prior to 1927 a can of shrimps weighed approximately 4¼ oz.; in 1927 and later years the weight was 5 or 5¾ oz. For this reason the data for the years 1921–25 were not used in the construction of the indexes for those years.

[d] Figures on clam chowder for 1914–23, included in this series, are not strictly comparable with those for later years because the figures for the earlier years include clam chowder manufactured by canners of vegetables and fruits whereas the figures for the later years do not.

FLAVORINGS		1929	1931	1933[b]	1935	1937
Adjusted index		100.0	101.3		[c]	[c]
Unadjusted index[a]		100.0	94.1		96.0	153.2
Product	*Item*					
Flavoring extracts	*q* Mil. gal.	4.27	4.43		4.46	6.20[d]
	v Mil. $	32.5	28.4		21.9	23.8
	p $ per gal.	7.61	6.42		4.91	3.84
Flavoring sirups, excl. chocolate sirups	*q* Mil. gal.	38.6	35.6		37.6	57.2
	v Mil. $	50.5	45.8		40.9	76.4
	p $ per gal.	1.31	1.29		1.09	1.34

FLAVORINGS (concluded)		1929	1931	1933[b]	1935	1937
Product	*Item*					
Flavoring concentrates,	*q* Mil. lb.	2.60	1.95		1.15	5.04
incl. grape concentrates	*v* Mil. $	4.54	2.30		2.10	9.84
	p $ per lb.	1.75	1.18		1.83	1.95
Flavoring powders	*q* Mil. lb.	7.02	3.03		9.78	13.9[d]
	v Mil. $	2.24	1.23		2.86	4.57
	p $ per lb.	.319	.404		.293	.330
Flavoring pastes	*q* Mil. lb.	2.07	2.20		2.21	18.1[d]
	v Mil. $	1.02	.679		.967	2.16
	p $ per lb.	.492	.309		.437	.119
Fruit juices[e]	*q* Mil. gal.	2.66	2.33		1.64	1.55
	v Mil. $	3.59	2.87		2.24	1.57
	p $ per gal.	1.35	1.23		1.36	1.01
Crushed fruit,	*q* Mil. gal.	2.05	2.04		1.88	3.12
for fountain use	*v* Mil. $	5.58	4.52		3.50	4.43
	p $ per gal.	2.73	2.21		1.86	1.42

[a] Percentages of coverage: Given year 1931: 72.0; Base year 1929: 77.4

[b] Detailed data on products were not collected in 1933.

[c] Because of a marked change in the definition of the industry between 1931 and 1933, no adjusted indexes for 1935 and 1937 were computed on the 1929 base. The adjusted index given above, extrapolated by the unadjusted index, is 103.3 for 1935. Further extrapolation, and adjustment for the change in coverage from 1935 (109.7 percent) to 1937 (104.2 percent), yields an index of 173.5 for 1937.

[d] Estimated in part.

[e] Not including grape juice and other fruit juices made for sale as beverages.

FLOUR		1899	1904	1909	1914	1919	1921	1923	1925	1927	1929	1931		1933	1935	1937
Adjusted index		93.7	97.5	102.5	107.9	113.5	93.9	106.2	101.7[b]	100.1	100.0	91.0		80.4	82.2	85.8
Unadjusted index[a]		89.9	93.2	97.1	102.2	108.9	91.8	101.0	98.8	99.1	100.0	92.4		81.7	82.2	84.6
Product	*Item*											*A*	*B*	*C*		
Wheat flour	*q* Mil. bbl.	99.8	104	106	116	132	111	114	115	118	120	115	110	97.2	102	105
	v Mil. $	334	480	550	544	1,436	872	663	910	820	737	451	433	429	665	617
	p $ per bbl.	3.35	4.62	5.20	4.67	10.84	7.86	5.80	7.94	6.94	6.14	3.91	3.92	4.41	6.49	5.86

For footnotes see next page.

Indexes of Physical Output, with Basic Data on Quantity, Value and Price of Products

FLOUR (concluded)		1899	1904	1909	1914	1919	1921	1923	1925	1927	1929	1931		1933	1935	1937
Product	*Item*											*A*	*B*	*C*		
Feeds, screenings, etc.	*q* Mil. t.							3.92	3.43	2.75	2.47	1.55	1.37	1.09	1.37	1.60
	v Mil. $							136	129	97.0	93.8	36.5	32.1	21.9	41.0	52.9
	p $ per t.							34.6	37.5	35.3	38.0	23.5	23.4	20.0	30.0	33.2
Feeds, screenings, etc., incl. prepared feeds for stock not separately reported	*q* Mil. t.				4.75	4.57										
	v Mil. $				137	263										
	p $ per t.				28.8	57.5										
Feeds, screenings, etc., incl. prepared feeds, and bran and middlings (combined)	*q*	7.16	7.93	9.24												
	v	99.7	152	230												
	p	13.9	19.2	24.9												
Bran and middlings	*q* Mil. t.				4.67	4.76	4.04	4.19	4.53	4.64	4.68	4.57	4.60	3.77	4.10	4.18
	v Mil. $				105	211	106	118	138	142	142	73.7	69.8	57.9	91.5	116
	p $ per t.				22.4	44.4	26.1	28.2	30.5	30.7	30.3	16.1	15.2	15.3	22.3	27.8
Corn meal and corn flour	*q* Mil. bbl.	27.8	23.6	21.6	16.3	10.7	10.9	12.2	9.71	9.87	11.1	8.89	7.38[e]	7.59[e]	7.52	7.26
	v Mil. $	52.2	56.4	66.9	55.0	82.1	39.7	52.0	48.3	44.8	55.5	28.0	23.5	19.5	32.5	34.2
	p $ per bbl.	1.87	2.39	3.11	3.37	7.68	3.63	4.28	4.97	4.54	5.01	3.15	3.18	2.57	4.32	4.71
Rye flour	*q* Mil. bbl.	1.44	1.50	1.53	1.94	2.53	1.33	1.63	1.60	1.72	1.68	1.57	1.49	1.81	1.51	1.42
	v Mil. $	4.15	5.89	6.38	7.85	21.2	8.91	6.71	9.15	9.30	9.18	5.34	5.06	5.97	5.91	6.71
	p $ per bbl.	2.87	3.92	4.17	4.05	8.40	6.67	4.11	5.73	5.39	5.47	3.40	3.41	3.30	3.92	4.71
Buckwheat flour	*q* Mil. lb.	143	175	176	126	90.1	65.4	49.2	47.9	44.6	38.5	31.1	23.0	16.3	25.2	26.6
	v Mil. $	3.19	4.38	4.66	3.75	5.24	2.57	1.92	1.91	1.67	1.57	.961	.771	.458	.657	.844
	p $ per lb.	.0223	.0250	.0265	.0299	.0582	.0393	.0390	.0400	.0376	.0408	.0309	.0336	.0282	.0261	.0318

A Comparable with all years except 1933. *B* Comparable with 1933. *C* Comparable with 1931.

[a] Percentages of coverage:

Given year	Base year	Given year	Base year	Given year	Base year	Given year	Base year
1899:98.4	1909:97.2	1914:97.1	1919:98.4	1923:93.2	1929:98.0	1931:99.6	1929:98.0
1904:98.0	1909:97.2	1919:85.6	1929:89.2	1925:95.2	1929:98.0	1933:94.3	1931:94.3
1909:97.2	1919:98.4	1921:87.2	1929:89.2	1927:97.1	1929:98.0	1935:98.0	1929:98.0
						1937:96.7	1929:98.0

[b] Between 1925 and 1927 establishments grinding grain for prepared feeds were transferred from flour to feeds.

[e] Corn meal only; there was no report for corn flour.

FRUITS and VEGETABLES, CANNED		1899	1904	1909	1914	1919	1921	1923	1925[b]		1927	1929	1931	1933	1935	1937
Adjusted index		16.9[d]	23.6[d]	28.6	41.8	54.8	37.6	66.8	82.5		81.8	100.0	91.2	87.8	127.3	150.8
Unadjusted index[a]		16.8[d]	26.6[d]	32.0	46.1	61.3	39.9	68.4	85.9		79.5	100.0	86.6	88.3	125.3	148.5
Product	*Item*								*A*	*B*						
Canned vegetables[c]																
Asparagus	*q* Mil. c.			.343	.638	1.01	.740	1.46	1.48	1.90	2.18	2.73	1.88	2.06	2.93	2.75
	v Mil. $			1.98	2.79	6.57	5.14	11.0	10.5	10.5	12.2	15.5	10.4	7.25	12.0	13.1
	p $ per c.			5.76	4.38	6.53	6.94	7.49	7.11	5.53	5.61	5.67	5.53	3.51	4.09	4.74
Beans	*q* Mil. c.	1.49	2.59	4.42	8.99	14.8	11.3	20.5	24.4	24.7	25.4	30.8	24.2	25.6	30.2	34.7
	v Mil. $	2.03	4.13	7.93	16.6	39.4	30.7	39.6	55.2	55.2	52.1	69.7	45.6	39.2	46.7	58.7
	p $ per c.	1.36	1.60	1.80	1.84	2.66	2.71	1.94	2.26	2.24	2.05	2.26	1.89	1.53	1.55	1.69
Beets	*q* Mil. c.			.126	.252	.584	.391	.545	1.21	1.56	.815	1.91	1.47	1.23	2.44	3.39
	v Mil. $			.261	.512	1.95	1.20	1.76	3.81	3.81	2.05	4.58	2.37	1.93	3.74	5.18
	p $ per c.			2.07	2.03	3.34	3.08	3.24	3.14	2.45	2.51	2.40	1.62	1.56	1.53	1.53
Corn	*q* Mil. c.	6.34	11.2	7.45	9.92	14.4	9.01	14.7	22.8	22.6	10.3	16.7	19.4	10.2	22.1	26.1
	v Mil. $	8.19	16.0	10.3	13.9	35.5	19.6	30.8	51.3	51.3	22.9	36.8	31.5	17.7	38.0	44.3
	p $ per c.	1.29	1.42	1.39	1.40	2.47	2.17	2.10	2.25	2.27	2.23	2.20	1.63	1.73	1.72	1.70
Peas	*q* Mil. c.	2.54	4.69	5.90	8.83	9.33	8.22	14.4	16.8	16.5	13.1	17.5	13.3	13.3	25.1	24.4
	v Mil. $	4.47	7.93	10.2	15.1	25.1	23.0	39.8	42.9	42.9	34.0	44.5	28.9	28.6	50.8	47.4
	p $ per c.	1.76	1.69	1.74	1.71	2.69	2.79	2.76	2.55	2.59	2.60	2.54	2.18	2.15	2.02	1.94
Spinach	*q* Mil. c.			.149	.392	.676	.581	1.88	1.53	2.05	2.46	4.82	1.77	2.55	3.58	5.43
	v Mil. $			.294	.737	2.34	2.09	4.98	5.46	5.46	6.23	12.1	3.86	4.93	6.44	9.86
	p $ per c.			1.97	1.88	3.46	3.59	2.65	3.56	2.67	2.53	2.52	2.18	1.94	1.80	1.81
Tomatoes	*q* Mil. c.	8.70	9.41	12.9	16.2	11.8	4.13	14.8	15.3	21.8	18.2	21.4	13.9	15.9	26.2	23.6
	v Mil. $	13.7	14.0	18.7	25.5	38.1	12.5	39.7	42.7	42.7	33.8	42.2	21.7	26.4	37.7	34.3
	p $ per c.	1.57	1.49	1.45	1.58	3.22	3.03	2.68	2.79	1.96	1.86	1.97	1.56	1.66	1.44	1.46
Kraut	*q* Mil. c.				1.18	1.04		2.07	1.95	2.40	3.10	4.22	3.65	3.34	4.40	4.58
	v Mil. $				1.57	2.85		5.15	4.57	4.57	5.46	8.42	5.43	5.21	5.82	7.25
	p $ per c.				1.32	2.73		2.48	2.35	1.91	1.76	1.99	1.49	1.56	1.32	1.58

For footnotes see p. 401.

Indexes of Physical Output, with Basic Data on Quantity, Value and Price of Products

FRUITS and VEGETABLES, CANNED (continued)		1899	1904	1909	1914	1919	1921	1923	1925[b]		1927	1929	1931	1933	1935	1937
Product	*Item*								*A*	*B*						
Canned vegetables[e] (concluded)																
Spaghetti	*q* Mil. c.									1.84	2.75	4.24	2.80	3.17	3.41	5.45
	v Mil. $									5.55	6.06	8.32	6.43	5.61	6.72	8.96
	p $ per c.									3.02	2.20	1.96	2.30	1.77	1.97	1.64
Hominy	*q* Mil. c.									1.13	1.69	1.77	1.08	1.17	1.25	1.65
	v Mil. $									1.52	2.18	2.53	1.35	1.44	1.83	2.15
	p $ per c.									1.34	1.29	1.43	1.26	1.23	1.46	1.31
Pimientos	*q* Mil. c.									.253	.487	.506	.274	.270	.712	.626
	v Mil. $									1.46	2.07	2.01	.981	.800	1.91	1.86
	p $ per c.									5.79	4.25	3.98	3.57	2.97	2.68	2.96
Pumpkin and squash	*q* Mil. c.									1.18	1.09	2.42	1.01	1.75	1.02	1.73
	v Mil. $									2.59	1.98	4.21	1.51	2.62	1.55	2.57
	p $ per c.									2.19	1.81	1.74	1.49	1.50	1.52	1.49
Tomato sauce	*q* Mil. c.									.580	.410	.952	.466	1.87	1.51	1.61
	v Mil. $									1.95	1.08	2.55	1.12	3.22	3.24	3.30
	p $ per c.									3.36	2.64	2.68	2.40	1.72	2.15	2.06
Tomato pulp and puree	*q* Mil. c.				1.50	1.52		2.01	2.72	3.63	2.46	2.89	1.48		2.57	3.91
	v Mil. $				1.45	3.82		3.87	6.64	6.64	3.86	5.29	1.72		3.65	5.44
	p $ per c.				.967	2.52		1.93	2.44	1.83	1.57	1.83	1.17		1.42	1.39
Tomato paste	*q* Mil. c.					.113		.219	.671	.623	.438	.606	.199	*q* 20.7	.921	2.38
	v Mil. $					1.30		1.99	2.81	2.81	2.30	3.84	.991	*v* 45.4	3.52	6.43
	p $ per c.					11.5		9.08	4.19	4.51	5.25	6.34	4.99	*p* 2.19	3.83	2.70
Other canned vegetables and soups	*q* Mil. c.									12.1	12.5	18.6	18.2		36.1	48.1
	v Mil. $									44.0	45.0	63.2	47.4		77.7	108
	p $ per c.									3.63	3.59	3.39	2.61		2.15	2.24

FRUITS and VEGETABLES, CANNED (continued)		1899	1904	1909	1914	1919	1921	1923	1925[b]		1927	1929	1931	1933	1935	1937
Product	*Item*								*A*	*B*						
Canned fruits																
Apples	*q* Mil. c.	.646	.490	1.21	1.51	2.45	2.24	2.73	2.60	3.47	2.94	3.59	2.07	2.55	2.05	2.77
	v Mil. $	1.13	.738	1.90	2.39	9.08	7.75	6.54	6.95	6.95	5.90	7.94	3.32	4.17	3.09	4.56
	p $ per c.	1.74	1.51	1.57	1.58	3.71	3.46	2.40	2.67	2.00	2.01	2.21	1.61	1.63	1.51	1.64
Apricots	*q* Mil. c.	.532	.540	.630	1.05	3.94	1.06	1.56	1.94	2.09	3.10	4.27	2.12	2.49	3.27	5.81
	v Mil. $	1.58	1.64	1.83	3.06	25.2	4.31	5.46	7.67	7.67	12.3	17.1	5.50	6.04	9.17	16.7
	p $ per c.	2.98	3.04	2.90	2.91	6.39	4.08	3.50	3.95	3.67	3.95	4.02	2.60	2.43	2.80	2.88
Berries, all	*q* Mil. c.	.600	.490	.816	1.33	2.35	1.26	2.45	2.50	2.12	2.37	2.52	2.64		2.65	3.37
	v Mil. $	1.09	1.06	1.75	3.10	16.4	5.78	10.4	9.08	9.08	9.81	10.8	7.98		7.52	10.4
	p $ per c.	1.82	2.16	2.15	2.33	7.01	4.60	4.25	3.63	4.28	4.13	4.27	3.03		2.84	3.08
Berries, excl. cranberries and "other" berries	*q* Mil. c											2.44		1.44		
	v Mil. $											10.5		3.62		
	p $ per c.											4.31		2.51		
Cherries	*q* Mil. c.	.114	.319	.390	.543	1.36	.780	2.12	1.88	1.49	1.23	2.14	1.90	2.55	2.96	2.84
	v Mil. $	.308	.826	1.02	1.63	8.45	4.48	10.7	7.25	7.25	6.49	11.8	5.56	6.45	7.48	9.06
	p $ per c.	2.69	2.58	2.61	3.00	6.20	5.75	5.02	3.86	4.88	5.28	5.50	2.92	2.52	2.53	3.19
Fruit cocktail and fruits for salad	*q* Mil. c.							.413	.914	.914	1.10	1.68	1.57	2.24	3.09	4.78
	v Mil. $							3.02	6.97	6.97	7.57	11.0	6.94	9.19	12.6	20.8
	p $ per c.							7.30	7.63	7.63	6.88	6.55	4.41	4.10	4.08	4.35
Grapefruit	*q* Mil. c.							.200	.0877	.0877	.455	1.17	1.60	2.28	2.96	4.93
	v Mil. $							.792	.330	.330	1.76	4.14	3.84	4.89	5.91	7.86
	p $ per c.							3.96	3.76	3.76	3.86	3.52	2.40	2.14	2.00	1.60
Peaches	*q* Mil. c.	1.45	1.30	1.47	3.41	7.71	5.42	7.04	9.90	10.5	11.3	8.72	8.62	10.5	11.5	13.6
	v Mil. $	4.28	3.90	3.75	9.59	46.5	23.9	26.3	38.6	38.6	36.2	35.7	22.6	24.5	30.4	40.1
	p $ per c.	2.96	2.99	2.56	2.81	6.04	4.41	3.73	3.90	3.66	3.21	4.09	2.63	2.34	2.65	2.95

For footnotes see p. 401.

Indexes of Physical Output, with Basic Data on Quantity, Value and Price of Products

FRUITS and VEGETABLES, CANNED (concluded)		1899	1904	1909	1914	1919	1921	1923	1925[b]		1927	1929	1931	1933	1935	1937
Product	*Item*								*A*	*B*						
Canned fruits (concluded)																
Pears	*q* Mil. c.	.672	.789	.638	1.06	2.02	1.17	1.82	3.59	3.88	2.95	4.93	3.92	4.85	4.73	5.17
	v Mil. $	2.19	2.19	1.83	3.85	14.2	7.54	9.39	20.9	20.9	13.1	24.4	12.1	13.1	13.4	15.0
	p $ per c.	3.25	2.78	2.87	3.63	7.03	6.47	5.17	5.82	5.39	4.42	4.96	3.09	2.70	2.84	2.91
Prunes	*q* Mil. c.					.274		.374	.505	.380	.519	1.07	.800	.810	1.71	1.83
	v Mil. $					1.27		.955	1.19	1.19	1.53	3.23	1.63	1.53	3.16	3.59
	p $ per c.					4.65		2.55	2.34	3.12	2.95	3.02	2.04	1.88	1.85	1.97
Olives, ripe	*q* Mil. c.									.193	.458	.934	.816	.433	.608	1.15
	v Mil. $									1.10	2.81	4.68	4.27	1.75	2.76	4.10
	p $ per c.									5.69	6.13	5.01	5.23	4.05	4.54	3.56
Dried fruits[d]																
Apples	*q* Mil. lb.	33.2	40.7	44.6	55.0	46.6	23.0	19.4	21.1	21.1	22.3	44.6	44.3	53.3	70.4	63.9
	v Mil. $	1.91	1.76	3.10	2.89	6.77	2.80	1.69	2.23	2.23	2.23	5.21	3.42	4.17	5.51	4.58
	p $ per lb.	.0574	.0432	.0695	.0526	.145	.122	.0873	.105	.105	.100	.117	.0771	.0782	.0783	.0716
Apricots	*q* Mil. lb.	5.47	19.6	29.2	39.4	24.2	21.8[e]	54.0	33.0	33.0	36.8	43.1	74.1	83.0	49.2	70.6
	v Mil. $	.455	1.41	2.28	3.62	6.03	3.39	5.19	5.43	5.43	5.44	7.32	7.35	6.82	6.76	7.77
	p $ per lb.	.0833	.0721	.0780	.0918	.249	.155	.0961	.164	.164	.148	.170	.0991	.0822	.138	.110
Peaches	*q* Mil. lb.	5.66	25.9	46.8	61.9	73.4	35.4	61.6	36.9	36.9	38.0	35.8	50.3	48.7	50.7	57.9
	v Mil. $	.312	1.70	2.42	2.92	12.1	4.17	6.47	3.55	3.55	3.90	4.31	3.54	2.78	3.75	4.17
	p $ per lb.	.0552	.0658	.0517	.0471	.165	.118	.105	.0964	.0964	.102	.120	.0704	.0570	.0739	.0720
Prunes	*q* Mil. lb.	25.4	118	138	139	136	124[e]	246	398	398	439	347	447	405	474	442
	v Mil. $	.971	3.30	5.13	9.00	18.3	10.1	22.4	29.0	29.0	23.7	30.4	19.9	18.1	20.0	19.4
	p $ per lb.	.0382	.0280	.0370	.0647	.134	.0811	.0909	.0729	.0729	.0541	.0874	.0446	.0447	.0421	.0438
Raisins	*q* Mil. lb.	15.0	121	196	226	293	275	380	534	534	435	421	392	376	414	449
	v Mil. $	1.06	6.35	6.91	13.9	35.5	47.6	36.2	28.8	28.8	25.8	23.5	20.5	13.8	17.4	21.7
	p $ per lb.	.0709	.0523	.0353	.0617	.121	.173	.0953	.0539	.0539	.0593	.0558	.0524	.0367	.0421	.0482
Other dried fruits	*q* Mil. lb.				47.2	41.5	25.0	30.9	31.8	31.8	41.6	46.6	76.5	48.0	61.7	77.0
	v Mil. $				2.41	6.69	3.16	2.47	3.14	3.14	3.04	5.18	5.78	2.75	3.50	4.25
	p $ per lb.				.0510	.161	.127	.0800	.0989	.0989	.0732	.111	.0755	.0574	.0568	.0551

A Comparable with earlier years. *B* Comparable with later years.

[a] Percentages of coverage:

Given year	Base year	Given year	Base year	Given year	Base year	Given year	Base year
1899:54.6	1909:61.5	1919:61.9	1925:57.6	1925:73.9	1929:71.0	1933:71.3	1929:70.9
1904:62.0		1921:56.2	1925:55.2	1927:69.0		1935:69.9	1929:71.0
1909:63.5	1919:63.4	1923:63.4	1925:64.4	1931:67.4		1937:69.9	
1914:65.0	1919:65.8						

[b] Prior to 1927 data were given in terms of both actual and standard cases, but in 1927 and thereafter only actual cases were given. Since the contents of an actual case vary, while those of a standard case do not, the figures on standard cases were used wherever possible. Because 1925 is the last year for which both figures are available, the indexes for 1919, 1921 and 1923 were computed on a 1925 base, and standard cases were used, whereas the indexes for 1925 and all later years were computed on a 1929 base, and actual cases were used. Separate indexes for the years 1919–25, based on actual and standard cases, were constructed by the National Research Project with 1925 as the base (see Magdoff, Siegel and Davis, *op. cit.*). The ratios of their indexes based on actual cases to those based on standard cases are .94 for 1919; .96 for 1921; .92 for 1923; 1.00 for 1925 (base).

[c] Data on cases of vegetables packed are collected annually by the National Canners Association. Sometimes these differ considerably from those given in the Census. In 1927 the Census lists the figures from both sources and explains the differences as follows. "At the biennial census, because of the fact that values as well as quantities were called for, it was in many cases more convenient for canners to report their sales rather than their production; but in connection with the annual canvass the difficulty in regard to values did not arise, and therefore the canners reported their actual packs during the year." *Biennial Census of Manufacturers, 1927*, p. 77. The ratios of the Census data to the National Canners Association annual data for certain vegetables are given below for 1927 and 1935.

Product	*1927*	*1935*
Beans, green	1.10	1.00
Beans, wax	1.14	1.10
Corn	1.01	1.07
Peas	1.04	1.06
Spinach	1.01	1.03
Tomatoes	.97	1.08
Lima beans	..	1.46
Beets	..	1.18

[d] In 1899 dried fruits completely processed on fruit farms were treated as agricultural products and such fruit farms were excluded. In 1904, however, the products of such farms were included when the Census canvassed the packing and shipping houses handling these products. In 1909 and later years they were again treated as agricultural products and excluded.

[e] Data for 1921 and earlier years are not comparable with 1923 and later years because of an enlargement in the scope of the canvass. The 1919–21 data were not used in the computation of the indexes for those years on the 1929 base.

Indexes of Physical Output, with Basic Data on Quantity, Value and Price of Products

ICE		*1899*	*1904*	*1909*	*1914*	*1919*	*1921*	*1923*	*1925*	*1927*	*1929*	*1931*	*1933*	*1935*	*1937*
Adjusted index		9.8	16.6	29.7	43.6	59.8	67.4	77.0	87.5	88.0	100.0	95.7	74.2	72.3	75.3
Unadjusted index[a]		9.7	16.2	28.4	41.2	56.9	66.7	76.5	87.3	87.8	100.0	95.2	73.9	71.6	74.8
Product	*Item*														
Ice, can and plate,	*q* Mil. t.	4.29	7.20	12.6	18.3	25.3	29.7	34.0	38.8	39.1	44.5	42.4	32.9	31.9	33.3
made for sale	*v* Mil. $	13.3	22.5	39.9	55.3	126	152	159	181	179	204	185	134	123	131
	p $ per t.	3.10	3.12	3.15	3.02	4.99	5.14	4.66	4.66	4.57	4.60	4.37	4.09	3.87	3.95

[a] Percentages of coverage:

Given year	Base year	Given year	Base year	Given year	Base year
1899:95.9, 1904:94.4	1909:92.9	1919:92.2, 1921:95.9, 1923:96.3, 1925:96.7	1929:96.9	1927:96.7, 1931:96.5, 1933:96.5, 1935:95.9, 1937:96.3	1929:96.9
1909:92.9, 1914:91.5	1919:92.2				

ICE CREAM		*1923*	*1925*	*1927*	*1929*	*1931*	*1933*	*1935*	*1937*
Adjusted index		76.6	83.9	87.8	100.0	83.3	60.2	81.7	109.0
Unadjusted index[a]		81.5	86.8	89.9	100.0	82.9	60.4	82.8	109.7
Product	*Item*								
Ice cream	*q* Mil. gal.				267	216	146	198	257[b]
	v Mil. $				315	251	139	184	240
	p $ per gal.				1.18	1.16	.951	.928	.934
Ice cream and ices, sherbets, frappes, etc. (combined)	*q*	222	241	248					
	v	270	295	305					
	p	1.22	1.22	1.23					
Ices, sherbets,	*q* Mil. gal.				5.16	4.92	4.86	6.24	9.09
frappes, etc.	*v* Mil. $				5.97	5.14	4.11	5.04	7.61
	$ per gal.				1.16	1.05	.845	.807	.838

ICE CREAM (concluded)		1923	1925	1927	1929	1931	1933	1935	1937
Product	*Item*								
Ice cream specialties	*q* Mil. gal.		3.08	4.14	7.34	9.92	15.1	22.8	33.9[c]
	v Mil. $		4.93	7.25	11.2	14.1	17.4	25.9	39.6
	p $ per gal.		1.60	1.75	1.53	1.42	1.15	1.14	1.17

[a] Percentages of coverage:

Given year	Base year	Given year	Base year
1923:104.0	1929:97.7	1933:101.4	1929:101.1
1925:104.7	1929:101.1	1935:102.5	1929:101.1
1927:103.6	1929:101.1	1937:101.8	1929:101.1
1931:100.6	1929:101.1		

[b] Includes ice milk, not reported separately prior to 1937.

[c] Includes ice milk specialties, not reported separately prior to 1937.

MACARONI		1927	1929	1931	1933[b]	1935	1937
Adjusted index		90.6	100.0	96.6		115.7	122.7
Unadjusted index[a]		84.6	100.0	96.1		110.4	122.8
Product	*Item*						
Macaroni, spaghetti, vermicelli, and noodles, plain or water	*q* Mil. lb.	451	498	478		537	564
	v Mil. $	36.7	38.7	28.9		37.4	39.5
	p $ per lb.	.0813	.0776	.0604		.0697	.0702
Egg noodles and other egg products	*q* Mil. lb.	31.8	55.0	53.2		68.1	94.6
	v Mil. $	5.49	8.20	6.97		7.85	10.6
	p $ per lb.	.173	.149	.131		.115	.112

[a] Percentages of coverage:

Given year	Base year
1927:93.0	1929:99.6
1931:99.0	1929:99.6
1935:95.0	1929:99.6
1937:99.6	1929:99.6

[b] Detailed data on products were not collected in 1933.

Indexes of Physical Output, with Basic Data on Quantity, Value and Price of Products

MEAT PACKING		1899	1904	1909	1914	1919	1921	1923	1925	1927	1929	1931		1933	1935	1937
Adjusted index		56.5	63.8	72.1	71.1	93.1	77.4	96.7	92.4	95.4	100.0	94.5		95.4	84.9	93.8
Unadjusted index[a]		58.6	65.0	71.1	70.2	93.6	79.7	98.7	94.0	96.8	100.0	94.2		93.6	78.8	89.2
Product[b]	*Item*											*A*	*B*	*C*		
Beef	*q* Mil. lb.	2,918	3,748	4,209	3,658	4,832	4,212	4,835	5,065	5,070	4,575	4,553	4,322	4,382	4,747	5,236
	v Mil. $	211	247	328	421	847	548	607	661	763	860	544	517	344	575	711
	p $ per lb.	.0723	.0659	.0778	.115	.175	.130	.126	.131	.150	.188	.119	.120	.0786	.121	.136
Veal	*q* Mil. lb.	84.5	154	253	195	423	419	499	576	550	511	530	487	496	662	779
	v Mil. $	7.71	12.9	25.1	26.3	83.9	63.9	71.7	87.2	98.5	107	67.6	61.9	40.8	80.2	105
	p $ per lb.	.0912	.0834	.0990	.135	.198	.152	.144	.151	.179	.210	.128	.127	.0823	.121	.135
Mutton and lamb	*q* Mil. lb.	401	461	495	629	500	566	511	522	547	602	772	744	716	767	775
	v Mil. $	32.7	36.9	50.7	74.7	120	103	114	128	130	145	117	113	81.8	113	128
	p $ per lb.	.0815	.0800	.102	.119	.240	.183	.223	.246	.238	.242	.151	.152	.114	.147	.165
Pork	*q* Mil. lb.	1,222	1,225	1,547	1,877	2,096	2,322	3,266	2,828	3,110	3,571	3,467	3,320	3,228	2,065	2,519
	v Mil. $	83.9	91.7	159	227	533	374	429	516	518	604	404	387	225	329	416
	p $ per lb.	.0687	.0749	.103	.121	.254	.161	.131	.183	.166	.169	.116	.117	.0698	.159	.165
Edible organs, tripe, and other fresh meat	*q* Mil. lb.	80.4	124	258[c]	280	507	392	518	540	569	585	567	554	506	567	648
	v Mil. $	7.81	9.58	16.4	17.6	56.1	33.3	39.1	51.0	55.0	64.9	45.2	44.0	29.3	50.7	59.3
	p $ per lb.	.0972	.0771	.0636	.0630	.111	.0849	.0756	.0943	.0967	.111	.0798	.0795	.0579	.0894	.0916
Cured meat, total	*q* Mil. lb.	3,276	3,060	2,956	3,021	4,276	3,064	3,975	3,380[d]	3,370	3,752	3,235	3,154	3,080	2,139	2,389
	v Mil. $	246	257	340	408	1,246	560	625	770	675	748	461	447	295	441	504
	p $ per lb.	.0752	.0840	.115	.135	.291	.183	.157	.228	.200	.199	.143	.142	.0957	.206	.211
Canned meat and canned sausage	*q* Mil. lb.	112		121	235	467	74.6	95.1[e]	119	144	169	105	105	150	202	267
	v Mil. $	9.17		15.3	36.3	125	16.3	19.7	24.3	27.8	42.5	23.6	23.6	20.7	39.5	53.9
	p $ per lb.	.0815		.126	.154	.267	.219	.207	.205	.193	.251	.225	.225	.138	.196	.202
Sausage (not canned), meat puddings, head cheese, etc.	*q* Mil. lb.				477	687	604	804	904	919	929	795	738	702	825	989
	v Mil. $				62.8	156	106	133	178	181	202	125	118	81.9	140	175
	p $ per lb.				.132	.227	.176	.166	.197	.197	.217	.158	.159	.117	.170	.177

MEAT PACKING (continued)		1899	1904	1909	1914	1919	1921	1923	1925	1927	1929	1931		1933	1935	1937
Product[b]	*Item*											*A*	*B*	*C*		
Sausage casings, total	*q* Mil. lb.				69.5	102	86.1	96.3	91.5	115	116	70.9	70.1	90.9	91.3	
	v Mil. $				9.08	16.8	12.0	13.7	18.7	22.3	21.8	8.97	8.83	12.3	13.6	
	p $ per lb.				.131	.164	.140	.143	.204	.194	.188	.126	.126	.135	.149	
Lard and other shortenings	*q* Mil. lb.				1,622	2,092[f]	2,196	2,682		2,494	2,706	2,332	2,289	2,318	1,561	1,622
	v Mil. $				166	593	258	334		319	328	197	194	128	201	193
	p $ per lb.				.103	.284	.117	.125		.128	.121	.0847	.0848	.0553	.129	.119
Lard and other shortenings, excl. lard compounds and other lard substitutes	*q* Mil. lb.								1,942		2,301					
	v Mil. $								317		281					
	p $ per lb.								.163		.122					
Lard, stearin, and oleo-margarine	*q* Mil. lb.			1,341		1,541										
	v Mil. $			147		462										
	p $ per lb.			.110		.300										
Lard alone	*q* Mil. lb.	1,020	1,169	1,244												
	v Mil. $	61.1	82.5	134												
	p $ per lb.	.0600	.0706	.108												
Cattle hides and calf skins, cured and uncured	*q* Mil. lb.	336	456	505	435	628	524[g]	627[g]	677	670	584	580	544	535	648	710
	v Mil. $	33.9	44.2	68.4	73.5	210	52.6	73.3	91.9	110	90.2	45.4	43.2	42.5	63.2	97.1
	p $ per lb.	.101	.0969	.136	.169	.334	.100	.117	.136	.165	.155	.0783	.0793	.0794	.0976	.137
Sheep and lamb pelts and other pelts	*q* Mil. skins									9.18	10.8	15.1	14.5	14.5	14.0	15.1
	v Mil. $									16.3	18.8	8.56	8.27	11.9	14.8	26.3
	p $ per skin									1.78	1.74	.568	.571	.818	1.06	1.74
Sheep and lamb pelts and other pelts, excl. other hides and skins, cured and uncured	*q* Mil. skins			11.7	15.9	12.2[h]	12.1	10.9	10.8		10.5					
	v Mil. $			11.4	13.6	33.7	8.31	17.9	22.6		18.4					
	p $ per skin			.974	.856	2.76	.685	1.64	2.08		1.76					

For footnotes see next page.

Indexes of Physical Output, with Basic Data on Quantity, Value and Price of Products

MEAT PACKING (concluded)		1899	1904	1909	1914	1919	1921	1923	1925	1927	1929	1931		1933	1935	1937
Product[b]	*Item*											*A*	*B*	*C*		
Pickled sheep	*q* Mil. lb.									17.0	13.2	23.4	23.3	27.9	29.1	31.1
and lamb	*v* Mil. $									4.27	4.01	1.90	1.90	2.65	3.38	6.57
skins	*p* $ per lb.									.252	.305	.0814	.0816	.0950	.116	.211
Wool	*q* Mil. lb.	13.2	16.4	21.9	26.4	29.9	32.2	30.9	32.2	30.4	35.9	43.9	43.8	49.4	41.7	40.4
	v Mil. $	3.33	5.23	8.33	7.94	20.1	9.89	19.1	23.4	18.5	19.9	12.5	12.5	15.1	15.9	23.4
	p $ per lb.	.253	.319	.381	.300	.671	.307	.617	.727	.607	.553	.286	.286	.305	.382	.579
Hair, hog and	*q* Mil. lb.					60.3	19.8	26.4	27.3	29.7	25.9	15.6	15.6	11.8	13.1	25.4
other	*v* Mil. $					4.06	.702	1.80	2.11	2.72	1.15	.516	.516	.372	.708	1.70
	p $ per lb.					.0673	.0354	.0681	.0774	.0917	.0445	.0330	.0330	.0315	.0541	.0668
Fertilizer	*q* Th. t.								181	176	135	115	107	88.6	87.0	35.4
materials	*v* Mil. $								6.90	7.77	6.23	2.88	2.77	1.93	2.32	1.31
	p $ per t.								38.1	44.2	46.2	25.1	26.0	21.8	26.6	36.9

A Comparable with all years except 1933. *B* Comparable with 1933. *C* Comparable with 1931.

[a] Percentages of coverage:

Given year	Base year	Given year	Base year	Given year	Base year	Given year	Base year
1899:88.9	1909:84.5	1914:93.5	1919:95.1	1923:96.6	1929:94.7	1931:94.7	1929:95.0
1904:86.1	1909:83.3	1919:95.2	1929:94.7	1925:95.0	1929:93.5	1933:89.5	1931:90.9
1909:86.3	1919:88.0	1921:97.5	1929:94.7	1927:96.4	1929:95.0	1935:88.2	1929:95.0
						1937:89.7	1929:94.4

[b] Does not include meat used in the production of cured and canned meat and sausage made in the same plants in which the animals are slaughtered. It does, however, include fresh meat sold to packers to be manufactured into cured and canned meat products. Such sales, which lead to some duplication in the data on the output of the industry, account for 15 to 20 percent of the quantity of fresh meat represented in the table. There appears to be no significant upward or downward trend in the degree of duplication.

[c] Includes poultry in 1909 and earlier years. In 1914, 16.6 mil. lb. of poultry at a value of 2.93 mil. dollars were produced.

[d] Prior to 1927 excludes some cooked hams.

[e] Prior to 1925 canned meat and canned sausage included a small amount of canned goods other than meat and sausage to avoid disclosing the operations of individual establishments.

[f] Prior to 1921 oleo oil was excluded from lard and other shortenings because the quantity was given in gallons.

[g] For 1923 and 1921 cattle hides included data for hides received as payment for custom slaughtering.

[h] Prior to 1921 sheep pelts included goat and kid skins.

MILK, CANNED		1899	1904	1909	1914	1919	1921	1923	1925	1927	1929	1931	1933	1935	1937
Adjusted index		[b]	10.9	17.9[c]	35.8	84.3	69.0	72.9	76.2	87.5	100.0	99.5	98.3	115.0	128.1
Unadjusted index[a]		7.2	11.7	18.6	32.8	79.7	67.4	71.9	73.0	85.2	100.0	94.5	95.0	111.4	126.9
Product	*Item*														
Condensed milk, sweetened	*q* Mil. lb.								431	379	533	399	275	257	260
	v Mil. $								38.7	34.3	42.9	23.9	14.6	14.9	16.2
	p $ per lb.								.0900	.0904	.0806	.0600	.0532	.0579	0622
Condensed and evaporated milk, unsweetened	*q* Mil. lb.	*q* 187	308	495	876	2,154	1,766	1,835	1,288	1,606	1,642	1,551	1,832	2,122	2,271
	v Mil. $	*v* 11.9	20.1	33.6	58.9	299	160	165	104	130	126	90.1	89.1	118	137
	p $ per lb.	*p* .0636	.0653	.0678	.0672	.139	.0904	.0900	.0807	.0809	.0768	.0581	.0487	.0555	.0604
Condensed and evaporated buttermilk	*q* Mil. lb.								95.4	113	136	100	61.6	65.0	93.5
	v Mil. $								2.70	3.73	4.20	1.90	.920	1.03	1.77
	p $ per lb.								.0283	.0330	.0309	.0189	.0149	.0158	.0190
Casein	*q* Mil. lb.	12.3	11.6	13.0	18.8	16.7	9.73	21.4	22.0	23.5	57.8	41.4	31.5	49.0	77.2
	v Mil. $	.384	.554	.796	.991	2.20	.620	2.50	2.30	3.05	5.73	2.27	2.56	4.27	8.36
	p $ per lb.	.0312	.0478	.0611	.0527	.132	.0638	.117	.105	.130	.0990	.0548	.0812	.0873	.108
Dried and powdered milk, cream, and buttermilk	*q* Mil. lb.				20.5	50.2	61.2	97.9	112	183	289	371	343	372	441
	v Mil. $				1.97	12.2	8.16	12.5	12.0	19.7	24.5	16.3	16.8	21.4	28.5
	p $ per lb.				.0962	.243	.133	.128	.107	.108	.0848	.0439	.0490	.0573	.0647
Ice cream mix	*q* Mil. lb.								113	114	137	162	108	199	310
	v Mil. $								12.4	13.8	15.3	13.5	8.85	15.0	26.7
	p $ per lb.								.109	.121	.111	.0835	.0818	.0754	.0863

[a] Percentages of coverage:

Given year	Base year	Given year	Base year	Given year	Base year	Given year	Base year
1904:100.9	1909:97.4	1919:92.2		1925:100.4	-	1933:101.3	
1909: 97.4	1919:88.6	1921:95.3	1929:97.6	1927:102.2	1929:104.9	1935:101.6	1929:104.9
1914: 89.4	1919:92.2	1923:96.3		1931: 99.6		1937:103.8	

[b] No adjusted index for 1899 could be computed because the industry is not shown separately in the Census for that year. The adjusted index given above, extrapolated by the unadjusted index, is 6.7 for 1899.

[c] Between 1909 and 1914 establishments making powdered milk and sugar of milk were transferred from chemicals, n.e.c., to milk, canned. The resulting discontinuity appears to be slight.

Indexes of Physical Output, with Basic Data on Quantity, Value and Price of Products

OLEOMARGARINE, not elsewhere made		*1925*	*1927*	*1929*	*1931*	*1933*	*1935*	*1937*
Adjusted index		72.0	79.2	100.0	71.2	62.8	94.5	126.1
Unadjusted index[a]		81.4	87.3	100.0	60.4	60.8	95.9	115.0
Product[b]	*Item*							
Oleomargarine	*q* Mil. lb.	168	180	206	125	125	198	237
	v Mil. $	34.4	33.0	35.5	14.8	9.43	25.1	31.0
	p $ per lb.	.205	.183	.172	.119	.0752	.127	.131

[a] Percentages of coverage:

Given year	Base year	Given year	Base year
1925:86.3 1927:84.1 1931:64.8	1929:76.4	1933:73.9 1935:77.5 1937:69.6	1929:76.4

[b] Data relate to products made within the oleomargarine industry alone.

RICE		*1899*	*1904*	*1909*	*1914*	*1919*	*1921*	*1923*	*1925*	*1927*	*1929*	*1931*	*1933*	*1935*	*1937*
Adjusted index		[c]	51.4	51.9	55.0	88.2	93.5	94.6	76.5	100.4	100.0	101.8		95.9	106.2
Unadjusted index[a]		20.6	51.5	51.1	55.0	86.1	93.2	94.7	76.5	100.2	100.0	101.7	89.1[d]	95.2	105.7
Product[b]	*Item*														
Clean rice	*q* Mil. lb.	243	624	626	675	1,063	1,154	1,172	948	1,247	1,243	1,263		1,182	1,305
	v Mil. $		15.4	20.7	21.7	83.5	39.0	44.8	51.1	51.8	46.1	38.4		41.6	43.4
	p ¢ per lb.		2.46	3.30	3.21	7.85	3.38	3.82	5.39	4.16	3.71	3.04		3.52	3.33
Polish	*q* Mil. lb.	15.1	33.3	29.8	31.1	36.2	42.4	39.9	32.7	34.6	34.4	33.0		27.8	32.9
	v Mil. $		.268	.362	.352	.966	.578	.535	.502	.452	.513	.331		.332	.500
	p ¢ per lb.		.804	1.21	1.13	2.67	1.36	1.34	1.53	1.31	1.49	1.00		1.20	1.52
Bran	*q* Mil. lb.	69.3	121	91.2	99.4	143	136	146	115	140	143	153		147	181
	v Mil. $		.501	.736	.772	2.50	1.02	1.28	1.32	1.15	1.65	1.10		1.39	2.18
	p ¢ per lb.		.415	.807	.777	1.75	.753	.874	1.15	.822	1.15	.720		.949	1.21

[a] Percentages of coverage:

Given year	Base year	Given year	Base year	Given year	Base year	Given year	Base year
1904:99.0	1909:97.4	1919:96.5	1929:98.9	1925:98.9	1929:98.9	1935:98.2	1929:98.9
1909:97.4	1919:96.5	1921:98.6		1927:98.7		1937:98.4	
1914:98.9		1923:99.0		1931:98.8			

[b] Data relate to products made within the rice industry alone.

[c] No adjusted index for 1899 could be computed because the percentage of coverage in that year could not be determined. In the computation of the index for 1899, quantities were multiplied by the price per pound in 1909. The adjusted index given above, extrapolated by the unadjusted index, is 20.6 for 1899; interpolated by the unadjusted index it is 89.5 for 1933.

[d] Detailed statistics of products were not collected by the Census in 1933. The unadjusted index for 1933 was estimated on the basis of shipments of milled rice from mills in Louisiana, Texas, Arkansas and Tennessee (data compiled by the U.S. Bureau of Agricultural Economics). These mills accounted for 79.1 percent of total United States production of clean rice in 1931 and 76.8 percent in 1935.

SAUSAGE, not elsewhere made		*1929*	*1931*	*1933*[b]	*1935*	*1937*
Adjusted index		100.0	107.6		153.8	182.4
Unadjusted index[a]		100.0	104.2		116.6	110.9
Product[c]	*Item*					
Fresh sausage	*q* Mil. lb.	346	387		438	387
	v Mil. $	78.3	62.7		74.2	69.1
	p $ per lb.	.226	.162		.169	.179
Dry sausage	*q* Mil. lb.	31.5	32.0		39.8	32.4
	v Mil. $	9.46	6.68		8.65	7.78
	p $ per lb.	.300	.209		.217	.240
Sausage casings	*q* Mil. lb.	57.9	29.5		28.9	
	v Mil. $	10.4	4.54		6.52	
	p $ per lb.	.179	.154		.225	

[a] Percentages of coverage:

Given year	Base year
1931:87.7	1929:90.6
1935:68.7	
1937:49.3	1929:81.0

[b] Detailed data on products were not collected in 1933.

[c] Data relate to products made within the sausage industry alone.

Indexes of Physical Output, with Basic Data on Quantity, Value and Price of Products

SHORTENINGS		*1927*	*1929*	*1931*	*1933*	*1935*	*1937*
Adjusted index		98.9	100.0	99.5	97.9	134.5	147.8
Unadjusted index[a]		98.5	100.0	100.1	90.4	127.5	141.8
Product[b]	*Item*						
Shortenings	*q* Mil. lb.	775	832	833	702	1,063	1,178
	v Mil. $	89.3	98.3	73.8	45.1	126	139
	p $ per lb.	.115	.118	.0886	.0642	.118	.118
Vegetable cooking oils	*q* Mil. lb.	468	422				
	v Mil. $	45.6	42.6				
	p $ per lb.	.0973	.101				
Vegetable cooking oils, vegetable salad oils, and other edible refined oils	*q* Mil lb.			556	564	705	789
	v Mil. $			37.4	30.8	67.6	80.8
	p $ per lb.			.0673	.0547	.0959	.102

[a] Percentages of coverage:

Given year	Base year	Given year	Base year
1927:90.8	1929:91.2	1933:88.5	1931:96.5
1931:64.0	1929:63.6	1935:90.9	
		1937:91.9	

(1933, 1935 and 1937 bracketed to base year 1931:96.5.)

[b] Data relate to products made within the shortenings industry alone.

TOTAL FOODS	*1899*	*1904*	*1909*	*1914*	*1919*	*1921*	*1923*	*1925*	*1927*	*1929*	*1931*	*1933*	*1935*	*1937*
Adjusted index	30.3	37.1	44.9	53.1	65.1	64.5	80.0	85.1	90.3	100.0	91.1	82.4	92.5	104.2
Unadjusted index[a,b]	40.3	47.9	56.8	64.0	79.3	68.2	81.7	86.5	90.3	100.0	91.0	82.2	92.4	103.1

[a] Percentages of coverage:

Given year	Base year	Given year	Base year	Given year	Base year
1899:63.5	1909:60.5	1919:58.3	1929:47.9	1927:93.0	1929:93.0
1904:61.7		1921:52.0	1929:49.2	1931:96.2	1929:96.3
1909:60.6	1919:58.2	1923:81.7	1929:80.0	1933:92.2	1929:92.4
1914:57.7		1925:90.0	1929:88.6	1935:93.8	1929:93.9
				1937:92.8	

(1899 and 1904 bracketed to 1909:60.5; 1909 and 1914 bracketed to 1919:58.2; 1935 and 1937 bracketed to 1929:93.9.)

[b] Indexes for the following industries and years were not used in the computation of the group indexes, chiefly because adequate information on value added was lacking: flavoring extracts, 1933–37; feeds, 1925.

The 1899 and 1904 indexes for cane sugar and cane-sugar refining were combined (with 1909 value added as weights) before inclusion in the group index because for these years the industries are given in combination by the Census, and separate values added are not available for 1899 and 1904. The combined indexes are as follows: 1899: 77.2; 1904: 84.6; 1909: 100.0. For the same reason the 1899 indexes for butter, cheese, and canned milk were combined, with 1909 value added weights. The combined indexes are as follows: 1899: 62.2; 1909: 100.0.

BEVERAGES

BEVERAGES, NONALCOHOLIC		1931	1933	1935	1937
Adjusted index		66.3	35.3	51.7	100.0
Unadjusted index[a]		63.4	36.1	51.8	100.0
Product	*Item*				
Carbonated beverages[b]	*q* Mil. gal.	291	196	291	565
	v Mil. $	170	110	159	276
	p $ per gal.	.583	.559	.545	.488
Cereal beverages	*q* Mil. gal.	95.8	12.1	3.64	2.58
	v Mil. $	33.6	4.11	1.11	1.06
	p $ per gal.	.351	.339	.304	.411

[a] Percentages of coverage:

Given year	Base year
1931: 95.7	
1933: 102.1	1937: 99.9
1935: 100.2	

[b] Figures for bottled carbonated beverages (reported in cases) were converted to gallons on the basis of size of bottles per case for 1935 and 1937; for 1931 and 1933, cases were converted to gallons by multiplication by average number of gallons per case. Data for carbonated beverages include also bulk goods, reported in gallons.

LIQUORS, DISTILLED		1899	1904	1909	1914	1919	1921	1923	1925	1927	1929	1931	1933	1935	1937
Adjusted index[a]															
Unadjusted index		2,573.8	2,892.2	3,356.1	4,257.4	108.3	116.8	91.8	55.0	47.5	100.0	94.3	322.0	6,985.8	10,696.3
Product[b]	*Item*														
Distilled spirits, excl. alcohol	*q* Mil. tax gal.	62.3	70.0	81.3	103	2.62	2.83	2.22	1.33	1.15	2.42	2.28	7.80	169	259

[a] No adjusted index could be computed because data are lacking on the value of output of the product listed.

[b] The quantity data are taken from the annual reports of the U.S. Bureau of Internal Revenue and cover fiscal years ending June 30. The data for 1921–37 relate to total production of distilled spirits, excluding alcohol produced in industrial alcohol plants. The 1909–19 data relate to total production of distilled spirits, excluding alcohol and commercial alcohol; the 1899–1904 data refer to total production of distilled spirits, excluding alcohol and pure, neutral, or cologne spirits.

Indexes of Physical Output, with Basic Data on Quantity, Value and Price of Products

LIQUORS, MALT		*1899*	*1904*	*1909*	*1914*	*1919*	*1921*	*1923*	*1925*	*1927*	*1929*	*1931*	*1933*	*1935*	*1937*
Adjusted index[a]															
Unadjusted index[b]		949.2	1,248.4	1,457.9	1,712.1	716.8	238.5	136.3	132.4	113.4	100.0	81.1	286.1	1,173.3	1,522.3
Product[c]	*Item*														
Fermented malt liquors	*q* Mil. bbl.[d]	36.7	48.3	56.4	66.2	27.7							9.80[e]	45.2	58.7
Cereal beverages	*q* Mil. bbl.[d]						9.22[f]	5.27[f]	5.12[f]	4.38	3.87	3.14	1.26	.131	.103[f]

[a] No adjusted index could be computed because data are lacking on the value of output of the product listed.

[b] Based on the total output, in terms of barrels, of fermented malt liquors and cereal beverages.

[c] The production figures are those compiled by the Bureau of Internal Revenue and cover fiscal years ending June 30. Production figures are reported in the Census for the calendar years 1933–37 alone.

[d] Barrels containing not more than 31 gallons.

[e] Alcoholic content limited to 3.2 percent by weight from April 7 to December 5, 1933. There was no legal production of fermented malt liquors during the period 1921–31.

[f] Reported in gallons and converted to barrels of 31 gallons each.

LIQUORS, VINOUS		*1923*	*1925*	*1927*	*1929*	*1931*	*1933*	*1935*	*1937*
Adjusted index[a]									
Unadjusted index		122.7	31.9	38.7	100.0	58.4	164.7	809.2	1,075.1
Product[b]	*Item*								
Still and sparkling wine	*q* Mil. wine gal.	14.0	3.64	4.41	11.4	6.66	18.8	92.3	123

[a] No adjusted index could be computed because data are lacking on the value of output of the product listed.

[b] The production figures (which represent "the amount removed by fermenters including wine that is removed for use as distilling material in the production of brandy") are those compiled by the Bureau of Internal Revenue and cover fiscal years ending June 30.

MALT		1925	1927	1929	1931	1933	1935	1937
Adjusted index		83.1	80.4	100.0	88.7	125.2[b]	213.2	245.1
Unadjusted index[a]		84.7	83.3	100.0	91.2	147.8	229.0	258.4
Product	*Item*							
Barley malt	q Mil. bu.	22.1	21.6	26.0	23.6	38.4	59.0	67.1
	v Mil. $	21.7	18.5	20.8	17.5	29.1	70.9[c]	88.5[c]
	p $ per bu.	.983	.857	.802	.738	.759	1.20	1.32
Rye and wheat malt and roasted malt	q Mil. bu.	.139	.221	.239	.236	.356	.921	.634
	v Mil. $	.232	.270	.291	.231	.350	1.235	.726
	p $ per bu.	1.67	1.22	1.22	.980	.984	1.34	1.14

[a] Percentages of coverage:

Given year	Base year
1925: 91.2	1929:89.5
1927: 92.6	
1931: 91.9	
1933: 105.6	
1935: 96.1	
1937: 94.3	

[b] Between 1933 and 1935 malthouses operated by breweries were transferred from liquors, malt, to malt.

[c] Estimated in part.

TOTAL BEVERAGES	1899	1904	1909	1914	1919	1921	1923	1925	1927	1929	1931	1933	1935	1937
Adjusted index	43.2	54.6	63.3	75.6	23.2							16.9	70.4	100.0
Unadjusted index[a,b]	53.0	66.0	76.9	91.2	24.1							16.9	70.4	100.0

[a] Percentages of coverage:

Given year	Base year	Given year	Base year	Given year	Base year
1899:92.3	1909:91.5	1909:91.5	1919:78.0	1935:100.0	1933:100.0
1904:91.1		1914:90.9		1937:100.0	
		1919:67.3	1937:65.0		

[b] No indexes are given for 1921–31 because of inadequate coverage.

TOBACCO PRODUCTS

Indexes of Physical Output, with Basic Data on Quantity, Value and Price of Products

CIGARETTES		*1899*	*1904*	*1909*	*1914*	*1919*	*1921*	*1923*	*1925*	*1927*	*1929*	*1931*	*1933*	*1935*	*1937*
Adjusted index									[b]	81.1	100.0	95.5	95.5	112.8	134.1
Unadjusted index[a]		3.1	2.8	5.6	13.8	43.4	42.6	54.5	67.2	81.6	100.0	95.6	93.9	114.4	138.9
Product[c]	*Item*														
Cigarettes	*q* Bil. cigarettes	3.74	3.43	6.84	16.9	53.2	52.1	66.7	82.3	99.8	122	117	115	140	170

[a] Percentages of coverage:

Given year	Base year	Given year	Base year
1927:89.0 1931:88.5 1933:86.9	1929:88.6	1935:89.7 1937:91.6	1929:88.6

[b] No adjusted indexes for 1899–1925 could be computed because data are lacking on the value of output of the product listed. The adjusted index given above, extrapolated by the unadjusted index, is 3.1 for 1899; 2.8 for 1904; 5.6 for 1909; 13.7 for 1914; 43.1 for 1919; 42.3 for 1921; 54.2 for 1923; 66.8 for 1925.

[c] The quantity data are taken from the annual reports of the Bureau of Internal Revenue and cover fiscal years ending June 30. No comparable value data are available in this source. While the Census does not present statistics for quantities, it does provide values for 1927 and later years. To obtain the percentages of coverage, we divided the values given in the Census for cigarettes made in all tobacco industries by the values of products for the cigarettes industry. The quantity and value statistics are not strictly comparable, but the differences are probably small. For the years 1933–37, for which quantity data are given by the Census, the ratios of Census calendar-year figures to the Internal Revenue fiscal-year figures are practically 1.00.

CIGARS		*1899*	*1904*	*1909*	*1914*	*1919*	*1921*	*1923*	*1925*	*1927*	*1929*	*1931*	*1933*	*1935*	*1937*
Adjusted index									[b]	100.4	100.0	81.8	65.6	70.4	79.8
Unadjusted index[a]		79.8	106.4	111.2	119.0	112.3	106.7	107.6	99.7	100.3	100.0	81.9	65.5	70.5	79.8
Product[c]	*Item*														
Cigars															
Excl. cigars made in bonded warehouses	*q* Mil. cigars	5,532	7,377	7,711	8,249	7,786	7,396								
Incl. cigars made in bonded warehouses	*q* Mil. cigars						7,428	7,493	6,944	6,988	6,964	5,706	4,565	4,913	5,556

[a] Percentages of coverage:

Given year	Base year	Given year	Base year
1927:99.1	1929:99.2	1935:99.5	1929:99.2
1931:99.4		1937:99.2	
1933:99.1			

[b] No adjusted indexes for 1899–1925 could be computed because data are lacking on the value of output of the product listed. The adjusted index given above, extrapolated by the unadjusted index, is 79.9 for 1899; 106.5 for 1904; 111.3 for 1909; 119.1 for 1914; 112.4 for 1919; 106.8 for 1921; 107.7 for 1923; 99.8 for 1925.

[c] The quantity data are taken from the annual reports of the Bureau of Internal Revenue and cover fiscal years ending June 30. No comparable value data are available in this source. While the Census does not present statistics for quantities, it does provide values for 1927 and later years. The percentages of coverage were secured in the same way as the percentages of coverage for cigarettes; for the method used, see footnote c to the table for the cigarettes industry. For 1937, the only year for which quantity data are given by the Census, the ratio of the Census calendar-year figure to the Internal Revenue fiscal-year figure is .96.

TOBACCO PRODUCTS, OTHER		*1899*	*1904*	*1909*	*1914*	*1919*	*1921*	*1923*	*1925*	*1927*	*1929*	*1931*	*1933*	*1935*	*1937*
Adjusted index								[b]	124.5	113.8	100.0	95.6	81.4	82.2	82.9
Unadjusted index[a]		77.3	92.8	113.2	115.7	111.2	101.5	108.3	108.6	104.0	100.0	97.4	89.8	89.9	89.3
Product[c]	*Item*														
Chewing and smoking tobacco, and snuff	*q* Mil. lb.	295	354	431	441	424	387	413	414	396	381	371	342	343	341

[a] Percentages of coverage:

Given year	Base year	Given year	Base year
1925:128.9	1929:147.8	1933:162.9	1929:147.8
1927:135.0		1935:161.8	
1931:150.5		1937:159.3	

[b] No adjusted indexes for 1899–1923 could be computed because data are lacking on the value of output of the product listed. The adjusted index given above, extrapolated by the unadjusted index, is 88.6 for 1899; 106.4 for 1904; 129.8 for 1909; 132.6 for 1914; 127.5 for 1919; 116.4 for 1921; 124.2 for 1923.

[c] The quantity data are taken from the annual reports of the Bureau of Internal Revenue and cover fiscal years ending June 30. No comparable value data are available in this source. While the Census does not present statistics for quantities, it does provide values for 1925 and later years. The percentages of coverage were secured in the same way as the percentages of coverage for cigarettes; for the method used see footnote c to the table for the cigarettes industry. For 1937, the only year for which quantity data are given by the Census, the ratio of the Census calendar-year figure to the Internal Revenue fiscal-year figure is 1.00.

Indexes of Physical Output, with Basic Data on Quantity, Value and Price of Products

TOTAL TOBACCO PRODUCTS	1899	1904	1909	1914	1919	1921	1923	1925	1927	1929	1931	1933	1935	1937
Adjusted index / Unadjusted index[a,b]	29.8	37.4	43.4	52.7	69.3	66.1	73.7	81.3	89.5	100.0	92.8	87.6	100.8	117.2

[a] Percentages of coverage: 100.0 in every year.

[b] The 1899, 1904 and the 1925 indexes for cigars and cigarettes were combined, with estimated value added as weights based on Census data for 1909 and 1923–27, because for these years the industries were given in combination by the Census. The combined indexes on the 1929 base are as follows: 1899: 22.1; 1904: 28.3; 1925: 75.1.

TEXTILE PRODUCTS

ARTIFICIAL LEATHER		1923	1925	1927	1929	1931	1933[b]	1935	1937
Adjusted index		101.7	108.6	104.3	100.0	58.7		91.0	118.1
Unadjusted index[a]		71.8	88.1	80.7	100.0	55.9		79.5	104.2
Product	*Item*								
Heavy goods, pyroxylin-	*q* Mil. sq.yd.	32.6	31.9	32.1	36.5	19.6		23.4	31.6
coated, made on	*v* Mil. $	19.0	20.9	19.3	22.1	8.76		9.67	13.0
textile base	*p* $ per sq.yd.	.583	.655	.602	.605	.446		.414	.412
Light goods, pyroxylin-	*q* Mil. sq.yd.	8.43	25.6	17.6	28.5	17.4		33.9	42.5
coated, made on	*v* Mil. $	2.88	9.76	5.15	8.35	4.59		7.46	9.51
textile base	*p* $ per sq.yd.	.341	.381	.293	.293	.264		.220	.224

[a] Percentages of coverage:

Given year	Base year	Given year	Base year
1923:65.2, 1925:74.9, 1927:71.4	1929:92.4	1931:87.8, 1935:80.7, 1937:81.5	1929:92.4

[b] Detailed data on products were not collected in 1933.

ASPHALTED-FELT-BASE FLOOR COVERING		1919	1921	1923	1925	1927	1929	1931	1933	1935	1937
Adjusted index		[b]	24.2	56.5	74.2	105.2	100.0	78.2	84.5	112.9	144.1
Unadjusted index[a]		25.7	26.9	58.3	59.1	92.9	100.0	73.0	85.8	107.4	131.5
Product	*Item*										
Piece goods	q Mil. sq.yd.			38.9	55.5	59.7	57.0	48.4		66.6	79.2
	v Mil. $			11.8	17.6	15.0	14.7	11.3		14.5	17.1
	p $ per sq.yd.			.302	.318	.251	.257	.234		.217	.216
Piece goods and rugs (bracketed together)	q	30.4	31.7						101		
	v	13.9	13.0						26.7		
	p	.458	.411						.264		
Rugs	q Mil. sq.yd.			32.2	22.4	52.1	60.9	39.2		61.4	76.8
	v Mil. $			18.5	12.4	19.9	22.3	10.3		16.8	18.3
	p $ per sq.yd.			.574	.553	.382	.365	.263		.274	.239

[a] Percentages of coverage:

Given year	Base year	Given year	Base year
1921: 128.5	1929: 115.8	1931: 108.2	1929: 115.8
1923: 119.6		1933: 117.6	
1925: 92.3		1935: 110.2	
1927: 102.3		1937: 105.8	

[b] No adjusted index for 1919 could be computed because the industry is not shown separately in the Census for that year. The adjusted index given above, extrapolated by the unadjusted index, is 23.1 for 1919.

CARPETS and RUGS, WOOL		1899	1904	1909	1914	1919	1921	1923	1925	1927	1929	1931	1933	1935	1937
Adjusted index		60.7	65.4	78.3[c]	71.1	61.9	59.1	101.2	95.5	89.2	100.0	62.8	60.6	85.8[d]	92.4
Unadjusted index[a]		51.0	56.1	68.8	61.9	55.1	59.2	102.6	97.0	89.1	100.0	60.4	57.4	78.2	87.1
Product[b]	*Item*														
Carpets and rugs															
Axminster and moquette	q Mil. sq.yd.	5.35	8.18	15.7	15.7										
	v Mil. $	5.10	8.48	17.4	18.6										
	p $ per sq.yd.	.953	1.04	1.11	1.18										
Wilton	q Mil. sq.yd.	3.93[e]	2.40	5.34	5.62										
	v Mil. $	4.58	4.71	10.1	11.9										
	p $ per sq.yd.	1.17	1.97	1.89	2.12										

For footnotes see p. 421.

Indexes of Physical Output, with Basic Data on Quantity, Value and Price of Products

CARPETS and RUGS, WOOL (continued)		1899	1904	1909	1914	1919	1921	1923	1925	1927	1929	1931	1933	1935	1937
Product[b]	*Item*														
Carpets and rugs (concluded)															
Brussels	*q* Mil. sq.yd.	2.69	3.02	4.44	2.70										
	v Mil. $	2.98	3.90	5.55	4.00										
	p $ per sq.yd.	1.11	1.29	1.25	1.48										
Tapestry velvet	*q* Mil. sq.yd.	4.28	8.03[e]	10.7[e]	13.2[e]										
	v Mil. $	3.74	7.75	9.03	12.9										
	p $ per sq.yd.	.875	.965	.847	.973										
Tapestry Brussels	*q* Mil. sq.yd.	8.76	16.1	17.1	13.6										
	v Mil. $	5.53	11.5	13.0	9.85										
	p $ per sq.yd.	.632	.712	.761	.724										
Ingrain carpets	*q* Mil. sq.yd.	39.9	33.6	17.8	5.80										
	v Mil. $	14.4	13.3	6.75	2.24										
	p $ per sq.yd.	.360	.396	.379	.387										
Ingrain art squares	*q* Mil. sq.yd.	2.72	7.14	6.13	3.18										
	v Mil. $	1.18	2.79	2.41	1.17										
	p $ per sq.yd.	.432	.390	.393	.367										
Smyrna rugs	*q* Mil. sq.yd.	3.65	3.83	1.40	.822										
	v Mil. $	3.68	4.13	1.66	.871										
	p $ per sq.yd.	1.01	1.08	1.19	1.06										
Other rugs	*q* Mil. sq.yd.	5.11	.406	2.68	5.64										
	v Mil. $	2.39	.350	1.08	3.18										
	p $ per sq.yd.	.468	.862	.403	.564										
Carpets															
Axminster and moquette	*q* Mil. sq.yd.				1.45	2.02	.763	4.29	4.59	2.94	6.88	2.29	2.21	5.42	5.09
	v Mil. $				1.85	4.97	2.05	11.5	9.81	7.57	14.8	4.12	3.33	8.92	11.2
	p $ per sq.yd.				1.27	2.45	2.68	2.69	2.14	2.57	2.15	1.79	1.50	1.65	2.20

CARPETS and RUGS, WOOL (continued)		1899	1904	1909	1914	1919	1921	1923	1925	1927	1929	1931	1933	1935	1937
Product[b]	*Item*														
Carpets (concluded)															
Wilton	*q* Mil. sq.yd.				1.90	1.23	2.23	2.82	3.40	3.80	4.21	2.00	1.32	2.39	4.10
	v Mil. $				3.55	4.52	7.75	13.0	15.5	15.1	16.8	6.23	3.18	6.69	13.7
	p $ per sq.yd.				1.87	3.68	3.47	4.63	4.55	3.98	3.98	3.12	2.41	2.80	3.34
Brussels	*q* Th. sq.yd.				694	149	125	52.7	25.5	20.2	120				
	v Th. $				1,030	219	488	160	71.7	69.8	645				
	p $ per sq.yd.				1.49	1.47	3.91	3.04	2.82	3.46	5.39				
Tapestry velvet	*q* Mil. sq.yd.				4.86	4.38	3.03	7.90	8.82	6.95	13.6	5.41	7.10	11.4	17.0
	v Mil. $				4.81	9.32	5.81	17.7	17.1	14.1	26.2	10.6	10.6	23.4	48.6
	p $ per sq.yd.				.991	2.13	1.92	2.24	1.94	2.03	1.93	1.97	1.49	2.05	2.86
Tapestry Brussels	*q* Mil. sq.yd.				2.61	2.00	1.11	1.32	1.27	1.64	1.28	.862			
	v Mil. $				1.71	2.66	1.70	1.59	1.32	1.50	1.34	.763			
	p $ per sq.yd.				.653	1.33	1.53	1.20	1.03	.915	1.04	.885			
Ingrain	*q* Mil. sq.yd.				5.80	1.20	.835	.693	.820	.266	.259	.0590	.028		
	v Mil. $				2.24	1.06	.678	.623	.653	.218	.165	.0482	.025		
	p $ per sq.yd.				.387	.880	.812	.898	.797	.822	.635	.816	.89		
All other	*q* Mil. sq.yd.					.989	4.96	4.66	2.93	1.25	1.09				
	v Mil. $					.831	1.92	6.88	4.58	2.22	1.92				
	p $ per sq.yd.					.840	.387	1.48	1.56	1.78	1.77				
Rugs made of sewed strips															
Axminster and moquette	*q* Mil. sq.yd.				9.64	7.21	9.31	10.9	6.04	2.84					
	v Mil. $				10.7	15.0	18.9	26.9	14.4	5.42					
	p $ per sq.yd.				1.11	2.08	2.03	2.47	2.38	1.91					
Wilton	*q* Mil. sq.yd.				3.57	2.95	1.24	6.63	5.93	4.49	2.03	.884	.844		
	v Mil. $				8.02	14.6	5.59	36.7	35.9	23.8	10.8	3.37	2.34		
	p $ per sq.yd.				2.24	4.94	4.51	5.53	6.04	5.29	5.31	3.81	2.77		
														q 1.04	.976
														v 2.78	2.65
														p 2.68	2.72
Other than Wilton	*q* Mil. sq.yd.									4.85	1.69	.455	1.30		
	v Mil. $									11.3	3.63	.640	2.05		
	p $ per sq.yd									2.34	2.15	1.41	1.58		

For footnotes see p. 421.

Indexes of Physical Output, with Basic Data on Quantity, Value and Price of Products

CARPETS and RUGS, WOOL (continued)		1899	1904	1909	1914	1919	1921	1923	1925	1927	1929	1931	1933	1935	1937
Product[b]	*Item*														
Rugs, woven whole															
Axminster and moquette	*q* Mil. sq.yd.				4.65	5.47	7.84	9.57	16.0	19.0	20.7				
	v Mil. $				6.07	15.5	18.4	22.2	38.2	45.0	44.8				
	p $ per sq.yd.				1.30	2.84	2.35	2.33	2.39	2.36	2.16				
Wilton	*q* Mil. sq.yd.				.141	.782	1.10	1.09	1.45	1.98	5.02				
	v Mil. $				.367	4.35	4.50	4.79	6.07	10.0	25.9				
	p $ per sq.yd.				2.61	5.57	4.10	4.41	4.19	5.06	5.17				
Tapestry velvet	*q* Mil. sq.yd.				5.46	4.20	5.60	9.83	8.88	9.39	7.55				
	v Mil. $				5.62	9.01	10.6	20.2	19.8	18.9	14.1				
	p $ per sq.yd.				1.03	2.15	1.88	2.06	2.23	2.01	1.86				
Tapestry Brussels	*q* Mil. sq.yd.				8.27	7.88	9.55	11.9	4.69	5.15	3.45				
	v Mil. $				6.27	9.90	12.5	15.9	6.26	5.60	3.53				
	p $ per sq.yd.				.758	1.26	1.31	1.34	1.34	1.09	1.02				
Chenille Axminster	*q* Mil. sq.yd.				.178	.310	.398	.552	.437	.329	.546				
	v Mil. $				.715	2.53	3.24	4.36	3.83	2.75	3.39				
	p $ per sq.yd.				4.01	8.15	8.14	7.89	8.75	8.35	6.21				
Wool and paper fiber (mixed)	*q* Mil. sq.yd.				4.17	6.83	1.63	6.02	1.85	1.34	.990				
	v Mil. $				1.54	6.25	1.58	3.08	1.59	.974	.830				
	p $ per sq.yd.				.370	.915	.969	.511	.860	.728	.838				
Sheen type															
Wilton	*q* Mil. sq.yd.										1.59	1.24	.398	.754	.512
	v Mil. $										12.1	6.97	2.07	3.44	2.49
	p $ per sq.yd.										7.61	5.61	5.20	4.56	4.86
Other than Wilton	*q* Mil. sq.yd.										.237	1.21	1.26	1.35	.901
	v Mil. $										2.49	5.74	4.83	4.69	3.83
	p $ per sq.yd.										10.5	4.73	3.84	3.47	4.25

CARPETS and RUGS, WOOL (concluded)		1899	1904	1909	1914	1919	1921	1923	1925	1927	1929	1931	1933	1935	1937
Product[b]	*Item*														
Rugs, woven whole (concluded)															
Other than sheen type															
Axminster	*q* Mil. sq.yd.										20.7	18.6	19.1	21.2	23.7
	v Mil. $										44.2	31.2	28.5	35.3	45.1
	p $ per sq.yd.										2.14	1.68	1.49	1.67	1.90
Wilton	*q* Mil. sq.yd.										3.44	1.15	1.12	2.14	1.62
	v Mil. $										13.9	4.24	3.18	5.75	6.19
	p $ per sq.yd.										4.04	3.70	2.83	2.68	3.82
Tapestry and velvet, all kinds	*q* Mil. sq.yd.										11.0	3.84	2.42	4.79	3.52
	v Mil. $										17.6	5.12	2.99	6.82	6.54
	p $ per sq.yd.										1.60	1.33	1.23	1.42	1.86
Chenille	*q* Mil. sq.yd.										.546	.245	.125	.468	
	v Mil. $										3.39	1.12	.401	.494	
	p $ per sq.yd.										6.21	4.56	3.21	1.05	

[a] Percentages of coverage:

Given year	Base year	Given year	Base year	Given year	Base year
1899:90.4	1914:93.6 (1899–1909)	1919:81.7	1927:91.8 (1919–1925)	1927:95.3	1929:95.4
1904:92.3		1921:92.0		1931:90.0	1929:94.5
1909:94.1		1923:93.1		1933:88.9	1929:93.8
1914:78.8	1927:90.4	1925:93.2		1935:85.3	1929:93.7
				1937:86.5	1929:91.8

[b] From 1909 to 1914 carpets and rugs were reported in combination. After 1914 carpets and rugs were reported separately and, in addition, rugs were divided into two categories, rugs, woven whole, and rugs made of sewed strips. In 1929 rugs, woven whole, were divided into two kinds, sheen type and other than sheen type. The data are therefore presented under three different classifications: first, that prevailing from 1899 to 1914; second, that prevailing from 1914 to 1929; and third that prevailing from 1929 to 1937.

[c] Between 1909 and 1914, 8 establishments manufacturing jute carpets were transferred from carpets and rugs, wool, to jute goods. The resulting discontinuity appears to be slight.

[d] Between 1935 and 1937 some establishments formerly classed with carpets and rugs, rag, were transferred to carpets and rugs, wool, and some establishments in the latter industry were transferred to woolen goods.

[e] Includes Wilton velvets.

Indexes of Physical Output, with Basic Data on Quantity, Value and Price of Products

CLOTH, KNIT		*1899*	*1904*	*1909*	*1914*	*1919*	*1921*	*1923*	*1925*	*1927*	*1929*	*1931*	*1933*	*1935*	*1937*
Adjusted index							b	57.7	63.5	73.8	100.0	148.1			
Unadjusted index[a]		9.4	12.1	7.9	14.0	39.7	59.7	60.7	66.1	74.7	100.0	150.7	c		
Product[d]	*Item*														
Jersey cloth, stockinette, and tricolette	*q* Mil. sq.yd.	4.49	3.35	3.11	10.6	35.4									
	v Mil. $	1.31	1.15	.784	4.38	45.9									
	p $ per sq.yd.	.291	.341	.252	.413	1.30									
Fleece lining (shoe and glove)	*q* Mil. sq.yd.	10.4	11.8	9.73	6.22	6.58									
	v Mil. $	2.20	1.25	1.21	.670	2.52									
	p $ per sq.yd.	.212	.106	.124	.108	.383									
Eider down	*q* Mil. sq.yd.		4.84	1.30	1.08	.941									
	v Mil. $		1.02	.442	.517	1.17									
	p $ per sq.yd.		.210	.341	.480	1.25									
Wool jersey	*q* Mil. sq.yd.									10.2	7.21	13.0			
	v Mil. $									11.3	7.74	7.62			
	p $ per sq.yd.									1.10	1.07	.588			
Other knit woolens	*q* Mil. sq.yd.									1.87	2.51	4.56			
	v Mil. $									2.73	4.41	5.08			
	p $ per sq.yd.									1.45	1.76	1.11			
	q					25.3	38.1	38.7	42.2						
	v					42.1	35.4	43.4	36.5						
	p					1.66	.929	1.12	.864						
Silk jersey, incl. milanese	*q* Mil. sq.yd.									3.51	4.13	6.03			
	v Mil. $									2.80	3.12	2.56			
	p $ per sq.yd.									.798	.755	.425			
Rayon tubing, incl. tricolette	*q* Mil. sq.yd.									28.8	49.9	74.1			
	v Mil. $									20.9	29.8	19.2			
	p $ per sq.yd.									.724	.596	.259			

CLOTH, KNIT (concluded)		1899	1904	1909	1914	1919	1921	1923	1925	1927	1929	1931	1933	1935	1937
Product[d]	*Item*														
Other knit rayons	*q* Mil. sq.yd.										1.61	3.30			
	v Mil. $										.891	1.40			
	$ per sq.yd.										.552	.425			
Cotton jersey	*q* Mil. sq.yd.										14.2	15.2			
	v Mil. $										4.76	2.16			
	p $ per sq.yd.										.334	.142			
Corset cloth	*q* Mil. sq.yd.										4.86	5.62			
	v Mil. $										4.49	2.83			
	p $ per sq.yd.										.925	.503			

[a] Percentages of coverage:

Given year	Base year
1923:64.9, 1925:64.3, 1927:62.5	1929:61.7
1931:77.0	1929:75.6

[b] No adjusted indexes for 1899–1921 could be computed because the industry is not shown separately in the Census for those years. Adjusted indexes were computed for the entire knit goods industry. The adjusted index given above, extrapolated by the unadjusted index, is 8.9 for 1899; 11.5 for 1904; 7.5 for 1909; 13.3 for 1914; 37.7 for 1919; 56.7 for 1921.

[c] In 1933 the unit of measurement was changed from the square yard to the pound. It was therefore impossible to compute index numbers for 1933–37 with 1929 as the base.

[d] For years prior to 1929 the detailed data relate to products made within the knit goods group alone, but for 1929 and subsequent years they relate to the total of products, wherever made.

CLOTHING, MEN'S[a]		1927	1929	1931	1933	1935	1937
Adjusted index		96.3[c]	100.0	74.9[d]	78.9	100.5[e]	98.6
Unadjusted index[b]		99.3	100.0	74.6	75.2	91.5	93.6
Product	*Item*						
Men's and youths' suits	*q* Mil.	23.8	23.5	17.5	16.7	21.4	18.9[f]
	v Mil. $	491	449	283	231	306	337
	p $ ea.	20.7	19.1	16.2	13.9	14.3	17.9

For footnotes see p. 425.

Indexes of Physical Output, with Basic Data on Quantity, Value and Price of Products

CLOTHING, MEN'S (concluded)		1927	1929	1931	1933	1935	1937
Product	*Item*						
Men's and youths' separate coats	*q* Mil.	1.15	1.26	.826	.470	.532	.488
	v Mil. $	8.04	13.0	7.85	3.84	3.26	3.59
	p $ ea.	6.97	10.4	9.50	8.18	6.14	7.35
Men's and youths' top coats and overcoats	*q* Mil.	6.53	7.32	4.53	4.23	5.51	6.17
	v Mil. $	129	132	68.3	54.4	73.3	96.2
	p $ ea.	19.8	18.0	15.1	12.8	13.3	15.6
Men's and youths' separate vests	*q* Mil.	.600	1.01	.532	.953	.511	
	v Mil. $	2.33	3.31	2.05	1.92	2.31	
	p $ ea.	3.88	3.29	3.85	2.01	4.51	
Boys' separate pants and knickers, incl. cotton	*q* Mil.	9.32	12.8	12.8	10.7	14.5	
	v Mil. $	14.1	16.0	15.4	9.90	11.4	
	p $ ea.	1.52	1.25	1.21	.929	.789	
Boys' overcoats and reefers	*q* Mil.	2.16	1.95	1.21	.654	.742	
	v Mil. $	19.5	12.6	6.49	3.36	5.49	
	p $ ea.	9.01	6.50	5.36	5.13	7.40	
Men's, youths' and boys' waterproof garments	*q* Mil.	7.65[g]	5.43[g]	2.62[g]	3.49	5.73	
	v Mil. $	21.8	17.6	7.10	7.44	12.8	
	p $ ea.	2.84	3.25	2.71	2.13	2.23	
Men's, youths' and boys' work clothing							
Overalls, overall jackets, and 1-piece overall suits	*q* Mil. doz.	6.90	6.45	5.86	7.50	6.58	6.01
	v Mil. $	88.8	79.7	46.9	55.9	60.2	61.1
	p $ per doz.	12.9	12.4	8.00	7.46	9.15	10.2
Work pants and breeches	*q* Mil. doz.	2.27	2.10	2.25	3.51	4.23	4.18
	v Mil. $	34.9	29.2	23.2	37.0	47.9	47.9
	p $ per doz.	15.4	13.9	10.3	10.5	11.3	11.5
Boys' play suits	*q* Mil. doz.	1.58	2.26	1.70	.818	1.02	1.34
	v Mil. $	12.9	15.9	10.5	4.15	5.55	6.52
	p $ per doz.	8.14	7.03	6.17	5.07	5.46	4.86

[a] Includes clothing, men's, work; clothing, men's, n.e.c.; clothing, men's, buttonholes; and cloth sponging and refinishing.

[b] Percentages of coverage:

Given year	Base year
1927:75.9	1929:73.6
1931:73.3	
1933:70.1	
1935:67.1	
1937:62.0	1935:59.5

[c] Between 1927 and 1929 establishments making sheep-lined clothing were transferred from fur goods to clothing, men's, work. The resulting discontinuity appears to be slight.

[d] Between 1931 and 1933 establishments making work shirts (including flannel shirts) were transferred from shirts to clothing, men's, work. The resulting discontinuity appears to be slight.

[e] Between 1935 and 1937 establishments making uniforms were transferred from flags and banners to clothing, men's, n.e.c.

[f] The figures for 1937, unlike those for preceding years, exclude the following series: two-piece suits with extra knickers; tuxedo and dress suits; cotton suits; mohair, silk, linen, etc., suits. The 1935 figures comparable with 1937 are: *q* 18.3 mil.; *v* 278 mil. dollars; *p* 15.2 dollars each.

[g] Includes data on a small number of garments made in the rubber goods industry.

CLOTHING, WOMEN'S, not elsewhere classified		*1927*	*1929*	*1931*	*1933*[b]	*1935*	*1937*[b]
Adjusted index		84.3[c]	100.0	102.6	90.8	108.7	124.7
Unadjusted index[a]		86.8	100.0	101.4	86.3	103.1	117.0
Product	*Item*						
Outerwear for women, misses, and juniors							
Dresses, 1-piece	*q* Mil.	109	163	167	145	172	177[d]
	v Mil. $	587	823	618	376	478	437
	p $ ea.	5.38	5.06	3.70	2.59	2.77	2.47
Suits	*q* Mil.	4.47	1.67	2.32	2.56	4.54	5.28[e]
	v Mil. $	68.1	34.9	29.1	26.1	50.9	56.2
	p $ ea.	15.2	20.9	12.5	10.2	11.2	10.7
Ensembles	*q* Mil.		1.16	1.96	.155	3.15	3.24
	v Mil. $		13.8	14.9	2.46	30.3	42.5
	p $ ea.		11.9	7.61	15.9	9.64	13.1
Separate coats	*q* Mil.	19.5	16.9	16.3	13.0	12.1	16.7[e]
	v Mil. $	395	333	252	149	140	209
	p $ ea.	20.3	19.8	15.5	11.5	11.6	12.5

For footnotes see p. 427.

Indexes of Physical Output, with Basic Data on Quantity, Value and Price of Products

CLOTHING, WOMEN'S, not elsewhere classified (continued)		1927	1929	1931	1933[b]	1935	1937[b]
Product	*Item*						
Outerwear for women, misses, and juniors (concluded)							
Separate skirts	*q* Mil.	.859	1.23	3.17	5.12	5.93	6.69
	v Mil. $	3.30	3.81	6.21	9.76	10.2	11.8
	p $ ea.	3.84	3.09	1.96	1.91	1.72	1.77
Blouses and shirt waists	*q* Mil.	7.16	5.09	8.68	10.5	17.1	22.0
	v Mil. $	14.1	10.7	13.8	13.4	23.8	25.3
	p $ ea.	1.97	2.10	1.59	1.27	1.39	1.15
Outerwear for children							
Dresses	*q* Mil.	32.1	42.5	40.4	39.3	42.3	48.4
	v Mil. $	47.2	53.2	37.6	29.4	35.1	40.3
	p $ ea.	1.47	1.25	.930	.749	.830	.832
Coats	*q* Mil.	7.07	6.19	4.71	2.80	2.96	4.03
	v Mil. $	43.8	34.5	20.3	13.2	13.7	20.2
	p $ ea.	6.20	5.58	4.31	4.72	4.63	5.00
Outerwear for infants	*q* Mil.	8.16	12.6	17.9	6.96	8.63	10.1
	v Mil. $	7.92	13.0	9.76	5.68	6.50	5.86
	p $ ea.	.970	1.03	.546	.816	.754	.578
Washable service apparel	*q* Mil.	4.15	3.81	4.49	4.19	4.72	7.55
	v Mil. $	8.03	8.62	7.01	4.75	6.92	9.42
	p $ ea.	1.93	2.26	1.56	1.13	1.47	1.25
Kimonos and bathrobes	*q* Mil.	6.49	5.40	4.71	3.77	4.25	12.9
	v Mil. $	21.4	19.1	14.4	7.32	11.7	24.5
	p $ ea.	3.30	3.54	3.07	1.94	2.76	1.90
Raincoats	*q* Mil.	4.38	3.60	1.96	1.60	1.43	1.89
	v Mil. $	13.8	12.3	4.96	3.68	3.30	4.75
	p $ ea.	3.15	3.42	2.53	2.30	2.31	2.51

CLOTHING, WOMEN'S, not elsewhere classified (concluded)		1927	1929	1931	1933[b]	1935	1937[b]
Product	*Item*						
Aprons	*q* Mil. doz.	.925	1.41	1.50	1.40	2.05	1.82
	v Mil. $	3.84	7.62	5.83	5.24	4.27	5.34
	p $ per doz.	4.15	5.42	3.88	3.74	2.08	2.93
Smocks	*q* Mil. doz.		.552	.217	.154	.180	.161
	v Mil. $		6.02	2.31	1.19	1.62	1.87
	p $ per doz.		10.9	10.6	7.74	9.02	11.6
Hoovers	*q* Mil. doz.		.259	.253	.360	.254	.322
	v Mil. $		2.40	1.95	1.36	1.93	2.22
	p $ per doz.		9.28	7.69	3.77	7.61	6.87
Neckwear and scarfs	*q* Mil. doz.		2.55	1.61	2.26	2.96	2.29
	v Mil. $		22.3	11.4	9.62	13.5	9.42
	p $ per doz.		8.75	7.10	4.26	4.55	4.11

[a] Percentages of coverage:

Given year	Base year	Given year	Base year
1927:86.9	1929:84.4	1935:82.7	1929:87.2
1931:86.1	1929:87.2	1937:81.8	1929:87.2
1933:82.9	1929:87.2		

[b] The 1933 and 1937 Censuses of this industry are reported by the Bureau of the Census as somewhat incomplete.

[c] Between 1927 and 1929 establishments making women's scarfs and other neckwear were transferred from trimmings to clothing, women's. The resulting discontinuity appears to be slight.

[d] Estimated in part.

[e] Coats and suits amounting in value to 2.04 mil. dollars were not reported separately for 1937.

CORDAGE and TWINE		1899	1904[b]	1909	1914	1919	1921	1923	1925	1927	1929	1931	1933	1935	1937
Adjusted index		66.8		82.3	98.4	92.8	74.9	96.1	94.6	94.6	100.0	68.6	70.6	72.5	92.1
Unadjusted index[a]		56.2		88.8	102.1	95.3	91.7	92.8	97.0	88.3	100.0	70.9	73.7	66.0	84.7
Product	*Item*														
Rope and cordage															
All rope, except cotton	*q* Mil. lb.	140		222											
	v Mil. $	12.5		16.8											
	p $ per lb.	.0890		.0758											

For footnotes see p. 429.

Indexes of Physical Output, with Basic Data on Quantity, Value and Price of Products

CORDAGE and TWINE (continued)		1899	1904[b]	1909	1914	1919	1921	1923	1925	1927	1929	1931	1933	1935	1937
Product	*Item*														
Rope and cordage (concluded)															
Abaca	*q* Mil. lb.			126	105	130	71.8	92.3	101	106	114	62.6	63.3	75.4	88.1
	v Mil. $			10.7	12.9	32.0	13.2	14.9	21.8	22.6	22.2	9.43	7.66	9.05	14.2
	p $ per lb.			.0852	.123	.245	.184	.162	.216	.214	.194	.151	.121	.120	.161
Sisal and henequen	*q* Mil. lb.			64.2	53.4	42.6	41.5	66.1	48.3	43.7	43.5	30.0	20.2	6.86	7.92
	v Mil. $			4.25	4.03	7.91	5.53	9.00	7.25	6.28	6.42	3.07	1.80	.547	.816
	p $ per lb.			.0662	.0755	.186	.133	.136	.150	.144	.148	.102	.0890	.0797	.103
Cotton (not elsewhere made)	*q* Mil. lb.	1.62		16.8	13.2	11.9					21.0	17.9	19.7	19.3	22.6
	v Mil. $	.247		3.01	2.54	6.12					6.33	3.68	3.94	5.09	6.12
	p $ per lb.	.153		.180	.192	.512					.301	.206	.200	.264	.271
Cotton (wherever made)	*q* Mil. lb.						17.3	24.5	25.9	27.4	28.1				
	v Mil. $						5.34	8.86	9.28	7.60	8.30				
	p $ per lb.						.308	.362	.358	.277	.295				
Twine															
Binder	*q* Mil. lb.	166		189	302	230	236	240	234	170	179	134	143	109	115
	v Mil. $	14.2		14.1	24.1	46.3	31.6	23.5	29.2	19.5	18.4	11.5	6.99	6.63	8.58
	p $ per lb.	.0857		.0744	.0797	.202	.134	.0980	.125	.115	.103	.0853	.0490	.0609	.0747
Hard-fiber and wrapping	*q* Mil. lb.										13.2	13.1	27.3	47.4	52.9
	v Mil. $										1.84	1.39	2.29	3.88	5.94
	p $ per lb.										.139	.106	.0840	.0818	.112
Cotton (made in this industry only)	*q* Mil. lb.	8.69		20.4	17.9	23.4		20.2	28.6	35.9	45.3	30.9	39.3	33.5	49.7
	v Mil. $	1.13		3.52	3.47	12.3		8.58	10.8	10.6	14.3	6.35	7.34	9.26	13.3
	p $ per lb.	.130		.172	.194	.524		.425	.378	.295	.316	.206	.187	.276	.267
Jute	*q* Mil. lb.	1.68		35.5	55.3	52.4				38.7	68.8	59.0	46.9	22.2	26.0
	v Mil. $	.118		2.56	5.27	10.9				5.61	9.44	6.35	4.69	2.62	4.07
	p $ per lb.	.0700		.0720	.0953	.208				.145	.137	.108	.0999	.118	.156

CORDAGE and TWINE (concluded)		1899	1904[b]	1909	1914	1919	1921	1923	1925	1927	1929	1931	1933	1935	1937
Product	*Item*														
Twine (concluded)															
Flax and hemp	*q* Mil. lb.									6.79	5.85	5.26	3.93	2.36	2.87
	v Mil. $									1.99	2.43	2.00	1.28	1.01	1.35
	p $ per lb.									.294	.415	.380	.325	.426	.471

[a] Percentages of coverage:

Given year	Base year	Given year	Base year	Given year	Base year
1899:74.4	1909:95.4	1921:74.0	1929:60.4	1931:91.9	1929:89.0
1909:90.9	1919:86.6	1923:73.5	1929:76.1	1933:92.9	1929:89.0
1914:87.5	1919:86.6	1925:78.0	1929:76.1	1935:81.1	1929:89.0
1919:86.6	1929:84.3	1927:83.1	1929:89.1	1937:81.8	1929:89.0

[b] Detailed data on products were not collected in 1904.

CORSETS		1927	1929	1931	1933	1935[b]	1937
Adjusted index		99.3	100.0	111.2	108.8		129.4
Unadjusted index[a]		96.7	100.0	112.6	109.9		134.8
Product	*Item*						
Brassieres and bandeau brassieres	*q* Mil.	25.0	24.7	32.7	36.3		43.6
	v Mil. $	15.1	18.4	14.9	12.1		14.7
	p $ ea.	.605	.747	.455	.334		.338
Corsets, girdles, and garter belts	*q* Mil.	14.0	18.1	25.0	23.7		28.2
	v Mil. $	31.8	32.8	35.0	29.6		36.0
	p $ ea.	2.26	1.82	1.40	1.25		1.28
Combinations or 1-piece garments	*q* Mil.	13.5	10.6	7.45	6.46		8.86
	v Mil. $	24.5	21.6	19.3	14.0		19.3
	p $ ea.	1.81	2.04	2.59	2.16		2.18

[a] Percentages of coverage:

Given year	Base year
1927:92.5	1929:95.0
1931:96.2	1929:95.0
1933:95.9	1929:95.0
1937:98.9	1929:95.0

[b] The data for 1935 are not comparable with those for other years because some leading manufacturers reported unsatisfactorily the detailed breakdown of their output in 1935.

Indexes of Physical Output, with Basic Data on Quantity, Value and Price of Products

COTTON GOODS		1899	1904	1909	1914	1919	1921	1923	1925	1927	1929	1931	1933	1935	1937
Adjusted index		49.1	53.5	67.5[b]	72.8	77.9[c]	69.5	93.3	93.0	103.9	100.0	77.6	87.1[d]	78.1	98.9
Unadjusted index[a]		56.1	61.3	77.0	81.9	84.3	75.6	99.9	97.2	104.4	100.0	72.9	84.6	78.2	102.9
Product[e]	*Item*														
Duck, incl. tire duck	*q* Mil. sq.yd.	129	123	162	251	336									
	v Mil. $	14.3	17.0	27.5	49.2	237									
	p $ per sq.yd.	.110	.139	.169	.196	.705									
Ounce duck, excl. tire duck	*q* Mil. sq.yd.					179	97.0	139	162	179	188	112	133	127	197
	v Mil. $					70.6	21.8	42.8	40.3	43.6	48.7	18.5	22.6	27.5	35.6
	p $ per sq.yd.					.395	.225	.307	.249	.244	.259	.166	.170	.217	.181
Numbered duck, excl. paper felts	*q* Mil. sq.yd.					34.5	38.2	27.9	31.4	39.7	42.1	25.0	19.5	22.6	24.3
	v Mil. $					23.4	13.1	14.4	13.5	14.4	16.4	6.22	5.66	8.37	8.31
	p $ per sq.yd.					.678	.345	.517	.430	.362	.389	.249	.290	.370	.342
Sheetings, shirtings, and muslins	*q* Mil. sq. yd.	2,794	2,991	3,709		3,194									
	v Mil. $	113	142	200		477									
	p $ per sq.yd.	.0405	.0473	.0539		.149									
Sheetings	*q* Mil. sq.yd.				2,666	1,369	1,601	1,696	1,638	1,857	1,693	1,360[f]	1,680[f]	1,390	1,826
	v Mil. $				133	220	158	208	180	168	146	76.9	98.9	108	151
	p $ per sq.yd.				.0500	.161	.0988	.123	.110	.0904	.0863	.0566	.0588	.0776	.0825
Shirtings, cotton and cotton mixtures	*q* Mil. sq.yd.				185	352	301	341	455	379	317	273	278		
	v Mil. $				15.9	83.3	51.7	72.3	75.8	55.4	45.8	24.4	25.2		
	p $ per sq.yd.				.0861	.237	.172	.212	.166	.146	.144	.0891	.0907		
Shirtings, cotton only	*q* Mil. sq.yd.										266			273	344
	v Mil. $										37.3			29.7	41.9
	p $ per sq.yd.										.140			.109	.122
Drills	*q* Mil. sq.yd.	237	195	239	290	315	192	303	286	348	324	185	192	179	282
	v Mil. $	11.9	12.6	17.8	21.3	73.3	22.0	46.8	42.4	40.7	39.7	15.1	15.3	18.6	27.5
	p $ per sq.yd.	.0500	.0647	.0743	.0733	.233	.115	.154	.148	.117	.123	.0820	.0795	.104	.0975

COTTON GOODS (continued)		1899	1904	1909	1914	1919	1921	1923	1925	1927	1929	1931	1933	1935	1937
Product[e]	*Item*														
Print cloth, voiles, lawns, muslins, tobacco and cheese cloths	*q* Mil. sq.yd.				1,153	1,655									
	v Mil. $				60.2	219									
	p $ per sq.yd.				.0522	.132									
Print cloth	*q* Mil. sq.yd.					997	1,158	1,578	1,166	1,584	1,703	1,586	1,710	1,610	2,121
	v Mil. $					123	82.0	144	98.5	110	121	74.5	80.0	101	133
	p $ per sq.yd.					.123	.0709	.0913	.0844	.0693	.0713	.0470	.0468	.0627	.0628
Lawns, nainsooks, cambrics, and similar muslins	*q* Mil. sq.yd.					418					227				
	v Mil. $					79.4					25.4				
	p $ per sq.yd.					.190					.112				
Lawns, nainsooks, cambrics, and similar muslins, incl. voiles	*q* Mil. sq.yd.						478	502	451	424	384	306	373	245	351
	v Mil. $						69.4	76.5	57.8	47.1	38.8	23.3	24.0	17.8	26.2
	p $ per sq.yd.						.145	.152	.128	.111	.101	.0760	.0644	.0729	.0745
Tobacco and cheese cloth, and gauze	*q* Mil. sq.yd.					240	274	402	452	660	617	587	634	642	903
	v Mil. $					17.0	10.0	20.1	16.3	19.3	18.1	9.78	11.0	12.8	17.9
	p $ per sq.yd.					.0708	.0366	.0500	.0360	.0292	.0293	.0166	.0173	.0199	.0198
Reps, poplins, broadcloths, pajama checks, and dimities	*q* Mil. sq.yd.									380	431	395	512	392	519
	v Mil. $									47.9	53.6	34.2	39.8	38.4	49.4
	p $ per sq.yd.									.126	.125	.0865	.0777	.0980	.0953
Osnaburgs	*q* Mil. sq.yd.						100	109	118	165	146	109	131	141	153
	v Mil. $						11.8	19.5	18.4	17.9	18.2	8.06	9.21	15.2	16.2
	p $ per sq.yd.						.118	.179	.156	.108	.125	.0739	.0704	.108	.106
Twills and sateens	*q* Mil. sq.yd.	236	366	388	392	424	385	489	533	414	284	201	274	265	333
	v Mil. $	14.3	23.7	34.3	32.9	101	51.8	91.6	84.1	50.3	37.4	16.8	23.2	31.6	39.8
	p $ per sq.yd.	.0606	.0647	.0883	.0839	.238	.135	.187	.158	.122	.132	.0833	.0845	.119	.120
Table damask	*q* Mil. sq.yd.					27.5	43.1	40.9	53.5	33.5	35.9	20.5	15.8	15.3	15.9
	v Mil. $					9.54	10.8	10.9	12.4	6.75	8.38	3.65	2.84	3.32	2.98
	p $ per sq.yd.					.347	.250	.265	.233	.201	.234	.178	.179	.216	.187

For footnotes see pp. 434–35.

Indexes of Physical Output, with Basic Data on Quantity, Value and Price of Products

COTTON GOODS (continued)		1899	1904	1909	1914	1919	1921	1923	1925	1927	1929	1931	1933	1935	1937
Product[e]	*Item*														
Tapestries, cotton	*q* Mil. sq.yd.	10.2	9.60	10.7	10.1	21.7	10.4	20.7	15.7	18.6	9.81	9.19	9.98	9.07	
	v Mil. $	4.16	4.24	4.72	5.41	17.3	13.9	20.9	17.4	16.6	13.0	7.24	4.79	3.70	
	p $ per sq.yd.	.409	.442	.443	.534	.797	1.34	1.01	1.10	.892	1.32	.788	.480	.408	
Napped fabrics	*q* Mil. sq.yd.	269	331	306	264	268	295	381	340	400	323	288	378	299[g]	455[g]
	v Mil. $	18.2	26.1	25.7	24.4	60.2	37.7	69.6	53.6	55.4	48.3	27.0	34.1	31.3	49.2
	p $ per sq.yd.	.0678	.0789	.0841	.0923	.224	.128	.183	.157	.138	.150	.0938	.0902	.105	.108
Blankets, all cotton, cotton and wool mixed, and crib blankets	*q* Mil. sq.yd.					96.6	91.5	88.1	92.1	107	94.1	72.0	103		
	v Mil. $					32.6	21.5	24.7	29.5	29.5	25.4	12.7	16.1		
	p $ per sq.yd.					.338	.235	.281	.321	.275	.270	.177	.156		
Blankets, all cotton, and crib blankets	*q* Mil. sq.yd.										66.1			58.0	110
	v Mil. $										16.4			10.9	19.0
	p $ per sq.yd.										.248			.188	.172
Denims, pin checks, tickings and ginghams	*q* Mil. sq.yd.			802	719	589	751	851	585	604	439	291	386	304	318
	v Mil. $			65.3	61.7	155	128	172	114	97.3	76.3	33.8	46.6	46.8	48.4
	p $ per sq.yd.			.0814	.0858	.264	.170	.202	.195	.161	.174	.116	.121	.154	.152
Ginghams	*q* Mil. sq.yd.	278	302	537											
	v Mil. $	16.2	22.5	37.9											
	p $ per sq.yd.	.0581	.0743	.0706											
Cottonades and other coverts	*q* Mil. sq.yd.					21.1	23.0	21.0	29.1	32.7	34.8	45.0	57.9	46.0	59.7
	v Mil. $					8.48	5.84	6.17	7.90	8.15	8.36	8.84	9.30	8.06	12.0
	p $ per sq.yd.					.401	.254	.294	.271	.249	.240	.197	.161	.175	.200
Toweling and terry weaves	*q* Mil. sq.yd.		40.3	52.8	75.8	75.2									
	v Mil. $		4.37	6.04	9.81	31.2									
	p $ per sq.yd.		.108	.114	.129	.415									
Towels, towelings and wash cloths	*q* Mil. sq.yd.					74.7	120	123	127	170	170	158	150	171	200
	v Mil. $					30.8	31.1	36.7	38.2	42.6	33.0	24.1	22.5	32.8	37.3
	p $ per sq.yd.					.412	.260	.299	.301	.251	.195	.152	.150	.192	.186

COTTON GOODS (continued)		1899	1904	1909	1914	1919	1921	1923	1925	1927	1929	1931	1933	1935	1937
Product[e]	*Item*														
Pillow tubing	*q* Mil. sq.yd.				15.2	12.1	28.1	17.3	30.5	26.7	21.3	12.5	9.65	11.8	17.5
	v Mil. $				1.48	2.56	4.95	3.35	5.47	4.42	3.99	1.62	1.40	1.60	2.05
	p $ per sq.yd.				.0975	.211	.176	.194	.179	.166	.188	.130	.145	.135	.117
Bedspread fabrics and quilts, cotton and other materials	*q* Mil. sq.yd.					24.1	31.8	35.7	52.6	71.3	52.9	55.9	50.5		
	v Mil. $					10.2	11.0	13.6	16.7	19.0	16.4	8.64	6.36		
	p $ per sq.yd.					.426	.346	.380	.317	.266	.310	.155	.126		
Bedspread fabrics and quilts, cotton	*q* Mil. sq.yd.										27.2			32.6	38.6
	v Mil. $										6.41			5.50	6.33
	p $ per sq.yd.										.236			.169	.164
Plushes, velvets and velveteens	*q* Mil. sq.yd.					20.3	11.5	27.7	33.5	42.7	52.9	23.8	18.2	20.6	24.4
	v Mil. $					22.8	14.4	35.6	40.7	45.7	40.9	15.9	10.2	11.9	16.2
	p $ per sq.yd.					1.12	1.25	1.29	1.22	1.07	.774	.668	.561	.580	.663
Plushes, velvets and velveteens, and corduroys (combined)	*q*	7.96	16.0	19.7	29.1										
	v	2.68	4.79	6.97	8.54										
	p	.337	.299	.353	.293										
Corduroys	*q* Mil. sq.yd.					19.9	16.4	27.4	21.6	23.2	27.1	15.7	24.6	31.8	30.2
	v Mil. $					13.9	6.70	12.0	9.55	8.68	9.50	3.98	5.46	10.0	8.90
	p $ per sq.yd.					.698	.410	.440	.442	.374	.350	.254	.222	.316	.294
Tire fabrics, incl. tire duck	*q* Mil. sq.yd.					160	95.7	227	242	226	303[h]	158[h]	146[h]		
	v Mil. $					176	102	106	106	81.0	112	41.2	31.8		
	p $ per sq.yd.					1.10	1.06	.468	.436	.358	.369	.261	.217		
	q Mil. lb.										251			194	261
	v Mil. $										112			64.3	75.1
	p $ per lb.										.446			.332	.288
Thread	*q* Mil. lb.	15.9	17.2	23.7	26.5	26.4	23.3	31.6	34.2	30.0	25.2	19.6	27.8	34.9	38.9
	v Mil. $	11.9	15.0	20.5	22.9	55.0	50.2	55.3	53.3	46.4	37.1	29.2	30.4	35.1	41.4
	p $ per lb.	.749	.876	.866	.865	2.08	2.16	1.75	1.56	1.55	1.47	1.49	1.09	1.01	1.06
Twine	*q* Mil. lb.	11.6	7.30	13.7	13.3	11.9	13.4	18.7	21.3	28.3	40.6	16.2	19.8	17.2	19.5
	v Mil. $	1.55	1.43	2.42	2.79	5.94	3.98	8.47	8.92	9.56	14.6	3.59	4.70	4.69	4.68
	p $ per lb.	.133	.196	.176	.210	.500	.296	.453	.419	.338	.360	.222	.238	.273	.240

For footnotes see pp. 434–35.

Indexes of Physical Output, with Basic Data on Quantity, Value and Price of Products

COTTON GOODS (concluded)		1899	1904	1909	1914	1919	1921	1923	1925	1927	1929	1931	1933	1935	1937
Product[e]	*Item*														
Waste, for sale	*q* Mil. lb.	271	248	311	317	315	272	379	417	484	444	316	361	339	515
	v Mil. $	5.56	10.1	10.9	14.4	36.3	13.3	37.3	40.6	26.8	32.6	10.6	12.8	21.0	25.1
	p $ per lb.	.0205	.0406	.0350	.0455	.115	.0490	.0985	.0974	.0553	.0734	.0337	.0354	.0621	.0487
Yarn, for sale	*q* Mil. lb.	332	365	470	498	618	484	621	626	664	648	414	498	390	534
	v Mil. $	55.2	79.9	109	127	454	219	349	313	254	253	112	131	134	176
	p $ per lb.	.166	.219	.232	.256	.734	.451	.562	.500	.382	.391	.270	.263	.342	.330
Batting, wadding and mattress felts	*q* Mil. lb.					68.5	49.9	101	90.7	130	149	114	93.9		
	v Mil. $					8.48	5.88	16.6	14.1	16.3	19.4	12.2	8.87		
	p $ per lb.					.124	.118	.166	.156	.126	.130	.107	.0945		
Card laps, silver and roving	*q* Mil. lb.					4.26	4.34	4.58	4.96	3.42	10.1	5.46	7.58	8.99	7.24
	v Mil. $					1.96	1.06	1.57	1.80	.980	1.76	.754	.938	.157	1.17
	p $ per lb.					.459	.245	.342	.363	.287	.174	.138	.124	.175	.161

[a] Percentages of coverage:

Given year	Base year	Given year	Base year	Given year	Base year
1899:80.9	1909:80.9	1919:89.0	1929:82.2	1927:88.2	1929:87.8 (1927–1933)
1904:82.1	1909:81.9	1921:91.7	1929:84.3 (1921–1925)	1931:82.5	
1909:86.4	1919:81.9	1923:90.3		1933:85.3	
1914:87.4	1919:84.1	1925:88.1		1935:84.9	1929:84.7
				1937:87.4	1929:83.9

[b] Prior to 1914 lace goods were distributed between cotton goods and cotton small wares in unknown proportions. The resulting discontinuity appears to be slight.

[c] Between 1919 and 1921 some establishments in the cotton goods industry engaged primarily in the manufacture of aircraft parts, other than engines and tires, were transferred to aircraft. The resulting discontinuity appears to be slight.

[d] In 1933 establishments making cotton-and-silk-mixed fabrics and cotton-and-rayon-mixed fabrics having a cotton warp (even though the material of chief value was silk or rayon) were transferred from silk and rayon to cotton goods and cotton output of the industry is concerned, the duplication arising from interplant movements of yarn and waste is not more than 5 percent. Between 1933 and 1935 some changes were made by the Bureau of the Census in the character and detail of the classification of the products of the cotton goods industry. Because of these changes, some of the individual series of products for 1935–37 are not strictly comparable with those for earlier years. Also, many of the series for 1935–37 shown above are composites of more detailed series given in the Censuses for these years.

[f] The figures for 1933 and 1931 are not strictly comparable,

small wares. On the other hand, establishments manufacturing cotton batting, wadding and mattress felts were transferred from cotton goods to upholstering materials, n.e.c. The resulting discontinuity appears to be slight.

[e] Fractions of cotton waste (varying from a maximum of 15 to 38 percent) and of cotton yarn (22 to 33 percent) produced for sale by establishments in the cotton goods industry were purchased by other establishments in the industry. For this reason there is duplication in the products of this industry. The extent of the duplication has not been constant, but no clear-cut upward or downward trend is apparent. Insofar as the total since the increase is due at least in part to a change in classification. In prior Censuses mills making sheets and pillowcases, or having them made on contract from cloth of their own weaving, did not report the sheeting used in the manufacture of such sheets and pillowcases. In the Census for 1933, however, data for sheeting used in the manufacture of sheets and pillowcases were included.

[g] Includes a small amount of duvetyn to avoid disclosing approximations of data for individual establishments.

[h] Estimated in part.

ELASTIC WOVEN GOODS, not elsewhere made		*1927*	*1929*	*1931*	*1933*[b]	*1935*	*1937*
Adjusted index		76.0	100.0	61.8		68.8[c]	63.0
Unadjusted index[a]		82.9	100.0	72.3		71.7	65.9
Product	*Item*						
Suspenders	*q* Mil. doz.pr.	1.35	1.79	1.22		1.70	1.87
	v Mil. $	5.29	7.55	5.08		5.46	6.59
	p $ per doz.pr.	3.92	4.21	4.17		3.20	3.52
Arm bands	*q* Mil. doz.pr.	.534	.416	.520		.126	.129
	v Mil. $	.516	.378	.410		.0943	.0985
	p $ per doz.pr.	.967	.908	.788		.749	.764
Garters							
Men's	*q* Mil. doz.pr.	3.55	4.23	2.72		1.89	1.29
	v Mil. $	8.00	8.15	5.24		3.05	2.65
	p $ per doz.pr.	2.25	1.93	1.92		1.61	2.06
Women's	*q* Mil. doz.pr.	5.50	6.36	5.49		5.37	4.79
	v Mil. $	8.05	6.56	4.18		2.76	2.35
	p $ per doz.pr.	1.46	1.03	.761		.514	.491

[a] Percentages of coverage:

Given year	Base year
1927:81.0 1931:86.8 1935:77.5 1937:77.7	1929:74.3

[b] Detailed data on products were not collected in 1933.

[c] Between 1935 and 1937 some establishments were transferred from cotton small wares to elastic woven goods, n.e.m.

Indexes of Physical Output, with Basic Data on Quantity, Value and Price of Products

GLOVES, TEXTILE, not elsewhere made		*1927*	*1929*	*1931*	*1933*[b]	*1935*	*1937*
Adjusted index		103.9	100.0	66.6		61.0	97.0
Unadjusted index[a]		105.8	100.0	68.0		72.5	104.8
Product	*Item*						
Gloves and mittens, total	*q* Mil. doz.pr.	16.9	16.0				
	v Mil. $	29.4	28.6				
	p $ per doz.pr.	1.74	1.79				
Gloves and mittens, cloth or cloth	*q* Mil. doz.pr.		16.0	10.8		11.6	
and leather combined, made from	*v* Mil. $		28.2	14.0		21.3	
purchased fabrics and leather	*p* $ per doz.pr.		1.77	1.29		1.84	
All-fabric cotton work gloves	*q* Mil. doz.pr.					7.19	11.7
	v Mil. $					8.70	14.0
	p $ per doz.pr.					1.21	1.19
Mittens, cotton	*q* Mil. doz.pr.					.241	.655
	v Mil. $					.350	.894
	p $ per doz.pr.					1.45	1.37
Gloves, leather and cloth combined	*q* Mil. doz.pr.					2.24	2.54
	v Mil. $					5.62	8.11
	p $ per doz.pr.					2.51	3.19

[a] Percentages of coverage:

Given year	Base year
1927: 97.5	1929:95.8
1931: 96.4 1935:112.2	1929:94.5
1937: 70.4	1935:77.4

[b] Detailed data on products were not collected in 1933.

HANDKERCHIEFS		*1927*	*1929*	*1931*	*1933*[b]	*1935*	*1937*
Adjusted index		99.4	100.0	75.2		78.1	85.6
Unadjusted index[a]		102.1	100.0	76.3		79.5[c]	84.4
Product	*Item*						
Men's handkerchiefs	*q* Mil. doz.	19.7	21.0	14.9		16.9	17.9
	v Mil. $	15.8	14.7	9.69		8.66	10.2
	p $ per doz.	.800	.699	.650		.513	.567
Women's and children's handkerchiefs	*q* Mil. doz.	21.2	19.0	15.7		14.9	15.8
	v Mil. $	15.6	13.9	8.74		9.46	8.63
	p $ per doz.	.736	.731	.558		.634	.546

[a] Percentages of coverage:

Given year	Base year
1927:99.2 1931:98.0 1935:98.3 1937:95.2	1929:96.6

[b] Detailed data on products were not collected in 1933.

[c] According to the Bureau of the Census, the 1935 data are not strictly comparable with those for other years because some leading manufacturers reported unsatisfactorily the detailed breakdown of their 1935 output.

HATS, CLOTH		*1927*	*1929*	*1931*	*1933*[b]	*1935*	*1937*[c]
Adjusted index		96.6	100.0	59.2		71.3	52.8
Unadjusted index[a]		101.8	100.0	61.6		68.3	50.5
Product	*Item*						
Cloth hats and caps	*q* Mil. doz.	4.62	4.54	2.80		3.10	2.29[d]
	v Mil. $	41.3	34.2	16.7		13.0	10.7
	p $ per doz.	8.95	7.52	5.97		4.19	4.65

[a] Percentages of coverage:

Given year	Base year	Given year	Base year
1927:100.3 1931: 99.1	1929:95.1	1935:91.2 1937:91.0	1929:95.1

[b] Detailed data on products were not collected in 1933.

[c] The Bureau of the Census states that the 1937 figures for hats, cloth, are not quite complete.

[d] Estimated in part.

Indexes of Physical Output, with Basic Data on Quantity, Value and Price of Products

HATS, FUR-FELT		*1899*	*1904*	*1909*	*1914*	*1919*	*1921*	*1923*	*1925*	*1927*	*1929*	*1931*	*1933*[b]	*1935*	*1937*
Adjusted index		79.3	106.1	125.8	90.6	94.4	80.7	93.3	86.4	104.4	100.0	77.8		94.1	100.0
Unadjusted index[a]		80.5	108.4	129.9	93.5	96.1	80.8	96.4	88.5	104.8	100.0	77.4		98.1	104.3
Product[c]	*Item*														
Finished hats															
Manufactured complete in plant	*q* Mil. doz.										.832	.525		.629	.630
	v Mil. $										42.3	20.1		19.0	22.6
	p $ per doz.	*q* 1.88	2.61	2.99	2.12	2.10	1.76	1.97	1.73	2.01	50.9	38.4		30.2	35.8
		v 25.4	34.3	43.4	33.6	71.1	44.0	62.4	62.2	73.1					
Finished from bodies purchased	*q* Mil. doz.	*p* 13.5	13.1	14.5	15.9	33.8	25.1	31.7	35.9	36.3	.938	.782		1.02	1.09
	v Mil. $										28.5	19.8		19.0	21.7
	p $ per doz.										30.3	25.3		18.7	20.0
Hat bodies and hats in the rough	*q* Mil. doz.	.165	.089	.366	.329	.518	.457	.813	.953	1.23	1.53	1.47		1.93	2.20
	v Mil. $	.993	.661	2.70	2.37	7.66	5.13	10.2	14.4	19.9	24.5	15.7		16.5	20.8
	p $ per doz.	6.02	7.43	7.38	7.20	14.8	11.2	12.5	15.1	16.2	16.0	10.6		8.52	9.47

[a] Percentages of coverage:

Given year	Base year	Given year	Base year	Given year	Base year
1899:94.9 1904:95.5	1909:96.4	1919:95.1 1921:93.5 1923:96.5 1925:95.7	1929:93.4	1927:93.8 1931:93.2 1935:97.3 1937:97.4	1929:93.4
1909:96.4 1914:96.3	1919:95.1				

[b] Detailed data on products were not collected in 1933.

[c] A considerable amount of duplication appears to have arisen from purchases by establishments in the industry of unfinished hats made by other establishments in the same industry. No accurate figures concerning the degree of duplication are available. The maximum amount of duplication was 3 percent in 1899 (in terms of value) and 16 percent in 1937. These figures suggest that our index of output overstates the rise in the output of the industry, free of such duplication, perhaps by as much as 10 or 15 percent.

HATS, STRAW, MEN'S	Item	*1927*	*1929*	*1931*	*1933*[b]	*1935*	*1937*
Adjusted index		122.2	100.0	99.4		143.1	158.4
Unadjusted index[a]		126.4	100.0	95.8		94.2	110.5
Product	*Item*						
Sewed-braid hats	*q* Mil. doz.	.705	.715	.654		.302	.524
	v Mil. $	13.6	13.3	8.63		3.23	5.37
	p $ per doz.	19.2	18.6	13.2		10.7	10.3
Woven-body hats, except harvest[c]	*q* Mil. doz.	.315	.135	.181		.397	.352
	v Mil. $	8.90	4.85	4.93		4.78	4.18
	p $ per doz.	28.2	35.9	27.3		12.0	11.9
Harvest hats, men's	*q* Mil. doz.	1.03	1.03	.619		.590	.743
	v Mil. $	3.26	3.30	1.77		1.31	1.33
	p $ per doz.	3.17	3.20	2.86		2.21	1.79

[a] Percentages of coverage:

Given year	Base year
1927:118.4	1929:114.5
1931:110.3	
1935: 75.4	
1937: 79.8	

[b] Detailed data on products were not collected in 1933.
[c] Includes a small number of women's hats.

HATS, WOOL-FELT	Item	*1899*	*1904*	*1909*	*1914*	*1919*	*1921*	*1923*	*1925*	*1927*[b] *A*	*1927*[b] *B*	*1929*	*1931*	*1933*[c]	*1935*	*1937*
Adjusted index		135.1	67.5	100.8	64.3	79.4	49.6	72.1	72.7	86.8		100.0	84.0		185.4	256.0
Unadjusted index[a]		139.4	74.1	102.8	66.8	74.1	48.4	72.2	70.5	86.3		100.0	85.2		189.9	249.9
Product	*Item*															
Hat bodies, carded, for sale as such	*q* Th. doz.	56.0	18.6	53.9	5.72	104	55.3	59.2	185	379	379	501	745		1,803	2,428
	v Th. $	120	100	309	13.0	165	245	479	1,347	2,734	2,734	3,621	2,982		6,796	9,668
	p $ per doz.	2.15	5.41	5.74	2.28	1.59	4.44	8.08	7.26	7.22	7.22	7.24	4.00		3.77	3.98

For footnotes see next page.

Indexes of Physical Output, with Basic Data on Quantity, Value and Price of Products

HATS, WOOL-FELT (concluded)		1899	1904	1909	1914	1919	1921	1923	1925	1927[b] A	1927[b] B	1929	1931	1933[c]	1935	1937
Product	*Item*															
Finished hats	*q* Mil. doz.	.811	.446	.591	.381	.402	.280	.454	.373	.386	.377	.400	.177		.322	.372
	v Mil. $	3.16	2.29	3.65	1.78	5.41	4.05	7.18	6.34	5.53	5.03	4.41	1.91		3.36	3.73
	p $ per doz.	3.90	5.13	6.17	4.66	13.5	14.4	15.8	17.0	14.3	13.4	11.0	10.8		10.4	10.0

A Comparable with earlier years. *B* Comparable with later years.

[a] Percentages of coverage:

Given year	Base year	Given year	Base year	Given year	Base year
1899:91.4, 1904:97.3	1909:90.3	1919:82.7, 1921:86.5, 1923:88.6, 1925:85.9	1927:88.1	1927:88.2, 1931:90.0, 1935:90.8, 1937:86.6	1929:88.7
1909:90.3, 1914:92.1	1919:82.7				

[b] The figures for 1927 were revised in 1929 to exclude data for 5 establishments engaged exclusively in finishing wool-felt hats.

[c] Detailed data on products were not collected in 1933.

HOSIERY, KNIT		1899	1904	1909	1914	1919	1921	1923	1925	1927	1929	1931	1933	1935	1937
Adjusted index							[c]	57.2	68.1	78.5	100.0	88.5	92.2[d]	102.3[e]	114.6
Unadjusted index[a,b]		9.1	13.6	19.7	34.7	44.4	49.0	59.1	69.5	80.6	100.0	88.8	93.5	104.5	113.5
Product[f]	*Item*														
Cotton															
Hose, full-fashioned	*q* Mil. doz.pr.					2.94	1.71	1.80	.728						
	v Mil. $					10.9	4.58	6.30	2.13						
	p $ per doz.pr.					3.71	2.67	3.51	2.92						
Hose, full-fashioned and seamless	*q*	15.0	24.2	32.5	37.0										
	v	13.3	22.8	34.1	38.4										
	p	.883	.942	1.05	1.04										
Hose, seamless	*q* Mil. doz.pr.					33.9	28.5	32.9	27.9						
	v Mil. $					94.8	58.1	64.4	51.9						
	p $ per doz.pr.					2.80	2.04	1.96	1.86						
Hose, full-fashioned, seamless and half-hose	*q*									43.2					
	v									66.4					
	p									1.54					
Half-hose	*q* Mil. doz.pr.	11.4	15.2	24.8	24.5	23.8	20.7	22.9	21.8						
	v Mil. $	7.91	11.8	21.8	21.2	47.9	31.6	35.2	33.8						
	p $ per doz.pr.	.697	.777	.880	.868	2.01	1.53	1.54	1.55						

HOSIERY, KNIT (continued)		*1899*	*1904*	*1909*	*1914*	*1919*	*1921*	*1923*	*1925*	*1927*	*1929*	*1931*	*1933*	*1935*	*1937*
Product[f]	*Item*														
Wool															
Hose	*q* Mil. doz.pr.	1.18	1.08	1.17	1.37	.395	1.12	.611	.279						
	v Mil. $	2.27	2.21	2.36	2.55	2.14	7.19	5.39	1.64						
	p $ per doz.pr.	1.93	2.03	2.02	1.86	5.41	6.40	8.83	5.87	*q* .565					
										v 2.69					
Half-hose	*q* Mil. doz.pr.	.940	1.31	1.06	.616	.652	.390	.567	.361	*p* 4.76					
	v Mil. $	1.74	3.40	2.09	1.33	3.26	1.69	2.77	1.94						
	p $ per doz.pr.	1.85	2.60	1.97	2.15	5.00	4.33	4.88	5.39						
Cotton and wool, mixed															
Hose	*q* Mil. doz.pr.	.437	.746	.834	.723	1.03	2.63	3.37	1.03						
	v Mil. $	.660	1.18	1.47	1.41	4.46	10.3	12.3	4.60						
	p $ per doz.pr.	1.51	1.58	1.76	1.95	4.33	3.91	3.64	4.48	*q* 4.20					
										v 11.6					
Half-hose	*q* Mil. doz.pr.	.958	1.61	2.02	2.34	3.16	1.84	4.52	3.21	*p* 2.77					
	v Mil. $	1.38	2.21	3.30	3.38	10.5	6.13	13.1	9.27						
	p $ per doz.pr.	1.45	1.37	1.63	1.45	3.33	3.34	2.90	2.89						
Silk															
Hose, full-fashioned	*q* Mil. doz.pr.					.935	.973	1.72	1.48						
	v Mil. $					12.4	19.2	25.2	22.0						
	p $ per doz.pr.				*q* 2.35	13.2	19.7	14.6	14.8						
					v 13.9										
Hose, seamless	*q* Mil. doz.pr.				*p* 5.88	.913	1.62	1.40	.260						
	v Mil. $					9.21	16.6	12.5	2.73						
	p $ per doz.pr.	*q* .0126	.0421	.434		10.1	10.3	8.90	10.5	*q* 3.57					
		v .186	.522	3.60						*v* 45.6					
Half-hose, full-fashioned	*q* Mil. doz.pr.	*p* 14.8	12.4	8.29		.0844	.0457	.0186	.209	*p* 12.8					
	v Mil. $					1.05	.323	.143	2.13						
	p $ per doz.pr.				*q* 1.31	12.4	7.08	7.68	10.2						
					v 4.70										
Half-hose, seamless	*q* Mil. doz.pr.				*p* 3.60	.996	1.49	1.50	.183						
	v Mil. $					5.80	8.06	8.18	.893						
	p $ per doz.pr.					5.82	5.39	5.44	4.87						

For footnotes see p. 443.

Indexes of Physical Output, with Basic Data on Quantity, Value and Price of Products

HOSIERY, KNIT (continued)		1899	1904	1909	1914	1919	1921	1923	1925	1927	1929	1931	1933	1935	1937
Product[f]	*Item*														
Rayon															
Hose	*q* Mil. doz.pr.				g	.741	1.60	2.17	.305						
	v Mil. $					3.74	5.62	8.39	1.19						
	p $ per doz.pr.					5.05	3.52	3.87	3.92	*q* .906					
										v 2.26					
Half-hose	*q* Mil. doz.pr.				g	.846	.451	.591	.252	*p* 2.50					
	v Mil. $					2.91	1.45	2.26	.586						
	p $ per doz.pr.					3.43	3.20	3.82	2.33						
Silk or rayon mixed with other fibers															
Hose, full-fashioned	*q* Mil. doz.pr.					2.34	4.80	6.04	9.98						
	v Mil. $					32.3	64.3	88.1	116						
	p $ per doz.pr.			h	*q* 2.79	13.8	13.4	14.6	11.6						
					v 6.94										
Hose, seamless	*q* Mil. doz.pr.				*p* 2.49	8.24	9.10	9.61	17.6						
	v Mil. $					46.8	43.4	56.4	100						
	p $ per doz.pr.					5.68	4.76	5.87	5.68	*q* 50.6					
										v 312					
Half-hose, full-fashioned	*q* Mil. doz.pr.					.871	.616	.819	.540	*p* 6.16					
	v Mil. $					7.90	3.38	6.30	4.07						
	p $ per doz.pr.			h	*q* 2.26	9.07	5.50	7.69	7.53						
					v 4.30										
Half-hose, seamless	*q* Mil. doz.pr.				*p* 1.90	2.83	2.67	6.88	13.7						
	v Mil. $					12.7	8.64	31.9	49.0						
	p $ per doz.pr.					4.49	3.24	4.64	3.59						
Men's hosiery, full-fashioned	*q* Mil. doz.pr.									1.24	.715	.697	.657	.210[i]	.222[i]
	v Mil. $									5.21	4.78	3.54	1.85	.861	.985
	p $ per doz.pr.									4.19	6.69	5.08	2.82	4.10	4.43
Men's hosiery, seamless	*q* Mil. doz.pr.									43.0	44.1	39.7	37.8	42.5	43.3
	v Mil. $									89.5	92.5	56.7	48.8	61.4	64.3
	p $ per doz.pr.									2.08	2.10	1.43	1.29	1.44	1.48

HOSIERY, KNIT (concluded)		1899	1904	1909	1914	1919	1921	1923	1925	1927	1929	1931	1933	1935	1937
Product[f]	*Item*														
Women's hosiery,	*q* Mil. doz.pr.									19.8	31.1	28.7	31.6	36.2	40.0
full-fashioned	*v* Mil. $									227	307	208	162	200	228
	p $ per doz.pr									11.5	9.86	7.24	5.12	5.52	5.71
Women's hosiery,	*q* Mil. doz.pr.									24.9	20.1	13.9	14.1	13.7	13.7
seamless	*v* Mil. $									86.9	65.4	28.7	23.2	24.7	26.2
	p $ per doz.pr.									3.48	3.25	2.06	1.65	1.80	1.91
Boys', misses', and	*q* Mil. doz.pr.									14.2	15.2	13.1	12.8	14.6	22.3[j]
children's hosiery,	*v* Mil. $									31.6	31.1	16.9	16.1	1.79	25.7
principally seamless	*p* $ per doz.pr.									2.22	2.05	1.29	1.26	1.23	1.15
Infants' hosiery,	*q* Mil. doz.pr.									6.84	6.17	5.53	6.14	5.49	6.00
principally seamless	*v* Mil. $									13.0	11.2	7.69	6.98	6.08	6.49
	p $ per doz.pr.									1.90	1.82	1.39	1.14	1.11	1.08

[a] Percentages of coverage:

Given year	Base year	Given year	Base year
1923:97.0	1925:95.9	1933:98.1	1929: 96.8
1925:95.9	1927:96.4	1935:98.6	1933: 97.9
1927:99.3 / 1931:97.1	1929:96.8	1937:97.3	1935:100.4

[b] Because some of the 1935 data are not comparable with those for 1929, the 1935 index was computed on the 1933 base. Because of a similar incomparability, the 1937 index was computed on the 1935 base. The 1925 index was computed on the 1927 base, and the indexes for 1919–23 were computed on the 1925 base.

[c] No adjusted indexes for 1899–1921 could be computed because the industry is not shown separately in the Census for those years. Adjusted indexes were computed for the entire knit goods industry. The adjusted index given above, extrapolated by the unadjusted index, is 8.8 for 1899; 13.2 for 1904; 19.1 for 1909; 33.6 for 1914; 42.9 for 1919; 47.4 for 1921.

[d] Between 1933 and 1935 plants engaged in dyeing and finishing of hosiery knitted by others were transferred from dyeing and finishing to hosiery, knit.

[e] A slight discontinuity arises from the fact that between 1935 and 1937 establishments engaged in commission knitting were excluded.

[f] Do not include athletic and golf hose which are classified in the outerwear industry.

Prior to 1929, the detailed data relate to products made within the knit goods group alone, while in 1929 and subsequent years they relate to the total of products, wherever made.

[g] Not reported separately in earlier years. Included in silk hose or silk half-hose.

[h] Not reported separately in earlier years. We assume that these products were included in silk hose or silk half-hose.

[i] Not strictly comparable with earlier data. Comparable figures for 1933 are as follows: men's full-fashioned: *q* 285 th. doz.pr., *v* $1.26 mil., *p* $4.44 per doz.pr., full-fashioned, total: *q* 31.9 mil.doz.pr., *v* $163 mil., *p* $5.11 per doz.pr.; seamless, total, except infants': *q* 64.7 mil.doz.pr., *v* $88.0 mil., *p* $1.36 per doz.pr.

[j] Not strictly comparable with earlier data. Comparable figures for 1935 are: *q* 18.3 mil.doz.pr., *v* $23.5 mil., *p* $1.28 per doz.pr.

Indexes of Physical Output, with Basic Data on Quantity, Value and Price of Products

JUTE GOODS		*1899*	*1904*[b]	*1909*	*1914*	*1919*	*1921*	*1923*	*1925*	*1927*	*1929*	*1931*	*1933*	*1935*	*1937*
Adjusted index		61.3		108.9[c]	138.4	116.8	77.4	103.7	104.6	97.4	100.0	79.4	89.4	99.9	143.4
Unadjusted index[a]		88.4		92.2	134.2	92.9	72.9	105.7	108.1	101.6	100.0	66.7	87.1	92.4	136.0
Product	*Item*														
Yarns produced for sale	*q* Mil. lb.	54.3		62.5	69.8	56.4				84.5	96.5	57.3	61.9	81.9	
	v Mil. $	3.23		4.36	7.36	11.6				14.6	14.9	6.96	6.83	9.76	
	p $ per lb.	.0595		.0698	.105	.205				.173	.154	.121	.110	.119	
Yarns produced for sale, incl. yarns other than jute	*q* Mil. lb.						54.1	99.1	97.5		97.9				116
	v Mil. $						9.86	19.2	19.5		15.5				14.8
	p $ per lb.						.182	.194	.200		.158				.128
Bagging for baling cotton, incl. other bagging	*q* Mil. sq.yd.	74.1		69.3	132	78.8									
	v Mil. $	3.46		3.51	6.44	12.0									
	p $ per sq.yd.	.0467		.0506	.0489	.152									
Bagging for baling cotton	*q* Mil. sq.yd.					75.2	54.5	37.4	45.9	48.3	27.9	31.5	64.9	40.0	61.7
	v Mil. $					11.3	4.51	2.77	5.05	5.20	3.13	2.00	3.37	2.84	5.83
	p $ per sq.yd.					.151	.0828	.0741	.110	.108	.112	.0635	.0520	.0710	.0945
Webbing (not over 12 in. wide)	*q* Mil. lin.yd.					25.4	17.5	47.1	38.4	45.9	43.7	22.7	21.1	27.5	
	v Mil. $					1.05	.484	1.37	1.12	1.35	1.12	.468	.432	.606	
	p $ per lin.yd.					.0414	.0277	.0292	.0292	.0295	.0257	.0206	.0205	.0220	

[a] Percentages of coverage:

Given year	Base year	Given year	Base year	Given year	Base year
1899:124.3	1909:72.9	1921:84.9	1929:90.2	1931:73.7	1929:87.6
1909: 72.9	1919:68.5	1923:91.9	1929:90.2	1933:85.3	1929:87.6
1914: 83.6	1919:68.5	1925:93.2	1929:90.2	1935:81.0	1929:87.6
1919: 69.6	1929:87.6	1927:91.4	1929:87.6	1937:80.6	1929:85.0

[b] Detailed data on products were not collected in 1904.

[c] Between 1909 and 1914, 8 establishments manufacturing jute carpets were transferred from carpets and rugs, wool, to jute goods. The resulting discontinuity appears to be slight.

KNIT GOODS, total	*1899*	*1904*	*1909*	*1914*	*1919*	*1921*	*1923*	*1925*	*1927*	*1929*	*1931*	*1933*	*1935*	*1937*
Adjusted index[b]	19.1	23.9	33.1[c]	45.1	55.4	59.2	74.7	76.8	83.0	100.0	92.4	99.6[d]	111.1	115.7
Unadjusted index[a,b]	20.2	25.3	35.5	46.6	56.4	61.1				100.0				

[a] Percentages of coverage:

Given year	Base year
1899: 92.6	1909: 94.0
1904: 93.0	1909: 94.2
1909: 94.2	1919: 89.3
1914: 92.0	1919: 90.6
1919: 90.3	1923: 88.8
1921: 91.7	1923: 88.8

[b] For the basic data, see the separate industries: hosiery, underwear, outerwear, and cloth, knit. For the years 1923–37 the adjusted index was computed from the 4 underlying adjusted indexes (3 for 1933–37), with values added as weights. For the earlier years the 4 component industries are treated as one in the Census; therefore we followed the usual procedure in the construction of the unadjusted and adjusted indexes.

[c] Between 1909 and 1914 some knitting mills, using as a material silk alone, were transferred from silk and rayon goods to knit goods.

[d] Between 1933 and 1935 plants engaged in the dyeing and finishing of hosiery knitted by others were transferred from dyeing and finishing to hosiery, knit. The resulting discontinuity appears to be slight.

LACE GOODS		*1914*	*1919*	*1921*	*1923*	*1925*	*1927*	*1929*	*1931*	*1933*[b]	*1935*	*1937*
Adjusted index		73.9	87.1	67.1	100.9	89.7	95.9	100.0	80.0		142.9	153.5
Unadjusted index[a]		69.6	85.9	64.2	114.3	96.5	95.0	100.0	81.1		135.8	167.2
Product	*Item*											
Levers laces	*q* Mil. sq.yd.	7.24	11.6	4.45	10.5	8.98						
	v Mil. $	3.68	6.61	3.99	8.03	6.55						
	p $ per sq.yd.	.509	.568	.896	.763	.729						
Levers laces, all-overs	*q* Mil. sq.yd.						3.02	4.96	7.08		9.68	15.2
	v Mil. $						2.47	4.37	4.78		5.67	7.96
	p $ per sq.yd.						.818	.881	.676		.586	.524
Nottingham lace curtains	*q* Mil. pr.	5.59	3.93	3.92	6.04	4.56	5.66	6.11	4.52		9.57	10.7
	v Mil. $	4.68	8.17	8.44	12.9	10.3	10.8	11.2	6.87		11.3	12.1
	p $ per pr.	.837	2.08	2.15	2.14	2.25	1.91	1.84	1.52		1.18	1.13

For footnotes see next page.

Indexes of Physical Output, with Basic Data on Quantity, Value and Price of Products

LACE GOODS (concluded)		1914	1919	1921	1923	1925	1927	1929	1931	1933[b]	1935	1937
Product	*Item*											
Nottingham lace-curtain nets	*q* Mil. lin.yd.	7.50	19.5	17.2	30.3	28.6	19.2	14.3	6.28		4.89	5.19
	v Mil. $	1.26	7.62	6.79	10.3	8.82	5.52	4.67	1.83		1.15	1.38
	p $ per lin.yd.	.168	.391	.394	.341	.308	.287	.327	.291		.235	.265

[a] Percentages of coverage:
Given year 1914:72.8, Base year 1919:76.2;
Given year 1919:53.7, Base year 1929:54.5;
Given year 1921:73.9, Base year 1919:76.2;
Given year 1923:87.4, 1925:83.2, Base year 1919:76.2;
Given year 1927:68.8, Base year 1929:69.4;
Given year 1931:70.4, 1935:65.9, 1937:75.6, Base year 1929:69.4.

[b] Detailed data on products were not collected in 1933.

LINEN GOODS		1899	1904[b]	1909	1914	1919	1921	1923	1925	1927	1929	1931	1933	1935	1937
Adjusted index		136.6		200.0	191.6	86.3	71.8	125.4	117.0	120.1	100.0	68.1	71.6	73.2	77.2
Unadjusted index[a]		128.1		204.2	186.4	169.2	72.7	123.0	104.6	104.6	100.0	84.9	95.9	89.3	89.6
Product	*Item*														
Linen thread	*q* Mil. lb.	4.02		6.53	5.71	4.28	1.49	4.06	2.86	2.71	3.10	2.11	2.57	2.65	2.96
	v Mil. $	2.33		3.41	3.41	6.69	2.87	5.72	4.69	4.21	4.51	2.39	2.38	3.14	3.57
	p $ per lb.	.580		.522	.597	1.56	1.92	1.41	1.64	1.56	1.45	1.13	.923	1.18	1.21
Woven goods, linen	*q* Mil. sq.yd.	6.87		10.5	10.8	14.3	7.68	6.54	7.85	8.53					
	v Mil. $	.796		1.57	1.77	3.80	3.47	2.81	2.93	2.70					
	p $ per sq.yd.	.116		.151	.164	.265	.452	.430	.374	.316					
Woven goods, linen and part-linen	*q* Mil. sq.yd.									12.4[c]	9.43	10.1	10.7	8.92	7.75
	v Mil. $									3.55	3.36	2.89	2.36	2.39	2.48
	p $ per sq.yd.									.287	.357	.286	.221	.268	.320

[a] Percentages of coverage:
Given year 1899:71.6, Base year 1909: 78.0;
Given year 1909:78.0, 1914:74.4, Base year 1919:149.9;
Given year 1919:149.9, 1921: 77.3, 1923: 74.9, Base year 1927:66.6;
Given year 1925: 68.4, Base year 1927:66.6;
Given year 1927: 70.4, 1931:100.9, Base year 1929:80.9;
Given year 1933:108.3, 1935: 98.7, 1937: 93.9, Base year 1929:80.9.

[b] Detailed data on products were not collected in 1904.

[c] Estimated in part.

LINOLEUM		1904	1909	1914	1919	1921	1923	1925	1927	1929	1931	1933	1935	1937
Adjusted index					b	81.9	98.8	86.2	91.6	100.0	45.3	42.3	60.5	82.7
Unadjusted index[a]		31.6	58.4	82.8	66.3	81.6	98.5	100.1	95.3	100.0	44.9	32.3	54.1	80.6
Product	*Item*													
Linoleum, plain	q Mil. sq.yd.						8.69	8.88	9.28	10.3	4.40		4.37	8.09
	v Mil. $						9.49	10.4	10.3	13.1	4.83		3.91	7.97
	p $ per sq.yd.						1.09	1.17	1.11	1.27	1.10		.895	.985
Linoleum, printed	q Mil. sq.yd.	q 14.8	26.2	33.3	22.1	26.2	21.5	18.3	15.2	11.5	2.26		2.20	2.45
	v Mil. $	v 4.22	7.85	10.0	17.1	20.5	12.9	10.8	7.95	6.24	1.28		1.00	1.16
	p $ per sq.yd.	p .286	.299	.302	.775	.781	.600	.591	.523	.544	.567		.455	.474
Cork carpet	q Mil. sq.yd.						.516	.490	.521	.408	.247	q 15.6	.215	.367
	v Mil. $						.583	.546	.515	.453	.244	v 12.4	.189	.376
	p $ per sq.yd.						1.13	1.11	.988	1.11	.988	p .797	.880	1.03
Inlaid, excluding inlaid linoleum rugs	q Mil. sq.yd.	2.13	4.46	8.48	9.83	12.6	17.9	19.2	18.2	23.2				
	v Mil. $	1.10	2.99	4.73	10.3	12.1	18.2	18.5	19.1	27.0				
	p $ per sq.yd.	.520	.671	.557	1.05	.966	1.01	.967	1.05	1.16	13.5		17.7	24.8
											13.1		13.2	20.1
Rugs	q Mil. sq.yd.						4.42	5.99	6.76	2.87	.969		.746	.808
	v Mil. $						3.44	4.24	4.17	1.93				
	p $ per sq.yd.						.778	.708	.618	.674				

[a] Percentages of coverage:

Given year	Base year	Given year	Base year
1921:84.8		1931:84.4	
1923:84.9	1929:85.1	1933:64.9	1929:85.1
1925:98.9		1935:76.1	
1927:88.6		1937:83.0	

[b] No adjusted indexes for 1904–19 could be computed because the industry is not shown separately in the Censuses for those years. The adjusted index given above, extrapolated by the unadjusted index, is 31.7 for 1904; 58.6 for 1909; 83.1 for 1914; 66.5 for 1919.

Indexes of Physical Output, with Basic Data on Quantity, Value and Price of Products

OILCLOTH		1904	1909	1914	1919	1921	1923	1925	1927	1929	1931	1933[b]	1935	1937
Adjusted index		36.0	62.3	61.0	38.0	46.1	61.3	66.1	79.1	100.0	76.8		76.3	65.7
Unadjusted index[a]		40.6	64.0	63.6	38.3	49.1	63.2	68.2	82.2	100.0	73.1		62.3	56.6
Product	*Item*													
Enameled	*q* Mil. sq.yd.	11.6	17.3	18.4	8.46	3.00	8.75	7.93	10.7	18.5	11.6		8.23	6.96
	v Mil. $	1.54	2.27	2.50	3.42	1.01	2.68	1.85	2.20	5.36	2.50		1.59	1.56
	p $ per sq.yd.	.133	.131	.136	.404	.336	.307	.234	.205	.290	.216		.194	.224
Table, wall, and shelf	*q* Mil. sq.yd.	38.0	61.2	59.4	39.1	62.2	72.3	79.4	94.6	107	81.5		72.1	66.4
	v Mil. $	3.54	5.64	6.03	12.5	13.9	16.0	17.0	16.6	18.3	11.1		9.36	9.74
	p $ per sq.yd.	.0931	.0922	.102	.320	.224	.222	.214	.175	.171	.137		.130	.147

[a] Percentages of coverage:

Given year	Base year	Given year	Base year	Given year	Base year
1904:115.4	1909:105.0	1919:103.3	1929:102.3	1927:106.4	1929:102.3
1909:105.0	1919:103.3	1921:109.0		1931: 97.4	
1914:106.6		1923:105.6		1935: 83.6	
		1925:105.5		1937: 88.2	

[b] Detailed data on products were not collected in 1933.

OUTERWEAR, KNIT		1899	1904	1909	1914	1919	1921	1923	1925	1927	1929	1931	1933	1935	1937
Adjusted index							[b]	119.0	84.6	83.5	100.0	108.3	119.0	141.5	117.4
Unadjusted index[a]		22.3	29.7	55.2	53.5	56.7	78.5	111.4	84.9	82.2	100.0	105.2	117.5	122.2	96.4
Product[c]	*Item*														
Sweaters, sweater coats, jerseys, etc.	*q* Mil. doz.	.594	.812	2.22	2.25	2.13	2.75	4.46	3.71	3.78	4.81	4.03	5.00	4.39	3.85
	v Mil. $	3.50	8.35	22.4	26.2	61.1	69.4	111	84.9	74.6	89.4	56.1	48.0	55.3	49.7
	p $ per doz.	5.89	10.3	10.1	11.6	28.6	25.3	25.0	22.9	19.7	18.6	13.9	9.59	12.6	12.9
Bathing suits	*q* Mil. doz.				.274	.301	.909	.972	.695	.740	1.02	.963	.833	.990	1.21
	v Mil. $				2.03	6.64	11.2	17.6	16.3	15.9	22.1	12.9	11.3	14.6	17.3
	p $ per doz.				7.41	22.0	12.3	18.1	23.5	21.4	21.6	13.4	13.6	14.7	14.4

OUTERWEAR, KNIT (concluded)		1899	1904	1909	1914	1919	1921	1923	1925	1927	1929	1931	1933	1935	1937
Product[c]	*Item*														
Scarfs and shawls, incl. mufflers	*q* Mil. doz.	.158	.435	.219	.0633	.298	.363	.980	.492	.188	.127	.0585	.178	.292	.121
	v Mil. $	.329	1.29	.916	.714	4.05	7.78	10.4	4.66	2.21	1.16	.554	1.09	1.72	.707
	p $ per doz.	2.09	2.97	4.19	11.3	13.6	21.5	10.6	9.47	11.8	9.16	9.47	6.10	5.89	5.84
Headwear, except infants'	*q* Mil. doz.	.343	.589	.888	.987	.558	.508	.843	.805	.700	.783	1.08	1.15	.969	.859
	v Mil. $	1.00	1.77	3.22	3.46	4.00	3.41	4.81	4.51	3.88	3.78	3.28	3.48	3.88	2.85
	p $ per doz.	2.92	3.01	3.62	3.50	7.17	6.71	5.71	5.60	5.53	4.83	3.04	3.03	4.00	3.32
Neckties	*q* Mil. doz.					.548	1.76	3.32	2.71	1.81	.628	.131	.0564	.255	.0694
	v Mil. $					5.10	9.14	12.3	8.96	5.85	1.72	.327	.219	.519	.157
	p $ per doz.					9.31	5.20	3.71	3.31	3.23	2.74	2.51	3.88	2.03	2.26
Athletic and golf hose	*q* Mil. doz.								.573	.950	1.11	2.13	2.30	3.08	2.01
	v Mil. $								3.96	4.28	4.77	4.88	3.70	4.79	3.09
	p $ per doz.								6.91	4.50	4.32	2.29	1.61	1.55	1.54
Dresses and suits	*q* Mil. doz.									.868	1.02	2.91	2.91	4.03	1.75
	v Mil. $									6.25	11.2	20.7	15.4	22.6	10.3
	p $ per doz.									7.20	10.9	7.12	5.30	5.60	5.89
Gloves and mittens, incl. sueded-cotton	*q* Mil. doz.	1.90	2.26	2.53	2.47	3.57	2.69	2.09	1.30	1.05					
	v Mil. $	4.24	5.56	7.30	10.5	19.5	25.2	16.8	9.08	7.34					
	p $ per doz.	2.24	2.46	2.89	4.26	5.47	9.39	8.01	6.98	6.99					

[a] Percentages of coverage:

Given year	Base year	Given year	Base year
1923:82.9	1927:87.2	1933:89.9	1929:91.1
1925:92.3	1927:90.6	1935:78.6	1929:91.1
1927:89.7	1929:91.1	1937:74.7	1929:91.1
1931:88.4	1929:91.1		

[b] No adjusted indexes for 1899–1921 could be computed because the industry is not shown separately in the Census for those years. Adjusted indexes were computed for the entire knit goods industry. The adjusted index given above, extrapolated by the unadjusted index, is 23.8 for 1899; 31.7 for 1904; 59.0 for 1909; 57.1 for 1914; 60.6 for 1919; 83.8 for 1921.

[c] For years prior to 1929 the detailed data relate to products made within the knit goods group alone, whereas for 1929 and subsequent years the data relate to the total of products wherever made.

Indexes of Physical Output, with Basic Data on Quantity, Value and Price of Products

SHIRTS and COLLARS, MEN'S		*1927*	*1929*	*1931*	*1933*	*1935*	*1937*
Adjusted index		100.8	100.0	99.3[b]	79.4	90.6	92.8
Unadjusted index[a]		103.5	100.0	94.4	83.9	89.0	105.8
Product	*Item*						
Men's and youths' shirts, excl. work shirts	*q* Mil. doz.	10.9	11.0	10.2	9.71	10.7	12.0
	v Mil. $	156	147	101	82.6	103	129
	p $ per doz.	14.4	13.4	9.92	8.51	9.64	10.7
Boys' blouses and shirts	*q* Mil. doz.	2.43	2.90	3.55	2.22	1.99	2.22
	v Mil. $	18.4	20.2	18.1	10.7	10.6	11.9
	p $ per doz.	7.58	6.96	5.10	4.83	5.33	5.37
Men's and youths' work shirts, incl. flannels	*q* Mil. doz.	6.77	5.70	5.53			
	v Mil. $	55.9	45.7	30.0			
	p $ per doz.	8.25	8.02	5.42			
Collars, men's	*q* Mil. doz.	8.05	5.70	3.05	1.98	1.21	
	v Mil. $	14.4	8.88	5.16	3.09	2.65	
	p $ per doz.	1.79	1.56	1.69	1.56	2.19	

[a] Percentages of coverage:

Given year	Base year	Given year	Base year
1927:96.0, 1931:88.8	1929:93.5	1933:78.4, 1935:72.8	1929:74.2
		1937:80.3	1929:70.4

[b] Between 1931 and 1933 establishments making work shirts, including flannel shirts, were transferred from shirts to clothing, men's, work; and establishments making men's nightwear were transferred from furnishings, men's, n.e.c., to shirts.

SILK and RAYON GOODS		*1899*	*1904*	*1909*	*1914*	*1919*	*1921*	*1923*[b]		*1925*	*1927*	*1929*	*1931*	*1933*	*1935*	*1937*
Adjusted index		22.1	29.9	39.6[c]	48.6	63.7	58.5	72.8		86.4	91.5	100.0	92.2	84.1	d	d
Unadjusted index[a]		20.2	25.7	34.4	43.7	58.6	54.4	69.3		83.2	89.2	100.0	88.5	76.8	121.3	127.8
Product[e]	*Item*							*A*	*B*							
Broad goods, all silk	*q* Mil. sq.yd.[b]	68.4	97.9	115	143	246	223	255	272	385	386	425	386	201	239	109
	v Mil. $	42.6	55.9	74.5	96.7	323	285	333	333	426	377	386	210	77.1	69.7	40.8
	p $ per sq.yd.	.622	.572	.648	.678	1.31	1.28	1.30	1.22	1.11	.978	.909	.543	.383	.291	.374

SILK and RAYON GOODS (continued)

Product[e]	Item	1899	1904	1909	1914	1919	1921	1923[b]		1925	1927	1929	1931	1933	1935	1937
								A	B							
Broad goods, other than all silk	q Mil. sq.yd.[b]	19.2	27.0	70.8	73.3	64.3	50.3	102	104	98.4	127	173			12.8[f]	27.3[f]
	v Mil. $	9.58	11.0	33.4	41.0	69.2	56.3	123	123	103	109	102			7.34	16.7
	p $ per sq.yd.	.499	.406	.472	.560	1.08	1.12	1.21	1.18	1.05	.854	.594			.574	.612
Broad goods, silk and rayon and silk and cotton mixed	q Mil. sq.yd.											59.5	22.4	35.4		
	v Mil. $											42.2	16.0	15.9		
	p $ per sq.yd.											.710	.717	.450		
Broad goods, all rayon	q Mil. sq.yd.											66.0	109	273	731	947
	v Mil. $											34.7	38.4	78.8	141	200
	p $ per sq.yd.											.526	.351	.289	.193	.211
Broad goods, rayon and cotton mixed	q Mil. sq.yd.											37.2	41.1	47.0	44.1[g]	54.8[g]
	v Mil. $											16.6	12.2	11.6	18.8	22.2
	p $ per sq.yd.											.446	.297	.246	.426	.405
Velvets, all	q Mil. sq.yd.[b]	5.12	7.26	10.1	16.3	16.2	11.5	17.1	9.11	6.08	5.48	9.65	7.35	7.86		
	v Mil. $	2.48	3.16	4.77	8.57	21.0	16.0	23.9	23.9	14.5	11.9	25.1	12.2	8.68		
	p $ per sq.yd.	.484	.435	.472	.525	1.30	1.39	1.39	2.62	2.39	2.17	2.60	1.67	1.11		
Plushes	q Mil. sq.yd.[b]	3.85	2.55	2.76	9.12	5.86	5.58	6.44	7.12	.925	1.31	1.96	1.88	1.06		
	v Mil. $	2.48	1.34	2.10	10.1	21.6	12.1	17.2	17.2	2.35	2.75	3.83	2.09	.764		
	p $ per sq.yd.	.644	.526	.763	1.11	3.69	2.17	2.67	2.42	2.54	2.10	1.96	1.11	.720		
Upholsteries and tapestries	q Mil. sq.yd.[b]	1.33	1.77	.227	.478	.516	.974	2.80	3.80	2.68	3.71	3.40	3.83	2.90		
	v Mil. $	1.01	1.56	.383	.840	2.16	3.83	10.6	10.6	5.04	8.30	6.12	2.59	1.06		
	p $ per sq.yd.	.757	.883	1.69	1.76	4.18	3.93	3.80	2.80	1.88	2.24	1.80	.675	.367		
Silk thread and yarn																
Organzine and tram	q Mil. lb.	2.47	2.03	2.74	4.07	4.50										
	v Mil. $	11.2	9.19	12.6	16.0	40.6										
	p $ per lb.	4.52	4.54	4.58	3.94	9.03										
Organzine, tram and crepe twist	q Mil. lb.					5.57	6.43	8.43	8.43	9.66	11.4	12.1	9.75	7.54	9.41	
	v Mil. $					52.6	47.1	67.4	67.4	66.5	70.2	69.7	32.2	17.0	20.9	
	p $ per lb.					9.45	7.32	7.99	7.99	6.88	6.16	5.75	3.30	2.25	2.22	

For footnotes see next page.

Indexes of Physical Output, with Basic Data on Quantity, Value and Price of Products

SILK and RAYON GOODS (continued)		1899	1904	1909	1914	1919	1921	1923[b]		1925	1927	1929	1931	1933	1935[d]	1937[d]
Product[e]	*Item*							*A*	*B*							
Silk thread and yarn (concluded)																
Spun silk	*q* Mil. lb.	.437	.571	.779	1.61	3.96	4.74	3.49	3.49	4.69	4.46	3.77	1.91	1.08	1.40	
	v Mil. $	1.03	1.66	2.10	4.58	23.8	17.1	14.7	14.7	20.4	15.7	12.9	5.27	2.50	2.43	
	p $ per lb.	2.35	2.91	2.70	2.85	6.02	3.61	4.23	4.23	4.34	3.52	3.43	2.75	2.32	1.74	
Machine twist	*q* Mil. lb.	.988	.933	1.09	.660	.774	.805	1.10	1.10	.860	.723	.515	.300	.271	.470	
	v Mil. $	6.00	5.52	6.34	4.04	10.6	8.65	11.4	11.4	8.97	6.47	4.82	1.55	1.35	1.97	
	p $ per lb.	6.07	5.92	5.82	6.12	13.8	10.7	10.4	10.4	10.4	8.95	9.36	5.17	4.99	4.19	
Sewing thread and embroidery and other floss silks	*q* Mil. lb.	.739	.812	.747	.902	.553	1.08	.652	.652	.764	.659	.335	.298	.193		
	v Mil. $	4.25	4.62	4.18	5.64	7.59	9.27	6.78	6.78	6.02	5.77	2.86	2.14	1.45		
	p $ per lb.	5.75	5.70	5.59	6.25	13.7	8.56	10.4	10.4	7.88	8.75	8.56	7.18	7.52		
Rayon yarns	*q* Mil. lb.									4.69	8.60	5.19	4.47	6.06		
	v Mil. $									10.2	15.8	8.77	5.79	6.44		
	p $ per lb.									2.18	1.84	1.69	1.29	1.06		

A Comparable with earlier years. *B* Comparable with later years.

[a] Percentages of coverage:

Given year	Base year	Given year	Base year	Given year	Base year
1899:75.1	1909:71.3	1919:77.1	1923:79.9	1927:83.0	1929:85.1
1904:70.5		1921:78.0		1931:80.5	1929:83.9
1909:71.3	1919:75.4	1923:79.9	1929:83.9	1933:76.6	
1914:73.8		1925:82.0	1929:85.1	1937:62.6	1935:61.0

[b] For years prior to 1923 data are presented only in linear yards; after 1923 data are presented in square yards; for 1923 alone data are available in both units.

[c] Between 1909 and 1914 some knitting mills using silk exclusively were transferred from silk and rayon to knit goods.

[d] According to the Bureau of the Census the detailed data on products for 1935 and 1937 are not comparable with those for earlier years. An unadjusted index for 1937 on the 1935 base was obtained by use of the production data; this was then chained to the materials consumption index and thus placed on the 1929 base. The adjusted index for 1937, relative to 1935, is 101.9. The adjusted index given above, extrapolated by the unadjusted index, is 132.8 for 1935; this index, spliced to the adjusted index for 1937 on the 1935 base, is 135.3 for 1937.

earlier years. The gap between 1933 and 1935 was bridged by means of Census data on silk and rayon consumed in the industry in 1935 and in 1931, the closest preceding year for which data are available. In combining the rayon and silk consumed, we multiplied the quantity of the former by .526, the unit value of rayon broad goods in 1929, and the quantity of the latter by .909, the unit value of silk broad goods in 1929. Comparison of a similar index based on consumption data for earlier years, with the unadjusted index based on production data, given above, yields the following ratios of the latter to the former; 1914: 1.19; 1919: 1.26; 1925: 1.01; 1927: 0.98; 1929 (base): 1.00; 1931: 0.89.

[e] There was a rise in the relative importance of receipts for contract work in the silk and rayon goods industry, from 2 percent of the total value of products in 1899 to 8 percent in 1929. This rise tended to increase the amount of duplication in the output of the industry, but it was counterbalanced by a decline in the duplication arising from the sale of silk yarns by one group of establishments in the industry to another group. The cost of purchased yarns amounted to 14 percent of the total value of products in 1899 and to 7 percent in 1929.

[f] All silk mixtures.

[g] All rayon mixtures.

UNDERWEAR, KNIT		*1899*	*1904*	*1909*	*1914*	*1919*	*1921*	*1923*	*1925*	*1927*	*1929*	*1931*	*1933*	*1935*	*1937*
Adjusted index							[b]	102.6	106.6	101.8	100.0	78.2	98.3	99.1	102.2
Unadjusted index[a]		91.1	100.8	129.7	139.8	148.4	123.1	139.5	124.6	97.8	100.0	74.5	92.7	90.6	80.1
Product[c]	*Item*														
Shirts and drawers, total	*q* Mil. doz.pieces										8.80		10.4	10.6	
	v Mil. $										37.7		25.8	29.0	
	p $ per doz.pieces										4.28		2.48	2.72	
All-cotton	*q* Mil. doz.pieces	12.1	17.1	22.6	19.7	14.7	10.3	11.6	9.37	7.18	7.18	6.45	9.08		
	v Mil. $	26.9	39.7	50.0	43.1	72.6	35.0	44.3	36.8	24.0	23.1	16.4	18.2		
	p $ per doz.pieces	2.23	2.32	2.22	2.18	4.95	3.40	3.84	3.93	3.35	3.22	2.54	2.01		
All-wool	*q* Mil. doz.pieces	1.08	.485	.178	.373	.316	.0738	.112	.0469	.0606	.0501	.0396	.054		
	v Mil. $	4.98	3.65	1.82	3.45	3.06	1.24	2.24	1.19	1.39	.816	.430	.530		
	p $ per doz.pieces	4.59	7.52	10.2	9.24	9.68	16.8	20.0	25.3	23.0	16.3	10.9	9.81		
Silk	*q* Mil. doz.pieces				.0698	.0859	.153	.251	.485	.150	.120	.137			
	v Mil. $				1.21	1.40	3.18	5.92	7.95	2.31	1.90	1.08			
	p $ per doz.pieces				17.4	16.4	20.7	23.6	16.4	15.4	15.9	7.86			
Rayon	*q* Mil. doz.pieces								.501	.754	1.00	.733	.557		
	v Mil. $								4.45	5.76	6.96	3.99	2.40		
	p $ per doz.pieces								8.87	7.64	6.95	5.44	4.31		

For footnotes see p. 455.

Indexes of Physical Output, with Basic Data on Quantity, Value and Price of Products

UNDERWEAR, KNIT (continued)		1899	1904	1909	1914	1919	1921	1923	1925	1927	1929	1931	1933	1935	1937
Product[c]	*Item*														
Shirts and drawers (concluded)															
Cotton and wool mixed	*q* Mil. doz.pieces	2.68	2.11	2.54	1.43	1.85	1.08	.723	.696	.373	.380	.159	.458		
	v Mil. $	13.3	13.0	17.1	9.23	19.6	9.30	8.19	8.72	4.70	4.30	1.58	3.33		
	p $ per doz.pieces	4.97	6.17	6.72	6.43	10.6	8.63	11.3	12.5	12.6	11.3	9.96	7.27		
Union suits, total	*q* Mil. doz.										8.89		8.17	6.28	7.22
	v Mil. $										70.8		39.3	35.9	43.5
	p $ per doz.										7.97		4.82	5.71	6.02
All-cotton	*q* Mil. doz.	.825	1.26	2.05	5.47	7.52	8.15	9.41	10.2	8.34	7.38	5.89	7.48		
	v Mil. $	2.24	4.48	9.71	25.6	71.1	59.5	74.1	73.7	59.3	50.4	31.3	32.6		
	p $ per doz.	2.72	3.55	4.74	4.68	9.46	7.30	7.88	7.19	7.11	6.83	5.31	4.35		
All-wool	*q* Th. doz.	9.50	68.1	50.1	147	76.7	28.6	25.2	69.7	104	136	26.3	78.0		
	v Mil. $	.202	.965	.683	2.49	2.00	.963	.936	2.45	2.97	3.08	.519	1.06		
	p $ per doz.	21.2	14.2	13.6	16.9	26.1	33.6	37.1	35.2	28.4	22.6	19.7	13.6		
Silk	*q* Th. doz.				31.7	49.4	147	93.2	125	53.2	30.6	27.1			
	v Mil. $				.886	1.31	5.46	2.54	2.66	.966	.803	.439			
	p $ per doz.				27.9	26.6	37.1	27.3	21.3	18.1	26.2	16.2			
Rayon	*q* Mil. doz.								.137	.442	.481	.399	.102		
	v Mil. $								2.58	4.97	4.30	2.55	.849		
	p $ per doz.								18.8	11.2	8.95	6.39	8.32		
Cotton and wool mixed	*q* Mil. doz.	.140	.105	.364	.486	1.13	.755	1.13	.808	.702	.811	.369	.417		
	v Mil. $	1.13	1.20	4.22	5.71	21.4	14.9	19.7	16.4	14.3	11.7	4.84	4.26		
	p $ per doz.	8.10	11.4	11.6	11.7	18.9	19.7	17.3	20.3	20.4	14.5	13.1	10.2		

UNDERWEAR, KNIT (concluded)		1899	1904	1909	1914	1919	1921	1923	1925	1927	1929	1931	1933	1935	1937
Product[c]	*Item*														
Bloomers and step-ins	*q* Mil. doz.									1.76	2.38	1.86	2.31	2.85	
	v Mil. $									17.4	18.3	8.07	8.08	8.70	
	p $ per doz.									9.89	7.69	4.33	3.50	3.05	
Slips and petticoats	*q* Mil. doz.									.218	.259	.109	.0821	.143	.125
	v Mil. $									3.03	2.12	1.36	.852	1.62	1.16
	p $ per doz.									13.9	8.19	12.4	10.4	11.3	9.29

[a] Percentages of coverage:

Given year	Base year	Given year	Base year
1923:86.6	1929:63.7	1933:78.3	1929:82.9
1925:83.2	1929:71.2	1935:78.2	1929:85.5
1927:81.3 } 1931:80.7 }	1929:84.7	1937:37.9	1929:48.4

[b] No adjusted indexes for 1899–1921 could be computed because the industry is not shown separately in the Census for those years. Adjusted indexes were computed for the entire knit goods industry. The adjusted index given above, extrapolated by the unadjusted index, is 67.0 for 1899; 74.1 for 1904; 95.4 for 1909; 102.8 for 1914; 109.1 for 1919; 90.5 for 1921.

[c] For years prior to 1929 the detailed data relate to products made within the knit goods industries alone; for 1929 and subsequent years they relate to knit goods wherever made.

WOOL SHODDY		1899	1904	1909	1914	1919	1921	1923	1925	1927	1929	1931	1933	1935	1937
Adjusted index		54.6	74.9	67.9	82.5	98.1	46.3	99.5	110.4	71.1	100.0	58.7	86.8	[b]	[b]
Unadjusted index[a]		60.0	82.9	73.7	84.0	103.3	48.0	96.7	118.7	71.7	100.0	58.9	76.0	95.2	103.1
Product	*Item*														
Recovered wool fiber[c]	*q* Mil. lb.			41.9	47.8	58.8	27.3	55.1	67.5	40.8	56.9	33.5	43.2	57.2[d]	62.0[d]
	v Mil. $			6.27	6.61	20.7	5.94	13.7	19.1	10.7	12.9	5.03	7.73	13.6	14.8
	p $ per lb.			.150	.138	.351	.218	.248	.282	.262	.227	.150	.179	.237	.238
Shoddy, mungo, and wool extract[e]	*q* Mil. lb.	44.0	60.8	54.0											
	v Mil. $	6.01	7.56	6.56											
	p $ per lb.	.137	.124	.122											

[a] Percentages of coverage:

Given year	Base year	Given year	Base year	Given year	Base year	Given year	Base year
1899:89.3 } 1904:89.9 }	1909:88.2	1909:91.5 } 1914:85.8 }	1919:88.8	1921:87.4 } 1923:81.9 } 1925:90.7 }	1929:84.3	1927:85.0 } 1931:84.5 } 1933:73.8 }	1929:84.3
		1919:88.8	1929:84.3				

Footnotes concluded next page.

Indexes of Physical Output, with Basic Data on Quantity, Value and Price of Products

WOOL SHODDY (concluded)

[b] No adjusted indexes for 1935 and 1937 could be computed because the industry is not shown separately in the Census for those years. The adjusted index given above, extrapolated by the unadjusted index, is 108.7 for 1935; 117.8 for 1937.

[c] Includes carbonized rags (wool extract).

[d] Includes recovered wool fiber made by establishments outside the industry. Similar data for 1929 are *q* 60.1 mil. lb.; *v* $13.4 mil.; *p* $.222 per lb.

[e] Prior to 1914 the industry included plants engaged in the manufacture of cotton shoddy, which was included with recovered wool fiber under the generic term "shoddy."

WOOLEN GOODS		*1909*	*1914*	*1919*	*1921*	*1923*	*1925*	*1927*	*1929*	*1931*
Adjusted index		78.1	82.8	91.9	79.5	114.7	112.4	104.6	100.0	70.2
Unadjusted index[a,b]		75.9	79.3	88.2	79.6	113.2	111.2	105.2	100.0	72.5
Product	*Item*									
Woven goods	*q* Mil. sq.yd.	216	229	254	224[c]	316	305	289	264	191
	v Mil. $	95.2	89.7	316	207	321	308	260	242	135
	p $ per sq.yd.	.442	.392	1.25	.924	1.02	1.01	.901	.916	.708
Yarns for sale, woolen, all-wool	*q* Mil. lb.	22.1	18.7	21.7	25.1	38.5	42.4	37.4	47.9	
	v Mil. $	5.40	6.34	23.8	16.9	24.7	32.8	26.2	32.9	
	p $ per lb.	.244	.339	1.09	.674	.641	.773	.700	.688	
Yarns for sale, worsted, all-wool	*q* Mil. lb.	.423	.841	.134	.620	2.19	4.78	6.03	6.16	5.04
	v Mil. $	.344	.401	.0531	.325	2.91	5.99	7.72	7.24	4.20
	p $ per lb.	.813	.477	.396	.525	1.33	1.25	1.28	1.18	.835
Noils and wool waste, for sale	*q* Mil. lb.	4.33	5.86	10.3	2.06	11.0	7.69	7.30	9.34	3.28
	v Mil. $	.271	.256	.940	.208	.811	.849	.770	.736	.254
	p $ per lb.	.0626	.0437	.0916	.101	.0736	.110	.105	.0788	.0775

[a] Percentages of coverage:

Given year	Base year	Given year	Base year
1909:94.5	1919:93.3	1923:96.0	1929:97.3
1914:93.1		1925:96.2	
1919:93.3	1929:97.3	1927:97.9	
1921:97.4		1931:88.7	1929:86.0

[b] Separate data for woolen goods are available only for the years for which indexes have been computed. For other years see woolen and worsted goods.

[c] For 1921 and earlier years the data for woven goods exclude upholstery materials. In 1923 upholstery materials constituted less than 2 percent of total woven goods produced.

WOOLEN and WORSTED GOODS		1899	1904	1909	1914	1919	1921	1923	1925	1927	1929	1931	1933	1935	1937
Adjusted index		71.3	85.9	102.8	101.7	97.5	92.7	119.9	107.9	102.8	100.0	81.1	86.8[b]	115.9[c]	114.4
Unadjusted index[a]		72.3	88.3	106.1	103.8	97.8	93.7	122.6	109.3	104.6	100.0	80.8	86.9	114.7	102.2
Product	*Item*														
Woven goods	q Mil. sq.yd.	427	506	571	565	536	494[e]	628	580	558	514	390	427		
	v Mil. $	183	235	296	269	739	551	745	674	584	571	331	306		
	p $ per sq.yd.	.430	.464	.519	.475	1.38	1.12	1.19	1.16	1.05	1.11	.849	.717		
Woven goods, excl. fabrics noted below[d]	q Mil. sq.yd.												423	559	
	v Mil. $												291	431	
	p $ per sq.yd.												.688	.771	
Woven goods, excl. fabrics, noted below[d]	q Mil. sq.yd.													543	500
	v Mil. $													457	489
	p $ per sq.yd.													.840	.977
Yarns for sale, woolen, all-wool	q Mil. lb.	32.7	42.9	28.5	26.1	28.4	30.7	47.9	43.7	41.8	48.8	33.7	32.8		
	v Mil. $	6.80	9.99	7.51	8.78	32.8	22.9	32.4	34.1	31.3	33.9	18.3	14.1		
	p $ per lb.	.208	.233	.263	.336	1.16	.744	.675	.781	.748	.694	.542	.428		
Yarns for sale, woolen and worsted, wool and cotton combined	q Mil. lb.	16.0	12.1	14.0	10.5	13.4	5.50	11.2	19.4	10.9	8.87	6.56	7.70	q 97.9[f]	75.4
	v Mil. $	4.67	5.00	5.67	4.86	16.1	7.35	17.3	25.9	9.78	7.25	4.77	4.96	v 102	98.8
	p $ per lb.	.292	.412	.404	.462	1.21	1.34	1.55	1.34	.897	.817	.728	.644	p 1.04	1.31
Yarns for sale, worsted, all-wool	q Mil. lb.		55.5	88.3	86.4	74.3	85.9	113	82.6	81.4	89.1	85.7	80.1		
	v Mil. $		40.1	80.4	69.8	185	126	191	144	125	140	93.1	80.3		
	p $ per lb.	q 43.0	.724	.910	.808	2.49	1.47	1.69	1.74	1.54	1.58	1.09	1.00		
		v 30.1													
Tops and slubbing, for sale	q Mil. lb.	p .700	4.77	11.3	8.99	9.90	10.3	21.1	18.1	18.3	14.0	16.1	24.4	9.38[g]	9.95[g]
	v Mil. $		2.86	8.03	4.93	14.5	7.44	23.9	23.6	20.8	15.7	11.7	16.9	7.02	7.38
	p $ per lb.		.598	.709	.548	1.47	.719	1.13	1.31	1.14	1.12	.726	.693	.749	.742
Yarns for sale, mohair and other yarns	q Mil. lb.									11.7	12.7	15.7	18.7		
	v Mil. $									17.8	18.3	13.0	12.7		
	p $ per lb.									1.52	1.44	.829	.676		

For footnotes see next page.

Indexes of Physical Output, with Basic Data on Quantity, Value and Price of Products

WOOLEN and WORSTED GOODS (concluded)		1899	1904	1909	1914	1919	1921	1923	1925	1927	1929	1931	1933	1935	1937
Product	*Item*														
Noils and wool waste, for sale	*q* Mil. lb.	20.3	33.3	51.9	50.4	52.1	40.6	55.1	42.6	48.5	46.4	35.6	41.5	15.4[h]	10.1[h]
	v Mil. $	4.58	7.31	12.5	10.1	24.8	9.58	19.3	17.9	18.5	15.6	7.24	9.47	6.75	5.74
	p $ per lb.	.225	2.19	.240	.201	.476	.236	.350	.420	.382	.336	.203	.228	.438	.566

[a] Percentages of coverage:

Given year	Base year	Given year	Base year	Given year	Base year	Given year	Base year
1899:96.1 1904:97.4	1909:97.8	1919:95.0 1921:95.8 1923:96.9 1925:95.1	1929:94.8	1927:98.7 1931:96.6 1933:97.1	1929:97.0	1937:72.7	1935:80.5
1909:97.8 1914:96.8	1919:95.0			1935:62.8	1933:63.6		

[b] A slight discontinuity arises from the fact that between 1933 and 1935 establishments making woven felts were transferred from felt goods to woolen and worsted goods, and establishments making batts, padding, and card rolls were transferred from woolen and worsted goods to upholstering materials, n.e.c.

[c] Between 1935 and 1937 some establishments were transferred from carpets and rugs, wool, to woolen and worsted goods.

[d] The woven goods data comparable for 1933 and 1935 exclude auto cloths (with pile), upholstery fabrics, drapery fabrics, and woven felts. The woven goods data comparable for 1935 and 1937 exclude bathrobe flannels, snow and ski suit cloths, undercollar cloths, miscellaneous apparel cloths, interlinings, necktie linings, other linings, blankets of less than 98 percent wool, and woven felts.

[e] For 1921 and earlier years the data for woven goods exclude upholstery materials. In 1923 upholstery materials constituted less than 2 percent of total woven goods produced.

[f] According to the Census, the 1935 data are not comparable with those for 1933. For this reason the 1935 data were not used in the computation of the 1935 index.

[g] Tops only; not used in the computation of the 1935 index.

[h] Noils only; not used in the computation of the 1935 index.

WORSTED GOODS		1909	1914	1919	1921	1923	1925	1927	1929	1931
Adjusted index		122.9	118.2	104.0	104.6	129.7	106.5	102.7	100.0	87.8
Unadjusted index[a,b]		129.6	123.7	105.7	106.5	128.7	105.8	104.8	100.0	85.6
Product	*Item*									
Woven goods	*q* Mil. sq.yd.	355	337	282	269[c]	312	275	269	250	199
	v Mil. $	201	179	423	343	424	365	324	329	196
	p $ per sq.yd.	.567	.531	1.50	1.27	1.36	1.33	1.20	1.32	.985
Yarns for sale, woolen, all-wool	*q* Mil. lb.	6.43	7.40	6.68	5.61	9.47	1.26	4.43	.944	
	v Mil. $	2.11	2.44	9.07	5.95	7.71	1.31	5.08	.968	
	p $ per lb.	.328	.329	1.36	1.06	.815	1.04	1.15	1.03	
Yarns for sale, worsted, all-wool	*q* Mil. lb.	87.9	85.6	74.2	85.2	111	77.8	75.4	82.9	80.7
	v Mil. $	80.1	69.4	185	126	188	138	118	133	88.9
	p $ per lb.	.911	.811	2.49	1.48	1.70	1.77	1.56	1.60	1.10
Tops and slubbing, for sale	*q* Mil. lb.	11.3	8.99	9.90	10.3	[d]	18.1	18.3[e]	14.0[e]	16.0
	v Mil. $	8.03	4.93	14.5	7.44		23.6	20.8	15.7	11.6
	p $ per lb.	.709	.548	1.47	.719		1.31	1.14	1.12	.726
Noils and wool waste, for sale	*q* Mil. lb.	47.6	44.5	41.8	38.6	44.1	34.9	41.2	37.0	32.3
	v Mil. $	12.2	9.88	23.9	9.37	18.5	17.0	17.8	14.9	6.99
	p $ per lb.	.257	.222	.571	.243	.419	.488	.431	.401	.216

[a] Percentages of coverage:

Given year	Base year	Given year	Base year
1909:97.1, 1914:96.4	1919:93.6	1923:91.4, 1925:91.5, 1927:93.9	1929:92.1
1919:93.6, 1921:93.8	1929:92.1	1931:89.6	1929:91.9

[b] Separate data for worsted goods are available only for the years for which indexes have been computed. For other years see woolen and worsted goods.

[c] For 1921 and earlier years the data for woven goods exclude upholstery materials. In 1923 upholstery materials constituted less than 2 percent of total woven goods produced.

[d] Not shown separately by the Census.

[e] These figures include a very small amount of wool card rolls, batts, and batting.

Indexes of Physical Output, with Basic Data on Quantity, Value and Price of Products

TOTAL TEXTILE PRODUCTS	*1899*	*1904*	*1909*	*1914*	*1919*	*1921*	*1923*	*1925*	*1927*	*1929*	*1931*	*1933*	*1935*	*1937*
Adjusted index	37.9	47.7	60.5	71.9	67.3	64.5	82.5	86.2	93.6	100.0	86.6	85.1	99.3	106.2
Unadjusted index[a,b]	43.3	50.5	63.7	71.6	74.6	68.9	90.8	90.6	93.9	100.0	85.4	86.1	100.8	109.7

[a] Percentages of coverage:

Given year	Base year	Given year	Base year	Given year	Base year
1899:54.2	1909:49.9	1919:53.9	1929:48.6	1927:81.1	1929:80.8
1904:48.9	1909:48.6	1921:52.0		1931:79.7	
1909:50.1	1919:52.8	1923:53.9	1929:48.9	1933:77.3	1929:76.4
1914:47.8	1919:53.2	1925:51.4		1935:80.4	1929:79.1
				1937:82.8	1929:80.2

[b] Indexes for the following industries and years were not used in the computation of the group indexes, chiefly because information on value added is lacking: wool shoddy, 1935 and 1937; corsets, 1935.

The combined index for woolen and worsted goods was used throughout. The combined index for knit goods was used prior to 1923. A combined index for linoleum and asphalted-felt-base floor covering was used for 1919. On the 1929 base this index is 46.9.

LEATHER PRODUCTS

BELTING, LEATHER		*1927*	*1929*	*1931*	*1933*	*1935*	*1937*
Adjusted index		79.8	100.0	46.0	47.5	76.3	86.5
Unadjusted index[a]		74.6	100.0	42.5	41.0	58.6	63.9
Product	*Item*						
Flat belting	*q* Mil. lb.	9.74	13.1	5.55	5.35[b]	7.65	8.34
	v Mil. $	16.8	23.5	8.84	8.47	10.9	13.6
	p $ per lb.	1.73	1.80	1.59	1.58	1.42	1.63

[a] Percentages of coverage:

Given year	Base year	Given year	Base year
1927:61.7		1935:50.7	1929:65.9
1931:60.9	1929:65.9	1937:48.7	
1933:56.9			

[b] Estimated in part.

GLOVES, LEATHER		1899	1904	1909	1914	1919	1921	1923[b]	1925[b]	1927	1929	1931	1933[b]	1935	1937
Adjusted index		84.8[c]	96.9	98.1	91.1	105.1	64.6		[d]	90.7	100.0	74.2		102.0	98.0
Unadjusted index[a]		81.2	94.5	94.5	86.5	101.4	59.4			92.2	100.0	76.6		104.8	103.3
Product	*Item*														
Gloves, mittens, and gauntlets	*q* Mil. doz.pr.	2.90	3.37	3.37	3.08	3.62									
	v Mil. $	16.0	17.1	22.5	20.3	44.8									
	p $ per doz.pr.	5.54	5.08	6.69	6.58	12.4									
Leather gloves and mittens															
Made in industry	*q* Mil. doz.pr.					3.02	1.77			2.74	2.98	2.28			
	v Mil. $					42.3	21.3			34.8	36.5	27.0			
	p $ per doz.pr.					14.0	12.1			12.7	12.3	11.8			
Wherever made	*q* Mil. doz.pr.										3.04			3.19	
	v Mil. $										37.0			27.3	
	p $ per doz.pr.										12.2			8.58	
All-leather work gloves, men's and boys'	*q* Mil. doz.pr.													.809	.894
	v Mil. $													4.97	5.53
	p $ per doz.pr.													6.14	6.19
Leather dress gloves															
Table-cut and pattern cut	*q* Mil. doz.pr.													.890	.857
	v Mil. $													12.8	14.3
	p $ per doz.pr.													14.4	16.7
Block cut	*q* Mil. doz.pr.													.831	.790
	v Mil. $													6.95	7.82
	p $ per doz.pr.													8.36	9.89

[a] Percentages of coverage:

Given year	Base year	Given year	Base year	Given year	Base year
1899:94.8 1904:96.5	1909:95.3	1919:90.0 1921:85.9 1927:94.8 1931:96.2	1929:93.3	1935:97.1	1929:94.6
1909:95.3 1914:93.9	1919:95.5			1937:90.2	1935:87.8

[b] Detailed data on products were not collected in 1923, 1925 or 1933.

[c] In 1899 a few establishments making gloves and mittens from materials other than leather were included in gloves, leather.

[d] In 1925 establishments manufacturing gloves and mittens of cloth and leather combined were transferred from gloves, leather, to gloves, textile, n.e.m.

Indexes of Physical Output, with Basic Data on Quantity, Value and Price of Products

LEATHER		1899	1904	1909	1914	1919	1921	1923	1925	1927	1929	1931	1933	1935	1937
Adjusted index[b]											100.0	81.0	85.2	103.5	112.1
Unadjusted index[a,c]		75.2	87.2	95.9	85.8	104.4	88.3	120.5	101.3	105.9	100.0	77.8	83.1	107.1	112.5
Product[d]	*Item*														
Upholstery leather (auto, furniture and carriage)															
Whole hide grains	*q* Mil. hides				.654	.934									
	v Mil. $				8.17	18.3									
	p $ per hide				12.5	19.6									
Whole hide grains and splits combined	*q*	.620	.827	1.40											
	v	5.75	7.78	14.3											
	p	9.28	9.41	10.2											
Whole hide splits	*q* Mil. hides				1.10	1.51									
	v Mil. $				6.16	14.0									
	p $ per hide				5.57	9.26									
Upper leather (other than patent)															
Cattle	*q* Mil. sides	8.14	6.85	7.95	8.25	16.7									
	v Mil. $	17.5	15.5	24.2	32.9	121									
	p $ per side	2.15	2.26	3.05	3.99	7.24									
Horse	*q* Mil. sides				.407	1.72									
	v Mil. $				1.36	10.6									
	p $ per side				3.34	6.14									
Horsehides and colt skins	*q* Mil. skins	.223	1.53	1.34											
	v Mil. $	.843	4.60	4.95											
	p $ per skin	3.77	3.01	3.69											
Finished splits	*q* Mil.	8.79	6.20	8.13	8.65	11.9									
	v Mil. $	6.74	5.99	7.41	8.55	16.5									
	p $ ea.	.767	.966	.911	.988	1.39									
Calf and kip skins	*q* Mil. skins	8.26	12.0	19.0	15.9	11.7									
	v Mil. $	14.6	22.5	42.4	41.8	92.6									
	p $ per skin	1.77	1.87	2.23	2.63	7.92									

LEATHER (continued)		1899	1904	1909	1914	1919	1921	1923	1925	1927	1929	1931	1933	1935	1937
Product[d]	*Item*														
Upper leather (other than patent) (continued)															
Goatskins,	*q* Mil. skins	47.0	45.7	47.9	29.9	51.5									
tanned and	*v* Mil. $	35.7	37.9	40.9	26.1	14.4									
finished	*p* $ per skin	.758	.829	.853	.874	2.79									
Sheepskins,	*q* Mil. skins	20.3	20.6	19.7	16.8	10.0									
tanned and	*v* Mil. $	8.35	11.2	12.2	10.9	16.5									
finished	*p* $ per skin	.412	.542	.622	.648	1.64									
Patent (other than upholstery)															
Sides	*q* Mil.				2.83	2.72									
	v Mil. $				9.56	23.4									
	p $ ea.				3.38	8.63									
Skins	*q* Mil.				4.87	.829									
	v Mil. $				5.51	3.18									
	p $ ea.				1.13	3.84									
Shoe (except	*q* Mil. sides	.237	1.36	2.71											
calf and kip)	*v* Mil. $	1.09	3.34	8.34											
	p $ per side	4.61	2.46	3.08											
Glove leather															
Skins	*q* Mil.				4.00	5.89									
	v Mil. $				2.90	11.5									
	p $ ea.				.725	1.96									
Sides	*q* Mil.				.344	5.37									
	v Mil. $				.998	8.89									
	p $ ea.				2.90	1.66									
Leather sold in the rough															
Rough leather,	*q* Mil. equiv. sides	1.40	2.05	.829	.585	.206									
for sale in the	*v* Mil. $	4.26	7.80	3.54	2.12	1.59									
rough	*p* $ per side	3.05	3.80	4.27	3.62	7.71									

For footnotes see p. 473.

Indexes of Physical Output, with Basic Data on Quantity, Value and Price of Products

LEATHER (continued)		*1899*	*1904*	*1909*	*1914*	*1919*	*1921*	*1923*	*1925*	*1927*	*1929*	*1931*	*1933*	*1935*	*1937*
Product[d]	*Item*														
Leather sold in the rough (continued)															
Rough grains (split leather)	*q* Mil. equiv. sides	.322	.259	.318	.144	.0955									
	v Mil. $	.806	.584	.719	.538	.499									
	p $ per side	2.50	2.26	2.26	3.73	5.22									
Rough splits, whole	*q* Mil. sides				1.14	1.05									
	v Mil. $				1.48	1.37									
	p $ per side				1.29	1.30									
Rough splits, butt splits	*q* Mil. butts				.292	.172									
	v Mil. $				.363	.251									
	p $ per butt				1.25	1.46									
Sole leather															
Hemlock	*q* Mil. equiv. sides	9.81	9.93	7.96	5.63	1.73									
	v Mil. $	29.3	32.7	32.2	31.0	16.2									
	p $ per side	2.99	3.29	4.05	5.51	9.34									
Oak	*q* Mil. equiv. sides	2.56	3.61	3.81	5.27	10.1									
	v Mil. $	13.4	19.2	26.1	38.4	118									
	p $ per side	5.21	5.31	6.85	7.29	11.7									
Union	*q* Mil. equiv. sides	3.10	4.40	5.76	6.59	7.31									
	v Mil. $	12.8	17.4	28.4	42.5	79.9									
	p $ per side	4.14	3.95	4.93	6.44	10.9									
Chrome	*q* Mil. equiv. sides	2.10		.279	.592	.583									
	v Mil. $	8.97		1.64	4.34	5.21									
	p $ per side	4.27		5.85	7.33	8.93									
Harness leather	*q* Mil. sides	3.44	4.37	3.95	2.78	1.72									
	v Mil. $	16.7	20.3	24.8	21.0	24.2									
	p $ per side	4.85	4.64	6.29	7.55	14.1									

LEATHER (continued) Product[d]	Item	1899	1904	1909	1914	1919	1921	1923	1925	1927	1929	1931	1933	1935	1937
Belting, oak, and chrome	q Mil. butts	.736	.430	.521	.647	1.48									
	v Mil. $	7.09	4.75	7.00	8.37	32.8									
	p $ per butt	9.64	11.1	13.4	12.9	22.1									
Case, bag, and strap	q Mil. sides				1.00	1.23									
	v Mil. $				5.38	11.9									
	p $ per side				5.36	9.69									
Sole and belting leather															
Oak and union	q Mil. backs, bends, or sides					17.4[e]	16.9	18.1	14.3	15.2	13.9				
	p $ per back, bend, or side					11.3					6.83				
Chrome sole	q Mil. backs, bends, or sides					.583[e]	.488	.629	.552	.635	.577				
	p $ per back, bend, or side					8.93					6.70				
Chrome sole, horse	q Mil. whole butts							.261	.141	.176	.331				
	p $ per whole butt										2.37				
Belting butts, curried	q Mil. butts and butt bends									.962	1.08				
	p $ per butt or butt bend										13.3				
Belting butts, rough	q Mil. butts and butt bends								.809	.929	.990				
	p $ per butt or butt bend										12.8				
Offal	q Mil. lb.					[f]	100	135	110	118	107				
	p $ per lb.					.305					.250				
Harness leather	q Mil. sides					1.72	.811	1.56	1.29	1.02	.642				
	p $ per side					14.1					8.18				
Bag, case, and strap leather	q Mil. sides					1.23	.821	1.20	1.18	1.10	.947				
	p $ per side					9.69					6.93				
Skirting leather	q Mil. sides							.142	.0779	.0688	.0479				
	p $ per side					q .582	.410				9.46				
						p 10.3									
Collar leather	q Mil. sides							.786	.581	.476	.309				
	p $ per side										4.29				

For footnotes see p. 473.

Indexes of Physical Output, with Basic Data on Quantity, Value and Price of Products

LEATHER (continued)		1899	1904	1909	1914	1919	1921	1923	1925	1927	1929	1931	1933	1935	1937
Product[d]	*Item*														
Latigo leather	*q* Mil. sides					.0232	.0249	.0318	.0253	.0385	.0204				
	p $ per side					10.7									
Lace leather	*q* Mil. sides					.496	.151	.211	.170	.148	.118				
	p $ per side					5.16					6.38				
Upholstery leather															
Whole hide grains and machine buffed	*q* Mil. hides						.414	.743	.626	.502	.414				
	p $ per hide										14.3				
Buffings, russet	*q* Mil. hides							.0745	.115	.153	.119				
	p $ per hide										5.63				
Splits, whole hide, main and second	*q* Mil. pieces					1.51	.676	1.23	.832	.938	.672				
	p $ each					9.26					6.99				
Upper leather, other than patent															
Cattle, incl. kip side	*q* Mil. sides					16.7	12.5	18.4	15.3	13.5	12.6				
	p $ per side					7.24					4.22				
Calf and kip, excl. kip side	*q* Mil. skins					11.7	14.8	18.0	13.6	16.1	14.5				
	p $ per skin					7.92					3.45				
Goat and kid	*q* Mil. skins					51.5	34.4	46.5	40.9	49.4	54.4				
	p $ per skin					2.79					1.29				
Sheep and lamb and cabretta	*q* Mil. skins					15.2	16.3	22.0	16.5	16.4	19.4				
	p $ per skin					1.78					1.08				
Kangaroo and wallaby	*q* Mil. skins						.963	1.28	.820	.705	.854				
	p $ per skin										1.61				
Horse and colt skins, fronts	*q* Mil. equiv. half fronts							.198	.108	.0913	.106				
	p $ per half front										3.70				

LEATHER (continued)		1899	1904	1909	1914	1919	1921	1923	1925	1927	1929	1931	1933	1935	1937
Product[d]	*Item*														
Upper leather, other than patent (continued)															
Horse and colt skins, butts	*q* Mil. whole butts							.570	.255	.376	.346				
	p $ per whole butt										2.15				
Horse and colt skins, shanks	*q* Mil. shanks							.331	.241	.295	.404				
	p $ per shank										.383				
Patent leather, other than upholstery															
Cattle, incl. foreign tanned kip	*q* Mil. sides					2.56	2.28	5.66	8.63	8.39	5.95				
	p $ per side					8.34					4.37				
Calf and kip, excl. foreign tanned kip	*q* Th. skins					45.0	37.4	163	4.98	121	37.0				
	p $ per skin					12.7									
Goat and kid	*q* Mil. skins					.730	.489	.446	.991	.430	.302				
	p $ per skin					3.13									
Horse and colt	*q* Mil. equiv. half fronts					.153	.195	1.08	.684	.416	.271				
	p $ per half front					13.5									
Glove leather															
Cattle grains, incl. foreign tanned kip	*q* Th. sides					43.2	16.5	113	66.8	18.3	63.6				
	p $ per side					7.23									
Calf and kip, excl. foreign tanned kip	*q* Th. skins					5.53	4.86	22.3	1.33	41.9	24.1				
	p $ per skin					4.94									
Horse	*q* Mil. equiv. half fronts					.969	.518	.930	1.15	1.46	1.86				
	p $ per half front					5.18					3.44				
Pig and hog	*q* Mil. skins					.217	.102	.0869	.114	.251	.573				
	p $ per skin					1.54									
Goat and kid	*q* Mil. skins					.123	.0479	.0803	.0667	.171	.138				
	p $ per skin					2.41									
Cabretta	*q* Mil. skins						.560	1.43	1.68	1.82	1.07				
	p $ per skin										2.18				

For footnotes see p. 473

Indexes of Physical Output, with Basic Data on Quantity, Value and Price of Products

LEATHER (continued)		1899	1904	1909	1914	1919	1921	1923	1925	1927	1929	1931	1933	1935	1937
Product[d]	*Item*														
Glove leather (continued)															
Sheep and lamb	*q* Mil. skins					4.98	3.81	7.79	5.33	7.58	8.63				
	p $ per skin					1.85					1.33				
Deer and elk	*q* Mil. skins					.324	.370	.540	.665	.595	.614				
	p $ per skin					3.17					2.63				
Fancy and bookbinder's leather															
Cowhide	*q* Mil. sides					.655	.0799	.232	.302	.202	.240				
	p $ per side					3.77					5.94				
Buffings, finished	*q* Th. hides						73.6	197	89.0	58.6	63.7				
	p $ per hide										8.02				
Goat and kid	*q* Mil. skins					.336	.165	.291	.541	.717	.889				
	p $ per skin					2.93					2.28				
Sheep and lamb and cabretta	*q* Mil. skins						1.99	3.04	2.08	2.86	2.78				
	p $ per skin										1.56				
Calf and kip	*q* Mil. skins					.277	.119	.281	.249	.674	.766				
	p $ per skin					6.82					4.02				
Chamois and roller leather	*q* Mil. doz.					.174	.287	.349	.327	.314	.244				
	p $ per doz.					17.3					17.0				
Shearlings	*q* Mil. skins					.544	1.24	2.56	1.98	2.73	3.99				
	p $ per skin					2.46					1.79				
Hat sweats	*q* Mil. doz.					.121	.0954	.140	.118	.0748	.0471				
	p $ per doz.					24.1					20.4				
Skivers, other than hat sweats	*q* Mil. doz.					.571	.206	.322	.274	.197	.165				
	p $ per doz.					16.4					13.8				
Fleshers, other than chamois	*q* Th. doz.					497	30.9	49.6	70.5	20.6	6.53				
	p $ per doz.					4.34					17.8				

LEATHER (continued)		1899	1904	1909	1914	1919	1921	1923	1925	1927	1929	1931		1933	1935	1937
Product[d]	*Item*											*A*	*B*	*C*		
Rough leather and rough grains, (split leather)	*q* Th. equiv. sides					302	105	58.1	48.2	29.8	12.6					
	p $ per side					6.93					5.63					
Sole and belting leather																
Oak and union sole	*q* Mil. backs, bends, or sides										13.8	11.7	11.6	11.3	16.0	18.3
	v Mil. $										93.9	55.0	54.3	38.5	62.0	80.1
	p $ per back, bend, or side										6.83	4.68	4.69	3.41	3.87	4.36
Chrome and combination sole	*q* Mil. backs, bends, or sides										.596	.447	.414	.559	1.19	1.05
	v Mil. $										3.99	2.17	2.00	1.99	4.25	4.00
	p $ per back, bend, or side										6.70	4.86	4.82	3.56	3.58	3.80
Belting butts, rough	*q* Mil. butts or butt bends										.705	.369			.494	.653
	v Mil. $										9.04	2.92			3.68	5.83
	p $ per butt or butt bend										12.8	7.90	*q*.621	.674	7.45	8.93
													*v*5.54	5.16		
Belting butts, curried	*q* Mil. butts or butt bends										.670	.266	*p*8.92	7.66	.466	.628
	v Mil. $										8.88	2.78			4.45	6.37
	p $ per butt or butt bend										13.3	10.5			9.54	10.1
Offal	*q* Mil. lb.										94.6	86.2	85.0	79.2	91.5	94.4
	v Mil. $										23.7	13.2	12.7	14.9	15.3	18.9
	p $ per lb.										.250	.153	.150	.188	.168	.201
Harness leather																
Union black	*q* Mil. sides										.284	.0963	.058	.119	.300	.303
	v Mil. $										2.48	.513	.364	.504	.153	1.82
	p $ per side										8.71	5.33	6.28	4.24	5.09	5.98
Oak black and russet	*q* Mil. sides										.461	.279	.256	.289	.513	.431
	v Mil. $										3.62	1.65	1.48	1.45	2.84	2.67
	p $ per side										7.85	5.93	5.79	5.00	5.54	6.21

For footnotes see p. 473.

Indexes of Physical Output, with Basic Data on Quantity, Value and Price of Products

LEATHER (continued)		1899	1904	1909	1914	1919	1921	1923	1925	1927	1929	1931		1933	1935	1937
Product[d]	*Item*											*A*	*B*	*C*		
Bag, case, and strap leather	*q* Mil. sides										1.05	.787	.725	.537	1.11	
	v Mil. $										7.31	3.66	3.40	2.50	5.62	
	p $ per side										6.93	4.65	4.69	4.66	5.08	
Skirting leather	*q* Th. sides										63.1	30.4	12	25	54.4	
	v Th. $										597	255	109	149	388	
	p $ per side										9.46	8.38	9.08	5.96	7.13	
Collar leather	*q* Mil. sides										.363	.180	.147	.207	.366	.376
	v Mil. $										1.55	.627	.499	.786	1.10	1.51
	p $ per side										4.29	3.48	3.39	3.80	3.02	4.02
Lace leather	*q* Mil. sides										.143	.128	.056	.070	.133	.152
	v Mil. $										.912	.575	.242	.236	.542	.735
	p $ per side										6.38	4.50	4.32	3.37	4.07	4.83
Upholstery leather																
Whole hide grains and machine buffed	*q* Mil. hides										.623	.318	.284	.134	.424	.658
	v Mil. $										8.91	2.89	2.55	1.10	4.37	7.04
	p $ per hide										14.3	9.09	8.98	8.22	10.3	10.7
Buffings, russet	*q* Mil. hides										.255	.138			.0314	.0573
	v Mil. $										1.44	.555			.117	.223
	p $ per hide										5.63	4.02			3.72	3.89
Splits, main and second	*q* Mil. pieces										.724	.410	.362	.279	.375	.577
	v Mil. $										5.06	1.75	1.59	.698	1.75	2.80
	p $ per piece										6.99	4.27	4.39	2.50	4.65	4.86
Upper leather																
Cattle, incl. kip side	*q* Mil. sides										12.3	12.5	12.5	15.9	21.0	20.0
	v Mil. $										52.0	32.5	32.4	39.8	51.9	64.5
	p $ per side										4.22	2.60	2.60	2.51	2.48	3.22

LEATHER (continued)		1899	1904	1909	1914	1919	1921	1923	1925	1927	1929	1931		1933	1935	1937
Product[d]	Item											A	B	C		
Upper leather (continued)																
Calf	q Mil. skins										12.9	10.3	10.2	12.1		
	v Mil. $										43.4	26.0	25.8	23.9		
	p $ per skin										3.35	2.53	2.53	1.98	q 12.8	12.3
															v 28.8	35.7
Kip, excl. kip side	q Mil. whole skins										1.32	.268	.268	.178	p 2.25	2.90
	v Mil. $										5.77	1.10	1.10	.474		
	p $ per whole skin										4.38	4.12	4.12	2.66		
Goat and kid	q Mil. skins										50.1	35.0	35.0	38.1	41.0	37.6
	v Mil. $										64.7	37.3	37.3	30.9	36.1	39.1
	p $ per skin										1.29	1.07	1.07	.810	.880	1.04
Sheep and lamb (shoe stock) and cabretta	q Mil. skins										14.3	9.99	9.86	8.72		
	v Mil. $										15.5	7.68	7.56	4.86		
	p $ per skin										1.08	.769	.767	.557		
Kangaroo and wallaby	q Mil. skins										.892	1.16			1.30	1.19
	v Mil. $										1.44	1.05			1.75	1.63
	p $ per skin										1.61	.906			1.35	1.37
Horse, half or whole fronts	q Mil. equiv. half fronts										.116	.0904	.084	.035	.110	
	v Mil. $										.429	.253	.240	.064	.191	
	p $ per half front										3.70	2.80	2.86	1.83	1.74	
																q 1.61
Glove and garment leather																v 3.86
Horse, half or whole fronts	q Mil. equiv. half fronts										1.86	1.51	1.50	1.27	1.49	p 2.39
	v Mil. $										6.38	3.26	3.25	2.21	3.01	
	p $ per half front										3.44	2.16	2.16	1.74	2.02	
Sheep and lamb, except shearlings	q Mil. skins										5.62	9.04	8.21	12.2	13.4	12.6
	v Mil. $										7.45	6.84	6.41	7.59	8.95	10.1
	p $ per skin										1.33	.756	.780	.622	.665	.800

For footnotes see p. 473.

Indexes of Physical Output, with Basic Data on Quantity, Value and Price of Products

LEATHER (continued)		1899	1904	1909	1914	1919	1921	1923	1925	1927	1929	1931		1933	1935	1937
Product[d]	*Item*											*A*	*B*	*C*		
Glove and garment leather (continued)																
Shearlings	*q* Mil. skins										3.03	2.00	1.37	1.56	2.38	
	v Mil. $										5.41	1.74	1.32	1.41	3.17	
	p $ per skin										1.79	.869	.964	.905	1.34	
Deer and elk	*q* Mil. skins										.181	.257			.0932	.131
	v Mil. $										.476	.386			.171	.214
	p $ per skin										2.63	1.50			1.84	1.63
Patent leather																
Cattle, incl. kip side	*q* Mil. sides										5.37	3.61	3.56	2.81		
	v Mil. $										23.5	10.8	10.7	7.26		
	p $ per side										4.37	2.99	3.00	2.58		
Fancy and bookbinder's leather																
Cowhide (cattle hide)	*q* Mil. sides										.157	.110			.197	.145
	v Mil. $										.930	.479			.865	.729
	p $ per side										5.94	4.34			4.40	5.04
Buffings, finished	*q* Th. hides										96.8	40.8	1	1	28.3	57.3
	v Th. $										777	281	9	13	196	324
	p $ per hide										8.02	6.90	9	13	6.92	5.66
Sheep and lamb and cabretta	*q* Mil. skins										3.97	2.81	2.81	2.11	1.57	
	v Mil. $										6.19	2.99	2.99	2.04	1.34	
	p $ per skin										1.56	1.06	1.06	.966	.849	
Calf and kip	*q* Mil. skins										.496	.249	.249	.308	.732	
	v Mil. $										1.99	.743	.743	.860	1.78	
	p $ per skin										4.02	2.99	2.99	2.79	2.43	
Splits, other than uphol-stery, finished	*q* Mil. side splits										21.2	14.8	14.5	17.8		
	v Mil. $										19.5	10.0	9.76	9.96		
	p $ per side split										.920	.678	.673	.560		

LEATHER (concluded)		1899	1904	1909	1914	1919	1921	1923	1925	1927	1929	1931		1933	1935	1937
Product[d]	*Item*											*A*	*B*	*C*		
Miscellaneous leather																
Roller leather	*q* Mil. skins										.979	.649				
	v Mil. $										1.71	1.03				
	p $ per skin										1.74	1.59				
Skivers, hat sweat and other	*q* Mil. doz.										.345	.192			.184	.226
	v Mil. $										5.46	1.68			1.91	2.30
	p $ per doz.										15.9	8.78			10.4	10.2
Chamois fleshers	*q* Mil. doz.										.196	.175				
	v Mil. $										3.00	2.29				
	p $ per doz.										15.3	13.1				
Rough splits	*q* Mil. equiv. side splits										1.21	1.22				
	v Mil. $										1.11	.284				
	p $ per side split										.916	.232				

A Comparable with all years except 1933. *B* Comparable with 1933. *C* Comparable with 1931.

[a] Percentages of coverage:

Given year	Base year	Given year	Base year
1899:85.7	1909:85.1	1931:87.5	1929:91.1
1904:83.7	1909:84.6	1933:84.0	1931:82.7
1909:81.1	1919:75.4	1935:80.5	1929:77.7
1914:84.5	1919:83.0	1937:73.5	1929:73.2

[b] No adjusted indexes for 1921–27 could be computed because data are lacking on the value of output of the products listed. For the years 1899–1919 percentages of coverage could be determined, since value figures are available, but a 1929 percentage of coverage comparable to the percentages of coverage for these years could not be determined. Consequently, adjusted indexes on the 1929 base were not computed for these years. The adjusted indexes on the 1919 base are: 1899: 66.6; 1904: 78.6; 1909: 85.5; and 1914: 80.8. The adjusted index given above, extrapolated by the unadjusted index for 1919–27, and by the adjusted index for 1899–1919, is 69.5 for 1899; 82.1 for 1904; 89.3 for 1909; 84.4 for 1914; 104.4 for 1919; 88.3 for 1921; 120.5 for 1923; 101.3 for 1925; 105.9 for 1927.

[c] Since values are not reported for the 1921–27 data or for the 1919 data which are comparable with 1929, we computed the indexes for these years by using an average of 1919 and 1929 unit values as price coefficients. Where the unit value for only one of these years was available, that was used, but it was adjusted to the price level represented by the 1919–29 average by means of the U.S. Bureau of Labor Statistics index of leather prices.

[d] Where only quantity figures are given they relate to leather, wherever processed. Where both quantity and value figures are given they relate to the leather industry alone.

[e] Reported in equivalent sides.

[f] A quantity figure is available, but it is not strictly comparable with that for 1929.

Indexes of Physical Output, with Basic Data on Quantity, Value and Price of Products

SHOES, LEATHER		*1899*	*1904*	*1909*	*1914*	*1919*	*1921*	*1923*	*1925*	*1927*	*1929*	*1931*	*1933*	*1935*	*1937*
Adjusted index[b]		60.1	67.7		81.2	89.2				96.4	100.0	84.4	94.0	103.3	112.3
Unadjusted index[a,c]		61.7	69.3	79.4	81.2	87.9	74.6	91.5	83.0	95.6	100.0	84.7	94.1	100.7	109.5
Product	*Item*														
Men's shoes	*q* Mil. pr.	67.7	83.4	93.9	98.0	95.0	69.5	100	86.5	93.0	101	79.2	88.7	96.6	104
	v Mil. $	108	142		220	430				299	313	204	175	210	251
	p $ per pr.	1.60	1.70		2.24	4.52				3.21	3.10	2.57	1.97	2.17	2.41
Youths' and boys' shoes	*q* Mil. pr.	21.0	21.7	23.8	22.9	26.5	18.5	22.2	21.0	26.9	22.6	19.5	17.3	18.5	19.1
	v Mil. $	20.7	24.3		32.9	72.9				60.8	49.1	31.1	23.0	27.9	29.8
	p $ per pr.	.986	1.12		1.43	2.75				2.26	2.17	1.59	1.33	1.51	1.56
Women's shoes	*q* Mil. pr.	65.0	69.5	86.6	80.9	105	101	110	105	124	136	115	134	146	151
	v Mil. $	81.8	98.3		148	447				394	432	295	252	281	320
	p $ per pr.	1.26	1.41		1.83	4.27				3.19	3.18	2.56	1.88	1.92	2.12
Misses' and children's shoes	*q* Mil. pr.	41.8	41.4	43.3	48.3	48.5	35.1	40.1	38.7	51.4	44.2	42.4	49.3	43.5	43.4
	v Mil. $	30.1	34.1		51.9	102				89.5	77.7	57.3	50.0	47.4	50.1
	p $ per pr.	.719	.822		1.07	2.10				1.74	1.76	1.35	1.01	1.09	1.15
Infants' shoes	*q* Mil. pr.				15.5	16.7	17.4	27.0	24.6	24.1	23.1	16.2	18.1	19.1	
	v Mil. $				7.57	18.2				25.3	24.2	13.7	12.1	13.3	
	p $ per pr.				.489	1.09				1.05	1.05	.846	.672	.699	
Athletic and sporting shoes	*q* Mil. pr.					.586	5.55	6.43	5.91	1.40	2.86	4.34	2.13	1.97	
	v Mil. $					2.08				4.16	8.83	9.42	4.09	4.49	
	p $ per pr.					3.56				2.96	3.09	2.17	1.92	2.28	
Slippers, all leather	*q* Mil. pr.				17.7	8.49			3.83	12.9	13.0	13.7	10.5	15.5[d]	
	v Mil. $				22.0	18.2				14.5	16.1	14.0	9.93	13.6	
	p $ per pr.				1.24	2.14				1.12	1.24	1.02	.944	.874	
	q	17.1	17.5	17.5											
	v	12.9	14.0												
	p	.757	.799												
Slippers, part leather	*q* Mil. pr.				6.94	13.3			20.1	21.7	25.1	20.7	25.2	23.5[d]	
	v Mil. $				4.06	15.2				16.0	19.7	12.4	13.1	11.7	
	p $ per pr.				.585	1.14				.738	.785	.597	.520	.499	

SHOES, LEATHER (concluded)		1899	1904	1909	1914	1919	1921	1923	1925	1927	1929	1931	1933	1935	1937
Product	*Item*														
Leather and fabric	*q* Mil. pr.					11.1				5.28	3.63	4.72	4.47	4.71	14.6
uppers with leather	*v* Mil. $					16.1				20.1	11.6	10.5	7.36	8.98	34.4
soles	*p* $ per pr.					1.45				3.80	3.21	2.22	1.65	1.91	2.36

[a] Percentages of coverage:

Given year	Base year	Given year	Base year	Given year	Base year
1899:98.0 1904:97.7	1914:95.5	1919:97.1 1927:97.7 1931:99.0	1929:98.6	1933:98.7 1935:96.1	1929:98.6
1914:97.0	1919:95.6			1937:89.1	1929:91.4

[b] For the years 1909, 1921, 1923 and 1925, only quantity figures are available and consequently no adjusted indexes were computed for these years. The adjusted index given above, interpolated by the unadjusted index, is 78.5 for 1909; 75.6 for 1921; 92.6 for 1923; 83.8 for 1925.

[c] In the absence of the necessary price figures, 1914 prices were used in the construction of the 1909 index, and 1929 prices in the construction of the 1921, 1923 and 1925 indexes. The indexes for 1899, 1904 and 1909 were constructed on the 1914 base.

[d] In 1935, there were 2.43 mil. pr. of slippers for which value and method of construction were not reported. In addition, the 1935 data include moccasins, which were not reported previously.

TOTAL LEATHER PRODUCTS	1899	1904	1909	1914	1919	1921	1923	1925	1927	1929	1931	1933	1935	1937
Adjusted index	64.0	73.7	82.8	80.8	90.1	74.6	94.7	84.6	97.0	100.0	80.1	86.0	99.7	108.4
Unadjusted index[a]	63.6	72.7	82.1	82.1	94.1	77.9	98.9	87.9	98.1	100.0	82.3	90.3	102.6	111.1

[a] Percentages of coverage:

Given year	Base year	Given year	Base year	Given year	Base year	Given year	Base year
1899:78.6 1904:78.0	1909:78.5	1919:82.8 1921:82.8	1929:79.2	1927:82.1 1931:83.4	1929:81.2	1935:83.5 1937:83.2	1929:81.2
1909:78.5 1914:80.3	1919:82.7	1923:80.2 1925:79.8	1929:76.8	1933:82.7	1929:78.7		

RUBBER PRODUCTS

Indexes of Physical Output, with Basic Data on Quantity, Value and Price of Products

RUBBER GOODS, OTHER		*1919*	*1921*	*1923*	*1925*	*1927*	*1929*	*1931*		*1933*	*1935*	*1937*
Adjusted index						79.7	100.0	82.9		80.1	95.5	111.9
Unadjusted index[a]					[b]	86.9	100.0	74.6		76.0	88.9	108.8
Product	*Item*							*A*	*B*	*C*		
Heels, made for sale as such	*q* Mil. pr.	138	137	289	342	318	293	248	247	273	278	295
	v Mil. $	16.1	14.5	23.7	26.1	25.5	17.9	11.6	11.6	11.1	11.6	16.3
	p $ per pr.	.116	.106	.0819	.0762	.0801	.0612	.0469	.0469	.0408	.0416	.0552
Soles, incl. composition or fiber, made for sale as such	*q* Mil. pr.	9.78	5.00	13.5	36.1	40.8	46.2	59.6	59.6	92.0	69.7	72.5
	v Mil. $	2.46	1.74	4.91	10.4	9.34	8.96	8.39	8.38	8.32	7.26	10.8
	p $ per pr.	.251	.348	.363	.288	.229	.194	.141	.141	.0904	.104	.148
Soling strips and top-lift sheets	*q* Mil. sq.ft.						4.31	8.92	8.90	10.8	9.94	8.07
	v Mil. $						1.72	1.98	1.97	1.71	2.67	2.08
	p $ per sq.ft.						.398	.222	.222	.159	.268	.257
Automobile and carriage fabrics	*q* Mil. sq.yd.	40.8	15.5	33.0	25.2	17.4	22.4	10.4	10.4	8.62	5.23	6.01
	v Mil. $	10.7	6.91	14.2	13.9	11.0	11.9	5.40	5.40	3.36	1.87	2.12
	p $ per sq.yd.	.262	.445	.429	.550	.636	.529	.518	.518	.390	.358	.353
Raincoat fabrics	*q* Mil. sq.yd.					23.7	25.6	15.1	15.0	18.1	20.0	21.4
	v Mil. $					9.74	9.68	4.24	4.21	5.46	4.36	4.87
	p $ per sq.yd.					.411	.379	.281	.281	.302	.218	.228
Hospital sheeting	*q* Mil. sq.yd.	*q* 47.2	19.7	18.1	25.8	3.42	3.05	2.68	2.68	2.24	2.51	2.98
	v Mil. $	*v* 13.7	4.31	6.57	7.76	1.84	1.44	1.05	1.05	.741	.839	1.07
	p $ per sq.yd.	*p* .291	.219	.363	.300	.538	.474	.390	.390	.331	.334	.360
All other rubberized fabrics	*q* Mil. sq.yd.					11.3	41.9	35.8	35.6	42.3	43.6	39.3
	v Mil. $					3.91	6.76	6.97	6.93	8.64	13.0	13.6
	p $ per sq.yd.					.345	.161	.195	.195	.204	.298	.346

RUBBER GOODS, OTHER (continued)		1919	1921	1923	1925	1927	1929	1931		1933	1935	1937
Product	*Item*							*A*	*B*	*C*		
Transmission belting (flat)	*q* Mil. lb.					23.2	21.6	14.5	14.5	13.7	15.5	21.8
	v Mil. $					12.6	13.1	6.72	6.72	6.51	8.98	13.4
	p $ per lb.					.544	.609	.463	.463	.474	.577	.614
All other rubber belting	*q* Mil. lb.					20.2	23.4	16.1	16.1	16.9	32.8	36.9
	v Mil. $					9.35	12.6	6.89	6.89	6.42	11.5	18.7
	p $ per lb.					.462	.539	.428	.428	.380	.351	.506
Rubber tubing	*q* Mil. lb.						16.2	5.71	5.43	13.3	13.6	23.0
	v Mil. $						3.49	1.18	1.15	1.31	2.24	4.49
	p $ per lb.						.215	.207	.211	.099	.164	.196
Rubber packing	*q* Mil. lb.					15.0	17.9	9.27	9.24	9.33	11.4	14.0
	v Mil. $					4.85	5.03	2.21	2.20	1.87	2.74	3.55
	p $ per lb.					.323	.281	.238	.238	.201	.240	.253
Washers, gaskets, etc.	*q* Mil. lb.					12.9	13.3	5.98	5.65	3.81	5.17	15.0
	v Mil. $					7.73	5.11	2.48	2.38	1.47	2.11	5.04
	p $ per lb.					.597	.383	.415	.422	.387	.408	.335
Rubber and friction tape	*q* Mil. lb.					17.0	20.4	14.9	14.8	11.4	12.4	21.1
	v Mil. $					4.04	4.95	2.82	2.80	2.13	2.85	4.54
	p $ per lb.					.238	.242	.189	.189	.187	.230	.215
Water bottles and fountain syringes	*q* Mil. doz.					.514	.693	.487	.485	.552	.580	.641
	v Mil. $					4.77	4.96	2.38	2.37	2.19	2.50	3.37
	p $ per doz.					9.28	7.16	4.89	4.89	3.97	4.31	5.27
Rubber bands	*q* Mil. lb.					1.74	3.49	3.44	3.44	3.31	3.88	4.27
	v Mil. $					1.42	1.96	1.16	1.16	.810	1.26	1.75
	p $ per lb.					.820	.560	.337	.337	.245	.326	.409
Rubber cement	*q* Mil. gal.					4.83	6.05	5.34	4.74	3.74	5.97	15.4
	v Mil. $					3.88	4.70	3.26	2.91	2.10	3.14	8.93
	p $ per gal.					.805	.776	.610	.613	.561	.526	.578

For footnotes see next page.

Indexes of Physical Output, with Basic Data on Quantity, Value and Price of Products

RUBBER GOODS, OTHER (concluded)		1919	1921	1923	1925	1927	1929	1931		1933	1935	1937
Product	*Item*							*A*	*B*	*C*		
Rubber flooring	*q* Mil. sq.ft.				12.0	8.78	8.57	7.52	7.52	4.32	5.91	8.77
	v Mil. $				6.12	4.50	4.27	2.92	2.92	1.24	1.70	2.66
	p $ per sq.ft.				.512	.513	.498	.389	.389	.286	.289	.304
Rubber thread	*q* Mil. lb.					5.28	5.73	5.50	5.50	4.81	5.42	5.62
	v Mil. $					5.34	5.19	2.90	2.90	2.24	2.55	3.48
	p $ per lb.					1.01	.906	.528	.528	.465	.471	.619
Jar rings	*q* Mil. gr.					6.77	8.44	11.0	11.0	7.44	7.57	6.12
	v Mil. $					3.05	3.00	3.11	3.11	1.78	2.07	1.95
	p $ per gr.					.451	.356	.284	.284	.240	.274	.320
Bathing caps	*q* Mil. doz.					.741	1.09	1.18	1.18	1.23	.945	.790
	v Mil. $					1.70	1.84	1.80	1.79	1.34	1.17	1.23
	p $ per doz.					2.30	1.69	1.52	1.52	1.09	1.24	1.56
Reclaimed rubber, for sale as such	*q* Mil. lb.		68.3	132	244	330	364	217	216	159		
	v Mil. $		7.42	11.7	23.0	27.4	23.9	9.98	9.96	5.96		
	p $ per lb.		.109	.0889	.0944	.0828	.0657	.0461	.0461	.0376		
Rubber gloves	*q* Mil. doz.pr.					.817	1.05	.997	.895	1.01	1.29	1.38
	v Mil. $					2.42	2.93	2.01	1.83	1.68	2.86	2.98
	p $ per doz.pr.					2.96	2.79	2.02	2.05	1.66	2.22	2.17

A Comparable with all years except 1933. *B* Comparable with 1933. *C* Comparable with 1931.

[a] Percentages of coverage:

Given year	Base year	Given year	Base year
1927:66.9	1929:61.4	1935:50.0	1929:53.8
1931:57.2	1929:63.5	1937:52.2	
1933:59.7	1931:56.6		

[b] No indexes are given for the period prior to 1927 because of inadequate coverage. For an index relating to rubber goods, other, and tires and tubes, 1919–37, see rubber goods, other, incl. tires and tubes, below.

RUBBER GOODS, OTHER, incl. TIRES and TUBES	1919	1921	1923	1925	1927	1929	1931	1933	1935	1937
Adjusted index[b]	48.4	37.1	66.6	83.2	88.3	100.0	71.1	69.1	78.6	90.1
Unadjusted index[a,b]	51.7	39.5	68.0	88.3	91.9	100.0				

[a] Percentages of coverage:

Given year	Base year	Given year	Base year
1919:77.0	1929:72.2	1923:76.1	1929:74.5
1921:79.3	1929:74.5	1925:79.5	1929:74.9
		1927:84.7	1929:81.4

[b] For the detailed data on products see the individual industries, rubber goods, other, and tires and tubes. For the years 1931–37 we computed the adjusted index from the two underlying adjusted indexes, using value added weights. In the earlier years the two component industries are treated as one in the Census; therefore we followed the usual procedure in constructing the unadjusted and adjusted indexes.

SHOES, RUBBER		1914	1919	1921	1923	1925	1927	1929	1931	1933	1935	1937
Adjusted index		68.6	115.0	91.0	111.0	91.2	119.9	100.0	58.3	71.3	82.7	95.1
Unadjusted index[a]		75.8	105.1	84.4	104.8	86.8	118.0	100.0	54.2	64.9	69.2	79.2
Product	*Item*											
Rubber-soled canvas shoes	*q* Mil. pr.		21.0	15.2	26.1	25.0	28.8	44.0	28.1	29.7	24.0	31.5
	v Mil. $		25.2	18.9	28.4	23.8	25.5	30.3	17.2	13.8	12.3	18.0
	p $ per pr.		1.20	1.24	1.09	.953	.884	.690	.611	.465	.515	.572
Rubber boots	*q* Mil. pr.	4.02	9.21	6.53	9.10	4.74	5.36	5.45	1.97	2.62	3.03	3.88
	v Mil. $	12.6	26.1	15.1	23.6	16.0	16.7	16.1	4.78	4.66	5.53	7.62
	p $ per pr.	3.14	2.83	2.31	2.59	3.38	3.12	2.96	2.42	1.78	1.83	1.96
Lumbermen's pacs	*q* Mil. pr.						3.77	1.82	.983	1.20	1.88	1.36
	v Mil. $						8.85	4.17	2.09	1.66	3.36	2.81
	p $ per pr.						2.35	2.30	2.12	1.38	1.79	2.07
Arctics and gaiters	*q* Mil. pr.	*q* 57.2	66.1	57.2	60.1	52.3	36.7	19.2	11.0	15.8	19.3	20.1
	v Mil. $	*v* 37.9	64.7	60.8	83.0	80.1	54.4	31.7	14.7	13.4	17.6	18.3
	p $ per pr.	*p* .662	.978	1.06	1.38	1.53	1.48	1.65	1.33	.846	.909	.912
Other shoes, rubbers, and footholds	*q* Mil. pr.						31.1	30.3	15.2	16.0	16.6	20.1
	v Mil. $						27.7	29.0	9.63	8.01	9.44	11.4
	p $ per pr.						.892	.957	.635	.501	.569	.569

[a] Percentages of coverage:

Given year	Base year	Given year	Base year	Given year	Base year	Given year	Base year
1914:93.8	1919: 77.6	1921:100.8		1927:106.9		1935:90.8	1929:108.6
1919:99.2	1929:108.6	1923:102.5	1929:108.6	1931:100.8	1929:108.6	1937:90.4	
		1925:103.4		1933: 98.8			

Indexes of Physical Output, with Basic Data on Quantity, Value and Price of Products

TIRES and TUBES	Item	1914	1919	1921	1923	1925	1927	1929	1931	1933	1935	1937
Adjusted index			[b]	39.0	68.8	87.9	91.2	100.0	66.9	64.9	72.0	81.3
Unadjusted index[a]		12.8	50.8	40.3	69.1	89.1	93.0	100.0	68.9	63.3	68.7	76.8
Product	*Item*											
Pneumatic tires and casings	*q* Mil.	8.02	32.8	27.3	45.4	58.8	63.6	69.8	49.1	45.4	48.8	54.1
(motor-vehicle, excl.	*v* Mil. $	106	604	378	458	656	634	574	314	221	322	413
motorcycle and bicycle)	*p* $ each	13.2	18.4	13.8	10.1	11.2	9.97	8.22	6.40	4.87	6.61	7.63
Pneumatic tires, casings	*q* Mil.	3.73	5.78	1.98	4.31	2.51	3.05	3.74	2.83	3.91	5.54[c]	8.45
and inner tubes (motor-	*v* Mil. $	6.91	14.8	4.26	5.69	3.96	3.70	3.63	2.41	2.30	4.51	5.77
cycle and bicycle)	*p* $ each	1.85	2.56	2.16	1.32	1.58	1.21	.973	.850	.589	.815	.682
Inner tubes (other than	*q* Mil.	7.91	33.3	32.1	57.2	77.4	70.9	74.0[d]	49.2[d]	42.9[d]	47.8[d]	52.6
motorcycle and bicycle)	*v* Mil. $	20.1	81.3	52.9	75.0	118	105	80.6	44.6	29.4	44.5	56.3
	p $ each	2.54	2.45	1.65	1.31	1.53	1.49	1.09	.907	.686	.930	1.07
Solid and cushion tires												
Motor-vehicle	*q* Mil.		1.45	.401	.944	1.04	.813	.590			.154	.255
	v Mil. $		43.9	14.7	29.1	43.9	35.0	18.0			2.39	2.42
	p $ each		30.2	36.7	30.8	42.4	43.1	30.5			15.5	9.51
Truck and bus only	*q* Mil.							.424	.112	.0850		
	v Mil. $							14.9	4.05	2.22		
	p $ each							35.1	36.1	26.2		

[a] Percentages of coverage:

Given year	Base year
1921:90.6, 1923:88.1	1929:87.7
1925:88.9, 1927:89.4	1929:87.7
1931:90.0, 1933:85.2	1929:87.3
1935:83.7, 1937:82.9	1929:87.7

[b] For years prior to 1921 no adjusted indexes could be computed because the industry is not shown separately in the Census for those years. The adjusted index given above, extrapolated by the unadjusted index, is 12.4 for 1914; 49.2 for 1919. For an adjusted index for tires and tubes, and rubber goods, other, 1919–37, see rubber goods, other, incl. tires and tubes.

[c] Includes a small amount of other inner tubes, which in 1937 amounted in value to not quite 8 percent of the total value of this item.

[d] Excludes a small quantity of inner tubes, other than for motor-vehicles, motorcycles and bicycles.

TOTAL RUBBER PRODUCTS	1919	1921	1923	1925	1927	1929	1931	1933	1935	1937
Adjusted index / Unadjusted index[a,b]	53.7	42.6	72.1	84.2	91.9	100.0	69.5	69.3	79.1	90.6

[a] Percentages of coverage: 100.0 in every year.

[b] A combined index for tires and tubes and rubber products, other, treated as a single industry for 1919–25, was used in the construction of the group index for that period. This index on the 1929 base is as follows: 1919: 48.4; 1921: 37.1; 1923: 66.6; 1925: 83.2.

No group index was computed for 1914 because of inadequacy of coverage and lack of data on value added for tires and tubes.

PAPER PRODUCTS

PAPER		1899	1904	1909	1914	1919	1921	1923	1925	1927	1929	1931	1933	1935	1937
Adjusted index									[b]	87.8	100.0	85.4	83.0	95.5	115.2
Unadjusted index[a]		20.7	29.4	39.7	49.8	57.6	50.5	74.1	82.8	89.2	100.0	84.3	82.6	94.3	114.3
Product[c]	*Item*														
Newsprint and similar papers	*q* Mil. t.	.624	.975	1.27	1.42	1.47	1.33	1.69	1.75	1.81	1.77	1.51	1.21	1.22	1.49
	v Mil. $	22.4	38.9	51.3	57.9	112	124	126	123	123	109	86.1	47.8	49.5	69.7
	p $ per t.	35.9	39.9	40.5	40.9	75.9	93.6	74.7	70.0	68.1	61.7	56.9	39.4	40.5	46.6
Book paper	*q* Mil. t.	.304	.454	.677	.913	.961	.807	1.21[d]	1.34	1.33	1.50	1.21	1.08	1.28	1.52
	v Mil. $	21.5	32.6	52.8	70.7	144	125	169	177	161	168	120	83.2	113	147
	p $ per t.	70.6	71.8	78.0	77.4	150	156	140	132	121	112	99.5	77.1	87.8	96.9
Cover paper	*q* Th. t.	18.7	22.2	17.6	21.7	22.2	16.4	20.6	24.3	26.3	28.1	23.5	12.7	20.8	24.4
	v Mil. $	1.67	2.02	1.98	2.81	5.64	4.11	4.97	5.81	5.94	6.43	4.37	2.10	3.71	4.44
	p $ per t.	88.8	91.4	113	130	255	251	241	239	225	229	186	166	178	182
Writing paper	*q* Mil. t.	.113	.147	.198	.248	.325	.231	.377	.474	.509	.608	.488	.478	.507	.578
	v Mil. $	15.9	22.2	29.1	34.1	87.7	61.3	89.1	105	105	113	77.9	61.3	70.6	87.3
	p $ per t.	141	152	147	137	270	266	236	223	207	186	160	128	139	151

For footnotes see p. 483.

Indexes of Physical Output, with Basic Data on Quantity, Value and Price of Products

PAPER (concluded)		1899	1904	1909	1914	1919	1921	1923	1925	1927	1929	1931	1933	1935	1937
Product[c]	*Item*														
Wrapping paper,[c] incl. tag stock	*q* Mil. t.	.535	.644	.763	.911	.858	.827	1.18	1.29	1.53	1.61	1.40	1.44	1.63	2.05
	v Mil. $	24.5	30.4	42.2	51.3	109	103	142	144	163	163	111	95.8	127	180
	p $ per t.	45.9	47.2	55.3	56.3	126	125	120	111	107	102	79.1	66.5	77.8	87.5
Tissue paper	*q* Th. t.	28.4	43.9	77.7	115	191	186	251	281	316	388	395	407	473	540
	v Mil. $	3.49	5.06	8.55	11.5	40.7	33.6	44.1	45.7	46.6	53.3	45.0	37.7	46.2	55.9
	p $ per t.	123	115	110	100	214	181	176	163	147	137	114	92.7	97.7	104
Absorbent paper[f]	*q* Th. t.								51.1	63.8	90.8	76.6	79.8	95.2	138
	v Mil. $								10.0	13.3	17.0	14.8	12.1	15.9	22.1
	p $ per t.								196	209	187	193	151	167	160
Blotting paper	*q* Th. t.	4.35	8.70	9.58	14.2	13.4	11.5	15.8	12.9	13.1	14.1				
	v Mil. $	.581	1.05	1.19	1.46	3.21	2.67	3.78	2.59	2.70	2.83				
	p $ per t.	133	120	124	103	239	231	239	200	206	200				
Building paper	*q* Th. t.	96.9	145	226	244	195	217	345[g]	582	626	659[h]	395	308	441	608
	v Mil. $	3.03	4.85	9.25	9.48	17.7	12.8	23.5	45.7	40.1	39.4	18.1	12.7	19.4	32.6
	p $ per t.	31.2	33.4	41.0	38.8	90.8	59.2	68.3	78.5	64.0	59.7	45.9	41.2	44.1	53.7
Paperboard	*q* Mil. t.	.394	.560	.883	1.29	1.87	1.74	2.79	3.29	3.77	4.45	3.85	4.08	4.70	5.80
	v Mil. $	12.1	19.7	29.5	44.9	124	104	183	193	211	228	149	161	200	277
	p $ per t.	30.6	35.2	33.4	34.7	66.5	60.0	65.5	58.7	56.0	51.2	38.8	39.5	42.6	47.8
Other paper[e,f]	*q* Th. t.	49.1	106	96.6	93.3	192	66.1	148[d]	95.6	20.9	39.3[h]	31.4	94.9	110	78.0
	v Mil. $	2.80	6.73	6.87	7.46	29.7	13.6	27.2	13.4	3.01	5.23	4.50	7.61	10.9	11.4
	p $ per t.	56.9	63.3	71.1	80.0	155	206	183	140	144	133	143	80.2	99.1	147

[a] Percentages of coverage:

Given year	Base year
1927:94.8, 1931:92.1, 1933:93.0	1929:93.4
1935:92.2, 1937:92.7	1929:93.4

[b] No adjusted indexes for 1899–1925 could be computed because the industry is not shown separately in the Census for those years. The adjusted index given above, extrapolated by the unadjusted index, is 20.4 for 1899; 28.9 for 1904; 39.1 for 1909; 49.0 for 1914; 56.7 for 1919; 49.7 for 1921; 72.9 for 1923; 81.5 for 1925. For an adjusted index for paper and pulp combined, 1899–1925, see paper and pulp.

[c] The data on products are available in much greater detail in the Census. Adjusted indexes computed from the more detailed data for the Census years 1927–37 are very close to those given above: the differences amount to less than 2 percent in each year.

[d] In 1923 a small quantity of book paper (plate, lithograph, map, and woodcut) was combined with "other paper." Book paper figures for 1929 comparable with those given for 1923 are *q* 1.48 mil. tons; *v* $166 mil.; *p* $112 per ton. Comparable "other paper" figures for 1929 are *q* 59.2 th. tons; *v* $7.63 mil.; *p* $129 per ton.

[e] Beginning in 1925 some wrapping paper which was included under "other paper" in earlier years was combined with wrapping paper.

[f] Prior to 1925 absorbent paper other than blotting was included with "other paper."

[g] The figures for building paper for 1923 and earlier years are not comparable with those for 1929. The comparable 1929 figures are: *q* .592 mil. tons; *v* $34.8 mil.; *p* $58.7 per ton.

[h] The 1929 data for building and "other paper" are not strictly comparable with those for 1931. Comparable 1929 data are: building paper, *q* .662 mil. tons; *v* $39.5 mil.; *p* $60 per ton; and "other paper," *q* 36.6 th. tons; *v* $5.12 mil.; *p* $140 per ton.

PAPER and PULP	*1899*	*1904*	*1909*	*1914*	*1919*	*1921*	*1923*	*1925*	*1927*	*1929*	*1931*	*1933*	*1935*	*1937*
Adjusted index[b]	19.4	27.5	36.5	44.5	52.7	44.5	65.7	75.3	87.5	100.0	85.9	84.0	97.6	119.8
Unadjusted index[a,b]	21.3	31.3	42.1	51.1	60.2	51.9	74.5	82.2		100.0				

[a] Percentages of coverage:

Given year	Base year
1899:109.7, 1904:113.5	1909:115.0
1909:115.0, 1914:114.6	1919:113.8
1919:113.8, 1921:116.4, 1923:113.0	1929: 99.7
1925:110.7	1929:101.4

[b] For the detailed data on products see the individual industries, paper, and pulp. For the years 1927–37 the adjusted index was computed from the two underlying indexes, with value added as weights. In the earlier years the two component industries are treated as one in the Census; therefore the usual procedure was followed in the construction of the unadjusted and adjusted indexes.

Indexes of Physical Output, with Basic Data on Quantity, Value and Price of Products

PULP		*1899*	*1904*	*1909*	*1914*	*1919*	*1921*	*1923*	*1925*	*1927*	*1929*	*1931*	*1933*	*1935*	*1937*
Adjusted index									b	86.3	100.0	88.1	88.9	106.6	141.0
Unadjusted index[a]		23.7	38.4	51.2	56.4	69.8	57.1	75.9	79.6	87.9	100.0	88.0	88.0	102.9	137.3
Product[c,d]	*Item*														
Sulphite-fiber, bleached	*q* Mil. t.				.385	.510	.421	.558	.613	.680	.840	.741	.726	.945	1.35
	v Mil. $				19.4	56.0	43.3	49.8	50.6	53.8	62.2	42.3	33.4	48.5	79.2
	p $ per t.	*q* .416	.756	1.02	50.3	110	103	89.3	82.6	79.2	74.0	57.1	45.9	51.4	58.7
		v 16.0	27.4	41.1											
Sulphite-fiber, unbleached	*q* Mil. t.	*p* 38.5	36.2	40.4	.766	.910	.721	.853	.791	.872	.842	.677	.601	.635	.792
	v Mil. $				29.0	71.2	55.3	52.9	44.0	44.8	40.8	28.1	21.1	21.9	30.7
	p $ per t.				37.8	78.2	76.7	62.0	55.7	51.3	48.5	41.5	35.2	34.5	38.8
Sulphate-fiber, bleached and unbleached	*q* Mil. t.				.0526	.120	.138	.312	.410	.603	.918	1.03	1.26	1.47	2.14
	v Mil. $				1.89	8.52	9.72	18.8	24.6	28.7	37.2	28.8	29.1	36.0	59.4
	p $ per t.				35.8	70.8	70.4	60.2	60.0	47.6	40.5	27.9	23.1	24.5	27.8
Soda-fiber	*q* Mil. t.	.177	.197	.299	.348	.412	.301	.445	.473	.487	.521	.374	.458[e]	.485[e]	.508
	v Mil. $	6.46	7.79	12.6	15.3	36.3	32.1	35.2	34.2	32.8	34.1	21.0	16.5	18.2	23.5
	p $ per t.	36.5	39.6	42.2	44.1	88.2	107	79.1	72.3	67.4	65.4	56.0	36.0	37.4	46.2
Mechanical	*q* Mil. t.	.586	.969	1.18	1.29	1.52	1.26	1.57	1.61	1.61	1.64	1.45	1.20	1.36	1.60
	v Mil. $	9.28	15.3	21.4	23.4	51.5	50.8	56.1	59.7	46.0	47.2	34.1	23.6	25.0	30.3
	p $ per t.	15.8	15.8	18.2	18.1	33.9	40.4	35.8	37.0	28.5	28.8	23.5	19.7	18.4	18.9

[a] Percentages of coverage:

Given year	Base year
1927: 94.5	
1931: 92.6	
1933: 91.8	1929: 92.7
1935: 89.5	
1937: 90.3	

[b] No adjusted indexes for 1899–1925 could be computed be-

[c] Prior to 1914 screenings were included in sulphite-fiber, soda-fiber, and mechanical pulp. Beginning in 1914 screenings were reported separately. The resulting incomparabilities are probably small (in 1914 the value of screenings was less than ½ of 1 percent of the total value of sulphite-fiber, soda-fiber, and mechanical pulp), and have therefore been ignored.

[d] Prior to 1927 quantities were reported both for total output and for output made for sale or interplant transfer, but values

cause the industry is not shown separately in the Census for those years. The adjusted index given above, extrapolated by the unadjusted index, is 23.3 for 1899; 37.7 for 1904; 50.3 for 1909; 55.4 for 1914; 68.5 for 1919; 56.1 for 1921; 74.5 for 1923; 78.2 for 1925. For an adjusted index for paper and pulp combined, 1899–1925, see paper and pulp.

were reported only for output made for sale or interplant transfer. Values for total output were obtained by multiplication of total output by prices derived from the sales figures.

[e] Includes semimechanical and other soda-fiber. The corresponding totals for 1929 are: *q* .561 mil. tons; *v* $34.9 mil.; *p* $62.1 per ton.

WALL PAPER		1929	1931	1933	1935	1937
Adjusted index		100.0	80.6	77.3	92.9	110.0
Unadjusted index[a]		100.0	80.6	77.3	92.1	110.0
Product	*Item*					
Wall paper	*q* Mil. rolls	374	301	289	344	411
	v Mil. $	30.0	20.2	15.8	19.5	26.8
	p $ per roll	.0802	.0670	.0546	.0566	.0651

[a] Percentages of coverage:

Given year	Base year
1931:100.0, 1933:100.0	1929:100.0
1935: 99.2, 1937:100.0	1929:100.0

TOTAL PAPER PRODUCTS	1899	1904	1909	1914	1919	1921	1923	1925	1927	1929	1931	1933	1935	1937
Adjusted index	18.3	26.1	36.7	46.3	52.8	50.5	70.2	77.0	89.0	100.0	86.5	84.5	101.9	122.0
Unadjusted index[a,b]	19.4	27.5	36.5	44.5	52.7	44.5	65.7	75.3	87.5	100.0	85.7	83.8	97.5	119.5

[a] Percentages of coverage:

Given year	Base year
1899:60.8, 1904:60.4	1909:57.0
1909:57.0, 1914:55.1	1919:57.3
1919:57.3, 1921:50.6, 1923:53.7, 1925:56.1, 1927:56.4	1929:57.4
1931:58.8, 1933:58.8, 1935:56.7, 1937:58.1	1929:59.3

[b] In computing the group indexes we combined the separate industries, paper and pulp, and treated them as a single industry for 1899–1925 because separate data on value added are lacking for these years. The combined indexes for the two industries for these years are exactly the same as the unadjusted group indexes given above.

PRINTING AND PUBLISHING

Indexes of Physical Output, with Basic Data on Quantity, Value and Price of Products

TOTAL PRINTING and PUBLISHING		*1899*	*1904*	*1909*	*1914*	*1919*	*1921*	*1923*	*1925*	*1927*	*1929*	*1931*	*1933*	*1935*	*1937*
Adjusted index[a]															
Unadjusted index[a]		17.1	26.3	35.5	47.2	54.0	52.2	73.3	82.2	90.5	100.0	84.2	72.2	87.0	101.6
Material and Item	*Unit*														
Newsprint															
Shipments from mills[b]	Th. t.	569	913	1,168	1,313	1,379	1,226	1,477	1,534	1,474	1,409	1,158	950	917	945
Imports[c]	Th. t.				315	628	792	1,309	1,448	1,987	2,423	2,067	1,794	2,383	3,317
Exports[c]	Th. t.				60.8	110	16.8	16.4	22.7	12.3	18.7	9.65	11.1	22.5	17.0
Stock changes															
At publishers[d]	Th. t.					−67.0[e]	−30.1	+64.3	−43.6	−14.2	+31.4	−35.0	+34.6	−45.3	+366
In transit[d]	Th. t.					+7.0[e]	−10.7	−12.9	−1.85	−5.29	+7.38	−.422	+16.7	+10.1	+19.1
Book paper															
Production[g]	Th. t.	304	454	677	913	961	807	1,208[f]	1,343	1,329	1,498	1,209	1,080	1,282	1,520
Fine paper															
Production[g]	Th. t.	113	147	198	248	325	231	377	474	509	608	488	478	507	578
Printing paper other than newsprint															
Imports	Th. t.				2.88	.080	.681	8.40	8.31	5.21	2.18	1.50	2.09	5.78	15.5
Exports	Th. t.				15.1	76.7	20.1	13.3	8.67	8.02	18.9	9.51	9.19	9.96	15.0

[a] Since data on production are lacking, the index of output is based on the physical volume of materials consumed. For this reason no adjusted index could be obtained.

[b] For years prior to 1919, figures represent production. The corresponding figure for 1919 is 1,324 th. tons.

stocks, minus signs decreases. The figures are as given by the Bureau of Foreign and Domestic Commerce, *Survey of Current Business* (Sept. 1938), p. 20, after adjustment to represent the whole industry on the basis of estimates of coverage of the sample provided in the *Survey*.

[c] The data are taken from December issues of *Monthly Summary of Foreign Commerce of the United States*. No foreign trade statistics are available for 1899, 1904 and 1909 on a calendar year basis. The 1909 figures for the fiscal year indicate that the role of imports and exports in the early years was negligible.

[d] Difference in stocks between December 31 of given year and December 31 of preceding year. Plus signs denote increases in

[e] Obtained from Magdoff, Siegel and Davis, *op. cit.*, Part III, p. 96.

[f] Excludes lithograph, wood-cut, and "other paper."

[g] The use of production instead of shipment figures probably introduces only a small error; the two sets of figures are almost identical whenever both are given.

CHEMICAL PRODUCTS

CARBON BLACK		*1914*	*1919*	*1921*	*1923*	*1925*	*1927*	*1929*	*1931*	*1933*	*1935*	*1937*
Adjusted index		10.0	22.9	23.7	47.4	70.0	66.9	100.0	74.6	74.3	94.4	133.2
Unadjusted index[a]		18.1	25.2	27.0	45.5	58.9	61.4	100.0	72.0	68.0	88.7	124.5
Product	*Item*											
Bone black	*q* Mil. lb.	44.5	47.5	53.1	49.7	64.1	59.4	54.3	33.2	23.1	32.9	35.6
	v Mil. $	1.53	2.37	4.01	2.42	2.54	2.52	2.49	1.29	.829	1.31	1.72
	p $ per lb.	.0344	.0499	.0754	.0486	.0396	.0425	.0459	.0388	.0358	.0399	.0483
Carbon black[b]	*q* Mil. lb.	22.9	52.1	59.8	138	177	198	366	281	273	353	511
	v Mil. $	.918	3.82	5.45	11.7	9.64	11.0	18.7	8.62	7.60	13.8	17.4
	p $ per lb.	.0401	.0733	.0911	.0846	.0543	.0552	.0511	.0307	.0278	.0390	.0341
Lamp black	*q* Mil. lb.	11.2[c]	9.83[c]	6.59	11.1	12.0	8.80	10.8	3.42	3.01	3.90	5.31
	v Mil. $	.504	1.39	.935	1.46	1.44	1.04	1.19	.321	.210	.386	.473
	p $ per lb.	.0450	.142	.142	.131	.119	.118	.110	.0937	.0697	.0988	.0890

[a] Percentages of coverage:

Given year	Base year	Given year	Base year
1914:201.8	1919:122.5	1927:101.8	1929:111.1
1919:122.5	1929:111.1	1931:107.3	1929:111.1
1921:127.0	1929:111.1	1933:101.6	1929:111.1
1923:106.6	1929:111.1	1935:104.3	1929:111.1
1925: 93.5	1929:111.1	1937:103.8	1929:111.1

[b] From reports of the Bureau of Mines.

[c] Figures given as estimates in the Census.

Indexes of Physical Output, with Basic Data on Quantity, Value and Price of Products

CHARCOAL[a]		1921	1923	1925	1927	1929	1931	1933[c]	1935	1937
Adjusted index		192.2	132.3	237.6	144.5	100.0	39.1		45.8	43.2
Unadjusted index[b]		322.4	214.2	170.0	170.5	100.0	59.3		69.8	72.6
Product	*Item*									
Charcoal, made in kiln or pit plants	*q* Mil. bu.	2.80	1.86	1.48	1.48	.870	.516		.608	.631
	v Mil. $	.419	.385	.289	.293	.163	.0806		.0987	.125
	p $ per bu.	.149	.206	.195	.197	.188	.156		.163	.197

[a] Because this industry contains a large proportion of small establishments, the degree to which it is covered by the Census probably varies from year to year.

[b] Percentages of coverage:

Given year	Base year	Given year	Base year
1921: 100.0 1923: 96.5 1925: 42.7	1929: 59.6	1927: 70.3 1931: 90.4 1935: 90.9 1937: 100.1	1929: 59.6

[c] Detailed data on products were not collected in 1933.

CHEMICALS, not elsewhere classified		1899	1904	1909	1914	1919	1921	1923	1925	1927	1929	1931		1933	1935	1937
Adjusted index									b	73.8	100.0[e]	81.2		79.8[d]	104.9	141.3
Unadjusted index[a]		17.6	22.8	31.4	30.6	50.4	36.0	67.4	68.1	77.4	100.0	77.2		79.6	93.5	119.3
Product	*Item*											*A*	*B*	*C*		
Acids																
Acetic	*q* Mil. lb.	26.7	27.1	56.9	70.6	53.5	34.5	57.7	65.6	46.3	66.4	62.6	62.6	65.2	102	132
	v Mil. $	.427	.569	1.34	1.27	4.26	1.79	4.15	4.44	5.05	6.89	3.54	3.54	4.30	5.46	6.61
	p $ per lb.	.0160	.0210	.0235	.0180	.0797	.0518	.0721	.0677	.109	.104	.0565	.0565	.0660	.0537	.0502
Citric[e]	*q* Mil. lb.	3.89[e]	2.27	2.10	2.66	3.16	3.85	5.69	7.60	7.06	10.8	8.38	8.38	5.70	10.5	18.1
	v Mil. $	.335	.599	.777	1.52	3.05	1.91	2.83	3.47	3.15	4.83	3.06	3.06	1.80	2.77	4.12
	p $ per lb.	.0863	.264	.370	.571	.963	.497	.497	.457	.446	.449	.365	.365	.315	.264	.227

CHEMICALS, not elsewhere classified (continued)		1899	1904	1909	1914	1919	1921	1923	1925	1927	1929	1931		1933	1935	1937
Product	*Item*											*A*	*B*	*C*		
Acids (continued)																
Hydrochloric[f]	*q* Th. t.	18.6	27.8	32.4	27.2	47.8	30.6	49.6	49.4	51.8	62.6	40.7	40.7	44.9	54.9	71.2
	v Mil. $	1.02	1.61	1.76	1.35	4.31	2.78	3.10	2.98	3.02	3.20	2.42	2.42	2.39	3.05	3.99
	p $ per t.	54.7	58.0	54.3	49.5	90.2	90.7	62.5	60.3	58.3	51.0	59.5	59.5	53.2	55.5	56.0
Nitric[f]	*q* Th. t.	14.6	21.9	12.9	13.9	18.4	7.84	20.6	25.4	27.1	33.0	31.4	31.4	29.6	24.5	35.4
	v Mil. $	1.45	2.25	1.36	1.59	2.98	1.32	2.74	3.56	3.56	3.49	3.38	3.38	2.43	2.14	3.05
	p $ per t.	99.5	103	105	115	162	168	133	140	131	106	108	108	82.1	87.5	86.2
Oleic	*q* Mil. lb.			16.4	21.9	44.4	47.9	48.8	53.3	55.7	56.9	29.9	25.7	27.9	43.8	38.1
	v Mil. $			.845	1.30	6.55	3.34	4.35	5.17	4.78	5.37	1.87	1.60	1.39	3.27	3.60
	p $ per lb.			.0516	.0593	.148	.0697	.0892	.0971	.0858	.0944	.0625	.0624	.0500	.0748	.0946
Phosphoric[g]	*q* Mil. lb.		.991	26.3	12.4	13.4	6.20	12.8	21.3	22.4	34.7	19.1	19.1	24.7	45.4	78.3
	v Mil. $		.0685	.508	.680	1.71	.899	.955	1.49	1.68	2.07	.761	.761	.892	1.33	1.79
	p $ per lb.		.0692	.0193	.0548	.128	.145	.0745	.0698	.0751	.0598	.0399	.0399	.0362	.0294	.0228
Stearic	*q* Mil. lb.			11.9	14.4	17.0	14.3	22.5	26.9	37.3	39.2	24.9	23.4	23.9	27.4	31.9
	v Mil. $			.975	1.24	3.80	1.51	2.75	3.38	3.83	5.49	2.06	1.92	1.88	2.78	3.66
	p $ per lb.			.0817	.0866	.224	.106	.122	.126	.103	.140	.0827	.0819	.0787	.101	.115
Sulphuric[h]	*q* Mil. t.	.338	.673	1.10	1.86	2.21	2.00	3.30	3.28	3.27	4.14	2.84	2.84	2.64	3.07	3.92
	v Mil. $	3.16	6.16	7.84	12.8	24.6	21.6	30.6	27.6	29.7	32.7	24.0	24.0	18.9	22.8	30.2
	p $ per t.	9.34	9.16	7.09	6.89	11.1	10.8	9.26	8.42	9.09	7.91	8.45	8.45	7.18	7.42	7.70
Ammonia																
Ammonia, anhydrous	*q* Mil. lb.					25.7	21.1	23.5	31.7	45.1	173	127	127	150	139	223
	v Mil. $					7.07	5.71	6.41	6.77	4.01	10.7	8.04	8.04	5.93	5.68	8.87
	p $ per lb.					.275	.270	.273	.213	.0889	.0616	.0633	.0633	.0395	.0409	.0398
Ammonia, anhydrous, incl. product of the manufactured gas industry	*q* Mil. lb.	2.44	5.75	12.0	16.7	27.5										
	v Mil. $	.438	1.18	2.54	3.14	7.22										
	p $ per lb.	.179	.205	.213	.189	.262										

For footnotes see p. 493.

Indexes of Physical Output, with Basic Data on Quantity, Value and Price of Products

CHEMICALS, not elsewhere classified (continued)		1899	1904	1909	1914	1919	1921	1923	1925	1927	1929	1931		1933	1935	1937
Product	*Item*											*A*	*B*	*C*		
Sodium compounds																
Sodium bicarbonate, refined	*q* Th. t.	68.9	68.9	82.8	90.2	142	101	145	123	121	140	128	128	129	137	142
	v Mil. $	1.33	1.14	1.52	1.44	3.70	2.64	3.74	3.65	3.65	4.06	3.73	3.70	3.59	3.66	3.61
	p $ per t.	19.4	16.5	18.3	16.0	26.1	26.2	25.7	29.6	30.0	29.0	29.2	29.0	27.7	26.8	25.4
Sodium chromate and bichromate	*q* Th. t.				11.8	23.0	18.2	26.9	27.8	31.5	39.3	24.7	24.7	29.2	42.3	48.7
	v Mil. $				1.13	5.34	3.82	3.99	3.53	3.78	5.14	3.16	3.16	3.28	4.76	5.93
	p $ per t.				95.2	232	210	149	127	120	131	128	128	112	113	122
Sodium borate, (borax)	*q* Th. t.	5.64	20.9	20.2	26.5	29.6	18.5	53.1	50.0	64.9	92.2	80.0	80.0	93.8	106	126
	v Mil. $	.502	2.12	1.76	2.07	4.62	2.75	5.10	4.08	5.08	3.28	2.43	2.43	3.16	3.69	3.42
	p $ per t.	89.1	102	87.2	78.2	156	148	96.1	81.7	78.3	35.6	30.4	30.4	33.7	34.8	27.1
Caustic soda, (sodium hydroxide)	*q* Th. t.	167	86.8	132	213	302	231	431	487	547	725	634	634	645	720	897
	v Mil. $	3.17	3.19	5.26	6.66	18.7	16.6	25.1	27.4	29.2	36.1	26.6	26.6	24.5	28.1	32.0
	p $ per t.	19.0	36.7	40.0	31.3	61.9	72.0	58.1	56.2	53.3	49.8	41.9	41.9	38.0	39.1	35.7
Sodium silicate[i]	*q* Th. t.	32.7		34.2	169	287	222	331	395	505	590	664	638	630	608	641
	v Mil. $	.416		.367	1.65	6.05	4.64	5.07	5.72	6.83	7.18	7.50	7.41	6.58	7.67	8.35
	p $ per t.	12.7		10.7	9.75	21.1	21.0	15.3	14.5	13.5	12.2	11.3	11.6	10.4	12.6	13.0
Soda ash	*q* Mil. t.	.391	.519	.646	.935	1.03	.776	1.26	1.37	1.47	1.81	1.51	1.51	1.65	1.87	2.32
	v Mil. $	4.86	8.20	10.4	10.9	31.2	29.3	32.4	32.2	29.9	34.6	22.5	22.5	24.2	28.4	33.8
	p $ per t.	12.4	15.8	16.0	11.7	30.2	37.8	25.8	23.6	20.4	19.1	14.9	14.9	14.6	15.2	14.5
Sodium sulphate, salt cake	*q* Th. t.				90.4	123	96.0	141	141	175	170	98.7	98.7	115	170	241
	v Mil. $				.842	1.93	2.05	2.97	2.34	2.79	2.01	1.53	1.53	1.47	1.86	2.37
	p $ per t.				9.31	15.7	21.3	21.1	16.6	15.9	11.8	15.5	15.5	12.8	11.0	9.81
Sodium sulphate, niter cake	*q* Th. t.			27.5	24.1	81.2	49.0	129	102	121	82.7	30.7	30.7	17.0	18.8	23.0
	v Th. $			53.7	31.6	281	274	588	401	625	1023	564	564	353	344	522
	p $ per t.			1.95	1.31	3.47	5.60	4.54	3.94	5.19	12.4	18.4	18.4	20.7	18.3	22.7

CHEMICALS, not elsewhere classified (continued)		1899	1904	1909	1914	1919	1921	1923	1925	1927	1929	1931		1933	1935	1937
Product	*Item*											*A*	*B*	*C*		
Miscellaneous products																
Potassium bitartrate	*q* Mil. lb.	11.0	15.6	15.6	12.6	4.85	5.78	5.97	7.07	7.59	7.85	6.88	6.88	5.79	3.86	5.08
(cream of tartar)	*v* Mil. $	2.12	2.89	2.93	3.12	2.62	1.63	1.75	1.47	1.75	1.93	1.57	1.57	.891	.642	.884
	p $ per lb.	.193	.185	.188	.247	.540	.282	.292	.208	.230	.246	.228	.228	.154	.167	.174
Aluminous	*q* Th. t.					11.3	9.18	20.4	16.4	19.8	33.2	7.40	7.40	7.66		
abrasives	*v* Mil. $					2.03	.903	2.13	1.79	1.97	3.45	1.15	1.15	1.52		
	p $ per t.					180	98.3	104	109	99.6	104	156	156	199		
Aluminum	*q* Th. t.			77.7	92.5	313	155	234	284	314	345	309	309	322	348	393
sulphate, incl.	*v* Mil. $			1.31	1.73	15.7	5.76	6.52	7.40	8.01	8.04	6.67	6.67	6.60	7.75	8.96
concentrated alum	*p* $ per t.			16.9	18.7	50.1	37.1	27.8	26.0	25.5	23.3	21.6	21.6	20.5	22.3	22.8
Concentrated alum	*q* Th. t.	51.5	40.5	27.4												
	v Mil. $	1.06	.973	.469												
	p $ per t.	20.6	24.0	17.1												
Coal-tar dyes[j]	*q* Mil. lb.				6.62	63.4	39.0	93.7	86.3	95.2	111	83.5	83.5	101	102	122
	v Mil. $				2.47	67.6	32.3	51.1	40.8	37.3	48.2	37.8	37.8	44.3	53.6	66.9
	p $ per lb.				.373	1.07	.827	.546	.472	.392	.432	.453	.453	.439	.526	.547
Pyroxylin plastics	*q* Mil. lb.							24.0	13.7	16.3	17.0	12.0	12.0	10.1	13.3	14.9
	v Mil. $							17.7	13.7	14.4	17.3	11.1	11.1	7.80	10.7	12.5
	p $ per lb.							.737	1.00	.884	1.02	.926	.926	.773	.801	.843
Butyl acetate	*q* Mil. gal.							.0646	.870	2.34	4.52	4.66	4.64	3.76	5.63	9.32
	v Mil. $							.193	1.58	3.61	5.68	3.49	3.33	2.58	3.69	5.08
	p $ per gal.							2.99	1.81	1.54	1.26	.749	.718	.685	.655	.546
Carbon bisulphide	*q* Mil. lb.					11.6	14.9	25.2	39.9	45.0	71.0	83.0	83.0	90.2	118	155
	v Mil. $					.640	.796	1.34	1.94	2.16	2.86	3.20	3.20	3.28	3.38	4.75
	p $ per lb.					.0552	.0533	.0531	.0486	.0480	.0403	.0385	.0385	.0364	.0287	.0306
Calcium chloride[k]	*q* Th. t.				44.8	74.7	79.0	90.8	171	191	277	232	232	158	227	264
	v Mil. $				.342	1.04	2.03	2.04	3.72	4.44	5.95	4.73	4.73	2.72	3.63	4.18
	p $ per t.				7.65	14.0	25.7	22.5	21.8	23.2	21.5	20.4	20.4	17.2	16.0	15.9

For footnotes see p. 493.

Indexes of Physical Output, with Basic Data on Quantity, Value and Price of Products

CHEMICALS, not elsewhere classified (continued)		1899	1904	1909	1914	1919	1921	1923	1925	1927	1929	1931	1931	1933	1935	1937
Product	*Item*											*A*	*B*	*C*		
Miscellaneous products (continued)																
Calcium phosphate	*q* Th. t.				12.1	22.1	23.2	38.8	35.8	34.0	38.1	41.0	41.0	42.2	40.6	43.8
	v Mil. $				1.30	4.73	4.12	4.39	4.45	4.91	5.56	5.59	5.59	5.33	5.12	5.44
	p $ per t.				107	214	178	113	124	145	146	136	136	126	126	124
Carbon tetra-chloride	*q* Mil. lb.					9.81		11.7	16.1	17.0	32.7	34.1	34.1	30.3	52.0	78.7
	v Mil. $					.804		.957	.978	1.04	1.73	1.72	1.72	1.35	2.15	3.07
	p $ per lb.					.0819		.0814	.0609	.0609	.0528	.0504	.0504	.0446	.0414	.0390
Copper sulphate	*q* Mil. lb.			36.5	37.2	35.3	27.2	32.3	32.3	56.7	78.7	61.0	60.8	56.1	54.8	78.9
	v Mil. $			1.53	1.60	3.16	1.77	1.78	1.68	2.77	4.34	2.18	2.18	1.41	2.00	3.88
	p $ per lb.			.0419	.0430	.0897	.0649	.0550	.0521	.0490	.0552	.0358	.0358	.0251	.0366	.0492
Ether, ethyl	*q* Mil. lb.	.263	.854	1.17	2.12	4.13	3.42	4.94	5.39	6.13	6.46	6.98	6.98	7.42	7.92	13.1
	v Mil. $	.130	.427	.190	.279	1.13	.921	.620	1.46	1.72	1.90	1.47	1.47	1.38	1.31	1.65
	p $ per lb.	.493	.500	.163	.132	.272	.270	.126	.271	.280	.294	.211	.211	.187	.165	.126
Ethyl acetate	*q* Mil. gal.					.354	.520	2.53	2.91	4.61	10.9	5.46	4.50	5.08	5.56	6.95
	v Mil. $					.340	.318	2.19	2.41	3.70	9.01	2.45	2.06	2.66	2.68	2.92
	p $ per gal.					.959	.611	.867	.828	.803	.824	.449	.458	.523	.482	.420
Glycerin, refined	*q* Mil. lb.				59.8	67.3	59.9	74.1	94.3	89.6	113	103	102	108	119	122
	v Mil. $				10.8	20.7	9.51	12.2	17.0	19.2	12.7	10.3	10.2	7.92	13.0	21.3
	p $ per lb.				.180	.308	.159	.165	.180	.214	.112	.101	.101	.0734	.109	.174
Glycerin, crude and refined	*q* Mil. lb.	26.5	47.0	79.7	76.4	88.7										
	v Mil. $	3.10	5.36	11.8	13.1	23.7										
	p $ per lb.	.117	.114	.148	.171	.267										
Ferro-alloys, electric furnace	*q* Th. t.						48.5	215	150	197	247	146	146	136	243	395
	v Mil. $						8.84	20.9	15.3	17.0	28.7	13.2	13.2	11.9	23.5	45.3
	p $ per t.						182	97.0	102	86.4	116	90.5	90.5	87.6	96.8	115
Sulphur, refined	*q* Th. t.			25.3	31.2	52.1	29.4	61.4	47.2	43.5	78.1	66.9	66.9	48.7	47.5	
	v Mil. $			.892	1.14	2.71	1.60	2.77	2.12	1.80	3.07	2.07	2.07	1.74	1.65	
	p $ per t.			35.3	36.6	52.1	54.4	45.0	44.9	41.4	39.2	30.9	30.9	35.7	34.7	

CHEMICALS, not elsewhere classified (concluded)		1899	1904	1909	1914	1919	1921	1923	1925	1927	1929	1931		1933	1935	1937
Product	*Item*											*A*	*B*	*C*		
Miscellaneous Products (concluded)																
Vanillin	*q* Th. lb.				121	135	191	228	215	300	317	172	128	196	237	
	v Mil. $				.525	1.37	1.49	1.33	1.13	1.92	1.86	.776	.590	.777	.685	
	p $ per lb.				4.35	10.1	7.81	5.82	5.27	6.42	5.86	4.52	4.61	3.97	2.89	
Amyl acetate	*q* Th. gal.			239	180	96.1	65.4	250	137	219	181	477	473	608	1,030	1,522
	v Mil. $			.443	.466	.351	.150	.996	.415	.436	.313	.401	.392	.442	.789	1.19
	p $ per gal.			1.85	2.58	3.65	2.29	3.99	3.02	1.99	1.72	.842	.829	.726	.769	.781

A Comparable with all years except 1933. *B* Comparable with 1933. *C* Comparable with 1931.

[a] Percentages of coverage:

Given year	Base year	Given year	Base year
1927:47.0 / 1931:42.6	1929:44.8	1935:39.5	1929:44.3
		1937:36.9	1929:43.7
1933:44.4	1931:42.3		

[b] No adjusted indexes for 1899–1925 could be computed because the industry is not shown separately in the Census for those years. For adjusted indexes for 1899–1925 see chemicals, n.e.c., incl. gases, compressed, and rayon (below). The adjusted index given above, extrapolated by the unadjusted index, is 16.8 for 1899; 21.7 for 1904; 29.9 for 1909; 29.2 for 1914; 48.1 for 1919; 34.3 for 1921; 64.3 for 1923; 64.9 for 1925.

[c] In 1931 establishments making molded plastics were transferred from chemicals, n.e.c., to pulp goods. The resulting discontinuity appears to be slight.

[d] In 1935 establishments making ethyl alcohol were transferred from liquors, distilled, to chemicals, n.e.c. The resulting discontinuity appears to be slight.

[e] For 1935–37, basis is 100 percent; for earlier years, as reported regardless of strength. In 1899 includes lactic acid.

[f] Basis is 100 percent. Reported quantities were converted, where necessary, on the basis of the ratio of actual tons to 100 percent equivalents in 1929. The ratios are: hydrochloric acid: 3.14; nitric acid: 1.06.

[g] For 1935–37, basis is 50 percent H_3PO_4. For 1933 and 1929, basis is 50 percent, in part P_2O_5 and in part H_3PO_4.

[h] Data for sulphuric acid include only the amount made in chemicals, n.e.c. For 1914–31, the data are given by the Census. For the other years, both quantities and values have been estimated: for the years 1933–37 on the basis of the average ratio for 1925–31 of sulphuric acid made in the industry to the total, wherever made, and for 1899–1909 on the basis of the average ratio for 1914–23.

[i] Basis is 40° for 1921–37. For earlier years, basis is not specified.

[j] Sources of data for production in 1914–37 are U.S. Tariff Commission reports on *Dyes and Other Synthetic Organic Chemicals*. Values of output in 1914–19 are taken from the same sources. Values of output in 1921–37 are based on prices calculated from quantity of sales and their values as given in these sources.

[k] Data for calcium chloride made by establishments engaged primarily in production of salt were included in 1929 and 1933, but not in 1935 and 1937. Such production in 1935, reported by 8 establishments, amounted to 8.04 th. tons valued at 50.4 th. dollars. In 1937 4 establishments reported production of 7.30 th. tons, valued at 66.6 th. dollars.

Indexes of Physical Output, with Basic Data on Quantity, Value and Price of Products

CHEMICALS, n.e.c., incl. RAYON and COMPRESSED GASES

	1899	1904	1909	1914	1919	1921	1923	1925	1927	1929	1931	1933	1935	1937
Adjusted index[c]	6.6	8.3	12.5[d]	20.2[e]	36.3[f]	27.0	54.7	55.8[g]	70.2	100.0	92.0	101.5[h]	130.2	171.6
Unadjusted index[a,b]	13.0	17.4	23.9	26.7	47.8	35.3	55.0	59.0		100.0				

[a] Percentages of coverage:

Given year	Base year	Given year	Base year
1899:42.7	1909:41.2	1919:46.7	1929:35.4
1904:45.1	1909:41.3	1921:50.0	1929:38.3
1909:46.1	1919:31.8	1923:56.2 }	1929:55.9
1914:46.4	1919:46.1	1925:59.2 }	

[b] For the basic data, see the separate industries: chemicals, n.e.c.; gases, compressed; and rayon. Rayon was not used in the computation of the combined index for the period prior to 1923 because the unit value of rayon was not available for this period.

[c] For the years 1927–37, the adjusted index was computed from the three underlying adjusted indexes. In the earlier years the three underlying industries were treated as one and the usual procedure was therefore followed.

[d] Between 1909 and 1914 establishments making powdered milk and sugar of milk were transferred from chemicals, n.e.c. to milk, canned. The resulting discontinuity appears to be slight.

[e] Between 1914 and 1919 establishments making artificial dyestuffs and mineral colors and dyes were transferred from tanning and dye materials to chemicals, n.e.c.

[f] Between 1919 and 1921 certain establishments were transferred from secondary metals, nonprecious, to chemicals, n.e.c. The resulting discontinuity appears to be slight.

[g] Between 1925 and 1927 Pintch gas plants were transferred from gas, manufactured, to gases, compressed. The resulting discontinuity appears to be slight.

[h] Between 1933 and 1935 establishments making ethyl alcohol were transferred from liquors, distilled, to chemicals, n.e.c. The resulting discontinuity appears to be slight.

COTTONSEED PRODUCTS

		1899	1904	1909	1914	1919	1921	1923	1925	1927	1929	1931	1933	1935	1937
Adjusted index		50.7	73.6	73.3	133.8	111.0	80.2	69.6	107.9	121.1	100.0	86.1	94.2	65.8	82.8
Unadjusted index[a]		41.2	59.5	58.9	108.5	75.7	56.9	63.0	105.1	118.5	100.0	90.6	88.8	70.1	88.2
Product[b]	*Item*														
Cottonseed oil,	*q* Mil. lb.	700	1004	982	1719	1211	930	980	1617	1888	1604	1442	1446	1109	1364
crude	*v* Mil. $	21.4	31.3	55.2	80.5	210	71.5	88.1	139	142	134	91.6	47.2	91.8	123
	p $ per lb.	.0306	.0312	.0562	.0468	.173	.0769	.0899	.0857	.0753	.0835	.0636	.0327	.0829	.0903

COTTONSEED PRODUCTS (concluded)		1899	1904	1909	1914	1919	1921	1923	1925	1927	1929	1931	1933	1935	1937
Product[b]	*Item*														
Cottonseed cake and meal	*q* Mil. t.	.884	1.36	1.33	2.65	1.82	1.35	1.52	2.60	2.84	2.28	2.16	2.09	1.61	2.03
	v Mil. $	16.0	27.8	35.9	57.7	119	49.9	59.3	81.5	72.5	90.7	58.6	29.5	54.0	65.8
	p $ per t.	18.1	20.4	27.1	21.8	65.5	36.8	39.1	31.4	25.5	39.8	27.1	14.1	33.5	32.4
Cottonseed hulls	*q* Mil. t.	1.17	1.21	1.19	1.68	1.14	.937	.941	1.55	1.85	1.37	1.30	1.31	.913	1.14
	v Mil. $	3.19	5.59	9.81	8.45	11.1	8.95	12.7	12.6	8.88	12.8	10.5	4.68	10.3	10.5
	p $ per t.	2.73	4.61	8.25	5.04	9.71	9.55	13.5	8.17	4.79	9.39	8.04	3.57	11.2	9.15
Cotton linters	*q* Mil. bale	.115	.236	.297	.820	.584	.382	.640	1.04	1.04	1.09	.824	.741	.805	1.13
	v Mil. $	1.80	4.61	4.77	6.15	12.3	6.62	22.0	23.2	16.7	27.8	8.97	5.93	21.6	29.7
	p $ per bale	15.7	19.6	16.1	7.50	21.1	17.3	34.4	22.2	16.0	25.6	10.9	8.00	26.8	26.4

[a] Percentages of coverage:

Given year	Base year	Given year	Base year	Given year	Base year
1899:72.2	1909:71.5	1919:60.6	1929:88.9	1927:87.0	1929:88.9
1904:71.9		1921:63.1		1931:93.6	
1909:71.5	1919:60.6	1923:80.5		1933:83.8	
1914:72.1		1925:86.6		1935:94.6	
				1937:94.7	

[b] The data for 1899 and 1904 are taken from *Cotton Production and Distribution*, an annual publication of the U.S. Bureau of the Census. For the period 1899–1925 the data for the industry relate to the year ending July 31 of the year following the one specified. For the period 1927–37 the data relate to the year ending July 31 of the year indicated. However, the possibility exists that in some years some firms may have reported their value of products for the calendar year.

EXPLOSIVES		1899	1904	1909	1914	1919	1921	1923	1925	1927	1929	1931	1933	1935	1937
Adjusted index		25.3	44.8	61.6	70.4	93.6	60.6	94.3	92.4	95.5	100.0	66.8	57.6	68.1	92.8
Unadjusted index[a]		29.5	49.3	67.1	77.1	99.8	65.7	98.5	97.5	100.2	100.0	66.9	55.0	66.9	89.6
Product	*Item*														
Dynamite	*q* Mil. lb.	85.8	131	220	224	213	167	262	282	295	306	192	148	191	257
	v Mil. $	8.25	12.9	21.0	20.6	37.2	28.5	35.9	36.2	38.3	37.0	22.0	15.2	19.7	27.0
	p $ per lb.	.0961	.0985	.0954	.0919	.175	.170	.137	.128	.130	.121	.115	.103	.103	.105

For footnotes see p. 497.

Indexes of Physical Output, with Basic Data on Quantity, Value and Price of Products

EXPLOSIVES (concluded)		1899	1904	1909	1914	1919	1921	1923	1925	1927	1929	1931	1933	1935	1937
Product	*Item*														
Permissible explosives	*q* Mil. lb.			9.61	18.1	30.6	36.8	67.3	60.7	65.2	70.6	51.6	51.6	48.0	71.3
	v Mil. $			.863	1.60	5.50	6.38	9.39	7.94	8.41	8.38	5.82	4.15	4.99	7.47
	p $ per lb.			.0898	.0886	.180	.173	.139	.131	.129	.119	.113	.0806	.104	.105
Nitroglycerin, sold as such, and consumed in shooting wells on contract[b]	*q* Mil. lb.	3.62	7.94	3.92	3.79	8.34	3.60	2.70	3.06	2.85	3.45	.679	1.11	2.48	3.43
	v Mil. $	.783	1.62	.863	.951	3.74	3.40	2.16	2.28	2.17	2.45	.434	.451	.819	1.64
	p $ per lb.	.216	.204	.220	.251	.448	.943	.800	.744	.762	.709	.639	.406	.330	.477
Blasting powder and pellet powder	*q* Mil. lb.	*q* 123	205	233	207	185	184	211	161	137	121	78.4	66.2	66.6	65.6
	v Mil. $	*v* 5.31	7.38	9.61	8.46	12.2	12.5	13.5	9.68	8.69	7.75	4.91	4.06	4.22	4.15
	p $ per lb.	*p* .0431	.0359	.0412	.0408	.0657	.0684	.0640	.0602	.0635	.0642	.0626	.0613	.0634	.0632
Gun powder	*q* Mil. lb.		10.4	12.9	7.69	11.7	.991	2.78	1.18	1.54	1.08	.443			
	v Mil. $		1.54	1.74	.977	2.10	.227	.548	.238	.316	.231	.105			
	p $ per lb.		.148	.135	.127	.179	.230	.197	.202	.206	.214	.237			
Smokeless powder	*q* Mil. lb.						2.53	5.15	4.05	5.73	6.62	*q* 26.5	*q* 20.7	28.4	39.1
	v Mil. $						2.44	3.59	2.77	3.86	4.54	*v* 6.68	*v* 4.98	4.68	8.13
	p $ per lb.						.964	.698	.683	.674	.686	*p* .252	*p* .240	.165	.208
Other explosives	*q* Mil. lb.	*q* 3.20	6.30	7.46	21.1	57.7	11.5	23.4	36.1	39.2	19.0				
	v Mil. $	*v* 2.61	4.26	3.91	7.10	24.9	1.98	2.53	4.14	3.90	2.20				
	p $ per lb.	*p* .815	.675	.524	.337	.432	.172	.108	.115	.0995	.115				
Fuse powder	*q* Mil. lb.						1.13	2.72	2.84	2.71	2.27	1.42	.992	1.48	2.44
	v Mil. $						.335	.532	.609	.562	.427	.293	.186	.232	.438
	p $ per lb.						.295	.195	.215	.208	.188	.206	.188	.157	.180
Sulphuric acid, 50° Baumé[c]	*q* Th. t.				.133	42.0	28.9	39.0	47.8	32.3	45.3	24.3			
	v Th. $				1.71	537	337	380	414	267	438	193			
	p $ per t.				12.9	12.8	11.6	9.76	8.66	8.26	9.67	7.93			

[a] Percentages of coverage:

Given year	Base year	Given year	Base year	Given year	Base year
1899:99.0 / 1904:93.6	1909:92.5	1919:93.2 / 1921:94.8 / 1923:91.3 / 1925:92.2 / 1927:91.7	1929:87.4	1931:87.5	1929:87.4
1909:94.6	1919:92.6			1933:82.7 / 1935:85.2 / 1937:83.8	1929:86.8
1914:95.7	1919:93.2				

[b] Amount received for shooting wells is treated as value of nitroglycerin used for this purpose.

[c] Published in the Census report for chemicals, n.e.c.

FERTILIZERS		*1899*	*1904*	*1909*	*1914*	*1919*	*1921*	*1923*	*1925*	*1927*	*1929*	*1931*		*1933*	*1935*	*1937*
Adjusted index		30.4	37.4	59.9	88.5	80.4	59.6	76.3	86.9	89.5	100.0	78.0		60.5	77.5	105.9
Unadjusted index[a,b]		30.9	40.5	60.6	91.9	85.1	60.2	77.5	85.8	86.4	100.0	74.6		56.8	69.7	98.0
Product[c]	*Item*											*A*	*B*	*C*		
Complete fertilizers	*q* Mil. t.						2.99	4.03	4.93	5.09	5.99	4.54	4.46	3.27	4.20	5.68
	v Mil. $						113	118	143	128	169	110	108	61.2	93.1	129
	p $ per t.	*q* 1.62	2.39	3.52	5.61	4.76	37.8	29.4	29.1	25.2	28.2	24.2	24.2	18.7	22.2	22.7
		v 28.8	44.3	74.1	122	200										
Ammoniated fertilizers	*q* Mil. t.	*p* 17.7	18.6	21.0	21.7	42.1	.339	.190	.132	.0748						
	v Mil. $						10.1	5.68	3.28	1.93						
	p $ per t.						29.9	29.9	24.9	25.8	*q* .462	.208	.188	.222	.213	.272
											v 15.9	3.91	3.78	5.40	4.47	5.86
Other fertilizers	*q* Mil. t.								.165	.154	*p* 34.4	18.8	20.1	24.3	21.0	21.5
	v Mil. $								2.54	3.08						
	p $ per t.								15.5	20.0						
Bone meal	*q* Mil. t.	*q* .328	.420	.600	1.06	.965	.693	.869	.0483	.0420	.0395	.0518	.0180	.0205	.0563	.0849
	v Mil. $	*v* 4.72	4.78	9.52	15.4	34.4	18.4	19.9	1.62	1.60	1.54	1.52	.676	.480	1.41	1.92
	p $ per t.	*p* 14.4	11.4	15.9	14.6	35.6	26.5	22.9	33.6	38.1	39.0	29.3	37.6	23.4	25.1	22.6
Potash superphosphate	*q* Mil. t.								.248	.234	.211	.149	.145	.0869	.142	.226
	v Mil. $								6.16	5.46	4.85	3.00	2.91	1.38	2.68	4.46
	p $ per t.								24.9	23.4	23.0	20.1	20.1	15.9	18.9	19.8

For footnotes see next page.

Indexes of Physical Output, with Basic Data on Quantity, Value and Price of Products

FERTILIZERS (concluded)		1899	1904	1909	1914	1919	1921	1923	1925	1927	1929	1931		1933	1935	1937
Product[c]	*Item*											*A*	*B*	*C*		
Sulphuric acid, 50° Baumé[d]	*q* Mil. t.	.0712	.0245	.153	.129	.309	.176	.265	.663	.775	.629	.583				
	v Mil. $	.438	.195	.929	.769	3.64	1.87	2.01	4.81	6.16	4.98	3.87				
	p $ per t.	6.15	7.94	6.05	5.96	11.8	10.7	7.56	7.26	7.94	7.92	6.63				
Fish scrap	*q* Mil. t.			.0785	.0629	.0475	.0447	.0762	.0721	.0958	.0847	.0457	.0380	.0469	.114	.127
	v Mil. $			2.01	1.92	3.17	1.72	2.72	2.93	3.35	3.24	1.44	1.17	1.49	2.91	4.60
	p $ per t.			25.6	30.4	66.7	38.5	35.7	40.6	35.0	38.3	31.6	30.7	31.7	25.5	36.2
Superphosphates, not ammoniated (16% available phosphoric acid)	*q* Mil. t.	.937	.787	1.22	1.69	2.40										
	v Mil. $	8.59	7.82	13.7	14.8	46.2										
	p $ per t.	9.17	9.94	11.2	8.73	19.3										
Superphosphates and concentrated phosphates (combined)	*q*						1.98	2.46	2.64	2.43	2.53	1.97	1.96	1.55	1.75	3.11
	v						33.6	33.2	35.2	30.0	28.4	20.7	20.6	12.9	16.5	27.8
	p						17.0	13.5	13.3	12.3	11.2	10.5	10.5	8.33	9.40	8.95
Concentrated phosphates	*q* Mil. t.			.270	.0676	.120										
	v Mil. $			2.71	1.37	3.83										
	p $ per t.			10.0	20.2	32.0										

A Comparable with all years except 1933. *B* Comparable with 1933. *C* Comparable with 1931.

[a] Percentages of coverage:

Given year	Base year	Given year	Base year	Given year	Base year
1899: 95.2, 1904: 101.0	1909: 94.6	1919: 103.6, 1921: 98.9, 1923: 99.4, 1925: 96.7	1927: 94.5	1927: 94.5, 1931: 93.7	1929: 97.9
1909: 99.1, 1914: 101.8	1919: 103.6			1933: 87.2	1931: 88.9
				1935: 86.2, 1937: 88.6	1929: 95.8

[b] In 1919, 1921 and 1923 the figures for "other fertilizers," bone meal, and potash superphosphates are given in combination. In 1929, for the first time, "other fertilizers" is combined with ammoniated fertilizers; it is therefore impossible to obtain a 1929 combination comparable to the combination for 1919, 1921 and 1923. Consequently, the indexes for these years, and also for 1925, were computed on the 1927 base, and the 1927 index was computed on the 1929 base.

[c] The industry's index of physical output is affected by a certain amount of duplication arising from the sale of superphosphates and other (less important) products by establishments in the industry to other establishments in the industry. In 1937, 3.1 mil. tons of superphosphates were made for sale, and 1.3 mil. were purchased. Intra-industry sales give rise to an overstatement of the industry's net sales in 1937: of superphosphates, 70 percent; of total output, about 6 percent. Corresponding figures for 1899 are not very different; the trend indicated by the index is therefore not distorted seriously.

[d] Published in the Census report for chemicals, n.e.c.

GASES, COMPRESSED		1899	1904	1909	1914	1919	1921	1923	1925	1927	1929	1931	1933	1935	1937
Adjusted index									c	68.3	100.0	81.7	71.1	95.0	138.1
Unadjusted index[a]		b	b	3.3	9.3	33.6	31.5	52.9	55.3	69.1	100.0	77.0	70.8	99.1	143.3
Product	*Item*														
Acetylene	*q* Mil. cu.ft.				122	311	291	522	526	682	970	743	754	1143	1511
	v Mil. $				2.32	7.14	7.50	13.1	13.5	16.2	16.6	12.9	11.0	14.7	19.2
	p $ per cu.ft.				.0190	.0229	.0258	.0250	.0257	.0237	.0171	.0174	.0146	.0129	.0127
Carbon dioxide[d]	*q* Mil. lb.	12.1	36.0	48.0	50.4	59.8	54.6	51.1	59.7	74.3	137	154	117	87.7	101
	v Mil. $	.719	1.34	2.35	2.32	6.57	6.37	4.99	5.13	6.05	6.93	6.23	4.47	4.54	4.94
	p $ per lb.	.0595	.0373	.0489	.0460	.110	.117	.0977	.0859	.0814	.0506	.0405	.0381	.0518	.0490
Chlorine[e]	*q* Mil. t.				.0611	.0172	.0286	.0381	.0525	.0901	.145	.128	.125	.207	.286
	v Mil. $				.473	1.43	3.19	2.78	4.24	6.68	7.11	5.25	4.49	7.96	10.4
	p $ per t.				77.4	82.9	111	73.0	80.7	74.1	49.1	41.1	36.0	38.4	36.4
Oxygen	*q* Mil. cu.ft.			3.81	105	1173	1060	2058	2074	2360	3140	2050	1822	2684	4441
	v Mil. $			.177	1.83	16.6	14.0	23.4	22.6	24.0	23.4	16.4	13.0	18.1	26.1
	p ¢ per cu.ft.			4.65	1.75	1.41	1.32	1.14	1.09	1.02	.746	.800	.713	.675	.587

[a] Percentages of coverage:

Given year	Base year	Given year	Base year
1927: 104.7 1931: 97.6 1933: 103.1	1929: 103.5	1935: 108.0 1937: 107.4	1929: 103.5

[b] Because of the small coverage in 1899 and 1904, no index is given.

[c] No adjusted indexes for 1909–1925 could be computed because the industry is not shown separately in the Census for those years. Adjusted indexes were computed for chemicals, n.e.c., including gases, compressed, and rayon. The adjusted index given above, extrapolated by the unadjusted index, is 3.3 for 1909; 9.2 for 1914; 33.2 for 1919; 31.1 for 1921; 52.3 for 1923; 54.7 for 1925.

[d] Excludes dry ice but includes carbon dioxide piped to plants making dry ice. Quantities thus piped, as estimated by the Census, are (in mil. lb.): 80.0 for 1931; 64.5 for 1933; 25.3 for 1935; 17.0 for 1937.

[e] Production for sale. Does not include chlorine made and consumed in the wood-pulp industry.

Indexes of Physical Output, with Basic Data on Quantity, Value and Price of Products

GLUE and GELATIN		*1927*	*1929*	*1931*	*1933*[b]	*1935*	*1937*
Adjusted index		95.8	100.0	85.2		110.2	138.7
Unadjusted index[a]		94.1	100.0	85.6		99.0	128.6
Product	*Item*						
Glue							
Animal	*q* Mil. lb.	112	106	89.4		90.3	121
	v Mil. $	15.5	15.1	13.4		9.22	17.4
	p $ per lb.	.138	.142	.150		.102	.144
Vegetable	*q* Mil. lb.	97.1	133	103		127	230
	v Mil. $	4.97	6.14	4.07		5.20	8.62
	p $ per lb.	.0512	.0461	.0397		.0410	.0375
Casein	*q* Mil. lb.		6.76[c]	4.79[c]		5.87	7.98
	v Mil. $		.876[c]	.468[c]		.668	1.07
	p $ per lb.		.130	.0978		.114	.134
Flexible and fish	*q* Mil. lb.	7.49	10.3	10.2		13.8	15.9
	v Mil. $	2.31	2.43	2.06		2.16	2.41
	p $ per lb.	.309	.236	.201		.156	.152
Gelatin							
Edible	*q* Mil. lb.	17.6	18.4	15.2		20.9	22.0
	v Mil. $	6.46	7.51	5.98		6.91	7.79
	p $ per lb.	.367	.408	.393		.331	.354
Inedible	*q* Mil. lb.	2.03	1.71	3.15		2.92	
	v Mil. $	.689	.543	1.83		1.28	
	p $ per lb.	.339	.317	.582		.439	

[a] Percentages of coverage:

Given year	Base year	Given year	Base year
1927: 96.1	1929: 97.9	1935: 90.4	1929: 100.6
1931: 101.0	1929: 100.6	1937: 91.7	1929: 98.9

[b] Detailed data on products were not collected in 1933.

[c] Revised by the Bureau of the Census, partly on the basis of estimates.

LINSEED PRODUCTS		1923	1925	1927	1929	1931	1933[b]	1935	1937
Adjusted index		83.4	100.0	94.6	100.0	66.8		63.4	86.0
Unadjusted index[a]		84.3	97.1	96.8	100.0	69.7		64.4	83.5
Product	*Item*								
Linseed oil	*q* Mil. lb.	635	715	724	742	509		483	638
	v Mil. $	76.8	94.0	73.6	66.7	43.5		43.3	59.8
	p $ per lb.	.121	.132	.102	.0900	.0855		.0896	.0938
Linseed cake and meal	*q* Th. t.	613	744	716	752	542		471	588
	v Mil. $	29.3	32.4	32.2	36.3	17.3		13.4	21.4
	p $ per t.	47.7	43.5	44.9	48.3	31.9		28.4	36.4

[a] Percentages of coverage:

Given year	Base year	Given year	Base year
1923:93.6 1925:90.0 1927:94.8	1929:92.6	1931:96.7 1935:94.0 1937:89.9	1929:92.6

[b] Detailed data on products were not collected in 1933.

PAINTS and VARNISHES		1899	1904	1909	1914	1919	1921	1923	1925	1927	1929	1931		1933	1935	1937
Adjusted index		22.2	27.9	37.5	41.2	52.2	45.2	67.0	75.8	87.0	100.0	68.9		62.5	87.4	109.0
Unadjusted index[a]		28.3	32.5	41.5	45.1	58.5	47.2	71.8	77.8	87.5	100.0	70.5		64.6	87.2	109.5
Product[b]	*Item*											*A*	*B*	*C*		
Pigments																
White lead, dry	*q* Mil. lb.	123	62.4	85.3	71.6	80.5	124	140	143	143	150	125	125	102	118	144
	v Mil. $	4.50	2.88	3.92	3.70	6.32	9.07	12.3	14.2	12.0	12.3	6.90	6.90	4.92	5.87	9.45
	p ¢ per lb.	3.66	4.61	4.60	5.16	7.85	7.33	8.80	9.92	8.38	8.18	5.51	5.51	4.84	4.99	6.55
Lead oxides	*q* Mil. lb.	62.4	63.5	65.8	58.6	162	130	214	249	232	262	165	165	165	218	256
	v Mil. $	2.86	3.51	3.80	3.28	12.7	9.32	20.6	27.3	20.0	21.5	9.03	9.03	8.41	11.7	18.9
	p ¢ per lb.	4.59	5.53	5.78	5.60	7.85	7.19	9.63	11.0	8.63	8.20	5.48	5.48	5.10	5.38	7.37

For footnotes see p. 505.

Indexes of Physical Output, with Basic Data on Quantity, Value and Price of Products

PAINTS and VARNISHES (continued)		1899	1904	1909	1914	1919	1921	1923	1925	1927	1929	1931	1931	1933	1935	1937
Product[b]	*Item*											*A*	*B*	*C*		
Pigments (continued)																
Zinc oxide	*q* Mil. lb.					279	117	323	319	348	437	240	240	247	256	322
	v Mil. $					24.1	9.03	23.5	22.7	22.3	26.9	14.3	14.3	12.1	13.1	15.3
	p ¢ per lb.					8.62	7.71	7.28	7.14	6.40	6.17	5.97	5.97	4.92	5.11	4.76
Iron oxides	*q* Mil. lb.	34.9	48.8	213	92.9	202	85.1	127	88.8	108	106	64.2	60.6	62.0	112	129
	v Mil. $	.368	.337	1.09	.798	3.78	1.95	3.13	2.38	3.36	3.37	1.94	1.83	2.07	3.08	4.07
	p ¢ per lb.	1.05	.689	.509	.859	1.87	2.29	2.47	2.69	3.10	3.20	3.03	3.02	3.34	2.74	3.16
Lithopone	*q* Mil. lb.				49.0	151	96.4	211	246	360	411	307	307	273	323	325
	v Mil. $				1.86	9.76	6.12	13.0	12.2	17.2	19.3	12.9	12.9	11.7	14.3	13.8
	p ¢ per lb.				3.79	6.45	6.35	6.18	4.95	4.77	4.69	4.20	4.20	4.28	4.43	4.23
Chrome yellow, orange and green	*q* Mil. lb.				13.8	9.49	13.4	26.3	28.7	33.1	42.7	38.8	38.8	37.4	42.6[c]	42.1[c]
	v Mil. $				1.32	2.08	2.58	4.67	4.99	5.56	6.45	5.85	5.85	5.73	4.70	6.25
	p ¢ per lb.				9.58	21.9	19.2	17.7	17.4	16.8	15.1	15.1	15.1	15.3	11.0	14.8
Other dry colors[d]	*q* Mil. lb.	159[e]	143[e]	164[e]	143[f]	78.3[g]	108[h]	90.1	157	202	211	160				
	v Mil. $	4.08	5.18	6.52	3.94	5.98	5.08	5.13	8.54	13.3	14.7	10.7				
	p ¢ per lb.	2.56	3.63	3.98	2.77	7.65	4.69	5.70	5.44	6.62	6.96	6.65				
Mortar colors	*q* Mil. lb.								62.6	62.2	41.5	15.4			*q* 283[i]	492[i]
	v Mil. $								1.09	1.10	.781	.264			*v* 26.3	38.7
	p ¢ per lb.								1.73	1.77	1.88	1.72	*q* 318	305	*p* 9.29	7.87
													v 11.8	11.0		
Other mineral colors	*q* Mil. lb.					38.3	51.8	145	41.1	29.2	17.3	2.81	*p* 3.72	3.62		
	v Mil. $					1.18	.710	2.35	.858	.344	.254	.0413				
	p ¢ per lb.					3.07	1.37	1.62	2.09	1.18	1.47	1.47				
Whiting	*q* Mil. lb.								236	221	202	152			126	124
	v Mil. $								1.98	1.67	1.51	1.07			.833	.867
	p ¢ per lb.								.837	.755	.749	.702			.663	.699

PAINTS and VARNISHES (continued)		1899	1904	1909	1914	1919	1921	1923	1925	1927	1929	1931		1933	1935	1937
Product[b]	*Item*											*A*	*B*	*C*		
Pigments (concluded)																
Pulp colors, sold moist	*q* Mil. lb.	20.1	25.5	28.6	22.1	30.1	9.52	18.8	16.2	14.4	15.6	10.5	10.1	7.59	7.82	
	v Mil. $	.862	.931	1.29	1.05	3.26	.973	1.24	1.38	1.30	1.39	1.03	1.01	.717	.807	j
	p ¢ per lb.	4.29	3.65	4.53	4.77	10.8	10.2	6.63	8.53	9.04	8.90	9.83	10.0	9.45	10.3	
Paints																
Water paints and calcimine, dry or paste	*q* Mil. lb.	14.4	28.5	47.5	61.9	107	87.7	122	111	122	156	123	117	100	125	151
	v Mil. $	.744	.937	1.92	2.06	4.55	4.40	5.53	4.64	6.32	7.09	5.27	5.02	3.95	5.30	7.62
	p ¢ per lb.	5.16	3.29	4.04	3.32	4.26	5.01	4.53	4.19	5.16	4.55	4.29	4.27	3.93	4.23	5.05
Paints in paste form	*q* Mil. lb.	310	364	412	420	398	428	426	435	409	402	243	236	184	257	270
	v Mil. $	17.9	20.7	26.7	29.0	49.2	46.6	50.6	55.7	49.6	46.7	26.2	25.4	16.9	23.3	28.5
	p ¢ per lb.	5.76	5.69	6.48	6.91	12.3	10.9	11.9	12.8	12.1	11.6	10.8	10.8	9.19	9.06	10.6
Paints, mixed, ready for use	*q* Mil. gal.	17.4	22.8	34.8	41.0	60.0	48.1	71.4	87.6	94.1	106	78.2	74.6	63.8	87.6	106
	v Mil. $	15.3	20.8	30.8	41.7	120	91.2	127	158	166	178	121	116	90.3	126	159
	p $ per gal.	.878	.913	.884	1.02	2.00	1.89	1.78	1.81	1.76	1.68	1.55	1.55	1.41	1.44	1.50
Varnishes, japans, and lacquers, incl. enamels																
Oleoresinous varnishes	*q* Mil. gal.	14.8	17.3	18.7	17.8	28.1	22.2	40.4	38.4	33.9	38.8	27.1	26.0	24.7	30.4	37.3
	v Mil. $	14.5	15.7	17.6	18.8	40.0	29.0	52.3	48.4	43.6	47.7	29.9	28.9	25.6	32.1	42.3
	p $ per gal.	.981	.906	.939	1.05	1.42	1.31	1.29	1.26	1.29	1.23	1.10	1.11	1.04	1.06	1.13
Spirit varnishes, not turpentine	*q* Mil. gal.	.553	1.54	1.27	2.96	2.97	3.08	5.61	7.12	6.82	7.38	5.89	5.53	5.09	7.92	8.45
	v Mil. $	.921	2.20	1.50	3.08	8.11	7.26	10.6	13.4	12.4	13.5	7.42	6.90	5.06	8.67	8.76
	p $ per gal.	1.66	1.43	1.18	1.04	2.73	2.35	1.89	1.88	1.83	1.83	1.26	1.25	.994	1.10	1.04
Other varnishes	*q* Mil. gal.			3.48	3.30	6.36	4.29	3.86	4.05	8.94	8.48	5.40	5.13	4.69	9.20	15.7
	v Mil. $			2.84	2.87	10.3	6.17	6.14	5.97	12.8	10.6	5.99	5.72	4.70	9.21	13.7
	p $ per gal.			.815	.869	1.62	1.44	1.59	1.47	1.43	1.25	1.11	1.11	1.00	1.00	.875

For footnotes see p. 505.

Indexes of Physical Output, with Basic Data on Quantity, Value and Price of Products

PAINTS and VARNISHES (continued)		1899	1904	1909	1914	1919	1921	1923	1925	1927	1929	1931	1933		1935	1937
Product[b]	Item											A	B	C		
Pyroxylin products																
Clear lacquers	q Mil. gal.									7.74	9.94	8.10	7.87	6.95	9.33	14.6
	v Mil. $									15.7	19.2	12.8	12.5	9.64	12.9	22.5
	p $ per gal.	q .171	.453	1.89	.853	.500	1.41	3.26		2.03	1.93	1.59	1.59	1.39	1.38	1.54
		v .188	.556	2.36	1.31	.923	3.09	6.94								
Lacquer enamels	q Mil. gal.	p 1.10	1.23	1.25	1.54	1.85	2.20	2.13	q 12.3	10.8	15.2	8.71	8.49	7.42	11.8	14.0
	v Mil. $								v 27.3	30.2	38.6	20.7	20.3	15.5	25.4	28.4
	p $ per gal.								p 2.22	2.81	2.54	2.38	2.39	2.09	2.16	2.02
Thinners for pyroxylin lacquers	q Mil. gal.									12.3	17.9	12.7			18.6	24.1
	v Mil. $									14.4	19.2	11.3			12.9	15.6
	p $ per gal.									1.16	1.07	.887			.692	.647
Drying japans and driers	q Mil. gal.	6.56	4.36	6.64	7.61	6.35	4.53	7.51	5.76	6.56	5.19	2.48	2.37	2.11	1.85	3.52
	v Mil. $	3.09	3.35	3.17	3.27	6.07	3.75	6.81	4.56	4.96	4.06	2.05	1.97	1.64	1.71	2.95
	p $ per gal.	.470	.769	.477	.430	.956	.828	.906	.792	.756	.782	.824	.832	.781	.921	.837
Baking japans	q Mil. gal.			2.98	4.89	5.38	3.46	6.47	6.06	4.99	4.04	2.39	2.31	2.23	3.52	3.27
	v Mil. $			2.08	2.96	5.88	4.25	6.20	4.77	4.45	3.48	1.82	1.75	1.57	2.15	2.51
	p $ per gal.			.697	.606	1.09	1.23	.958	.787	.893	.862	.760	.755	.704	.611	.768
Enamels, oil and varnish base	q Mil. gal.						6.38	13.4	15.0	14.5	20.0	15.5	15.1	17.9	31.5	42.4
	v Mil. $						14.8	27.5	32.2	32.1	40.2	29.8	29.1	32.8	55.1	75.3
	p $ per gal.						2.31	2.06	2.14	2.22	2.01	1.93	1.93	1.83	1.75	1.78
Fillers																
Liquid	q Mil. gal.	.124	1.06	1.17	.966	2.61	.984	.846	.722	.566	.495	.204			.293	.252
	v Mil. $	.113	.787	.828	.670	1.84	1.05	.940	.922	.722	.683	.236			.343	.236
	p $ per gal.	.914	.742	.710	.694	.705	1.07	1.11	1.28	1.28	1.38	1.15			1.17	.937
Paste and dry	q Mil. lb.			65.1	49.6	17.0	21.5	34.5	42.0	41.5	30.6	19.5			17.2	30.5
	v Mil. $			1.20	1.32	1.55	1.60	2.04	2.30	2.11	1.95	.975			.816	1.87
	p ¢ per lb.			1.84	2.66	9.14	7.43	5.91	5.49	5.08	6.38	5.00			4.75	6.15
Putty	q Mil. lb.	17.3	43.9	67.8	69.8	66.7	65.9	92.7	101	103	99.2	69.9	56.3	47.4	71.8	90.5
	v Mil. $	.238	.728	1.17	1.25	3.16	2.64	3.77	3.93	4.26	4.25	2.99	2.43	1.74	2.87	3.68
	p ¢ per lb.	1.38	1.66	1.73	1.79	4.75	4.01	4.07	3.88	4.14	4.29	4.28	4.32	3.67	4.00	4.07

PAINTS and VARNISHES (concluded)		1899	1904	1909	1914	1919	1921	1923	1925	1927	1929	1931		1933	1935	1937
Product[b]	*Item*											*A*	*B*	*C*		
Bleached shellac	*q* Mil. lb.			3.91	8.65	8.80	8.80	15.3	11.1	10.6	11.1	10.7	10.7	11.2	12.5	14.6
	v Mil. $			.772	1.81	5.96	5.37	9.57	5.99	5.01	5.43	2.62	2.62	1.88	2.42	2.66
	p ¢ per lb.			19.8	20.9	67.7	61.0	62.6	53.8	47.3	48.8	24.4	24.4	16.8	19.4	18.2
Stains																
Varnish	*q* Mil. gal.									2.41	2.16	1.73	1.66	1.95	1.76	2.16
	v Mil. $									4.71	4.38	2.54	2.46	2.44	2.93	3.57
	p $ per gal.									1.95	2.03	1.47	1.48	1.25	1.66	1.65
Other than varnish	*q* Mil. gal.								3.32	3.83	3.53	3.04			3.08	3.88
	v Mil. $								4.68	4.77	4.54	3.96			3.31	4.15
	p $ per gal.								1.41	1.24	1.28	1.30			1.08	1.07

A Comparable with all years except 1933. *B* Comparable with 1933. *C* Comparable with 1931.

[a] Percentages of coverage:

Given year	Base year	Given year	Base year	Given year	Base year
1899:94.4, 1904:86.5	1909:82.1	1919: 96.0	1929:85.7	1927: 98.6, 1931:100.3	1929:98.1
1909:87.6	1919:88.8	1921: 97.0, 1923: 99.5	1929:92.8	1933: 93.5	1931:92.6
1914:86.5	1919:88.6	1925:100.0	1929:97.3	1935: 97.8, 1937: 98.6	1929:98.1

[b] Duplication arises in the industry's output because some of the dry colors and pigments sold by some establishments in the industry are purchased by other establishments in the industry for use in paint manufacture. The value of all colors and pigments sold in 1937 was 16 percent of the total value of output of the industry, but the amount of duplication was less than 16 percent since some colors were sold to other industries (wall paper, ink, etc.). There does not appear to have been any serious change in the degree of duplication.

[c] Includes reduced chrome green in 1935 and 1937.

[d] Includes barytes, and, from 1899 through 1919, coal-tar color lakes. The resulting incomparability is probably negligible.

[e] Includes also lithopone, chrome yellow, orange and green, prussian blue, and ultramarine. The 1919 figures corresponding to these totals (except that they exclude ultramarine) are: *q* 240 mil. lb.; *v* $18.5 mil.; *p* 7.70¢ per lb.

[f] Includes lampblack and other carbon blacks made by paint and varnish establishments.

[g] Includes a small amount of carbon black.

[h] Includes a small amount of lampblack.

[i] Includes all color-pigments not included in any other group (with the exception of other fine colors and coal-tar color lakes). The corresponding 1929 figures are: *q* 270 mil. lb.; *v* $15.7 mil.; *p* 5.83¢ per lb.

[j] Pulp colors, sold moist, are distributed among other items in 1937. The resulting incomparability is insignificant.

Indexes of Physical Output, with Basic Data on Quantity, Value and Price of Products

RAYON		1914	1919	1921	1923	1925	1927	1929	1931	1933	1935	1937
Adjusted index				b	28.3	40.3	60.5	100.0	138.3	201.2	253.3	310.4
Unadjusted index[a]		2.0	6.8	12.3	28.8	42.1	62.2	100.0	124.3	175.9	212.2	265.0
Product[c]	*Item*											
Rayon, yarns	*q* Mil. lb.	2.42	8.28	15.0	35.0	51.0	75.6	121	151	213	258	322
	v Mil. $				56.6	86.6	106	147	112	129	146	205
	p $ per lb.				1.62	1.70	1.41	1.21	.744	.605	.567	.637

[a] Percentages of coverage:

Given year	Base year	Given year	Base year
1923:95.8 1925:98.3 1927:96.9 1931:84.7	1929:94.2	1933:82.3 1935:78.9 1937:80.4	1929:94.2

We obtained these percentages by dividing the derived values (see footnote c) by the total value of products as reported in the Census, and multiplying by 100. The total value of products for 1929 we adjusted to represent production rather than sales by multiplying by the ratio of rayon yarn production (Textile Economics Bureau) to rayon yarn sales (Census).

[b] For adjusted indexes prior to 1923 see chemicals, n.e.c., including gases, compressed, and rayon. The adjusted index given above, extrapolated by the unadjusted index, is 2.0 for 1914; 6.7 for 1919; 12.1 for 1921.

[c] The sources of the data on quantities are the Census for 1927 and 1931–37 and the Textile Economics Bureau, Inc., *Rayon Organon*, for other years. The data relate to production of rayon filament yarn and rayon staple fiber exclusively and take no account of waste and other minor primary rayon items. The data on unit values were derived from the Census; these are not available for years prior to 1923. The data on values were derived by multiplication of the quantities by the unit values.

SALT	1899	1904	1909	1914	1919	1921	1923	1925	1927	1929	1931	1933	1935	1937
Adjusted index		b	67.4	72.2	88.2	70.7	86.6	87.7	91.7	100.0	91.1	84.2	86.8	96.9
Unadjusted index[a]	54.4	57.8	68.8	72.5	88.2	72.5	90.6	92.8	91.8	100.0	86.5	89.7	88.4	99.0

SALT (concluded)		1899	1904	1909	1914	1919	1921	1923	1925	1927	1929	1931	1933	1935	1937
Product[c]	*Item*[d]														
Salt, by method of manufacture															
Evaporated, in open pans or grainers	*q* Mil. t.						.693	.769	.735	.704	.771	.589	.573	.466	.493
	v Mil. $						7.15	7.43	6.69	6.15	6.60	4.54	4.63	3.74	4.09
	p $ per t.						10.3	9.67	9.10	8.74	8.55	7.71	8.08	8.02	8.29
Evaporated, in vacuum pans	*q* Mil. t.						.916	1.04	1.04	1.10	1.20	1.16	1.31	1.39	1.60
	v Mil. $						7.39	8.30	8.04	7.87	8.41	7.50	8.12	8.84	9.42
	p $ per t.	*q* 1.92	1.91	2.16	2.16	2.39	8.07	8.02	7.71	7.18	7.00	6.48	6.20	6.35	5.88
		v		6.62	7.58	19.4									
Solar evaporated	*q* Mil. t.	*p*		3.07	3.51	8.12	.224	.308	.321	.312	.401	.326	.322	.347	.363
	v Mil. $						1.20	1.39	1.25	1.31	1.52	1.15	1.18	1.30	1.34
	p $ per t.						5.34	4.51	3.90	4.20	3.78	3.52	3.65	3.74	3.70
Pressed blocks from evaporated salt	*q* Mil. t.						.0976	.128	.135	.150	.172	.130	.153	.126	.120
	v Mil. $						1.11	1.26	1.07	1.25	1.39	.984	1.13	.900	.967
	p $ per t.						11.3	9.86	7.90	8.33	8.09	7.57	7.40	7.14	8.05
Rock	*q* Mil. t.						1.45	2.07	2.31	2.11	2.07	1.82	1.75	1.73	2.00
	v Mil. $						6.52	7.56	7.24	6.15	6.80	5.54	5.40	5.35	6.21
	p $ per t.	*q* .356	.612	.831	1.06	1.64	4.49	3.66	3.14	2.91	3.28	3.05	3.08	3.09	3.10
		v		1.29	2.02	6.22									
Pressed blocks from rock salt	*q* Mil. t.	*p*		1.55	1.91	3.80	.0201	.0380	.0357	.0344	.0409	.0345	.0305	.0247	.0290
	v Mil. $						.169	.281	.207	.230	.331	.193	.169	.156	.240
	p $ per t.						8.40	7.39	5.79	6.68	8.10	5.60	5.53	6.32	8.29
Salt in brine (sold or used as such)	*q* Mil. t.	.488	.561	1.23	1.65	2.85	1.58	2.79	2.82	3.16	3.88	3.30	3.46	3.84	4.63
	v Mil. $			.439	.590	1.42	1.02	1.57	1.67	1.85	2.29	1.63	1.68	1.55	1.86
	p $ per t.			.357	.357	.499	.645	.562	.591	.587	.588	.494	.486	.405	.402

[a] Percentages of coverage:

Given year	Base year	Given year	Base year	Given year	Base year
1909:73.7 1914:72.5	1919:72.2	1919:72.2 1921:74.1 1923:75.5 1925:76.4	1929:72.2	1927:72.3 1931:68.5 1933:76.9 1935:73.5 1937:73.7	1929:72.2

[b] Values are not available for 1899 and 1904. For this reason, 1909 prices were used to compute the unadjusted index numbers for 1899 and 1904. For the same reason no adjusted indexes could be computed. The adjusted index given above, extrapolated by the unadjusted index, is 53.3 for 1899; 56.6 for 1904.

[c] The data are those compiled by the Bureau of Mines and published in *Minerals Yearbook*.

[d] Statistics on quantity for 1899–1909 were quoted in barrels of 280 pounds each, and converted to short tons.

Indexes of Physical Output, with Basic Data on Quantity, Value and Price of Products

SOAP		1904	1909	1914	1919	1921	1923	1925	1927	1929	1931		1933	1935	1937
Adjusted index		45.7	61.4	70.4	89.4	79.0	86.6	86.3	93.1	100.0	98.0		97.6	100.1	109.0
Unadjusted index[a]		46.0	59.6	68.4	76.5	75.6	81.7	85.8	92.1	100.0	97.6		96.0	103.2	109.2
Product	*Item*										*A*	*B*	*C*		
Hard soaps															
Toilet soap	*q* Mil. lb.						240	272	288[b]	324	306	299	315	353	361
	v Mil. $						53.1	49.4	53.6	60.0	53.1	52.2	44.1	53.3	62.8
	p $ per lb.						.221	.181	.186	.185	.174	.174	.140	.151	.174
Foots soap	*q* Mil. lb.						25.2	13.1	15.8	21.8	20.0	4.10	3.02		
	v Mil. $						1.83	1.16	1.37	1.92	1.21	.227	.172		
	p $ per lb.						.0728	.0890	.0867	.0878	.0606	.0553	.0570		
Soap chips	*q* Mil. lb.				*q* 1836	1752	219	325	373	388	351	327	399	459	390
	v Mil. $				*v* 203	164	25.4	36.3	39.4	41.8	30.4	28.7	24.9	36.3	38.0
	p $ per lb.				*p* .111	.0936	.116	.112	.106	.108	.0865	.0877	.0624	.0792	.0973
Laundry soap, white and yellow	*q* Mil. lb.	*q* 1387	1794	2064				1431	1486	1465	1431	1404	1258	1134	1122
	v Mil. $	*v* 58.0	91.1	104				97.1	91.7	91.9	68.4	66.9	44.5	51.3	61.4
	p $ per lb.	*p*.0418	.0508	.0506			*q* 1516	.0678	.0617	.0628	.0478	.0477	.0354	.0453	.0547
							v 99.6								
Other hard soaps	*q* Mil. lb.						*p*.0657	67.9	56.1	51.3	43.3	25.2	17.4		
	v Mil. $							7.47	5.37	4.24	3.19	1.91	.894		
	p $ per lb.							.110	.0957	.0826	.0738	.0757	.0513		
Granulated and powdered soap	*q* Mil. lb.							142	216	337	422	404	370	503	743
	v Mil. $							15.8	21.0	35.7	41.0	39.5	31.4	45.3	68.4
	p $ per lb.				*q* 473	580	655	.111	.0973	.106	.0971	.0977	.0850	.0900	.0920
					v 24.2	29.4	39.8								
Soap powders, cleansing powders, washing powders	*q* Mil. lb.				*p*.0512	.0507	.0608	548	484	506	427	396	366	453	411
	v Mil. $							25.9	24.0	23.4	18.4	16.9	12.3	15.4	16.3
	p $ per lb.							.0472	.0496	.0463	.0432	.0427	.0336	.0341	.0396

SOAP (concluded)		1904	1909	1914	1919	1921	1923	1925	1927	1929	1931		1933	1935	1937
Product	*Item*										*A*	*B*	*C*		
Soft soap	*q* Mil. lb.	43.9	60.0	57.0	64.5	63.3	67.8	61.2	79.8	66.1	42.3				
	v Mil. $	.761	1.27	1.70	3.93	2.72	2.47	2.51	4.23	3.95	2.25				
	p $ per lb.	.0173	.0211	.0298	.0609	.0430	.0364	.0411	.0530	.0597	.0531				
Liquid soap	*q* Mil. lb.				10.0	10.5	17.9	22.0	24.9	35.3	33.6			29.3[c]	29.9
	v Mil. $				1.26	1.27	1.67	2.12	3.24	3.50	2.42			1.97	2.44
	p $ per lb.				.125	.120	.0932	.0963	.130	.0992	.0720			.0674	.0815

A Comparable with all years except 1933. *B* Comparable with 1933. *C* Comparable with 1931.

[a] Percentages of coverage:

Given year	Base year
1904:86.1	1909:82.9
1909:82.9, 1914:83.0	1919:73.0
1919:73.4, 1921:82.2, 1923:81.0	1929:85.9
1925:85.4, 1927:85.0, 1931:85.5	1929:85.9
1933:79.1	1931:80.1
1935:85.2, 1937:82.8	1929:82.6

[b] Data for shaving soap (but not for shaving cream or shaving powder) are included in the figures for 1927 and earlier years and excluded from those for 1929.

[c] Estimated in part.

TANNING and DYE MATERIALS		1899	1904	1909	1914	1919	1921	1923	1925	1927	1929	1931		1933	1935	1937
Adjusted index		25.9	37.6	53.7	79.2[c]	81.7	68.8	95.2	87.2	88.2	100.0	77.7		73.6	100.4	101.4
Unadjusted index[a]		23.9	37.5	49.2	65.5	96.4	74.6	107.2	92.9	89.9	100.0	78.1		69.3	76.7	88.8
Product	*Item*											*A*	*B*	*C*		
Tanning materials, extracts																
Oak, liquid and solid	*q* Mil. lb.[d]						11.0	11.7	8.66	9.48	7.83	5.12	4.50	4.95	11.1	12.7
	v Mil. $						.428	.454	.288	.358	.295	.167	.139	.124	.270	.346
	p $ per lb.						.0390	.0388	.0332	.0378	.0377	.0327	.0309	.0251	.0244	.0273
Oak and chestnut combined	*q*	29.0	157	267	328	508										
	v	.530	2.41	4.32	4.13	18.7										
	p	.0183	.0154	.0162	.0126	.0367										
Chestnut, liquid and solid	*q* Mil. lb.[d]						250	434	294	310	270	229	229	236	303	364
	v Mil. $						5.93	8.41	5.07	5.31	4.00	3.64	3.64	3.52	4.59	4.97
	p $ per lb.						.0237	.0194	.0172	.0172	.0148	.0159	.0159	.0149	.0152	.0137

For footnotes see p. 512.

Indexes of Physical Output, with Basic Data on Quantity, Value and Price of Products

TANNING and DYE MATERIALS (continued)		1899	1904	1909	1914	1919	1921	1923	1925	1927	1929	1931		1933	1935	1937
Product	*Item*											*A*	*B*	*C*		
Tanning materials, extracts (concluded)																
Sumac, liquid and solid[b]	*q* Mil. lb.[d]	4.35	4.09	3.15	4.51	4.51	5.03	6.11	4.21	5.52	5.28	5.81	5.81	6.45	3.55	3.36
	v Mil. $	.103	.0960	.107	.130	.253	.346	.309	.261	.277	.344	.370	.370	.301	.204	.169
	p $ per lb.	.0237	.0234	.0341	.0287	.0562	.0687	.0506	.0621	.0501	.0651	.0636	.0636	.0467	.0574	.0504
Quebracho, liquid	*q* Mil. lb.[d]						65.6	104	82.4	125	100	76.5	75.7	33.7	81.2	
	v Mil. $						2.45	3.35	2.40	3.01	3.23	1.86	1.83	.763	1.40	
	p $ per lb.						.0373	.0322	.0291	.0242	.0323	.0243	.0242	.0226	.0173	
Hemlock, liquid and solid[e]	*q* Mil. lb.[d]	26.0	18.8	12.6	19.0	19.7	9.39	9.32	8.62	6.60						7.71
	v Mil. $	.564	.407	.280	.340	.879	.347	.287	.284	.210						.195
	p $ per lb.	.0217	.0216	.0223	.0179	.0446	.0369	.0308	.0329	.0318						.0253
Natural dyes, dyewood extracts																
Logwood, liquid and solid	*q* Mil. lb.	39.3	29.8	22.3	29.0	32.8	22.9	26.2	13.7	18.2	19.3	17.0	17.0	10.8	8.71	8.22
	v Mil. $	1.49	1.47	.992	1.31	3.29	2.55	1.97	1.20	1.47	1.84	1.25	1.25	.870	.744	.832
	p $ per lb.	.0379	.0494	.0444	.0453	.101	.111	.0755	.0880	.0808	.0953	.0734	.0734	.0804	.0855	.101
Fustic, liquid and solid	*q* Mil. lb.				4.51	3.84	4.48	4.02	3.60	2.78	2.63				1.36	1.22
	v Mil. $				.223	.355	.490	.324	.294	.219	.254				.100	.107
	p $ per lb.				.0494	.0924	.109	.0804	.0815	.0788	.0964				.0738	.0874
Quercitron	*q* Mil. lb.				3.84	6.75	2.19	5.67	4.17	4.07	2.42	1.44	1.44	1.45		
	v Mil. $				.113	.303	.134	.323	.251	.212	.172	.0632	.0632	.0680		
	p $ per lb.				.0294	.0450	.0611	.0569	.0602	.0520	.0710	.0439	.0439	.0468		
Mordants																
Tannic acid	*q* Mil. lb.[f]				.760	.666	.718	.970	1.44	1.30	1.45	.667	.667	.682	.725	1.02
	v Mil. $				.235	.528	.287	.357	.586	.593	.504	.251	.251	.236	.305	.382
	p $ per lb.				.309	.794	.400	.368	.407	.457	.347	.376	.376	.346	.421	.376

TANNING and DYE MATERIALS (continued)		1899	1904	1909	1914	1919	1921	1923	1925	1927	1929	1931 A	1931 B	1933 C	1935	1937
Product	*Item*															
Assistants																
Turkey red oil	*q* Mil. lb.	2.21	3.02	1.81	11.7	2.48	10.4	23.7	14.3	15.6	24.3	13.6	13.0	17.6		
	v Mil. $	.0148	.160	.108	.820	.319	.995	2.31	1.55	1.56	2.54	1.29	1.24	1.73		
	p $ per lb.	.00668	.0528	.0597	.0702	.129	.0956	.0973	.108	.100	.105	.0953	.0952	.0982		
Softeners	*q* Mil. lb.						19.0	29.6	25.3	23.3	31.6	33.1	26.5	23.0		
	v Mil. $						1.32	2.20	2.01	1.80	2.25	1.97	1.64	1.27		
	p $ per lb.						.0695	.0744	.0793	.0770	.0711	.0596	.0618	.0554		
Softeners, incl. soluble oils and greases	*q* Mil. lb.														52.0[g]	63.5
	v Mil. $														4.60	5.22
	p $ per lb.														.0886	.0823
Sulphonated oils and fats																
Castor	*q* Mil. lb.														18.4	25.7
	v Mil. $														1.79	2.48
	p $ per lb.														.0974	.0967
Olive	*q* Mil. lb.														8.11	5.06
	v Mil. $														1.10	.635
	p $ per lb.														.135	.125
Cod	*q* Mil. lb.														7.61	9.67
	v Mil. $														.491	.661
	p $ per lb.														.0645	.0683
Tallow	*q* Mil. lb.														8.73	17.0
	v Mil. $														.554	.992
	p $ per lb.														.0635	.0583

For footnotes see p. 512.

Indexes of Physical Output, with Basic Data on Quantity, Value and Price of Products

TANNING and DYE MATERIALS (concluded)		1899	1904	1909	1914	1919	1921	1923	1925	1927	1929	1931		1933	1935	1937
Product	*Item*											*A*	*B*	*C*		
Sizes																
Dextrins	*q* Mil. lb.				18.9	49.3	31.0	57.6	56.4	31.9	33.5	25.2	25.1	24.2	29.5	26.9
	v Mil. $				.706	3.79	1.64	3.29	3.34	2.09	2.04	1.51	1.44	1.45	1.59	1.60
	p $ per lb.		*q* 6.65	16.1	.0373	.0769	.0531	.0571	.0592	.0656	.0610	.0601	.0575	.0599	.0539	.0593
			v .232	.611												
Gums, other than rosin	*q* Mil. lb.		*p* .0348	.0378	3.83	8.68	13.2	12.7	44.4	16.0	20.1	22.3			4.57[g]	8.98
	v Mil. $				.205	.635	.745	.843	2.28	.920	1.40	1.21			.583	.656
	p $ per lb.				.0536	.0731	.0566	.0663	.0514	.0573	.0696	.0542			.127	.0730
Rosin	*q* Mil. lb.				20.7	57.1	60.0	104	147	158	201	144	*q* 191	169[h]		
	v Mil. $				.373	2.89	1.61	2.77	5.50	5.87	6.11	2.90	*v* 6.21	4.78		
	p $ per lb.				.0180	.0506	.0268	.0267	.0374	.0372	.0303	.0202	*p* .0325	.0283	*q* 185[g]	198
															v 5.44	8.16
Starches, glue, and other sizes	*q* Mil. lb.						52.7	45.3	28.4	31.0	42.4	29.6			*p* .0294	.0413
	v Mil. $						3.09	2.18	1.59	2.41	3.61	2.42				
	p $ per lb.						.0587	.0482	.0560	.0776	.0853	.0820				

A Comparable with all years except 1933. *B* Comparable with 1933. *C* Comparable with 1931.

[a] Percentages of coverage:

Given year	Base year	Given year	Base year	Given year	Base year
1899:36.7	1909:36.4	1919:57.7	1929:49.0	1931:71.5	1929:71.1
1904:43.9	1909:40.2	1921:77.8	1929:71.8	1933:64.0	1931:68.3
1909:40.2	1919:51.8	1923:80.9		1935:45.3	1929:59.3
1914:41.6	1919:59.4	1925:76.5		1937:76.2	1935:66.5
		1927:73.1			

[b] No solid sumac was reported, 1925–33.

[c] Between 1914 and 1919 artificial dyestuffs and mineral colors and dyes were transferred from tanning and dye materials to chemicals, n.e.c.

[d] For 1935 and 1937, basis is 25 percent tannin; for 1933 and earlier years, not reported according to strength.

[e] The figures for 1921–37 were not used in the computation of the indexes for these years because no comparable figures are available for the base year, 1929.

[f] For 1935 and 1937, basis is 100 percent; for 1933 and earlier years, not reported according to strength.

[g] Estimated in part.

WOOD-DISTILLATION PRODUCTS		1899	1904	1909	1914	1919	1921	1923	1925	1927	1929	1931	1933[b]	1935	1937
Adjusted index		28.2	40.2	54.1	57.9	74.6	30.9	80.2	85.3	91.7	100.0	55.9		72.7	101.3
Unadjusted index[a]		39.0	61.6	72.6	70.1	81.3	34.3	86.6	89.1	95.6	100.0	53.7		72.4	99.1
Product	*Item*														
Methanol (wood alcohol), crude	*q* Mil. gal.[c]	4.95	6.81	6.77	7.20	6.98	3.29	7.04	5.85	5.73	5.10	2.10		1.95	1.17
	v Mil. $	1.98	2.20	1.77	1.61	5.59	1.11	4.11	2.03	2.07	1.79	.288		.316	.185
	p $ per gal.	.400	.323	.262	.223	.801	.338	.584	.346	.361	.352	.137		.162	.158
Methanol (wood alcohol), refined	*q* Mil. gal.[d]	3.04	5.92	6.73	6.24	6.98	2.72	5.04	5.87	5.00	6.68	2.74		3.65	3.97
	v Mil. $	2.30	3.46	3.10	2.71	8.38	1.92	4.82	3.39	2.95	3.91	.885		1.15	1.13
	p $ per gal.	.756	.584	.460	.435	1.20	.709	.957	.577	.590	.585	.323		.315	.286
Acetate of lime	*q* Mil. t.[e]	.0434	.0552	.0707	.0818	.0770	.0277	.0723	.0727	.0690	.0582	.0258		.0259	.0225
	v Mil. $	.981	1.53	2.12	2.14	2.68	.737	4.76	3.44	4.02	4.70	.870		.826	.721
	p $ per t.	22.6	27.7	29.9	26.2	34.9	26.6	65.9	47.3	58.3	80.7	33.7		31.9	32.0
Turpentine	*q* Mil. gal.		.442	.707	.576	1.53	.442	2.61	3.17	4.33	4.62	3.15		4.61	8.72
	v Mil. $		.177	.250	.194	1.21	.233	2.01	2.08	1.67	1.71	1.03		1.85	2.25
	p $ per gal.		.399	.353	.337	.787	.528	.773	.657	.386	.371	.327		.402	.258
Tar	*q* Mil. gal.			1.57	1.48	2.14	1.44	3.14	5.52	4.58	6.90	1.86		3.37	8.14
	v Mil. $			.113	.146	.482	.198	.461	.840	.798	.879	.225		.599	.894
	p $ per gal.			.0721	.0988	.225	.137	.147	.152	.174	.127	.121		.178	.110
Charcoal, hardwood and softwood distillation	*q* Mil. bu.	17.2	29.9	40.0	44.8	48.0	19.9	45.1	42.4	40.8	44.5	22.4		25.2	26.8
	v Mil. $	.727	1.49	2.43	2.83	8.22	4.05	8.60	5.60	5.98	5.31	3.07		2.95	3.70
	p $ per bu.	.0424	.0497	.0607	.0631	.171	.204	.191	.132	.147	.119	.137		.117	.138
Rosin	*q* Mil. bbl.				.0290	.131	.0293	.201	.287	.452	.479	.334		.529	.800
	v Mil. $				.198	2.74	.199	1.37	3.38	5.23	5.44	1.90		4.17	10.4
	p $ per bbl.				6.83	20.9	6.79	6.81	11.8	11.6	11.4	5.71		7.89	13.0
Methyl acetone	*q* Mil. lb.					.930	.587	6.37	3.64	2.60	4.68	1.93			
	v Mil. $					.134	.0590	.879	.458	.353	.575	.126			
	p $ per lb.					.144	.100	.138	.126	.136	.123	.0653			

For footnotes see next page.

Indexes of Physical Output, with Basic Data on Quantity, Value and Price of Products

WOOD-DISTILLATION PRODUCTS (concluded)		1899	1904	1909	1914	1919	1921	1923	1925	1927	1929	1931	1933[b]	1935	1937
Product	*Item*														
Tar oils	*q* Mil. gal.					.803	.401	1.19	1.43	1.56	.997	.859		1.09	1.02
	v Mil. $					.241	.0924	.217	.329	.323	.201	.119		.194	.209
	p $ per gal.					.300	.230	.182	.231	.207	.201	.139		.179	.206
Pine oil	*q* Mil. gal.							1.26	2.03	2.89	2.72	2.15		3.44	4.54
	v Mil. $							.587	.827	1.25	1.27	1.01		1.53	2.40
	p $ per gal.							.465	.407	.432	.467	.472		.443	.528
Pitch	*q* Mil. lb.								26.4	19.6	8.59	10.9			
	v Mil. $								.328	.376	.102	.0942			
	p $ per lb.								.0124	.0192	.0119	.00867			

[a] Percentages of coverage:

Given year	Base year	Given year	Base year	Given year	Base year
1899: 99.7	1909:96.7	1919:91.2	1929:83.6 (1919, 1921)	1927:92.0	1929:88.3 (1927, 1931)
1904:113.2	1909:99.3	1921:92.9		1931:84.8	
1909:100.4	1919:81.6	1923:95.0	1929:88.0	1935:85.7	1929:86.0 (1935, 1937)
1914:100.0	1919:90.1	1925:92.2	1929:88.3	1937:84.1	

[b] Detailed data on products were not collected in 1933.

[c] Strength, 82 percent; not reported before 1935.

[d] Strength, 100 percent; not reported before 1935.

[e] Strength, 80 percent; not reported before 1935.

TOTAL CHEMICAL PRODUCTS	1899	1904	1909	1914	1919	1921	1923	1925	1927	1929	1931	1933	1935	1937
Adjusted index	18.6	22.6	31.4	42.5	51.5	42.0	64.5	69.6	82.9	100.0	87.0	83.8	100.7	123.9
Unadjusted index[a]	16.9	19.8	30.4	42.1	54.3	41.6	65.6	70.4	81.8	100.0	84.6	86.7	105.5	134.6

[a] Percentages of coverage:

Given year	Base year	Given year	Base year	Given year	Base year	Given year	Base year
1899:48.9	1909:52.1	1919:68.3	1929:64.7	1927:65.7	1929:66.6 (1927, 1931)	1935:69.8	1929:66.6 (1935, 1937)
1904:56.3	1909:62.3	1921:64.2	1929:64.8	1931:64.8		1937:72.4	
1909:62.3	1919:67.8	1923:67.0	1929:65.8 (1923, 1925)	1933:66.1	1929:63.9		
1914:64.0	1919:68.1	1925:66.5					

PETROLEUM AND COAL PRODUCTS

COKE-OVEN PRODUCTS		1899	1904	1909	1914	1919[d] A	1919[d] B	1921	1923	1925	1927	1929	1931	1933	1935	1937
Adjusted index		18.2	22.8	38.3	37.7	61.4		43.3	89.4	80.9	83.6	100.0	55.0	43.1	58.1	87.3
Unadjusted index[a]		19.5	24.9	41.8	41.7	63.3		40.6	85.8	82.8	85.6	100.0	57.2	45.7	60.8	89.1
Product[b,c]	*Item*					*A*	*B*									
Coke																
Made in bee-hive ovens	q Mil. t.	q 19.6	22.7	33.1	23.3	19.0	19.0	5.54	19.4	11.4	7.21	6.47	1.13	.877	.917	3.16
	v Mil. $	v 34.6	43.3	69.5	50.3	98.1	98.1	30.9	116	51.7	30.3	22.6	3.52	2.53	3.58	13.6
	p $ per t.	p 1.76	1.91	2.10	2.15	5.15	5.15	5.58	5.98	4.56	4.20	3.49	3.12	2.89	3.91	4.31
Made in by-product ovens	q Mil. t.		2.47	6.25	11.2	25.1	23.9	19.0	36.6	38.8	41.9	50.2	28.8	23.6	31.0	45.7
	v Mil. $		6.96	20.4	38.1	160	151	111	248	202	217	234	135	102	153	224
	p $ per t.		2.82	3.27	3.39	6.37	6.32	5.85	6.76	5.21	5.17	4.66	4.67	4.33	4.93	4.90
Screenings and breeze	q Mil. t.							.212	.734	.907	.752	.945	.644	.618	.684	.686
	v Mil. $							.499	2.86	3.20	2.11	2.62	1.59	1.19	1.40	1.55
	p $ per t.							2.36	3.90	3.53	2.81	2.77	2.46	1.92	2.04	2.25
By-products																
Gas	q Bil. cu.ft.	1.17	4.46	15.8	61.4	193	183	136	277	325	356	441	260	200	275	377
	v Mil. $	.225	.844	2.61	6.01	16.6	10.5	19.8	42.7	49.1	53.7	61.1	45.3	34.8	42.8	52.7
	p $ per th. cu.ft.	.192	.189	.165	.0979	.0863	.0574	.145	.154	.151	.151	.138	.174	.174	.155	.140
Tar	q Mil. gal.	10.5	26.2	60.1	110	218	205	128	201	226	278	291	222	195	263	341
	v Mil. $	.208	.613	1.41	2.87	6.92	6.43	5.27	8.68	11.1	14.6	14.7	9.98	7.15	10.8	16.4
	p $ per gal.	.0199	.0234	.0234	.0261	.0318	.0313	.0410	.0432	.0492	.0523	.0504	.0449	.0367	.0409	.0480
Ammonia liquor (NH_3 content)	q Mil. lb.						45.1	30.0	51.0[e]	47.1	49.0	51.8	34.0	36.2	38.8	48.0
	v Mil. $						5.11	3.05	5.14	4.39	2.34	2.69	1.39	1.09	1.16	1.48
	p $ per lb.						.113	.102	.101	.0931	.0476	.0519	.0409	.0300	.0299	.0309
Ammonium sulphate	q Mil. lb.	12.0	31.5	123[f]	171	557	551	530	885	986	1,226	1,350	905	590	895	1,246
	v Mil. $	.331	.818	3.23	4.70	21.1	20.8	13.1	26.0	22.5	23.9	24.2	11.5	5.36	8.52	13.5
	p $ per th. lb.	27.6	25.9	26.2	27.5	37.8	37.8	24.7	29.3	22.8	19.5	17.9	12.7	9.08	9.51	10.9

For footnotes see next page.

Indexes of Physical Output, with Basic Data on Quantity, Value and Price of Products

COKE-OVEN PRODUCTS (concluded)		1899	1904	1909	1914	1919[d] A	1919[d] B	1921	1923	1925	1927	1929	1931	1933	1935	1937
Product[b,c]	*Item*					*A*	*B*									
By-products (concluded)																
Crude light oil	*q* Mil. gal.							2.26	6.23	9.72	8.26	10.3	5.72	4.70	9.22	8.32
	v Mil. $							.214	.642	1.00	.955	1.27	.479	.450	.779	.708
	p $ per gal.							.0944	.103	.103	.116	.124	.0836	.0957	.0844	.0850
Light-oil derivatives	*q* Mil. gal.						66.6	59.7	102	113	124	150	95.1	73.4	103	150
	v Mil. $						12.3	11.1	18.1	20.4	23.9	29.3	13.5	11.5	13.6	19.1
	p $ per gal.						.184	.187	.177	.182	.193	.196	.142	.156	.131	.127

A Comparable with earlier years. *B* Comparable with later years.

[a] Percentages of coverage:

Given year	Base year	Given year	Base year	Given year	Base year
1899: 99.5	1909:101.6	1921:88.3	1929:94.3	1931: 98.0	1929:94.3
1904:101.6		1923:90.5		1933:100.2	
1909:101.6	1919: 95.7	1925:96.5		1935: 98.6	
1914:102.6		1927:96.5		1937: 96.3	
1919: 96.2	1929: 93.4				

[b] The data relate to coke and by-products made in all industries except the illuminating gas industry. The data for the years 1933, 1935 and 1937 are taken from the Bureau of Mines, *Minerals Yearbook;* the 1919 data comparable with those for later years are taken from the Bureau of Mines, *Mineral Resources, 1925.*

[c] For coke the data relate to production; for screenings and breeze and all by-products they relate to sales.

[d] Because of a change in the classification of a number of establishments producing by-product coke, it was necessary to introduce an additional set of data for 1919. Coke and its by-products made in city-owned gas plants were included in coke-oven products in the first set of 1919 figures and in earlier years, and in the illuminating gas industry in the second set of 1919 figures and in later years.

[e] Includes data for an unknown quantity of sulphate sold on the basis of NH_3 content.

[f] Includes data for an unknown quantity of ammonia liquor.

FUEL BRIQUETTES		1909	1914	1919	1921	1923	1925	1927	1929	1931	1933	1935	1937
Adjusted index		7.9	15.5	21.0	28.8	54.5	58.6	72.3	100.0	50.1	36.9	63.8	79.0
Unadjusted index[a]		11.5	20.7	24.4	32.9	57.5	69.2	80.0	100.0	57.6	43.8	71.0	82.1
Product[b]	*Item*												
Fuel briquettes	*q* Mil. t.	.140	.251	.296	.399	.697	.839	.970	1.21	.698	.530	.861	.996
	v Mil. $	.453	1.15	2.30	3.63	5.90	7.13	7.99	9.52	5.26	3.50	5.48	6.39
	p $ per t.	3.24	4.61	7.78	9.10	8.47	8.49	8.23	7.85	7.53	6.60	6.36	6.42

[a] Percentages of coverage:

Given year	Base year	Given year	Base year
1909:145.6	1919:116.6	1925:118.4	1929:100.2
1914:133.8	1919:116.6	1927:110.8	1929:100.2
1919:116.6	1929:100.2	1931:115.2	1929:100.2
1921:114.3	1929:100.2	1933:118.8	1929:100.2
1923:105.6	1929:100.2	1935:111.5	1929:100.2
		1937:104.2	1929:100.2

[b] The data are those collected by the Bureau of Mines, and relate to fuel briquettes, wherever made.

PETROLEUM REFINING		1899	1904	1909	1914	1919	1921	1923	1925	1927	1929	1931	1933	1935	1937
Adjusted index		5.9	7.2	11.0	17.0	34.0	40.3	55.7	72.8	81.2	100.0	90.7	86.3	99.1	119.2
Unadjusted index[a]		6.0	6.9	10.7	16.8	33.7	39.6	54.8	72.4	81.0	100.0	89.9	84.2	97.4	117.6
Product	*Item*														
Light products of distillation[b]	*q* Bil. gal.	.281	.291	.540	1.46	4.11	5.35	7.80	11.3	13.4	18.4	17.6	16.4	18.8	22.9
	v Mil. $	16.0	21.3	39.8	122	755	878	924	1265	1102	1610	854	775	1041	1470
	p $ per th. gal.	57.0	73.4	73.6	83.5	184	164	119	112	82.3	87.5	48.5	47.2	55.3	64.0
Illuminating oils	*q* Bil. gal.	1.26	1.36	1.67	1.94	2.31	1.94	2.24	2.37	2.22	2.34	1.75	1.95	2.19	2.51
	v Mil. $	74.7	91.4	94.5	96.8	236	152	147	162	148	165	72.7	78.1	94.2	124
	p $ per th. gal.	59.3	67.3	56.5	50.0	102.	78.2	65.6	68.4	66.7	70.5	41.7	40.1	42.9	49.3
Fuel oils, total	*q* Bil. gal.	.305	.360	1.70	3.73	7.77	9.75	12.0	14.6	15.4	16.4	14.2	13.3	15.9	19.2
	v Mil. $	7.55	9.21	36.5	84.0	318	377	346	489	457	385	272	253	359	513
	p $ per th. gal.	24.8	25.5	21.4	22.5	41.0	38.7	28.9	33.5	29.6	23.5	19.1	19.0	22.6	26.7

For footnotes see p. 519.

Indexes of Physical Output, with Basic Data on Quantity, Value and Price of Products

PETROLEUM REFINING (continued)			1899	1904	1909	1914	1919	1921	1923	1925	1927	1929	1931	1933	1935	1937
Product	*Item*															
Partially refined oils, sold for rerunning	*q* Bil. gal.						.428	.394	1.30	1.50	1.58	1.47	1.31	1.13	1.04	1.15
	v Mil. $						29.3	24.2	55.0	65.3	62.2	49.1	28.5	23.7	31.7	38.7
	p $ per th. gal.						68.3	61.3	42.3	43.6	39.3	33.5	21.7	21.0	30.4	33.7
Lubricating oils	*q* Mil. gal.		170	315	537	518	822	949	1151	1361	1382	1554	1148	1047	1274	1517
	v Mil. $		10.9	23.6	38.9	55.8	196	195	204	252	245	305	197	142	187	246
	p $ per th. gal.		63.9	74.8	72.4	108	239	205	178	185	177	196	172	136	146	162
Liquid asphaltic road oils	*q* Mil. gal.						98.0	168	199	274	205	323	378	300	407	481
	v Mil. $						4.49	7.83	7.86	12.5	9.31	11.0	10.4	8.34	13.3	16.4
	p $ per th. gal.	*q*	29.8	159	89.4	135	45.8	46.5	39.5	45.6	45.4	34.2	27.6	27.8	32.8	34.1
		v	.688	3.14	2.22	4.02										
Residuum or tar	*q* Mil. gal.	*p*	23.1	19.7	24.8	29.8	29.2	40.1	80.1	125	118	104	67.5	65.0	88.5	20.4
	v Mil. $						1.52	1.83	3.19	5.58	5.12	3.15	1.66	1.27	1.70	.853
	p $ per th. gal.						52.2	45.7	39.9	44.6	43.2	30.2	24.7	19.6	19.2	41.8
Petrolatum, mineral jelly, etc.	*q* Mil. gal.					6.08	10.2	9.03	12.9	13.9	15.3	13.7	17.0	14.7	18.3	23.1
	v Mil. $					1.24	3.75	2.55	2.79	3.56	2.97	2.55	2.22	1.85	2.61	3.93
	p $ per gal.	*q*	28.6	10.1	6.92	.205	.367	.283	.216	.257	.194	.186	.131	.126	.142	.170
		v	2.45	1.39	1.57											
Lubricating greases, incl. axle grease[c]	*q* Mil. gal.	*p*	.0858	.138	.227	7.93	17.9	15.4	22.1	32.0	29.6	38.4	28.9	27.2	31.6	38.8
	v Mil. $					2.29	8.15	7.20	8.00	10.4	9.99	14.1	10.2	7.40	10.1	13.3
	p $ per gal.					.289	.455	.467	.362	.324	.338	.368	.352	.272	.321	.342
Paraffin wax	*q* Mil. gal.		38.7	39.7	47.3	57.5	68.0	58.4	69.5	89.8	94.3	84.6	79.5	72.9	76.5	90.6
	v Mil. $		7.79	10.0	9.39	8.90	28.3	11.8	12.9	30.6	23.4	22.3	13.4	12.2	14.4	19.2
	p $ per gal.		.201	.252	.198	.155	.417	.201	.186	.341	.249	.264	.168	.168	.189	.212
Acid oil	*q* Mil. gal.						45.6	65.4	67.4	59.6	90.6	34.8	84.6	85.6	94.3	57.6
	v Mil. $						.993	1.48	1.47	1.14	1.85	.663	1.12	1.01	1.22	1.02
	p $ per gal.						.0218	.0226	.0218	.0191	.0204	.0191	.0132	.0118	.0129	.0176

PETROLEUM REFINING (concluded)

Product	Item	1899	1904	1909	1914	1919	1921	1923	1925	1927	1929	1931	1933	1935	1937
Asphalt, other than liquid asphalt	*q* Mil. t.			.233	.465	.927	1.17	2.13	2.28	2.64	3.12	2.46	1.79	2.15	2.97
	v Mil. $			2.72	4.87	12.5	16.6	23.3	30.5	37.9	34.5	21.8	17.9	23.2	31.4
	p $ per t.			11.7	10.5	13.5	14.2	10.9	13.4	14.3	11.1	8.83	10.0	10.8	10.6
Petroleum coke	*q* Mil. t.				.214	.798	.531	.647	.924	1.24	1.26	2.03	1.75	1.44	1.33
	v Mil. $				.819	3.93	3.72	4.80	6.44	7.17	5.46	7.18	5.58	5.76	5.05
	p $ per t.				3.83	4.92	6.99	7.41	6.97	5.77	4.32	3.54	3.19	3.99	3.80

[a] Percentages of coverage:

Given year	Base year	Given year	Base year	Given year	Base year
1899:96.9	1909:94.0	1919:97.9	1929:98.8	1927:98.6	1929:98.8
1904:91.6	1909:94.2	1921:97.1		1931:97.9	
1909:95.3	1919:96.5	1923:97.0		1933:96.4	
1914:96.2	1919:96.7	1925:98.2		1935:97.1	
				1937:97.4	

[b] Includes gasoline, naphtha, benzine, tops (except in 1937) and, prior to 1919, other light products of distillation. In 1919, other light products of distillation amounted to 97.3 mil. gallons, valued at 11.0 mil. dollars. The 1937 quantity data are not shown completely in the final 1937 Census report; they are taken from the 1937 preliminary Census release on this industry.

[c] Production in petroleum refineries only.

TOTAL PETROLEUM and COAL PRODUCTS

	1899	1904	1909	1914	1919	1921	1923	1925	1927	1929	1931	1933	1935	1937
Adjusted index	8.7	10.2	16.1	21.4	39.1	40.9	63.7	75.1	83.4	100.0	84.2	77.7	91.9	113.6
Unadjusted index[a]	7.5	9.3	14.8	19.8	37.8	40.7	62.4	74.1	81.6	100.0	83.1	77.7	91.0	113.1

[a] Percentages of coverage:

Given year	Base year	Given year	Base year	Given year	Base year
1899:82.0	1909:87.0	1919:92.0	1929:95.1	1927:93.1	1929:95.1
1904:86.3		1921:94.7		1931:93.8	
1909:87.0	1919:92.0	1923:93.1		1933:95.1	
1914:88.0		1925:93.8		1935:94.1	
				1937:94.7	

STONE, CLAY AND GLASS PRODUCTS

Indexes of Physical Output, with Basic Data on Quantity, Value and Price of Products

ASBESTOS PRODUCTS		1927	1929	1931	1933	1935	1937
Adjusted index		72.6	100.0	68.0	56.2	77.7[b]	126.0
Unadjusted index[a]		91.4	100.0	60.2	48.0	64.5	106.8
Product	*Item*						
Asbestos textiles							
Yarn	*q* Mil. lb.	12.2	15.4	9.51	8.49	8.04	14.0
	v Mil. $	3.86	5.17	2.47	1.55	1.84	3.46
	p $ per lb.	.317	.336	.260	.183	.229	.248
Cloth	*q* Mil. lb.	8.28	6.67	4.63	4.65	7.30	7.81
	v Mil. $	3.22	2.77	1.41	1.07	1.79	2.19
	p $ per lb.	.389	.415	.305	.230	.245	.280
Tape, listings and tubular lagging	*q* Mil. lb.	1.97[c]	2.23	2.35	1.74	1.98	3.27
	v Mil. $	1.01	1.20	.881	.581	.740	1.32
	p $ per lb.	.514	.540	.375	.335	.374	.404
Brake lining, not molded	*q* Mil. ft.		110	56.1	35.8	36.7	46.5
	v Mil. $		16.4	8.37	4.54	4.69	6.31
	p $ per ft.		.149	.149	.128	.128	.136
Clutch facings	*q* Mil. pieces	14.8[c]	38.1	21.3	18.9	26.5	
	v Mil. $	2.60	3.91	1.80	1.60	2.72	
	p $ per piece	.176	.103	.0842	.0849	.102	
Asbestos building materials							
Asbestos shingles	*q* Mil. sq.	1.01	.894	.566	.408	1.17	2.10
	v Mil. $	6.45	5.28	3.27	1.83	5.23	11.5
	p $ per sq.	6.39	5.90	5.77	4.47	4.47	5.48
Asbestos lumber, plain and corrugated	*q* Mil. sq.ft.	48.4	35.4	16.9	14.2	18.3	34.9
	v Mil. $	4.17	3.09	1.56	1.03	1.50	2.82
	p $ per sq.ft.	.0861	.0874	.0924	.0727	.0822	.0807

ASBESTOS PRODUCTS (concluded)		1927	1929	1931	1933	1935	1937
Product	*Item*						
Molded asbestos brake lining	*q* Mil. ft.		22.4	24.2	24.4	23.1	60.0
	v Mil. $		2.53	2.82	3.42	4.67	8.22
	p $ per ft.		.113	.117	.140	.202	.137
Molded 85% magnesia blocks	*q* Mil. board ft.		21.5	11.7	9.71	13.7	21.4
	v Mil. $		2.46	1.21	.853	1.07	1.95
	p $ per board ft.		.114	.103	.0878	.0780	.0913
Table mats and protectors	*q* Mil. lb.	1.43[c]	1.62	1.17		.700	.898
	v Mil. $	.638	.766	.404		.372	.457
	p $ per lb.	.446	.474	.344		.531	.509

[a] Percentages of coverage:

Given year	Base year	Given year	Base year
1927:49.7	1929:39.5	1935:64.5	1929:77.7
1931:68.8	1929:77.7	1937:60.0	1929:70.7
1933:65.3	1929:76.3		

[b] Between 1935 and 1937 some establishments were transferred from cotton small wares to asbestos products.

[c] Estimated in part.

CEMENT		1899	1904	1909	1914	1919	1921	1923	1925	1927	1929	1931	1933	1935	1937
Adjusted index		[b]	18.8	43.3	61.1	57.0	59.8	77.4[c]	94.4	100.5	100.0	74.8	36.2	44.3	68.5
Unadjusted index[a]		6.6	17.1	38.4	51.5	47.1	57.5	80.3	94.6	101.4	100.0	73.8	37.0	45.0	68.3
Product[d]	*Item*														
Portland cement	*q* Mil. bbl.	5.65	26.5	65.0	88.2	80.8	98.8	137	162	173	171	125	63.5	76.7	116
	v Mil. $	8.07	23.4	52.9	81.8	138	187	261	286	281	253	139	84.5	116	172
	p $ per bbl.	1.43	.881	.813	.927	1.71	1.89	1.90	1.77	1.62	1.48	1.11	1.33	1.51	1.48
Natural, puzzolan, and masonry cement	*q* Mil. bbl.[e]	10.2	5.17	1.70	.820	.529	.539	1.33	1.73	2.12	2.21	1.24	.511	1.01	1.90
	v Mil. $	5.08	2.68	.752	.415	.584	.897	2.03	2.52	2.84	3.02	1.64	.690	1.43	2.62
	p $ per bbl.	.498	.518	.443	.506	1.10	1.66	1.53	1.46	1.33	1.37	1.32	1.35	1.42	1.38

For footnotes see next page.

Indexes of Physical Output, with Basic Data on Quantity, Value and Price of Products

CEMENT (concluded)

[a] Percentages of coverage:

Given year	Base year	Given year	Base year	Given year	Base year
1904:87.1	1909:84.8	1921:92.2	1929:95.8	1931:94.5	1929:95.8
1909:84.8	1919:79.1	1923:99.5		1933:98.0	
1914:80.8		1925:96.0		1935:97.2	
1919:79.1	1929:95.8	1927:96.7		1937:95.5	

[b] No adjusted index for 1899 could be computed because the industry is not shown separately in the Census for that year. The adjusted index given above, extrapolated by the unadjusted index, is 7.3 for 1899.

[c] Beginning with 1925 quantity data are reported for production and shipments, but value data are reported only for shipments. Prices, secured from the data for shipments, have been assumed to relate to production also. The value of production was computed by multiplication of barrels produced by these prices.

[d] A slight incomparability arises from the changing manner of treatment of the value of containers. For all years except 1923 the value of containers is included with the value of products of the industry.

[e] The unit for natural, puzzolan, and masonry cement is inconstant through 1919. See *Mineral Resources, 1915*, Part II, p. 190.

CLAY PRODUCTS, not elsewhere classified

		1899	*1904*	*1909*	*1914*	*1919*	*1921*	*1923*	*1925*	*1927*	*1929*	*1931*	*1933*	*1935*	*1937*
Adjusted index				[b]	83.1	63.0	56.7	99.1[c]	105.6	106.8	100.0[d]	48.3	28.0	40.0	65.7
Unadjusted index[a]		83.4	92.2	109.9	89.9	70.0	61.3	103.7	109.6	108.3	100.0	47.3	26.3	36.1	60.6
Product	*Item*														
Common brick	*q* Bil.	7.65	8.68	9.79	7.15	4.75	4.45	7.28	7.56	7.06	5.51	2.31	1.02	1.81	3.25
	v Mil. $	39.7	51.2	57.2	43.8	63.6	57.1	94.5	88.6	78.4	58.7	21.7	8.82	18.2	34.0
	p $ per th.	5.18	5.90	5.85	6.12	13.4	12.8	13.0	11.7	11.1	10.7	9.35	8.65	10.1	10.5
Fire brick, block or tile	*q* Bil.	.801[e]	.678[e]	.838[e]	.817[e]	.963[e]	.621[e]	1.11	.990	.866	.938	.416	.373	.482	.701
	v Mil. $	8.64	11.8	16.6	16.4	38.0	24.8	45.4	40.7	34.3	36.2	15.7	13.1	19.5	32.8
	p $ per th.	10.8	17.3	19.8	20.1	39.5	40.0	41.0	41.1	39.6	38.6	37.7	35.2	40.5	46.8
Face brick	*q* Bil.	.451[f]	.626[f]	.822[f]	.810	.791	.873	1.93	2.47	2.41	2.14	.903	.270	.473	.938
	v Mil. $	5.17	7.34	9.89	9.29	16.0	18.1	38.9	45.4	41.5	36.1	13.3	3.81	7.01	14.4
	p $ per th.	11.5	11.7	12.0	11.5	20.3	20.8	20.1	18.4	17.2	16.9	14.7	14.1	14.8	15.3

CLAY PRODUCTS, not elsewhere classified (continued)		1899	1904	1909	1914	1919	1921	1923	1925	1927	1929	1931	1933	1935	1937
Product	*Item*														
Vitrified brick, block, for paving	*q* Mil.	591[g]	716[g]	1024[g]	931[g]	393	469	539	448	406	274	179	53.8	71.8	84.7
	v Mil. $	4.83	7.26	11.3	12.5	9.37	11.2	13.0	10.4	9.14	5.97	3.84	1.11	1.72	2.05
	p $ per th.	8.17	10.1	11.0	13.4	23.9	23.9	24.2	23.1	22.5	21.8	21.5	20.6	24.0	24.2
Sewer pipe	*q* Mil. t.					1.16	1.36	1.78	2.14	2.12	1.68	.823	.451	.670	.973
	v Mil. $					16.8	22.2	29.1	30.4	29.4	21.3	9.45	4.91	8.62	13.7
	p $ per t.					14.5	16.3	16.4	14.2	13.9	12.7	11.5	10.9	12.9	14.1
Hollow building tile	*q* Mil. t.					2.33	2.02	3.76	4.22	4.11	4.16	1.93	.608	.913	1.65
	v Mil. $					18.0	14.8	28.3	29.3	26.5	30.1	11.2	2.84	5.47	10.8
	p $ per t.					7.71	7.36	7.51	6.93	6.44	7.24	5.80	4.67	5.99	6.51
Silica brick	*q* Mil.					211	105	258	236	246	294	104	111	150	220
	v Mil. $					10.9	5.22	12.9	11.3	12.8	15.2	5.13	4.65	8.18	12.8
	p $ per th.					51.6	49.7	49.8	47.8	51.9	51.5	49.6	42.0	54.7	58.2
Architectural terra cotta	*q* Th. t.						68.4	138	152	156	134	54.7	25.6	17.6	28.7
	v Mil. $						9.07	16.5	19.1	16.6	13.9	5.49	1.83	1.53	2.91
	p $ per t.						133	119	126	107	104	100	71.5	87.1	101
Wall tile	*q* Mil. sq.ft.					7.50	10.9	26.3	30.4	39.5	30.4	17.7	9.93	10.7	10.1
	v Mil. $					2.61	4.39	10.2	10.2	12.5	11.3	4.99	1.55	3.09	2.69
	p $ per sq.ft.					.349	.401	.387	.337	.316	.370	.282	.156	.289	.268
Enameled brick	*q* Mil.					14.2	12.7	19.5	16.9	18.1	17.1	8.60	4.00		
	v Mil. $					.847	1.20	1.67	1.51	1.37	1.26	.484	.172		
	p $ per th.					59.8	94.7	85.7	89.0	76.0	73.5	56.3	43.0		
Drain tile	*q* Mil. t.					1.24	.976	.616	.661	.734	.859	.253	.168	.264	.444
	v Mil. $					10.9	8.37	5.10	4.96	5.51	6.52	1.67	1.13	2.00	3.59
	p $ per t.					8.82	8.57	8.28	7.51	7.50	7.59	6.58	6.71	7.58	8.09
Roofing tile	*q* Th. sq.					94.1	132	231	290	368	371	285	103	135	228
	v Mil. $					1.28	2.31	4.02	5.16	5.35	3.94	3.13	.911	1.15	2.05
	p $ per sq.					13.6	17.5	17.4	17.8	14.5	10.6	11.0	8.82	8.49	8.99

For footnotes see p. 525.

Indexes of Physical Output, with Basic Data on Quantity, Value and Price of Products

CLAY PRODUCTS, not elsewhere classified (continued)		1899	1904	1909	1914	1919	1921	1923	1925	1927	1929	1931	1933	1935	1937
Product	*Item*														
Floor tile	*q* Mil. sq.ft.					7.79	7.79	13.3	19.2	20.4	15.9	12.2	5.79	7.55	13.2
	v Mil. $					1.54	2.38	3.05	4.36	4.59	3.77	2.05	.887	1.08	1.75
	p $ per sq.ft.					.197	.306	.229	.227	.224	.238	.168	.153	.143	.132
Ceramic mosaic	*q* Mil. sq.ft.					7.47	10.6	21.0	20.3	20.5	18.1	8.74	4.23	6.42	11.7
	v Mil. $					1.82	2.57	4.99	4.09	4.55	3.74	1.78	.699	1.32	2.37
	p $ per sq.ft.					.244	.243	.238	.201	.222	.207	.204	.165	.205	.202
Vitrified brick, block, not for paving	*q* Mil.					96.7	93.0	161	90.6	97.6	93.5	28.7	9.30	11.5	
	v Mil. $					2.24	1.67	2.54	1.53	1.62	1.53	.422	.118	.171	
	p $ per th.					23.2	17.9	15.8	16.8	16.6	16.4	14.7	12.7	15.0	
Enameled and faience tile	*q* Mil. sq.ft.					1.55	1.04	1.86	4.92	10.2	19.4	21.4	8.40	12.6	29.2
	v Mil. $					.881	.902	1.58	3.29	5.78	10.1	7.75	2.39	3.86	9.07
	p $ per sq.ft.					.569	.864	.847	.670	.569	.524	.362	.284	.306	.311
Clay sold, raw or prepared	*q* Mil. t.							.648	.657	.487	.464	.214	.192	.253	.394
	v Mil. $							3.18	3.48	2.60	2.20	.970	1.01	1.19	1.68
	p $ per t.							4.91	5.30	5.33	4.74	4.53	5.27	4.71	4.27
Aluminum brick	*q* Mil.							28.6	4.97	11.4	23.9	7.02	9.55	13.2	27.5
	v Mil. $							1.31	.436	1.19	2.11	.734	.718	1.07	2.13
	p $ per th.							45.6	87.8	104	88.4	104	75.2	81.0	77.7
Stove lining	*q* Th. t.							54.7	25.9	13.6	16.8	8.88	5.83	7.61	12.2
	v Mil. $							1.22	.656	.503	.468	.317	.224	.236	.310
	p $ per t.							22.3	25.4	36.9	27.9	35.7	38.5	31.0	25.5
Magnesite and chrome brick	*q* Mil.							13.0	12.7	13.9	17.4	8.36	9.03	12.1	22.8
	v Mil. $							4.06	3.75	3.87	5.63	2.23	2.58	3.42	6.73
	p $ each							.311	.295	.278	.324	.267	.286	.283	.296

CLAY PRODUCTS, not elsewhere classified (concluded)		1899	1904	1909	1914	1919	1921	1923	1925	1927	1929	1931	1933	1935	1937
Product	*Item*														
Refractory cement, clay and nonclay	q Th. t.							95.8	78.5	106	138	74.2	68.5	76.2	173
	v Mil. $							1.84	2.27	2.48	3.11	2.27	2.19	2.68	4.74
	p $ per t.							19.2	28.9	23.4	22.5	30.6	31.9	35.2	27.5

[a] Percentages of coverage:

Given year	Base year	Given year	Base year	Given year	Base year
1914:60.3	1919:62.0	1923:96.9	1929:92.6	1931:89.9	1929:91.7
1919:93.5	1929:84.1	1925:96.1		1933:86.1	
1921:95.9	1929:88.8	1927:94.0		1935:82.3	1929:91.3
				1937:83.7	1929:90.8

[b] No adjusted indexes for the period prior to 1914 could be computed because of a serious change in the definition of the industry between 1909 and 1914. The adjusted index given above, extrapolated by the unadjusted index, is 77.1 for 1899; 85.2 for 1904; 101.6 for 1909.

[c] Between 1923 and 1925 establishments making clay crucibles were transferred from crucibles to clay products. The resulting discontinuity appears to be slight.

[d] Beginning in 1931 crucibles are included in clay products, n.e.c. Since overlapping figures are available for 1929, the adjusted index for years prior to 1929 was computed from the value of products excluding the crucibles industry, and for years following 1929 from the value of products including the crucibles industry.

[e] Including high-alumina brick. The corresponding totals for 1929 are: q 962 mil.; v \$38.3 mil.; p \$39.8 per th.

[f] Including fancy or ornamental brick. The corresponding totals for 1919 are: q 793 mil.; v \$16.1 mil.; p \$20.3 per th.

[g] Including vitrified brick "for other purposes." The corresponding totals for 1919 are: q 489 mil.; v \$11.6 mil.; p \$23.7 per th.

CONCRETE PRODUCTS[a]		1925	1927	1929	1931	1933	1935	1937
Adjusted index		75.4	94.0	100.0	60.6	24.8	57.2	91.5
Unadjusted index[b]		83.1	96.9	100.0	49.5	18.3	40.5	64.2
Product	*Item*							
Building materials								
Block and tile, except roofing tile	q Mil. t.	4.18	5.01	4.33	1.66	.514	1.24	2.34
	v Mil. $	31.2	37.2	30.5	10.6	3.02	7.20	14.9
	p $ per t.	7.46	7.42	7.04	6.38	5.88	5.80	6.34

For footnotes see p. 527.

Indexes of Physical Output, with Basic Data on Quantity, Value and Price of Products

CONCRETE PRODUCTS (continued)		1925	1927	1929	1931	1933	1935	1937
Product	*Item*							
Building materials (concluded)								
Brick	*q* Th. t.	364	227	163	52.4	4.18	18.0	49.4
	v Mil. $	2.53	1.64	1.06	.342	.0280	.144	.348
	p $ per t.	6.96	7.20	6.55	6.53	6.70	8.03	7.04
Cast stone	*q* Th. t.	354	320	332	131	30.5	74.4	92.3
	v Mil. $	12.8	13.7	12.9	4.82	.847	1.63	2.26
	p $ per t.	36.3	42.8	38.9	36.9	27.8	21.9	24.5
Roofing tile	*q* Th. t.	132[c]	118	137	31.9	12.0	43.1	74.1
	v Mil. $	4.01	3.18	2.87	.862	.339	.862	1.95
	p $ per t.	30.4	26.9	20.9	27.1	28.3	20.0	26.3
Circular structures	*q* Th. t.	111	152	213	78.2	25.5	55.9	63.7
	v Mil. $	1.42	1.72	2.22	.815	.385	.703	1.52
	p $ per t.	12.8	11.4	10.4	10.4	15.1	12.6	23.8
Conduits and pipes								
Culvert pipe	*q* Th. t.	349[d]	345[d]	358	403	233	411	573
	v Mil. $	4.48	4.41	4.38	4.65	2.56	4.97	6.70
	p $ per t.	12.8	12.8	12.2	11.5	11.0	12.1	11.7
Draintile	*q* Th. t.	79.9	95.0	75.6	56.4	12.5	21.9	71.1
	v Th. $	704	840	715	543	138	245	639
	p $ per t.	8.81	8.84	9.46	9.64	11.0	11.1	9.00
Electric conduits	*q* Th. t.	1.86	11.5	12.6	6.70		5.41	1.65
	v Th. $	43.8	267	296	151		117	31.5
	p $ per t.	23.6	23.3	23.5	22.6		21.6	19.1
Irrigation pipe	*q* Th. t.	139[d]	94.4[d]	255	140	65.8	109	171
	v Mil. $	1.78	1.25	3.05	1.59	.691	1.37	2.00
	p $ per t.	12.9	13.3	12.0	11.4	10.5	12.6	11.7

CONCRETE PRODUCTS (concluded)		1925	1927	1929	1931	1933	1935	1937
Product	*Item*							
Conduits and pipes (concluded)								
Pressure pipe	*q* Th. t.	46.5[d]	78.2[d]	112	147	4.38	82.4	206
	v Mil. $	1.83	2.16	2.29	3.14	.115	1.92	4.32
	p $ per t.	39.4	27.6	20.5	21.4	26.2	23.2	21.0
Sewer pipe	*q* Mil. t.	.400[d]	.820[d]	1.00	.481	.188	.371	.535
	v Mil. $	5.16	10.4	12.4	5.32	2.09	4.15	5.72
	p $ per t.	12.9	12.6	12.3	11.1	11.1	11.2	10.7
Laundry trays	*q* Th. t.	60.5	36.4	36.4	19.4	9.96	15.9	29.3
	v Mil. $	1.62	1.20	1.10	.547	.281	.403	.683
	p $ per t.	26.8	33.0	30.2	28.1	28.2	25.3	23.3
Vaults	*q* Th. t.	34.5	52.0	82.6	68.5	56.0	89.9	110
	v Mil. $	1.68	2.09	3.27	2.76	2.04	3.06	3.68
	p $ per t.	48.7	40.1	39.6	40.3	36.5	34.0	33.5
Paving materials	*q* Th. t.	28.4	55.7	54.2	22.6	7.62	54.8	157
	v Th. $	423	650	695	295	84.6	243	673
	p $ per t.	14.9	11.7	12.8	13.0	11.1	4.43	4.27
Poles and posts	*q* Th. t.	21.9	37.5	28.2	16.1	5.38	15.3	16.0
	v Mil. $	1.34	1.81	1.41	.693	.197	.299	.493
	p $ per t.	61.1	48.2	50.1	43.0	36.6	19.5	30.9
Septic tanks	*q* Th. t.	13.8	13.5	27.4	8.87		8.71	9.05
	v Th. $	435	450	963	316		184	216
	p $ per t.	31.5	33.4	35.2	35.6		21.1	23.8

[a] Because this industry contains many small establishments, the degree to which it is covered by the Census probably varies from year to year.

[b] Percentages of coverage:

Given year	Base year	Given year	Base year
1925: 95.1	1929: 86.2	1933: 62.5	1929: 84.9
1927: 88.9	1929: 86.2	1935: 61.1	1929: 86.2
1931: 70.4	1929: 86.2	1937: 60.5	1929: 86.2

[c] Estimated in part.

[d] These are possibly understated because part of the production of such pipe may have been reported as conduits and pipes "hand-made" and "machine-made" for 1927, or as conduits and pipes "machine-made" for 1925; 412 th. tons of hand and machine-made pipe valued at 4.9 mil. dollars were reported for 1927, and 262 th. tons of machine-made pipe valued at 3.62 mil. dollars were reported for 1925. These classifications were not used in subsequent years.

Indexes of Physical Output, with Basic Data on Quantity, Value and Price of Products

GLASS		1899	1904	1909	1914	1919	1921	1923	1925	1927	1929	1931		1933	1935	1937
Adjusted index									83.9	91.7	100.0	80.9		77.7	118.4	162.6
Unadjusted index[a]								[b]	100.5	96.2	100.0	78.0		80.6	112.6	150.3
Product	*Item*											*A*	*B*	*C*		
Plate glass, polished	*q* Mil. sq.ft.	16.9	27.3	47.4	60.4	56.8	56.2	94.5	117	118	149	87.0			177	
	v Mil. $	5.16	7.98	12.2	14.8	33.3	37.3	66.1	57.2	44.3	50.2	25.8			41.8	
	p $ per sq.ft.	.306	.292	.258	.245	.587	.663	.700	.487	.375	.337	.296			.236	
Window glass	*q* Mil. sq.ft.	217	243	346	401	369	260	510	567	481	403	267	258	249	429	617
	v Mil. $	10.9	11.6	11.7	17.5	41.1	24.0	42.6	37.5	26.8	26.0	10.3	10.0	10.5	18.2	31.4
	p $ per sq.ft.	.0501	.0479	.0339	.0436	.111	.0924	.0835	.0662	.0557	.0645	.0386	.0387	.0419	.0424	.0509
Obscured glass, incl. cathedral and skylight glass, and opalescent sheet glass	*q* Mil. sq.ft.	12.5	21.9	22.8	43.0	33.8	20.9	46.4	54.0	41.5	34.3	17.8			14.4	27.7
	v Mil. $	.732	.972	1.36	2.42	4.30	2.55	5.11	6.92	5.09	5.26	2.39			1.64	3.97
	p $ per sq.ft.	.0585	.0444	.0595	.0562	.127	.122	.110	.128	.123	.153	.134			.114	.143
													q 30.5	19.9		
Wire glass													*v* 3.85	2.59		
Rough (for sale as such)	*q* Mil. sq.ft.				14.0	14.5	13.9	28.8	28.7	25.8	38.9	14.2	*p* .126	.130		
	v Mil. $				1.06	2.27	2.11	3.88	3.55	2.75	4.28	1.25				
	p $ per sq.ft.				.0756	.157	.151	.135	.123	.106	.110	.0879			*q* 12.0	21.3
															v 1.37	2.72
Polished	*q* Mil. sq.ft.				1.71	1.23	2.21	2.80	4.17	3.32	3.89	1.45			*p* .114	.127
	v Mil. $				.534	.636	1.21	1.65	2.26	1.63	1.71	.551				
	p $ per sq.ft.				.313	.517	.547	.589	.543	.491	.440	.380				
Glassware, except containers																
Pressed tumblers and goblets	*q* Mil. doz.								29.7	27.3	17.5	8.33	8.14	11.3		
	v Mil. $								8.68	7.77	5.67	2.69	2.50	4.27		
	p $ per doz.								.292	.285	.323	.323	.308	.380		
Lenses, motor-vehicle	*q* Mil. doz.										2.32	1.40	1.24	.675	1.95	2.83
	v Mil. $										2.03	.884	.824	.421	1.12	1.76
	p $ per doz.										.876	.633	.665	.624	.572	.620

GLASS (continued)		1899	1904	1909	1914	1919	1921	1923	1925	1927	1929	1931		1933	1935	1937
Product	*Item*											*A*	*B*	*C*		
Glassware, except containers (concluded)																
Lamp chimneys	*q* Mil. doz.								3.44	2.99	3.02	1.60	1.16	1.88	2.43	2.21
	v Mil. $								2.66	2.28	1.95	1.10	.868	.990	1.29	1.38
	p $ per doz.								.773	.763	.646	.689	.751	.528	.532	.625
Lantern globes	*q* Th. doz.								1080	869	942	404	301	281	616	276
	v Th. $								867	636	672	383	239	230	495	462
	p $ per doz.								.803	.732	.713	.948	.794	.819	.803	1.68
Tubing	*q* Mil. lb.								16.9	21.5	23.1	17.3	17.2	14.3	27.3	38.9
	v Mil. $								3.93	4.02	4.75	3.14	3.12	2.58	3.67	4.87
	p $ per lb.								.233	.187	.206	.182	.181	.180	.134	.125
Miscellaneous types[c]																
Food product containers																
Narrow-neck and wide-mouth bottles and jars (packers' ware)	*q* Mil. gr.										9.45	8.98	8.95	9.36	11.2	13.2
	v Mil. $										33.2	25.8	25.7	25.5	33.1	38.7
	p $ per gr.										3.51	2.87	2.87	2.72	2.96	2.93
Pressed ware (packers' ware)	*q* Mil. gr.									.763	.761	.822				
	v Mil. $									2.45	2.59	1.86				
	p $ per gr.									3.21	3.40	2.26				
													q 2.90	1.54		
													v 17.0	9.37		
													p 5.84	6.08		
Fruit-jars (home-pack)	*q* Mil. gr.								1.29	1.52	1.15	2.08			1.39	1.16
	v Mil. $								6.64	11.4	8.53	15.1			10.1	6.72
	p $ per gr.								5.15	7.50	7.39	7.25			7.26	5.81
Milk bottles	*q* Mil. gr.								2.09	2.18	2.61	2.14	2.14	1.96	2.12	2.68
	v Mil. $								10.6	11.5	11.7	10.0	10.0	9.18	11.0	14.3
	p $ per gr.								5.07	5.26	4.48	4.69	4.70	4.68	5.17	5.33
Beverage containers	*q* Mil. gr.									4.15	4.57	4.12	4.11	6.53	9.11	16.5
	v Mil. $									17.7	18.5	15.6	15.6	21.6	33.1	57.5
	p $ per gr.									4.27	4.04	3.80	3.80	3.30	3.63	3.49

For footnotes see next page.

Indexes of Physical Output, with Basic Data on Quantity, Value and Price of Products

GLASS (concluded)		1899	1904	1909	1914	1919	1921	1923	1925	1927	1929	1931		1933	1935	1937
Product	*Item*											*A*	*B*	*C*		
Medicinal and toilet preparation containers (both pressed and blown)	*q* Mil. gr.										15.8	12.8	12.8	14.1	14.6	18.3
	v Mil. $										41.5	30.3	30.3	29.8	30.3	36.2
	p $ per gr.										2.63	2.37	2.37	2.11	2.08	1.97
General-purpose containers (carboys, pantry jars)	*q* Mil. doz.										16.3	12.3	12.1	15.9	23.1	22.8
	v Mil. $										5.73	6.62	6.52	4.00	5.24	5.75
	p $ per doz.										.352	.536	.540	.252	.227	.252

A Comparable with all years except 1933. *B* Comparable with 1933. *C* Comparable with 1931.

[a] Percentages of coverage:

Given year	Base year	Given year	Base year	Given year	Base year
1925:47.6	1929:39.7	1931:71.1	1929:73.8	1935:68.4	1929:71.9
1927:49.0	1929:46.6	1933:63.0	1931:58.5	1937:64.0	1935:65.9

[b] For 1899–1923 the detailed data on products relate to the different varieties of building glass alone, and account for only about 30 percent of the total value of products. Because of the low coverage no indexes were computed.

[c] The miscellaneous types are as follows:

	Tumblers, Goblets and Barware					
	Machine-made, pressed and blown		Hand-made, pressed		Hand-made, blown	
Item	*1935*	*1937*	*1935*	*1937*	*1935*	*1937*
q Mil. doz.	33.6	39.7	1.87	.924	4.02	4.51
v Mil. $	12.4	12.6	2.90	1.42	5.55	6.38
p $ per doz.	.370	.317	1.55	1.54	1.38	1.42

	Plates, Dishes, Cups and Saucers and Other Tableware				*Other Tableware*	
	Machine-made, pressed and blown		Hand-made, pressed		Hand-made, blown	
Item	*1935*	*1937*	*1935*	*1937*	*1935*	*1937*
q Mil. pieces	398	531	19.4	43.8	5.38	4.40
v Mil. $	10.9	15.1	2.47	4.68	.462	.898
p $ per th. pieces	27.5	28.5	127	107	85.9	204

LIME		1904	1909	1914	1919	1921	1923	1925	1927	1929	1931	1933[b]	1935	1937
Adjusted index		80.7	90.8	94.8	76.8	58.2	92.7	101.8	101.4	100.0	77.5		67.4	101.7
Unadjusted index[a]		65.9	84.9	82.8	75.7	59.5	94.0	101.7	109.6	100.0	76.2		66.4	94.0
Product[c]	*Item*													
Quicklime	q Mil. t.								2.33	1.95	1.48		1.47	2.14
	v Mil. $								21.4	15.7	9.46		10.4	14.8
	p $ per t.		q 3.28	2.87	2.30	1.67	2.51	2.61	9.17	8.06	6.39		7.06	6.93
			v 12.9	11.0	20.5	18.7	25.7	26.3						
Agricultural lime	q Mil. t.	q 2.71	p 3.95	3.85	8.90	11.2	10.2	10.1	.317	.756	.307		.253	.397
	v Mil. $	v 9.95							1.54	2.48	1.43		1.47	2.19
	p $ per t.	p 3.68							4.85	3.28	4.66		5.80	5.53
Hydrated lime	q Mil. t.		208	.515	.770	.726	1.26	1.45	1.47	1.31	1.14		.841	1.12
	v Mil. $		.913	2.24	7.16	7.49	13.9	15.5	14.2	11.4	7.14		7.10	9.70
	p $ per t.		4.40	4.35	9.30	10.3	11.0	10.7	9.62	8.71	6.24		8.45	8.66

[a] Percentages of coverage:

Given year	Base year	Given year	Base year	Given year	Base year
1904:67.5	1909:77.1	1921:84.5	1929:82.6	1931:81.2	1929:82.6
1909:77.1	1919:81.4	1923:83.7		1935:81.3	
1914:72.1		1925:82.5		1937:76.4	
1919:81.4	1929:82.6	1927:89.2			

[b] Detailed data on products were not collected by the Census in 1933. Data for this industry are available, however, in a somewhat different form in the *Minerals Yearbook* for 1933 and for other years as well. An index for 1925–37 computed from these data did not agree closely with our index, and it was decided, therefore, not to use these data to compute an index for 1933.

[c] For 1927 and later years data relate to products wherever made; for other years they relate to products made within the industry.

Indexes of Physical Output, with Basic Data on Quantity, Value and Price of Products

ROOFING		1929	1931	1933[b]	1935	1937
Adjusted index		100.0	61.5		82.9	110.4
Unadjusted index[a]		100.0	60.7		80.3	100.9
Product	*Item*					
Asphalt-roll roofing	*q* Mil. roofing sq.	28.4	17.5		22.6	25.6
	v Mil. $	36.1	20.3		25.7	29.3
	p $ per roofing sq.	1.27	1.16		1.14	1.15
Asphalt shingles	*q* Mil. roofing sq.	11.7	6.56		7.73	9.09
	v Mil. $	42.3	22.6		26.8	35.0
	p $ per roofing sq.	3.62	3.44		3.47	3.85
Saturated felt	*q* Mil. t.	.206	.144		.226	.406
	v Mil. $	9.80	6.03		8.05	12.6
	p $ per t.	47.7	42.0		35.7	30.9
Asphalt roof cements, solid	*q* Mil. t.	.0352	.0166		.107	.133
	v Mil. $	.842	.334		1.45	2.24
	p $ per t.	24.0	20.1		13.6	16.8
Fibrous plastic roof cement	*q* Mil. lb.	52.8	29.5		33.2	55.8
	v Mil. $	2.34	1.35		1.31	1.73
	p $ per lb.	.0443	.0457		.0396	.0310
Fibrous liquid roof coating	*q* Mil. gal.	4.94	4.98		5.52	8.13
	v Mil. $	2.12	2.04		1.53	2.35
	p $ per gal.	.428	.410		.278	.289
Nonfibrous liquid roof coating	*q* Mil. gal.	1.93	1.42		5.58	9.07[c]
	v Mil. $	1.02	.577		2.51	2.44
	p $ per gal.	.527	.406		.449	.269

[a] Percentages of coverage: Given year 1931:90.2, 1935:88.5, 1937:83.5; Base year 1929:91.3

[b] Detailed data on products were not collected in 1933.

[c] Estimated in part.

SAND-LIME BRICK		1914	1919	1921	1923	1925	1927	1929	1931	1933	1935	1937
Adjusted index		58.9	52.1	33.9	75.5	114.2	115.2	100.0	53.5	8.7	26.5	66.5
Unadjusted index[a]		64.0	54.5	34.5	76.2	115.7	118.6	100.0	53.3	8.5	22.9	51.3
Product[b]	*Item*											
Sand-lime brick	*q* Mil.	173[c]	147[c]	93.0	205	312	320	270	144	22.9	61.8	138
	v Mil. $	1.06	1.71	1.21	2.38	3.73	3.65	2.91	1.24	.195	.555	1.22
	p $ per th.	6.13	11.6	13.1	11.6	12.0	11.4	10.8	8.61	8.53	8.98	8.84

[a] Percentages of coverage:

Given year	Base year	Given year	Base year	Given year	Base year
1914:106.5	1919:102.5	1923: 98.8	1929:97.9	1931:97.6	1929:97.9
1919:102.5	1929: 97.9	1925: 99.2		1933:95.2	
1921: 99.5		1927:100.8		1935:84.8	
				1937:75.6	

[b] For 1914, 1919 and 1927, the data relate to sand-lime brick, wherever made, whereas for the other years they relate to sand-lime brick made within the industry. Very little sand-lime brick is made outside the industry, if one may judge from the figures for the years for which both sets of data are available.

[c] For the years 1914 and 1919 data relate to sand-lime brick marketed during the year. According to the data for 1927–31, marketings paralleled production quite closely.

WALL PLASTER and BOARD		1927	1929	1931	1933[b]	1935	1937
Adjusted index		100.0	100.0	64.6		63.6	111.8
Unadjusted index[a]		90.2	100.0	59.8		54.7	100.4
Product	*Item*						
Gypsum plasters							
Sanded	*q* Th. t.	555	336	180		74.6	166
	v Mil. $	4.14	2.24	1.44		.594	1.18
	p $ per t.	7.47	6.67	8.01		7.96	7.09
Neat, fibered and unfibered	*q* Mil. t.	2.42	2.38	1.17		.770	1.19
	v Mil. $	18.1	14.0	10.5		7.82	10.8
	p $ per t.	7.46	5.87	8.99		10.2	9.03

For footnotes see p. 535.

Indexes of Physical Output, with Basic Data on Quantity, Value and Price of Products

WALL PLASTER and BOARD (continued)		1927	1929	1931	1933[b]	1935	1937
Product	*Item*						
Gypsum plasters (concluded)							
Molding and gauging	*q* Th. t.		72.5	90.6		83.7	124
	v Mil. $		.959	1.35		1.15	1.60
	p $ per t.	*q* 349	13.2	14.9		13.8	13.0
		v 4.34					
Industrial (terra-cotta,	*q* Th. t.	*p* 12.4	226	115		77.7	120
plate-glass, pottery, casting, dental, etc.)	*v* Mil. $		2.07	1.28		.636	1.31
	p $ per t.		9.16	11.1		8.19	10.9
Plasters other than gypsum							
Magnesite stucco and	*q* Th. t.	64.4	66.2	25.9		18.4	20.3
Portland-cement stucco	*v* Mil. $	2.10	2.18	.776		.350	.322
	p $ per t.	32.6	32.9	29.9		19.0	15.8
Other nongypsum plasters	*q* Th. t.	56.8	107	14.9		61.9	
	v Mil. $	1.25	3.07	.553		1.13	
	p $ per t.	22.0	28.6	37.2		18.3	
Gypsum board							
Wallboard	*q* Mil. sq.ft.	659	626	376		332	393
	v Mil. $	15.9	12.2	10.0		7.41	8.36
	p $ per sq.ft.	.0242	.0195	.0266		.0223	.0213
Plaster board and lath	*q* Mil. sq.ft.	271	351	216		219	739
	v Mil. $	4.29	5.47	3.32		3.42	9.32
	p $ per sq.ft.	.0158	.0156	.0154		.0156	.0126
Fiber wallboard, fiber	*q* Mil. sq.ft.	404	605	477		506	1003
insulating board, and	*v* Mil. $	15.7	19.4	13.4		13.9	28.1
flexible fiber insulations[c]	*p* $ per sq.ft.	.0389	.0320	.0281		.0274	.0280

WALL PLASTER and BOARD (concluded)		1927	1929	1931	1933[b]	1935	1937
Product	*Item*						
Magnesite floor composition	q Th. t.		17.7	11.4		7.46	5.38
	v Mil. $		1.19	.754		.669	.410
	p $ per t.		67.5	66.3		89.7	76.2

[a] Percentages of coverage:

Given year	Base year
1927:78.5	1929:87.1
1931:79.5, 1935:73.9	1929:85.9
1937:73.4	1929:81.7

[b] No comparable figures are available for 1933.

[c] These figures relate to wall and insulating board and insulating materials other than gypsum, produced in the wall plaster industry alone.

TOTAL STONE, CLAY and GLASS PRODUCTS	1925	1927	1929	1931	1933	1935	1937
Adjusted index	91.2	99.5	100.0	67.4	46.9	68.6	99.6
Unadjusted index[a,b]	93.4	98.3	100.0	66.4	45.8	66.8	99.8

[a] Percentages of coverage:

Given year	Base year	Given year	Base year
1925:60.9	1929:59.4	1933:59.0	1929:60.4
1927:65.2	1929:66.0	1935:68.0, 1937:70.0	1929:69.9
1931:68.8	1929:69.9		

[b] Indexes are not given for this group for years prior to 1925 because of inadequate coverage.

FOREST PRODUCTS

Indexes of Physical Output, with Basic Data on Quantity, Value and Price of Products

BOXES, WOODEN, CIGAR		1927	1929	1931	1933	1935	1937
Adjusted index		98.5	100.0	83.9	65.3	64.5	82.9
Unadjusted index[a]		103.6	100.0	87.4	67.0	66.0	79.9
Product[b]	*Item*						
Size one-tenth	*q* Mil.	4.23	11.1	2.39		2.78	4.95
(100 cigars)	*v* Mil. $	.558	1.40	.287		.303	.435
	p $ ea.	.132	.127	.120		.109	.0878
Size one-twentieth	*q* Mil.	78.7	67.4	68.9		50.3	60.4
(50 cigars)	*v* Mil. $	9.67	7.94	6.55		4.39	4.79
	p $ ea.	.123	.118	.0951	*q* 66.2	.0874	.0793
					v 5.70		
Size one-fortieth	*q* Mil.	12.9	13.0	8.33	*p* .0861	8.72	10.8
(25 cigars)	*v* Mil. $	1.51	1.53	.831		.752	1.00
	p $ ea.	.118	.118	.0998		.0862	.0934
Size not specified and	*q* Mil.	7.19	7.36	7.80		4.29	3.12
miscellaneous sizes	*v* Mil. $	1.03	.849	1.01		.487	.237
	p $ ea.	.144	.115	.129		.114	.0759

[a] Percentages of coverage: Given year 1927: 99.0; 1931: 98.0; 1933: 96.5; 1935: 96.3; 1937: 90.7. Base year 1929: 94.1.

[b] Quantities are estimated in part.

CASKETS and COFFINS		1927	1929	1931	1933[b]	1935	1937
Adjusted index		77.3	100.0	88.6		97.3	104.1
Unadjusted index[a]		78.2	100.0	91.1		100.7	108.0
Product[c]	*Item*						
Caskets and coffins[d]							
Wood, including metal lined	*q* Mil.	1.20	1.32	1.09		1.15	1.22
	v Mil. $	43.2	45.4	34.3		32.4	34.7
	p $ ea.	36.0	34.3	31.4		28.2	28.4
Metal	*q* Th.	82.3	179	199		250	280
	v Mil. $	10.4	17.0	15.7		15.0	17.8
	p $ ea.	127	95.4	78.9		60.0	63.7
Wooden shipping and outer cases[d]	*q* Th.	507	592	537		581	512
	v Mil. $	4.18	4.72	3.74		3.44	3.01
	p $ ea.	8.24	7.98	6.97		5.92	5.88
Metal grave vault and shipping cases	*q* Th.	114	144	146		157	164
	v Mil. $	4.66	5.70	5.49		5.29	5.88
	p $ ea.	41.0	39.6	37.7		33.7	35.9

[a] Percentages of coverage:

Given year	Base year
1927: 83.4	1929: 82.5
1931: 84.8	
1935: 85.4	
1937: 85.6	

[b] Detailed data on products were not collected in 1933.

[c] Quantities are estimated in part.

[d] In some manufacturers' returns data on shipping and outer cases were included with those on caskets and coffins.

Indexes of Physical Output, with Basic Data on Quantity, Value and Price of Products

COOPERAGE		1927	1929	1931	1933	1935	1937
Adjusted index		97.9	100.0	68.4	55.6	59.6	63.1
Unadjusted index[a]		100.7	100.0	68.8	54.6	58.7	60.6
Product	*Item*						
Cooperage, slack and tight[b]	q Mil.	82.3	81.7	56.2	44.6	48.0	49.5
	v Mil. $	65.7	61.9	37.6	33.4	43.7	46.0
	p $ ea.	.799	.757	.669	.749	.912	.930

[a] Percentages of coverage: Given year 1927:98.2, 1931:96.0, 1933:93.8, 1935:93.9, 1937:91.6; Base year 1929:95.4

[b] Quantities are estimated in part.

EXCELSIOR		1925	1927	1929	1931	1933	1935	1937
Adjusted index			[b]	100.0	63.0	51.1	60.0	69.5
Unadjusted index[a]		99.2	96.6	100.0	66.3	40.2	55.3	70.0
Product	*Item*							
Excelsior[c,d]	q Th. t.	195	190	196	130	78.9	109	138
	v Mil. $			3.50	2.20	1.15	1.58	2.14
	p $ per t.			17.8	16.9	14.6	14.5	15.5

[a] Percentages of coverage: Given year 1931:73.7, 1933:54.9, 1935:64.4, 1937:70.5; Base year 1929:69.9

[b] No adjusted indexes for 1925 and 1927 were computed because the percentages of coverage in those years could not be determined.

[c] Quantities for 1929–37 are estimated in part.

[d] Includes excelsior produced and used as a material in plants manufacturing excelsior pads, wrappers, etc., as well as excelsior produced as such.

LUMBER-MILL PRODUCTS, not elsewhere classified		1899	1904	1909	1914	1919	1921	1923	1925	1927	1929	1931	1933	1935	1937
Adjusted index		107.0	95.8	104.6	[c]	97.0[d]	80.4	98.7	105.7	97.3	100.0	50.6	40.5	55.0	72.3
Unadjusted index[a,b]		98.6	96.1	125.8	103.3	95.4	73.6	100.8	104.2	101.7	100.0	50.0	36.9	56.0	73.5
Product[e]	*Item*														
Rough lumber															
Softwood, total production[f]	*q* Bil. ft.b.m.	26.2	27.4	33.9	29.4	27.4	22.2	30.9	31.7	28.4	29.8	13.9	11.9	16.2	21.6
	v Mil. $	269	320	477		778	485	931	821	668	725	232	202	310	496
	p $ per th.ft.	10.3	11.7	14.1	13.2[e]	28.4	21.8	30.1	25.9	23.5	24.3	16.7	16.9	19.1	23.0
Hardwood, total production[f]	*q* Bil. ft.b.m.	8.63	6.78	10.6	7.94	7.14	4.78	6.26	6.63	6.09	7.07	2.67	2.06	3.29	4.41
	v Mil. $	117	116	207		266	148	249	253	224	269	74.8	57.4	89.1	134
	p $ per th.ft.	13.5	17.1	19.5	17.5[e]	37.2	30.9	39.8	38.2	36.7	38.0	28.0	27.8	27.1	30.5
Softwood and hardwood, sold or transferred[g]	*q* Bil. ft.b.m.								17.2	15.5	17.2	8.13	5.32	9.20	11.3
	v Mil. $								483	400	464	151	98.7	188	274
	p $ per th.ft.								28.0	25.8	26.9	18.6	18.6	20.4	24.2
Lath	*q* Bil.	2.52	2.65	3.70		1.72	1.97	3.33	3.16	2.37	1.71	.614	.408	.620	.839
	v Mil. $	4.69	5.43	9.96		8.29	8.61	15.2	13.5	8.07	5.90	1.63	1.04	2.06	2.88
	p $ per th.	1.86	2.05	2.69		4.81	4.37	4.56	4.28	3.40	3.46	2.65	2.54	3.33	3.43
Shingles	*q* Mil. sq.[h]	15.1	18.2	18.6		11.5	8.55	9.38	9.16	8.05	7.64	3.39	3.66	4.42	5.65
	v Mil. $	18.9	24.0	30.3		38.5	19.4	23.9	21.8	16.3	18.0	4.99	6.96	10.4	14.5
	p $ per sq.	1.25	1.32	1.62		3.35	2.27	2.54	2.38	2.02	2.36	1.47	1.90	2.35	2.57
Dressed lumber, incl. flooring, ceiling, partition, and siding	*q* Bil. ft.b.m.								14.3	15.9	13.7	7.35	6.04	8.25	11.6
	v Mil. $								413	423	363	134	108	179	291
	p $ per th.ft.								28.8	26.7	26.5	18.3	17.9	21.7	25.0
Doors, for general construction	*q* Mil.								7.98	4.21	5.21	3.13	2.11	2.10	2.40
	v Mil. $								18.8	14.0	15.2	5.93	2.34	2.56	4.35
	p $ ea.								2.36	3.33	2.92	1.90	1.11	1.22	1.82
Sash	*q* Mil.								7.17	5.65	2.08	1.26	.863	.817	1.60
	v Mil. $								2.17	1.76	.870	.518	.356	.382	1.11
	p $ ea.								.304	.311	.419	.410	.412	.468	.696

For footnotes see next page.

Indexes of Physical Output, with Basic Data on Quantity, Value and Price of Products

LUMBER-MILL PRODUCTS, not elsewhere classified (concluded)		1899	1904	1909	1914	1919	1921	1923	1925	1927	1929	1931	1933	1935	1937
Product[e]	*Item*														
Window and door frames	*q* Mil.								1.95	1.51	.971	.535	.224	.288	.515
	v Mil. $								3.69	2.40	1.75	.777	.295	.489	.850
	p $ ea.								1.89	1.59	1.80	1.45	1.32	1.70	1.65

[a] Percentages of coverage:

Given year	Base year	Given year	Base year	Given year	Base year
1899:73.7; 1904:80.2	1909:96.2	1919:78.6; 1921:73.2; 1923:81.6	1929:79.9	1927:71.3; 1931:67.4; 1933:62.1; 1935:69.5; 1937:69.4	1929:68.2
1909:96.2	1919:78.6	1925:67.2	1929:68.2		

[b] Data on the output of sawed lumber are available in two forms. Figures for all lumber cut are given for the entire period 1899–1937. Beginning with 1925 there are available data on rough lumber, not remanufactured in the same plants. In order to avoid duplication we used for 1925–37 the latter series and the series for the other final products, lath, shingles, dressed lumber, doors, sash, and window and door frames. For 1899–1923 we used the data for all lumber cut, hardwood and softwood, and for lath and shingles. (The 1925 and 1927 figures for rough lumber sold or transferred are estimates; see footnote g.)

[c] Prices for 1915 were used in the computation of the 1914 index since no 1914 prices were available, and for this reason no adjusted index could be computed. The adjusted index given above, interpolated by the unadjusted index, is 95.5 for 1914.

[d] Between 1919 and 1921 establishments engaged primarily in the manufacture of aircraft parts, other than engines and tires, were transferred from lumber-mill products, n.e.c., to aircraft. The resulting discontinuity appears to be slight.

[e] Quantities and average prices for softwood, hardwood, lath, and shingles are given in Census reports; values were derived from quantities and prices.

[f] Data for 1925–37 were not used in the computation of the index.

[g] Quantities were estimated by division of the value shown by the average price of all rough lumber. Value data for 1925 and 1927 were obtained by multiplication of the value of all lumber cut by the average of the 1929–37 ratios of rough lumber sold or transferred to all lumber cut. These ratios, expressed in percentage form, are as follows: 46.7 for 1929; 49.2 for 1931; 38.1 for 1933; 47.1 for 1935; 43.5 for 1937.

[h] Reported in thousands prior to 1933, and converted on the basis of 800 shingles to the square.

PLANING-MILL PRODUCTS, not elsewhere made		1925	1927	1929	1931	1933	1935	1937
Adjusted index		119.2	97.1	100.0[b]	55.0[c]	32.3	45.8	64.4
Unadjusted index[a]		123.9	96.5	100.0	48.6	29.4	45.0	67.5
Product[d]	*Item*							
Dressed lumber, incl.	*q* Bil. ft.b.m.	4.79	3.49	4.11	1.93	1.08	1.76	2.41
flooring, ceiling,	*v* Mil. $	160	133	131	49.5	27.1	46.4	72.8
partition, and siding	*p* $ per th.ft.b.m.	33.4	38.0	31.8	25.6	25.0	26.4	30.3
Doors, for general	*q* Mil.	15.1	12.1	12.0	5.37	4.15	5.15	9.12
construction	*v* Mil. $	60.5	43.9	44.1	14.8	8.07	13.4	26.1
	p $ each	4.00	3.62	3.67	2.76	1.95	2.60	2.87
Sash	*q* Mil.	40.7	34.2	27.0	17.5	11.9	19.2	29.6
	v Mil. $	41.3	28.0	24.4	10.1	6.39	11.6	19.3
	p $ each	1.02	.819	.903	.580	.538	.605	.654
Window and door	*q* Mil.	10.8	10.4	8.20	4.09	2.01	2.99	5.26
frames	*v* Mil. $	38.8	30.6	26.0	10.3	4.35	7.07	14.8
	p $ each	3.59	2.95	3.16	2.52	2.17	2.36	2.82

[a] Percentages of coverage:

Given year	Base year	Given year	Base year
1925: 42.3	1929: 40.7	1933: 36.9	1929: 40.7
1927: 40.4		1935: 40.0	
1931: 35.9		1937: 42.6	

[b] Between 1929 and 1931, when dairymen's supplies was abandoned as a separate classification, some establishments producing these products were transferred to planing-mill products, n.e.m.

[c] In 1933 establishments making horsedrawn lunch wagons were transferred from carriages, wagons and sleighs to planing-mill products, n.e.m. The resulting discontinuity appears to be slight.

[d] Data relate only to the production of independent planing mills.

Indexes of Physical Output, with Basic Data on Quantity, Value and Price of Products

TURPENTINE and ROSIN		*1899*	*1904*	*1909*	*1914*	*1919*	*1921*	*1923*	*1925*	*1927*	*1929*	*1931*[e]	*1933*	*1935*	*1937*
Adjusted index				[b]	81.8	75.6	73.7	88.3	91.1	107.2	100.0	[b]			80.6
Unadjusted index[a,b]		121.8	98.6	92.4	83.5	57.2	81.3	88.7	78.5	103.4	100.0	78.8	84.1	81.7	85.4
Product[c]	*Item*														
Turpentine	*q* Mil. gal.[d]	37.7	30.7	29.0	27.0	17.7	24.4	27.2	23.9	31.5	31.3	24.3	25.5	24.8	25.9
	v Mil. $				9.10	13.9	12.9	21.0	15.7	12.2	11.6	7.97	9.88[f]	10.1[f]	7.47[f]
	p $ per gal.				.337	.787	.528	.773	.657	.386	.371	.327	.388	.408	.288
Rosin	*q* Mil. bbl.	2.43	1.96	1.83	1.62	1.14	1.66	1.79	1.58	2.07	1.98	1.57	1.70	1.65	1.71
	v Mil. $				11.0	23.8	11.3	12.2	18.6	24.0	22.5	8.97	9.67[f]	11.4[f]	22.0[f]
	p $ per bbl.				6.83	20.9	6.79	6.81	11.8	11.6	11.4	5.71	5.69	6.92	12.9

[a] Percentages of coverage:

Given year	Base year	Given year	Base year	Given year	Base year
1914: 95.9	1919:71.2	1923:94.4	1929:94.0	1937:99.6	1929:94.0
1919: 71.2	1929:94.0	1925:80.9			
1921:103.7		1927:90.6			

[b] Since unit values are not available for 1899–1909, we computed the unadjusted indexes for these years by using 1914 unit values. Because data on values are lacking, no adjusted indexes could be computed for 1899–1909. No adjusted indexes for 1931–35 were computed because the total value of products of the industry is incomplete for these years. The adjusted index given above, extrapolated and interpolated by the unadjusted index, is 119.3 for 1899; 96.6 for 1904; 90.5 for 1909; 77.7 for 1931; 81.7 for 1933; 78.3 for 1935.

[c] For 1935 and 1937 statistics on quantities were compiled from data collected by the Bureau of Chemistry and Soils (Department of Agriculture); for 1933, from data collected by the Control Committee of the Marketing Agreement for Gum Turpentine and Gum Rosin Processors; for 1925, from data compiled by the Turpentine and Rosin Producers' Association, and for all other years by the Bureau of the Census. These data refer to the calendar year for each of the years 1899–1919 and 1933, and to the crop year ending March 31 of the following year for each of the years 1921–31, 1935 and 1937. For the years 1914–31 inclusive the unit value figures were derived from the quantity and value figures given for turpentine and for rosin made in the wood distillation industry. The values given above for these years were derived by multiplication of the quantities by the unit values.

[d] Reported as barrels, 1933–37, and converted to gallons calculated at 50 gallons to the barrel.

[e] According to the Bureau of the Census the 1931 data are somewhat incomplete because some establishments failed to report.

[f] Estimated.

TOTAL FOREST PRODUCTS	1899	1904	1909	1914	1919	1921	1923	1925	1927	1929	1931	1933	1935	1937
Adjusted index	82.0	76.5	83.0	82.3	78.6	83.4	90.9	103.1	99.3	100.0	63.4	46.4	59.2	76.2
Unadjusted index[a]	107.7	96.0	104.0	95.0	96.1	80.2	98.4	108.5	96.6	100.0	54.6	40.0	55.4	71.8

[a] Percentages of coverage:

Given year	Base year	Given year	Base year	Given year	Base year
1899:58.8, 1904:56.2	1909:56.1	1919:54.2, 1921:42.6, 1923:47.9	1929:44.3	1927:60.2, 1931:53.3	1929:61.9
1909:56.0, 1914:51.6	1919:54.6	1925:60.8	1929:57.8	1933:51.1	1929:59.4
				1935:57.9, 1937:58.3	1929:61.9

IRON AND STEEL PRODUCTS

BLAST-FURNACE PRODUCTS		1899	1904	1909	1914	1919	1921	1923	1925	1927	1929	1931	1933	1935	1937
Adjusted index		32.4	37.8	58.1	53.0	69.8	38.8	93.3	84.4	84.4	100.0	44.0	31.7	50.6	87.8
Unadjusted index[a]		33.6	38.6	59.6	54.1	71.7	39.1	94.5	85.1	85.0	100.0	43.4	31.4	50.2	87.0
Product	*Item*														
Pig iron	q Mil. l.t.					30.5			36.1	35.7	41.8	17.9	13.0	20.8	36.1
	v Mil. $					786			712	655	703	279	192	338	605
	p $ per l.t.					25.7			19.8	18.3	16.8	15.5	14.7	16.3	16.8
Pig iron and Ferro-alloys combined	q	14.4	16.6	25.7	23.3		16.6	40.2							
	v	207	229	388	313		409	985							
	p	14.3	13.8	15.1	13.4		24.6	24.5							
Ferro-alloys	q Mil. l.t.					.324			.430	.502	.648	.341	.234	.389	.629
	v Mil. $					31.9[b]			32.4	33.5	41.6	17.6	12.3	21.2	37.3
	p $ per l.t.					98.4			75.4	66.7	64.2	51.7	52.7	54.4	59.3

[a] Percentages of coverage:

Given year	Base year	Given year	Base year	Given year	Base year
1899:99.9, 1904:98.7	1909:99.1	1919:99.2, 1921:97.3, 1923:97.8, 1925:97.3	1929:96.5	1927:97.1, 1931:95.1, 1933:95.5, 1935:95.8, 1937:95.6	1929:96.5
1909:99.1, 1914:98.5	1919:99.2				

[b] Covers also the value of some other products, not exceeding 0.3 mil. dollars.

Indexes of Physical Output, with Basic Data on Quantity, Value and Price of Products

CAST-IRON PIPE		1914	1919	1921	1923	1925	1927	1929	1931	1933	1935	1937
Adjusted index		61.5	43.6	47.6	93.2	112.6	114.0	100.0	69.1	30.9	46.5	68.5
Unadjusted index[a]		56.0	39.3	40.3	82.7	101.6	102.2	100.0	68.9	31.2	46.4	69.3
Product	*Item*											
Bell and spigot pipe	*q* Mil. t.	.829	.375	.493	1.03	1.32	1.39	1.22	.868	.341	.459	.628
	v Mil. $	16.7	19.3	21.4	50.1	59.6	54.3	44.7	27.6	10.9	19.1	29.3
	p $ per t.	20.1	51.3	43.5	48.9	45.2	39.1	36.6	31.8	31.8	41.7	46.6
Flanged pipe	*q* Th. t.	27.3	23.8	19.6	15.2	16.2	17.6	22.5	9.73	6.99	5.76	11.2
	v Mil. $	.707	1.71	1.58	1.00	1.08	1.03	1.18	.601	.381	.391	.761
	p $ per t.	25.9	72.1	80.6	66.0	66.8	58.8	52.7	61.8	54.5	67.8	68.1
Culvert pipe	*q* Th. t.	11.0	5.66	4.65	7.49	9.36	14.2	21.4	18.1	4.63	12.4	10.1
	v Mil. $	.247	.344	.190	.394	.563	.777	1.11	.783	.143	.447	.398
	p $ per t.	22.4	60.8	40.8	52.6	60.1	54.9	51.8	43.3	30.8	35.9	39.5
Soil and plumbers' pipe and fittings	*q* Mil. t.	.212	.255	.211	.425	.524	.489	.358	.237	.129	.222[b]	.352[b]
	v Mil. $	6.17	20.4	11.7	24.0	26.4	25.7	18.8	10.9	4.81	10.0	16.1
	p $ per t.	29.2	80.1	55.3	56.5	50.4	52.5	52.5	46.1	37.3	45.3	45.8
Pipe fittings, other than reported as soil and plumbers'	*q* Th. t.	41.9	43.2	39.3	92.3	89.0	85.0	180[b]	122[b]	62.7[b]	98.8[b]	163[b]
	v Mil. $	2.18	6.81	5.33	12.4	9.70	9.40	20.1	11.2	6.45	10.4	19.6
	p $ per t.	52.1	157	136	134	109	111	112	92.4	103	105	120

[a] Percentages of coverage:

Given year	Base year	Given year	Base year	Given year	Base year
1914:97.5	1919: 96.6	1923:94.9	1929:107.0	1931:106.6	1929:107.0
1919:96.6	1929:107.0	1925:96.5		1933:108.2	
1921:90.7		1927:95.9		1935:106.7	
				1937:108.3	

[b] Estimated in part.

FILES		1929	1931	1933	1935	1937
Adjusted index		100.0	62.6	65.0	72.0	105.5
Unadjusted index[a]		100.0	61.6	65.9	71.7	103.2
Product	*Item*					
Metal-working files and rasps	q Mil. doz.	8.25	5.09	5.43[b]	5.93[b]	8.54[b]
	v Mil. $	13.0	6.66	6.92	8.47	12.4
	p $ per doz.	1.58	1.31	1.27	1.43	1.45
Woodworking files and rasps	q Th. doz.	74.1	38.7		36.5	42.7
	v Th. $	116	50.8		56.5	76.1
	p $ per doz.	1.57	1.31		1.55	1.78

[a] Percentages of coverage:

Given year	Base year
1931:91.7	1929:93.1
1933:93.6	1929:92.3
1935:92.8 } 1937:91.1 }	1929:93.1

[b] Estimated in part.

FIREARMS		1919	1921	1923	1925	1927	1929	1931	1933	1935	1937
Adjusted index			51.5	77.0	70.2	92.8	100.0	55.6	55.5	72.0	107.1
Unadjusted index[a]		b	70.0	90.2	80.7	100.6	100.0	47.6	33.2	66.4	114.1
Product	*Item*										
Pistols and revolvers	q Mil.		.451	.284	.283	.229	.225	.115	.0553	.0713	.139
	v Mil. $		6.20	3.62	3.26	2.89	2.97	1.52	.873	1.16	2.52
	p $ ea.		13.8	12.7	11.5	12.6	13.2	13.2	15.8	16.2	18.1
Rifles	q Mil.	.679	.127	.380	.323	.416	.458	.355	.313	.694	.913
	v Mil. $	7.89	1.29	3.71	3.06	4.44	4.57	2.33	1.78	4.31	7.37
	p $ ea.	11.6	10.1	9.75	9.46	10.7	9.99	6.58	5.69	6.20	8.07

For footnotes see next page.

Indexes of Physical Output, with Basic Data on Quantity, Value and Price of Products

FIREARMS (concluded)		1919	1921	1923	1925	1927	1929	1931	1933	1935	1937
Product	*Item*										
Shotguns	*q* Mil.	.432	.294	.485	.423	.623	.589	.198	.123	.253	.552
	v Mil. $	6.17	5.59	8.12	6.72	8.42	8.87	2.94	1.47	3.52	7.27
	p $ ea.	14.3	19.0	16.8	15.9	13.5	15.0	14.9	11.9	13.9	13.2

[a] Percentages of coverage:

Given year	Base year	Given year	Base year
1921: 101.6 1923: 87.5 1925: 85.9 1927: 81.0	1929: 74.7	1931: 64.0 1933: 44.7 1935: 69.0 1937: 79.6	1929: 74.7

[b] For 1919 value data alone are available for pistols and revolvers, the most important product of the industry in this year. For this reason no index is given, although the coverage is slightly in excess of 40 percent.

STEEL-MILL PRODUCTS		1899	1904	1909		1914	1919	1921	1923	1925	1927	1929	1931	1933	1935	1937
Adjusted index		23.5	29.0	43.3		43.8	63.2	38.0	80.8	81.9	81.1	100.0	47.2	43.0	63.5	97.0
Unadjusted index[a]		25.8	31.4	47.0		46.7	66.4	35.3	82.9	81.1	77.1	100.0	42.8	37.5	54.4	84.9
Product[b,c]	*Item*			*A*	*B*											
Unrolled steel																
Ingots	*q* Mil. l.t.	.104	.196	.143[d]	.143	.0634	.713	.331	.551	.535	.437	.661	.243	.133	.237	.643
	v Mil. $	2.78	3.99	3.59	3.59	1.38	33.3	14.4	18.9	16.4	12.7	17.1	5.55	3.93	9.47	21.1
	p $ per l.t.	26.8	20.3	25.2	25.2	21.8	46.7	43.5	34.3	30.6	29.0	25.9	22.8	29.6	40.0	32.9
Direct steel castings	*q* Mil. l.t.	.177	.287	.505	.448	.562	.683	.396	1.05	.938	.888	1.21	.371	.222	.405	1.04
	v Mil. $	14.6	20.6	38.9	34.7	44.2	129	70.8	163	144	145	191	59.6	32.3	67.4	185
	p $ per l.t.	82.5	71.7	77.0	77.5	78.7	189	179	154	154	163	158	161	145	167	178

STEEL-MILL PRODUCTS (continued)		1899	1904	1909		1914	1919	1921	1923	1925	1927	1929	1931	1933	1935	1937
Product[b,c]	*Item*			*A*	*B*											
Semifinished rolled products																
Blooms, billets and slabs[e]	q Mil. l.t.				4.97	4.06	6.23	2.78	7.27	6.98	6.27	7.63	3.18	3.09	4.53[f]	7.65[f]
	v Mil. $				111	82.3	261	104	290	251	211	255	93.6	81.5	133	257
	p $ per l.t.				22.3	20.3	41.9	37.5	39.8	35.9	33.6	33.4	29.5	26.4	29.4	33.6
Blooms, billets and slabs and sheet and tin plate bars (combined)	q	4.17	4.82	6.62[d]												
	v	96.3	110	149												
	p	23.1	22.7	22.4												
Sheet and tin plate bars	q Mil. l.t.				1.65	2.24	2.86	1.90	4.06	4.35	3.99	5.06	2.44	2.37	2.87	2.64
	v Mil. $				37.7	45.4	118	69.6	160	152	133	162	67.3	56.0	75.8	78.6
	p $ per l.t.				22.8	20.2	41.1	36.6	39.3	34.9	33.4	32.1	27.6	23.6	26.4	29.8
Muck and scrap bar	q Mil. l.t.	.204	.151	.174[d]	.174	.108	.173	.0309	.0989	.0534	.0474	.0865	.0169	.0120	.0183	.0221
	v Mil. $	5.94	3.94	4.99	4.99	2.97	10.8	1.94	6.06	2.77	2.36	3.89	.778	.423	.874	1.02
	p $ per l.t.	29.2	26.1	28.6	28.6	27.4	62.2	62.8	61.3	51.8	49.7	45.0	45.9	35.4	47.8	46.2
Finished rolled products																
Rails	q Mil. l.t.	2.25	2.19	2.86	2.84	1.84[g]	2.08	2.10	2.73	2.69	2.70	2.67	1.13	.393	.692	1.41
	v Mil. $	46.5	58.3	81.1	80.7	54.0	92.6	98.6	114	114	115	114	48.2	15.2	25.5	53.7
	p $ per l.t.	20.7	26.5	28.4	28.4	29.3	44.5	47.0	41.7	42.4	42.4	42.7	42.6	38.6	36.9	38.1
Rail joints and fastenings, tie plates, etc.	q Mil. l.t.		.174	.397	.392	.349[g]	.456	.383	.768	.815	.893	.872	.379	.198	.270	.460
	v Mil. $		5.66	14.5	14.3	11.5	27.4	24.3	43.2	46.7	50.4	47.8	19.1	9.32	12.9	23.8
	p $ per l.t.		32.5	36.5	36.5	33.0	60.0	63.5	56.2	57.4	56.4	54.8	50.3	47.1	47.7	51.6
Structural steel, light and heavy	q Mil. l.t.	.857	.955	2.12	2.10	2.08[g]	2.45	1.18	3.29	3.41	3.50	4.47	1.98	.992	1.62	3.11
	v Mil. $	29.4	32.7	65.6	64.7	57.5	148	57.3	162	155	148	189	71.7	35.2	67.3	149
	p $ per l.t.	34.3	34.3	30.9	30.9	27.6	60.3	48.6	49.2	45.4	42.4	42.3	36.1	35.5	41.6	47.7

For footnotes see p. 551.

Indexes of Physical Output, with Basic Data on Quantity, Value and Price of Products

STEEL-MILL PRODUCTS (continued)		1899	1904	1909		1914	1919	1921	1923	1925	1927	1929	1931	1933	1935	1937
Product[b,c]	*Item*			*A*	*B*											
Finished rolled products (continued)																
Concrete reinforcing bars	*q* Mil. l.t.				.191	.270[g]	.301	.202	.617	.709	.783	.972	.617	.357	.523	.814
	v Mil. $				5.59	7.75	18.4	10.3	32.4	35.1	35.4	42.4	23.1	12.3	22.2	36.8
	p $ per l.t.				29.2	28.7	61.1	50.8	52.6	49.5	45.2	43.6	37.4	34.5	42.6	45.2
Merchant bars, mill shafting, etc.																
Open-hearth and Bessemer steel bars	*q* Mil. l.t.							1.38	4.97	4.82[h]	4.17	6.07	2.17	2.22	3.19[i]	4.19[i]
	v Mil. $							76.8	281	265	209	305	93.2	91.7	156	236
	p $ per l.t.	*q* 2.49	2.44	3.98				55.5	56.5	55.0	50.2	50.3	43.0	41.3	48.7	56.2
		v 101	84.1	127												
Electric and crucible steel bars	*q* Mil. l.t.	*p* 40.3	34.4	32.0				.0317	.104	.110[h]	.0831	.161	.0642	.0575	.122[i]	.178[i]
	v Mil. $					*q* 2.33	4.19	9.68	35.5	36.2	31.3	53.3	18.4	16.2	31.7	51.1
	p $ per l.t.					*v* 79.4	332	305	341	330	376	331	287	281	259	287
						p 34.1	79.4									
Iron bars	*q* Mil. l.t.				*q* 3.15			.208	.400	.255	.202	.187	.0526	.0452	.0512	.0709
	v Mil. $				*v* 102			14.4	29.4	16.9	13.6	13.3	3.70	3.35	3.62	6.58
	p $ per l.t.				*p* 32.4			69.0	73.6	66.3	67.4	71.0	70.3	74.0	70.8	92.7
Bolt, nut, spike and chain rods	*q* Mil. l.t.					.0492	.0221	.0302	.0920	.0633	.0948	.121	.0198	.0340	.0398	.0371
	v Mil. $					1.67	1.89	1.78	5.24	3.31	4.38	5.68	.843	1.36	1.80	1.74
	p $ per l.t.					34.0	85.4	59.1	56.9	52.3	46.2	47.0	42.5	40.1	45.2	46.8
Wire rods	*q* Mil. l.t.	.917	1.79	2.30	.976	.979	1.13[j]	.666	1.24	1.11	1.02	1.16	.650	.736	.920	1.04
	v Mil. $	35.5	53.0	61.9	27.0	25.5	58.7	33.1	62.0	54.7	46.1	49.0	23.4	26.2	36.0	49.2
	p $ per l.t.	38.8	29.6	27.0	27.7	26.0	51.9	49.6	50.2	49.5	45.0	42.5	36.0	35.6	39.1	47.3

STEEL-MILL PRODUCTS (continued)		1899	1904	1909		1914	1919	1921	1923	1925	1927	1929	1931	1933	1935	1937
Product[b,c]	*Item*			*A*	*B*											
Finished rolled products (continued)																
Plates, no. 12 and thicker, not coated																
Crucible and electric plates, steel and saw plates	*q* Th. l.t.							2.57	10.9	9.60	5.07	4.13	3.45	7.41		
	v Mil. $							1.03	3.01	3.14	1.76	1.65	.971	1.53		
	p $ per l.t.							399	276	328	348	401	282	206		
Boiler and other plate	*q* Th. l.t.	*q*1,488	1,856	3,333	2,869	2,933	5,466	1,713	4,212	3,853	3,776	5,215	1,983	1,396	*q*1,745	3,334
	v Mil. $	*v* 68.1	77.8	133	111	97.9	427	91.8	217	178	163	227	74.9	50.9	*v* 78.8	171
	p $ per l.t.	*p* 45.8	41.9	40.0	38.7	33.4	78.1	53.6	51.6	46.1	43.1	43.4	37.8	36.5	*p* 45.1	51.3
Sheets no. 13 and thinner, not coated																
Plain and automobile body	*q* Th. l.t.							1,005	2,597	2,914	2,923	3,898	1,907	2,555	3,457	4,789
	v Mil. $							84.2	239	234	223	297	118	125	182	272
	p $ per l.t.							83.8	91.9	80.4	76.4	76.1	62.0	48.9	52.6	56.7
Black, for tinning	*q* Mil. l.t.	.394	.504	.631	.631	1.01	.563	.0434	.128	k	.0593	.143	.114	.123	.416	.779
	v Mil. $	21.0	25.3	31.0	31.0	43.1	49.2	3.63	10.4		4.38	10.2	7.65	7.08	27.4	44.7
	p $ per l.t.	53.2	50.2	49.0	49.0	42.6	87.4	83.6	81.0		73.9	71.1	67.1	57.7	65.9	57.4
Strips, bands, flats, scroll and hoops, narrower than 24 inches	*q* Mil. l.t.						.744	.427	1.28	1.38[h]	1.22	2.01	1.06	1.15	1.77	2.29
	v Mil. $						62.7	30.8	99.8	83.3	64.1	95.1	47.9	46.5	90.6	138
	p $ per l.t.						84.8	72.0	78.0	60.1	52.5	47.4	45.2	40.4	51.2	60.1
			q.337	.341	.341	.604										
			*v*12.8	10.4	10.4	19.9										
			*p*37.8	30.6	30.6	33.0										
Cotton ties for sale	*q* Mil. l.t.	*q*1.20					.0427	.0241	.0345	.0506	.0428	.0382	.0476	.0457	.0238	.0621
	v Mil. $	*v*49.2					3.51	1.34	2.77	2.78	2.23	1.84	1.93	1.49	1.07	3.33
	p $ per l.t.	*p*41.1					82.2	55.6	80.2	54.9	52.1	48.2	40.6	32.5	45.1	53.6
Skelp	*q* Mil. l.t.		1.56	2.08	.683	.777	.923	.682	1.38	1.28	1.24	1.27	.619	.468	.702	1.14
	v Mil. $		46.8	64.5	21.9	21.7	53.8	31.6	69.2	54.4	50.6	50.1	21.3	15.2	25.2	45.1
	p $ per l.t.		30.0	31.0	32.1	27.9	58.3	46.3	50.1	42.5	40.8	39.4	34.4	32.5	35.9	39.4

For footnotes see p. 551.

Indexes of Physical Output, with Basic Data on Quantity, Value and Price of Products

STEEL-MILL PRODUCTS (concluded)		1899	1904	1909		1914	1919	1921	1923	1925	1927	1929	1931	1933	1935	1937
Product[b,c]	*Item*			*A*	*B*											
Finished rolled products (concluded)																
Axles, rolled and forged	*q* Mil. l.t.	.103	.0836	.102	.0935	.0894[g]	.0978	.0363	.197	.135	.119	.150	.0269	.0546	.0428	.127
	v Mil. $	4.48	2.88	3.83	3.50	3.41	9.75	3.38	15.4	11.4	10.7	12.0	2.24	2.79	3.04	11.4
	p $ per l.t.	43.7	34.4	37.4	37.4	38.1	99.7	93.3	78.2	84.5	90.1	80.0	83.2	51.1	71.0	90.2
Car and locomotive wheels, rolled and forged	*q* Mil. l.t.						.118	.0829	.237	.147	.155	.209	.0844	.0693	.0827	.172
	v Mil. $						17.0	10.8	23.3	15.3	15.2	19.4	7.69	6.49	7.91	15.5
	p $ per l.t.						145	130	98.3	104	98.0	92.5	91.1	93.6	95.7	90.1
Armor plate and ordnance for sale	*q* Th. l.t.	15.3	24.4	26.8	26.8	38.7	101	70.8	8.84	1.07	7.75	9.94	17.2	7.51	21.3	19.7
	v Mil. $	7.53	10.6	10.6	10.6	19.9	55.7	39.7	1.92	.424	2.61	3.29	6.18	2.08	8.85	8.46
	p $ per l.t.	492	432	397	397	516	551	561	217	396	337	331	359	361	416	429
Scrap iron and steel	*q* Mil. l.t.		.877	1.24[d]	1.24	1.45	2.11	1.16	2.22	2.22	2.45	2.83	1.41	1.03	1.54	2.94
	v Mil. $		11.1	18.2	18.2	16.3	37.4	16.8	37.1	37.6	35.8	42.1	16.6	10.3	17.3	53.8
	p $ per l.t.		12.6	14.7	14.7	11.3	17.7	14.4	16.7	17.0	14.6	14.9	11.8	9.95	11.3	18.3
Rerolled or renewed rails	*q* Mil. l.t.		.0995	.106	.106	.0637	.0956	.0538	.113	.0703	.0885	.0568		.0183	.0197	.0322
	v Mil. $		2.48	2.68	2.68	1.44	4.74	2.16	5.12	2.65	3.10	1.93		.537	.685	1.35
	p $ per l.t.		24.9	25.2	25.2	22.6	50.0	40.2	45.4	37.7	35.1	34.0		29.4	34.7	42.1

A Comparable with earlier years. *B* Comparable with later years.

[a]Percentages of coverage:

Given year	Base year	Given year	Base year	Given year	Base year	Given year	Base year
1899:80.7	1909:79.7	1914:69.4	1919:68.4	1923:67.4		1931:59.5	1929:65.6
1904:83.3	1909:83.3	1919:69.0	1929:65.7	1925:65.1	1929:65.7	1933:57.2	
1909:70.6	1919:68.4	1921:61.0		1927:62.4		1935:56.2	1929:65.7
						1937:57.5	

[b] Two sets of 1909 data are presented, one comparable with earlier years and one with later years. Unless otherwise noted, the 1899–1909 data relate to total production, i.e., production for sale, interplant transfer and consumption within the plant; and the 1909–37 data relate to production for sale and interplant transfer only.

[c] Some of the establishments in the industry transfer unrolled steel and semifinished products (such as blooms and billets) to other steel producers classified in the industry. In 1899 transfers of this kind accounted for some 15 percent of the total value of products, but in 1937 for only about 7 percent. The decline in this percentage suggests a corresponding decline in the degree of duplication in the output of the industry; and an understatement, by our index, of the rise in the final output of the industry.

[d] The figures for 1899, 1904 and 1909 relate to production for sale and interplant transfer.

[e] Includes small amounts of hammered charcoal blooms in the years 1919–37, which came to less than one-tenth of 1 percent of the total for 1929.

[f] Not strictly comparable with earlier data because of the exclusion of piercing billets, rounds, and blanks in 1935 and 1937, which constituted less than 5 percent of the earlier totals.

[g] Contains a small but indeterminate amount produced and consumed in the same plant.

[h] The figures for 1925 and earlier years are not strictly comparable with those for 1927and 1929, because the "for sale" figures for 1925 and earlier years include data on cold-rolled steel, whereas the data for 1927 and 1929 on all the tonnage intended for cold-rolling are included in the "produced and consumed in same works" item.

[i] Stainless steel bars, which were probably included in the figures for open-hearth and Bessemer, and electric and crucible steel bars, were reported separately in 1935 and 1937. The 1935 quantity figure for stainless-steel bars (for sale and interplant transfer) was 7.04 th.l. tons, valued at 3.74 mil. dollars.

[j] The 1919 figure is not comparable with those for later years; the latter include rolled wire rods in coils or bars, of crucible, electric or cementation steel. Total production of this product amounted to 15.4 th.l. tons, valued at 4.77 mil. dollars in 1919, and no production was reported in 1914 or earlier years.

[k] In 1925 all black plate for tinning was consumed within the plant producing it.

Indexes of Physical Output, with Basic Data on Quantity, Value and Price of Products

TIN CANS and TINWARE, not elsewhere classified		1927	1929	1931	1933	1935	1937
Adjusted index		87.2[b]	100.0[c]	91.5	94.4	119.0[b]	160.2
Unadjusted index[a]		88.1	100.0	96.0	97.8	123.3	153.0
Product	*Item*						
Packers' cans							
Venthole-top cans	*q* Bil.	1.18	1.71	1.45	1.74	1.77	1.80
	v Mil. $	17.8	20.7	14.5	14.7	17.2	16.1
	p $ per th.	15.0	12.1	9.99	8.48	9.69	8.96
Sanitary cans, incl.	*q* Bil.	4.29	5.53	4.85	5.44	7.61	9.59
sweetened-condensed-	*v* Mil. $	97.7	122	93.8	94.8	152	169
milk cans	*p* $ per th.	22.8	22.1	19.3	17.4	19.9	17.6
Ice-cream cans	*q* Mil.	.694	1.10	.701	.540	.760	1.00
	v Mil. $	1.29	1.82	.825	.399	.412	.536
	p $ ea.	1.85	1.66	1.18	.739	.542	.536
Dairy milk cans	*q* Mil.	1.18	1.70	.976[d]	.973[d]	1.20[d]	1.58
	v Mil. $	4.25	3.98	2.58	2.56	3.58	5.04
	p $ ea.	3.62	2.33	2.64	2.63	2.98	3.20
Other cans and packages[d]	*q* Bil.	3.22	3.11	3.36	3.08	3.57	4.47
	v Mil. $	119	130	108	89.3	111	130
	p $ per th.	36.8	41.6	32.1	29.0	31.1	29.1

[a] Percentages of coverage:

Given year	Base year	Given year	Base year
1927:94.6 1931:98.2 1933:97.0	1929:93.7	1935:97.1 1937:89.5	1929:93.7

[b] Between 1927 and 1929 establishments making stamped tinware were transferred from tin cans and tinware to stamped and enameled ware, and between 1935 and 1937 they were transferred back to tin cans and tinware. The resulting discontinuities appear to be slight.

[c] Between 1929 and 1931, when dairymen's supplies was abandoned as a separate classification, some establishments making these products were transferred to tin cans and tinware.

[d] Estimated in part.

WIRE, not elsewhere made		1909	1914	1919	1921	1923	1925	1927	1929[b]			1931	1933	1935	1937
Adjusted index		66.5	64.0	69.1	50.8	97.0	91.6	98.4[c]	100.0			49.6	46.5	67.2	89.5
Unadjusted index[a]		78.2	75.8	83.5	56.9	108.3	94.1	101.5	100.0			50.8	45.5	55.1	73.2
Product[b]	*Item*								*A*	*B*	*C*				
Iron and steel wire															
Plain wire[d]	*q* Mil. t.	.189	.207	.245	.136	.257	.195	.229	.354	.305	1.07	.531	.611	.750	.921
	v Mil. $	11.4	12.9	28.5	12.6	25.5	20.1	20.7	31.3	26.8	79.0	35.7	39.9	53.2	76.0
	p $ per t.	60.1	62.6	116	92.9	99.3	103	90.6	88.4	87.8	73.5	67.1	65.2	70.9	82.5
Galvanized wire[d]	*q* Th. t.			173	72.8	96.7	50.2	50.8	86.9	72.7	233	172[e]	168[e]	175	201
	v Mil. $			15.8	5.77	7.20	4.27	4.85	8.09	6.77	17.0	11.0	9.94	12.7	16.3
	p $ per t.	*q* 155	156	91.4	79.3	74.5	85.1	95.6	93.1	93.1	72.9	63.8	59.2	72.7	80.9
		v 7.47	7.12												
Other coated wire, for sale and interplant transfer	*q* Th. t.	*p* 48.2	45.7	20.6	14.3	31.1	28.9	34.4	36.0	36.0	52.2	43.4	33.6	36.8	46.4
	v Mil. $			2.72	1.64	4.46	4.04	5.36	5.45	5.45	8.14	5.16	4.18	4.65	7.03
	p $ per t.			132	115	144	139	156	152	152	156	119	125	126	152
Copper wire															
Bare, for sale and interplant transfer	*q* Th. t.		54.2	60.8	45.3	126	131	140	98.7	98.7	272	94.0	49.6	71.8	129
	v Mil. $		16.2	26.9	13.4	44.5	44.0	43.3	41.8	41.8	119	22.9	10.3	19.5	43.1
	p $ per t.	*q* 102	298	442	297	354	335	309	424	424	436	244	208	272	334
		v 30.7													
Insulated wire and cable	*q* Th. t.	*p* 300	32.4	32.7											
	v Mil. $		10.9	21.8											
	p $ per t.		335	668											
Brass wire[d]	*q* Th. t.						3.52	3.21	4.71[f]	4.53[f]	40.7[g]	21.8	25.0	29.2	36.2
	v Mil. $						1.69	1.49	2.57	2.50	19.1	7.29	6.89	10.1	15.3
	p $ per t.		*q* 4.85	2.45	1.12	5.24	479	464	546	553	469	334	275	346	423
			v 2.02	2.05	.949	3.55									
Other wire, for sale and interplant transfer	*q* Th. t.		*p* 416	835	849	677	1.55	1.15	2.20	2.20	24.2	13.4	7.81[h]	10.4[h]	23.1[h]
	v Mil. $						1.77	2.29	4.79	4.79	23.6	10.2	6.76	9.79	14.5
	p $ per t.						1,143	1,990	2,176	2,176	973	764	865	940	627

For footnotes see pp. 554–55

Indexes of Physical Output, with Basic Data on Quantity, Value and Price of Products

WIRE, not elsewhere made (concluded)		1909	1914	1919	1921	1923	1925	1927	1929[b]			1931	1933	1935	1937
Product[b]	*Item*								*A*	*B*	*C*				
Wire products, iron and steel															
Nails and spikes	q Mil. 100 lb. kegs	3.45	3.21	3.68	3.34	3.70	2.26	2.34	1.96	1.96	13.6	8.18	9.10	9.58	11.1
	v Mil. $	7.14	6.05	15.1	12.4	12.8	8.08	8.23	6.65	6.65	44.9	22.5	24.3	30.6	35.7
	p $ per 100 lb. keg	2.07	1.88	4.10	3.72	3.47	3.57	3.52	3.39	3.39	3.30	2.76	2.67	3.20	3.22
Barbed wire, plain and coated	q Th. t.	76.3	69.2	82.1	37.9	46.6	31.1	32.6	39.3	39.3	222	162	182	196	188
	v Mil. $	3.34	2.82	7.31	3.05	3.60	2.23	2.22	2.65	2.65	13.8	8.28	8.61	10.8	11.2
	p $ per t.	43.8	40.8	89.0	80.5	77.1	71.6	68.0	67.4	67.4	62.3	51.2	47.2	55.0	59.6
Rope, cable, and strand	q Th. t.	34.1	43.2	55.6	29.8	67.0	69.0	75.0	88.3	88.3	202	92.9	69.1	101	139
	v Mil. $	5.45	6.88	12.2	6.18	15.7	17.2	18.1	19.8	19.8	52.5	21.7	15.7	29.7	40.8
	p $ per t.	160	159	219	208	234	250	241	225	225	260	234	227	294	293
Woven-wire fence and poultry netting, plain and coated	q Th. t.	q 116	128	97.1	83.1	117	85.2	97.9	89.5	89.5	412	274	233	267	334
	v Mil. $	v 6.72	6.76	10.3	9.88	11.9	8.31	9.37	8.84	8.84	38.6	22.1	17.6	21.5	29.4
	p $ per t.	p 58.0	52.7	106	119	102	97.5	95.7	98.7	98.7	93.6	80.4	75.8	80.6	88.1
Other woven-wire products	q Th. t.		8.61	13.4											
	v Mil. $		.915	2.18											
	p $ per t.		106	163											
Other fabricated iron and steel wire products, incl. cold-rolled flat wire and washers	q Th. t.	71.9	54.2	63.1											
	v Mil. $	6.13	4.95	11.7											
	p $ per t.	85.3	91.2	185											

A Comparable with 1909–19. *B* Comparable with 1921–27. *C* Comparable with 1931–37.

[a] Percentages of coverage:

Given year	Base year	Given year	Base year	Given year	Base year
1909:92.7	1919:95.3	1921:66.0	1929:58.9	1931:200.0	1929:195.3
1914:94.7	1919:96.5	1923:65.8		1933:191.1	
1919:74.5	1929:61.7	1925:60.5		1935:159.0	1929:194.0
		1927:60.8		1937:158.8	

[b] The data are not necessarily comparable for all years. Data for 1929 *A* relate to production for sale and interplant transfer, for 1929 *B* to production for sale, for 1929 *C* to production in all industries.

[c] Between 1927 and 1929 certain large establishments engaged primarily in rolling nonferrous metal and manufacturing nonferrous wire were transferred from wire, n.e.m., to nonferrous-metal products, n.e.c. In addition, a somewhat different method of handling data on the custom drawing of nonferrous wire was adopted in that year.

[d] Data for 1909–19 relate to production for sale and interplant transfer. For 1921–29, data relate to production for sale only.

[e] Data relate to production for sale and interplant transfer. The comparable 1929 figures are: *q* 269 th. tons; *v* $19.7 mil.; *p* $73.1 per ton.

[f] Because complete breakdowns are not available, these figures were estimated on the basis of the proportions obtaining in 1927 and 1929.

[g] For the years 1929–37, the data include a small amount of bronze wire.

[h] Estimated in part.

WROUGHT PIPE, not elsewhere made		*1925*	*1927*	*1929*	*1931*	*1933*	*1935*	*1937*
Adjusted index		76.8	68.4	100.0	62.8	31.4	55.8	91.0
Unadjusted index[a]		69.3	65.1	100.0	63.1	30.0	48.0	83.2
Product[b]	*Item*							
Oil-country casing,	*q* Mil. l.t.		.219	.493	.434	.0822	.170	.307
tubing and pipe	*v* Mil. $		19.2	39.7	33.2	6.20	14.4	26.6
	p $ per l.t.		87.6	80.4	76.4	75.4	84.3	86.8
Other black pipe	*q* Mil. l.t.	.330	.434	.531	.266	.187	.262	.485
	v Mil. $	28.9	41.7	45.2	21.7	13.5	25.2	40.2
	p $ per l.t.	87.8	96.2	85.0	81.5	72.3	96.2	82.9
Galvanized pipe	*q* Mil. l.t.	.150	.159	.172	.117	.0774	.126	.190
	v Mil. $	15.2	18.6	19.2	11.6	6.88	13.4	20.0
	p $ per l.t.	101	117	112	99.0	89.0	106	105
Mechanical tubing	*q* Th. l.t.		39.4	98.3	32.1	31.9		
	v Mil. $		9.44	14.6	5.35	5.21		
	p $ per l.t.		240	149	167	163		

[a] Percentages of coverage:

Given year	Base year	Given year	Base year
1925:46.6	1929:51.7	1935:71.7	1929:83.5
1927:90.6	1929:95.2	1937:76.3	1929:83.5
1931:95.6	1929:95.2		
1933:91.0	1929:95.2		

[b] Data relate to production in all industries other than steel-mill products.

Indexes of Physical Output, with Basic Data on Quantity, Value and Price of Products

TOTAL IRON and STEEL PRODUCTS	*1899*	*1904*	*1909*	*1914*	*1919*	*1921*	*1923*	*1925*	*1927*	*1929*	*1931*	*1933*	*1935*	*1937*
Adjusted index	20.9	28.9	43.9	48.3	58.9	45.6	84.3	87.0	87.2	100.0	54.4	44.6	61.4	89.3
Unadjusted index[a]	24.9	30.4	45.6	46.0	63.6	39.1	83.1	83.1	82.9	100.0	50.5	44.6	64.7	98.0

[a] Percentages of coverage:

Given year	Base year	Given year	Base year	Given year	Base year
1899:59.6	1909:52.0	1919:58.3	1929:53.9	1931:55.4	1929:59.6
1904:52.6		1921:46.8	1929:54.5	1933:59.7	
1909:54.3	1919:56.6	1923:53.7		1935:62.8	
1914:50.7	1919:57.6	1925:53.6	1929:56.2	1937:65.5	
		1927:56.4	1929:59.3		

NONFERROUS-METAL PRODUCTS

CLOCKS, WATCHES and MATERIALS		*1927*	*1929*	*1931*	*1933*	*1935*	*1937*
Adjusted index		113.4	100.0	63.5	48.4	77.8	139.2
Unadjusted index[a]		110.4	100.0	66.8	48.4	78.4	152.0
Product	*Item*						
Clocks							
Electric clocks	*q* Mil.	.0873	.447	3.80	2.01	2.68	4.27
	v Mil. $	1.62	5.19	12.9	4.82	7.45	12.7
	p $ ea.	18.6	11.6	3.40	2.40	2.78	2.96
Alarm clocks	*q* Mil.	10.5	9.46	5.68	6.70	8.39	10.7
	v Mil. $	13.1	10.8	5.11	5.16	6.91	9.08
	p $ ea.	1.25	1.14	.900	.770	.824	.851
Clock movements for other instruments	*q* Mil.		.239	.149	.0938	.475	1.13
	v Mil. $		1.63	.567	.254	.859	1.48
	p $ ea.		6.83	3.80	2.71	1.81	1.31

CLOCKS, WATCHES and MATERIALS (concluded)		1927	1929	1931	1933	1935	1937
Product	*Item*						
Clocks (concluded)							
Time stamps, watchmen's clocks, time switches, time locks, interval timers, etc.	*q* Mil.		.129	.0382	.0357	.155	.429
	v Mil. $		1.79	.982	.738	1.12	1.78
	p $ ea.		13.8	25.7	20.7	7.22	4.15
Time-recording clocks	*q* Th.		47.4	19.7	11.9	23.2	46.3
	v Mil. $		5.16	1.48	.511	1.53	2.50
	p $ ea.		109	75.3	43.0	66.2	54.1
Watches							
Nonjeweled watches	*q* Mil.	8.89	9.48	5.14	5.75	8.61	11.9
	v Mil. $	7.90	9.67	4.54	5.18	8.24	10.4
	p $ ea.	.888	1.02	.884	.902	.956	.875
Jeweled watches	*q* Mil.	2.28	1.52	.859	.688	1.41[b]	3.94
	v Mil. $	21.9	23.8	10.3	7.04	20.0	42.2
	p $ ea.	9.62	15.6	12.0	10.2	14.2	10.7

[a] Percentages of coverage:

Given year	Base year	Given year	Base year
1927:62.1	1929:63.8	1935:75.4	1929:74.9
1931:78.7	1929:74.9	1937:81.8	1929:74.9
1933:74.9	1929:74.9		

[b] Estimated in part.

COLLAPSIBLE TUBES		1925	1927	1929	1931	1933	1935	1937
Adjusted index		94.1	102.7	100.0	102.2	107.9	109.6	123.8
Unadjusted index[a]		80.2	87.0	100.0	108.2	111.2	105.1	114.3
Product	*Item*							
Collapsible tubes	*q* Mil. gross	2.76	3.00	3.45	3.73	3.83	3.62	3.94
	v Mil. $	7.73	9.24	8.56	7.77	6.86	7.83	8.15
	p $ per gross	2.80	3.08	2.48	2.08	1.79	2.16	2.07

[a] Percentages of coverage:

Given year	Base year	Given year	Base year
1925: 81.8	1929:96.1	1933: 99.0	1929:96.1
1927: 81.4	1929:96.1	1935: 92.1	1929:96.1
1931:101.8	1929:96.1	1937: 88.7	1929:96.1

Indexes of Physical Output, with Basic Data on Quantity, Value and Price of Products

COPPER		*1899*	*1904*	*1909*	*1914*	*1919*	*1921*	*1923*	*1925*	*1927*	*1929*	*1931*	*1933*	*1935*	*1937*
Adjusted index[a]															
Unadjusted index[b]		21.6	31.1	46.8	51.8	59.9	34.1	68.7	78.3	82.4	100.0	54.1	29.9	48.2	80.4
Product[c]	*Item*														
Copper, primary and secondary, produced at primary refineries	*q* Bil. lb.	.592[d]	.851[d]	1.41	1.57	1.84	1.06	2.11	2.40	2.54	3.07	1.66	.913	1.47	2.45
Gold	*q* Th. fine oz.				265	187	52.8	272	348	368	458	215	106	227	496
Silver	*q* Mil. fine oz.			18.3	14.8	12.9	4.78	14.7	18.1	14.6	17.9	9.57	5.84	12.7	20.4
Nickel	*q* Th. t.	.011	.012		.423	.511[e]	.111	.100	.272	.860	.340	.373	.126	.160	.219
Sulphuric acid	*q* Th. t.				349	365	286	401[f]	393[f]	470	633	436	301	160	292
Copper sulphate	*q* Mil. lb.			31.0	34.4	31.1	26.1	31.4	26.5	36.0	40.3	35.3	25.4	26.5	46.0

[a] No adjusted indexes were computed because value data are not available for some of the products, and therefore the percentages of coverage could not be determined; and also because the aggregate value reported for the industry's products is seriously affected by duplication.

[b] The unadjusted index was computed by means of aggregates of quantities, with 1929 prices used as coefficients. These prices are: copper, $.176 per lb.; gold, $20.7 per fine oz.; silver, $.533 per fine oz.; nickel $874 per ton; sulphuric acid, $9.63 per ton; and copper sulphate, $.055 per lb. The source of these prices is the *Minerals Yearbook.*

[c] Bureau of Mines, *Minerals Yearbook*, chapters on the respective products. The quantities of gold and silver represent the gold or silver content of the domestic copper ore mined during the year specified.

[d] Does not include secondary copper produced in primary refineries. The comparable 1929 figure is 2.74 bil. lb.

[e] Includes an indeterminate amount of nickel refined from other ores.

[f] These figures, taken from the Census of Manufactures, relate to sales, not production.

LEAD		1899	1904	1909	1914	1919	1921	1923	1925	1927	1929	1931	1933	1935	1937
Adjusted index[a]															
Unadjusted index[b]		38.5	50.8	63.0	72.3	62.8	59.9	83.3	99.4	101.4	100.0	57.5	36.2	43.2	58.3
Product[c]	*Item*														
Lead, primary and secondary, produced at primary refineries[d]	q Th. t.	298[e]	393[e]	447[e]	553	495	463	655	802	835	840	487	305	369	497
Gold	q Th. fine oz.				74.5	41.9	61.9	38.1	50.4	41.5	37.2	17.6	13.5	23.1	25.6
Silver	q Mil. fine oz.			17.0	19.3	14.4	14.9	20.1	18.8	15.8	11.7	6.12	3.92	3.35	4.77

[a] No adjusted indexes were computed because value data are not available for some of the products, and therefore the percentages of coverage could not be determined; and also because the aggregate value reported for the industry's products is seriously affected by duplication.

[b] The unadjusted index was computed by means of aggregates of quantities, with 1929 prices used as coefficients. These prices are: lead, $126 per ton; gold, $20.7 per fine oz.; and silver, $.533 per fine oz.

[c] Bureau of Mines, *Minerals Yearbook*, chapters on the respective products. The quantities of gold and silver represent the gold or silver content of the domestic lead ore mined during the year specified.

[d] Does not include antimonial lead.

[e] Does not include secondary pig lead produced at primary refineries. The comparable 1929 figure is 775 th. tons.

NONFERROUS-METAL PRODUCTS, not elsewhere classified		1925	1927	1929	1931	1933	1935	1937
Adjusted index		70.4	71.9[b]	100.0	58.9	43.1	61.6	88.5
Unadjusted index[a]		72.7	72.2	100.0	60.7	40.3	59.7	83.1
Product	*Item*							
Ingots and pigs[c]								
Copper, secondary	q Th. t.	15.0	.410	5.91	.459	.113	.134	.028
	v Th. $	4,049	123	1,864	65.6	16.1	22.6	6.67
	p $ per t.	270	299	316	143	143	169	238

For footnotes see p. 563.

Indexes of Physical Output, with Basic Data on Quantity, Value and Price of Products

NONFERROUS-METAL PRODUCTS, not elsewhere classified (continued)		1925	1927	1929	1931	1933	1935	1937
Product	*Item*							
Ingots and pigs[c] (concluded)								
Lead, secondary	*q* Th. t.	24.7	24.3	45.1	51.6	13.9	24.6	9.41
	v Mil. $	4.78	3.02	6.55	4.27	1.16	2.18	1.16
	p $ per t.	193	125	145	82.7	83.2	88.2	123
Tin, secondary	*q* Th. t.			1.80	2.07	1.07	.267[d]	.829
	v Mil. $			1.50	.766	.737	.264	.839
	p $ per t.			834	370	686	988	1012
Zinc, secondary	*q* Th. t.	.593	.836	1.66	.236	.420		
	v Th. $	105	102	197	17.8	36.7		
	p $ per t.	177	122	119	75.3	87.3		
Brass and bronze	*q* Th. t.	25.7	30.1	33.2	26.7	10.2	13.6[d]	14.0
	v Mil. $	6.61	7.29	10.1	4.71	1.39	2.62	3.46
	p $ per t.	257	243	305	176	137	193	248
Antifriction-bearing metal	*q* Th. t.	35.6	23.3	42.8	8.57	7.84	18.7[d]	26.8
	v Mil. $	15.3	12.0	16.1	2.23	2.65	5.70	7.63
	p $ per t.	431	516	376	260	337	305	285
Solders	*q* Th. t.	38.3	38.6	40.5	24.2	12.8	27.0	34.2
	v Mil. $	22.8	22.8	21.3	7.02	5.39	11.6	16.7
	p $ per t.	595	590	527	290	420	429	489
Type metal	*q* Th. t.	25.6	26.3	30.4	19.6	14.4	19.6[d]	23.6
	v Mil. $	5.45	5.13	5.52	2.37	1.78	2.93	4.25
	p $ per t.	213	195	181	121	123	149	180

NONFERROUS-METAL PRODUCTS, not elsewhere classified (continued)		1925	1927	1929	1931	1933	1935	1937
Product	*Item*							
Plates and sheets[e]								
Brass and bronze, made for sale	*q* Th. t.	189	165[f]	216	107	107	145	178
	v Mil. $	71.0	60.8	91.0	31.6	26.2	42.3	72.4
	p $ per t.	375	369	422	296	245	291	407
Copper	*q* Th. t.	81.2	92.6	128	72.0	69.3	93.0	104
	v Mil. $	35.2	39.2	59.5	23.3	17.2	26.1	36.3
	p $ per t.	434	424	466	323	249	281	348
Lead	*q* Th. t.	25.6	26.3	35.8	16.6	12.3	17.3	22.5
	v Mil. $	5.68	4.81	6.49	2.23	1.54	2.31	3.78
	p $ per t.	222	183	181	134	125	133	168
Zinc	*q* Th. t.			54.1	56.6	25.0	49.9	63.7
	v Mil. $			9.54	8.10	4.31	8.13	12.3
	p $ per t.			176	143	173	163	194
Nickel alloys	*q* Th. t.		18.5	27.2	13.6	10.6	14.9	17.9
	v Mil. $		12.6	18.3	8.20	5.71	7.71	10.8
	p $ per t.		680	675	603	537	518	603
Other metals	*q* Th. t.			2.42	2.53	1.50	2.29[d]	
	v Mil. $			1.49	1.40	.981	1.18	
	p $ per t.			615	553	655	518	
Rods[e]								
Brass and bronze	*q* Th. t.	80.4	91.7	125	101	68.8	94.3	140
	v Mil. $	26.5	28.2	45.9	22.6	14.3	23.9	43.2
	p $ per t.	330	308	366	225	207	253	309
Copper	*q* Th. t.	113	110	227	90.4	80.5	111	199
	v Mil. $	36.5	32.5	81.1	18.6	12.6	22.4	44.1
	p $ per t.	322	295	357	205	156	201	221
Nickel alloys and other nonferrous metals	*q* Th. t.			10.9	4.14	5.00	7.82	
	v Mil. $			8.93	3.35	4.23	6.40	
	p $ per t.			822	810	846	819	

For footnotes see p. 563.

Indexes of Physical Output, with Basic Data on Quantity, Value and Price of Products

NONFERROUS-METAL PRODUCTS, not elsewhere classified (continued)		1925	1927	1929	1931	1933	1935	1937
Product	*Item*							
Tubing, seamless and pipe[e]								
Brass and bronze	*q* Th. t.	51.3	62.3	71.3	49.0	38.7	47.8	78.9
	v Mil. $	24.7	25.9	36.2	16.8	10.8	16.6	34.9
	p $ per t.	483	416	508	343	278	348	442
Copper	*q* Th. t.	29.0	36.2	49.1	32.3	29.6	34.0	58.0
	v Mil. $	14.9	17.9	25.8	12.1	9.05	12.0	26.3
	p $ per t.	515	494	525	374	306	354	453
Lead	*q* Th. t.	52.9	43.8	37.0	22.2	13.5	16.8	23.0
	v Mil. $	11.9	8.29	7.00	2.91	1.95	2.46	3.93
	p $ per t.	224	189	189	131	145	146	171
Nickel alloys	*q* Th. t.			1.79	1.23	.792	1.30	1.92
	v Mil. $			2.54	1.29	.600	1.52	2.16
	p $ per t.			1421	1052	758	1167	1129
Other metal	*q* Th. t.			3.69	2.83	1.59	1.29[d]	
	v Mil. $			2.34	1.55	1.53	.872	
	p $ per t.			635	549	967	676	
Castings, rough								
Brass and bronze	*q* Mil. lb.	340[d]	344[d]	414	209	73.1	180[d]	253
	v Mil. $	66.0	66.3	98.9	33.5	11.9	33.5	49.4
	p $ per lb.	.194	.193	.239	.160	.163	.186	.195
Copper	*q* Mil. lb.	4.91	4.51	9.80	3.29	2.73	6.68[d]	7.80
	v Mil. $	1.31	1.31	2.69	.951	.664	1.41	2.21
	p $ per lb.	.266	.291	.275	.289	.243	.212	.284
Heat-corrosion-resistant nonferrous alloys, and nickel alloys other than heat-corrosion-resistant	*q* Mil. lb.			5.23	4.07	6.63	5.18[d]	8.47
	v Mil. $			2.94	2.23	2.84	2.90	4.49
	p $ per lb.			.563	.547	.428	.559	.530

NONFERROUS-METAL PRODUCTS, not elsewhere classified (concluded)		1925	1927	1929	1931	1933	1935	1937
Product	*Item*							
Castings, rough (concluded)								
Other metals	q Mil. lb.			17.6	10.3	2.97	8.12[d]	
	v Mil. $			5.94	2.16	.610	1.74	
	p $ per lb.			.337	.210	.206	.215	

[a] Percentages of coverage:

Given year	Base year	Given year	Base year
1925:59.5	1929:57.6	1933:58.6	1929:62.6
1927:59.9	1929:59.6	1935:60.7	1929:62.6
1931:64.6	1929:62.6	1937:56.8	1929:60.6

[b] In 1929 certain large establishments engaged primarily in rolling nonferrous metal and manufacturing nonferrous wire were transferred from wire, n.e.m., to nonferrous-metal products, n.e.c. In addition, a somewhat different method of handling data on the custom drawing of nonferrous wire was adopted in that year.

[c] For the years 1931–37 values are given for the combined production of ingots and pigs in the nonprecious secondary metals industry and in nonferrous-metal products, n.e.c. The value figures for nonferrous-metal products, n.e.c., were estimated by multiplication of the given quantity figure by a price obtained by division of the combined value figure for both industries by the combined production figure for both industries.

[d] Estimated in part.

[e] Except where otherwise indicated, the data relate to production for sale and interplant transfer.

[f] Production for sale and interplant transfer. The comparable 1929 data are: q 234 th. tons; v $98.5 mil.; p $421 per ton.

SECONDARY METALS, NONPRECIOUS		1925	1927	1929	1931	1933	1935	1937
Adjusted index		78.3	84.0	100.0	57.6	67.2	86.7	124.3
Unadjusted index[a]		59.4	78.6	100.0	59.4	64.3	73.7	114.6
Product[b]	*Item*							
Copper	q Th. t.	24.1	16.4	44.2	25.8	29.2	29.1	39.9
	v Mil. $	6.66	4.13	14.6	3.69	4.16	4.91	9.49
	p $ per t.	277	252	331	143	143	169	238

For footnotes see next page.

Indexes of Physical Output, with Basic Data on Quantity, Value and Price of Products

SECONDARY METALS, NONPRECIOUS (concluded)		*1925*	*1927*	*1929*	*1931*	*1933*	*1935*	*1937*
Product[b]	*Item*							
Lead	*q* Th. t.	44.8	84.4	108	87.1	105	105	116
	v Mil. $	7.91	11.7	15.0	7.20	8.76	9.25	14.3
	p $ per t.	176	139	139	82.7	83.2	88.2	123
Tin	*q* Th. t.			1.36	1.27	1.38	2.52[c]	4.10
	v Mil. $			1.17	.472	.950	2.49	4.14
	p $ per t.			858	370	686	988	1,012
Zinc	*q* Th. t.	39.2	49.0	38.2	18.9	22.9		
	v Mil. $	6.41	5.88	5.32	1.42	2.00		
	p $ per t.	164	120	139	75.3	87.3		
Brass and bronze	*q* Th. t.	73.7	94.8	112	54.2	48.5	61.8[c]	125
	v Mil. $	17.0	22.2	33.4	9.54	6.63	12.0	30.9
	p $ per t.	230	234	298	176	137	193	248
Solders	*q* Th. t.	4.41	10.2	15.9	10.9	13.9	16.6[c]	24.4
	v Mil. $	2.89	7.06	7.27	3.15	5.86	7.12	11.9
	p $ per t.	656	691	456	290	420	429	489
Antifriction-bearing metal	*q* Th. t.	13.3	15.2	11.6	5.99	4.98	6.59[c]	14.2
	v Mil. $	6.48	5.44	4.21	1.56	1.68	2.01	4.05
	p $ per t.	487	357	363	260	337	305	285
Type metal	*q* Th. t.	4.47	10.8	11.8	9.63	7.98	10.2[c]	11.1
	v Mil. $	1.06	2.21	2.37	1.16	.983	1.52	2.01
	p $ per t.	238	204	200	121	123	149	180

[a] Percentages of coverage:

Given year	Base year	Given year	Base year
1925:58.9, 1927:72.7	1929:77.7	1933:75.4	1929:78.8
1931:81.3	1929:78.8	1935:62.7, 1937:67.9	1929:73.7

[b] For the years 1931–37 values are given for the combined production in the nonprecious secondary metals industry and in nonferrous-metal products, n.e.c. The value figures for secondary metals, nonprecious, were estimated by multiplication of the given quantity figure by a price obtained by division of the combined value figure for both industries by the combined production figure for both industries.

[c] Estimated in part.

ZINC		1899	1904	1909	1914	1919	1921	1923	1925	1927	1929	1931	1933	1935	1937
Adjusted index[a]															
Unadjusted index[b]		20.6	29.9	40.7	56.7	73.9	33.9	82.3	90.5	94.0	100.0	48.4	49.6	64.3	86.1
Product[c]	*Item*														
Zinc, primary and secondary, produced at primary refineries[d]	*q* Th. t.	129[e]	187[e]	256[e]	360	477	210	530	586	606	637	297	321	434	581
Gold	*q* Th. fine oz.				1.91	.086	.076	3.32	.375	1.56	1.35	0	.254	.163	1.88
Silver	*q* Th. fine oz.			314	145	39.5	6.16	2171	182	1686	1577	6.02	70.7	51.9	557
Sulphuric acid	*q* Th. t.[g]				412[f]	447[f]	320[f]	384[fh]	1082	1091	1274	808	598	534	693

[a] No adjusted indexes were computed because value data are not available for some of the products, and therefore the percentages of coverage could not be determined; and also because the aggregate value reported for the industry's products is seriously affected by duplication.

[b] The unadjusted index was constructed by means of aggregates of quantities, with 1929 prices used as coefficients. These prices are: zinc, $132 per ton; gold, $20.7 per fine oz.; silver $.533 per fine oz.; and sulphuric acid, $9.63 per ton. The source of these prices is the *Minerals Yearbook*.

[c] Bureau of Mines, *Minerals Yearbook*, chapters on the respective products. The quantities of gold and silver represent the gold or silver content of the domestic zinc ore mined during the year specified.

[d] Data on redistilled zinc at primary refineries, 1921–27, supplied in a special tabulation prepared by the Bureau of Mines.

[e] Does not include redistilled zinc produced at primary refineries. Comparable 1929 figure: 625 th. tons.

[f] Sulphuric acid made from zinc blende only. The comparable 1929 figure is 627 th. tons.

[g] 60° Baumé equivalent. The 1921 figure is estimated in part (see Bureau of Mines, *Mineral Resources of the United States, 1925*, Part I, p. 335).

[h] Figure relates to sales, not production.

TOTAL NONFERROUS-METAL PRODUCTS	1925	1927	1929	1931	1933	1935	1937
Adjusted index	79.2	84.5	100.0	64.4	47.1	66.0	89.4
Unadjusted index[a,b]	75.9	81.5	100.0	58.0	43.4	61.5	91.5

[a] Percentages of coverage:

Given year	Base year	Given year	Base year
1925:40.8	1929:42.6	1933:43.8	1929:47.6
1927:45.8	1929:47.5	1935:44.4	1929:47.6
1931:42.8	1929:47.6	1937:48.6	1929:47.6

[b] Indexes are not given for this group for years prior to 1925 because of inadequate coverage.

MACHINERY

Indexes of Physical Output, with Basic Data on Quantity, Value and Price of Products

AGRICULTURAL IMPLEMENTS		1921	1923	1925	1927	1929	1931		1933	1935	1937
Adjusted index		68.3	63.6	61.2	72.8	100.0	30.5		b	c	c
Unadjusted index[a]		51.4	56.3	55.6	75.3	100.0	24.9		b	40.7	79.8
Product	*Item*						*A*	*B*	*C*		
Plows and listers											
Moldboard plows											
Horse, walking, 1-horse	*q* Th.	133	217	227	202	242	75.6	64.9	54.1	159	147
	v Mil. $	.882	1.38	1.28	1.21	1.42	.365	.294	.232	.835	.839
	p $ each	6.66	6.35	5.64	5.98	5.87	4.83	4.53	4.29	5.25	5.69
2-horse and larger	*q* Th.	180	285	182	164	205	54.8	50.4	50.2	160	156
	v Mil. $	2.45	3.09	2.32	2.25	2.65	.666	.607	.561	1.86	1.84
	p $ each	13.6	10.9	12.7	13.7	12.9	12.2	12.0	11.2	11.6	11.8
Horse, sulky, 1-bottom	*q* Th.	28.7	26.5	17.3	24.2	22.8	3.80	3.52	2.20	6.67	5.20
	v Mil. $	1.57	1.12	.964	1.29	1.19	.179	.164	.101	.341	.266
	p $ each	54.8	42.2	55.6	53.2	52.4	47.1	46.5	46.0	51.2	51.1
2-bottom and larger	*q* Th.	19.2	33.4	29.5	34.0	33.6	1.53[d]	1.28	1.82	4.96[d]	7.67
	v Mil. $	1.59	2.31	3.08	3.36	3.17	.129	.107	.126	.374	.647
	p $ each	83.2	69.2	104	98.9	94.3	84.2	83.6	69.3	75.3	84.3
Tractor, 1- and 2-bottom	*q* Th.	13.1	60.0	53.5	64.9	66.8	19.9	19.6	4.75	46.7	125
	v Mil. $	1.03	3.42	3.45	4.12	4.14	1.26	1.23	.272	3.16	9.13
	p $ each	78.4	57.0	64.6	63.5	61.9	63.3	62.8	57.3	67.7	73.1
3-bottom and larger	*q* Th.	10.8	5.17	4.66	16.7	56.1	6.88	6.85	1.20	11.2	24.1
	v Mil. $	1.60	.409	.416	1.85	6.94	.828	.824	.105	1.31	2.81
	p $ each	148	79.1	89.3	110	124	120	120	87.8	118	117
Listers (middle busters) horse, 1-bottom	*q* Th.	20.6	34.6	30.5	23.8	37.3	6.86			15.0[e]	20.1[e]
	v Mil. $	.686	.879	.748	.510	.913	.130			.415	.650
	p $ each	33.3	25.4	24.5	21.4	24.5	18.9			27.6	32.3

AGRICULTURAL IMPLEMENTS (continued)		1921	1923	1925	1927	1929	1931		1933	1935	1937
Product	*Item*						*A*	*B*	*C*		
Plows and listers (continued)											
Listers (middle busters) tractor-drawn	*q* Th.					2.97	4.68	4.68	.784		
	v Mil. $					.417	.439	.439	.047		
	p $ each					141	93.7	93.8	60.0		
Disk plows, tractor	*q* Th.					16.4	2.04	1.86	.958	3.64	11.2
	v Mil. $					2.13	.314	.302	.182	.668	1.66
	p $ each					130	154	162	190	183	148
1-way disk tillers	*q* Th.					23.0	7.08	7.02	.430	6.98	15.0
	v Mil. $					4.52	1.24	1.22	.0560	1.10	2.39
	p $ each					196	176	174	130	158	159
Harrows, rollers, pulverizers, and stalk cutters											
1-horse (spike- and spring-tooth)	*q* Th.					30.9	16.9	16.6	10.8		
	v Th. $					162	68.6	68.0	38.0		
	p $ each					5.24	4.07	4.10	3.52		
Harrow sections, spike-tooth	*q* Th.	176	195	177	242	339	103	95.5	37.2	163	247
	v Mil. $	1.42	1.22	1.43	1.72	2.31	.727	.657	.216	1.18	1.90
	p $ each	8.09	6.29	8.09	7.11	6.80	7.07	6.88	5.81	7.20	7.68
spring-tooth	*q* Th.	82.5	120	109	117	126	44.0	39.2	27.9	113	153
	v Mil. $	1.04	1.49	1.00	1.24	1.45	.491	.400	.205	1.07	1.63
	p $ each	12.6	12.4	9.13	10.6	11.4	11.2	10.2	7.34	9.51	10.6
Disk harrows, horse	*q* Th.	80.4	91.2	66.6	76.9	81.4	20.1	18.2	8.09		
	v Mil. $	3.13	3.23	2.82	3.30	3.48	.796	.711	.210		
	p $ each	38.9	35.4	42.3	43.0	42.8	39.6	39.1	25.9	*q* 82.8	136
										v 5.19	9.74
tractor	*q* Th.	38.1	35.4	29.1	45.8	57.4	26.8	25.4	3.30	*p* 62.8	71.9
	v Mil. $	3.41	2.36	2.32	3.75	5.23	2.27	2.09	.217		
	p $ each	89.5	66.7	79.7	81.8	91.0	85.0	82.5	65.8		

For footnotes see p. 572.

Indexes of Physical Output, with Basic Data on Quantity, Value and Price of Products

AGRICULTURAL IMPLEMENTS (continued)		1921	1923	1925	1927	1929	1931		1933	1935	1937
Product	*Item*						*A*	*B*	*C*		
Harrows, rollers, pulverizers, and stalk cutters (concluded)											
Soil pulverizers and packers	*q* Th.	7.28[f]	11.9	6.76	22.8	18.8	5.89			7.24	19.5
	v Mil. $	.446	.566	.352	1.21	.880	.308			.404	1.02
	p $ each	61.2	47.7	52.1	53.2	46.7	52.3			55.7	52.2
Stalk cutters	*q* Th.					11.7	2.30	1.95	.379	5.16	7.51
	v Th. $					439	86.1	73.0	13.0	166	264
	p $ each					37.6	37.5	37.5	34.3	32.1	35.1
Planting and fertilizing machinery											
Corn planters, horse, 1-row	*q* Th.					19.4	8.21			14.7	21.7
	v Th. $					335	183			213	338
	p $ each					17.3	22.3			14.5	15.6
Corn planters, horse or tractor, 2-row	*q* Th.	35.8	41.3	41.2	42.5	55.4[g]	27.7	25.5	4.26	19.8	53.9
	v Mil. $	1.76	2.12	2.39	2.37	3.09	1.54	1.44	.211	1.15	3.04
	p $ each	49.2	51.2	58.1	55.6	55.8	55.7	56.8	49.6	58.2	56.4
Combination corn and cotton planters, 1-row	*q* Th.	33.1	34.8	52.1	39.6	81.0	11.0	10.8	5.97	38.4	67.1
	v Mil. $	.625	.711	1.33	.804	1.65	.204	.200	.0910	.666	1.09
	p $ each	18.9	20.4	25.5	20.3	20.4	18.6	18.5	15.2	17.4	16.2
2-row	*q* Th.	1.87	8.95	10.8	4.89	13.0	4.43	4.43	.497	11.1	11.7
	v Th. $	110	406	719	294	914	305	305	28.0	588	675
	p $ each	59.0	45.4	66.7	60.2	70.5	68.7	68.7	56.3	52.9	57.9
Combined listers and drills with planting attachments	*q* Th.	12.4	4.46	20.2	9.23	7.00	2.03	1.84	1.38	4.64	6.86
	v Mil. $	.510	.238	1.39	.674	.604	.140	.120	.0860	.470	.629
	p $ each	41.1	53.4	68.8	73.1	86.2	69.1	65.4	62.4	101	91.7
Grain drills, horse	*q* Th.	41.1	29.4	31.8	52.5	51.1	8.89	8.17	3.44		
	v Mil. $	3.37	2.82	3.46	5.78	6.68	.964	.890	.159		
	p $ each	82.0	95.9	109	110	131	108	109	46.2	*q* 32.4	57.0
										v 4.13	7.04
tractor	*q* Th.	1.46	1.15	.805	6.12	19.3	2.49	2.39	.415	*p* 127	124
	v Mil. $	.130	.112	.106	.862	3.36	.456	.420	.0600		
	p $ each	88.8	98.1	132	141	174	183	176	145		

AGRICULTURAL IMPLEMENTS (continued)		1921	1923	1925	1927	1929	1931		1933	1935	1937
Product	*Item*						*A*	*B*	*C*		
Planting and fertilizing machinery (concluded)											
Fertilizer distributors, horse and tractor	*q* Th.	19.6	38.4	68.1	53.4	92.7[g]	21.1	16.3	6.84	33.5	55.4
	v Th. $	230	593	585	433	720	152	110	48.0	439	500
	p $ each	11.7	15.4	8.59	8.10	7.76	7.20	6.74	7.01	13.1	9.02
Lime spreaders	*q* Th.					12.3	3.23	2.61	.423	2.01	12.8
	v Th. $					346	129	110	13.0	74.6	434
	p $ each					28.2	40.1	42.2	30.7	37.1	33.8
Manure spreaders	*q* Th.	44.1	36.5	53.8	67.7	61.0	19.7	19.5	6.36	31.5	60.1
	v Mil. $	4.99	3.83	6.33	8.30	7.19	2.10	2.08	.581	3.62	7.22
	p $ each	113	105	118	123	118	107	107	91.4	115	120
Potato planters, except hand	*q* Th.	6.46	5.76	3.54	6.36	8.54	4.13			3.52	4.85
	v Th. $	591	364	238	440	573	361			292	587
	p $ each	91.6	63.1	67.1	69.2	67.1	87.4			82.9	121
Cultivators and weeders											
Cultivators, horse-drawn except disk											
1-horse	*q* Th.	86.3	155	156	132	203	58.0	49.6	48.6	129	138
	v Th. $	500	822	822	698	979	295	250	210	650	786
	p $ each	5.79	5.31	5.29	5.28	4.83	5.09	5.04	4.32	5.04	5.69
1-row, walking	*q* Th.	33.0	54.1	52.0	34.5	51.7	8.82	8.11	5.56	16.7	28.8
	v Mil. $	.683	1.27	1.56	1.09	1.67	.253	.234	.152	.562	.951
	p $ each	20.7	23.5	29.9	31.6	32.3	28.7	28.8	27.3	33.6	33.0
1-row, riding	*q* Th.	105	137	122	86.7	115	40.5	37.6	15.2	34.3	48.6
	v Mil. $	4.16	4.74	5.14	3.31	4.24	1.46	1.34	.488	1.35	1.95
	p $ each	39.7	34.5	42.1	38.2	36.8	36.1	35.6	32.2	39.5	40.1
2-row	*q* Th.	23.5	27.8	50.5	41.0	54.5	10.4	9.01	1.91	5.84	1.88
	v Mil. $	1.62	1.73	4.11	3.50	4.49	.874	.774	.138	.451	.108
	p $ each	69.1	62.0	81.4	85.4	82.3	84.0	85.9	72.1	77.1	57.2
Cultivators, tractor-drawn	*q* Th.					34.6	15.6	13.5	3.37	54.5[h]	127[h]
	v Mil. $					2.90	1.79	1.54	.284	4.47	10.9
	p $ each					83.8	115	115	84.3	82.1	86.0

For footnotes see p. 572.

Indexes of Physical Output, with Basic Data on Quantity, Value and Price of Products

AGRICULTURAL IMPLEMENTS (continued)		1921	1923	1925	1927	1929	1931		1933	1935	1937
Product	*Item*						*A*	*B*	*C*		
Cultivators and weeders (concluded)											
Weeders	*q* Th.					25.2	14.7	13.2	3.69		
	v Th. $					449	213	164	50.0		
	p $ each					17.8	14.5	12.4	13.5		
Harvesting machinery											
Potato-digging machines (elevator type)	*q* Th.	7.71	10.0	4.59	12.1	9.40	3.91	3.33	1.40	3.40	5.70
	v Th. $	745	760	352	940	753	326	258	70.0	349	657
	p $ each	96.6	75.9	76.7	77.4	80.1	83.5	77.5	50.0	103	115
Grain binders	*q* Th.	72.3	62.8	42.4	71.1	65.1	15.4[i]			47.1	31.3
	v Mil. $	9.34	8.61	6.65	10.8	10.7	2.45			7.50	5.37
	p $ each	129	137	157	152	164	160			159	172
Combines	*q* Th.	5.03	4.01	5.13	18.3	37.0	5.91	5.83	.349	3.87	29.4
	v Mil. $	4.68	4.91	7.28	26.9	50.7	9.19	9.18	.323	3.96	21.3
	p $ each	931	1,224	1,420	1,469	1,371	1,556	1,574	926	1,024	724
Haying machinery											
Mowers	*q* Th.	104	130	112	111	126	43.3	42.4	36.7	119	126
	v Mil. $	5.17	6.58	6.04	6.01	7.05	2.38	2.31	1.77	6.89	8.02
	p $ each	49.8	50.4	53.8	54.3	55.8	54.9	54.5	48.1	58.0	63.7
Rakes, sulky (dump)	*q* Th.	54.2	46.4	61.0	51.1	58.1	17.8	17.5	5.07	40.7	50.4
	v Mil. $	1.46	1.19	1.81	1.49	1.78	.514	.512	.155	1.29	1.60
	p $ each	26.8	25.6	29.6	29.3	30.7	28.9	29.3	30.6	31.7	31.8
Loaders	*q* Th.	21.5	23.3	15.7	25.1	24.9	10.0	10.0	.953	8.81	27.3
	v Mil. $	1.53	1.80	1.24	2.02	1.99	.828	.828	.0750	.655	2.56
	p $ each	71.4	77.2	78.9	80.4	79.9	82.4	82.4	78.7	74.3	93.9

AGRICULTURAL IMPLEMENTS (continued)		1921	1923	1925	1927	1929	1931		1933	1935	1937
Product	*Item*						*A*	*B*	*C*		
Haying machinery (concluded)											
Rakes, sweep	*q* Th.	14.4	16.0	11.1	12.3	18.3	7.12			5.24	7.09
	v Th. $	445	529	415	440	707	260			215	407
	p $ each	30.8	33.1	37.5	35.9	38.7	36.6			40.9	57.4
Stackers	*q* Th.	8.82	3.65	3.72	3.34	6.28	2.37			1.26	1.41
	v Th. $	634	278	361	285	528	190			97.2	135
	p $ each	71.9	76.2	97.1	85.3	84.1	80.2			77.0	95.2
Machines for preparing crops for market or use											
Grain threshers, wood and steel	*q* Th.					13.8	3.95	3.79	.369	4.62[j]	5.00[j]
	v Mil. $					12.4	3.11	3.02	.302	3.59	4.05
	p $ each					894	787	795	818	777	810
Grain threshers (steel)											
Width of rear 46 in. or under	*q* Th.	5.29	6.33	10.5	12.9	12.2					
	v Mil. $	3.88	4.48	9.61	11.4	10.5					
	p $ each	734	707	917	886	863					
47 in. or over	*q* Th.	1.36	1.68	1.90	1.60	1.38					
	v Mil. $	1.78	2.33	2.87	2.32	1.67					
	p $ each	1,312	1,388	1,510	1,446	1,212					
Ensilage cutters (silo fillers)	*q* Th.	12.3[k]	12.8[k]	8.77	9.25	8.06	3.16	3.07	1.49[l]	7.29	10.2
	v Mil. $	2.09	2.07	1.97	1.93	1.69	.598	.581	.301	1.55	2.18
	p $ each	171	162	225	208	210	189	189	202	213	214
Corn shellers, power, cylinder	*q* Th.	1.10	1.75	1.34	1.49	2.15	1.05			1.15	3.61
	v Th. $	387	610	541	547	768	270			197	532
	p $ each	352	349	402	367	357	256			171	147
Corn huskers and shredders	*q* Th.					.972	.631			1.30	1.95
	v Th. $					460	294			648	960
	p $ each					473	465			497	493

For footnotes see next page.

Indexes of Physical Output, with Basic Data on Quantity, Value and Price of Products

AGRICULTURAL IMPLEMENTS (concluded)		1921	1923	1925	1927	1929	1931 A	1931 B	1933 C	1935	1937
Product	*Item*										
Machines for preparing crops for market or use (concluded)											
Hay presses, engine	*q* Th.	2.91	3.01	1.74	2.05	2.17	1.31			3.21	4.48
	v Mil. $	1.13	1.26	.814	.859	.904	.545			1.29	1.94
	p $ each	388	419	467	419	416	416			400	433
Feed grinders and crushers, power	*q* Th.	15.3	53.0	33.3	40.7	53.1	17.1			6.71	8.23
	v Mil. $	.371	1.70	1.37	1.85	3.08	.714			.238	.313
	p $ each	24.2	32.0	41.3	45.4	58.1	41.7			35.5	38.1
Grain cleaners and graders (for small grains only)	*q* Th.	3.96	7.15	17.3	15.2	11.6	3.64				4.29
	v Th. $	271	376	944	991	646	147				232
	p $ each	68.4	52.6	54.5	65.0	55.5	40.2				54.1

A Comparable with all years except 1933. *B* Comparable with 1933. *C* Comparable with 1931.

[a] Percentages of coverage:

Given year	Base year	Given year	Base year
1921:44.2	1929:58.8	1927:60.8	1929:58.8
1923:52.0		1931:51.7	1929:63.2
1925:53.5			

[b] No index for 1933 was computed because of inadequate coverage (27.3 percent).

[c] No adjusted indexes for 1935 and 1937 were computed because of a serious change in the definition of the industry in 1935. The adjusted index given above, extrapolated by the unadjusted index, is 49.9 for 1935; 97.7 for 1937.

[d] Figures relate to 2-bottom sulkies only.

[e] After 1931, figures relate to horse- or tractor-drawn listers.

[f] Figures for 1921 include corrugated rollers.

[g] Prior to 1931 the figures relate only to horse-drawn planters or distributors.

[h] Figures include both tractor-drawn and mounted cultivators.

[i] A small number of rice binders is included with the grain binders.

[j] Rice and alfalfa threshers are included in 1935 and 1937, although they are not included in 1929. An examination of the 1931 data in which the figures for rice and alfalfa threshers are given separately indicated that they constituted less than 5 percent of the aggregate value shown. The data were therefore treated as comparable with the 1929 figures.

[k] Includes data for fodder cutters.

[l] Estimated in part.

PHONOGRAPHS		1899	1904[b]	1909	1914	1919	1921	1923	1925	1927	1929[b]
Adjusted index		8.3		29.3	37.8	181.5	80.5	104.6	80.3	113.6	100.0
Unadjusted index[a]		8.2		32.7	46.2	195.8	88.9	114.3	81.6	121.2	100.0
Product	*Item*										
Phonographs (including dictating machines) and radio-phonograph combinations	*q* Th.	151		345	514	2,230	596	997	642	1,050	755
	v Mil. $	1.24		5.41	15.3	91.6	38.6	57.0	22.6	49.2	43.0
	p $ ea.	8.19		15.7	29.7	41.1	64.8	57.2	35.2	47.1	57.0
Records and blanks											
Disk records	*q* Mil.			8.57	23.3	101					
	v Mil. $			2.57	10.4	42.9					
	p $ ea.			.300	.445	.425					
Disk and cylinder records and blanks	*q*	2.76					105	98.1	82.1	106	105
	v	.539					47.8	36.4	26.8	31.8	34.1
	p	.195					.455	.371	.326	.301	.325
Cylinder records and blanks	*q* Mil.			18.6	3.91	5.91					
	v Mil. $			2.44	.734	1.76					
	p $ ea.			.131	.188	.298					

[a] Percentages of coverage:

Given year	Base year	Given year	Base year
1899:79.2	1909:88.8	1919:85.9	
1909:88.8	1919:85.9	1921:88.0	
1914:97.4		1923:87.0	1929:79.7
		1925:80.9	
		1927:85.0	

[b] No quantity data are available for 1904 or for 1931–37.

RADIOS		1923	1925	1927	1929	1931	1933	1935	1937
Adjusted index[a]									
Unadjusted index[b]		3.8	47.1	39.7	100.0	73.8	74.6	106.0	144.2
Product	*Item*								
Receiving sets (except crystal and short wave)	*q* Mil.	.190	2.35	1.98	4.98	3.78[c,d]			
	v Mil. $	13.3	93.4	95.2	253	118			
	p $ ea.	70.0	39.8	48.1	50.8	31.2			

For footnotes see next page.

Indexes of Physical Output, with Basic Data on Quantity, Value and Price of Products

RADIOS (concluded)		1923	1925	1927	1929	1931	1933	1935	1937
Product	*Item*								
Receiving sets (concluded)									
For home and general use	*q* Mil.					3.65	2.95[c]	4.45[c]	5.84
	v Mil. $					113	56.2	105	132
	p $ ea.					31.1	19.0	23.5	22.5
Automobile sets, except police	*q* Th.					92.8	698	1,219	1,885
	v Mil. $					2.96	13.6	25.3	38.3
	p $ ea.					31.9	19.4	20.8	20.3
Radio-phonograph combinations	*q* Th.				152	73.6	30.1	23.4	57.8
	v Mil. $				22.2	6.31	1.41	2.46	4.57
	p $ ea.				146	85.7	46.8	105	79.0
Radio receiving tubes, for replacement	*q* Mil.					24.3	36.4	36.8	41.5
	v Mil. $					13.7	15.9	13.0	15.5
	p $ ea.					.564	.435	.352	.373

[a] No adjusted index could be computed because prior to 1931 the industry was part of the electrical machinery industry, and from 1931 on it was combined with phonographs.

[b] The indexes for 1933, 1935 and 1937 were computed on the 1931 base.

[c] Estimated in part.

[d] Includes all receiving sets.

REFRIGERATORS, MECHANICAL		1921	1923	1925	1927	1929	1931	1933	1935	1937
Adjusted index[a]										
Unadjusted index[b]		0.6	2.0	8.4	43.8	100.0	118.0	130.3	211.5	317.3
Product[c]	*Item*									
Household refrigerators										
Electric	*q* Th.	5	18	75	390	840	965	1,080	1,722	2,559
Gas	*q* Th.					50	85	80	160	265

[a] No adjusted index was computed because continuous value data for the individual products or for the industry as a whole are not available.

[b] The index was obtained simply by summation of the two products. Prior to 1929 the number of gas refrigerators sold was negligible.

[c] Data on gas refrigerators were obtained from the Statistical Department of the American Gas Association, and on electric refrigerators from *Air Conditioning and Refrigeration News* and *Electrical Merchandising*. Quantities relate to sales, not to production.

SCALES and BALANCES		*1927*	*1929*	*1931*	*1933*	*1935*	*1937*
Adjusted index		82.7	100.0	60.4	34.8	61.7	86.9
Unadjusted index[a]		83.6	100.0	62.5	33.9	69.5	106.3
Product	*Item*						
Scales							
Automatic, industrial	*q* Th. scales		21.2	6.61	4.26	15.3	12.5
	v Mil. $		4.59	1.83	1.18	3.30	4.11
	p $ per scale	*q* 60.7 (automatic and calculating combined)	217	277	277	216	330
		v 10.9					
Calculating and computing	*q* Th. scales	*p* 180	58.0	32.1	21.0	30.4	62.8
	v Mil. $		9.07	4.02	2.13	3.60	4.84
	p $ per scale		156	125	102	118	77.0
Beam, including steelyards	*q* Th. scales	161	155	102	42.8	88.1	186
	v Mil. $	4.46	5.08	2.37	1.38	2.02	4.00
	p $ per scale	27.6	32.8	23.3	32.3	22.9	21.5
Spring, other than computing	*q* Th. scales		620	496	518	1131	1390
	v Mil. $		2.18	1.47	1.10	1.91	2.46
	p $ per scale		3.52	2.97	2.12	1.68	1.77
Coin operated	*q* Th. scales		8.64	20.0	2.86	5.70	9.87
	v Mil. $		1.45	1.41	.189	.286	.662
	p $ per scale		168	70.7	65.9	50.3	67.1

[a] Percentages of coverage:

Given year	Base year
1927:62.3	1929:61.7
1931:76.3, 1933:71.8	1929:73.7
1935:83.0, 1937:90.0	1929:73.7

Indexes of Physical Output, with Basic Data on Quantity, Value and Price of Products

SEWING MACHINES		1927	1929	1931	1933	1935	1937
Adjusted index		101.0	100.0	48.9	26.0	56.8	100.5
Unadjusted index[a]		99.5	100.0	45.0	25.1	55.7	86.2
Product	*Item*						
Sewing machines							
Household type							
Electric	q Th.	310	323	166		221	
	v Mil. $	12.7	16.5	6.13		7.86	
	p $ each	41.0	51.0	36.9	q 128	35.5	q 548
					v 4.39		v 13.8
Foot and hand	q Th.	454	346	65.4	p 34.3	122	p 25.3
	v Mil. $	9.09	8.61	1.49		1.97	
	p $ each	20.0	24.9	22.8		16.2	
Industrial type							
Electric, foot and hand	q Th.	103	123	67.0	42.9	65.3	115
	v Mil. $	10.4	12.0	7.63	5.89	8.42	10.7
	p $ each	101	97.9	114	137	129	93.3

(The 1931 and 1935 figures for the two household types are bracketed together against the combined household-type figures shown for 1933 and 1937.)

Percentages of coverage:

Given year	Base year	Given year	Base year
1927:81.1	1929:82.3	1933:79.5	1929:82.3
1931:75.7		1935:80.6	
		1937:70.6	

TYPEWRITERS		1921	1923	1925	1927	1929	1931	1933	1935	1937
Adjusted index[a]										
Unadjusted index[b]		51.4	73.9	78.0	90.7	100.0	53.5	43.3	82.9	108.7
Product	*Item*									
Typewriters, portable	q Th.				307[c]	375[c]	214	144	352	537
	v Mil. $						5.84	2.91	8.87	11.6
	p $ ea.						27.3	20.2	25.2	21.7
Typewriters, portable and standard combined	q	489[c]	698[c]	742[c]						
Typewriters, standard, including long carriage	q Th.				555	588	305	265	459	558
	v Mil. $				31.8	31.3	12.1	10.4	19.7	22.9
	p $ ea.				57.2	53.3	39.7	39.2	42.9	41.1

[a] Because reliable data on the value of portable and standard typewriters are lacking for 1921–29 (see footnote c), and also because there was a serious change in the definition of the industry after 1929, no adjusted index on the 1929 base could be computed. An adjusted index on the 1931 base is available for 1931–37: 100.0 for 1931; 81.7 for 1933; 149.5 for 1935; 215.4 for 1937.

The percentages of coverage for 1931–37 are:

Given year	Base year
1933:80.7	1931:81.4
1935:84.3	
1937:76.8	

[b] The 1931–37 indexes were computed on the 1931 base. The 1927–31 indexes were computed on the basis of 1931 unit values. The 1921–25 indexes were computed on the 1927 base.

[c] Includes bookkeeping-billing types. This inclusion affects the comparability of the number only slightly (by less than 4.8 percent of the quantity of portable typewriters, according to detailed 1931 data). The effect on the value is serious, however, and for this reason we do not show the value, aggregate or average.

Indexes of Physical Output, with Basic Data on Quantity, Value and Price of Products

WASHING and IRONING MACHINES		1927	1929	1931	1933	1935	1937
Adjusted index		73.1	100.0	79.0	91.8	131.6	146.4
Unadjusted index[a]		79.5	100.0	83.2	106.3	124.7	154.6
Product	*Item*						
Washing machines for household use							
Electric (standard size)	*q* Mil.	.760[b]	.956[b]	.795	1.02	1.19	1.48
	v Mil. $	55.6	59.9	39.0	37.5	43.0	53.8
	p $ ea.	73.1	62.7	49.1	36.9	36.1	36.4

[a] Percentages of coverage: Given year 1927:79.1, 1931:76.7, 1933:84.3 — Base year 1929:72.8; Given year 1935:69.0, 1937:76.9 — Base year 1929:72.8

[b] In 1927 and 1929 data for apartment-size washing machines were included with those for electric (standard size); the resulting incomparability is very slight.

TRANSPORTATION EQUIPMENT

AUTOMOBILES, incl. BODIES and PARTS		1899	1904	1909	1914	1919	1921	1923	1925	1927	1929	1931	1933	1935	1937
Adjusted index[a]															
Unadjusted index[a]		0.05	0.25	1.8	8.5	28.2	24.6	63.0	72.0	63.0	100.0	44.1	35.2	74.1	90.1
Product[b]	*Item*														
Total, complete vehicles and chassis[c]	*q* Mil.	.00372	.0217	.127	.573	1.89	1.60	3.90	4.18	3.35	5.29	2.29	1.85	3.92	4.73
	v Mil. $	4.55	23.8	165	465	1745	1332	2617	2951	2547	3412	1386	929	2153	2849
	p Th. $ ea.	1.22	1.09	1.30	.807	.920	.832	.670	.707	.759	.644	.604	.502	.549	.602

AUTOMOBILES, incl. BODIES and PARTS (continued)		1899	1904	1909	1914	1919	1921	1923	1925	1927	1929	1931	1933	1935	1937
Product[b]	*Item*														
Open passenger cars, 2-door	*q* Th.		12.1	40.8	81.6	174	197	432	390[d]	198	298	104	10.2	10.3	12.7
	v Mil. $		8.83	30.4	45.9	141	120	222	181	116	151	47.7	4.97	6.87	9.44
	p Th. $ ea.		.728	.746	.562	.811	.612	.513	.464	.587	.506	.459	.487	.665	.746
4-door	*q* Th.		7.22	76.1	451	1226	903	1783	1095	211	146	21.4	7.01	9.53	7.63
	v Mil. $		11.8	113	346	981	679	962	516	113	78.3	12.5	3.46	6.00	5.94
	p Th. $ ea.		1.63	1.49	.767	.800	.752	.540	.471	.536	.535	.586	.493	.630	.778
Closed passenger cars,															
2-door	*q* Mil.										2.21	1.01	.863	1.77	2.09
	v Mil. $										1193	495	383	870	1130
	p Th. $ ea.										.539	.490	.443	.491	.542
2-door and 4-door (bracketed)	*q*					.156	.304	1.20	2.08	2.41					
	v					201	329	1067	1787	1918					
	p					1.28	1.08	.888	.859	.797					
4-door	*q* Mil.										1.70	.776	.653	1.42	1.74
	v Mil. $										1345	564	362	869	1151
	p Th. $ ea.										.789	.727	.554	.613	.661
Closed cars and public conveyances	*q* Th.			5.20	11.1	158									
	v Mil. $			12.7	22.4	204									
	p Th. $ ea.			2.45	2.01	1.29									
Government and municipal vehicles	*q* Th.			.042	.728	2.79									
	v Mil. $			.104	3.94	13.6									
	p Th. $ ea.			2.47	5.41	4.89									
Public conveyances, total[e]	*q* Th.					1.88	2.25	12.9	15.3	8.97	26.1				
	v Mil. $					3.10	5.75	24.7	43.7	28.0	58.4				
	p Th. $ ea.					1.65	2.55	1.92	2.86	3.12	2.24				
Motor busses															
Under 21 passengers	*q* Th.										5.64	.630	.407	1.16	1.24
	v Mil. $										7.45	.983	.860	1.41	3.07
	p Th. $ ea.										1.32	1.56	2.11	1.22	2.48
21 to 32 passengers	*q* Th.										2.33	1.95	.886	2.32	4.32
	v Mil. $										13.6	8.02	4.55	13.4	22.3
	p Th. $ ea.										5.82	4.12	5.14	5.77	5.15

For footnotes see p. 581.

Indexes of Physical Output, with Basic Data on Quantity, Value and Price of Products

AUTOMOBILES, incl. BODIES and PARTS (continued)		1899	1904	1909	1914	1919	1921	1923	1925	1927	1929	1931	1933	1935	1937
Product[b]	*Item*														
Motor busses (concluded)															
Over 32 passengers	*q* Th.										1.10	1.13	.281	1.34	2.11
	v Mil. $										10.6	8.62	1.54	12.3	21.8
	p Th. $ ea.										9.62	7.65	5.47	9.24	10.4
Taxicabs and other commercial vehicles	*q* Th.										20.4	6.08	5.28	3.20	4.36
	v Mil. $										28.4	8.71	5.24	3.57	3.64
	p Th. $ ea.										1.40	1.43	.993	1.11	.834
Truck tractors	*q* Th.										.181	.400	1.63	2.46	1.79
	v Mil. $										.494	1.53	3.20	5.03	2.78
	p Th. $ ea.										2.73	3.84	1.96	2.04	1.56
Light delivery trucks (under 1 ton)	*q* Th.		.251	1.86	4.39	18.1	15.1	28.0	36.0[e]	61.0[e]	124	79.8	78.9	202	305
	v Mil. $		.455	1.92	4.75	16.6	10.7	17.1	24.1	33.9	64.2	35.7	30.4	84.7	141
	p Th. $ ea.		1.81	1.03	1.08	.914	.707	.611	.669	.556	.516	.447	.385	.419	.464
Heavy trucks (1-ton and over)	*q* Th.		.160	1.37	19.5	102	90.3	253	304	266	261	164	135	303	297
	v Mil. $		.491	3.17	34.7	194	86.4	203	258	220	205	124	80.4	186	215
	p Th. $ ea.		3.07	2.32	1.78	1.90	.957	.803	.849	.826	.785	.754	.596	.615	.724
Hearses and undertaker's wagons	*q* Th.					.587	.519	.872	2.01	2.20	2.32	1.14	.825	1.68	2.60
	v Mil. $					1.75	2.00	2.56	5.36	4.47	5.66	2.95	1.91	3.77	6.21
	p Th. $ ea.					2.98	3.85	2.93	2.66	2.03	2.44	2.58	2.32	2.24	2.38
Ambulances	*q* Th.					.391	.134	.197	.129	.219	.361	.196	.418	.253	.467
	v Mil. $					.614	.557	.820	.528	.670	1.01	.449	.520	.589	1.15
	p Th. $ ea.					1.57	4.15	4.16	4.09	3.06	2.79	2.29	1.25	2.33	2.47
Fire department apparatus	*q* Th.					.759	.815	.910	1.02	1.14	1.35	.666	.244	.538	.985
	v Mil. $					6.94	8.53	8.72	9.59	9.96	7.86	4.99	1.48	2.81	5.87
	p Th. $ ea.					9.14	10.5	9.58	9.40	8.70	5.82	7.49	6.05	5.23	5.96

AUTOMOBILES, incl. BODIES and PARTS (concluded)		1899	1904	1909	1914	1919	1921	1923	1925	1927	1929	1931	1933	1935	1937
Product[b]	*Item*														
Other vehicles and apparatus	*q* Th.					1.64	.182	.085	.084	.235	.249	.292	.046	.124	.397
	v Mil. $					6.07	.371	.511	.370	.893	1.29	.725	.219	.762	1.04
	p Th. $ ea.					3.71	2.04	6.01	4.40	3.80	5.17	2.48	4.77	6.15	2.61
Chassis Passenger	*q* Th.						38.8	53.3	87.8	56.1	76.4	7.56	8.76	40.6	36.4
	v Mil. $						18.8	25.1	39.9	27.2	32.4	3.74	3.87	13.5	12.7
	p Th. $ ea.						.484	.472	.455	.484	.424	.495	.443	.331	.349
Commercial	*q* Th.					*q* 192					433	119	81.8	152	226
	v Mil. $					*v* 182					259	66.6	41.6	71.7	113
	p Th. $ ea.					*p* .945	40.5	122	153	122	.599	.559	.508	.473	.501
							64.5	76.4	81.6	68.1					
Bus	*q* Th.						1.59	.626	.533	.556	2.71	.393	.183	.739	1.72
	v Mil. $										7.02	.805	.219	.785	1.80
	p Th. $ ea.										2.59	2.05	1.20	1.06	1.05
Trailers	*q* Th.					15.7	3.77	11.5	12.8	19.7	22.4				
	v Mil. $					6.63	2.07	4.37	4.94	7.21	10.8				
	p Th. $ ea.					.423	.550	.381	.385	.365	.483				

[a] Because of the intimate relation between the two industries—automobiles, and automobile bodies and parts—and because of frequent shifts of establishments from one to the other, the two were combined and one index was computed for both. In the computation of this index only finished automobiles and chassis were considered. Bodies and parts were not included because no separate data for replacement bodies and parts are available; replacement bodies and parts are combined with a percentage, unknown and varying, of the bodies and parts used in the manufacture of new automobiles. The omission from the index of replacement bodies and parts probably results in an understatement of the long-term growth of the industry, and an exaggeration of the cyclical fluctuations of the index of output. The coverage of the index is undoubtedly high (certainly exceeding 60 percent), but no exact percentages can be given, nor can an adjusted index be computed.

[b] For the years 1904, 1909 and 1914 the detailed data, and for 1899 and 1904 the data for the total, relate to products made within the automobile industry, while for all other years the data relate to the total of products wherever made.

[c] Not used in the computation of the index except for 1899. Tractors are included from 1899 through 1919. Trailers are included prior to 1929; the 1929 figures for complete vehicles and chassis, including trailers, are: *q* 5.31 mil.; *v* $3,421 mil.

[d] The 1925 figures for 2-door open cars and light delivery trucks are not strictly comparable with those for 1927.

[e] Public conveyances include only motor busses and taxicabs.

Indexes of Physical Output, with Basic Data on Quantity, Value and Price of Products

CARRIAGES and SLEDS, CHILDREN'S		1925	1927	1929	1931	1933	1935	1937
Adjusted index		92.3	90.0	100.0	71.2	58.6	70.4	88.7
Unadjusted index[a]		91.9	91.7	100.0	71.5	69.9	80.6	98.2
Product	*Item*							
Baby carriages	*q* Mil.	.345[b]	.402[b]	.399[b]				
	v Mil. $	6.00	6.38	6.69				
	p $ each	17.4	15.8	16.8	*q* .541[b]	.397[b]	.372[b]	.541[b]
					v 5.69	3.79	3.87	5.22
Gocarts, strollers and sulkies	*q* Mil.	.359	.276	.309	*p* 10.5	9.55	10.4	9.64
	v Mil. $	3.05	2.36	2.36				
	p $ each	8.50	8.55	7.63				
Doll carriages and doll carts	*q* Mil.	1.21	1.09	1.37[b]	.795[b]	.737[b]	.799[b]	.905[b]
	v Mil. $	2.82	2.97	3.67	1.91	1.60	1.64	2.14
	p $ each	2.33	2.72	2.68	2.40	2.17	2.06	2.37
Velocipedes and tricycles	*q* Mil.	.567	.641	.905	.667	1.03	1.20	1.36
	v Mil. $	2.76	3.54	4.70	2.80	2.66	3.82	4.27
	p $ each	4.88	5.52	5.19	4.20	2.58	3.18	3.13
Sidewalk cycles	*q* Th.		56.9	80.3	75.2	35.3	35.1	83.4
	v Th. $		523	730	646	257	340	637
	p $ each		9.19	9.09	8.60	7.28	9.66	7.64
Children's wagons	*q* Mil.	1.41[b]	1.42	1.89[b]	1.41[b]	1.90	1.93[b]	
	v Mil. $	4.05	3.34	4.01	1.89	1.85	2.55	
	p $ each	2.88	2.36	2.13	1.34	.974	1.32	

CARRIAGES and SLEDS, CHILDREN'S (concluded)		*1925*	*1927*	*1929*	*1931*	*1933*	*1935*	*1937*
Product[b]	*Item*							
Children's automobiles	*q* Mil.	.216	.144	.205	.149[b]	.112[b]	.198	
	v Mil. $	1.77	1.17	1.02	.627	.562	1.09	
	p $ each	8.16	8.10	4.97	4.20	5.01	5.49	
Scooters	*q* Mil.	1.28	1.30	.471	.168	.211	.418	.597
	v Mil. $	3.45	3.28	.656	.227	.197	.631	.922
	p $ each	2.69	2.52	1.39	1.35	.933	1.51	1.54
Three-wheel play cars (with or without pedals)	*q* Mil.	.667	.482	.580	.206	.167	.303	.220
	v Mil. $	1.28	.723	.966	.258	.175	.318	.228
	p $ each	1.92	1.50	1.66	1.25	1.05	1.05	1.03
Sleds	*q* Mil.	.879	1.25	.888[b]	.847[b]	.620[b]	1.10[b]	1.39[b]
	v Mil. $	.919	1.74	.872	.801	.541	1.28	1.64
	p $ each	1.05	1.40	.981	.946	.873	1.16	1.18
Baby walkers and tenders	*q* Mil.	.237	.276	.332	.249	.216	.365	.580
	v Mil. $	.744	.799	.788	.618	.394	.783	1.12
	p $ each	3.14	2.90	2.38	2.48	1.82	2.15	1.93

[a] Percentages of coverage:

Given year	Base year
1925: 88.9	1929: 89.3
1927: 93.5; 1931: 92.2; 1933: 109.5; 1935: 105.2	1929: 91.8
1937: 82.3	1929: 74.4

[b] Estimated in part.

Indexes of Physical Output, with Basic Data on Quantity, Value and Price of Products

CARRIAGES, WAGONS and SLEIGHS		*1899*	*1904*	*1909*	*1914*	*1919*	*1921*	*1923*	*1925*		*1927*	*1929*	*1931*	*1933*	*1935*	*1937*
Adjusted index		1316.6	1392.0	1333.2	1123.1	647.2	182.2	300.0	215.8		173.3	100.0[b]	36.1	40.0	59.2	71.3
Unadjusted index[a]		2176.1	2340.5	2088.8	1586.8	856.3	171.2	362.0	262.7		160.4	100.0	25.9	49.2	91.9	102.2
Product[c]	*Item*								*A*	*B*						
Horse-drawn vehicles																
Farm wagons	*q* Th.										50.8	40.7	10.3		48.7	57.6
	v Mil. $										4.43	3.79	.755		2.95	3.66
	p $ each										87.1	93.1	73.2		60.5	63.5
Farm trucks	*q* Th.	*q* 570[d]	644[d]	588[d]	534[d]	*q* 303	52.6	169	141	172	48.3	61.0	16.0	*q* 52.8[e]	49.6	48.6
	v Mil. $	*v* 31.1	37.2	39.9	34.5	*v* 27.6	4.72	14.5	11.3	13.1	1.93	2.52	.623	*v* 2.35	1.53	1.85
	p $ each	*p* 54.5	57.8	68.0	64.7	*p* 90.9	89.6	85.5	80.5	76.3	39.9	41.3	38.9	*p* 44.5	30.9	38.1
Business vehicles, incl. mail carriers' wagons, public conveyances, and lunch wagons[f]	*q* Th.					39.4	14.2	23.8	15.7	24.2	13.2	4.61[e]	1.18[e]			
	v Mil. $					6.62	3.44	4.37	2.44	4.96	4.59	3.88	1.39			
	p $ each					168	243	183	155	205	348	841	1183			
Carriages, buggies, and sulkies[g]	*q* Th.	905	937	828	538	216	34.4	39.8	14.8	21.5	7.63	3.60	.711		1.01	.900
	v Mil. $	51.3	55.8	47.8	33.3	19.7	3.66	3.37	1.24	1.98	.687	.347	.0682		.0843	.110
	p $ each	56.7	59.5	57.6	61.9	91.2	106	84.6	84.2	92.0	90.1	96.4	96.0		83.4	123
Two-wheeled carts	*q* Th.								1.91	3.20	4.31	3.32	1.71	*q* 1.07	.913	1.05
	v Mil. $								.112	.165	.147	.145	.0530	*v* .0612	.0346	.0449
	p $ each								58.8	51.6	34.1	43.7	30.9	*p* 57.0	37.9	42.8

CARRIAGES, WAGONS and SLEIGHS (concluded)		1899	1904	1909	1914	1919	1921	1923	1925		1927	1929	1931	1933	1935	1937
Product[c]	*Item*															
Horse-drawn vehicles (concluded)									*A*	*B*						
Public convey-	*q* Th.	2.22	2.71	2.24	1.22	.194	.161	.237	.087							
ances	*v* Th. $	1114	1315	939	280	77.0	49.2	134	28.8							
	p $ each	502	485	419	229	397	305	564	331							
Sleighs and	*q* Th.	117	127	101	52.0	36.0	5.68	2.56	1.87	2.68	5.47	4.37[e]	.657		.697	1.16
bobsleds	*v* Mil. $	2.29	2.69	2.07	1.21	1.24	.227	.100	.0626	.0892	.183	.126	.0187		.0236	.0303
	p $ each	19.6	21.1	20.5	23.2	34.4	40.0	39.3	33.5	33.3	33.4	28.8	28.4		33.9	26.2
Handcarts and	*q* Th.					11.6			10.6	12.7	9.64	14.1	5.47		1.00	2.13
pushcarts	*v* Th. $					296			99.2	121	135	268	73.1		21.3	32.7
	p $ each					25.5			9.33	9.57	14.0	19.0	13.4		21.2	15.3

A Comparable with earlier years. *B* Comparable with later years.

[a] Percentages of coverage:

Given year	Base year	Given year	Base year	Given year	Base year
1899:75.5	1909:71.4	1919:66.3	1925:61.0	1927:62.3	1929:67.3
1904:76.6		1921:46.8	1925:60.6	1931:48.3	
1909:71.4	1919:60.3	1923:60.1		1933:50.8	1929:41.3
1914:64.4		1925:81.9	1929:67.3	1935:67.8	1929:43.7
				1937:62.6	

[b] Between 1929 and 1931 carriage and wagon materials was abandoned as a separate classification and establishments making materials and parts other than turned-wood products were transferred to carriages, wagons and sleighs. The resulting discontinuity appears to be slight.

[c] Data for 1899–1925 relate to products made within the industry, whereas data for later years relate to products wherever made. Since overlapping data are available for 1925, this year was introduced as an additional base year.

[d] Include also patrol wagons, ambulances, handcarts and pushcarts. Comparable figures for 1919 are: *q* 357 th. wagons; *v* $35.2 mil.; *p* $98.6 ea.

[e] Estimated in part.

[f] Data for 1919–25 do not include mail or mail carriers' wagons or public conveyances.

[g] Data for 1899–1925 do not include sulkies.

Indexes of Physical Output, with Basic Data on Quantity, Value and Price of Products

CARS, RAILROAD, not elsewhere made		1899	1904	1909	1914	1919	1921	1923	1925	1927	1929[b]		1931	1933[c]	1935	1937
Adjusted index		119.4	122.3	113.7	154.1	170.7	96.1	229.2	138.8	101.3	100.0		31.4		29.5	93.4
Unadjusted index[a]		136.8	147.6	109.8	161.3	176.0	76.1	218.8	137.7	96.7	100.0		19.3		11.0	93.8
Product[b]	*Item*										A	B			C	C
Passenger service																
Day coaches	q Th.	.331	.428	.957	1.65	.078	.668	1.16	.593	.967	.342					
	v Mil. $	1.98	2.96	7.21	19.6	1.29	16.2	25.2	14.0	22.6	6.82					
	p Th. $ each	5.97	6.91	7.53	11.9	16.5	24.3	21.7	23.6	23.4	19.9		q.115			
													v3.09			
Baggage and express	q Th.						.222	.282	.349	.265	.369		p26.8			
	v Mil. $						4.47	4.57	5.68	5.20	6.48					
	p Th. $ each						20.1	16.2	16.3	19.6	17.6	q1.36			q .142	.513
												v35.0			v 4.32	24.6
Chair, parlor, dining and buffet, mail, and sleeping	q Th.	q.648	1.60	.644	1.79	.156	.383	.321	1.03	.545	.521	p25.6			p 30.4	47.9
	v Mil. $	v5.39	15.2	6.62	24.4	3.57	12.0	9.14	32.1	19.2	18.3					
	p Th. $ each	p8.32	9.48	10.3	13.6	22.9	31.4	28.5	31.3	35.1	35.1		q.077			
													v2.47			
Other passenger service[d]	q Th.						.075	.075	.152	.188	.196		p32.1			
	v Mil. $						1.47	1.35	3.13	5.40	8.81					
	p Th. $ each						19.6	18.0	20.6	28.7	45.0					
Freight service																
Box	q Th.	47.8	38.2	29.7	50.5	59.7	13.8	60.0	49.2	19.6	34.2	34.2	3.04		1.81	35.3
	v Mil. $	25.6	28.5	24.0	41.0	161	40.5	119	101	45.3	81.0	81.0	6.35		4.62	85.5
	p Th. $ each	.534	.747	.807	.811	2.70	2.93	1.98	2.05	2.31	2.37	2.37	2.09		2.55	2.42

CARS, RAILROAD, not elsewhere made (continued)		1899	1904	1909	1914	1919	1921	1923	1925	1927	1929[b]		1931	1933[c]	1935	1937
Product[b]	Item										A	B			C	C
Freight service (concluded)																
Caboose	q Th.	.193	.160	.537[e]	.340[e]		.362	.552	.242	.186	.458	.458				.267
	v Mil. $	.185	.151	.526	.421		1.57	1.41	.691	.717	1.36	1.36				.913
	p Th. $ each	.958	.944	.979	1.24		4.33	2.56	2.85	3.86	2.96	2.96	q .473			3.42
													v 1.82			
Flat	q Th.	4.53	5.41	3.23	4.78	4.03	1.49	2.95	2.31	1.66	2.84	2.84	p 3.84		q .547	1.54
	v Mil. $	1.92	2.89	2.03	3.12	7.59	2.39	4.07	3.23	2.84	5.15	5.15			v 1.49	3.45
	p Th. $ each	.425	.535	.629	.653	1.88	1.61	1.38	1.40	1.71	1.81	1.81			p 2.72	2.24
Gondola	q Th.	11.8	9.52	19.6	25.1	54.8	10.0	29.3	21.4	10.5	12.6	12.6	.876			15.7
	v Mil. $	6.87	5.52	18.1	22.8	119	27.2	55.1	42.0	20.0	29.4	29.4	1.51			39.1
	p Th. $ each	.581	.580	.925	.910	2.17	2.71	1.88	1.96	1.91	2.33	2.33	1.73			2.50
Hopper	q Th.	28.9	28.0	11.5	9.75	16.7	10.2	36.6	3.24	8.73	10.1	10.1	2.68		4.37	19.9
	v Mil. $	18.4	21.4	9.42	10.7	45.8	25.0	67.0	5.87	19.9	24.7	24.7	5.97		9.48	45.2
	p Th. $ each	.638	.763	.821	1.10	2.74	2.44	1.83	1.81	2.28	2.44	2.44	2.23		2.17	2.27
Refrigerator	q Th.	2.35	3.35	2.62	5.80	.629	5.86	19.9	4.70	9.00	5.16	5.16	3.33			6.08
	v Mil. $	1.96	3.04	2.75	8.08	1.24	23.6	52.3	14.7	25.6	20.0	20.0	9.97			20.2
	p Th. $ each	.831	.907	1.05	1.39	1.97	4.02	2.63	3.13	2.85	3.88	3.88	3.00			3.32
Stock	q Th.	2.76	4.24	2.35	3.93	.410	1.87	3.32	3.31	1.02	2.47	2.47				.822
	v Mil. $	1.43	2.45	1.59	2.59	.960	4.31	5.24	5.88	1.88	4.74	4.74				1.54
	p Th. $ each	.517	.579	.675	.658	2.34	2.31	1.58	1.78	1.85	1.92	1.92	q 1.78[f]		q 2.08	1.88
													v 3.83		v 5.41	
Tank	q Th.				1.25	11.6	3.83	6.01	5.40	5.46	3.29	3.29	p 2.15		p 2.60	
	v Mil. $				1.26	26.5	11.0	14.1	10.7	10.4	6.14	6.14				q11.1
	p Th. $ each				1.00	2.29	2.87	2.34	1.98	1.92	1.87	1.87				v25.2
Other	q Th.											15.1				p2.27
	v Mil. $											28.1				
	p Th. $ each											1.86				

For footnotes see next page.

Indexes of Physical Output, with Basic Data on Quantity, Value and Price of Products

CARS, RAILROAD, not elsewhere made (concluded)		1899	1904	1909	1914	1919	1921	1923	1925	1927	1929[b]		1931	1933[c]	1935	1937
Product[b]	*Item*										*A*	*B*			*C*	*C*
Electric railroad cars, total	*q* Th.		4.38	2.52	2.54	1.90	1.42	2.88	1.83	1.29	.473	.697[g]	.333		.229[g]	.676[g]
	v Mil. $		9.30	6.63	8.79	13.5	10.1	26.2	19.4	19.8	5.94	13.5	6.97		3.23	9.81
	p Th. $ each		2.12	2.62	3.46	7.11	7.13	9.09	10.6	15.3	12.6	19.3	20.9		14.1	14.5

A Comparable with 1931 and earlier years. *B* Comparable with 1935 and 1937. *C* Comparable with second 1929 column.

[a] Percentages of coverage:

Given year	Base year	Given year	Base year	Given year	Base year	Given year	Base year
1899:65.1	1909:54.9	1914:69.3	1919:68.3	1923:63.7	1929:66.7	1931:42.1	1929:68.7
1904:74.9	1909:60.0	1919:68.3	1929:66.3	1925:66.2		1935:28.4	1929:75.9
1909:59.6	1919:63.5	1921:52.8	1929:66.7	1927:63.7		1937:76.2	

[b] Data for 1935 and 1937 relate to steam and electric railroad cars wherever made; data for other years relate to cars made within the steam and electric railroad car industry. Therefore two sets of data for 1929 were used, one comparable with 1935 and 1937, and one comparable with the earlier years.

[c] No index was computed for 1933 because quantity data are available for only two products, the value of which is only 7.5 percent of the total value of products for the industry for that year. The data available for 1933 are: freight service, box and tank cars: *q* 1.12 th. cars; *v* $2.00 mil.; *p* $1.78 th. each; freight service, other: *q* .813 th. cars; *v* $1.47 mil.; *p* $1.81 th. each.

[d] Does not include self-propelled cars after 1929.

[e] These figures were not used in the computation of the indexes for 1909 and 1914 because no comparable figures for the base year, 1919, are available.

[f] Data include "other freight service." In computing the index for 1931 we used comparable figures for 1929; they are: *q* 8.24 th. cars; *v* $17.5 mil.; *p* $2.12 th. each.

[g] Includes self-propelled cars.

LOCOMOTIVES, not elsewhere made		1899	1904	1909	1914	1919	1921	1923	1925	1927	1929	1931	1933	1935	1937
Adjusted index								[b]	136.6	104.7	100.0	23.3			55.2
Unadjusted index[a]		245.5	341.3	263.1	189.8	299.1	162.8	383.4	127.2	110.7	100.0	15.5	[c]	[c]	46.9
Product[d]	*Item*														
Standard-gage steam locomotives	*q* Number	1,991	2,768	2,134	1,539	2,426	1,320	3,109	1,032	898	811	126	10	47	380
	v Mil. $								40.6	54.1	56.0	9.82			40.8
	p Th. $ ea.								39.4	60.3	69.0	78.0			107

[a] Percentages of coverage:

Given year	Base year
1925: 62.1	1929: 66.7
1927: 70.6	
1931: 44.4	
1937: 56.6	

[b] Adjusted indexes for 1899–1923 could not be computed because data are lacking on the value of steam locomotives; see footnote d. The adjusted index given above, extrapolated by the unadjusted index, is 263.6 for 1899; 366.5 for 1904; 282.5 for 1909; 203.8 for 1914; 321.2 for 1919; 174.8 for 1921; 411.7 for 1923.

[c] No indexes are given for these years because the coverage is too small. The value of all types of locomotives constituted only 32.2 percent of the industry's value of products in 1935, and 10.2 percent in 1933.

[d] The quantity data for 1921–37 are taken from special monthly reports of the U.S. Bureau of the Census and refer to shipments of locomotives made within the industry. The basic source of earlier data is *Railway Age.* It was necessary to adjust these data because of the inclusion of Canadian production in 1909, 1914 and 1919, the inclusion of railway repair shop production in 1914 and 1919, and the inclusion of electric locomotives in all years.

Value data are not given in the special Census reports or in *Railway Age.* For the years 1925, 1927, 1929, 1931 and 1937 unit values of standard-gage steam locomotives could be derived from data presented in the Census of Manufactures. The aggregate values were derived by multiplication of the quantities by the unit values.

MOTORCYCLES and BICYCLES		1899	1904	1909	1914	1919	1921	1923	1925	1927	1929	1931	1933	1935	1937
Adjusted index		141.1	31.6[c]	64.0	120.6	179.6	81.2	128.2	97.7	87.0	100.0				
Unadjusted index[a]		170.6	38.0	56.8	150.4	170.0	77.5	143.6	111.6	97.4	100.0[d]				
Product[b]	*Item*														
Motorcycles	*q* Th.	.160	2.30	18.6	62.2	59.1	27.0	41.9	39.4	35.2	31.9				
	v Mil. $	.0337	.355	3.02	12.2	16.2	6.44	10.0	8.88	8.00	7.54				
	p $ each	210	154	162	196	274	239	239	226	227	236				

For footnotes see next page.

Indexes of Physical Output, with Basic Data on Quantity, Value and Price of Products

MOTORCYCLES and BICYCLES (concluded)		1899	1904	1909	1914	1919	1921	1923	1925	1927	1929	1931	1933	1935	1937
Product[b]	*Item*														
Bicycles	q Mil.	1.11	.225	.169	.299	.471	.216	.486	.303	.255	.308	.260	.320[e]	.657	1.13
	v Mil. $	22.1	3.20	2.44	3.76	12.7	6.22	10.7	7.03	5.80	6.18	4.73	5.40	12.1	22.2
	p $ each	19.9	14.2	14.4	12.6	27.0	28.7	22.1	23.2	22.7	20.1	18.2	16.9	18.4	19.7

[a] Percentages of coverage:

Given year	Base year	Given year	Base year
1899:69.4, 1904:69.1	1909:51.0	1923:64.3, 1925:65.6, 1927:64.3	1929:57.4
1909:51.0, 1914:71.6	1919:54.4		
1919:54.4, 1921:54.8	1929:57.4		

[b] Prior to 1923 data relate to products made within the industry, in 1923 and following years to products wherever made.

[c] Between 1904 and 1909 children's tricycles and velocipedes were transferred from motorcycles and bicycles to toys and games, n.e.c.

[d] Separate data for motorcycles are not available for years following 1929. For this reason, no index for the industry was computed for 1931–37.

[e] Estimated in part.

SHIPS and BOATS		1899	1904	1909	1914	1919	1921	1923	1925	1927	1929	1931	1933	1935[b]	1937
Adjusted index		97.0	80.5	73.9	73.9	551.2	213.1	99.4	90.1	109.7	100.0	78.3	22.7		80.5
Unadjusted index[a]		119.0	132.2	97.1	90.7	1,205.1	377.9	96.0	83.8	106.4	100.0	98.9	21.0		111.8
Product[c]	*Item*														
Vessels of 5 gross tons and over															
Steel	q Th. gr.t.[d]	263	328	255	243	3,734[e]	1,207	281	242	309	289	315	68.1		359
	v Mil. $	25.5	43.4	30.0	36.3	1,277	273	73.8	52.4	65.2	71.5	85.3	32.7		127
Wood	q Th. gr.t.[d]	425	350	212	182	756	119	113	110	135	131	32.3	3.56		27.3
	v Mil. $	10.3	9.72	7.68	6.25	110	5.13	6.65	12.1	14.9	19.0	7.06	.893		9.20

[a] Percentages of coverage:

Given year	Base year	Given year	Base year	Given year	Base year
1899:48.0, 1904:64.2	1909:51.4	1919:85.5, 1921:69.4, 1923:37.7, 1925:36.4	1929:39.1	1927:37.9, 1931:49.4, 1933:36.2, 1937:54.3	1929:39.1
1909:51.4, 1914:48.0	1919:85.5				

[b] No quantity data are available for 1935.

[c] Tonnage figures relate to the vessels launched during the year, whether or not work on these vessels was all done within the year or had been begun previously. Value figures relate to the value of all work done during the year on new vessels whether launched or not. For these reasons average values per unit derived for any particular Census year have no real meaning. Over a long period, however, quantity and value figures may be assumed to relate to identical objects, i.e., all vessels launched. The unit values used in the computation of the indexes relate to the entire period 1899–1937, and are as follows: steel, $277.69 per ton; wood, $84.378 per ton.

[d] Gross tonnage represents internal cubic capacity, with 100 cubic feet equal to 1 ton. The combined tonnage includes, in almost every year, a certain amount of displacement tonnage, measured by the weight of the volumn of water displaced. No adjustment is possible, since the quantitative relationship between the two measures is not known. Displacement tonnage as a percentage of total tonnage (including displacement tonnage) is as follows for those years for which figures are presented by the Census of Manufactures:

1904:25.0	1923: 4.9	1929:15.5
1919: 2.7	1925:11.7	1931:18.4
1921: 3.0	1927: 9.3	1933:41.3

[e] Includes concrete vessels with gross tonnage of 18.0 th.tons, and a corresponding value of 7.02 mil. dollars.

TOTAL TRANSPORTATION EQUIPMENT	*1899*	*1904*	*1909*	*1914*	*1919*	*1921*	*1923*	*1925*	*1927*	*1929*	*1931*	*1933*	*1935*	*1937*
Adjusted index	7.3	7.5	10.7	20.3	60.8	37.9	75.5	75.8	67.5	100.0	45.7	33.4	72.0	90.7
Unadjusted index[a]	6.9	7.1	10.2	20.1	61.6	38.2	76.2	76.8	68.2	100.0	45.4	34.1	71.2	88.7

[a] Percentages of coverage:

Given year	Base year	Given year	Base year	Given year	Base year
1899:92.1, 1904:92.0	1909:93.2	1919:98.7, 1921:98.3, 1923:98.4	1929:97.4	1931:97.0	1929:97.6
				1933:94.0	1929:91.8
1909:92.9, 1914:96.3	1919:98.7	1925:99.4, 1927:99.2	1929:98.1	1935:89.1	1929:90.1
				1937:95.5	1929:97.6

MISCELLANEOUS PRODUCTS

Indexes of Physical Output, with Basic Data on Quantity, Value and Price of Products

BROOMS		1927	1929	1931	1933	1935	1937
Adjusted index		92.8	100.0	87.7	75.5	90.5	81.4
Unadjusted index[a]		99.4	100.0	88.3	76.8	97.0	87.4
Product	*Item*						
Household brooms, made of broomcorn	q Mil. doz.		3.09	2.75		2.86	2.44
	v Mil. $		15.6	10.7		11.7	9.05
	p $ per doz.	q 3.13	5.06	3.89	q 2.40	4.08	3.71
		v 16.5			v 7.47		
Household brooms, made of bassine	q Mil. doz.	p 5.28	.0417	.0384	p 3.11	.112	.147
	v Mil. $		.274	.203		1.09	.907
	p $ per doz.		6.57	5.29		9.77	6.18
Whisk brooms	q Mil. doz.	.490	.535	.518	.384	.466	.570
	v Mil. $	1.06	1.17	.916	.512	.742	.814
	p $ per doz.	2.15	2.19	1.77	1.33	1.59	1.43
Toy and hearth brooms	q Th. doz.		68.0	70.6	81.0	63.8	60.3
	v Th. $		102	89.5	100	79.0	71.9
	p $ per doz.		1.50	1.27	1.23	1.24	1.19
Industrial brooms	q Mil. doz.		.264	.196	.210	.290	.281
	v Mil. $		1.54	.999	.930	1.44	1.36
	p $ per doz.		5.84	5.19	4.43	4.98	4.85
Street-sweeping-machine brooms	q Th.	2.16	1.80	1.69		1.21	1.61
	v Th. $	54.6	40.4	35.0		19.2	22.6
	p $ each	25.3	22.4	20.7		15.8	14.0

[a] Percentages of coverage:

Given year	Base year	Given year	Base year
1927: 95.5	1929:89.3	1935:104.9	1929:97.8
1931: 98.6	1929:97.8	1937:105.2	
1933: 99.3	1929:97.6		

BUTTONS		1904[b]	1909[b]	1914	1919	1921[d]		1923	1925	1927	1929	1931	1933[b]	1935	1937
Adjusted index				96.3	121.4	77.5		113.4	110.7	91.0	100.0	88.1		121.3	126.2
Unadjusted index[a]				93.4	124.4	82.5		117.1	117.2	94.6	100.0	84.2		121.0	123.4
Product[c]	*Item*					*A*	*B*								
Buttons															
Galalith	q Mil. gross									.357	1.19	1.82		10.8	12.3
	v Mil. $									.398	.715	1.06		3.86	3.38
	p $ per gross									1.12	.600	.584		.356	.274
Synthetic-resin	q Mil. gross							5.53	7.34		6.08	4.84		9.07	9.41
	v Mil. $							.716	1.27		1.11	.624		3.24	4.34
	p $ per gross							.129	.173		.183	.129		.357	.462
Cellulose compounds	q Mil. gross			.623	2.21	1.07				.340	.391	.497		.725	.327
	v Mil. $			.724	3.32	1.59				1.03	1.18	1.21		1.58	.717
	p $ per gross			1.16	1.50	1.49				3.03	3.02	2.43		2.18	2.19
Metal, embossed with a design	q Mil. gross			.258	.338	.172					2.84	1.84		3.06	2.08
	v Mil. $			.283	.434	.276					1.21	.703		1.50	1.12
	p $ per gross			1.10	1.28	1.60					.426	.383		.489	.536
	q						q 2.47	7.62	6.11	6.36					
	v						v .816	1.94	1.73	2.29					
	p						p .331	.255	.284	.361					
Other metal	q Mil. gross			.615	.433	.226					4.92	4.01		3.20	3.92
	v Mil. $			.172	.183	.0713					1.07	.881		.566	1.50
	p $ per gross			.280	.423	.315					.217	.219		.177	.383
Glass	q Th. gross			217	571	69.8	69.8	52.5	197	129	114				
	v Th. $			100	261	50.0	50.0	48.1	171	120	83.7				
	p $ per gross			.461	.457	.717	.717	.917	.869	.933	.735				
Bone	q Mil. gross	.956		2.20	2.17	1.69									
	v Mil. $	.124		.330	.509	.488									
	p $ per gross	.130		.150	.235	.288									
Covered with fabric	q Mil. gross	2.99		3.02	2.87	1.39	1.39	1.02	1.69	.717	1.18	1.46		6.74	4.77
	v Mil. $	.766		1.60	1.77	1.10	1.10	.627	.917	.559	.759	.863		2.22	2.12
	p $ per gross	.256		.530	.616	.789	.789	.617	.544	.781	.642	.591		.329	.445

For footnotes see pp. 594–95.

Indexes of Physical Output, with Basic Data on Quantity, Value and Price of Products

BUTTONS (concluded)		1904[b]	1909[b]	1914	1919	1921[d]		1923	1925	1927	1929	1931	1933[b]	1935	1937
Product[c]	*Item*					*A*	*B*								
Buttons (concluded)															
Vegetable-ivory	*q* Mil. gross			3.22	7.84	4.68	7.43	9.49	12.0	9.22	6.83	5.11		3.38	3.14
	v Mil. $			1.84	7.68	3.44	5.13	6.34	7.47	5.70	4.05	2.51		1.85	1.61
	p $ per gross			.572	.980	.736	.691	.668	.623	.619	.593	.492		.547	.511
Horn	*q* Mil. gross			.537	2.57	1.84	1.84	3.70	1.92	1.80	1.23				
	v Mil. $			.299	1.11	.966	.966	1.09	.598	.538	.228				
	p $ per gross			.558	.431	.524	.524	.295	.311	.299	.186				
Trouser	*q* Mil. gross			6.69	8.11	5.60									
	v Mil. $			2.34	2.81	2.27									
	p $ per gross			.349	.347	.406									
Pearl or shell, ocean, clothing and shoe	*q* Mil. gross	1.74		4.52	5.89	5.20	5.20	8.14	6.15	5.10	6.81	5.14		5.32[e]	7.84[e]
	v Mil. $	1.51		2.49	6.56	4.90	4.90	5.69	4.48	4.35	5.71	3.38		2.89	4.65
	p $ per gross	.870		.551	1.11	.944	.944	.699	.729	.852	.839	.656		.543	.593
Pearl or shell, fresh-water, clothing and shoe	*q* Mil. gross	11.4		21.7	24.0	17.4	17.4	22.4	23.5	22.5	22.0	18.0		15.3[e]	17.2[e]
	v Mil. $	3.36		4.88	8.20	6.60	6.60	8.13	8.49	8.07	7.14	5.06		4.46	4.78
	p $ per gross	.295		.225	.342	.379	.379	.363	.361	.359	.324	.281		.291	.278
Shoe, other than pearl or shell	*q* Mil. gross			15.5	5.30	1.21	1.21	4.02	2.47	1.02	.670				
	v Mil. $			.611	.632	.291	.291	.496	.349	.194	.120				
	p $ per gross			.0394	.119	.241	.241	.123	.141	.190	.179				

A Comparable with earlier years. *B* Comparable with later years.

[a] Percentages of coverage:

Given year	Base year	Given year	Base year	Given year	Base year
1914:75.7, 1919:80.0	1921:83.1	1921:74.8	1929:70.3	1927:79.9	1929:76.8
		1923:76.6, 1925:78.5	1929:74.1	1931:75.7, 1935:79.0, 1937:77.4	1929:79.2

[b] Detailed data on products were not collected in 1909 and 1933. Because of the small coverage in 1904, no index is given for that year.

[c] The second set of 1921 figures and those for later years relate to buttons, wherever made. The first set of 1921 figures and those for earlier years relate to buttons made within the industry alone.

[d] Because of changes in classification within the industry in 1921 it was necessary to introduce two sets of 1921 data, one set comparable with 1929 and the other comparable with 1914 and 1919. In the 1921 data comparable with those for 1929, trouser buttons are not classified separately but are included in the figures for vegetable-ivory and metal buttons. In the 1921 data comparable with those for 1919, trouser buttons are separately classified. In addition the 1921 data for cellulose compounds are comparable with 1914 and 1919 but not with 1929. The indexes for 1914 and 1919 were computed on the 1921 base.

[e] The figures for 1935 and 1937 relate only to pearl clothing buttons; 1929 figures relating only to pearl clothing buttons were used in the computation of the indexes for these years. For pearl or shell, fresh-water, they are: *q* 21.4 mil. gross; *v* $6.89 mil.; *p* $.321 per gross. For pearl or shell, ocean, they are: *q* 6.05 mil. gross; *v* $5.25 mil.; *p* $.868 per gross.

ORGANS		*1899*	*1904*	*1909*	*1914*	*1919*	*1921*	*1923*	*1925*	*1927*	*1929*	*1931*	*1933*[c]	*1935*	*1937*[d]
Adjusted index		b	167.7	124.4	130.0	92.5	125.1	96.0	103.9	125.1	100.0	54.2		31.0	
Unadjusted index[a]		143.3	167.7	136.7	108.2	92.4	114.2	100.1	110.1	136.7	100.0	50.9		27.8	
Product	*Item*														
Pipe organs	*q* Th.	.564	.901	1.22	1.18	1.15	1.95	1.71	1.96	2.47	1.80	.917		.479	
	v Mil. $	1.18	1.99	2.71	3.62	4.19	8.72	9.65	12.8	16.8	11.2	5.28		1.44	
	p Th. $ ea.	2.09	2.21	2.22	3.06	3.64	4.47	5.64	6.55	6.79	6.20	5.76		3.00	
Reed organs	*q* Th.	107	113	64.1	40.5	26.4	7.88	7.77	4.36	3.09	2.70	1.28		1.69	
	v Mil. $	4.04	4.16	2.60	1.72	1.89	.748	.539	.442	.385	.375	.168		.115	
	p $ ea.	37.9	36.8	40.5	42.4	71.5	95.0	69.3	101	125	139	131		67.9	

[a] Percentages of coverage:

Given year	Base year	Given year	Base year
1904:101.8	1909:111.9	1923:106.1	1929:101.8
1909:111.9	1919:101.7	1925:107.9	
1914: 84.8		1927:111.2	
1919:101.7	1929:101.8	1931: 95.5	
1921: 92.9		1935: 91.4	

[b] No adjusted index for 1899 could be computed because the industry is not shown separately in the Census for that year. The adjusted index given above, extrapolated by the unadjusted index, is 143.3 for 1899.

[c] No comparable figures are available for 1933.

[d] Only data for the production of all organs combined are available for 1937. Because of the large difference between the prices of pipe organs and of reed organs, it was considered inadvisable to compute an index for that year.

Indexes of Physical Output, with Basic Data on Quantity, Value and Price of Products

PENCILS		*1929*	*1931*	*1933*[b]	*1935*	*1937*
Adjusted index		100.0	73.7		134.1	129.6
Unadjusted index[a]		100.0	90.3		142.3	135.0
Product	*Item*					
Pencils, other than mechanical	*q* Mil. gross	5.85	4.76		6.24	6.73
	v Mil. $	13.6	10.0		10.4	11.0
	p $ per gross	2.32	2.10		1.67	1.64
Mechanical pencils						
Cellulose compounds (pyroxylin)	*q* Th. gross	50.7	81.0		125	134
	v Mil. $	4.28	3.75		3.66	4.60
	p $ per gross	84.5	46.2		29.3	34.4
Plated	*q* Th. gross	47.2	4.73 }			
	v Mil. $	1.35	.153 }			
	p $ per gross	28.7	32.4 }		214	95.0
			}		1.16	1.17
Other	*q* Th. gross	67.3	60.7 }		5.45	12.3
	v Mil. $	3.25	1.27 }			
	p $ per gross	48.3	20.9 }			

[a] Percentages of coverage: Given year 1931:88.0, 1935:76.3, 1937:74.9; Base year 1929:71.9

[b] Detailed data on products were not collected in 1933.

PENS and POINTS		*1929*	*1931*	*1933*[b]	*1935*	*1937*
Adjusted index		100.0	83.1		143.7	220.6
Unadjusted index[a]		100.0	72.3		129.0	205.3
Product	*Item*					
Fountain and stylographic pens	*q* Th. gross	99.4	73.8		142	229
	v Mil. $	22.7	14.6		11.0	13.6
	p $ per gross	228	198		77.7	59.6

PENS and POINTS (concluded)		1929	1931	1933[b]	1935	1937
Product	*Item*					
Steel and brass pen points, made for sale as such	*q* Mil. gross	2.01	1.22		1.44	1.52
	v Mil. $	1.30	.506		.918	1.16
	p $ per gross	.647	.413		.638	.765
Fountain-pen desk sets	*q* Mil.	.394	.224		.176[c]	.380
	v Mil. $	2.38	.861		.407	.832
	p $ ea.	6.04	3.83		2.32	2.19

[a] Percentages of coverage: Given year 1931:67.0, 1935:69.1, 1937:71.7; Base year 1929:77.0

[b] Comparable figures are not available for 1933.
[c] Estimated in part.

PIANOS		1899	1904	1909	1914	1919	1921	1923	1925	1927	1929	1931	1933[c]	1935	1937
Adjusted index		[b]	113.9	156.1	156.5	188.7	128.1	210.1	197.8	150.6	100.0	43.1		39.6	66.0
Unadjusted index[a]		75.2	123.7	168.4	168.2	204.2	136.9	236.7	219.3	157.9	100.0	44.1		52.7	73.1
Product	*Item*														
Upright pianos															
Other than player	*q* Th.	167	252	321	228	138	88.7	106	87.3	69.9	49.0	18.3		32.2	
	v Mil. $	25.3	37.4	45.2	31.4	29.4	17.6	21.7	16.9	12.3	7.87	2.58		3.85	
	p $ each	152	148	141	138	213	198	205	193	176	160	141		120	
Player	*q* Th.					166	102	171	144	76.4	17.3	1.69		.418	*q* 75.2
	v Mil. $					49.3	29.9	46.3	38.2	20.0	4.12	.274		.0601	*v* 10.5
	p $ each	*q* .224	1.87	34.5	84.5	297	294	271	265	262	237	162		144	*p* 139
		v .0447	.417	9.28	18.9										
Player, reproducing type	*q* Th.	*p* 200	223	269	224	11.5	5.31	12.7	5.48	4.10	1.44	.146			
	v Mil. $					4.07	2.84	4.65	2.19	1.42	.460	.0342			
	p $ each					354	534	367	400	347	318	234			

For footnotes see p. 599.

Indexes of Physical Output, with Basic Data on Quantity, Value and Price of Products

PIANOS (concluded)		1899	1904	1909	1914	1919	1921	1923	1925	1927	1929	1931	1933[c]	1935	1937
Product	*Item*														
Grand pianos															
Baby, other than player	*q* Th.					18.0	15.6	38.0	40.4	43.8	36.9	24.7		27.0	
	v Mil. $					8.65	7.76	16.1	16.2	17.5	12.9	7.01		6.84	
	p $ each					481	497	423	403	401	348	284		254	
Baby, player	*q* Th.					1.20	.348	1.40	5.29	.490	.384				
	v Mil. $					.662	.280	.937	2.04	.306	.160				
	p $ each					554	804	671	386	625	416				
Baby, player, reproducing type	*q* Th.					.839	2.26	5.37	7.60	7.22	5.90	.168			
	v Mil. $					1.05	2.58	4.49	6.32	5.55	2.67	.0944			
	p $ each					1250	1140	836	832	768	452	562			
Parlor, other than player	*q* Th.	*q* 4.25	7.37	8.74	10.5	2.17	2.56	5.90	9.17	8.76	7.77	5.52		1.36	*q* 27.9
	v Mil. $	*v* 1.70	3.66	4.04	4.62	1.11	1.61	3.83	5.43	5.32	4.16	2.38		.757	*v* 9.09
	p $ each	*p* 400	497	462	439	511	628	650	592	607	536	431		556	*p* 326
Parlor, player	*q* Th.					.012	.021	.106	.156	.042	.042				
	v Mil. $					.00975	.0204	.108	.104	.0304	.0302				
	p $ each					813	971	1016	665	724	718				
Parlor, player, reproducing type	*q* Th.					.113	1.43	2.63	2.54	1.18	2.16	.311			
	v Mil. $					.110	1.51	2.96	3.53	1.70	2.14	.260			
	p $ each					970	1,058	1124	1387	1434	986	836			
Concert	*q* Th.					.087	.101	.666	.579	.293	.234	.068			
	v Mil. $					.0541	.0726	.932	.453	.290	.155	.0444			
	p $ each					621	719	1400	782	990	662	653			

[a] Percentages of coverage:

Given year	Base year	Given year	Base year
1904:88.4	1909:87.9	1925:90.3	1929:81.4
1909:87.9	1919:88.1	1927:85.4	1929:81.4
1914:87.5	1919:88.1	1931:82.9	1929:81.0
1919:88.1	1929:81.4	1935:90.7	1929:68.2
1921:87.0	1929:81.4	1937:90.2	1929:81.4
1923:91.7	1929:81.4		

[b] No adjusted index for 1899 could be computed because the industry is not shown separately in the Census for that year. The adjusted index given above, extrapolated by the unadjusted index, is 69.2 for 1899.

[c] Comparable figures are not available for 1933.

SPORTING GOODS, not elsewhere classified		*1929*	*1931*	*1933*[b]	*1935*	*1937*
Adjusted index		100.0	96.2		69.4	91.1
Unadjusted index[a]		100.0	106.4		72.4	96.3
Product	*Item*					
Golf goods						
Balls	*q* Mil. doz.	2.82	2.30		1.54	1.72
	v Mil. $	7.46	5.99		3.97	4.39
	p $ per doz.	2.65	2.61		2.58	2.55
Clubs	*q* Mil.	3.17	4.13		1.67	2.35
	v Mil. $	9.72	12.0		4.41	6.24
	p $ ea.	3.07	2.90		2.65	2.66
Shafts	*q* Mil.	2.22	4.66		2.24	3.15
	v Mil. $	1.57	3.07		1.14	1.72
	p $ ea.	.709	.658		.511	.545
Caddy bags	*q* Mil.	.480[c]	.522[c]		.136[c]	.221[c]
	v Mil. $	1.91	1.83		.660	1.17
	p $ ea.	3.97	3.50		4.86	5.28

For footnotes see p. 601.

Indexes of Physical Output, with Basic Data on Quantity, Value and Price of Products

SPORTING GOODS, not elsewhere classified (continued)		1929	1931	1933[b]	1935	1937
Product	*Item*					
Fishing tackle						
Rods	*q* Mil.	1.50	1.34		1.55	2.08
	v Mil. $	2.45	1.91		2.28	3.45
	p $ ea.	1.64	1.43		1.47	1.66
Reels	*q* Mil.	1.14	1.05		1.89	2.39
	v Mil. $	1.82	1.54		2.19	3.36
	p $ ea.	1.60	1.47		1.16	1.40
Baseball goods						
Balls, including play-ground balls	*q* Mil. doz.	.710	.759		.592	.628
	v Mil. $	3.26	2.73		2.59	2.30
	p $ per doz.	4.60	3.60		4.38	3.66
Bats, including indoor bats	*q* Mil.	1.82	2.58		2.98	2.83
	v Mil. $	1.05	1.14		1.13	1.06
	p $ ea.	.577	.422		.380	.375
Masks	*q* Th.	35.7	31.7		16.6	23.3
	v Th. $	111	93.9		38.2	42.3
	p $ ea.	3.11	2.96		2.30	1.81
Mitts and gloves	*q* Mil.	.932	.908		.720	.786
	v Mil. $	1.82	1.36		1.02	.950
	p $ ea.	1.95	1.50		1.41	1.21
Footballs	*q* Mil.	.531	1.06		.973	1.44
	v Mil. $	1.41	1.32		.910	1.09
	p $ ea.	2.66	1.24		.935	.754

SPORTING GOODS, not elsewhere classified (concluded)		1929	1931	1933[b]	1935	1937
Product	*Item*					
Basketballs and other inflated balls	*q* Mil.	1.38	.679[c]		.239	.539
	v Mil. $	1.64	.967		.749	1.12
	p $ ea.	1.19	1.42		3.13	2.08
Striking bags	*q* Th.	71.0	48.9		65.7	95.1
	v Th. $	193	90.5		106	145
	p $ ea.	2.72	1.85		1.62	1.52
Boxing gloves	*q* Th.	244	271		171	318
	v Th. $	441	254		144	227
	p $ ea.	1.81	.938		.842	.716
Skates						
Roller	*q* Mil. pr.	2.61	1.75		2.68	2.90[c]
	v Mil. $	2.92	1.81		2.30	2.69
	p $ per pr.	1.12	1.04		.858	.927
Ice	*q* Mil. pr.	.685	.547		.528	1.19
	v Mil. $	1.78	.851		1.04	1.94
	p $ ea.	2.60	1.55		1.98	1.63

[a] Percentages of coverage: Given year 1931:75.0, 1935:70.8, 1937:71.7; Base year 1929:67.9

[b] Detailed data on products were not collected in 1933.

[c] Estimated in part.

TOTAL MANUFACTURING

Indexes of Physical Output

TOTAL MANUFACTURING	*1899*	*1904*	*1909*	*1914*	*1919*	*1921*	*1923*	*1925*	*1927*	*1929*	*1931*	*1933*	*1935*	*1937*
Indexes derived by combination of adjusted indexes of individual industries[a]														
Adjusted index	25.1	31.4	40.3	48.5	60.5	51.9	77.5	81.7	86.5	100.0	71.1	62.3	83.3	104.5
Unadjusted index[b]	29.0	34.3	43.7	52.5	65.7	53.4	79.8	83.8	87.0	100.0	73.8	67.0	84.8	102.6
Indexes derived by combination of adjusted indexes of groups[c]														
Adjusted index[d]	27.5	34.2	43.4	51.1	61.0	53.5	76.9	81.9	87.1	100.0	72.0	62.8	82.8	103.3
Unadjusted index[e]	29.6	36.1	45.8	54.1	62.8	55.7	79.2	83.7	88.3	100.0	74.2	65.6	82.9	100.4

[a] When adjusted indexes were not available, unadjusted indexes were used.

[b] Percentages of coverage:

Given year	Base year	Given year	Base year	Given year	Base year	Given year	Base year
1899:55.7	1909:52.2	1914:55.1	1919:55.3	1923:57.3	1929:55.7	1931:69.5	1929:67.0
1904:53.8	1909:53.4	1919:56.2	1929:51.8	1925:61.3	1929:59.7	1933:68.2	1929:63.5
1909:54.1	1919:54.1	1921:54.1	1929:52.5	1927:66.8	1929:66.4	1935:66.2	1929:65.1
						1937:64.6	1929:65.8

[c] Plus adjusted indexes (or, if not available, unadjusted indexes) of industries not covered by group indexes.

[d] This index we considered the most accurate.

[e] Percentages of coverage:

Given year	Base year	Given year	Base year	Given year	Base year	Given year	Base year
1899:79.9	1909:78.4	1914:80.6	1919:78.6	1923:79.4	1929:77.1	1931:86.2	1929:83.7
1904:79.2	1909:79.3	1919:78.9	1929:76.6	1925:84.7	1929:82.8	1933:86.1	1929:82.4
1909:79.5	1919:77.6	1921:80.3	1929:77.1	1927:84.7	1929:83.6	1935:82.9 1937:80.5	1929:82.8

Appendix C

Value Added by Manufacturing Industries, Census Years, 1899–1937

Appendix C

Value Added by Manufacturing Industries, Census Years, 1899–1937

EXPLANATORY NOTE

This appendix consists of three tables. The first is a detailed tabulation showing the value added by each manufacturing industry in each Census year from 1899 to 1937 inclusive. The industries are arranged in groups which proceed in the order previously established for major groups of manufacturing industries. Within the groups, the order of the individual industries is not alphabetical, as it was in Appendix B, but is designed to bring closely related industries together for convenience in presentation. A second table assembles the group totals and shows the grand total for all manufacturing industries combined, and a third table reconciles the grand total arrived at in the present study with the grand total given in each Census volume.[1] As stated in Appendix A, the composition of total manufacturing in this study differs somewhat from that of the Census, as do also the composition and order of our major groups.

The basic source of information on value added is the Census of Manufactures prepared by the United States Bureau of the Census. In order to obtain accurate and comparable data, we have had to take figures from many different Census volumes. Furthermore, we have sometimes combined series in a manner slightly different from that followed in the Census, and for this reason the reader may occasionally find it difficult to locate in the Census volumes certain figures presented by us. The industry titles used here are short titles; complete Census titles will be found in the index at the end of this volume.

Footnotes explain pertinent changes in classification and coverage. Breaks or discontinuities in series have been indicated by footnote symbols at the point in the series where the discontinuity occurs; and symbols are repeated in a series if breaks occur at more than one point in that series. When possible the continuity of a

[1] The 1899 and 1904 Census totals were taken from the 1909 Census report.

series has been preserved, at least in part, by the provision of two figures for the year in which a change in composition took place, one figure comparable with earlier years and the other comparable with later years. The footnotes that give details concerning the various changes in the definition of an industry are necessarily condensed. For example, footnote i, p. 609, reads: "Between 1909 and 1914 powdered milk and sugar of milk were transferred from *chemicals, n.e.c.,* to *milk, canned.*" In more precise terms, the statement means that up to and including 1909 establishments whose chief product was powdered milk or sugar of milk were classified under *chemicals, n.e.c.,* whereas in 1914 and later years they were classified under *milk, canned.*

We use *n.e.c.* as the abbreviation for *not elsewhere classified, n.e.m.* for *not elsewhere made,* and *n.e.d.* for *not elsewhere done.* Italicized figures represent duplications (such as totals) of other figures in the same column, though not necessarily on the same page. Group totals are not italicized. Census titles of industries are italicized in footnotes.

Value Added by Manufacturing Industries (Unit: $1,000,000)

FOODS	Establishments with Products Valued at $500 or More					Establishments with Products Valued at $5,000 or More									
	1899	*1904*	*1909*	*1914*	*1919*	*1919*	*1921*	*1923*	*1925*	*1927*	*1929*	*1931*	*1933*	*1935*	*1937*
Industry															
Meat packing[a]	102.8	108.6	164.8	210.3	463.4	463.4	332.7	409.8	425.1	393.5	460.5	341.6	287.5	332.4	402.2
Sausage, n.e.m.	1.4	2.6	3.6	5.2	12.7	12.6	15.6	18.5	20.9	21.3	26.9	25.1	23.7	26.7	32.4
Oleomargarine, n.e.m.	4.9	1.2	1.7	4.8	13.8	13.8	11.1	10.2	11.5	12.1	15.6	7.5	4.5	9.1	13.6
Shortenings			b	9.2	10.4	10.4	2.4	6.4	11.3[e]	11.4	15.5	15.5	17.7	34.8	35.2
Flour	73.3	93.1	116.0	125.4	253.3	252.4	185.9	162.6	172.6[d]	176.0	191.4	137.0	134.3	137.0	133.6
Cereals			b	23.2	41.4	41.3	43.5	48.3	57.5	63.8	73.8	72.2	56.0	64.2	69.6
Feeds	15.0	23.5[e]	4.8	7.9	21.2	21.2	13.9	19.9	29.4[d]	55.1	74.8	47.2	39.3	58.1	76.7
Food, n.e.c.			36.6	57.2[b] 19.9	52.0	51.8	41.5	53.5	65.8	68.7[f]	75.5	57.4	52.1	64.2	77.9
Rice	1.1	3.0	2.9	2.4	13.4	13.4	7.0	6.9	7.7	7.6	10.4	8.5	8.0	9.9	8.0
Macaroni			b	4.9	11.9	11.8	11.0	12.9	16.0	17.9	19.7	15.9	15.5	15.8	17.5
Biscuits and crackers	80.3	113.6	158.8	45.8	100.9	100.1	104.5	122.4	137.3	141.1	167.4	141.2	93.0	93.3	110.5
Bread and cake				171.8	337.8	335.2	386.9	426.0	462.9	560.4	621.6	543.4	399.3	472.1	588.7
Fish, canned	7.0	7.7	10.8	12.7	26.3	26.2	14.1	19.5	21.9	22.2	27.6	13.9	14.3	21.4	29.7
Fruits and vegetables, canned	28.6[g]	39.6[g]	44.4	71.1	189.4	188.5	128.0	216.3	230.5	217.2	288.3	191.0	171.6	240.5	290.4
Vinegar and cider	2.8	3.4	3.5	3.4	9.2	8.8	8.4	5.1	5.4	4.9	4.4	3.3	2.7	3.8	2.7
Butter	21.9	17.2	25.4	30.8	68.8	68.8	72.2	90.9	80.2	101.7	110.5	70.2	68.7	78.2	79.8
Cheese		3.9	5.2	5.0	14.0	14.0	12.8	20.7	15.1	17.7	17.9	14.0	10.5[h]	14.8	17.2
Milk, canned		4.2	8.4[i]	13.4	56.9	56.9	44.3	33.1	31.2	40.4	45.3	39.2	34.4	40.5	44.1
Ice cream			j	23.2	73.1	72.7	92.1	114.7	145.3	151.0	172.4	158.0	92.1	108.5	138.5
Beet sugar[k]	2.5	9.9	20.9	21.2	62.1	62.1	17.2	47.5	45.3	25.9	37.6	23.3	51.0	24.0	38.4
Cane sugar, n.e.m.[k]	18.3	32.5[e]	9.3	5.7	13.6	13.6	6.0	6.2	1.8	2.2	6.1	4.0	6.6	8.0	8.4
Cane-sugar refining			22.3	25.3	68.8	68.8	40.0	44.4	56.7	45.9	69.0	59.4	55.5	41.0	62.0
Chewing gum	25.3	38.3	53.6	9.8	26.0	25.8	19.0	25.4	29.9	34.8	36.9	34.5	29.1	32.8	39.8
Confectionery				60.0	195.3	194.3	139.9	163.5	173.6[l]	173.6	178.1	139.4	97.7[l]	106.2[l]	123.1

FOODS (concluded)	Establishments with Products Valued at $500 or More					Establishments with Products Valued at $5,000 or More									
	1899	*1904*	*1909*	*1914*	*1919*	*1919*	*1921*	*1923*	*1925*	*1927*	*1929*	*1931*	*1933*	*1935*	*1937*
Industry															
Chocolate	2.8	4.7	6.9	11.2	37.5	37.5	32.5	34.7	33.1[l]	32.3	40.0	37.3	26.2[l]	26.6[l]	28.2
Corn products	9.3	7.1	11.9	12.4	55.9	55.9	29.2	42.1	39.8	43.6	61.7	44.7	45.9	33.4	39.4
Flavorings	3.6	5.2	8.7	12.8	26.5	26.4	31.8	36.0	47.1	56.1	73.6[m]	70.7[n]	33.8	38.7	71.6
Baking powder	7.4	10.1	11.4	11.4	19.6	19.6	28.2	30.0	30.0	31.1	29.7	26.3	18.9	17.9	16.9
Ice	10.5	17.8	31.6	42.6	94.1	93.4	107.7	118.0	142.2	144.0	171.1	156.9	112.3	100.4	109.1
TOTAL	418.8	547.2	763.5	979.6 1,002.8	2,369.3	2,360.7	1,979.4	2,345.5	2,547.1	2,673.5	3,123.3	2,498.6	2,002.2	2,254.3	2,705.2

[a] For 1899–1919 *meat packing* includes *lard, not made in meat packing establishments*. After 1919 *lard* was not treated as a separate industry.

[b] Prior to 1914 *cereals*, *macaroni*, and *shortenings* were combined with *food, n.e.c.*

[c] Between 1925 and 1927 vegetable cooking oils were transferred from *oils, n.e.c.*, and other classifications to *shortenings*.

[d] Between 1925 and 1927 grain ground for prepared feeds was transferred from *flour* to *feeds*. The comparability of the figures for the latter industry appears to have been seriously affected by this shift.

[e] Between 1904 and 1909 some establishments compounding sirups were transferred from *cane-sugar refining* to *food, n.e.c.*

[f] Between 1927 and 1929 canned poultry products were transferred from *food, n.e.c.*, to *poultry products*. The latter we do not consider to be a manufacturing industry.

[g] Packing and shipping houses that handled dried fruits completely processed on fruit farms were included in *canned fruits and vegetables* in 1904 only.

[h] The 1933 Census of this industry is considered by the Bureau of the Census to be somewhat incomplete.

[i] Between 1909 and 1914 powdered milk and sugar of milk were transferred from *chemicals, n.e.c.* to *milk, canned*.

[j] Prior to 1914 *ice cream* was not considered a manufacturing industry and was not canvassed.

[k] Figures for 1931–37 for *beet sugar* and *cane sugar, n.e.m.*, were requested by the U.S. Bureau of the Census for the seasons beginning in the respective Census years, and for earlier Census years for the seasons ending in those years. Thus the figure given for 1931 applies to the season 1931–32, whereas the figure for 1921 refers to the season 1920–21. In 1925, 1927 and 1929, however, most of the establishments in *cane sugar, n.e.m.*, and a few of the establishments in *beet sugar* reported for the seasons 1925–26, 1927–28 and 1929–30, instead of 1924–25, 1926–27 and 1928–29.

[l] Chocolate departments operated by confectionery manufacturers are classified under *chocolate*. In 1935 and prior to 1927 some confectionery manufacturers failed to make separate returns for their chocolate departments, which were consequently included in the statistics on *confectionery*. Only 5 establishments failed to make separate reports in 1935.

[m] Between 1929 and 1931 *dairymen's supplies* was abandoned as a separate classification, and the products were divided among *flavorings* and other classifications.

[n] Between 1931 and 1933 malt extracts and sirups were transferred from *flavorings* to *liquors, malt*.

Value Added by Manufacturing Industries (Unit: $1,000,000)

BEVERAGES	Establishments with Products Valued at $500 or More					Establishments with Products Valued at $5,000 or More									
	1899	*1904*	*1909*	*1914*	*1919*	*1919*	*1921*	*1923*	*1925*	*1927*	*1929*	*1931*	*1933*	*1935*	*1937*
Industry															
Beverages, nonalcoholic															
Excl. near beer	14.7	20.2	27.0	31.6	66.8	64.4	54.5								
Incl. near beer								129.2	139.3	147.3	167.3	136.5	69.4	97.2	164.6
Liquors, malt[a]															
Incl. near beer	185.3	223.4	278.1	312.4	285.1	285.1	67.0								
Excl. near beer													266.8		
Excl. near beer and tax													*153.8*[b]	280.2	335.4
Malt	4.6	6.7	7.8	8.9	7.7	7.7	3.5	3.3	4.1	3.1	4.7	5.3	7.3[b]	18.7	18.5
Liquors, vinous	2.9	5.4	6.5	7.1	9.3	9.1	3.1	2.9	1.7	1.5	1.8	0.6[c]	14.8[c]	21.1	19.2
Liquors, distilled[a,d]	81.6	105.6[e]	168.7	165.8	12.2	12.2	6.5	15.2	19.1	14.7	19.2	8.6	36.9[f]		
Excl. tax													*19.7*	76.4	39.9
TOTAL	289.1	361.3	488.1	525.8	381.1	378.5	134.6	150.6	164.2	166.6	193.0	151.0	395.2		
													265.0	493.6	577.6

[a] The figures for 1899–1931 and the higher figure for 1933 for *liquors, malt*, and *liquors, distilled*, include internal revenue taxes in value added, whereas the 1935–37 figures and the lower figure for 1933 do not include these taxes.

Between 1931 and 1933 malt extracts and sirups were transferred from *flavorings* to *liquors, malt*.

[b] Between 1933 and 1935 malthouses were transferred from *liquors, malt*, to *malt*.

[c] Prior to 1933 internal revenue taxes were included in the value added by *liquors, vinous*. In 1933 internal revenue taxes were excluded in part and in 1935 and 1937 they were excluded entirely.

[d] The 1933 Census of this industry is considered by the Bureau of the Census to be somewhat incomplete.

[e] Beginning with 1909 the internal revenue tax was included in the value of products of *liquors, distilled*, whether such tax was paid by the manufacturer at the time the report was made, or whether the liquors were still held in bond pending the payment of the tax; in 1899 and 1904 this tax was included only when it was actually paid and reported by the manufacturer.

[f] Between 1933 and 1935 ethyl alcohol was transferred from *liquors, distilled*, to *chemicals, n.e.c.*

TOBACCO PRODUCTS[a]	Establishments with Products Valued at $500 or More					Establishments with Products Valued at $5,000 or More									
	1899	1904	1909	1914	1919	1919	1921	1923	1925	1927	1929	1931	1933	1935	1937
Industry															
Cigarettes[b]	102.1	133.2	25.7	48.8	208.2	204.8	176.6	269.3	543.5	439.2	536.8	566.6	490.4	594.5	709.2
Cigars[b]			131.7	135.6	212.2	208.8	177.9	182.4		191.0	173.3	123.6	92.5[c]	84.6	94.9
Tobacco products, other	68.7	71.8	82.1	98.7	109.0	108.8	85.3	76.6	121.8	112.9	106.8	102.3	85.0	83.2	83.3
TOTAL	170.8	205.0	239.5	283.1	529.4	522.4	439.8	528.3	665.3	743.1	816.9	792.5	667.9	762.3	887.4

[a] Prior to 1933 internal revenue taxes were included in the value added figures published by the Census for the tobacco products industries; in 1933–37 they were excluded. We have included them throughout.

[b] For the years 1909, 1914 and 1919 the Census gives figures for a small industry, *cigars and cigarettes*. The value added by this industry was distributed between the industries *cigars* and *cigarettes* in proportion to the value added by the two industries. The value added by the *cigars and cigarettes* industry in 1921 and 1923 was combined by the Census with the value added by *cigarettes* to avoid disclosure of the figures for individual establishments.

[c] In 1933 the coverage of *cigars* was incomplete. On the basis of U. S. Bureau of Internal Revenue data the coverage may be estimated as about 81.5 percent; the value added figure for this year has been raised accordingly.

TEXTILE PRODUCTS[a]	Establishments with Products Valued at $500 or More					Establishments with Products Valued at $5,000 or More									
	1899	1904	1909	1914	1919	1919	1921	1923	1925	1927	1929	1931	1933	1935	1937
Industry															
Cotton goods[b]	157.8	159.9	251.2[c]	243.5	843.8	843.8[d]	566.5	742.2	629.5	687.1	617.7	393.3	377.2[e,f]	370.5[g]	546.7
Cotton small wares	3.3	3.8	6.2[c]	5.3	16.9	16.9	13.2[h]	34.6	32.9	32.6	31.5	22.3	21.3[e,i]	21.9[j]	21.9
Lace goods			[c]	7,5	16.3	16.3	14.7	21.2	17.5	15.9	19.1	13.0	11.1	17.9	18.1
Woolen goods	47.4	54.4	41.5	40.1	146.9	146.9	110.7	162.7	141.9	128.6	125.1	74.3	71.2[k,f]	119.2[l]	127.0
Worsted goods	43.2	56.1	104.8	92.9	252.9	252.9	244.9	277.1	195.5	187.3	199.4	143.3	127.2[f]	147.7	166.2
Haircloth		[m]	0.6	0.7	1.1	1.1	1.1	1.2	0.8	0.9	1.3	1.0	1.1	1.4	
Wool pulling	0.5	0.8	1.1	1.6	4.6	4.6	1.6	3.9	1.6	2.2	2.7	2.0	3.1	3.4	4.0
Wool scouring	0.7	0.8[n]	1.2	1.4	6.5	6.5	3.5	3.7	3.3	3.7	3.2	3.5	3.2	3.9	2.6
Silk and rayon goods[b]	38.2	50.6	77.1[o]	95.0	256.9	256.8	215.2	252.0	283.3	266.4	282.2	177.2	129.4[e]	156.4[j,p]	156.5
Dyeing and finishing	27.0	31.2	48.3	52.6	149.2	149.2	135.6	167.5	187.8	195.4	230.1	161.1	136.1[e,q]	130.9[r]	156.1

For footnotes see pp. 614–15.

Value Added by Manufacturing Industries (Unit: $1,000,000)

TEXTILE PRODUCTS[a] (continued)	Establishments with Products Valued at $500 or More					Establishments with Products Valued at $5,000 or More									
	1899	1904	1909	1914	1919	1919	1921	1923	1925	1927	1929	1931	1933	1935	1937
Industry															
Hosiery, knit[b]	43.5	59.6	87.7[o]	109.0	277.5	277.3	264.5	156.3	183.4	221.3	269.8	175.2	143.3[q]	168.6[p]	201.7
Underwear, knit[b]								74.9	76.0	81.2	69.8	44.9	47.3	42.1	54.3
Outerwear, knit[b]								91.5	62.8	59.1	68.9	52.5	41.9	59.9	50.8
Cloth, knit[b]								20.8	18.1	19.7	20.5	16.4	16.5	20.6	23.7
Carpets and rugs, rag[s]	1.1	1.4	1.9	2.1	3.6	3.3	3.2	4.0	3.8	4.3	3.9	2.3	1.2	2.5[l]	0.7
Carpets and rugs, wool	21.0	23.6	31.6[t]	26.8	56.1	56.1	53.8	102.0	83.6	81.3	90.3	49.3	41.4	59.2[l]	79.5
Mats and matting	0.6	0.7	1.4	1.1	2.8	2.8	1.3	2.4	2.0	0.9	1.0	0.6	0.4	1.3	1.9
Asphalted-felt-base floor covering	3.0	3.6	5.7	6.4	22.3	22.3	6.4	16.1	17.6	17.9	17.6	10.8	13.2	15.8	16.0
Linoleum							16.6	25.2	25.0	23.2	29.8	15.1	12.3	12.7	20.4
Cordage and twine	11.2	11.9	12.6	16.2	43.7	43.7	28.9	34.6	33.6	33.1	36.9	23.2	20.4	23.2	28.5
Jute goods	2.4	4.0	4.5[t]	3.9	16.7	16.7	8.6	13.1	13.0	11.4	9.9	7.0	7.7	8.9	12.4
Linen goods	1.8	2.1	2.4	2.7	2.8	2.8	3.7	5.3	4.8	5.0	4.5	2.7	2.2	2.2	2.6
Clothing, men's, work[b]	104.4	135.6	192.4	190.4	449.1	448.0	390.7	59.7	53.8	60.8[u]	53.0	35.6[v]	50.5	62.8[w]	71.5
Clothing, men's, n.e.c.								423.8	381.1	390.5	380.6	230.6[v]	182.4		
Clothing, men's, buttonholes[x]	0.6	0.6	0.7	0.5	1.0	0.9	0.6	0.7	0.6	0.8	0.5	0.3	0.2	257.7[y]	284.4
Cloth sponging and refinishing	0.5	1.0	1.5	1.4	3.5	3.5	3.8	4.4	3.7	3.3	3.3	2.4	2.8		
Furnishings, men's, n.e.c.	10.9	14.6[z]	15.9	20.9	43.1	43.0	30.3	45.7	51.0[aa]	62.6	67.3	44.7[v]	24.2	34.4	33.4[bb]
Gloves, textile, n.e.m.					12.1	12.1	5.0	9.8[cc]	11.6	12.8	10.6	5.6	7.3	8.6	13.9

TEXTILE PRODUCTS[a] (continued)	Establishments with Products Valued at $500 or More					Establishments with Products Valued at $5,000 or More									
	1899	1904	1909	1914	1919	1919	1921	1923	1925	1927	1929	1931	1933	1935	1937
Industry															
Shirts[b]															
Incl. contract work	24.2	25.3													
Excl. contract work		*22.3*	32.2	39.2	67.2	67.0	66.7	84.6	80.2	95.8	93.3	68.2[v]	51.3	64.9 }	80.2 (Shirts and Collars combined)
Collars, men's	9.8	7.9	11.2	12.0	28.1	28.1	17.2	24.3	15.8	7.4	5.1	3.9	1.6	0.9 }	
Clothing, women's, n.e.c.[b]	69.4	110.0	165.8	205.7	475.7	474.8	393.4	453.4	440.9	537.0[dd]	622.1	459.1	301.1[ee]	439.6	488.7[bb]
Corsets	8.1	8.7	17.6	21.0	36.7	36.7	36.7	39.6	39.3	41.8	40.8	40.2	29.1	35.7[p]	38.9
Embroideries										24.5	18.7	15.7	8.9	12.5	13.6
Millinery	13.8 (Embroideries, Millinery, Trimmings combined)	24.5[z]	40.9	56.5	122.8	121.9	137.5	147.6	156.5[aa,ff]	106.0	97.6	72.8	42.7[ee]	49.2	47.6[bb]
Trimmings, n.e.m.										31.1[dd]	24.4	16.5	11.2	14.3[j]	18.3
Handkerchiefs									[aa]	13.4	13.2	8.5	6.9	8.9	7.8
Elastic woven goods, n.e.m.		[z]	11.4	9.2	24.4	24.4	17.7[h]	10.4	11.0	10.7	12.6	7.2	4.8	6.2[j]	6.4
Hats, fur-felt	14.3	20.7	25.8	20.4	42.6	42.6	26.4	40.8	39.9	48.1	46.7	30.1	21.3	28.4	32.4
Hats, cloth	10.5 (Hats, cloth and straw combined)	6.6	7.0	9.3	20.4	20.2	18.5	20.6	21.1	20.5	19.0	8.7	6.5	7.5	6.0[bb]
Hats, straw, men's		4.8	10.0	11.4	15.3	15.3	14.1	16.2	13.0[ff]	9.9	10.0	6.6	4.7	5.5	6.9
Hats, wool-felt	1.5	1.1	1.9	1.0	3.0	3.0	2.5	4.2	3.8	4.3	4.4	3.1	2.5	5.8	7.0
Hat and cap materials	1.1	2.2	2.9	1.9	9.9	9.8	4.8	6.6	6.8	7.7	7.7	4.5	3.5	4.8	5.4
Fur goods	11.6	15.9	24.2	19.8	67.5	67.1	54.8	71.9	95.0	104.3[u]	101.5	62.1	30.5	55.2	50.4[bb]
Furs, dressed	0.9	1.6	1.6	2.0	14.0	14.0	13.1	18.2	18.1	20.6	21.6	21.7	15.4	14.8	15.4
Artificial leather	1.6	2.2	*2.0*[gg]												
			1.1	2.0	8.1	8.1	4.3	10.9	9.7	12.4	10.7	6.1	5.4	7.3	9.5
Awnings	3.9	4.6	6.1	8.0	18.7	18.4	15.7	20.0	21.1	23.5	23.9	16.6	10.8[hh]	10.3[hh]	13.0
Bags, textile, n.e.m.	3.2	6.6	8.5	12.0	38.0	38.0	16.0	23.5	25.0	26.2	25.9	25.8	22.6	23.7	26.4
Belting, woven, n.e.m.	0.3	1.1	1.9	1.6	7.5	7.5	3.0[h]	1.6	1.5	1.7	1.5	0.6	0.5		
Housefurnishings, n.e.c.	5.1	5.4[jj]	6.1[kk]	9.1	20.4	20.3	19.4	24.7	27.6	35.0	51.0	34.8	29.0[ee]	36.4[j,r] (Belting, Housefurnishings, Horse blankets combined)	51.7
Horse blankets	0.5	0.8	1.4	1.6	2.6	2.6	1.2	2.4	1.4	1.5	1.4	0.5	0.7		
Felt goods	2.7	3.2	4.9	5.4	16.4	16.4	12.9	18.1	17.4	18.6	19.2	15.3	15.3[k]	10.2	11.0

For footnotes see pp. 614–15.

Value Added by Manufacturing Industries (Unit: $1,000,000)

TEXTILE PRODUCTS[a] (concluded)	Establishments with Products Valued at $500 or More					Establishments with Products Valued at $5,000 or More									
	1899	*1904*	*1909*	*1914*	*1919*	*1919*	*1921*	*1923*	*1925*	*1927*	*1929*	*1931*	*1933*	*1935*	*1937*
Industry															
Flags and banners	0.5	0.4	0.9	1.9	2.1	2.1	1.8	1.8	2.3	2.3	2.1	1.4	1.1 } [y]	4.3[y]	4.2
Regalia	1.5	2.7	3.4	2.8	5.1	5.0	5.9	6.3	5.7	4.7	4.7	3.6	1.8 }		
Oilcloth	0.9	1.1	2.1	1.5	4.3	4.3	4.4	5.6	4.3	5.8	8.2	5.7	5.8	3.8	3.5
Nets and seines	0.6	0.6	0.5	0.8	1.5	1.5	1.1	1.5	1.7	2.1	2.4	1.4	0.8	0.9	1.2
Upholstering materials, n.e.c.	2.6	2.5	*3.6*[m] 3.0	2.6	3.9	3.9	1.4	3.1	2.9	3.1	4.2	2.5	1.4[f]	9.8	13.0
Wool shoddy	1.9	2.4	*2.4*[ll] 2.3	2.4	7.2	7.2	2.3	6.1	6.1	4.6	5.2	2.6	4.2 }	14.0[ii]	11.8
Waste	1.0	1.6	*2.6*[ll] 2.7	2.5	8.0	8.0[mm]	4.2[mm]	8.5	9.2	10.3	10.4	6.1	5.9 }		
TOTAL	710.6	880.8 877.8	1,288.6 1,287.7	1,385.6	3,700.8	3,695.7	3,021.4	3,828.9	3,596.9	3,844.2	3,960.0	2,662.1	2,143.4	2,628.6	3,065.1

[a] In 1935 the industrial classification used in the major group, *textile products*, was changed considerably. We use the old classification consistently.

[b] Prior to 1935, the Bureau of the Census calculated value added by deducting cost of materials from value of products. In 1935 the Bureau of the Census calculated value added by deducting the sum of cost of materials and cost of contract work from value of products for all industries in which cost of contract work was equal to 10 percent or more of cost of materials. In 1937 the Bureau of the Census calculated value added for all industries by the second method. For the sake of consistency, we have modified the figures somewhat. Whenever the figures for cost of contract work were available for an entire series or for a good part of it, and cost of contract work was important, we followed the second method of calculation for all years. In this group the industries affected are: *cotton goods* (except for 1909); *clothing, men's, n.e.c.*; *clothing, men's, work*; *clothing, women's, n.e.c.*; *shirts* (except for 1899); the four knit goods industries; and *silk and rayon goods*. The value added in all other industries includes the cost of contract work. This statement applies also to the figures for 1935 and 1937 presented here: the value added as calculated by the Census was increased by the cost of contract work deducted by the Census.

[c] Prior to 1914 *lace goods* was included in *cotton small wares* and *cotton goods*. For 1899 and 1904, however, separate figures for *lace goods* can be obtained from a *and rayon goods*, in *corsets*, and in *hosiery, knit*. In the last industry commission knitting also was excluded after 1935.

[q] Between 1933 and 1935 dyeing and finishing of hosiery knitted by others were transferred from *dyeing and finishing* to *hosiery, knit*.

[r] Between 1935 and 1937 some establishments in *dyeing and finishing* were transferred to *fabricated textile products, n.e.c.* (combination of *housefurnishings, n.e.c.*, *belting, woven, n.e.m.*, and *horse blankets*).

[s] Because *carpets and rugs, rag*, contains a large proportion of small establishments, the degree to which it is covered in the Census probably varies from year to year.

[t] Between 1909 and 1914, 8 establishments manufacturing jute carpets were transferred from *carpets and rugs, wool*, to *jute goods*.

[u] Between 1927 and 1929 sheep-lined clothing was transferred from *fur goods* to *clothing, men's, work*.

[v] Between 1931 and 1933 children's play suits, windbreakers, lumberjacks and oiled waterproof outer garments were transferred from *clothing, men's, n.e.c.*, to *clothing, men's, work*; sheep-lined and blanket-lined coats were transferred from *clothing, men's, work*, to *clothing, men's, n.e.c.*; workshirts (including flannel shirts) were transferred from *shirts* to *clothing, men's, work*; and men's nightwear was transferred from *furnishings, men's, n.e.c.*, to *shirts*.

special Census report: value added was 2.0 million dollars in 1899 and 4.1 million dollars in 1904. Since there is no indication of the proportion of *lace goods* in each of the other industries in these two years, we cannot determine the value added in *cotton small wares* and in *cotton goods* excluding *lace goods*.

[d] Between 1919 and 1921 establishments engaged primarily in the manufacture of aircraft parts, other than engines and tires, were transferred from *cotton goods* and other industries to *aircraft*.

[e] Between 1933 and 1935 dyeing and finishing departments of textile mills making cotton, rayon, and silk goods were transferred to *dyeing and finishing*; and cotton-and-silk-mixed fabrics and cotton-and-rayon-mixed fabrics having a cotton warp, even though the material of chief value was silk or rayon, were transferred from *silk and rayon goods* to *cotton goods* and to *cotton small wares*. The Bureau of the Census states that the combined figures for the latter two industries for 1935 are "roughly, but not exactly" comparable with the figures for 1933 and prior years and that the 1935 figures for *silk and rayon goods* are not comparable with the figures for earlier years.

[f] Between 1933 and 1935 cotton batting, wadding, and mattress felts were transferred from *cotton goods* to *upholstering materials, n.e.c.*; and batts, padding, and card rolls were transferred from *woolen goods* and *worsted goods* to *upholstering materials, n.e.c.* The comparability of the figures for *upholstering materials, n.e.c.*, appears to have been seriously affected by these shifts.

[g] In 1935 the amount of processing tax was not included in value added in *cotton goods*, but in 1937 the tax was included.

[h] Between 1921 and 1923 belting manufactured in textile mills and elastic webbing manufactured in textile mills were transferred to *cotton small wares*, the former from *belting, woven, n.e.m.*, and the latter from *elastic woven goods, n.e.m.* The comparability of the figures for *cotton small wares* appears to have been seriously affected by the shift.

[i] Between 1933 and 1935 *cotton small wares* was expanded to include some mixed fabrics with a cotton warp. According to the Bureau of the Census, the figures are still comparable.

[j] Between 1935 and 1937 some establishments were transferred from *cotton small wares* to each of the following industries: *asbestos products*, *fabricated textile products, n.e.c.* (combination of *housefurnishings, n.e.c.*, *belting, woven, n.e.m.*, and *horse blankets*), *silk and rayon goods*, *elastic woven goods, n.e.m.*, and *trimmings, n.e.m.*

[k] Between 1933 and 1935, woven felts were transferred from *felt goods* to *woolen goods*.

[l] Between 1935 and 1937 some establishments in *carpets and rugs, rag*, were transferred to *carpets and rugs, wool*, and some establishments in the latter industry were transferred to *woolen goods*.

[m] Prior to 1909 *haircloth* was combined with *upholstering materials, n.e.c.*

[n] Prior to 1909 contract work alone was included in *wool scouring*, whereas some of the establishments included in later Censuses reported also work done on purchased skins and wool.

[o] Between 1909 and 1914 some knitting mills using silk as the sole material were transferred from *silk and rayon goods* to *knit goods*.

[p] After 1935 transfer charges were excluded from contract work in part of *silk*

[w] For 1935 and 1937 the statistics for *clothing, men's, work*, are not comparable because of a change in the constitution of the industry.

[x] Because *clothing, men's, buttonholes*, contains a large proportion of small establishments, the degree to which it is covered in the Census probably varies from year to year.

[y] Between 1935 and 1937 uniforms were transferred from *flags and banners* to *clothing, men's, n.e.c.* In 1935, moreover, some establishments in *flags and banners* reported their merchandising activities with their manufacturing activities.

[z] Prior to 1909 suspenders, garters and elastic woven goods were classified with *furnishings, men's, n.e.c.*, *rubber goods, other*, and *millinery*. In 1909 they were grouped under a new classification, *elastic woven goods, n.e.m.*

[aa] After 1925 *millinery and lace goods, n.e.c.*, was abandoned as a separate classification and divided among *embroideries*, *millinery*, and *trimmings, n.e.m.* Ladies' handkerchiefs (formerly part of *millinery and lace goods, n.e.c.*) were classified with men's handkerchiefs (formerly in *furnishings, men's, n.e.c.*) under the title *handkerchiefs*.

[bb] The 1937 Census of this industry is reported by the Bureau of the Census to be incomplete.

[cc] Between 1923 and 1925 certain establishments manufacturing gloves and mittens of cloth and leather combined were transferred from *gloves, leather*, to *gloves, textile, n.e.m.*

[dd] Between 1927 and 1929 women's scarfs and other neckwear were transferred from *trimmings, n.e.m.*, to *clothing, women's, n.e.c.*

[ee] The 1933 Census of this industry is considered by the Bureau of the Census to be somewhat incomplete.

[ff] Between 1925 and 1927 women's and children's straw hats, other than harvest hats, were transferred from *hats, straw, men's*, to *millinery*.

[gg] Prior to 1909 *excelsior* was combined with *artificial leather*. Overlapping figures for 1909 are available for *artificial leather*.

[hh] Between 1933 and 1935 more than 300 establishments whose values of products were reported as between $5,000 and $20,000 were eliminated from *awnings* by the Census of Manufactures. More than 100 such establishments were not eliminated in 1933–35, however, because in some previous Censuses they had reported values of products above $20,000. In 1937 these establishments also were eliminated.

[ii] After 1935 establishments reporting wiping rags as their primary product, formerly classified under *waste*, were not canvassed by the Bureau of the Census.

[jj] Between 1904 and 1909 establishments manufacturing signs and advertising novelties were transferred from *housefurnishings, n.e.c.*, and other classifications, to a new classification, *signs*.

[kk] Prior to 1914 *aluminum manufactures* was included in *housefurnishings, n.e.c.*, and other industries.

[ll] Between 1909 and 1914 a few establishments making cotton or mattress shoddy and a few small establishments engaged in the cutting of flocks were transferred from *wool shoddy* to *waste*.

[mm] *Oakum* was combined with *all other industries* in 1921 and with *waste* in other Census years.

Value Added by Manufacturing Industries (Unit: $1,000,000)

LEATHER PRODUCTS	Establishments with Products Valued at $500 or More					Establishments with Products Valued at $5,000 or More									
	1899	*1904*	*1909*	*1914*	*1919*	*1919*	*1921*	*1923*	*1925*	*1927*	*1929*	*1931*	*1933*	*1935*	*1937*
Industry															
Leather	49.0	61.4	79.6	83.0	282.1	282.0	105.6	167.1	155.2	162.3	143.7	98.4	99.0	110.4	115.8
Shoes, leather	90.3	122.7	165.2	191.4	439.8	439.7	389.0	472.6	443.8	450.2	450.9	316.3	267.1	310.6	352.7
Shoe cut stock, n.e.m.	5.4	6.1	7.7	8.5	27.3	27.3	15.8	20.7	18.7	23.1	25.9	15.6	12.7	35.5	36.8
Shoe findings, n.e.m.	2.8	3.6	7.2	8.0	22.4	22.3	16.2	20.4	22.8	25.6	26.7	19.2	18.8		
Belting, leather	3.1	4.9	8.1	7.6	12.3	12.3	6.1	13.2	12.9	11.1	15.0	7.2	7.9	10.0	12.4
Gloves, leather	7.4[a]	7.7	10.4	9.4	20.7	20.6	11.0	17.9[b]	15.5	17.4	18.9	14.9	12.1	14.7	15.6
Leather goods, n.e.c.	5.6	8.0[c]	8.5	8.7	22.9	22.8	24.0	20.5	20.0	21.8	17.9	14.0	9.2	13.1	40.1
Pocketbooks	1.2	1.8	1.7	1.6	7.0	6.9	6.9	16.5	20.7	27.7	33.3	20.5	13.0	20.7	
Luggage	6.5	9.5	13.4	12.8	30.7	30.5	22.7	30.2	29.8	30.8	32.3	13.5	8.0	13.3	18.2
Saddlery and harness	13.9	18.3	21.0	20.5	31.3	30.1	12.5	17.7	11.3	10.8	9.5				
Whips[d]	1.5	1.9	2.4	1.8	1.9	1.9	0.6	0.4	0.2	0.1	0.1	4.1	4.2	5.6	5.3
TOTAL	186.7	245.9	325.2	353.3	898.4	896.4	610.4	797.2	750.9	780.9	774.2	523.7	452.0	533.9	596.9

[a] In 1899 a few establishments making gloves and mittens from materials other than leather were included with *gloves, leather*.

[b] Between 1923 and 1925 some establishments manufacturing gloves and mittens of cloth and leather combined were transferred from *gloves, leather*, to *gloves, textile, n.e.m.*

[c] Between 1904 and 1909 establishments manufacturing signs and advertising novelties were transferred from *leather goods, n.e.c.*, and other classifications to a new classification, *signs*.

[d] Because this industry contains a large proportion of small establishments, the degree to which it is covered in the Census probably varies from year to year.

RUBBER PRODUCTS	Establishments with Products Valued at $500 or More					Establishments with Products Valued at $5,000 or More									
	1899	*1904*	*1909*	*1914*	*1919*	*1919*	*1921*	*1923*	*1925*	*1927*	*1929*	*1931*	*1933*	*1935*	*1937*
Industry															
Shoes, rubber	18.4[a]	38.1[a]	20.1	29.9	66.6	66.6	61.9	86.5	75.4	81.2	68.1	35.6	27.9	32.4	37.2
Tires and tubes	21.2	29.9[b]	54.5[c]	108.1	477.3	477.3	204.6	279.0	365.1	370.5	340.6	232.7	159.9	180.6	209.0
Rubber goods, other							60.5	91.9	96.1[d,e] *98.6*	113.0	130.1	93.1	73.5	96.1	123.1
TOTAL	39.6	68.0	74.6	138.0	543.9	543.9	327.0	457.4	536.6 539.1	564.7	538.8	361.4	261.3	309.1	369.3

[a] In 1904 some establishments in *shoes, rubber*, reported list price values of products, rather than sales or production values.

[b] Prior to 1909 *rubber goods, other*, included some suspenders, garters and elastic woven goods. Between 1904 and 1909 these three products were brought together in a new classification in the textile group, *elastic woven goods, n.e.m.*

[c] Between 1909 and 1914 rubber combs and hairpins were transferred from *combs, n.e.c.*, to *rubber goods, other*.

[d] Between 1925 and 1927 rubber cement was transferred from *mucilage* to *rubber goods, other*. Overlapping figures for 1925 are provided by the Bureau of the Census.

[e] Between 1925 and 1927 rubber toy balloons were transferred from *toys and games* to *rubber goods, other*. Overlapping figures for 1925 are provided by the Bureau of the Census.

PAPER PRODUCTS	Establishments with Products Valued at $500 or More					Establishments with Products Valued at $5,000 or More									
	1899	*1904*	*1909*	*1914*	*1919*	*1919*	*1921*	*1923*	*1925*	*1927*	*1929*	*1931*	*1933*	*1935*	*1937*
Industry															
Paper	56.8	77.5	102.2	119.0	320.6	320.6	221.4	333.6[a]	366.0	347.1	392.6	300.6	249.2	282.7	390.7
Pulp										66.9	90.2	55.9	52.8	71.0	93.5
Bags, paper, n.e.m.	2.3	3.5	5.3	5.4	13.9	13.9	11.4	12.9	16.0	16.8	21.4	20.9	20.1[b]	23.8	29.1
Boxes, paper, n.e.c.	15.6	20.2	28.7	38.4	105.3	105.2	86.0	120.1	130.2	138.1	134.4	104.6	96.7	130.1	171.6
Cardboard, n.e.m.	0.6	0.6	1.1	1.4	4.2	4.2	3.7	4.0	3.8	2.7	3.0	1.9	1.4	1.7	2.5
Card cutting and designing	0.3	0.6	0.7	0.6	3.0	3.0	2.5	3.5	3.8	9.3	10.4	9.3	6.1	9.5	11.8
Envelopes	2.6	4.2	5.9	8.2	17.7	17.7	19.9	23.2	23.8	27.0	31.4	24.5	18.0	22.9	26.4
Labels and tags	0.7	1.5	2.8	3.7	13.0	12.9	10.7	13.9	15.0	18.1	17.5	c			
Paper goods, n.e.c.	7.0	9.4	16.9	20.8	42.0	42.0	34.3	49.2	53.5	62.2	82.3	70.9 *77.7*[d]	 64.9	 85.9	 114.1
Stationery goods, n.e.c.	2.9	4.9[e]	8.9	11.1	30.2	30.2	35.0	43.0[f]	36.7	30.0	41.9	25.1 *15.0*[d]	 7.4	 b	
Wall paper	4.6	6.0	6.8	7.4	9.9	9.9	12.8	17.8	15.1	15.4	16.5	11.0	8.9	9.8	14.9
TOTAL	93.4	128.4	179.3	216.0	559.8	559.6	437.7	621.2	663.9	733.6	841.6	624.7 621.4	 525.5	 637.4	 854.6

[a] Between 1923 and 1925 some establishments were transferred from *roofing* to *paper and pulp*.

[b] Between 1933 and 1935 *stationery goods, n.e.c.*, was abandoned as a classification and the products were divided among *bags, paper, n.e.m.*, and other classifications.

[c] Between 1929 and 1931 *labels and tags* was abandoned as a classification and the products were divided among *printing and publishing, book and job*; *lithographing; engraving, other*; and *miscellaneous articles*.

[d] Between 1931 and 1933 papeteries were transferred from *stationery goods, n.e.c.*, to other industries, principally *paper goods, n.e.c.* Overlapping figures for 1931 are provided by the Bureau of the Census.

[e] Between 1904 and 1909 establishments manufacturing signs and advertising novelties were transferred from *stationery goods, n.e.c.* and other classifications to a new industry, *signs*.

[f] Between 1923 and 1925 manifolding machinery was transferred from *stationery goods, n.e.c.*, to *foundry and machine-shop products, n.e.c.*

Value Added by Manufacturing Industries (Unit: $1,000,000)

PRINTING AND PUBLISHING	Establishments with Products Valued at $500 or More					Establishments with Products Valued at $5,000 or More									
	1899	*1904*	*1909*	*1914*	*1919*	*1919*	*1921*	*1923*	*1925*	*1927*	*1929*	*1931*	*1933*	*1935*	*1937*
Industry															
Printing and publishing, book and job[a]	78.6	120.7	162.9	195.6	355.5	348.6	444.5	487.0	538.6	604.5	678.0[b]	533.1	344.9[c]	464.8	526.2
Printing and publishing, music[a]	1.5	2.8	3.7	4.7	9.8	9.7	8.9	9.3	10.5	11.4	11.0	8.0			
Printing and publishing, periodical[a]	161.7	222.7	286.2	345.8	573.0	557.5	687.3	829.2	982.5	1,067.6	1,241.3	1,023.3	757.7	889.9	1,003.0
Bookbinding and blank-book making	13.1	16.1	20.1	24.8	42.8	42.3	44.0	53.9	57.5	61.5	72.0	58.4	40.3	52.2	66.3
Engravers' materials	0.1	0.1	0.3	0.2	0.8	0.8	0.8	0.9	0.8	0.9	1.3	1.2	0.8	[e]	
Engraving, steel and copper	3.9	4.4	7.2	9.9	17.2	17.0	21.2	24.6	24.5	28.8	35.3	21.0	12.6	15.5	21.7
Engraving, wood[d]	0.6	0.6	0.6	0.6	0.9	0.8	0.5	0.5	0.5	0.6	0.7				
Engraving, other[d]	1.3	2.0	1.9	2.5	5.4	4.8	3.5	6.3	6.4	5.9	8.4[b]	4.2	2.5	5.0	6.2
Lithographing	14.4	16.9	22.2	25.1	45.4	45.3	49.0	60.7	66.6	64.3	82.0[b]	60.8	46.7	62.0	92.2
Photo-engraving, n.e.d.	3.5	6.0	9.5	12.6	24.4	24.3	30.3	37.1	50.2	58.4	66.4	48.6	32.0	45.5	64.5
Printing materials, n.e.c.	0.7	0.8	1.2	1.3	3.3	3.3	3.6	3.6	4.7	5.0	6.4	4.3	4.2	[e]	
Type founding	2.0	2.0	1.7	1.4	1.1	1.1	1.4	1.8	1.7	1.9	2.0	1.0			
Stereotyping, n.e.d.	3.0	4.0	4.6	5.9	11.7	11.7	13.6	16.8	18.1	20.9	29.1	21.0	17.4	23.1	26.4
TOTAL	284.4	399.1	522.1	630.4	1,091.3	1,067.2	1,308.6	1,531.7	1,762.6	1,931.7	2,233.9	1,784.9	1,259.1 1,254.1	1,558.0	1,806.5

[a] Value added in all years excludes payments for contract work. See footnote b, p. 614.

[b] Between 1929 and 1931 *labels and tags* was abandoned as a separate classification and its products were divided among *printing and publishing, book and job*; *ithographing*; *engraving, other*; and *miscellaneous articles*.

[c] Between 1933 and 1935 *stationery goods, n.e.c.*, was abandoned as a separate classification and the products were divided among *printing and publishing, book and job*; *printing and publishing, music*; and other classifications.

[d] Because this industry contains a large proportion of small establishments, the degree to which it is covered in the Census probably varies from year to year.

[e] After 1933 *printing materials, n.e.c.*; *type founding*; and *engravers' materials* were transferred to *foundry and machine-shop products, n.e.c.*

CHEMICAL PRODUCTS	Establishments with Products Valued at $500 or More					Establishments with Products Valued at $5,000 or More									
	1899	*1904*	*1909*	*1914*	*1919*	*1919*	*1921*	*1923*	*1925*	*1927*	*1929*	*1931*	*1933*	*1935*	*1937*
Industry															
Chemicals, n.e.c.[a]								279.7[e]	287.6[f]	275.4	374.5[g]	287.1	255.0[h]	339.3	478.2
Gases, compressed	25.6	37.3	58.1[b]	77.1[c]	312.7	312.7[d]	212.0			38.8[f]	37.7	31.7	23.4	30.8	42.2
Rayon								47.0[e]	69.6	84.1	116.2	96.5	112.9	120.7	174.1
Druggists' preparations	11.9	18.4	26.1	25.1	59.5	59.3	47.1	45.8	59.4	69.8	81.0	77.2[i]	203.1	237.4	284.8
Patent medicines	41.0	53.2	56.9	66.5	123.3	122.1	106.3	148.7	162.8	193.6	224.1	186.1[i]			
Toilet preparations	4.0	6.4	8.6	9.4	33.5	33.3	44.5	62.6	82.6	108.5	135.1	111.6[i]	63.9	75.0	78.6
Drug grinding	1.0	2.1	2.6	2.9	5.4	5.3	3.3	4.0	3.5	3.5	4.0	3.7	3.0	2.5	3.2
Cottonseed products[j]	13.6	16.4	28.0	31.2	86.1	86.1	22.4	28.9	51.4	56.3	49.4	34.2	26.0	27.3	46.3
Linseed products	2.8	4.4	5.7	5.3	20.1	20.1	12.6	10.5	18.8	13.8	18.5	12.6	6.6	11.5	16.0
Oils, essential	0.2	0.4	0.5	0.7	1.8	1.7	0.9	0.9	1.5	1.2	2.8	0.8	0.9	0.9	1.0
Ammunition	5.6	9.3	10.6	14.6	49.9	49.9	16.3	23.8	18.9	24.7	24.0	17.4	17.4	20.0	25.6
Fireworks	1.2	1.2	1.4	1.1	2.5	2.5	2.8	3.1	3.6	3.3	4.1	2.3	1.5		
Blackings	2.3	2.8	4.2	4.8	11.2	11.2	9.1	15.6	15.3	13.4	16.3	13.4	12.1	9.5	11.2
Bluing	0.3	0.4	0.6	0.7	1.2	1.2	0.9	0.8	1.1	1.1	0.9	0.8	0.7	0.6	0.8
Carbon black	0.3	0.4	0.6	0.8	3.3	3.3	4.4	9.3	8.9	7.7	11.1	4.5	4.5	9.5	11.6
Candles	20.1	1.0	1.0	0.6	1.2	1.2	1.7	2.7	2.3	3.4	3.4	2.9	2.3	2.3	2.7
Soap		24.6	39.2	39.1	78.2	78.2	89.8	102.9	93.4	114.8	129.8	135.9	106.6	99.7	116.2
Hardwood distillation products	2.5	3.0	3.9	3.4	12.5	12.5	2.5	9.9	4.9	6.6	8.5	2.8	2.2	3.0	3.8
Softwood distillation products							0.3	2.3	4.2	5.4	6.1	2.1	3.7	5.0	11.0
Charcoal[k]	0.7	0.6	0.4	0.2	0.3	0.3	0.2	0.2	0.4	0.2	0.2	0.1	0.1	0.1	0.1
Cleaning preparations	1.2	1.4	3.6	5.3	13.8	13.6	12.2	21.8	21.3	26.0	31.4	31.0	26.3	25.1	34.3
Explosives	6.8	12.4	17.3	15.8	46.6	46.6	28.5	35.5	31.8	35.6	40.8	26.7	22.4	23.7	34.0
Fertilizers	15.7	17.3	34.4	45.2	96.1	96.1	35.4	55.1	69.0	52.2	72.7	47.9	25.9	47.0	65.7

For footnotes see next page.

Value Added by Manufacturing Industries (Unit: $1,000,000)

CHEMICAL PRODUCTS (concluded)	Establishments with Products Valued at $500 or More					Establishments with Products Valued at $5,000 or More									
	1899	*1904*	*1909*	*1914*	*1919*	*1919*	*1921*	*1923*	*1925*	*1927*	*1929*	*1931*	*1933*	*1935*	*1937*
Industry															
Glue and gelatin	1.6	3.8	6.2	4.4	12.9	12.9	7.9	9.8	10.4	12.0	13.5	12.1	8.8	13.1	17.3
Grease and tallow	3.2	6.4	7.9	7.8	19.5	19.3	9.4	17.4	17.7	18.0	21.5	11.7	12.1	17.6	19.4
Ink, printing	1.5	3.2	4.7	7.0	11.6	11.6	10.2	14.6	18.5	21.7	23.5	17.7	13.6	15.9	22.2
Ink, writing	0.7	1.0	1.4	1.5	3.1	3.1	2.9	3.5	3.7	3.1	2.6	2.1	1.3	2.0	2.0
Mucilage	0.9	1.3	1.6	2.4	4.1	4.1	4.9	4.6	5.4 *4.3*[l]	3.7	3.0	1.7	1.2	1.9	2.0
Paints and varnishes	24.8	31.5	45.9	57.1	123.2	123.2	102.9	155.2	176.8	211.3	234.8	157.0	136.4	185.0	226.5
Salt	4.6	5.3	6.1	7.8	21.5	21.4	16.8	20.4	20.4	19.7	23.7	20.6	19.9	18.8	21.6
Tanning and dye materials	2.6	4.1	6.3	7.4[c]	19.2	19.2	8.2	11.9	12.0	12.6	14.5	10.9	9.8	13.9	13.1
TOTAL	196.7	269.6	383.8	445.2	1,174.3	1,172.0	816.4	1,148.5	1,277.2 1,276.1	1,441.5	1,729.7	1,363.1	1,123.6	1,359.1	1,765.5

[a] *Blast-furnace products* and *chemicals, n.e.c.*, each include part of *ferro-alloys*, which was listed as a separate industry in 1919.

[b] Between 1909 and 1914 powdered milk and sugar of milk were transferred from *chemicals, n.e.c.*, to *milk, canned*.

[c] Between 1914 and 1919 artificial dyestuffs and mineral colors and dyes were transferred from *tanning and dye materials* to *chemicals, n.e.c.*

[d] Between 1919 and 1921 some establishments were transferred from *secondary metals, nonprecious*, to *chemicals, n.e.c.*

[e] Between 1923 and 1925 rayon and allied products were transferred from *chemicals, n.e.c.*, to a new classification, *rayon*. The rayon data for 1923 were secured from a special tabulation made by the Bureau of the Census for the Bureau of Foreign and Domestic Commerce from the original returns for 1923; see the *Commerce Year Book, 1932*, vol. I, p. 423. To obtain the 1923 figure for *chemicals, n.e.c.*, we subtracted the figure for *rayon* from the figure given for 1923.

[f] Between 1925 and 1927 compressed and liquefied gases were transferred from *chemicals, n.e.c.*, and Pintsch gas plants from *gas, manufactured*, to a new classification, *gases, compressed*.

[g] Between 1929 and 1931 molded plastics were transferred from *chemicals, n.e.c.*, and other industries to *pulp goods*.

[h] Between 1933 and 1935 ethyl alcohol was transferred from *liquors, distilled*, to *chemicals, n.e.c.*

[i] Between 1931 and 1933 *druggists' preparations* and *patent medicines* were combined into a single industry, *drugs and medicines*. At the same time some establishments were shifted from the latter industry to *toilet preparations* and vice versa.

[j] Data on *cottonseed products* for 1925 and prior years relate to the 12-month period ending July 31 following the year specified, although in the early Census returns some firms may have reported for the calendar year. The figures for 1927–37 relate to the 12-month period ending July 31 of the year indicated, but may also include a few reports prepared on a calendar-year basis.

[k] Because this industry contains a large proportion of small establishments, the degree to which it is covered in the Census probably varies from year to year.

[l] Between 1925 and 1927 rubber cement was transferred from *mucilage* to *rubber goods, other*. Overlapping figures are provided for 1925 by the Bureau of the Census.

PETROLEUM AND COAL PRODUCTS	Establishments with Products Valued at $500 or More					Establishments with Products Valued at $5,000 or More									
	1899	*1904*	*1909*	*1914*	*1919*	*1919*	*1921*	*1923*	*1925*	*1927*	*1929*	*1931*	*1933*	*1935*	*1937*
Industry															
Petroleum refining	21.1	35.6	37.7	71.1	384.6	384.6	345.3	368.6	487.0	389.7	608.3	313.8	314.2	360.4	489.4
Lubricants, n.e.m.	0.4	0.5	0.7	2.2	4.1	4.1	3.6	5.3	6.4	5.3[a]	30.0	18.9	11.9	15.3	18.7
Oils, n.e.c.	7.7	8.6	9.7	11.6	37.2	37.2	18.7	34.0	32.6[b]	30.7[a]	8.3	6.0	6.6	10.8	13.4
Coke-oven products	15.9	21.8	31.7	30.1	92.2	92.2	52.5	162.9	100.9	95.3	134.8	63.7	42.5	58.1	84.6
Fuel briquettes		[c]	0.2	0.3	0.6	0.6	0.9	1.7	2.1	2.3	3.6	1.5	1.1	1.5	2.1
TOTAL	45.1	66.5	79.8 80.0	115.3	518.7	518.7	421.0	572.5	629.0	523.3	785.0	403.9	376.3	446.1	608.2

[a] Between 1927 and 1929 lubricating oils were transferred from *oils, n.e.c.*, to *lubricants, n.e.m.* The comparability of the figures for both industries appears to have been seriously affected by this change.

[b] Between 1925 and 1927 vegetable cooking oils were transferred from *oils, n.e.c.*, and other industries to *shortenings*.

[c] In 1904 no establishments were reported as engaged primarily in the manufacture of products classified under *fuel briquettes*; in 1899 this industry was included with *all other industries*.

STONE, CLAY AND GLASS PRODUCTS	Establishments with Products Valued at $500 or More					Establishments with Products Valued at $5,000 or More									
	1899	*1904*	*1909*	*1914*	*1919*	*1919*	*1921*	*1923*	*1925*	*1927*	*1929*	*1931*	*1933*	*1935*	*1937*
Industry															
Asbestos products			[a]	1.5	11.0	11.0	6.9	16.8	17.0	22.6	30.8	21.3	14.5	21.0[b]	34.3
Steam and other packing	1.9	5.1	5.5[a]	6.0	17.8	17.8	13.1	17.1	23.5	23.3	23.8	14.1	11.1[c]		
													10.6	12.5	17.6
Roofing	6.8	9.0[d]	6.7[a]	10.4	33.3	33.3	31.2	28.8[e]	45.0	55.9	42.1	26.3	20.9	31.8	39.9
Cement	} 17.6	17.7	33.9	49.8	95.8	95.8	101.3	163.3	186.7	173.6	172.3	92.7	60.0	77.5	113.2
Lime		9.3	11.2	10.8	19.7	19.5	16.8	27.5	30.7	24.3	21.9	13.3	9.7	14.4	21.8
Wall plaster and board		5.4	6.8	8.6	15.1	15.0	16.2[f]	40.7	51.4	51.9	42.4	33.9	17.7[c]		
													78.2	32.3	51.3
Concrete products[g]	} 42.1	2.7	11.6	13.0	19.8	18.0	18.3	33.1	47.4	59.3	58.9	30.8	11.2	24.9	41.0
Marble and granite		58.3[d]	75.7	69.3	79.6	78.1	84.2	124.7	126.1	134.9	134.5	85.0	37.3	38.2	52.7
Emery wheels	0.9	1.4	4.1	4.1	18.7	18.7	6.4	14.6	14.6	13.3	19.7				
Hones	0.1	0.2	0.2	0.2	0.5	0.5	0.2	0.4	0.4	0.5[h]	0.5 }[i]	19.9	18.8	33.1	48.6
Sandpaper	0.5	0.4	2.0	1.6	4.2	4.2	2.9	6.9	8.3	6.8	8.8				

For footnotes see next page.

Value Added by Manufacturing Industries (Unit: $1,000,000)

STONE, CLAY AND GLASS PRODUCTS (concluded)	Establishments with Products Valued at $500 or More					Establishments with Products Valued at $5,000 or More									
	1899	1904	1909	1914	1919	1919	1921	1923	1925	1927	1929	1931	1933	1935	1937
Industry															
Pulp goods	0.6	0.7	0.8	2.3	12.2	12.2	15.0[f]	9.2	10.0	12.6	15.2	8.1[j] / *16.4*	15.7	29.1	45.8
Sand-lime brick			k	0.6	1.1	1.1	0.7	1.5	2.5	2.5	2.0	0.8	0.1	0.4	1.1
China firing and decorating, n.e.d.[g]	0.3	0.2	0.5	0.4	0.6	0.6	0.7	0.9	0.9	1.0	0.9	0.6	0.4	0.6	0.9
Pottery	32.3	47.6	54.2[l]	24.9	54.1	54.0	59.0	80.8	77.2	77.0	83.6	49.5	31.5	48.8	69.3
Clay products, n.e.c.	40.3	54.8	69.0[k, l]	93.2	142.9	142.3	126.1	230.1[m]	233.7	220.0	213.2 }	90.4	44.6	73.2	128.4
Crucibles	0.9	0.6	0.8	0.6	1.1	1.1	1.1	2.2[m]	1.3	1.2	1.9 }				
Graphite	0.2	0.2	0.7	1.0	1.1	1.1	0.8	1.1	1.2	1.6	2.3	1.0	0.7	1.2[n]	0.3
Minerals and earths	2.1	2.6	2.6	5.7	29.8	29.7	14.7	22.0	25.2	23.6[o]	8.5	3.5	5.3	12.9	15.8
Statuary and art goods	p	2.0	2.8	3.1	3.6	3.5	5.0	5.7	7.3	7.8	8.0	4.4	1.9	2.2	2.3
Glass	39.8	53.5	60.0	77.1	171.1	171.1	127.4	196.2	182.3	172.5	200.5	142.7	128.5	173.9	247.3
Glass products, n.e.m.	5.2	8.5	9.9	9.3	14.1	13.9	11.4	13.2	14.6	13.5	17.0 }	19.1	14.3	39.6	47.4
Mirrors	3.0	3.0	3.7	4.2	8.3	8.3	6.7	13.4	15.2	15.2	16.2 }				
TOTAL	194.6	281.2 / 283.2	362.7	397.7	755.5	750.8	666.1	1,050.2	1,122.5	1,114.9	1,125.0	657.4 / 665.7	444.2	667.6	979.0

[a] Prior to 1914 *asbestos products* was included with *steam and other packing* and *roofing*.

[b] Between 1935 and 1937 some establishments were transferred from *cotton small wares* to *asbestos products* and other classifications.

[c] Between 1933 and 1935 mineral wool was transferred from *steam and other packing* to *wall plaster and board*. Overlapping figures for 1933 are provided by the Bureau of the Census.

[d] Between 1904 and 1909 roofing slate was transferred from *roofing* to *marble and granite*.

[e] Between 1923 and 1925 some establishments were transferred from *roofing* to *paper and pulp*.

[f] Between 1921 and 1923 wall board, other than gypsum wall board, was transferred from *pulp goods* to *wall plaster and board*.

[g] Because this industry contains a large proportion of small establishments, the degree to which it is covered in the Census probably varies from year to year.

[h] After 1927 *hones* was limited to establishments which did not quarry the stone but purchased it in the rough and prepared it for the market.

[i] Between 1929 and 1931 there was a change in the classification of an important manufacturer of abrasives. The Bureau of the Census believes that this change renders the statistics for the 3 abrasives industries for that year incomparable with those for prior years.

[j] Between 1929 and 1931 molded plastics were transferred principally from *electrical machinery*, but also from *miscellaneous articles*, *chemicals, n.e.c.*, *machine-tool accessories, n.e.c.*, and *phonographs*, to *pulp goods*. Overlapping figures for 1931 are given for *pulp goods*.

[k] Prior to 1914 *sand-lime brick* was included with *clay products, n.e.c.*

[l] Between 1909 and 1914 terra cotta and fire clay products were transferred from *pottery* to *clay products, n.e.c.* The comparability of the figures for both industries appears to have been seriously affected by this change.

[m] Between 1923 and 1925 clay crucibles were transferred from *crucibles* to *clay products, n.e.c.*

[n] Between 1935 and 1937 some establishments were transferred from *graphite* to other industries. The comparability of the figures for *graphite* appears to have been seriously affected by the shift.

[o] After 1927 establishments performing manufacturing operations alone were included in *minerals and earths*; in prior years mining establishments were also included. The change appears to have had a serious effect upon the comparability of the figures.

[p] Between 1899 and 1904 establishments engaged in manufacturing statuary and art goods were transferred from *plastering and stuccowork* (a classification abandoned by the Bureau of the Census in 1904) and *miscellaneous articles* to a new classification, *statuary and art goods*.

FOREST PRODUCTS	Establishments with Products Valued at $500 or More					Establishments with Products Valued at $5,000 or More									
	1899	*1904*	*1909*	*1914*	*1919*	*1919*	*1921*	*1923*	*1925*	*1927*	*1929*	*1931*	*1933*	*1935*	*1937*
Industry															
Lumber-mill products, n.e.c.[a, b]															
Incl. contract work	312.4	396.1													
Excl. contract work		*367.7*	456.7	401.6	879.0	861.1[c]	493.6	880.2	810.4	692.2	830.9	273.0	218.7	329.2	502.7
Planing-mill products, n.e.m.	68.2 (Planing-mill products and Window and door screens combined)	104.3 (combined)	131.3 (combined)	123.4	201.2	200.0[c]	190.6	291.6	307.6	260.2	257.6[d]	109.9[e]	56.4	87.6	138.5
Window and door screens				4.9	6.0	5.9	5.9	11.7	12.9	13.3	13.9	7.8	3.4	4.6	7.4
Wood turned and shaped, n.e.c.	10.6	16.2	18.3	15.1	29.9	29.5[c]	26.1	32.5[f]	31.1	34.5	41.2[d, g]	31.8	23.8	33.7	37.6
Baskets	2.3	3.4	3.4	3.6	6.9	6.7	6.0	8.6	9.9	12.5	14.0	10.0	7.5	8.8	9.7
Boxes, wooden, cigar	2.8	4.0	4.2	4.1	6.8	6.8	7.5	8.5	7.5	7.3	7.2	5.4	3.7	3.9	4.5
Boxes, wooden, other	15.4	23.6	28.9	33.7	74.9	74.7	49.3	68.8	65.9	58.2	60.9	35.0	25.9	31.2	41.0
Cooperage	16.3	18.3	17.5	17.1	29.7	29.4	16.0	24.8	23.6	23.1	23.3	14.8	12.7	16.6	17.7
Furniture	72.0	100.4	129.6	147.5	314.2	313.5	296.7	434.4	483.8	490.3[h]					
										493.1	521.7	264.4	155.1[i]	226.5	352.2
Billiard tables	0.9	1.3	2.5	2.4	9.6	9.6	4.0	4.0	3.8	4.7	5.6	2.4	0.6	2.1	3.7
Mirror and picture frames	6.1	8.3	8.0	6.5	11.2	11.0	9.8	12.5	12.3	12.4	12.7	7.4	4.3	5.7	7.6
Caskets and coffins	7.0	10.8	12.6	13.1	32.8	32.7	27.8	34.0	37.6[j]	41.6	48.9	41.3	33.1	36.2	38.2
Cork products	2.0	2.0	2.5	3.1	7.1	7.1	6.2	7.5	8.8	8.0	10.4	8.3	6.3	7.0	8.3
Excelsior		[k]	0.9	1.1	2.4	2.4	1.5	2.6	2.3	2.3	2.6	1.6	1.2	1.4	1.7
Lasts	1.4	1.8	2.8	3.2	8.5	8.5	8.0	6.7	6.3	5.0	5.4	4.1	3.7	4.1	3.8
Matches	2.6	2.4	6.8	7.4	11.6	11.6	17.0	12.2	10.8	13.0	7.8	7.6	14.7	11.4	10.7
Turpentine and rosin[l, m, n]	14.2	20.2	20.4	15.5	39.1	38.9	17.1	26.2	30.5	27.7	26.0	10.7	11.9	13.7	15.8
Wood preserving	0.6	0.9	4.8	5.0	10.0	10.0	13.0	20.9	24.5	43.0	43.2	21.4	12.9	20.6	32.1
TOTAL	534.8	714.0													
		679.0	850.3												
			851.2	808.3	1,680.9	1,659.4	1,196.1	1,887.7	1,889.6	1,749.3					
										1,752.1	1,933.3	856.9	595.9	844.3	1,233.2

For footnotes see next page.

Value Added by Manufacturing Industries (Unit: $1,000,000)

FOREST PRODUCTS (concluded)

[a] Sawmills are unaffected by the restriction, prevailing since 1919, of the Bureau of the Census inquiries to establishments reporting products valued at $5,000 or more. For Census purposes a mill which saws less than 200,000 feet of lumber or 1,000,000 lath or 2,000,000 shingles is treated as an establishment with products valued at less than $5,000.

[b] Value added excludes payments for contract work except for years noted. See footnote b, p. 614.

[c] Between 1919 and 1921 establishments engaged primarily in the manufacture of aircraft parts, other than engines and tires, were transferred from *lumber-mill products, n.e.c., planing-mill products, n.e.m., wood turned and shaped, n.e.c.,* and *cotton goods* to *aircraft.*

[d] Between 1929 and 1931 *dairymen's supplies* was abandoned as a separate classification, and the products were divided among *planing-mill products, n.e.m., wood turned and shaped, n.e.c.,* and other classifications.

[e] Between 1931 and 1933 horsedrawn lunch wagons were transferred from *carriages, wagons and sleighs* to *planing-mill products, n.e.m.*

[f] Between 1923 and 1925 *rules* was abandoned as a separate industry, and the products were divided among *wood turned and shaped, n.e.c.,* and other industries.

[g] Between 1929 and 1931 *carriage and wagon materials* was abandoned as a separate classification, and turned wood products, such as hubs, felloes, and spokes, were transferred to *wood turned and shaped, n.e.c.*

[h] Between 1927 and 1929 sewing machine cases, cabinets, and tables were transferred from *sewing machines* to *furniture.* Overlapping figures for 1927 are provided by the Census.

[i] Between 1933 and 1935 the composition of *dental goods and equipment* was changed to include, among other items, dental chairs and cabinets formerly classed with *furniture.*

[j] Between 1925 and 1927 metal burial vaults were transferred from *safes and vaults* to *caskets and coffins.*

[k] Prior to 1909 *excelsior* was combined with *artificial leather.*

[l] In 1937 the salaries and wages of those employees in *turpentine and rosin* who were engaged in the production and gathering of crude gum were added by the Bureau of the Census to cost of materials and deducted from value added, and only the employees at the still were considered as engaged in manufacturing. We have restored these data to value added in order to preserve as much comparability with 1935 as possible. The percentage of coverage of total production fell below 100 after 1929. The percentage of coverage is not given for 1931; in 1933 it was 85, and in 1935 it was 87. The value added figures for these two years have been raised accordingly. In 1937 estimates were made by the Bureau of the Census for producers who failed to report.

[m] For the period 1921–31, the statistics for *turpentine and rosin* relate to the crop year ending March 31. Thus the data for 1921 refer to the crop year 1921–22. In preceding years, however, and again in 1933, 1935, and 1937, the canvasses were made to cover the calendar year, in order to bring the statistics into line with those for other industries. The statistics for the calendar year differ only slightly from those for the crop year.

[n] The Census states that for the period 1925–33 the cost of turpentine rights (i.e., for the rental of pine forests) may not have been included in all cases in the cost of materials. If these costs were not included in cost of materials, the value added reported for these years was higher than it otherwise would have been. Whether value added in other years may have been similarly affected is not stated in the Census.

IRON AND STEEL PRODUCTS	Establishments with Products Valued at $500 or More					Establishments with Products Valued at $5,000 or More									
	1899	*1904*	*1909*	*1914*	*1919*	*1919*	*1921*	*1923*	*1925*	*1927*	*1929*	*1931*	*1933*	*1935*	*1937*
Industry															
Blast-furnace products[a]	75.3	52.9	70.8	53.1	180.4	180.4	58.7	180.0	147.9	129.3	161.1	52.2	29.7	74.0	127.6
Steel-mill products	206.3	232.8	328.2	327.8	1,148.3	1,148.3	476.5	1,109.9	1,134.1	1,090.2	1,461.7	571.0	451.8	820.9	1,499.7
Bolts and nuts, n.e.m.	5.9	6.9	11.7	10.5	45.5	45.5	17.2	42.6	37.4	37.6	58.2	22.6	17.5	28.4	54.4
Forgings, n.e.m.	5.5	6.9	10.8	15.5	93.5	93.5	39.8	87.2	67.3	52.9	84.6	25.0	15.6	31.6	60.5
Galvanizing, n.e.d.	0.8	1.7	1.6	2.2	3.9	3.9	1.9	3.0	3.0	3.2	3.7	2.4	1.5	3.2	3.5
Nails and spikes, n.e.m.	6.2	4.2	4.2	3.6	8.7	8.7	5.3	6.3	6.7	6.6	6.9	3.8	4.3	5.3	6.3
Springs, steel, n.e.m.	2.7	3.0	4.3	5.5	23.5	23.5	15.7	27.6	20.9[b]	19.2	21.3	7.6 *6.2*[c]	4.9	7.2	11.1
Structural metal work, n.e.m.	28.9	43.5	56.6	71.8	126.2	125.9	99.1	180.6	183.3	196.9	232.3	106.4	44.4	68.2	125.9
Wire, n.e.m.	2.4	7.9	23.9	25.4	59.3	59.3	37.2	62.5	57.2	62.6[d]	87.8	38.2	35.9	58.9	82.0
Wirework, n.e.c.	9.0	15.2	17.5	17.7	39.8	39.6	29.3	48.0	55.8	65.4	78.7	46.4	39.3	61.9	87.1
Wrought pipe, n.e.m.	5.8	4.7	7.9	11.4	30.7	30.7	19.6	32.9	35.6	42.4	54.5	32.7	14.1	31.8	45.5
Cast-iron pipe		[e]	10.3	9.7	24.8	24.8	20.4	43.9	52.1	46.9	46.0	27.0	11.9	23.1	35.7
Doors, metal	0.2	0.9	1.7	3.2	6.3	6.3	8.2	9.8	28.5	39.7	42.0	21.0	7.4	12.8	30.5
Heating apparatus	11.9	14.5	31.5	37.0	88.3	88.3	77.2	138.7	151.6	148.3	155.6	72.8	49.2	74.3	263.2 (heating apparatus and stoves and ranges)
Stoves and ranges	2.1	*3.9*[f] 39.9	49.5	55.4	122.2	122.2	82.1	165.7	168.4	165.2	171.0[g]	107.3	71.5	109.7	
Plumbers' supplies, n.e.c.	7.5	11.6	22.8	24.7	32.2	32.2	43.4[h]	81.2	104.3	89.6	80.6	44.9	29.3	43.8	64.3
Screw-machine products	2.9	3.2	5.8	8.1	34.9	34.9	15.7	31.4	34.5	34.1	66.5	27.6	20.0	36.4	61.3
Cutlery, n.e.c.	9.7	12.6	15.7	17.4	47.2	47.1	34.4	55.3	59.7	58.5	63.9	43.4	30.1	38.6	49.7
Files	2.2	3.1	4.1	4.0	13.4	13.4	5.3	9.7	10.0	9.8	11.1	6.1	5.8	6.9	10.3
Saws	3.8	5.8	6.6	7.8	19.7	19.6	11.7	21.0	16.5	15.0	15.7	7.5	6.9	8.4	12.5
Tools, other	8.7	13.2	19.3	21.7	98.4	98.0	45.0	80.0[i]	82.2	80.4[j] *48.5*	67.4	28.7	23.7	33.8	49.7
Firearms	4.1	6.5	6.5	7.9	22.6	22.6	10.2	14.0	12.0	14.4	17.9	8.1	7.0	9.6	17.2
Hardware, n.e.c.	23.7	32.1	42.6	46.5	105.8	105.7	79.0	135.4	147.5	136.4	153.0	77.6	55.0	90.3	133.2
Safes and vaults	2.2	4.6	5.0	4.6	8.7	8.7	12.3	12.0	14.8[k]	11.2	13.0	7.5	2.0	2.1	3.2
Tin cans and tinware, n.e.c.	[l]	15.6	19.5	28.1	68.8	68.7	59.6	80.0	84.6	84.1[m]	101.9[g]	74.5	70.9	86.4[m]	113.8
TOTAL	427.8	491.7 543.3	768.1 778.4	820.6	2,453.1	2,451.8	1,304.8	2,658.7	2,715.9	2,639.9 2,608.0	3,256.4	1,462.3 1,460.9	1,049.7	1,767.6	2,948.2

For footnotes see next page.

Value Added by Manufacturing Industries (Unit: $1,000,000)

IRON AND STEEL PRODUCTS (concluded)

[a] *Blast-furnace products* and *chemicals, n.e.c.*, each include part of *ferro-alloys*, listed as a separate industry in 1919.

[b] Between 1925 and 1927 motor vehicle spring bumpers were transferred from *springs, steel, n.e.m.*, to *automobile bodies and parts.*

[c] After 1931 establishments engaged in the repairing and replacing of motor vehicle springs, formerly classified under *springs, steel, n.e.m.*, were not canvassed by the Bureau of the Census. Overlapping figures for 1931 are provided by the Bureau of the Census.

[d] Between 1927 and 1929 certain large establishments engaged primarily in rolling nonferrous metal and manufacturing nonferrous wire were transferred from *wire, n.e.m.* to *nonferrous-metal products, n.e.c.*

[e] Prior to 1909 *cast-iron pipe* was combined with *foundry and machine-shop products, n.e.c.*

[f] After 1899 stoves and hot-air furnaces were transferred from *foundry and machine-shop products, n.e.c.* to *stoves and ranges.* Overlapping figures are provided for 1904.

[g] Between 1929 and 1931 *dairymen's supplies* was abandoned as a separate classification, and the products were divided among *stoves and ranges, tin cans and tinware, n.e.c.*, and other classifications.

[h] Between 1921 and 1923 enameled bathtubs, sinks, etc. were transferred from *stamped and enameled ware* to *plumbers' supplies, n.e.c.*

[i] Between 1923 and 1925 *rules* was abandoned as a separate classification, and the products were divided among *tools, other*, and other classifications.

[j] Between 1927 and 1929 a new classification, *machine-tool accessories, n.e.c.*, was established. Establishments thus classified were formerly classified with *tools, other*, and other industries. For *tools, other*, overlapping figures for 1927 are provided by the Bureau of the Census.

[k] Between 1925 and 1927 metal burial vaults were transferred from *safes and vaults* to *caskets and coffins.*

[l] In 1899 *tin cans and tinware, n.e.c.*, was combined with *sheet-metal work, n.e.c.*

[m] Between 1927 and 1929 stamped tinware was transferred from *tin cans and tinware, n.e.c.*, to *stamped and enameled ware.* In 1937 it was transferred back to *tin cans and tinware, n.e.c.*

NONFERROUS-METAL PRODUCTS	Establishments with Products Valued at $500 or More					Establishments with Products Valued at $5,000 or More									
	1899	*1904*	*1909*	*1914*	*1919*	*1919*	*1921*	*1923*	*1925*	*1927*	*1929*	*1931*	*1933*	*1935*	*1937*
Industry															
Copper	43.0	44.0[a]	45.3	64.9	66.7	66.7	29.0	71.3	92.0	81.5	74.4	42.9	15.9	37.5	70.4
Lead	31.3	16.9[a]	15.4	17.6	17.4	17.4	16.5	20.4	28.2	22.3	28.2	12.0	9.9	15.2	19.6
Zinc	4.9	7.8	9.0	14.0	34.1	34.1	13.2	30.0	34.9	31.7	44.1	18.0	15.5	25.6	40.9
Secondary metals, nonprecious	1.9	3.6	4.9	8.7	14.7	14.7[b]	8.1	7.5	12.9	11.9	22.4	6.1	9.7	10.6	19.0
Secondary metals, precious	0.9	1.2	1.6	2.9	5.7	5.7	4.9	6.8	6.4	3.8	6.4	4.5	5.6	6.3	6.9
Aluminum manufactures			[c]	5.2[d]	26.0	26.0	19.9	40.3	42.8	43.7	59.4	34.7	27.4	45.6	69.9
Collapsible tubes	} 0.5	0.9	1.1	1.4	4.9	4.9	4.8	9.0	{ 3.8	4.2	3.5	3.5	3.1	3.5	3.9
Tin and other foils									{ 5.0	5.6	7.4	4.8	3.7	5.3[e]	6.6
Electroplating [f]	1.9	2.2	3.3	3.4	7.8	7.5	6.1	9.7	9.9	10.6	18.9	10.3	7.7	13.7	20.0
Fire extinguishers	0.1	0.4	0.4	0.7	2.9	2.9	2.2	2.8	3.9	4.0	4.4	2.7	2.1	2.9	5.3
Gold leaf and foil	1.1	1.2	1.1	1.0	1.8	1.8	2.0	1.7	1.9	1.9	2.0	1.2	0.7	0.8	1.1
Lighting equipment	11.9	15.5	24.6	23.3	41.7	41.6	39.3	66.3	71.9	72.2	87.0	44.7	26.9	45.8	60.3
Needles and pins	2.0	3.2	4.4[g]	4.6	19.1	19.1	12.7	14.4	12.2	14.4	15.8	15.5	16.9	23.5	26.1

NONFERROUS-METAL PRODUCTS (concluded)	Establishments with Products Valued at $500 or More					Establishments with Products Valued at $5,000 or More									
	1899	*1904*	*1909*	*1914*	*1919*	*1919*	*1921*	*1923*	*1925*	*1927*	*1929*	*1931*	*1933*	*1935*	*1937*
Industry															
Nonferrous-metal products, n.e.c.	30.5	40.9	56.5	52.2[d]	191.7	191.5	91.0	191.1	192.2	203.4[h]	309.4	136.1	110.8	173.5	279.2
Plated ware	6.7	6.7	10.3	10.2	23.9	23.9	21.5	34.1	34.3	36.5	38.7 }	34.0	21.9	28.1	34.2
Silverware	7.7	11.7	13.6	11.5	16.1	16.1	15.4	16.3	19.4	19.5	20.3 }				
Sheet-metal work, n.e.c.	28.5[i]	*44.5* / 28.9	42.5	44.7	79.4	77.2	72.9	95.4[j]	91.0	92.7[j]	109.8[k]	60.1	33.3	51.6	74.0
Stamped and enameled ware	11.9	20.4	27.1[e]	34.2	80.4	80.4	53.8[l]	90.0	81.3	82.0[m]	116.7	69.1	62.7	107.5[m]	148.1
Clocks	4.1	5.8	8.5	7.0	16.2	16.2	11.2	20.4	20.5	28.1	31.5 }				
Watch and clock materials	0.2	0.3	0.5	0.7	0.8	0.8	0.7	0.9	1.0	1.0	0.7 }	32.7	22.2	38.7	59.7
Watches	5.5	9.6	9.6	11.6	25.7	25.7	19.2	21.8	30.1	26.4	23.9 }				
Watchcases	3.4	4.2	5.5	3.8	11.4	11.4	8.2	10.3	8.7	8.4	8.9	2.9	1.9	4.2	6.2
Jewelry	23.9	29.0	43.7	41.9	93.5	92.7	69.2	90.1	86.9	87.9	97.6	46.4	25.9	40.7	54.1
Jewelers' findings												4.9	3.7	6.2	7.2
TOTAL	221.9	270.0 / 254.4	328.9	365.5	781.9	778.3	521.8	850.6	891.2	893.7	1,131.4	587.1	427.5	686.8	1,012.7

[a] In 1909 the copper and lead departments of an important copper and lead smelting and refining establishment were reported together under *copper*, whereas in 1904 the lead department was included with *lead*.

[b] Between 1919 and 1921 certain establishments were transferred from *secondary metals, nonprecious*, to *chemicals, n.e.c.*

[c] Prior to 1914 *aluminum manufactures* was included among *miscellaneous articles, housefurnishings, n.e.c.*, and *stamped and enameled ware*.

[d] Between 1914 and 1919 aluminum castings were transferred from *nonferrous-metal products, n.e.c.*, to *aluminum manufactures*. The comparability of the figures for the latter industry appears to have been considerably affected by this change.

[e] Between 1935 and 1937 several establishments were transferred from *tin and other foils* to other industries.

[f] Because this industry contains a large proportion of small establishments, the degree to which it is covered in the Census probably varies from year to year.

[g] Between 1909 and 1914 metal hairpins were transferred from *combs, n.e.c.*, to *needles and pins*.

[h] Between 1927 and 1929 certain large establishments engaged primarily in rolling nonferrous metal and manufacturing nonferrous wire were transferred from *wire, n.e.m.*, to *nonferrous-metal products, n.e.c.*

[i] In 1899 *tin cans and tinware, n.e.c.*, was combined with *sheet-metal work, n.e.c.*

[j] Sheet-metal shops in which some manufacturing was carried on in connection with building construction or repair contracts were not canvassed for 1925 and 1927, unless the value of the manufactured products exceeded $20,000. Previously such shops were canvassed if the value of their manufactured products amounted to $5,000 or more. After 1927 all sheet-metal shops were covered with respect to work done in the shop; outside work was not included.

[k] After 1929 *dairymen's supplies* was abandoned as a separate classification, and the products were divided among *sheet-metal work, n.e.c.*, and other classifications.

[l] Between 1921 and 1923 enameled bathtubs, sinks, etc. were transferred from *stamped and enameled ware* to *plumbers' supplies*.

[m] Between 1927 and 1929 stamped tinware was transferred from *tin cans and tinware, n.e.c.*, to *stamped and enameled ware*. Between 1935 and 1937 it was transferred back to *tin cans and tinware, n.e.c.*

Value Added by Manufacturing Industries (Unit: $1,000,000)

MACHINERY	Establishments with Products Valued at $500 or More					Establishments with Products Valued at $5,000 or More									
Industry	*1899*	*1904*	*1909*	*1914*	*1919*	*1919*	*1921*	*1923*	*1925*	*1927*	*1929*	*1931*	*1933*	*1935*	*1937*
Foundry and machine-shop products, n.e.c.[a]	345.6	*444.7*[b]													
		408.1	*526.9*[c]												
			516.6	*561.4*[d]											
				509.5	1,589.6[e]										
					1,345.3	1,342.1	913.7	1,404.8[f]	1,371.5[g]	1,408.8					
										1,390.8[h]	1,756.2[i]	814.1			
												806.4[j]	506.3		
													507.8[k,l,m]	879.6	
														870.3[n]	1,462.6
Agricultural implements	57.3	63.7	86.0	90.6	160.4	160.3	76.5	87.8	95.6	117.1	163.9	52.0	18.6[o]		
													36.0	151.8	280.4
Business machines	4.8	8.4	20.2	26.5	72.6	72.6	44.1	82.6	87.2	95.7	99.2[p]	51.2	36.2		
													43.0[m]	81.0	117.2
Typewriters										45.4	54.6[p]	18.3	13.2	25.2	31.6
Carbon paper	5.5 (typewriters and carbon paper)	8.8	15.6	19.0	36.6	36.6	31.0	38.5	47.9	7.8	9.3	7.4	6.1	7.2	8.7
Electrical machinery	43.0	74.0[r]	112.7	180.4	572.9	572.7	489.9	744.4	903.3[g]	991.5	1,329.9	755.9			
												657.9[t]	340.9[u, v]	597.0	990.7
Phonographs	1.4	6.1	8.6	20.1	98.8	98.8	57.2	62.1	36.2	57.8	59.5[s]	6.7[t]			
Radios and phonographs												*104.7*[t]	63.3	97.5	124.2
Engines and tractors			d	40.7	247.2	247.2	87.8	142.5	167.8	202.7	254.3	111.4 (engines and tractors and windmills)	50.6[o]		
Windmills	2.2	2.5	3.3	2.9	5.0	5.0	3.1	3.7	4.6	4.3	5.1				
Engines and windmills, excl. tractors													*33.2*[o]	57.9	111.2
Steel barrels				e	*9.8*	9.8	5.3	8.4	7.2	9.4	15.9	8.7	12.4	13.6	18.0
Machine tools				e	*153.4*	153.3	43.8	96.2	100.4	113.4					
										102.7[h]	180.3	59.4	30.6	85.5	183.4
Machine-tool accessories, n.e.c.										*60.6*[h]	117.4[s]	52.7	33.5	69.9	118.1
Pumps	0.7	1.7	3.1	*3.6*[d]											
				14.8	49.3	49.3	43.2	58.5	69.8	77.8	97.2	50.6	28.7	51.7	
														67.0[n]	114.2
Textile machinery				e	*76.5*	76.4	84.0	91.0	82.6	80.7	85.9	47.6	41.9	45.7	72.1

MACHINERY (continued)	Establishments with Products Valued at $500 or More					Establishments with Products Valued at $5,000 or More									
	1899	*1904*	*1909*	*1914*	*1919*	*1919*	*1921*	*1923*	*1925*	*1927*	*1929*	*1931*	*1933*	*1935*	*1937*
Industry															
Gas machines and meters	2.4	3.0	8.3	9.1	15.6	15.6	13.0	19.9	21.3	21.1	25.4	15.8	8.8[l]		
Refrigerators and ice-making machinery											j	*110.9*	71.2	107.8	169.4
Refrigerators, nonmechanical	2.8	4.1	5.8	7.7	14.1	14.1	16.7	28.4	32.9	33.1	34.0	20.7	j		
Refrigerators, mechanical									g	53.9	89.2	82.5	j		
Scales and balances	3.7	4.4	6.1	6.6	13.6	13.6	11.2	17.6	19.9	17.2	22.9	10.9	6.2	9.6	12.1
Sewing machines	11.7	15.4	16.8	17.0	33.5	33.5	20.7	28.2	27.7	28.4[q]					
										25.7	28.6	14.1	10.1	16.6	25.9
Washing and ironing machines	1.6	1.6	3.0	3.5	17.4	17.4	13.6	24.6	36.8	35.7	41.6	26.4	20.2	25.4	28.7
TOTAL	482.7	637.8													
		601.8	816.4												
			806.1	948.4	2,926.6										
					2,922.0	2,918.3	1,954.8	2,939.2	3,112.7	3,401.8					
										3,431.0	4,470.4	2,206.4	1,298.8		
													1,298.3	2,323.0	3,868.5

[a] *Foundry and machine-shop products, n.e.c.*, includes *iron and steel, processed* (shown separately by the Census, 1919–29) and *vault, sidewalk, and floor lights, coal covers, and ventilating equipment* (shown separately by the Census from 1899 to 1923).

[b] After 1899 stoves and hot-air furnaces were transferred from *foundry and machine-shop products, n.e.c.*, to *stoves and ranges*. Overlapping figures are provided for 1904.

[c] Prior to 1909 *cast-iron pipe* was combined with *foundry and machine-shop products, n.e.c.* Overlapping figures are provided for 1909.

[d] Prior to 1914 the industry *engines and tractors*, and establishments engaged in the production of power pumps were included in *foundry and machine-shop products*. Overlapping figures are provided for 1914. Automobile repairing was first treated as a manufacturing industry in 1914. Prior to that year no special effort was made to canvass this industry but some reports were received in 1909 and were included with *foundry and machine-shop products, n.e.c.*

[e] Prior to 1919 *steel barrels, textile machinery, iron and steel, welded*, and *machine tools* were included in *foundry and machine-shop products, n.e.c.* Overlapping figures are provided for 1919.

[f] Between 1923 and 1925 manifolding machinery was transferred from *stationery goods, n.e.c.*, to *foundry and machine-shop products, n.e.c.*

[g] Between 1925 and 1927 a new classification, *refrigerators, mechanical*, was set up. Establishments there classified were formerly in *electrical machinery* and *foundry and machine-shop products, n.e.c.*

[h] Between 1927 and 1929 a new classification, *machine-tool accessories, n.e.c.*, was set up. Establishments there classified were formerly in *machine tools*, *foundry and machine-shop products, n.e.c.*, and *tools, other*. Overlapping figures are provided for 1927. We obtained the 1927 figures for *machine tool accessories, n.e.c.*, by subtracting the revised figures published in the 1929 Census of Manufactures for *foundry and machine-shop products, n.e.c.*, *tools, other*, and *machine tools* from the respective unrevised figures, published in the 1927 volume, and then totaling the differences.

[i] Between 1929 and 1931 *dairymen's supplies* was abandoned as a separate classification, and the products were divided among *foundry and machine-shop products, n.e.c.* and other classifications.

[j] Between 1931 and 1933 *refrigerators, mechanical*, *refrigerators, nonmechanical*, and ice-making apparatus, which was previously in *foundry and machine-shop products, n.e.c.*, were combined under *refrigerators and ice-making machinery*. Overlapping figures are provided for 1931.

[k] Between 1933 and 1935 *printing materials, n.e.c.*, *type founding*, and *engravers materials* were combined with *foundry and machine-shop products, n.e.c.*

[l] Between 1933 and 1935 *gas machines and meters* was abandoned as a separate classification. Gas and water meters were transferred to *instruments, professional*, and gas generators to *machine shops*, part of *foundry and machine-shop products, n.e.c.* Overlapping figures are provided for 1933.

Footnotes continued on next page.

Value Added by Manufacturing Industries (Unit: $1,000,000)

MACHINERY (concluded)

[m] Between 1933 and 1935 addressing and mailing machines, check-writing and canceling machines and duplicating or manifolding machines were transferred from *foundry and machine-shop products, n.e.c.*, to *business machines*, and numbering machines from *hand stamps and stencils* to *business machines*. Overlapping figures for 1933 are provided by the Bureau of the Census.

[n] Between 1935 and 1937 air compressors and dry vacuum pumps were transferred from *foundry and machine-shop products, n.e.c.*, to *pumps*. Overlapping figures are provided for 1935.

[o] Between 1933 and 1935 tractors were transferred from *engines* to *agricultural implements*. Overlapping figures are provided for 1933.

[p] Between 1929 and 1931 certain establishments manufacturing typewriter-bookkeeping-billing machines were transferred from *typewriters* to *business machines*.

[q] Between 1927 and 1929 sewing machine cases, cabinets and tables were transferred from *sewing machines* to *furniture*. Overlapping figures for 1927 are provided by the Census.

[r] Between 1904 and 1909 establishments manufacturing signs and advertising novelties were transferred from *electrical machinery* and other classifications to a new one, *signs*.

[s] Between 1929 and 1931 molded plastics were transferred principally from *electrical machinery*, but also from *phonographs*, *machine-tool accessories, n.e.c.*, and other classifications, to *pulp goods*.

[t] In 1931 a new classification, *radios and phonographs*, was set up. Establishments there classified were formerly in *electrical machinery* and *phonographs*. Overlapping figures for 1931 are provided for *electrical machinery* by the Bureau of the Census.

[u] *Electrical machinery* includes *beauty shop equipment*, listed separately by the Bureau of the Census after 1933. Most of the establishments in the latter industry were formerly classified in *electrical machinery* or in *miscellaneous articles*.

[v] Between 1933 and 1935 the composition of *dental goods and equipment* was changed to include certain electrical devices formerly in *electrical machinery*.

TRANSPORTATION EQUIPMENT

	Establishments with Products Valued at $500 or More					Establishments with Products Valued at $5,000 or More									
Industry	*1899*	*1904*	*1909*	*1914*	*1919*	*1919*	*1921*	*1923*	*1925*	*1927*	*1929*	*1931*	*1933*	*1935*	*1937*
Aircraft[a]	15.1 (Aircraft and motorcycles combined)	2.5[b]	5.6	0.7	7.2	7.2[c]	4.2	9.1	9.7	13.6	43.8	27.2	18.5	31.3	70.1
Motorcycles and bicycles				11.3	27.1	27.1	12.8	14.3	12.1	11.3	12.6	8.2	5.9	10.3	16.4
Automobile bodies and parts	d	1.9	31.5	66.0	330.1	329.4	194.1	449.0	660.6[e]	510.1	687.3[f]	428.5	318.8	547.8	807.8
Automobiles	2.9	15.0	86.1	210.6	809.3	809.2	564.3	1,015.9	1,089.9	959.0	1,315.0[f]	523.1	329.2	577.0	702.7
Carriage and wagon materials	12.0	14.2	16.5	11.3	12.0	12.0	4.7	3.3	2.5	1.5	1.3	g			
Carriages and sleds, children's	2.3	3.5	4.7	6.1	12.8	12.8	12.2	18.2	16.6	14.8	15.3	9.7	5.3	8.1	9.8

TRANSPORTATION EQUIPMENT (concluded)	Establishments with Products Valued at $500 or More					Establishments with Products Valued at $5,000 or More									
	1899	*1904*	*1909*	*1914*	*1919*	*1919*	*1921*	*1923*	*1925*	*1927*	*1929*	*1931*	*1933*	*1935*	*1937*
Industry															
Carriages, wagons and sleighs	59.8	64.8	62.4	*55.0*[h]											
				52.7	37.8	36.3	11.9	18.7	12.1	8.8	8.0[g]	3.3[i]			
												2.7	2.4	3.2	4.5
Cars, railroad, n.e.m.	32.1	41.0	48.5	66.7	188.5	188.5	128.6	190.7	124.7	103.4	104.3	39.9	18.8	38.8	109.0
Locomotives, n.e.m.	15.0	31.8	16.5	19.8	83.9	83.9	46.6	91.1	23.7	31.0	31.1	7.2	2.7	7.9	32.9
Ships and boats[j]	41.1	45.3	42.1	50.1	911.8	911.4	231.5	128.7	110.9	132.5	145.5	114.7	61.5	94.4	150.2
TOTAL	180.3	220.0	313.9	497.6											
				495.3	2,420.5	2,417.8	1,210.9	1,939.0	2,062.8	1,786.0	2,364.2	1,161.8			
												1,161.2	763.1	1,318.8	1,903.0

[a] Some degree of incomparability may have been introduced by the following changes in the questionnaire for *aircraft:* For 1937, aircraft were reported as "begun and completed in 1937"; for 1935, as "begun and completed in 1935"; for 1933, as "built in 1933"; for 1931, as "built in 1931"; for 1929, as "completed in 1929."

[b] Between 1904 and 1909 children's tricycles and velocipedes were transferred from *motorcycles and bicycles* to *toys and games, n.e.c.*

[c] Between 1919 and 1921 establishments engaged primarily in the manufacture of aircraft parts, other than engines and tires, were transferred from *cotton goods, lumber-mill products, n.e.c., planing-mill products, n.e.m.*, and *wood turned and shaped, n.e.c.*, to *aircraft.*

[d] In 1899 no establishments reported that they were engaged chiefly in the manufacture of automobile bodies and parts. The Bureau of the Census doubts that there were any such establishments at that time.

[e] Between 1925 and 1927 motor vehicle spring bumpers were transferred from *springs, steel, n.e.m.*, to *automobile bodies and parts.*

[f] Between 1929 and 1931 trailers were transferred from *automobiles* to *automobile bodies and parts.* The resulting discontinuity is slight.

[g] In 1931 *carriage and wagon materials* was abandoned as a separate classification. Turned products, such as hubs, felloes, and spokes were transferred to *wood turned and shaped, n.e.c.*, and other materials and parts were transferred to *carriages, wagons and sleighs.*

[h] Prior to 1914 establishments engaged in repair work were included with *carriages, wagons and sleighs.* Overlapping figures are available for 1914.

[i] Between 1931 and 1933 horsedrawn lunch wagons were transferred from *carriages, wagons and sleighs* to *planing-mill products, n.e.m.* A 1933 figure comparable with earlier years is provided for *carriages, wagons and sleighs.*

[j] Does not include government shipyards.

Value Added by Manufacturing Industries (Unit: $1,000,000)

MISCELLANEOUS PRODUCTS	Establishments with Products Valued at $500 or More					Establishments with Products Valued at $5,000 or More									
	1899	*1904*	*1909*	*1914*	*1919*	*1919*	*1921*	*1923*	*1925*	*1927*	*1929*	*1931*	*1933*	*1935*	*1937*
Industry															
Organs		4.0	3.0	3.6	3.8	3.7	6.5	6.8	8.5	10.9	8.2	4.1	1.2	1.1	3.2
Pianos	23.7	27.3	33.8	33.7	52.7	52.7	35.0	57.0	51.9	41.6	23.6	9.4	4.4	7.1	12.0
Organ and piano parts		6.8	9.3	10.4	20.1	20.1	10.4	21.8	21.5	12.6	7.6	2.1	1.1	2.0	2.9
Musical instruments, n.e.c.	2.2	2.4	2.3	2.6	8.1	7.9	9.0	11.3	14.8	13.3	10.4	5.9	3.5	6.3	8.2
Artificial flowers	3.5	3.2	4.4	4.4	9.1	9.1	8.3	11.0	10.6	11.7	8.9	5.6	3.9	5.7	8.2
Feathers and plumes			5.9	5.3	8.7	8.6	4.6	4.5	2.3	0.9	0.8	1.3	0.6	1.0	1.1
Artists' materials	0.2	0.5	1.0	1.2	2.8	2.8	3.0	4.3	4.5	4.4	5.3	3.7	2.9		
													7.1[a]	1.2	1.5
Pencils	1.2	2.6	3.8	3.8	15.1	15.1	14.1	15.9	15.9	14.6	17.0	8.8	7.5		
													9.3[a]	11.7	12.6
Brooms	8.9	10.1	6.0	6.2	12.8	12.4	7.8	11.3	10.5	9.3	9.5	6.9	4.5	6.9	5.3
Brushes			7.5	8.6	19.4	19.3	16.9	24.9	23.8	25.3	23.9	16.6	12.4	23.5	20.6
Buttons	4.9	7.0	13.2	12.0	25.1	24.9	16.1	19.6	20.1	17.9	17.5	13.2	13.8	17.0	18.0
Dairymen's supplies	b	3.3	9.4	9.7	18.9	18.8	14.6	21.9	21.8	21.1	25.9	c			
Dental goods and equipment	1.6	2.3	2.7	5.4	13.0	12.9	12.3	15.3	17.6	20.8					
										14.2[d]	17.9	14.6	9.5[e]	13.9[f]	18.2
Miscellaneous articles	5.0[g]	7.1[h]	7.0[i]	9.2	31.5	31.3	27.0	34.7	40.6	48.3	50.2	32.8[j,k]	24.7[l]	29.0	
Ivory work, etc.	0.9	1.5[m]	0.9	0.9	1.5	1.5	1.3	1.3	1.2	0.6	0.7				30.2
Combs, n.e.c.	1.0	1.4[m]	4.4[n]	2.6	3.4	3.4	2.4	4.2	2.9	2.6	1.5	1.1	0.4	0.4	
Foundry supplies	0.5	0.4	1.0	1.0	4.3	4.3	2.2	5.4	5.8	5.1	4.9	1.9	1.5	3.1	3.9
Hair work[o]	0.9	1.1	5.1	1.8	3.1	3.0	4.2	5.7	3.0	1.4	1.2	0.9	0.7	1.7	1.5
Hand stamps and stencils	1.9	2.1	2.5	3.1	6.2	6.0	6.3	8.0	11.3	10.4	11.2	7.7	5.8[p]	6.7	7.3
Instruments, professional	3.5	4.0	7.6	11.9	38.6	38.5	28.8	45.0	55.9[q]	58.9	61.3	30.6	19.0		
													26.3[r]	47.8[f]	66.6
Optical goods	3.1	3.8	7.5	11.6	35.9	35.8	27.8	35.4[s]	23.7[q]	23.9	28.7	20.4	18.1	22.5	33.1

MISCELLANEOUS PRODUCTS (continued)	Establishments with Products Valued at $500 or More					Establishments with Products Valued at $5,000 or More									
	1899	*1904*	*1909*	*1914*	*1919*	*1919*	*1921*	*1923*	*1925*	*1927*	*1929*	*1931*	*1933*	*1935*	*1937*
Industry															
Jewelry and instrument cases	0.7	1.4	1.9	2.2	4.6	4.6	4.3	6.1	6.3	5.5	5.5	3.0	2.0	4.0 *4.6*[t]	7.3
Lapidary work	1.1	1.4	2.6	1.4	10.7	10.6	1.5	3.2	2.8	3.2	3.7	1.1	0.3	0.8	1.1
Mattresses and bed springs, n.e.c.	7.7	12.4	15.3	16.3	34.7	34.4	32.6	46.1	48.2[u]	46.7	61.8	40.0	27.2	35.9	50.0
Models and patterns, n.e.c.[o]	3.0	3.6	6.0	6.6	18.9	18.5	11.7	19.0	17.6	18.8	25.3	13.4	7.1	12.1	18.1
Paving materials	2.4	2.4	2.8	21.5	29.7	29.3	36.7	46.6	57.2	65.2[v]	15.7 *10.1*[v]	7.4	4.7	7.9	10.7
Pens and points	1.3	2.0	3.0[w]	6.0	12.3	12.3	8.6	14.4	18.0	15.3	22.8	16.6	7.5	12.1	14.6
Photographic supplies	4.4	8.9	15.9	*26.3*[x] 27.5	54.6	54.5	47.8	52.6	52.9	61.8	72.4	58.6	41.9	47.8	79.5
Pipes, tobacco	1.4	1.5	2.9	1.9	8.1	8.0	4.3	5.9	4.6	4.6	3.8	3.7	2.3	4.2	5.2
Signs		h	8.8	15.7	27.3	26.8	34.5	44.6	63.8	67.6	82.3	53.4	31.8	40.1	49.1
Soda-water apparatus	2.0	2.7	4.1	4.9	8.6	8.5	8.9	11.5	13.4	13.5	14.0	9.4	3.4	4.1	6.8
Sporting goods, n.e.c.	1.8	4.1	5.5	6.3	11.9	11.8	16.4	23.3	24.8	25.5	33.8	29.2	14.7	18.3	22.9
Surgical equipment	3.3	4.4	7.0	9.0	23.8	23.5	19.9	23.3	31.5	29.9	35.6	28.1	22.6	25.7	32.1
Theatrical equipment			y	0.2	0.6	0.6	0.7	1.0	2.1	3.4	3.4	1.8	1.4	1.2	1.5
Toys and games, n.e.c.	2.3	3.3[z]	4.7	8.0	25.8	25.6	20.9	32.2	34.9 *33.5*[aa]	38.2	44.8	32.1	20.1[bb]	28.5	35.5
Umbrellas and canes	5.3	5.0	5.8	5.2	9.7	9.6	9.1	10.4	10.7	9.1	7.1	4.0	3.3	3.9	5.3
Window shades	2.5	3.0	5.9	5.6	10.9	10.8	11.8	18.1	16.6	16.0	17.2	9.4	7.1	8.1	10.3
TOTAL	102.2	147.0	230.5	285.9 287.3	626.3	621.5	528.3	723.6	773.6 772.2	779.9 773.3	785.4 779.8	498.8	332.9 340.2	463.3 463.9	604.4

For footnotes see next page.

Value added by Manufacturing Industries (Unit: $1,000,000)

MISCELLANEOUS PRODUCTS (concluded)

[a] Between 1933 and 1935 crayons were transferred from *artists' materials* to *pencils*. Overlapping figures for 1933 are provided by the Bureau of the Census.

[b] In 1899 *dairymen's supplies* was combined with other industries.

[c] In 1931 *dairymen's supplies* was abandoned as a separate classification, and the products were divided among *flavorings*, *planing-mill products, n.e.m.*, *sheet-metal work, n.e.c.*, *tin cans and tinware, n.e.c.*, *wood turned and shaped, n.e.c.*, *foundry and machine-shop products, n.e.c.*, and *stoves and ranges*.

[d] After 1927 dental laboratories operating on a custom basis, previously included in *dental goods and equipment*, were not canvassed. Overlapping figures for 1927 are provided by the Bureau of the Census.

[e] Between 1933 and 1935 the composition of *dental goods and equipment* was changed to include certain electrical devices formerly in *electrical machinery*, and dental chairs and cabinets formerly in *furniture*.

[f] Between 1935 and 1937 establishments manufacturing dental instruments as their major product were transferred from *instruments, professional* to *dental goods and equipment*.

[g] Between 1899 and 1904 establishments engaged in manufacturing statuary and art goods were transferred from *miscellaneous articles* and *plastering and stucco work* (an industry abandoned by the Bureau of the Census in 1904) to a new classification, *statuary and art goods*.

[h] Between 1904 and 1909 establishments manufacturing signs and advertising novelties were transferred from *housefurnishings, n.e.c.*, *leather goods, n.e.c.*, *stationery goods, n.e.c.*, *electrical machinery* and *miscellaneous articles* to *signs*.

[i] Prior to 1914 aluminum manufactures were included among *miscellaneous articles* and other classifications.

[j] Between 1929 and 1931 molded plastics were transferred principally from *electrical machinery*, but also from *miscellaneous articles* and other classifications to *pulp goods*.

[k] Between 1929 and 1931 *labels and tags* was abandoned as a separate classification and the products were divided among *miscellaneous articles* and other classifications.

[l] Between 1933 and 1935 *stationery goods, n.e.c.*, was abandoned as a classification and the products were divided among *miscellaneous articles* and other classifications. At the same time, some establishments making beauty shop equipment were transferred from *miscellaneous articles* to a new classification, *beauty shop equipment*, treated by us as part of *electrical machinery*.

[m] Between 1904 and 1909 many important establishments making horn, celluloid and other combs were transferred from *ivory work* to *combs, n.e.c.* Hairpins also were transferred from *ivory work* and other industries to *combs, n.e.c.*

[n] Between 1909 and 1914 rubber combs and hairpins were transferred from *combs, n.e.c.*, to *rubber goods, other*; metal hairpins were transferred from *combs, n.e.c.*, to *needles and pins*.

[o] Because this industry contains a large proportion of small establishments, the degree to which it is covered in the Census probably varies from year to year.

[p] Between 1933 and 1935 numbering machines were transferred from *hand stamps and stencils* to *business machines*.

[q] Between 1925 and 1927 surveyors' nautical instruments and similar instruments were transferred from *optical goods* to *instruments, professional*.

[r] Between 1933 and 1935 *gas machines and meters* was abandoned as a separate classification and gas and water meters were transferred to *instruments, professional*. Overlapping figures are provided for 1933.

[s] After 1923 establishments grinding lenses for spectacles and eyeglasses from prescriptions, classified under *optical goods*, were not canvassed by the Bureau of the Census. The comparability of the data for the industry appears to have been seriously affected by this omission.

[t] Because of changes in the classification of certain establishments between 1935 and 1937, the 1937 statistics for *jewelry and instrument cases* are not comparable with those for previous years. Comparable figures for 1935 are provided by the Bureau of the Census.

[u] After 1925 establishments engaged in renovating mattresses, classified under *mattresses and bedsprings, n.e.c.*, were not canvassed by the Census of Manufactures.

[v] Establishments formerly in *paving materials* and engaged primarily in quarrying and crushing stone were not canvassed after 1927. The data on the industry appear to have been seriously affected by this change. Crushed slag was not canvassed after 1929. The 1929 figure for *paving materials* has been revised to make it comparable with that for 1931.

[w] Between 1909 and 1914 there was a change in the classification of certain establishments, listed under *pens and points*, which manufactured gold pens and other products.

[x] In 1914 motion picture machines were included in *photographic supplies*, whereas in previous years they were included in *motion pictures*. Overlapping figures for 1914 are provided for *photographic supplies*.

[y] Canvassed for the first time in 1914.

[z] Between 1904 and 1909 children's tricycles and velocipedes were transferred from *motorcycles and bicycles* to *toys and games, n.e.c.*

[aa] Between 1925 and 1927 rubber toy balloons were transferred from *toys and games, n.e.c.*, to *rubber goods, other*. Overlapping figures for 1925 are provided by the Bureau of the Census.

[bb] The 1933 Census of this industry is considered by the Bureau of the Census as somewhat incomplete.

MAJOR GROUPS AND TOTAL MANUFACTURING	Establishments with Products Valued at $500 or More					Establishments with Products Valued at $5,000 or More									
	1899	*1904*	*1909*	*1914*	*1919*	*1919*	*1921*	*1923*	*1925*	*1927*	*1929*	*1931*	*1933*	*1935*	*1937*
Group															
Foods	418.8	547.2	763.5	979.6 1,002.8	2,369.3	2,360.7	1,979.4	2,345.5	2,547.1	2,673.5	3,123.3	2,498.6	2,002.2	2,254.3	2,705.2
Beverages	289.1	361.3	488.1	525.8	381.1	378.5	134.6	150.6	164.2	166.6	193.0	151.0	395.2 265.0	493.6	577.6
Tobacco products	170.8	205.0	239.5	283.1	529.4	522.4	439.8	528.3	665.3	743.1	816.9	792.5	667.9	762.3	887.4
Textile products	710.6	880.8 877.8	1,288.6 1,287.7	1,385.6	3,700.8	3,695.7	3,021.4	3,828.9	3,596.9	3,844.2	3,960.0	2,662.1	2,143.4	2,628.6	3,065.1
Leather products	186.7	245.9	325.2	353.3	898.4	896.4	610.4	797.2	750.9	780.9	774.2	523.7	452.0	533.9	596.9
Rubber products	39.6	68.0	74.6	138.0	543.9	543.9	327.0	457.4	536.6 539.1	564.7	538.8	361.4	261.3	309.1	369.3
Paper products	93.4	128.4	179.3	216.0	559.8	559.6	437.7	621.2	663.9	733.6	841.6	624.7 621.4	525.5	637.4	854.6
Printing and publishing	284.4	399.1	522.1	630.4	1,091.3	1,067.2	1,308.6	1,531.7	1,762.6	1,931.7	2,233.9	1,784.9	1,259.1 1,254.1	1,558.0	1,806.5
Chemical products	196.7	269.6	383.8	445.2	1,174.3	1,172.0	816.4	1,148.5	1,277.2 1,276.1	1,441.5	1,729.7	1,363.1	1,123.6	1,359.1	1,765.5
Petroleum and coal products	45.1	66.5	79.8 80.0	115.3	518.7	518.7	421.0	572.5	629.0	523.3	785.0	403.9	376.3	446.1	608.2
Stone, clay and glass products	194.6	281.2 283.2	362.7	397.7	755.5	750.8	666.1	1,050.2	1,122.5	1,114.9	1,125.0	657.4 665.7	444.2	667.6	979.0
Forest products	534.8	714.0 679.0	850.3 851.2	808.3	1,680.9	1,659.4	1,196.1	1,887.7	1,889.6	1,749.3 1,752.1	1,933.3	856.9	595.9	844.3	1,233.2
Iron and steel products	427.8	491.7 543.3	768.1 778.4	820.6	2,453.1	2,451.8	1,304.8	2,658.7	2,715.9	2,639.9 2,608.0	3,256.4	1,462.3 1,460.9	1,049.7	1,767.6	2,948.2

Value Added by Manufacturing Industries (Unit: $1,000,000)

MAJOR GROUPS AND TOTAL MANUFACTURING (concluded)	Establishments with Products Valued at $500 or More					Establishments with Products Valued at $5,000 or More									
	1899	*1904*	*1909*	*1914*	*1919*	*1919*	*1921*	*1923*	*1925*	*1927*	*1929*	*1931*	*1933*	*1935*	*1937*
Group															
Nonferrous-metal products	221.9	270.0													
		254.4	328.9	365.5	781.9	778.3	521.8	850.6	891.2	893.7	1,131.4	587.1	427.5	686.8	1,012.7
Machinery	482.7	637.8													
		601.8	816.4												
			806.1	948.4	2,926.6										
					2,922.0	2,918.3	1,954.8	2,939.2	3,112.7	3,401.8					
										3,431.0	4,470.4	2,206.4	1,298.8		
													1,298.3	2,323.0	3,868.5
Transportation equipment	180.3	220.0	313.9	497.6											
				495.3	2,420.5	2,417.8	1,210.9	1,939.0	2,062.8	1,786.0	2,364.2	1,161.8			
												1,161.2	763.1	1,318.8	1,903.0
Miscellaneous products	102.2	147.0	230.5	285.9											
				287.3	626.3	621.5	528.3	723.6	773.6						
									772.2	779.9					
										773.3	785.4				
											779.8	498.8	332.9		
													340.2	463.3	
														463.9	604.4
TOTAL MANUFACTURING	4,579.5	5,933.5													
		5,897.5	8,015.3												
			8,015.5	9,196.3											
				9,218.6	23,411.8										
					23,407.2	23,313.0	16,879.1	24,030.8	25,162.0	25,768.6					
										25,762.1	30,062.5				
											30,056.9	18,596.6			
												18,599.6	14,118.6		
													13,990.2	19,053.8	
														19,054.4	25,785.3

RECONCILIATION WITH CENSUS TOTAL	Establishments with Products Valued at $500 or More					Establishments with Products Valued at $5,000 or More									
	1899	1904	1909	1914	1919	1919	1921	1923	1925	1927	1929	1931	1933	1935	1937
CENSUS TOTAL	4,831.1	6,293.7	8,529.3	9,878.3	25,041.7	24,935.0	18,316.7	25,850.3	26,778.1	27,585.2	31,885.3	19,866.8	14,538.0	19,136.4	25,173.5
Add or Deduct:															
Revisions by Census							+15.6	−35.2	−24.3	−37.2		−5.0	−4.0	−4.9	
REVISED CENSUS TOTAL	4,831.1	6,293.7	8,529.3	9,878.3	25,041.7	24,935.0	18,332.3	25,815.1	26,753.8	27,548.0	31,885.3	19,861.8	14,534.0	19,131.5	25,173.5
Deduct															
Contract work deducted by NBER[a]															
Textile products	41.6	52.5	70.4	78.9	226.8	226.8	216.1	334.1	304.3	318.0	312.5	257.2	184.7	15.4	
Printing and publishing	18.8	28.4	35.7	40.2	85.8	85.8	107.0	118.0	139.7	173.2	169.9	134.7	96.4		
Forest products		35.0	31.1	31.8	37.5	37.5	31.0	41.2	31.3	28.5	23.0	10.1	8.3	14.3	
Value added by industries excluded by NBER															
Butter reworking	0.8	1.0	0.8	0.8	0.2	0.2[b]									
Coffee and spices	14.4 (Coffee and spices and Peanuts combined)	18.3	27.3	34.2	60.9	60.8	59.8	72.7	[c]	99.6	92.2	76.0	[d]		
Peanuts		0.9	1.1	2.4	4.9	4.9	2.6	3.0	2.4	10.1	10.1	11.2	[d]		
Poultry				1.7[e]	5.7	5.7	5.4	4.6	6.7	[c,r]	23.3	19.9	14.3	16.3	18.4
Rectified spirits														42.4[e]	72.1
Flax and hemp	0.1	0.1	0.1	0.1	0.7	0.7	0.1	0.1	0.2	0.2	0.1	[d]			
Wood carpet	0.6	0.4	0.3	0.2	[f]										
Gas, illuminating	55.1	88.0	114.4	143.5	171.7	171.7	208.9	259.0	277.0	304.9	324.2	315.2	216.3	248.1	[d]
Grindstones	0.8	0.5	1.2	0.6											
Grindstones and millstones					1.2	1.2	1.0	1.5	1.3	1.4	[d]				
Pulpwood	[g]	[g]	[g]	0.3	[f]										
Pulp, other than wood	0.1	[g]	[g]	[g]	0.1	0.1									
Iron and steel, welded				[h]	4.6	4.4	3.8	4.0	[d]						
Tinplate and terneplate	5.2	3.9	6.1	10.4	24.0	24.0	[i]								
Automobile repairing			[j]	20.8	137.0	125.9	[d]								
Carriage and wagon repairing			[k]	2.3	6.0	5.8	4.3	[d]							

For footnotes see p. 639.

Value Added by Manufacturing Industries (Unit: $1,000,000)

RECONCILIATION WITH CENSUS TOTAL (continued)	Establishments with Products Valued at $500 or More					Establishments with Products Valued at $5,000 or More									
	1899	*1904*	*1909*	*1914*	*1919*	*1919*	*1921*	*1923*	*1925*	*1927*	*1929*	*1931*	*1933*	*1935*	*1937*
Deduct (concluded)															
Railroad repair-shop products	113.7	166.7	223.0	291.2	806.6	806.5	760.8	888.7	769.0	744.2	721.6	441.9	314.1	232.6	d
Dental laboratory work										6.6[l]					
Motion pictures			2.0[e]	m	17.1	17.1	46.2	55.8	60.4	99.5	145.7	d			
Ordnance	1.4	0.4	g	g	42.9	42.9[i]	6.0	f							
Rules	0.1	0.2	0.1	0.5	0.3	0.3	0.4	0.5[n]							
Straw goods	0.02	0.1	g												
All other industries	0.2	0.2	0.3	0.7	0.2	0.2	0.4	1.9[i]	f						
Add:															
Contract work included by NBER[a]														11.8	131.2
Internal revenue taxes included by NBER (Tobacco products)[o]													400.8	477.9	561.7
Correction of value added in:															
Turpentine and rosin[p]													1.8	1.8	9.3
Cigars[q]													17.1		
ADJUSTED CENSUS TOTAL	4,578.2	5,897.1	8,015.4	9,217.7	23,407.5	23,312.5	16,878.5	24,030.0	25,161.5	25,761.8	30,062.7	18,595.6	14,119.6	19,053.9	25,785.2
NBER TOTAL	4,579.5	5,897.5	8,015.5	9,218.6	23,407.2	23,313.0	16,879.1	24,030.8	25,162.0	25,762.1	30,062.5	18,596.6	14,118.6	19,053.8	25,785.3
Unexplained difference	+1.3	+0.4	+0.1	+0.9	−0.3	+0.5	+0.6	+0.8	+0.5	+0.3	−0.2	+1.0	−1.0	−0.1	+0.1

[a] See footnote *b* p. 614.

[b] Between 1919 and 1921 *butter reworking* was combined with *all other industries*, and was not listed thereafter.

[c] Not canvassed.

[d] No longer canvassed.

[e] Canvassed for the first time.

[f] In 1919 *wood carpet* and *pulpwood*, in 1923 *ordnance*, and in 1925 *all other industries* were abandoned as separate classifications.

[g] Included in *all other industries*.

[h] Prior to 1919 *iron and steel, welded*, was included in *foundry and machine-shop products, n.e.c.*

[i] In 1921 *tinplate and terneplate* was combined with *ordnance* and in 1923 with *all other industries*. Since 1923 all the products of this industry have been made by the *steel-mill products* and the *tin cans and tinware, n.e.c.*, industries as secondary products.

[j] Automobile repairing was first treated as a manufacturing industry in 1914. Prior to that year no special effort was made to canvass this industry but some reports were received in 1909 and were included with *foundry and machine-shop products, n.e.c.*

[k] Prior to 1914 carriage repair work was included in *carriages, wagons, and sleighs*.

[l] After 1927 dental laboratories operating on a custom basis, and previously included in *dental goods and equipment*, were not canvassed.

[m] In 1914 motion-picture machines were included in *photographic supplies*, whereas in 1909 they were included with *motion pictures*.

[n] Between 1923 and 1925 *rules* was abandoned as a separate industry, and the products were divided among *tools, other*; *wood turned and shaped, n.e.c.*; and other industries, according to the character of the products.

[o] Prior to 1933 internal-revenue taxes were included in the figures on value added published by the Census for the tobacco products industries; in 1933–37 they were excluded. We have included them throughout.

[p] In 1937 the salaries and wages of those employees in *turpentine and rosin* who were engaged in the production and gathering of crude gum were added by the Bureau of the Census to cost of materials and deducted from value added, and only the employees at the still were considered as engaged in manufacturing. We have restored these data to value added in order to preserve as much comparability with 1935 as possible. The percentage of coverage of total production fell below 100 after 1929. The percentage of coverage is not given for 1931; in 1933 it was 85, and in 1935 it was 87. The value added figures for these two years have been raised accordingly.

[q] In 1933 the coverage of *cigars* was incomplete. On the basis of Bureau of Internal Revenue data the coverage may be estimated at about 81.5 percent; the value added figure for this year has been raised accordingly.

[r] Between 1927 and 1929 canned poultry products were transferred from *food, n.e.c.*, to *poultry products*.

Appendix D

Comparison of the National Bureau Indexes of Physical Output with Indexes Prepared by Other Agencies

Appendix D

Comparison of the National Bureau Indexes of Physical Output with Indexes Prepared by Other Agencies

CHARACTER OF THE INDEXES COMPARED

THE three indexes of manufacturing output compared in this appendix—the National Bureau index, the Day-Thomas index, and the National Research Project index—are all based primarily on the Census of Manufactures, but they differ from one another with respect to both technical methods of construction and coverage of industries and time-periods.[1]

The National Bureau index, as explained in Chapter 2 and Appendix A, was constructed with the use of the Edgeworth formula. Indexes were derived for four overlapping periods (1899–1909, 1909–1919, 1919–1929, and 1929–1937), and these were spliced together to produce indexes on the 1929 base. Adjustments were made for changes in coverage. Value of products per unit was employed as the price coefficient in the computation of indexes for individual industries; value added per unit was the price coefficient in the computation of indexes for industrial groups and for all manufacturing industries combined.

The Day-Thomas index was constructed on the basis of a weighted geometric mean of relatives of output quantities. The

[1] The "Day-Thomas index" is the index computed for 1899–1914 by W. M. Persons and E. S. Coyle; for 1914–1925 by E. E. Day and Woodlief Thomas; for 1927–31 by Aryness Joy; for 1933–35 by V. S. Kolesnikoff; and for 1937 by C. L. Dedrick. See E. E. Day and Woodlief Thomas, *The Growth of Manufactures, 1899 to 1923,* Census Monograph VIII (Bureau of the Census, 1928), pp. 23, 34; V. S. Kolesnikoff, "Index of Manufacturing Production Derived from Census Data, 1935," *Journal of the American Statistical Association* (Dec. 1937), pp. 713–14; and *Biennial Census of Manufactures, 1937* (1939), Part I, pp. 12, 17.

The National Research Project index was constructed by H. Magdoff, I. H. Siegel and M. B. Davis, and published in *Production, Employment and Productivity in 59 Manufacturing Industries, 1919–36,* Report No. S–1 (National Research Project, May 1939).

base was 1909 for the period 1899–1914, and 1919 for the period 1914–1937. For the indexes of output of individual industries the weight was value of products; for the indexes of groups and total manufacturing the weight was value added. The 1909 value was used for the 1899–1914 index, and the average of 1919 and the given year was employed similarly for the 1914–1937 index. No adjustments were made for changes in coverage, but imputed weights were used.[2]

For the National Research Project index the Laspeyres formula was used with 1929 as the base. The price coefficient employed in the computation of the indexes for most individual industries was value of product per unit. The remaining indexes for individual industries and the index for all manufacturing were constructed with employment per unit as the price coefficient. No adjustment was made for coverage changes, nor were imputed weights used.

Although the differences in construction are pronounced, the major source of variation among the indexes is to be traced to differences in coverage. These are shown in Table D–1, following. Indexes computed by the three agencies for the same individual industry are usually similar to one another. The more outstanding differences between the trends indicated by the three indexes for the same industry are described briefly in the notes below. These contain, also, brief descriptions of the indexes for industries or periods covered by Day-Thomas or National Research Project indexes but not by indexes constructed by the National Bureau of Economic Research.[3]

[2] See Appendix A, p. 372.

[3] There is still another index of manufacturing output based largely on Census data. This index, to which the present study owes much, was constructed at the National Bureau under the direction of Frederick C. Mills (see *Economic Tendencies in the United States* [1932], and *Prices in Recession and Recovery* [1936]). The index published in the present volume differs in certain technical respects from Dr. Mills' index. First, the number of industries covered by Dr. Mills' index is smaller, partly because the minimum coverage accepted by him as adequate for his purpose was 60 percent rather than the 40 percent specified by us and because less use was made of non-Census data by Dr. Mills than by us. Second, Dr. Mills used the Fisher "ideal" formula while we used the Edgeworth. Third, Dr. Mills' base periods are 1914 and 1927, rather than 1909, 1919 and 1929, selected in the present study. Fourth, the procedure of passing from output in the sample to output in all manufacturing industries differed: Dr. Mills used a modified type of imputed weighting, plus an adjustment based on employment and value added, while we used

TABLE D–1
Industrial and Time Coverage of Three Indexes of Physical Output of Manufacturing Industries

Industry and Group	*Census Years Covered by Index of Physical Output*[a]		
	National Bureau of Economic Research	Day-Thomas[b]	National Research Project[c]
Foods			
Meat packing	99–37	99–35	19–35 (Meat packing and Sausage combined)
Sausage, not elsewhere made	29–37	....	
Oleomargarine, not elsewhere made	25–37	....	....
Shortenings	27–37	....	....
Flour	99–37	99–35	19–35
Feeds	25–37	....	....
Cereals	25–37	....	....
Rice	99–37	14–31[d]	....
Macaroni	27–37	....	....
Bread and cake	23–37	....	23–35
Biscuits and crackers	23–37	....	23–35
Fish, canned	99–37	14–35	19–35
Fruits and vegetables, canned	99–37	99–35	19–35
Milk, canned	99–37	99–35 (Milk, Butter and Cheese combined)	....
Butter	99–37		....
Cheese	99–37		....
Ice cream	23–37	....	19–35
Beet sugar	99–37	99–35	19–35
Cane sugar, not elsewhere made	99–37	....	....
Cane-sugar refining	99–37	99–35	19–35
Confectionery	25–37	....	25–35
Chocolate	21–37	....	....
Corn products	09–37	14–35	....
Flavorings	29–37	....	....
Baking powder	27–37	....	....
Ice	99–37	14–35	19–35
TOTAL	99–37	99–35	....

For footnotes *see p. 650.*

only an adjustment based simply on value added (see Appendix A for a more detailed statement of this difference). Fifth, it was frequently possible for us, in the course of our study of Dr. Mills' indexes and the re-examination of the basic Census reports, to expand the scope of the data utilized by Dr. Mills in the computation of the indexes for individual industries by the inclusion of additional products, and to improve the homogeneity of the data by utilizing more detailed classes of products. There are a few other, minor, differences between the two indexes which need not be mentioned in detail.

TABLE D–1 (continued)

Industry and Group	*Census Years Covered by Index of Physical Output*[a]		
	National Bureau of Economic Research	Day-Thomas[b]	National Research Project[c]
Beverages			
Liquors, malt	99–37	99–19	....
Liquors, distilled	99–37		....
Malt	25–37	....	....
Liquors, vinous	23–37	....	....
Beverages, nonalcoholic	31–37	....	....
TOTAL	99–37	99–19[e]	....
Tobacco products			
Cigarettes	99–37	99–35	19–35
Cigars	99–37	99–35	19–35
Tobacco products, other	99–37	99–35	19–35
TOTAL	99–37	99–35	....
Textile products			
Cotton goods	99–37	99–35	19–35
Lace goods	14–37	....	....
Woolen and worsted goods	99–37	99–35	19–35
Silk goods	99–37	99–35	19–35
Rayon goods		....	
Hosiery, knit	99–37	99–35	19–35
Underwear, knit	99–37		19–35
Outerwear, knit	99–37		19–35
Cloth, knit	99–31		19–31
Carpets and rugs, wool	99–37	99–35	....
Asphalted-felt-base floor covering	19–37	14–31[d]	....
Linoleum	04–37		....
Oilcloth	04–37		....
Cordage and twine	99–37	99–35	....
Jute goods	99–37		....
Linen goods	99–37		....
Clothing, men's, incl. work clothing	27–37	....	....
Gloves, textile, not elsewhere made	27–37	....	....
Shirts and collars, men's	27–37	....	....
Clothing, women's, not elsewhere classified	27–37	....	....
Corsets	27–37	....	....
Handkerchiefs	27–37	....	....

For footnotes see p. 650.

TABLE D-1 (continued)

Industry and Group	*Census Years Covered by Index of Physical Output*[a]		
	National Bureau of Economic Research	Day-Thomas[b]	National Research Project[c]
Textile products (concluded)			
Elastic woven goods, not elsewhere made	27–37	....	....
Hats, fur-felt	99–37	99–31[d]	....
Hats, cloth	27–37	....	....
Hats, straw, men's	27–37	....	....
Hats, wool-felt	99–37	....	....
Artificial leather	23–37	....	....
Wool shoddy	99–37	....	....
TOTAL	99–37	99–35	....
Leather products			
Leather	99–37	99–35	19–35
Shoes, leather	99–37	99–35	19–35
Gloves, leather	99–37	99–14	....
Belting, leather	27–37	....	....
TOTAL	99–37	99–35	....
Rubber products			
Tires and tubes	14–37	14–35	21–35
Shoes, rubber	14–37	14–35	}21–35 (Shoes, rubber and Rubber goods, other)
Rubber goods, other	27–37	....	
TOTAL	19–37	09–35	....
Paper products			
Pulp	99–37	}99–35 (Pulp and Paper)	{19–35
Paper	99–37		{19–35
Wall paper	29–37	....	....
Boxes, paper	....	14–35	....
TOTAL	99–37	99–35	....
Printing and publishing			
TOTAL	99–37	14–35	19–35
Chemical products			
Chemicals, not elsewhere classified	99–37	99–35	}19–35 (Chemicals, not elsewhere classified and Gases, compressed)
Gases, compressed	09–37	....	
Rayon	14–37	....	19–37
Cottonseed products	99–37	99–35	....
Linseed products	23–37	....	....
Carbon black	14–37	....	....

For footnotes see p. 650.

TABLE D–1 (continued)

Industry and Group	Census Years Covered by Index of Physical Output[a]		
	National Bureau of Economic Research	Day-Thomas[b]	National Research Project[c]
Chemical products (concluded)			
Soap	04–37	14–35	....
Wood-distillation products	99–37	....	....
Charcoal	21–37	....	....
Explosives	99–37	99–35	....
Fertilizers	99–37	99–35	19–35
Glue and gelatin	27–37	....	....
Paints and varnishes	99–37	99–35	19–35
Salt	99–37	14–35	....
Tanning and dye materials	99–37	....	....
TOTAL	99–37	99–35[f]	....
Petroleum and coal products			
Petroleum refining	99–37	99–35	19–35
Coke-oven products	99–37	99–35	19–35
Fuel briquettes	09–37	....	....
Gas, illuminating and heating	....	99–35[g]	19–35
TOTAL	99–37	[f]	....
Stone, clay and glass products			
Asbestos products	27–37	....	....
Roofing	29–37	....	....
Cement	99–37	99–35	19–35
Lime	04–37	14–31[d]	....
Wall plaster and board	27–37	....	....
Concrete products	25–37	....	....
Sand-lime brick	14–37	....	....
Clay products	99–37	99–35	19–35
Glass	25–37	99–35	19–35
TOTAL	25–37	99–35	....
Forest products			
Lumber-mill products	99–37	99–35	19–35
Planing-mill products	25–37	....	19–35
Boxes, wooden, cigar	27–37	....	....
Cooperage	27–37	....	....
Caskets and coffins	27–37	....	....
Excelsior	25–37	....	....
Turpentine and rosin	99–37	99–35[h]	....
Furniture	....	....	19–35
TOTAL	99–37	99–35	....

For footnotes see p. 650.

Table D–1 (continued)

Industry and Group	*Census Years Covered by Index of Physical Output*[a]		
	National Bureau of Economic Research	Day-Thomas[b]	National Research Project[c]
Iron and steel products			
Blast-furnace products	99–37	99–35	19–35
Steel-mill products	99–37	99–35	19–35
Wire, not elsewhere made	09–37	....	....
Wrought pipe, not elsewhere made	25–37	....	....
Cast-iron pipe	14–37	....	....
Files	29–37	....	....
Firearms	21–37	....	....
Tin cans and tinware	27–37	....	....
TOTAL	99–37	99–35[k]	....
Nonferrous-metal products			
Copper	99–37	14–35 (Copper, Lead, Zinc)	19–35
Lead	99–37		
Zinc	99–37		
Secondary metals, nonprecious	25–37	....	19–35
Collapsible tubes	25–37	....	....
Nonferrous-metal products, not elsewhere classified	25–37	14–35	19–35
Clocks, watches and materials	27–37	....	....
Industries consuming nonferrous metals	....	99–35[k]	....
TOTAL	25–37	99–35	....
Machinery			
Agricultural implements	21–37	14–23[i]	21–35
Phonographs	99–29	14–23[i]	....
Radios	23–37	....	....
Refrigerators, mechanical	21–37	....	....
Scales and balances	27–37	....	....
Sewing machines	27–37	....	....
Typewriters	21–37	....	....
Washing and iron machines	27–37	....	....
Electrical machinery	....	14–23[i]	21–31[j]
Textile machinery	....	19–23[i]	....
Machine tools	....	19–23[i]	....
Engines and waterwheels	....	14–23[i]	....
TOTAL	....	....	....

For footnotes see p. 650.

Table D–1 (concluded)

Industry and Group	*Census Years Covered by Index of Physical Output*[a] National Bureau of Economic Research	Day-Thomas[b]	National Research Project[c]
Transportation equipment			
Automobiles, incl. bodies and parts	99–37	99–35	19–35
Carriages, wagons and sleighs	99–37	99–35	....
Cars, railroad, not elsewhere made	99–37	99–35	....
Locomotives, not elsewhere made	99–37	14–35	....
Ships and boats	99–37	99–35	....
Motorcycles and bicycles	99–29	....	....
Carriages and sleds, children's	25–37	....	....
TOTAL	99–37	99–35	....
Miscellaneous products			
Organs	99–35	....	....
Pianos	99–37	14–23[i]	....
Buttons	14–37	....	....
Brooms	27–37	....	....
Pencils	29–37	....	....
Pens and points	29–37	....	....
Sporting goods, not elsewhere classified	29–37	....	....
TOTAL	....	....	....

[a] Years are inclusive. In a few cases some years between the end years are not covered.

[b] The Bureau of the Census extended the Day-Thomas index through 1937, but published only the index for all manufacturing combined (*Census of Manufactures: 1937,* Part I, pp. 12, 17).

[c] The National Research Project is engaged in extending its index through 1937. (The index for rayon, 1937, has already been published.)

[d] Excluded 1919–31, in revision by Kolesnikoff.

[e] An index for 1933–37 was computed by the Bureau of the Census and included in the revised Day-Thomas index published by it (*loc. cit.*).

[f] Petroleum and coal products combined with chemical products.

[g] Excluded 1919–35, in revision by the Bureau of the Census.

[h] Included by Day-Thomas in the chemical products group.

[i] Considered "experimental" or "doubtful" by Day and Thomas. Not included in general index.

[j] "Electric lamps" only. Based on a special Bureau of Labor Statistics study.

[k] Output measured by the total volume of nonferrous metals consumed in the United States.

NOTES ON DIFFERENCES

Foods

Canned fish. From 1919 to 1929 the NBER index for canned and preserved fish rose only 18 percent, while the Day-Thomas index rose 47 percent. The latter index does not include data for cured fish, which dropped nearly 30 percent in the 10 years.

Canned fruits and vegetables. Our index for canned fruits and vegetables agrees closely with the Day-Thomas index, except for one decade, 1899–1909. For that period our index indicates a rise of 69 percent, much smaller than the increase of 122 percent shown by the Day-Thomas index. The divergence appears to be due to the adjustment made by us for an increase that occurred in the coverage of the sample of products of the industry; to the use, by Day and Thomas, of three simple aggregates (canned vegetables, canned fruits, and dried fruits) whereas we used data for individual fruits or vegetables, combining them by means of price coefficients; and to the employment by Day and Thomas of 1909 weights, as contrasted with our use of the average of weights for 1899–1909.

Ice cream. The National Research Project index for the ice cream industry covers the period 1919–36, but our index applies only to 1923–37. The two indexes agree closely for the overlapping period, since they are derived from substantially the same statistics. For 1919–23 the National Research Project index is based on a sample of reports from ice cream manufacturers collected by the Department of Agriculture. The sample for these years appears, however, to be subject to an upward bias of unknown magnitude,[4] and for this reason we begin our index with 1923, the first year covered by Census data.

Corn products. The Day-Thomas index for corn products indicates a rise of 133 percent from 1919 to 1929. The products covered by this index increased considerably in relative importance, if we may judge from their value in relation to the total

[4] U. S. Department of Agriculture, "Production and Consumption of Manufactured Dairy Products," by E. E. Vial, *Technical Bulletin No. 722* (April 1940), p. 23.

value of products of the industry. No adjustment for this change in the coverage of the sample was made by Day and Thomas. Our index, on the other hand, is adjusted for the increase, and shows a more moderate rise of 44 percent.

The group total. Our indexes for the foods group compare as follows with the Day-Thomas index:

	Percentage Change				
	1899–1935	1899–1909	1909–1919	1919–1929	1929–1935
NBER index					
Adjusted	+205	+48	+45	+54	−8
Unadjusted	+129	+41	+40	+26	−8
Day-Thomas index	+123	+41	+34	+32	−10

The differences between the NBER unadjusted index and the Day-Thomas index are slight, although the number of industries covered by our index is greater than the number covered by the Day-Thomas index. It is therefore the adjustment for changes in coverage, made by us but not by Day and Thomas, that accounts for the difference between the final NBER index—the adjusted index—and the Day-Thomas index.

Tobacco Products

Other tobacco products. Our index declines more than do the indexes computed by Day and Thomas and by the National Research Project because we make an adjustment for changes in coverage beginning with 1925.

Textile Products

Silk and rayon goods. The NBER index shows a rise of 33 percent from 1929 to 1935, whereas the Day-Thomas index indicates a fall of 17 percent and the NRP index a rise of 8 percent. The Day-Thomas index does not cover rayon goods, which rose while silk goods fell. The NRP index includes both rayon and silk goods, but is based on production data described by the Bureau of the Census as incomparable between 1933 and 1935. We bridged the gap between these two years by using Census data on materials consumed, which appear to be more comparable than the Census data on output. Because of changes in the Census classification of this industry, no great precision can be claimed for any index based on the Census data.

Knit goods. The Day-Thomas knit goods index differs widely from the NBER index:

	Percentage Change				
	1899–1935	1899–1909	1909–1919	1919–1929	1929–1935
NBER index	+482	+73	+67	+80	+11
Day-Thomas index	+182	+96	+15	+30	–4

There appear to be two main sources of difference: (1) Our index is based on data more detailed than those used by Day-Thomas (see the following note on hosiery). (2) The weights we used in combining the indexes for the four sub-branches are the value added by each for 1923–35 (the only years for which value added is available for sub-branches), and the value of products of each for other years; Day and Thomas used value of products for all years. See also the note below on knit underwear, another component branch of the industry.

Knit hosiery. The Day-Thomas index is based on a single series, representing the aggregate number of hose produced, but our index is based on several series of different types of hose, which we combined by using the respective prices of the various types. This factor explains the major part of the differences between the two indexes:

	Percentage Change				
	1899–1935	1899–1909	1909–1919	1919–1929	1929–1935
NBER index	+1,063	+116	+125	+125	+2
Day-Thomas index	+259	+110	+35	+31	–4

Knit underwear. The unadjusted index of knit underwear production—wherever made—fell from 140 in 1923 (1929: 100) to 80 in 1937, while the adjusted index—which relates to the "knit underwear industry"—fell from 103 in 1923 to 102 in 1937. The adjustment explains the discrepancy between our index and the corresponding National Research Project index.

Wool carpets and rugs. Our index of output for this industry takes into account the trend toward more expensive grades. If the index were based on output measured merely in terms of square yards, as is the Day-Thomas index, the 1899–1937 rise in output would be less than the figure quoted by us. Indeed, according to the Day-Thomas index, output in 1914 was 12 percent higher than in 1935; according to our index, output in 1914 was 17 percent lower than in 1935.

Cordage and twine. Our index for cordage and twine fell 28 percent from 1929 to 1935, whereas the Day-Thomas index rose 8 percent during this period. The difference may be attributable to a revision made by Kolesnikoff, based on unpublished Census data, but no information on this point is available.

The group total. Our textile index compares as follows with the Day-Thomas index:

	Percentage Change				
	1899–1935	1899–1909	1909–1919	1919–1929	1929–1935
NBER index					
Adjusted	+162	+60	+11	+49	−1
Unadjusted	+133	+47	+17	+34	+1
Day-Thomas index	+88	+51	+9	+30	−12

The differences are substantial, especially in the last two periods. The Day-Thomas index includes the output of cotton goods, knit goods, silk manufactures, woolen and worsted goods, wool carpets and rugs, and cordage and twine. The principal omissions from the Day-Thomas index are rayon manufactures and clothing, both included in the NBER index.

Leather Products

Leather. The National Bureau index for the leather industry differs somewhat from the Day-Thomas index:

	Percentage Change				
	1899–1935	1899–1909	1909–1919	1919–1929	1929–1935
NBER index	+49	+28	+17	−4	+4
Day-Thomas index	+12	+12	+11	−16	+7

The index we have computed is based on detailed data, whereas the Day-Thomas index differentiates only four classes of leather.

The group total. Despite the rather considerable differences between our index of leather output and the Day-Thomas index our unadjusted index of output for the entire leather products group differs only slightly from the Day-Thomas index:

	Percentage Change				
	1899–1935	1899–1909	1909–1919	1919–1929	1929–1935
NBER index					
Adjusted	+56	+29	+9	+11	0
Unadjusted	+61	+29	+15	+6	+3
Day-Thomas index	+53	+27	+14	+3	+3

The substantial differences between the two leather indexes are counterbalanced by relatively slight differences of opposite sign between the two shoe indexes. (The shoe indexes are, of course, weighted much more heavily than the leather indexes.) Our adjusted index differs somewhat from the Day-Thomas index, although the 1899–1935 net changes are very close to one another.

Rubber Products

Tires and tubes. The NRP index is based on the aggregate weight of the rubber, textiles and chemicals consumed in the production of tires and tubes. Our index is based on the number of tires and tubes produced. Because the average physical weight per tire was increasing in the period 1921–29, the NRP index rose in relation to our index:

	Percentage Change	
	1921–1929	1929–1935
NBER index	+156	–28
NRP	+212	–19

Rubber shoes. The aggregate production of rubber shoes—wherever made—fluctuated in relation to the output of the rubber shoes industry. The adjustment made by us for this fluctuation explains in part the difference between our index for the industry and the Day-Thomas index:

	Percentage Change		
	1914–1919	1919–1929	1929–1935
NBER index	+68	–13	–17
Day-Thomas index	+32	+8	–26

The Day-Thomas index, moreover, treats rubber heels as a product of this industry, while we class this item as a product of the industry called "other rubber goods."

The group total. Our index agrees fairly well with the Day-Thomas index:

	Percentage Change		
	1909–1919	1919–1929	1929–1935
NBER index	...	+86	−21
Day-Thomas index	+376	+80	−25

The 1909–19 figure in the Day-Thomas index relates presumably to rubber imports. No statement concerning the underlying data could be found in the Day-Thomas publications.

Paper Products

Paper boxes. Day and Thomas constructed an index of output of the paper box industry by using the output of paper boards in the paper industry.

The group total. Our unadjusted index for the paper products group differs appreciably from the Day-Thomas index only for the 1919–29 period. Our adjusted index differs for this period and also for the period 1899–1909:

	Percentage Change				
	1899–1935	1899–1909	1909–1919	1919–1929	1929–1935
NBER index					
Adjusted	+457	+100	+44	+89	+2
Unadjusted	+403	+88	+44	+90	−2
Day-Thomas index	+356	+91	+43	+69	−1

Chemical Products

Chemicals, not elsewhere classified. There are some differences between the NBER index for chemicals, n.e.c., and the Day-Thomas index:

	Percentage Change				
	1899–1935	1899–1909	1909–1919	1919–1929	1929–1935
NBER index	+524	+78	+61	+108	+5
Day-Thomas index	+613	+100	+110	+105	−17

The Day-Thomas index covers 10 chemicals and acids, while our index covers as many as 15 products in 1899, 35 in 1929 and 32 in 1937.

Soap. The Day-Thomas index is based on the output of hard soaps only. For this reason it shows a drop from 1929 to 1935 (−14 percent), whereas our index, which covers the output of all types of soap, remains unchanged.

The group total. See petroleum and coal products.

Petroleum and Coal Products

Coke-oven products. The Day-Thomas index is based on the output of coke alone. The NBER index is based on the output of coke plus by-products. Since the latter were increasing in relation to the former, our index indicates a greater rate of growth than does the Day-Thomas index:

	Percentage Change				
	1899–1935	1899–1909	1909–1919	1919–1929	1929–1935
NBER index	+219	+110	+60	+63	−42
Day-Thomas index	+72	+97	+11	+35	−42

Illuminating and heating gas. This industry is considered here as a nonmanufacturing industry, because it was excluded from the 1937 Census of Manufactures.

The group total. The index for the petroleum and coal products group must be combined with the index for chemical products if it is to be compared with the Day-Thomas index. The comparison follows:

	Percentage Change				
	1899–1935	1899–1909	1909–1919	1919–1929	1929–1935
NBER index					
Adjusted	+545	+72	+80	+112	−2
Unadjusted	+683	+84	+99	+112	0
Day-Thomas Index	+395	+95	+70	+87	−20

The Day-Thomas index advanced more rapidly than the NBER index in the first decade only. In the three later periods it advanced less rapidly, or fell more rapidly. The Day-Thomas index covers illuminating and heating gas, which we exclude.

Stone, Clay and Glass Products

Cement. The Day-Thomas index shows a rise of 320 percent in cement output between 1899 and 1909, whereas our index indicates an increase of 497 percent. The Day-Thomas index is based on the total output of all types of cement, aggregated without allowance for the relatively greater price of Portland cement. As a result the rate of growth shown by the Day-Thomas index is slower than the rate shown by a weighted index like ours.

Glass. The Day-Thomas index of glass production begins in 1899. It represents plate and window glass for the years 1899–1935, and in addition two series on bottles and jars, and pressed and blown glass for 1899–1914. In our opinion the output of the entire glass industry could not be measured adequately by these series: for 1914–25, because of inadequate coverage; and for 1899–1914, because the bottles and jars and pressed and blown glass series are excessively heterogeneous. Quantities of the individual bottles, jars, etc. are known, but values are not; therefore we concluded that no properly weighted indexes of the output of these glass products could be constructed.

The National Research Project index begins in 1919. For 1919–25 it is based on the Census data for window glass and plate glass; on Bureau of Labor Statistics data for glass containers (unweighted aggregates of different types); on Census data for 5 series of pressed and blown ware—equal in value to one third of the total value of pressed and blown ware and available for 1919 and 1925 only. Beginning with 1925 the National Research Project index is based on Census data of about the same detail as the data utilized by us.

The group total. The Day-Thomas index for the group begins in 1899. It is based on the output of cement, clay products and glass. Concerning the index for glass see above. The Day-Thomas index agrees closely with ours for the years 1929 to 1935.

Forest Products

Lumber-mill products. The Day-Thomas index for lumber shows a fairly sharp peak in 1909. The rise from 1899 to 1909 was 29 percent, and the fall from 1909 to 1919, 27 percent. In

other respects the index agrees well with the index worked out in the present study. The differences stem from the fact that the Day-Thomas index relates to the *product,* lumber, while our index relates to the *industry,* lumber-mill products. It seems that between 1899 and 1909 there was a considerable shift of processing operations from the lumber-mill products industry to the planing-mill products industry, followed by a shift in the other direction from 1909 to 1919.

Planing-mill products. For 1919–25 the National Research Project index for planing-mill products is based on the value of the industry's products deflated by an index of dressed lumber prices. We did not compute an index for this period.

Furniture. The National Research Project index for furniture is based on the value of the industry's products deflated by the Bureau of Labor Statistics prices of furniture.

Turpentine and rosin. The NBER index is adjusted for changes in the degree to which the products, turpentine and rosin, are made within the industry, "turpentine and rosin." This fact explains the differences between it and the Day-Thomas index.

The group total. The National Bureau indexes for the forest products group differ in several respects from the Day-Thomas index:

	Percentage Change				
	1899–1935	1899–1909	1909–1919	1919–1929	1929–1935
NBER index					
Adjusted	−28	+1	−5	+27	−41
Unadjusted	−49	−3	−8	+4	−45
Day-Thomas index	−46	+29	−27	+8	−47

The difference between the NBER unadjusted index and the Day-Thomas index is large in the first two decades. On this divergence see lumber-mill products above. The adjusted index differs also in the third decade, for the reason cited in footnote 4, Chapter 17, above.

Iron and Steel Products

The group total. Our indexes for iron and steel products rose more rapidly than the Day-Thomas index:

	Percentage Change				
	1899–1935	1899–1909	1909–1919	1919–1929	1929–1935
NBER index					
Adjusted	+193	+110	+34	+70	−39
Unadjusted	+160	+83	+40	+57	−35
Day-Thomas index	+113	+74	+33	+58	−42

Nonferrous-Metal Products

Secondary metals. The NRP index for secondary metals for 1919–25 was obtained by deflation of the value of the industry's products by an index of the prices of secondary metals. The index shows a rise of 72 percent from 1919 to 1925.

Nonferrous-metal products, not elsewhere classified. An index of output of this industry was computed by Day and Thomas for the period beginning in 1914. This index was based on the total weight of semifinished products. Examination of the underlying Census data reveals broad changes in the Census definition of semifinished products, and these changes destroy the continuity of the series. Thus the 1919, 1921 and 1923 output of semifinished products includes castings and machinery fittings; the 1914 output excludes castings and machinery fittings; and the 1925 output excludes finished castings. Because of these shifts we did not compute an index for the period 1914–15.[5]

The NRP index for nonferrous-metal products, not elsewhere classified, begins in 1919. The index for 1919–25 is based on fragmentary Census data subjected to rather elaborate adjustments and processes of estimate. It is difficult to judge the reliability of the index for this period. The rise between 1919 and 1925 shown by the NRP index is 70 percent.

The group total. The Day-Thomas index of output of nonferrous-metal products begins in 1899. It is based for 1899–1914 on the consumption of copper, zinc, lead, silver, and gold; and for 1914–35, on the consumption of these five nonferrous metals, on the production of the five metals (primary output), and on the output of nonferrous-metal products, not elsewhere

[5] During the examination of the Day-Thomas indexes it was found that the indexes for 1921 and 1923 were based on unrevised data. Revisions published in the 1925 Census report would reduce the 1921 Day-Thomas index by about 2 percent, and the 1923 index by about 11 percent.

classified. With respect to the output of the last-named industry, see above. The change in the Day-Thomas index for 1929–35 agrees closely with the trend shown by our index.

Machinery

The several "experimental" indexes computed by Day and Thomas for electrical machinery, textile machinery, machine tools, and engines and waterwheels are based on Census data. These data are inadequate on two counts: first, they are insufficiently subclassified, and therefore appear in heterogeneous classes; second, the products for which there are quantity data constitute small fractions of the total production of the respective industries, measured in terms of value. These criticisms cannot be leveled, at least in the same degree, against the data for agricultural implements, and phonographs. For this reason, we present indexes for these two industries, although corresponding indexes by Day and Thomas are also labeled "experimental."

Transportation Equipment

The group total. Because of the diversity of trends within the group, our group index disagrees with the Day-Thomas index:

	Percentage Change				
	1899–1935	1899–1909	1909–1919	1919–1929	1929–1935
NBER index					
Adjusted	+886	+47	+468	+64	–28
Unadjusted	+932	+48	+504	+62	–29
Day-Thomas index	+958	+190	+696	–4	–52

The difference in 1899–1909 arises mainly from the greater weight assigned to automobiles in the Day-Thomas index. Day and Thomas employed the 1909 value added as the weight, whereas we used what amounts to the average of value added for 1899 and 1909. The differences between the group indexes in the next two decades arise presumably from differences between the indexes for ships and boats: our index is adjusted to cover repair work. The divergence in the last period reflects the use of 1919 value added as a component in the weights used in the Day-Thomas index. As a result the declining industries are weighted more in the latter index, and the rising industries less, than we weight them.

Index

Full Census titles of industries are given in parentheses after the abbreviated titles used in this volume. N.e.c. denotes not elsewhere classified; n.e.m., not elsewhere made; and n.e.d., not elsewhere done.

PUBLICATIONS OF THE NATIONAL BUREAU OF ECONOMIC RESEARCH

INCOME IN THE UNITED STATES
Wesley C. Mitchell, W. I. King, F. R. Macaulay and *O. W. Knauth*

*1 Volume I, SUMMARY (1921) 152 pp.

2 Volume II, DETAILS (1922) 420 pp., $5.15

3 DISTRIBUTION OF INCOME BY STATES IN 1919 (1922)
O. W. Knauth 30 pp., $1.30

*4 BUSINESS CYCLES AND UNEMPLOYMENT (1923)
National Bureau Staff and *Sixteen Collaborators* 405 pp.

*5 EMPLOYMENT, HOURS AND EARNINGS, UNITED STATES, 1920–22 (1923)
W. I. King 147 pp.

6 THE GROWTH OF AMERICAN TRADE UNIONS, 1880–1923 (1924)
Leo Wolman 170 pp., $2.50

7 INCOME IN THE VARIOUS STATES: ITS SOURCES AND DISTRIBUTION, 1919, 1920 AND 1921 (1925) *Maurice Levin* 306 pp., $3.50

8 BUSINESS ANNALS (1926)
W. L. Thorp, with an introductory chapter, Business Cycles as Revealed by Business Annals, by *Wesley C. Mitchell* 380 pp., $2.50

9 MIGRATION AND BUSINESS CYCLES (1926)
Harry Jerome 256 pp., $2.50

10 BUSINESS CYCLES: THE PROBLEM AND ITS SETTING (1927)
Wesley C. Mitchell 489 pp., $5.00

*11 THE BEHAVIOR OF PRICES (1927) *Frederick C. Mills* 598 pp.

12 TRENDS IN PHILANTHROPY (1928) *W. I. King* 78 pp., $1.00

13 RECENT ECONOMIC CHANGES (1929)
National Bureau Staff and *Fifteen Collaborators* 2 vols., 950 pp., $7.50

INTERNATIONAL MIGRATIONS

14 Volume I, STATISTICS (1929), compiled by *Imre Ferenczi* of the International Labour Office, and edited by
W. F. Willcox 1,112 pp., $7.00

18 Volume II, INTERPRETATIONS (1931), edited by
W. F. Willcox 715 pp., $5.00

*15 THE NATIONAL INCOME AND ITS PURCHASING POWER (1930)
W. I. King 394 pp.

16 CORPORATION CONTRIBUTIONS TO ORGANIZED COMMUNITY WELFARE SERVICES (1930)
Pierce Williams and *F. E. Croxton* 347 pp., $2.00

* *Out of print.*

17 PLANNING AND CONTROL OF PUBLIC WORKS (1930)
Leo Wolman 260 pp., $2.50

*19 THE SMOOTHING OF TIME SERIES (1931)
Frederick R. Macaulay 172 pp.

20 THE PURCHASE OF MEDICAL CARE THROUGH FIXED PERIODIC PAYMENT (1932)
Pierce Williams 308 pp., $3.00

*21 ECONOMIC TENDENCIES IN THE UNITED STATES (1932)
Frederick C. Mills 639 pp.

22 SEASONAL VARIATIONS IN INDUSTRY AND TRADE (1933)
Simon Kuznets 455 pp., $4.00

23 PRODUCTION TRENDS IN THE UNITED STATES SINCE 1870 (1934)
A. F. Burns 363 pp., $3.50

24 STRATEGIC FACTORS IN BUSINESS CYCLES (1934)
J. Maurice Clark 238 pp., $1.50

25 GERMAN BUSINESS CYCLES, 1924–1933 (1934)
C. T. Schmidt 288 pp., $2.50

26 INDUSTRIAL PROFITS IN THE UNITED STATES (1934)
R. C. Epstein 678 pp., $5.00

27 MECHANIZATION IN INDUSTRY (1934)
Harry Jerome 484 pp., $3.50

28 CORPORATE PROFITS AS SHOWN BY AUDIT REPORTS (1935)
W. A. Paton 151 pp., $1.25

29 PUBLIC WORKS IN PROSPERITY AND DEPRESSION (1935)
A. D. Gayer 460 pp., $3.00

30 EBB AND FLOW IN TRADE UNIONISM (1936)
Leo Wolman 251 pp., $2.50

31 PRICES IN RECESSION AND RECOVERY (1936)
Frederick C. Mills 561 pp., $4.00

32 NATIONAL INCOME AND CAPITAL FORMATION, 1919–1935 (1937)
Simon Kuznets 100 pp., 8¼ x 11¾, $1.50

33 SOME THEORETICAL PROBLEMS SUGGESTED BY THE MOVEMENTS OF INTEREST RATES, BOND YIELDS AND STOCK PRICES IN THE UNITED STATES SINCE 1856 (1938)
F. R. Macaulay 586 pp., $5.00
The Social Sciences and the Unknown Future, a reprint of the introductory chapter to Dr. Macaulay's volume: 35 cents; in orders of 10 or more, 25 cents.

34 COMMODITY FLOW AND CAPITAL FORMATION, Volume I (1938)
Simon Kuznets 500 pp., 8¼ x 11¾, $5.00

35 CAPITAL CONSUMPTION AND ADJUSTMENT (1938)
Solomon Fabricant 271 pp., $2.75

36 THE STRUCTURE OF MANUFACTURING PRODUCTION, A CROSS-SECTION VIEW (1939) *C. A. Bliss* 234 pp., $2.50

37 THE INTERNATIONAL GOLD STANDARD REINTERPRETED, 1914–34 (1940)
William Adams Brown, Jr. 1420 pp., $12

* *Out of print.*

38 RESIDENTIAL REAL ESTATE, ITS ECONOMIC POSITION AS SHOWN BY VALUES, RENTS, FAMILY INCOMES, FINANCING, AND CONSTRUCTION, TOGETHER WITH ESTIMATES FOR ALL REAL ESTATE (1940)
D. L. Wickens 320 pp., 8¼ x 11¾, $3.50

39 THE OUTPUT OF MANUFACTURING INDUSTRIES, 1899–1937 (1940)
Solomon Fabricant 685 pp., $4.50

FINANCIAL RESEARCH PROGRAM

I *A Program of Financial Research*

1 REPORT OF THE EXPLORATORY COMMITTEE ON FINANCIAL RESEARCH (1937) 91 pp., $1.00

2 INVENTORY OF CURRENT RESEARCH ON FINANCIAL PROBLEMS (1937) 253 pp., $1.50

II *Studies in Consumer Instalment Financing*

1 PERSONAL FINANCE COMPANIES AND THEIR CREDIT PRACTICES (1940)
Ralph A. Young and *Associates* 170 pp., $2.00

2 SALES FINANCE COMPANIES AND THEIR CREDIT PRACTICES (1940)
Wilbur C. Plummer and *Ralph A. Young* 298 pp., $3.00

3 COMMERCIAL BANKS AND CONSUMER INSTALMENT CREDIT (1940)
John M. Chapman and *Associates* 318 pp., $3.00

4 INDUSTRIAL BANKING COMPANIES AND THEIR CREDIT PRACTICES (1940)
R. J. Saulnier 192 pp., $2.00

5 GOVERNMENT AGENCIES OF CONSUMER INSTALMENT CREDIT (1940)
J. D. Coppock 216 pp., $2.50

6 THE PATTERN OF CONSUMER DEBT, 1935–36 (1940)
Blanche Bernstein 238 pp., $2.50

7 THE VOLUME OF CONSUMER INSTALMENT CREDIT, 1929–38 (1940)
Duncan McC. Holthausen in collaboration with
Malcolm L. Merriam and *Rofl Nugent* 137 pp., $1.50

CONFERENCE ON RESEARCH IN NATIONAL INCOME AND WEALTH

STUDIES IN INCOME AND WEALTH (Volumes I–III together, $7.50)
Volume I (1937), 368 pp., $2.50; Volume II (1938), 342 pp., $3.00; Volume III (1939), 500 pp., $3.50.

CONFERENCE ON PRICE RESEARCH

1 REPORT OF THE COMMITTEE ON PRICES IN THE BITUMINOUS COAL INDUSTRY (1938) 144 pp., $1.25

2 TEXTILE MARKETS—THEIR STRUCTURE IN RELATION TO PRICE RESEARCH (1939) 304 pp., $3.00

3 PRICE RESEARCH IN THE STEEL AND PETROLEUM INDUSTRIES (1939) 224 pp., $2.00

NATIONAL BUREAU OF ECONOMIC RESEARCH
1819 Broadway, New York, N. Y.
European Agent: Macmillan & Co., Ltd.
St. Martin's Street, London, W.C.2